The Black–Scholes equation has quite a unique status in modern science: it is simultaneously extraordinarily important and woefully flawed. The present book, which musters an exceptional lineup of experts, reflects this duality. Some chapters celebrate the golden age, when mathematical finance explored all the nooks and crannies of the Black–Scholes world while too often turning a blind eye to its glaring inadequacies. Other contributions bite the bullet and present new and exciting modelling avenues, ever closer to the complexity of real markets.

Jean-Philippe Bouchaud
Chairman and Head of Research, Capital Fund Management, and
Member, Académie des Sciences, Paris

Gershon, Lipton, Rosenbaum, and Wiener have commemorated the landmark achievement of Black, Scholes, and Merton with an exceptional collection of works by most of the leading lights of the world of derivatives pricing and risk management. This volume conveys the continuing richness and vibrancy of the subject area. Anyone following developments in this field will want to have a copy.

Darrell Duffie
The Adams Distinguished Professor of Management, and
Professor of Finance, Stanford University

In the half century since the Black–Scholes–Merton theory was published, the world of finance has seen extraordinary advances boosting market activity by orders of magnitude. Despite unrealistic simplicities, the BSM model showed practitioners effective new ways of thinking, providing the key signposts needed to develop ever improving models and protocols for managing the risks and opportunities in the markets. With unparalleled gains in computing and data accessibility, we now stand at the threshold of a second great revolution in finance, and this book gathers the current research and thinking of the global leaders of financial engineering at this critical juncture, engineers who were brought together at Options: 45 Years After the Publication of the Black Scholes Merton Model. It is not known which combinations of neural nets, big data and machine intelligence, rough volatility and jump models, or synthetic hedging will lead us through these advances. But when we look back fifty years on, it will be clear that these works contain the key signposts for this next advance.

Patrick S. Hagan
Quantitative Trader, XBTQ Group, and
Managing Director, Gorilla Science

This book is a remarkable accomplishment. It is a financial history masterpiece, written by those who made that history possible. The names of Scholes, Lipton, Hull, Dupire, Wilmott, Carr, Avellaneda, El Karoui, ... are legendary in our industry, and an inspiration for generations to come. Any person with a remote interest in financial engineering must read this book, for what it says, and for who says it.

Marcos Lopez de Prado
Global Head of Quantitative R&D, Abu Dhabi Investment Authority, and
Professor of Practice, Cornell University

Options — 45 years since the Publication of the Black–Scholes–Merton Model

The Gershon Fintech Center Conference

World Scientific Lecture Notes in Finance

ISSN: 2424-9939

This series provides high quality lecture note-type texts in all areas of finance, for courses at all levels: undergraduate, MBA and PhD. These accessible and affordable lecture notes are better aligned with today's classrooms and are written by expert professors in their field with extensive teaching experience. Students will find these books less formal, less expensive and also more enjoyable than many textbooks. Instructors will find all the material that they need, thus significantly reducing their class preparation time. Authors can prepare their volumes with ease, as they would be based on already existing, and actively used, lecture notes. With these features, this book series will make a significant contribution to improving the teaching of finance worldwide.

Published:

Vol. 6 *Options — 45 years since the Publication of the Black–Scholes–Merton Model: The Gershon Fintech Center Conference*
edited by David Gershon (The Hebrew University of Jerusalem, Israel), Alexander Lipton (Abu Dhabi Investment Authority, UAE & The Hebrew University of Jerusalem, Israel), Mathieu Rosenbaum (École Polytechnique, France) and Zvi Wiener (The Hebrew University of Jerusalem, Israel)

Vol. 5 *Lecture Notes in Investment: Investment Fundamentals*
by Eliezer Prisman (York University, Canada)

Vol. 4 *Lecture Notes in Market Microstructure and Trading*
by Peter Joakim Westerholm (The University of Sydney, Australia)

Vol. 3 *Lecture Notes in Behavioral Finance*
by Itzhak Venezia (Tel Aviv-Yaffo Academic College, Israel & The Hebrew University of Jerusalem, Israel)

Vol. 2 *Lecture Notes in Fixed Income Fundamentals*
by Eliezer Z. Prisman (York University, Canada)

Vol. 1 *Lecture Notes in Introduction to Corporate Finance*
by Ivan E. Brick (Rutgers Business School at Newark and New Brunswick, USA)

More information on this series can also be found at https://www.worldscientific.com/series/wslnf

World Scientific Lecture Notes in Finance – **Vol. 6**

Options — 45 years since the Publication of the Black–Scholes–Merton Model

The Gershon Fintech Center Conference

David Gershon
The Hebrew University of Jerusalem, Israel

Alexander Lipton
Abu Dhabi Investment Authority, UAE &
The Hebrew University of Jerusalem, Israel

Mathieu Rosenbaum
École Polytechnique, France

Zvi Wiener
The Hebrew University of Jerusalem, Israel

NEW JERSEY • LONDON • SINGAPORE • BEIJING • SHANGHAI • HONG KONG • TAIPEI • CHENNAI • TOKYO

Published by

World Scientific Publishing Co. Pte. Ltd.
5 Toh Tuck Link, Singapore 596224
USA office: 27 Warren Street, Suite 401-402, Hackensack, NJ 07601
UK office: 57 Shelton Street, Covent Garden, London WC2H 9HE

Library of Congress Cataloging-in-Publication Data
Names: Gershon, David, editor. | Lipton, Alexander, editor. |
Rosenbaum, Mathieu, editor. | Wiener, Zvi, editor.
Title: Options — 45 years since the publication of the Black-Scholes-Merton model : the Gershon Fintech Center conference / edited by David Gershon, The Hebrew University of Jerusalem, Israel, Alexander Lipton, Abu Dhabi Investment Authority, UAE & The Hebrew University of Jerusalem, Israel, Mathieu Rosenbaum, École Polytechnique, France, Zvi Wiener, The Hebrew University of Jerusalem, Israel.
Other titles: Options — fourty five years since the publication of the Black-Scholes-Merton model
Description: New Jersey : World Scientific, 2023. | Series: World scientific lecture notes in finance, 2424-9939 ; volume 6 | Includes bibliographical references and index.
Identifiers: LCCN 2022020945 | ISBN 9789811255861 (hardcover) |
ISBN 9789811259142 (ebook) | ISBN 9789811259159 (ebook other)
Subjects: LCSH: Options (Finance) | Finance--Data processing. | Corporations--Finance.
Classification: LCC HG6024.A3 O647 2023 | DDC 332.64/53--dc23/eng/20220716
LC record available at https://lccn.loc.gov/2022020945

British Library Cataloguing-in-Publication Data
A catalogue record for this book is available from the British Library.

For any available supplementary material, please visit
https://www.worldscientific.com/worldscibooks/10.1142/12822#t=suppl

Desk Editors: Soundararajan Raghuraman/Pui Yee Lum

Typeset by Stallion Press
Email: enquiries@stallionpress.com

This book is dedicated
to the memory of
Professor Marco Avellaneda (1955–2022)
and
Professor Peter Carr (1958–2022)

https://doi.org/10.1142/9789811259142_fmatter

Preface

On December 4–5, 2019, the Gershon Fintech Center organized the international conference entitled *Options: 45 Years After the Publication of the Black Scholes Merton Model*, hosted at the Hebrew University of Jerusalem. It celebrated the original Black–Scholes–Merton formula published in 1973 and tremendous progress in option pricing since then. In addition to keynotes presented by Myron Scholes and Robert Merton, some of the most distinguished and respected financial engineering experts delivered 22 lectures.

We feel that *Options: 45 Years After the Publication of the Black Scholes Merton Model* was a significant event that deserves to be remembered, and we hope this book will accomplish this goal. Unfortunately, COVID-19 prevented its timely publication, but, as they say, "better late than never". In addition to Scholes' keynote (Chapter 1), this book contains 23 chapters, covering a broad spectrum of options pricing and hedging topics. As a result, we expect that the readers will benefit from deep and timely insights into this exciting and vital field.

https://doi.org/10.1142/9789811259142_fmatter

About the Editors

David Gershon is a Professor at the Hebrew University Business School, an entrepreneur, and a philanthropist. In 2000, after a decade of working on Wall Street and in the city of London as head of options trading, he founded SuperDerivatives, one of the world's first financial technology (fintech) companies and the first company that offered a financial system for financial institutions over the internet. SuperDerivatives revolutionized the options market by generating price transparency with a new option pricing model that David invented, replacing the celebrated Black-Scholes model.

For over a decade, David has been named one of the most influenceable individuals in fintech by various organizations and publications. From 2005 to 2010 David was ranked among the "Online Finance 40" annual list — "The Financial Technology Sector's Top 40 individuals", by Institutional Investor magazine, and from 2011 to 2014 he was ranked among "The Tech 50" — "The 50 most influential individuals in Financial Technology" by Institutional Investor magazine. In 2012, David was included in the "Inside Market Data Hall of Fame", celebrating his achievement in establishing SuperDerivatives as a global leading vendor of financial data.

In 2014, SuperDerivatives was acquired by InterContinental Exchange. In 2017, David put his world-class expertise in financial options to good use and returned to academia, to teach at the Hebrew University Business School. He continued to develop his options pricing model in a series of articles.

In 2018, David donated funds to establish the Hebrew University Fintech Center, named after his parents, Sima and Shlomo Gershon. The Gershon Fintech Center was founded as a bridge between academia and the fintech ecosystem, helping entrepreneurs and startup companies, as well as researchers in the field. Since its foundation, the Gershon Fintech Center has organized numerous workshops, conferences, seminars, and courses — significantly contributing to the dramatic growth and success of the fintech sector in Israel.

Alexander Lipton is a Global Head, Research & Development at Abu Dhabi Investment Authority, Professor of Practice at Khalifa University, Visiting Professor and Dean's Fellow at the Jerusalem Business School of the Hebrew University of Jerusalem, and Connection Science Fellow at MIT. Alex is an advisory board member of several fintech companies worldwide. From 2006 to 2016, Alex was Co-Head of the Global Quantitative Group and Quantitative Solutions Executive at Bank of America. Earlier, he was a senior manager at Citadel, Credit Suisse, Deutsche Bank, and Bankers Trust. At the same time, Alex held visiting professorships at EPFL, NYU, Oxford University, Imperial College, and the University of Illinois. Prior to becoming a quant, Alex was a Full Professor of Mathematics at the University of Illinois, and a Consultant at the Los Alamos National Laboratory. In 2000, he was awarded the Inaugural Quant of the Year Award and in 2021 the Buy-side Quant of the Year Award by *Risk Magazine*. Alex authored/edited 11 books and more than a 100 scientific papers on thermonuclear physics, astrophysics, applied mathematics, financial engineering, and distributed ledgers. He frequently gives keynote presentations on Quantitative Finance and FinTech at conferences and forums worldwide. In 2021, Alex published three books *Blockchain and Distributed Ledgers: Mathematics, Technology, and Economics* (with A. Treccani), *Building the New Economy* (with A. Pentland and T. Hardjono), and *Generalized Integral Transforms in Mathematical Finance* (with A. Itkin and D. Muravey).

Mathieu Rosenbaum is a Full Professor at École Polytechnique, where he holds the chair "Analytics and Models for Regulation" and is co-head of the quantitative finance (El Karoui) master program. His research mainly focuses on statistical finance problems, regulatory issues and risk management of derivatives. He published more than 70 articles on these subjects in the best international journals and supervised about 20 PhD students. He is notably one of the most renowned experts on the quantitative analysis of market microstructure and high-frequency trading. On this topic, he co-organizes every two years in Paris the conference "Market Microstructure, Confronting Many Viewpoints". He is also at the origin (with Jim Gatheral and Thibault Jaisson) of the development of rough volatility models. Mathieu Rosenbaum has collaborations with various financial institutions (investment banks, hedge funds, regulators, exchanges, etc.), notably BNP-Paribas since 2004, the French Financial Markets Authority (AMF), Euronext and Jump Trading. He also has several editorial activities as he is one of the editors in chief of the journal "*Market Microstructure and Liquidity*" and is an associate editor for 10 other journals. He received the Europlace Award for Best Young Researcher in Finance in 2014, the European Research Council Grant in 2016, the Louis Bachelier prize in 2020 and the Quant of the Year award in 2021.

Zvi Wiener is a Professor and former Dean of the Hebrew University Business School (2016–2020). He is an expert in risk management, financial engineering and the valuation of complex financial products. Zvi is one of the founders of Professional Risk Managers' International Association (PRMIA, see www.prmia.org), has served as a co-chair of the worldwide Education and Standards Committee of PRMIA and is currently a co-director of PRMIA Israel.

His research was published in leading financial journals including *The Journal of Finance*, *The Review of Financial Studies*, *Journal of Banking and Finance*, *Journal of Derivatives*, *Journal of Corporate*

Finance and many others and can be found at his academic website: http://pluto.mscc.huji.ac.il/~mswiener.

Zvi was a Visiting Professor at the Washington University in St. Louis and the University of Southern California in Los Angeles. In 2014, he was awarded the Teva Prize for research on dividend policy, in 2012 he received the PRMIA award for Outstanding Service and Leadership, in 1997, he received the Alon Fellowship and in 1994 the Rothschild Fellowship. In the years 1996, 2005, 2013, 2015 and 2016 he received research grants from the Israel Academy of Sciences.

Zvi Wiener has rich consulting experience. He consulted the Ministry of Finance, the Bank of Israel, the Israel Securities Authority, the Tel Aviv Stock Exchange, credit rating companies, banks, insurance firms and pension funds, as well as leading law and accounting firms on various financial issues. In addition, Zvi is an angel investor in several young companies.

https://doi.org/10.1142/9789811259142_fmatter

Contents

https://doi.org/10.1142/9789811259142_fmatter

Introduction

Derivative securities, including options, forwards, and futures, are as old as the Egyptian pyramids. Contracts for the future delivery of commodities originated in Mesopotamia about 4,000 years ago. For example, the Code of Hammurabi contains laws regulating such agreements. From Mesopotamia, usage of derivatives expanded to Egypt, Greece, and the Roman and Byzantine Empires. Sephardic Jews have practiced derivative trading since Roman times in the Iberian Peninsula. After the Jews were expelled from Spain and Portugal following the Alhambra Decree in 1492, they brought their derivatives trading skills to the Low Countries, first to Antwerp and then, after its sack by the Spanish in 1576, to Amsterdam. It is not a coincidence that the first stock trading manual was published in Amsterdam by Joseph de la Vega, who was fascinated by options; see [1]. From the Low Countries, the great arc of financial innovation expanded to Great Britain, France, Germany, the United States, and Asia. Weber presents an interesting, albeit brief, history of derivative security markets; see [2].

As nonlinear instruments, options come in many favors, including vanilla calls and puts with hockey-stick payoffs, European options with more complicated payoffs, various American, Bermudan, Asian, barrier options, etc. Moreover, they can be written on various underliers, including stocks, bonds, currencies, commodities.

While in the nineteenth century, several authors published option trading manuals, the original scientific approaches to option valuation were developed much later; see [3–6] among others. In retrospect, Bachelier's and Bronzin's results look particularly remarkable, given that they anticipated subsequent developments in financial engineering by 60–70 years. For example, it is worth mentioning that

Bachelier introduced a mathematical description of the Brownian motion 5 years ahead of Einstein. Thus, his work can be viewed as an antecedent to all the subsequent developments in stochastic calculus and financial engineering. However, only Black–Scholes's and Merton's theory of rational option pricing gained universal acceptance; see [7,8]. Not surprisingly, it became an indispensable tool of modern financial engineering because it ties together pricing and hedging. In 1997, Scholes and Merton received the Nobel Memorial Prize in Economics. Unfortunately, Black passed away in 1995.

Black–Scholes and Merton started a revolution that changed financial engineering and finance at large beyond recognition. Yet, their approach is not without limitations since it is based on several assumptions, which hold only in the ideal world. The key assumptions are as follows:

- Markets are efficient and frictionless.
- There are no restrictions on short sales, frequency of trading, or the number of shares bought and sold.
- A lognormal stochastic process governs the stock price with time-independent parameters.

When these assumptions are valid, it is possible to construct a perfect delta hedge for a contingent claim and price it under a risk-neutral measure. The following stochastic differential equation governs the stock price S:

$$\frac{dS}{dt} = (r - d)\, dt + \sigma dW, \tag{1}$$

where r is the risk-free interest rate, d is the dividend rate, σ is the stock volatility, and W is the standard Wiener process. Thus, for option pricing purposes, every stock has the risk-neutral drift $r-d$, so the only specific parameter is volatility σ. This simple but profound observation differentiates the Black–Scholes–Merton approach from its predecessors. It is easy to show that prices of vanilla calls and puts with maturity T and strike K have the form:

$$V\left(t, S, T, K; r, d, \sigma\right) = \omega e^{-r(T-t)} \left[F\mathcal{N}\left(\omega d_{+}\right) - K\mathcal{N}\left(\omega d_{-}\right)\right], \tag{2}$$

where $F = e^{(r-d)(T-t)}S$ is the forward price, ω is the so-called call/put indicator, $\omega = 1$ for calls, and $\omega = -1$ for puts, $\mathcal{N}(.)$ is the cumulative normal distribution, and

$$d_{\pm} = \frac{\ln(F/K) \pm \frac{1}{2}\sigma^2 (T-t)}{\sigma\sqrt{T-t}}. \tag{3}$$

In the Black–Scholes–Merton framework, the prices of exotic options can be computed either analytically or numerically.

Thus, Black–Scholes and Merton were the first to introduce the no-arbitrage concept to option pricing and develop a closed-form solution/expression for option pricing. Even though they used some idealized assumptions, their formula is still broadly used in practice, at least as a leading-order approximation.

Practitioners realized almost immediately that idealized assumptions of Black–Scholes–Merton are invalid in real markets, so different vanilla options on a given underlier have to be priced using different maturity- and strike-dependent implied volatilities $\sigma_{\mathrm{IMP}}(T, K)$. In other words, every underlier is characterized by an implied volatility surface rather than single volatility.

When the idealized assumptions are dropped, considerable ingenuity is required for pricing vanilla and exotic options consistent with the market.

Several extensions of the standard Black–Scholes–Merton theory have been developed:

- Local volatility models assume that the stock price is governed by Equation (1), with the constant volatility σ replaced by the so-called local volatility $\sigma_{\mathrm{LOC}}(t, S)$. Since these models extend the standard Black–Scholes framework in a limited way, they are complete, allow for a perfect hedge, and match market prices perfectly. Unfortunately, experience suggests that local volatility models do not generate realistic implied volatility dynamics and, as a result, tend to misprice exotic options.
- Jump-diffusion models assume that stock price is subject to Poissonian jumps in addition to regular diffusion. Since jumps cannot be delta hedged, these models are incomplete. For many underliers, models combining local volatility and jump-diffusion reasonably agree with the market.
- Stochastic volatility models assume that a separate stochastic process drives volatility. Such models are incomplete and cannot be

delta hedged. Though imperfect, these models are adequate for many markets, including forex.
- Rough volatility models extend stochastic volatility models by using fractional Brownian motion as a driver for volatility, thus providing a better description of the volatility micro moves.
- Universal volatility models, combining the best features of local, jump-diffusion, and stochastic volatility models, produce reliable prices and hedges for vanilla and many exotic options.
- Over time, the option pricing model became widely used in corporate finance, leading to the famous Merton's model that is essential to many corporate decisions and allows to attribute the value of assets to different stakeholders of a firm.

Given the importance of the original Black–Scholes–Merton discovery and tremendous progress in the field of option pricing achieved since then, the Gershon Fintech Center organized the international conference entitled "Options: 45 Years After the Publication of the Black Scholes Merton Model", hosted at the Hebrew University of Jerusalem, on December 4–5, 2019. We invited some of the most influential researchers, who developed important option pricing models, and provided a stage for them to describe the most significant developments and the current state of option pricing. Myron Scholes and Robert Merton presented keynotes. Besides, 22 lectures were delivered in person by some of the most distinguished and respected financial engineering experts.

We feel that it was a significant event that deserves to be remembered, and we hope this book will do it justice. Unfortunately, COVID-19 prevented its timely publication, but, as they say, "better late than never". In addition to Scholes' keynote (Chapter 1), this book contains 24 chapters, covering a broad spectrum of options pricing and hedging topics.[a]

With very heavy hearts, we must inform the readers that two speakers passed away in the interim — Professor Marco Avellaneda (1955–2022) and Professor Peter Carr (1958–2022). We shall never

[a]Madan's lecture (Chapter 22) was not delivered during the conference for technical reasons.

forget their extraordinary achievements as scientists and practitioners and their great human qualities. We dedicate this volume to their memory.

References

[1] de la Vega, J. (1688). *Confusion de Confusiones.* Amsterdam.
[2] Weber, E.J. (2009). A short history of derivative security markets. In *Vinzenz Bronzin's Option Pricing Models: Exposition and Appraisal,* W. Hafner and H. Zimmermann, Springer-Verlag, Berlin, pp. 431–466.
[3] Bachelier, L. (1900). Théorie de la spéculation, *Annales de l'Ecole Normale Supérieure,* 17, 21–86.
[4] Bronzin, V. (1908). *Theorie der Prämiengeschäfte.* Franz Deuticke, Leipzig.
[5] Boness, A.J. (1964). Elements of a theory of a stock option value, *Journal of Political Economy,* 72(2), 163–175.
[6] Samuelson, P.A. (1965). Rational theory of warrant pricing, *Industrial Management Review,* 6, 13–32.
[7] Black, F. and Scholes, M. (1973). The pricing of options and corporate liabilities, *Journal of Political Economy,* 81(3), 637–659.
[8] Merton, R.C. (1973). Theory of rational option pricing, *Bell Journal of Economics and Management Science,* 4, 141–183.

https://doi.org/10.1142/9789811259142_0001

Chapter 1

Using Option Pricing Information to Time Diversify Portfolio Returns

M. S. Scholes

Frank E. Buck Professor of Finance, Emeritus, Stanford University

msscholes@gmail.com

Keywords: Tail risk, extreme events, average returns, volatility, option prices, risk.

1. Average Returns are the Main Focus

> Compound returns, not average returns or performance relative to a benchmark, should be our major focus. They are enhanced most by mitigation of tail losses and participation in tail gains, each period of time. The options market prices provide valuable information about the risk of each period's gains and losses.
>
> — Myron Scholes, Nobel Prize recipient in Economics, 1997

> "Much of the real world is controlled as much by the 'tails' of distributions as by means or averages: by the exceptional, not the mean; by the catastrophe, not the steady drip.... We need to free ourselves from 'average' thinking".
>
> — Philip Anderson, Nobel Prize recipient in Physics, 1997

---

*Gershon Fintech Center Inauguration, December, 2018.

2. Compound Return Facts: Tail Risks Dominate!

Figure 1: Hypothetical growth of $1 invested in US large cap equities (1/1/1857–12/31/2016).

The risk of returns is much more important than the average return, with tail risk playing the dominant role.

Example: The realized return of US equities can be explained by the extreme tail gains or extreme tail losses; see Figure 1.

- Take out the extreme tail gains, realized return falls to almost zero.
- Take out the extreme tail losses, realized return nearly doubles.
- All the little moves up or down don't matter.
- One run of time.

3. Compound Returns a Function of Risk

Terminal Wealth $(TW) = (1 + R_1)(1 + R_2) \cdots (1 + R_n)$.

$$TW = \text{Exp}[\ln(1 + R_1) + \ln(1 + R_2) \cdots \ln(1 + R_n)].$$

Now by Taylor series: $\ln(1 + R) = R - \frac{1}{2}R^2 + \frac{1}{3}R^2 - \frac{1}{4}R^4$.

Compound Return is expectation: E[ln (1 +R)].

If normal, all the other moments than volatility would have expectations zero => no skewness, third moment, no fat tails, fourth moment. Maybe, changing distributions but ignored by most.

Can't ignore risk terms.

Strategic portfolio provides best cross-sectional allocation of risk.

> Diversification is Only Free Lunch in Finance.
>
> — Malkiel

E(R^2) = Variance for normal distribution
E(R^3) = The third moment or skew of the distribution.

Distributions are not constant and non-normal. Risk is dynamic.

4. Big Problem: Tail Events More Frequent than Normal Distribution

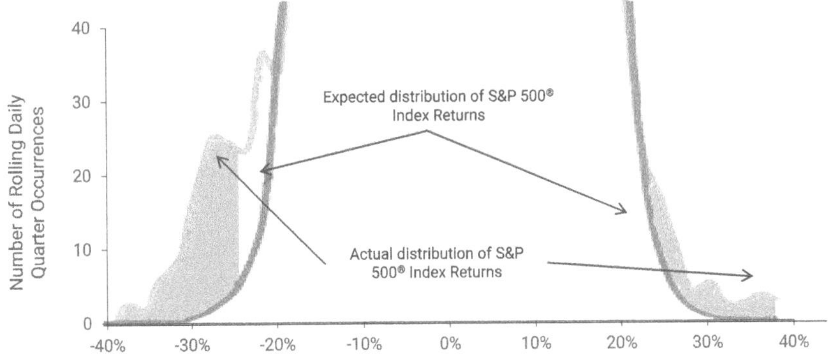

Figure 2: Unexpected equity tail risk based on Actual vs Expected S&P 500 index returns (June 1960–December 2015).

Figure 2 plots a histogram of the S&P 500's *actual* rolling compound 65-day returns (i.e., quarters) and the *expected* distribution of returns based on a normal distribution assumption with the same return and variance using standard Monte Carlo methods.

The actual frequency of severe losses occurred 72× more frequently than expected, see Table 1.

Table 1: Number of Quarterly Occurrences

Severe Quarterly Losses (%)	Actual S&P 500 Returns	Expected S&P 500 Returns*	Unexpected Left Tail Risk Events**
−26	29	1	+28
−28	20		+20
−30	10		+10
−32	7		+7
−34	2		+2
−36	3		+3
−38			
−40	1		+1
Total	72	1	+71

Notes: 7/1/1960–12/31/2015.
*Assuming a normal distribution of returns.
**Visually depicted as the gold region in the chart to the left.

5. Think Tails of the Distribution: Concentrate on Normal Events

- Quantity theory of money: Output (Growth Assets) × Inflation = Money × velocity.
- Cambridge extension: Investors want to hold safety assets (cushion) (bonds) vs macro risks.
- With shocks all growth assets nearly perfectly correlated, all safety assets perfectly correlated, and all inflation assets perfectly correlated:
  - These theories are a good approximation to understand the macro economy. Assets become redundant.
  - Diversification is not a "free lunch" in investment.

- However, need to estimate how these three asset classes correlate with each other in the tails:
  - Over long periods of time, bonds exhibit low correlation with equities.
  - Over long periods of time, inflation assets exhibit low correlation with equities.
  - But, with shocks could be highly positive or negatively correlated.
- Central Bankers (macros theory) concentrate on expectations of growth and inflation not tails.

6. Relative Performance Evaluation

Tracking-error constraints.

Convert investment from absolute to relative returns (benchmarks, information ratio or Sharpe ratio). Stay close to the herd.

Why?

Controls cheating and reduces explicit monitoring costs. But, with potential implicit costs in lost returns. Passive investments are active investments.

Trust issues: How to garner investor trust to not use benchmarks?

- Active managers concentrate on idiosyncratic risk: Rough waters, they diversify to benchmark.
- Trust allows for greater deviations from benchmarks.
- Big data and AI elevate this problem or eliminate short-term active management? (Take all the fish).
- Active fees too great for the returns available.

Trustees and boards use policy portfolios. Asset allocators don't want to lose their jobs with deviations from benchmarks.

7. Investment Strategies — Asset Allocation Static Constraints are Costly

Static asset allocation strategies — Common approach — Benchmark and tracking error.

- For example, 40% bonds and 60% stock. Based on static weights that, on average, provide a risk profile. Buckets are filled within the bond/stock allocations (e.g., private investments, ETFs and hedge funds).
- Dynamics only through readjustment to static weights (60/40). Mean reversion (static rules to rebalance). Not static risk, however.
- **Other static methods**: Life-cycle products (based on age and glide paths), index fund products, or factor products (smart betas) (small vs big, etc.) also ignore risk dynamics. What do these approaches do for savers?

> The one who follows the crowd will usually get no further than the crowd. The one who walks alone is likely to find himself in places no one has ever been.
>
> — Albert Einstein

8. Factors that Affect Terminal Wealth

8.1 *Fact 1*

Compound returns less than average returns even for a normal distribution. The *more risk*, and especially left tail risk, *the smaller compound returns.* Compound returns affect the level of terminal wealth.

- Average returns (and risks) are misleading. Averages are only one part of compound returns.
- The urns are not constant, not normally distributed. Average volatility vs next period's distribution of returns.

8.2 *Fact 2*

Performance over *every period matters* to compounding returns. It is not enough to say "I am a long-term investor;" therefore, no need to worry about what happens in the short run → *false*. **One run of time.**

The *more variability* in risk levels around target levels, the smaller the compound return vs the average return → excess risk drag (turns out to be very important, even for ETF could be 0.5% to 0.75% a year). S&P 500 low fees and no tracking error, but not risk managed. Not passive.

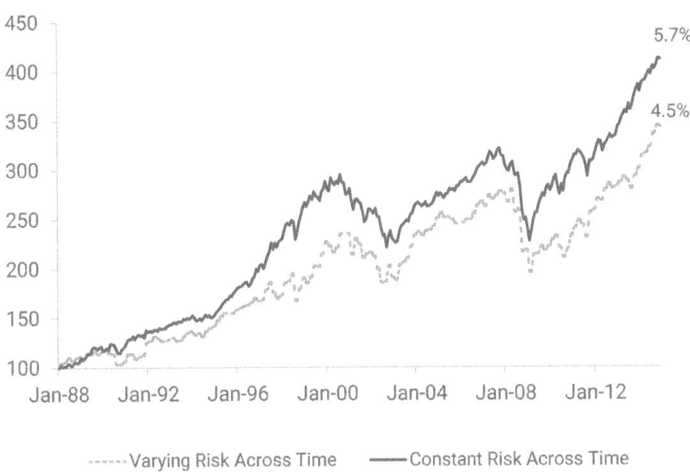

Figure 3: Growth of $100 invested in the S&P 500 Index.

Time diversification: One run of time; see Figure 3.

Strategy 1: 0.5 in stocks, 0.5 in bonds all of the time.

$$E(R) = 0.5E(R_m) + 0.5E(R_b).$$

Strategy 2: Randomly in stock 50% of time and bonds 50% of time, no selection skills => Both strategies have same expected return.

Volatility with normal and constant distribution for stocks and with zero volatility of bonds:

Strategy 1 $\sigma_1^2 = 0.5^2\sigma_m^2; \quad \sigma_1 = 0.5\sigma_m.$

Strategy 2 $\sigma_2^2 = [\sigma_m^2 + 0 + \sigma_m^2 + 0 + \cdots]; \, \sigma_2 = 0.71\sigma_m.$

A non-time diversified strategy (e.g., Strategy 2) has more risk (volatility) and therefore less compound return. Time diversification is a free lunch for sure.

8.3 *Fact 3*

Risk of return *much more important* than average return: Over the short run, average return plays little or no role:

- Annual Sharpe ratio = 0.25, monthly = 0.07 → close to zero.
- Moreover, volatility is easier to measure than Expected Returns (100 years for E(R)?).
- Controlling Volatility and Tails is the most important to Enhancing Compound Returns.

> Do we worry about expected returns changing or forecasting them for next month or next quarter?
>
> We worry about risk in the short run.
>
> We worry about CBs, Fiscal Issues and....

8.4 *Fact 4*

- Compound returns are *asymmetric* — larger losses require even larger gains to break-even; see Figure 4.
- Skewness of the distribution of future returns are important.
- Risk management is not only concentrating on reducing downside but also *participating in the upside.*

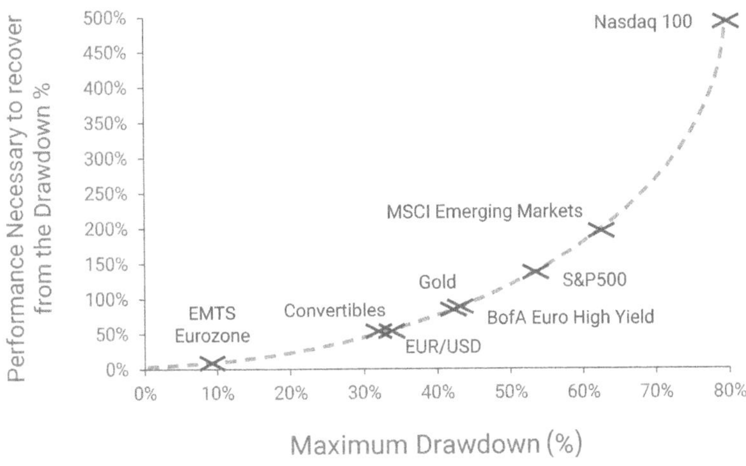

Figure 4: The (nonlinear) base effect.
Sources: Active Asset Allocation, Bloomberg.

8.5 *Fact 5*

Don't ignore tails of the distribution

- Differs from belief that if have a long horizon don't worry about risk. No, every period matters. Better to adjust if can measure risk.

> ... most of what we do in terms of portfolio theory and models of risk and expected return works for Mandelbrot's stable distribution class, as well as for the normal distribution.... **For passive investors, none of this matters, beyond being aware that outlier returns are more common than would be expected if return distributions were normal.**
>
> — Eugene Fama, Nobel Prize recipient in Economics, 2013.

Can **most** investors hold have given future consumption promises to family?

8.6 *Fact 6*

Prices of put options are like "insurance". Predictive markets: Poon and Granger (2003) options best estimate.

Generally: Three types of options; see Figure 5.

(1) Out-of-the-money put options protect you against very large losses. The higher their price the larger the left tail.
(2) At-the-money (ATM) options benefit from both large and small moves. Their price can tell you about the distribution of small moves (volatility) (e.g., VIX).
(3) Out-of-the-money call options are "lotto" tickets on the large gains. The higher their price the larger the right tails.

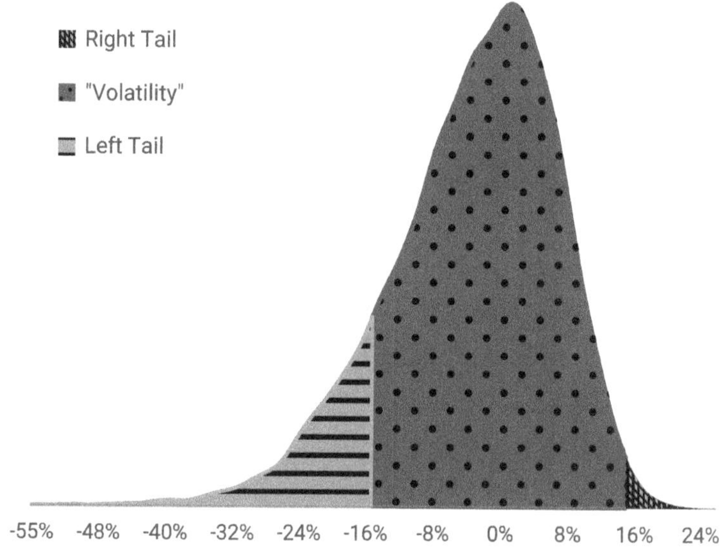

Figure 5: Hypothetical Outcome Distribution.

9. Measuring Tail Risk Using Market Prices

WAZE: Crowd-sourcing information from option prices; see Figure 6. Market prices impound information: Efficient market.

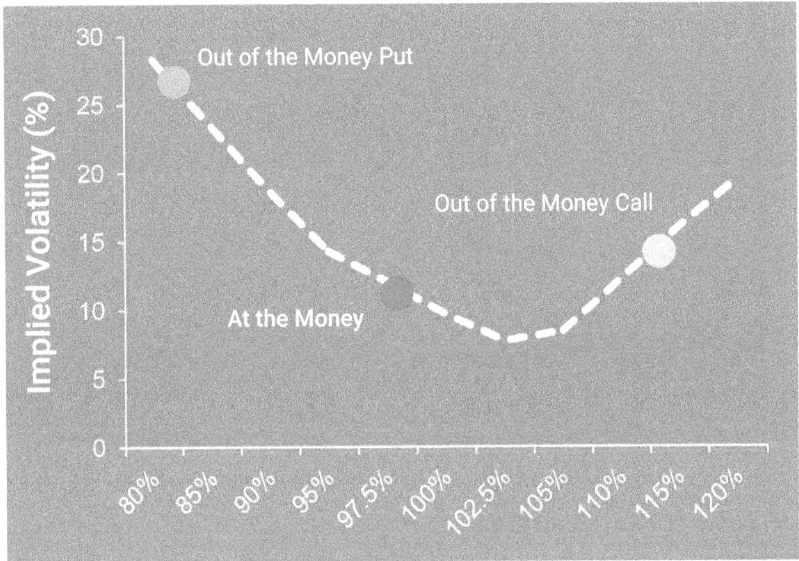

Figure 6: Moneyness of 3-month options.

10. Tail Gains/Losses from Opiton Prices

Combine the distributions. Stitch conditionals together to build unconditional arbitrage free distributions. Following Breeden-Litzenberger, Figlewski, and others; see Figures 7, 8, and 9.

Arbitrage free distributions of returns.

Historically, forecasting returns with accuracy has shown to be futile.... Risk Management is a more productive path of managing risk to improve compound returns.

Target the following *outcomes* to improve the shape of the distribution.

- Reduce risk of drawdown (left tails).
- Participate in rising markets (right tails, skewness).

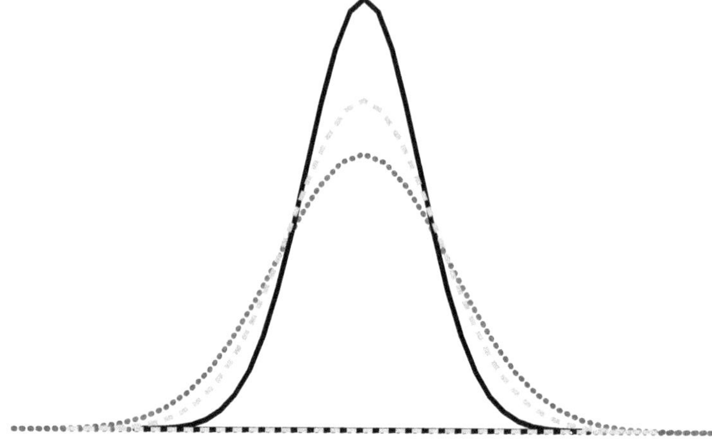

Figure 7: Future returns (3-month) of underlying assets.

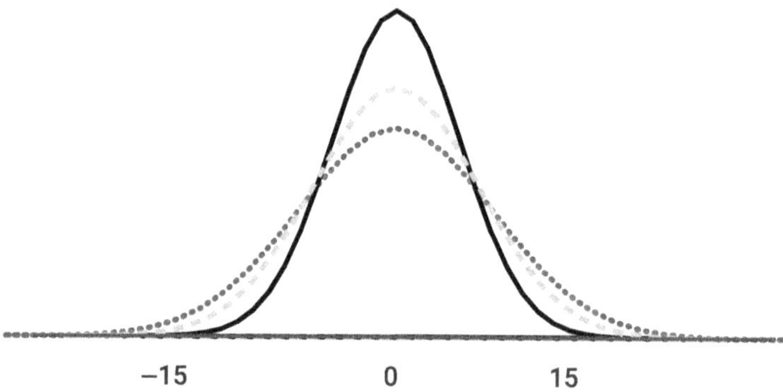

Figure 8: Future (3-month) returns of underlying assets (%).

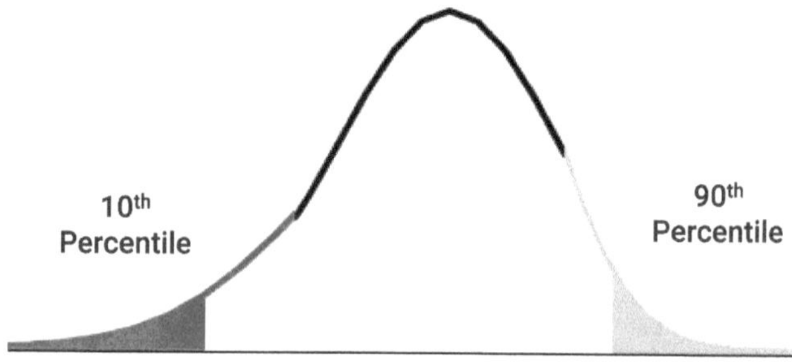

Figure 9: Future (3-month) returns of underlying assets.

11. Enhancing Compound Returns Through Dynamic Risk Management (1996–2015)

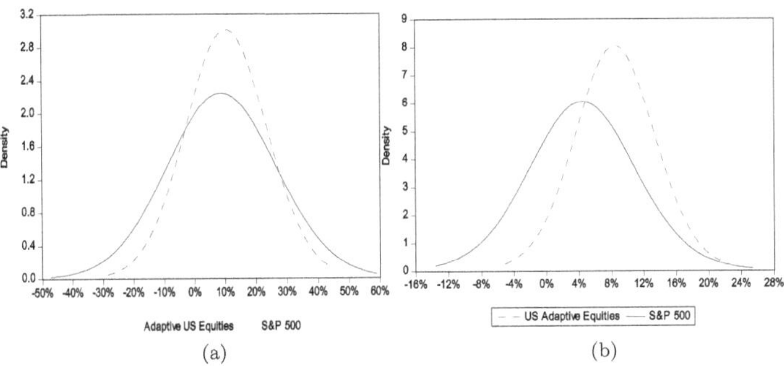

Figure 10: (a) Distribution of 1 year simulated (annual) compound returns. (b) Distribution of 5 year simulated annualized compound returns.

Risk managed S&P 500 (1996–2015) using Option Price risk information. (Could be ACWI or CSI 300, etc.) Global 60/40: 60% MSCI All Country World Index/40% Bloomberg Barclays Global Aggregate Index in red. Bootstrap results: Dashed line distribution is risk managed using option pricing information: Red is standard 60%/40%; see Figure 10.

12. Using Option Prices to Forecast Risk Changing Risk Proactively

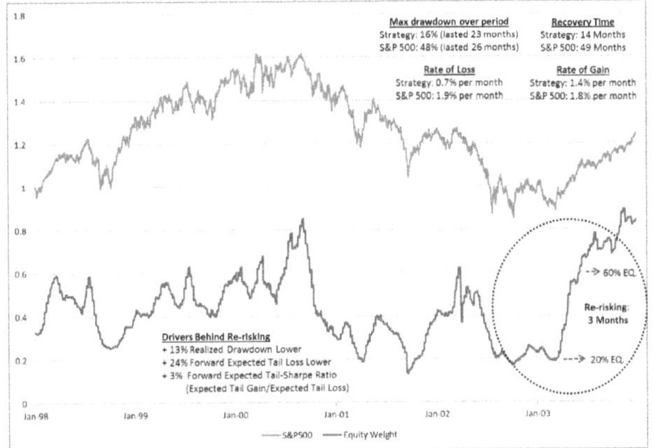

Figure 11: Internet Bubble/Bust.

Option prices can be used to manage risk proactively; see Figure 11.

13. Using Option Prices to Measure Risk

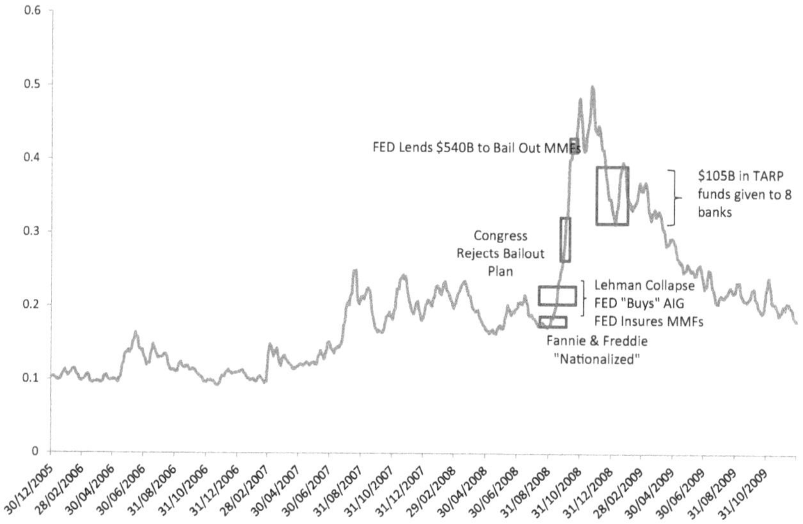

Figure 12: Implied expected tail loss to S&P 500.

Implied expected tail loss to S&P 500 is shown in Figure 12.

14. Uncertainty of the Distribution of Returns

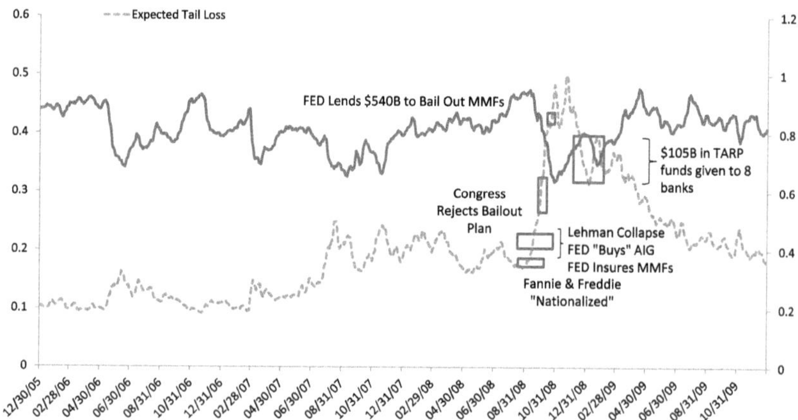

Figure 13: Implied left and right tail risks to S&P 500.

Implied left and right tail risks to S&P 500 are shown in Figure 13.

15. Adaptive Strategy — Pre and Post "2008" Crisis

Positive skewness achieved by de-risking and re-risking proactively and quickly; see Figure 14.

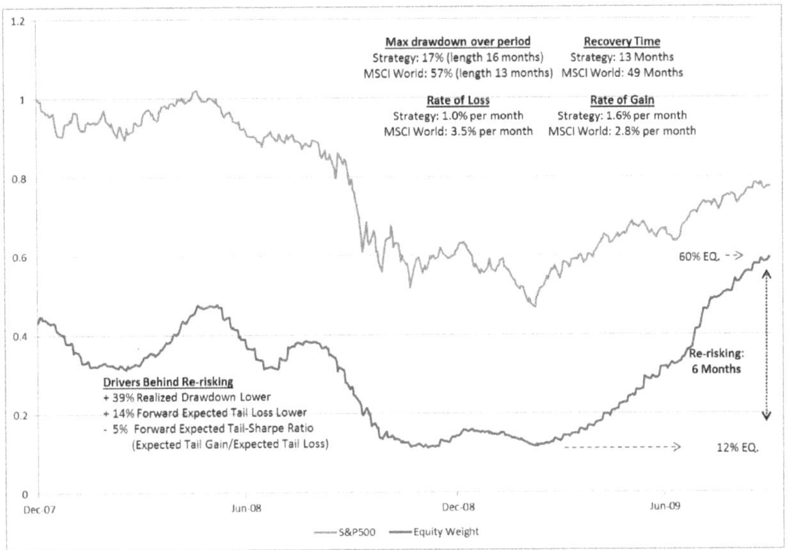

Figure 14: Great financial crisis and recovery.

16. Issues

- Macro prudential models of risk using market prices.
- Market prices vs historical moldening and scanarios.
- Understanding the effects of intermediation and liquidity provision through the prices of risk.
- Option prices have a important role in providing the market's estimates of risk.

https://doi.org/10.1142/9789811259142_0002

Chapter 2

How Good is Black–Scholes–Merton, Really?*

P. Wilmott

Burnham Court, Moscow Road London, UK

mathmax@cix.co.uk

Abstract

I consider the Black–Scholes–Merton option-pricing model from several angles, including personal, technical and, most importantly, from the perspective of a paradigm-shifting mathematical formula.

Keywords: Black–Scholes–Merton, partial differential equation, hedging, volatility, mathematical biology.

1. Introduction

A lot of people — including me — have spent a lot of time trying to improve the Black–Scholes–Merton option-pricing model (BSM). How bad can it be to justify so many man hours' work? Pretty bad, I guess.

*This chapter was first presented at the enlightening and often frankly hilarious (for all the best reasons) *Options: 45 Years after the Publication of the Black Scholes Merton Model* conference in the Hebrew University Fintech Center, Jerusalem 4–5 December 2018. I would like to thank David Gershon for inviting me.

Let me describe some of the things I like and dislike about BSM. And then we'll look at some of the technical aspects of BSM. Maybe this will help to decide whether all that effort has been helpful.

2. Things I Like About BSM

There's a lot I like about BSM. Some of it is because of the changes it has made to the financial world, and some of it because of the changes it has made to *my* world.

Here are a few words about some of these reasons.

- **Without BSM there would not be so many financial instruments:** Having the model and similar models for other financial quantities has played a large part in the development of new products and even new markets. And having a method for eliminating or reducing risk has been of great benefit.
- **Stochastic calculus is now taught at undergraduate level:** In my day stochastic calculus was not emphasised, I have no idea in which subject they hid it. And for a mathematical modeler that was a big shame.
- **One can use many types of mathematics in this field:** In this respect it is different from many, more classical, subjects.
- **There still continue to be many avenues for research:** Even after all these years!
- **The mathematical tools one picks up can be used in many other subjects:** Again, it would have been nice if I'd known this earlier in my mathematics career.

3. Things I Don't Like About BSM

On the other hand, there are many things I am not too keen on …

- **Without BSM there would not be so many financial instruments:** The other side of the coin. There are definitely some instruments that the world could have done without. Naming no names.
- **There is too much stating the obvious in papers:** It's highly tedious having to read through the same pages and pages about

sigma algebras and filtration to find that there is only one paragraph of interest in a paper.

- **"Risk neutrality" gets abused:** By this I mean that people will say something like "We replace μ with r because of risk neutrality" even when risk neutrality is not relevant.
- **There are too many Masters in Quantitative Finance degrees:** And they churn out too many brainwashed students who really don't know as much as they think they do. In particular they come out of their degree thinking they are "mathematicians" because they know Ito's lemma.
- **Too many closed-form solutions:** Speaks for itself. But just to be certain, you wouldn't build an airplane using mathematical models chosen for tractability, would you?
- **Too many topics are trendy:** Calibration. Eugh. Insistence on no arbitrage, even though it's clearly nonsense. Arbitrage is everywhere otherwise we'd still all be living in caves.
- **Important topics are not trendy:** For example how to make money.
- **Most researchers don't have enough experience outside quantitative finance:** There is so much to modeling than stochastic calculus. As a trivial example, I can't believe that almost no one in finance knows what phase-plane analysis is. For several years now I have been recommending a book to all financial modelers, it's *Mathematical Biology* by Jim Murray [7].

Ok, so those are my personal feelings. But how good is BSM technically?

4. Technically Speaking

Here are a few of my thoughts and experiences. There are several aspects to how good BSM is. For example, how well does it cope with new contracts and markets? And how much does it need to be changed because assumptions are obviously wrong?

4.1 *Coping with new markets and contracts*

BSM copes very well with non-vanilla contracts. Digital options? Change the final condition for the PDE. Barrier options? Add a boundary condition for the PDE. American options? It's just the same PDE with an obstacle constraint.

What about something more exotic? Lookback options? An extra dimension but same PDE. Discretely sampled exotics? More dimensions but same PDE, you just need jump conditions.

The worst case is often that you just need to add an extra term to the BSM PDE to cope with path dependency.

And even then thanks to the whole BSM continuous-hedging argument and risk elimination you can always hit the problem with a Monte Carlo simulation, that's if you don't like PDEs.

Conclusion: BSM copes very well with new contracts.

What about other markets? It doesn't look so good here. If I had to give BSM a score for how good it is for options with equity underlyings it would be seven out of 10. For fixed income it would be three out of 10. And that's mainly because there isn't really an underlying with which to hedge. And that raises the ugly issues of market price of risk and calibration. Yeugh.

And for credit markets? Am I allowed to give negative marks?! 'nuff said.

4.2 *Dropping assumptions*

Moving on to the assumptions, which ones of them are wrong and how much does it matter?

The first bit of that is easy to answer, all of them. But the second part is harder. In some cases it's easy to drop the assumptions to change the model.

For example, adding dividends on the underlying can be quite a small change. Although it can also be interesting from a modeling perspective, changing dividends when the stock falls, you don't want negative stock prices. Anyway, it's usually the same BSM PDE.

Other assumptions are more problematic. Constant/Known volatility, continuous hedging, transaction costs, cost of short selling, etc.

Well, it's quite easy to modify BSM to allow for all of these. I won't go into any of the mathematics, but probably everything you need is contained in *PWOQF2* [2].

But in words

- **Different volatility model:** You can make the volatility a function of asset and time, doesn't change the PDE, just means no more closed-form solutions (see above comment). Make volatility uncertain by making it a function of gamma, and look at worst-case valuation. Or make volatility stochastic and introduce a second variable. These all add some numerical complexity to the problem but nothing fundamental changes.
- **Discrete hedging:** BSM assumes that you hedge continuously, which is obviously impossible. Hedging error can be large but does it matter? Yes, and no. The good news is that, *ceteris paribus*, it's zero on average. The bad news is that the distribution is very asymmetrical. I know people tend to go on a lot about fat tails, but when it comes to derivatives they miss the point. They should be looking at the tails of the *square* of the returns distribution. Then you'll see that a long gamma might lose you money far, far more often than you make it thanks to discrete hedging but that when you make it back it is with big moves in the underlying. But there is more good news. If you know how to hedge optimally then you don't need to hedge all that frequently to reduce risk dramatically. See Figure 1 and Ahn and Wilmott [2].

  To emphasise these points I have long recommended that any junior quant should be given on their first day on the job the simple task of hedging one vanilla option for just one day to see how different are theory and practice.
- **Transaction costs:** Cost of hedging is the reason why getting close to continuous hedging is not possible. And obviously these costs don't average out to zero. But from a mathematical modeling perspective they are particularly interesting because transaction cost models tend to modify the BSM PDE by adding a new, nonlinear gamma-dependent term. So even if the cost of hedging is going to hurt you at least you can get a measure of the cost and it does lead to some interesting mathematics. (And if you are into fat tails then you should be looking at the tails of the *absolute value* of returns).
- **Cost of short selling:** A similar issue crops up when there is a cost of borrowing stock for short selling. Again this is something which leads to an interesting nonlinear mathematical problem, the coefficient of the drift term in the BSM PDE becomes a function of the first asset derivative.

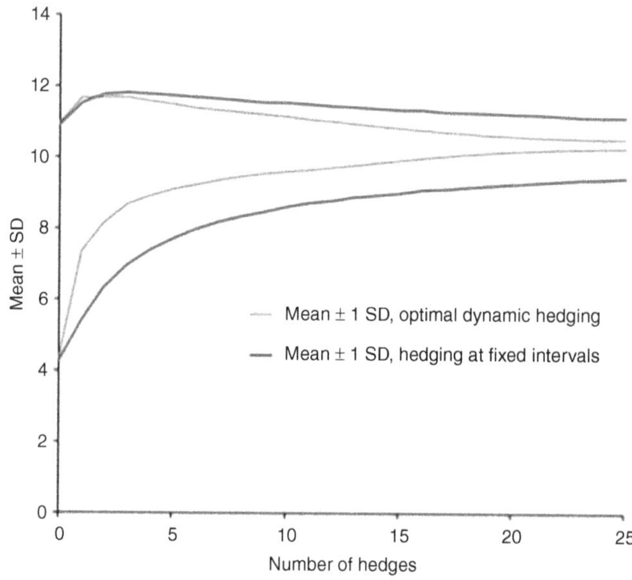

Figure 1: Risk reduction when hedging: Fixed time interval and optimally.

Ok, so BSM is pretty robust to contracts and assumptions, at least in the sense that the BSM PDE doesn't change too much when assumptions are dropped. But is it even necessary to change the basic BSM model? Is all the research justified?

4.3 *Robustness with respect to volatility*

Out of all the topics I've mentioned above the one that gets far and away the most research attention is volatility. So it's natural, surely, to ask whether that work is needed. Or is it just padding out academic CVs?!

In Ref. [3], we looked at how to make money (yes, really!) when options are incorrectly priced. The idea is simple, if you see a vanilla option with an implied volatility of 20% and you believe volatility will be 40% then buying the option and hedging should make you money. But do you hedge with a delta based on implied volatility or on forecast volatility? You'll have to read the paper to find out the answer, which really should be covered in Lecture 2 of any course on derivatives but isn't. However we also looked at what happens when you hedge with a volatility that is different from either of these two volatilities. This analysis was a proxy for studying the question "Does the volatility model matter?"

The results we found can be explained via Figure 2. In this figure are shown four profit curves, expected profit, standard deviation of profit, minimum and maximum profits, all plotted against hedging volatility.

Two things stand out from this. First, if there is any theoretical profit that can be made — here represented by the difference between implied and forecast volatilities — then this will obviously give a lot of leeway for hedging errors ("wrong" volatility, transaction costs, etc.). Second, even hedging with wildly wrong volatility the average profit is virtually unchanged. (A caveat would be that this wouldn't necessarily be true for very long-dated options or when asset drift is extreme).

In a nutshell, it is perhaps better to focus on having a nicely diversified portfolio of derivatives and then hedge reasonably well, rather than to obsess over calibration and valuation of every single

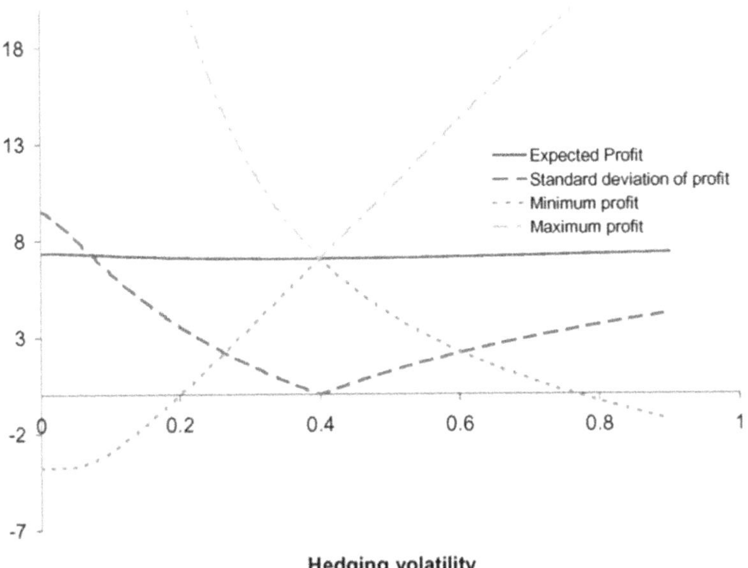

Figure 2: Expected profit, standard deviation of profit, minimum and maximum profits: $S = E = 100$, $\mu = 0$, $r = 0.1$, $D = 0$, $T = 1$, actual volatility is 40% and implied volatility is 20%.

contract to n decimal places. That is unless your whole financial career hinges on a single option, which would be unlikely and silly.

Similar and complementary results are found in the Ahn and Wilmott trilogy [2,4,5]. The conclusions are then that even in the presence of jumps just hedge exotic contracts with a few vanillas, and as often as possible with the underlying, but not so much that costs kill you. And you'll be fine.

But the mathematics isn't really the reason why BSM is so successful. To understand this one needs to not take the mathematics so seriously but take the position of what really matters. And I mean what really matters to everyone on the planet. And that is sales and marketing. For without those where would we be? Still in those caves again.

5. Derivations of BSM

Over the years [8] I have collected a dozen or more different derivations of BSM (equation, formulae...) using different types of mathematics. (I got a good start on this thanks to the eight derivations in Andreasen *et al.*, [6].) Some of those are simple to understand, some are easy to generalize, some give give insights, and some are quite frankly a waste of ink and paper. But only one derivation captures the most important features of BSM. It is a derivation that explains why it has been so successful while everything else in economics has been a flop.

6. The Marketing Department's Derivation

And now to one derivation, as weird as it is wonderful.

Imagine it's the start of 1973, with options about to be traded on the CBOE. These are, for those times, complex products. Traders need to be able to value them easily otherwise they will be ignored.

Now imagine a meeting between a mathematician and the marketing team of a bank.

Marketing: There could be big money in options. How are we going to get some of it?

Mathematician: We need a robust theoretical foundation for valuation.

Marketing: How long will this take?

Mathematician: A year or two. I'll need some PhD students. A postdoc. A budget for conferences. Add another couple of years for writing the paper, being refereed. Maybe five years.

Marketing: You've got one hour. We've got a reporter from the *Wall Street Journal* coming to interview you. Oh, and put on a decent pair of shoes.

The pressure is on. The mathematician has to come up with something, anything, in the next hour.

Let's think this through. How does a stock behave? Well, it sort of bounces around seemingly randomly. Good. What's a simple model for something bouncing around? I guess Brownian motion. And mathematically this is what? The Diffusion Equation. Back to the conversation.

Mathematician: The general form of the linear diffusion equation is [WRITING ON WHITEBOARD] $\frac{\partial V}{\partial t} + a\frac{\partial^2 V}{\partial S^2} + b\frac{\partial V}{\partial S} + cV = d$.

Marketing: Ok, I get the V, S and t. But what's with the as and bs? And that swirly d thing?

Mathematician: There are three unknown parameters, an unknown forcing term, and the swirly ds are partial derivatives.

Marketing: I dunno what half of that means, but you got to get rid of those unknowns.

To the whiteboard.... No payoff, no value. So get rid of that d. We now have

$$\frac{\partial V}{\partial t} + a\frac{\partial^2 V}{\partial S^2} + b\frac{\partial V}{\partial S} + cV = 0.$$

What simple contract should satisfy this? Cash/bond! So $V = e^{-r(T-t)}$ should be a solution. Plug it in and we find that $c = -r$. Now we have

$$\frac{\partial V}{\partial t} + a\frac{\partial^2 V}{\partial S^2} + b\frac{\partial V}{\partial S} - rV = 0.$$

Anything else? Stock! $V = S$ should be a solution. Plug that in and get $b = rS$. Now

$$\frac{\partial V}{\partial t} + a\frac{\partial^2 V}{\partial S^2} + rS\frac{\partial V}{\partial S} - rV = 0.$$

Mathematician: I've got it down to one parameter.
Marketing: Great work. But you still got those funny ds. And I need a number. You know, like \$10. How is this a number?
Mathematician: You have to solve the equation numerically. Maybe finite differences.
Marketing: Gimme a formula. You know, like Einstein.

Seeing the coefficient of the first S derivative is proportional to S suggests to our mathematician that going to a logarithmic S scale might help in finding a solution. But that has implications for the coefficient of the second-derivative coefficient. And so the mathematician figures the only way to get a nice formula is to have

$$a = \frac{1}{2}\sigma^2 S^2.$$

And so we have

$$\frac{\partial V}{\partial t} + \frac{1}{2}\sigma^2 S^2 \frac{\partial^2 V}{\partial S^2} + rS\frac{\partial V}{\partial S} - rV = 0.$$

And the formula for a call is then

$$SN(d_1) - E^{-r(T-t)}N(d_2),$$

where $d_1 = \cdots$. You know the rest.

The marketing man is ecstatic. He knows he can spin that σ:

- Too many unknown parameters? Who's got the time to figure them all out? The formula wouldn't get used.
- No unknown parameters? That's the very last thing we need. If everyone agrees on the value of something there'll be no market in it!

One parameter is absolutely perfect!

- An understandable formula.
- An equation mathematicians can solve for a variety of problems
- Only second-year undergraduate mathematics.
- *Crucially there is just the one parameter, a parameter that is just about understandable, that is almost measurable but not quite, is easy to interpret but also easy to argue over.*

From a business perspective it could not be better. I struggle to think of anything else in economics that is as useful and robust.

Marketing: You deserve a prize. Lemme buy you a beer. But first the shoes.

7. Conclusion

I hope you can see what I have concluded from my little journey here, a journey which encompasses and summarizes some of my own personal derivatives journey.

Even though the title of this chapter is meant to be ambiguous my conclusions aren't. To put it simply, Black–Scholes–Merton

- is very flexible.
- works well in most situations.
- is generally robust.

References

[1] Wilmott, P. (2006). *Paul Wilmott On Quantitative Finance*, 2nd Edition, John Wiley.
[2] Ahn, H. and Wilmott, P. (2009). A Note on Hedging: Restricted but Optimal Delta Hedging, Mean, Variance, Jumps, Stochastic Volatility, and Costs, *Wilmott*, June.
[3] Ahmad, R. and Wilmott, P. (2005). Which Free Lunch Would You Like Today, Sir? Delta Hedging, Volatility Arbitrage and Optimal Portfolios, *Wilmott*, November.
[4] Ahn, H. and Wilmott, P. (2007). Jump Diffusion, Mean and Variance: How to Dynamically Hedge, Statically Hedge and to Price, *Wilmott*, May.
[5] Ahn, H. and Wilmott, P. (2008). Dynamic Hedging is Dead! Long Live Static Hedging! *Wilmott*, January.
[6] Andreasen, J., Jensen, B., and Poulson, R. (1998). Eight valuation methods in financial mathematics: The Black–Scholes formula as an example. *Mathematical Scientist*, 23, 18–40.
[7] Murray, J.D. (2001). *Mathematical Biology*, Springer.
[8] Wilmott, P. (2007). *Frequently Asked Questions in Quantitative Finance*, 2nd Edition, John Wiley.

https://doi.org/10.1142/9789811259142_0003

Chapter 3

Probabilistic Interpretation of Black Implied Volatility

P. Carr[*,§], **L. Wu**[†,¶], **and Y. Zhang**[‡,||]

[*] *New York University, Tandon School of Engineering, New York*

[†] *Zicklin School of Business, Baruch College, City University of New York, New York*

[‡] *Rutgers Business School, The State University of New Jersey, New Jersey*

[§] *pc73@nyu.edu*

[¶] *Liuren.wu@baruch.cuny.edu*

[||] *yzhang@business.rutgers.edu*

Abstract

We use a market model of implied volatility to develop an implied volatility smile. The implied variance rate is given a simple probabilistic representation.

Keywords: Implied volatility, implied variance, implied volatility smile, probabilistic interpretation, financial interpretation.

1. Assumptions

For some fixed option maturity date T, assume zero interest rates and zero dividends for a stock over the time period $[0, T]$. Further assume that the spot price process S for the underlying stock is a strictly positive local martingale under a risk-neutral probability measure $\mathbb{Q}$. Under these conditions, the results of Merton can be used to produce arbitrage free ranges for option prices and hence implied volatilities.

The restrictions on option prices are fairly weak and simple to state geometrically. For example, call prices must lie between intrinsic value and stock price and must be decreasing convex functions of strike price. The corresponding restrictions on implied volatility are also fairly weak, but difficult to state geometrically. For example, implied volatility can be concave in strike price but not too concave.

In an effort to reduce the range of arbitrage-free implied volatilities and to simplify their geometric properties, dynamical restrictions on assets prices can be imposed. For example, one can further require that the stock price never jumps. In this case, there exists a bounded stochastic process σ_t, called the instantaneous volatility of the stock, such that S_t is the unique solution of the following stochastic differential equation (SDE):

$$dS_t = \sigma_t S_t dW_t, \quad t \geq 0,$$

where W is standard Brownian motion (SBM) under $\mathbb{Q}$. We allow the increments of σ to be correlated with those of S, but we do not directly specify the σ process. Instead, we will partially specify the risk-neutral dynamics of Black implied volatility (IV) across a continuum of positive strike prices at one fixed maturity date. When coupled with the stock price dynamics, the assumed dynamics for implied volatilities restrict the set of arbitrage-free dynamics for the option prices.

For our fixed maturity date T, let $I_t(K)$ be the Black IV at strike price $K > 0$. Suppose that three or more IV's are known. The goal is to develop an IV curve $I_t(K), K > 0$, which has five properties:

1. When exactly 3 IV's are given, $I_t(K), K > 0$ interpolates the three given implied volatilities.
2. For $K > 0$, $k \equiv \ln(K/S)$, and fixed S, $v_t^2(k) \equiv I_t^2(K)$ is a simple explicit algebraic function of k.
3. For $k \in \mathbb{R}$, $v_t^2(k)$ has a simple probabilistic interpretation.
4. $I_t(K), K > 0$ is free of factor-based arbitrage.
5. For $k \in \mathbb{R}$, $v_t^2(k)$ is testable, i.e., it can be rejected using data.

The third desired property is the main contribution of this chapter. The graph of implied variance rates across moneyness is well-defined, widely studied, but not well understood. In fact, the authors of this chapter have never seen a probabilistic interpretation of all implied variance rates at a given maturity. At-the money (ATM) IV has been argued to be the best forecast of subsequent realized volatility. A convex combination of all of the implied variance rates has been argued to be the best forecast of the subsequent realized variance rate. The slope and curvature of ATM IV in moneyness have been argued to say something about skewness and excess kurtosis of the underlying stock index. However, option traders and options quants would both be hard pressed to provide an exact direct probabilistic interpretation of each of the uncountably infinite number of IV's at each strike price and maturity date that an arbitrage-free model produces.

The fourth desired property of an IV smile is the absence of factor-based arbitrage. Factor-based arbitrage could potentially arise as a consequence of an assumption that all co-terminal IV's are continuous semi-martingales driven by a single factor called Z. Z is assumed to be an SBM under risk-neutral measure $\mathbb{Q}$. We let the increments of Z be correlated with those of S. The correlation coefficient is an unspecified stochastic process $\rho_t \in [-1, 1]$ at each $t \in [0, T]$. Thus all option prices are driven by just two SBM's W and Z. At each time $t \in [0, T]$, the IV's need to be set such that the instantaneous profit from setting up a delta-neutral and vega-neutral portfolio is always zero. Put another way, all option prices must be $\mathbb{Q}$ local martingales over $[0, T]$. For $t \in [0, T]$, let $C_t(K)$ be the market price of a call and for $S > 0, \sigma > 0$, let $B(S, \sigma, t)$ be the Black call pricing formula, where the strike price K and maturity date T are suppressed for notational simplicity:

$$
\begin{aligned}
B(S, \sigma, t) = SN &\left(\frac{\ell}{\sigma\sqrt{T-t}} + \frac{\sigma\sqrt{T-t}}{2} \right) \\
- KN &\left(\frac{\ell}{\sigma\sqrt{T-t}} - \frac{\sigma\sqrt{T-t}}{2} \right), \qquad (1)
\end{aligned}
$$

where $\ell \equiv -k = \ln(S/K)$ and as usual, $N(z) \equiv \int_{-\infty}^{z} \frac{e^{-\frac{x^2}{2}}}{\sqrt{2\pi}} dx$ is the standard normal cumulative distribution function. By the definition of IV, $C_t(K) = B(S_t, I_t(K), t)$ for all $t \in [0, T]$ and for all $K > 0$. Under $\mathbb{Q}$ and for fixed $T > 0$, we assume that $I_t(K)$ is the unique solution of the following SDE:

$$
dI_t(K) = \mu_t(I_t(K))I_t(K)dt + \omega_t I_t(K)dZ_t, \quad t \geq 0, \;\; K > 0. \qquad (2)
$$

The vol vol ω is assumed to be the same stochastic process across all strike prices $K > 0$. Like the instantaneous volatility σ_t and the correlation coefficient ρ_t, the vol vol ω_t does not depend on strike price $K > 0$ or the IV $I(K) > 0$. In contrast, the proportional risk-neutral drift coefficient μ_t is allowed to depend on $I_t(K)$, as indicated in (2). We assume that this dependence is such that IV's are always strictly positive, i.e., $I_t(K) > 0$ for all $t \in [0, T]$. For $t \in [0, T]$, let $\gamma_t \equiv \sigma_t \rho_t \omega_t$ be the stochastic process capturing the covariation rate between $\ln S$ and $\ln I$. Since σ_t, ρ_t, and ω_t do not depend on K or $I_t(K)$, neither does the covariation rate γ_t. The four stochastic processes $\sigma_t, \gamma_t, \omega_t$, and $\mu_t(I_t(K))$ are all unspecified, but must evolve in a way consistent with the dynamics in (2) governing IV. For example, the four stochastic processes should have continuous sample paths because the results of our analysis will imply that a jump in any of the 4 processes would induce a jump in each IV. Recall that we are assuming that we only observe three IV's. To obtain a unique IV smile, we will choose the proportional risk-neutral drift coefficient μ_t to depend on $\sigma_t, \gamma_t, \omega_t$, and $I_t(K)$ such that our arbitrage-free IV smile has a simple probabilistic interpretation. The particular restriction that we impose is

$$\mu_t(I_t(K)) = \frac{\omega_t^2}{8} I_t^2(K) - \frac{\gamma_t}{2}, \quad t \in [0, T], \ K > 0. \tag{3}$$

The fifth desired property is advantageous on the view that the input data is clean and that the option market is sometimes inefficient when quoting option prices or IV's. When the factor-arbitrage-free family of IV curves does not fit the market IV quotes, one can either take the view that our assumed factor model is wrong, or else take the view that market option prices are failing to reflect the actual known factor structure. On the latter view, portfolios can be formed which at least have positive risk-neutral drift and which at best also zero out the martingale components of P&L.

2. Probabilistic Interpretation of the Implied Variance Rate

In this section, we develop a probabilistic interpretation of the implied variance rate, I_t^2 at each positive strike price $K > 0$ and for fixed maturity date $T > 0$. In a world of zero interest rates and zero dividends before T, the implied variance rate $I_t^2(K), K > 0, t \in [0,T]$ can be defined as the ratio of negated theta to cash gamma. Cash gamma is defined as the product of the squared stock price, i.e., S^2 and the second partial derivative of the option price with respect to S, i.e., gamma. As its name suggests, cash gamma has the same units as the option premium, e.g, dollars. Cash gamma in the Black model depends on $S > 0, \sigma > 0$, and $t \in [0,T]$ as follows:

$$S^2 B_{11}(S,\sigma,t) = \frac{K}{\sigma\sqrt{T-t}} N'\left(\frac{\ell}{\sigma\sqrt{T-t}} - \frac{\sigma\sqrt{T-t}}{2}\right), \tag{4}$$

where subscripts of B denote partial derivatives and recall $\ell \equiv \ln(S/K)$. Still in the Black model, define cash vega as $\sigma B_2(S,\sigma,t)$, cash vanna as $S\sigma B_{12}(S,\sigma,t)$, and cash volga as $\sigma^2 B_{22}(S,\sigma,t)$. All 3 of these cash Greeks have the same units as cash gamma, e.g., dollars, and moreover are simply the product of a dimensionless quantity and cash gamma

$$\sigma B_2(S,\sigma,t) = \sigma^2(T-t) \times S^2 B_{11}(S,\sigma,t), \tag{5}$$

$$\sigma S B_{12}(S,\sigma,t) = (k + \sigma^2(T-t)/2) \times S^2 B_{11}(S,\sigma,t), \tag{6}$$

$$\sigma^2 B_{22}(S,\sigma,t) = (k^2 - \sigma^4(T-t)^2/4) \times S^2 B_{11}(S,\sigma,t). \tag{7}$$

Zeroing out the risk-neutral drift of a call's price implies that the call's theta must negate the P&L contributions from cash vega, cash gamma, cash vanna, and cash volga. As a result, the absence of factor arbitrage implies that negated theta is an inner product of a four vector of dynamical coefficients governing proportional changes, $[\mu_t(I_t(K)), \frac{\sigma_t^2}{2}, \gamma_t, \frac{\omega_t^2}{2}]^T$ with a four vector of cash greeks $[I_t(K)B_2, S_t^2 B_{11}, S_t I_t(K) B_{12}, I_t^2(K) B_{22}]^T$:

$$\begin{aligned} -B_3 = \mu_t(I_t(K)) I_t(K) B_2 + \frac{\sigma_t^2}{2} S_t^2 B_{11} + \gamma_t S_t I_t(K) B_{12} \\ + \frac{\omega_t^2}{2} I_t^2(K) B_{22}. \end{aligned} \tag{8}$$

Dividing (8) by halved cash gamma, $S^2 B_{11}/2 > 0$, and using (5) to (7) implies

$$\begin{aligned} I_t^2(K) = 2\mu_t(I_t(K)) I_t^2(K)(T-t) + \sigma_t^2 + 2\gamma_t(k + I_t^2(K)(T-t)/2) \\ + \omega_t^2(k^2 - I_t^4(K)(T-t)^2/4). \end{aligned} \tag{9}$$

Substituting (3) in (9) simplifies it so that the implied variance rate $v_t^2(k) \equiv I_t^2(K)$ is quadratic in $k \equiv \ln(K/S)$

$$v_t^2(k) = \sigma_t^2 + 2\gamma_t k + \omega_t^2 k^2, \quad k \in \mathbb{R}, \tag{10}$$

where recall $\gamma_t \equiv \sigma_t \rho_t \omega_t$. This is the simple explicit formula for the implied variance rate that we seek. Since $|\rho_t| \leq 1$, this quadratic function of k is positive everywhere. Since $\omega_t^2 > 0$ our quadratic function must open upwards. It follows that under our assumptions, IV's must smile everywhere and can never frown anywhere. When no dynamical restrictions are imposed, IV's can frown and yet be free of arbitrage. For example, if instead of our continuous time dynamics, the final stock price S_T takes only 2 values, $S_0 u$ for $u > 1$ and S_0/u, then the absence of arbitrage leads to negative curvature of IV in strike price K at every $K \in (S_0/u, S_0 u)$ (and for every $k \in (\ln S_0 - \ln u, \ln S_0 + \ln u)$. In contrast, under our market model, the absence of arbitrage leads positive curvature at every strike price and time.

Our arbitrage-free implied variance rate smile (10) can also be expressed as

$$v_t^2(k)dt = (\sigma_t dW_t + k\omega_t dZ_t)^2. \tag{11}$$

This is the simple probabilistic interpretation of the implied variance rate that we seek. When $k = 0$, then the ATM implied variance rate is the instantaneous variance rate of the underlying stock return, since $\frac{dS_t}{S_t} = \sigma_t dW_t$. When $k \neq 0$, then the away from-the-money Black implied variance rate is a variance rate, but not just of the underlying stock return. Rather the away from-the-money Black implied variance rate is the variance rate of a linear combination of the increments of the two SBM's W and Z driving option prices. The further away from the money the option is, the greater the weight $k\omega_t$ on the SBM Z driving IV's.

Our simple explicit formula (10) for the implied variance rate can be tested empirically, so long as three or more IV's are given by the market. When exactly 3 IV's are given, one can always fit a quadratic function to them. Notice that the implied variance rate in (10) is linear in σ_t^2, γ_t and ω_t^2. Given three option IV's, one can square them to get implied variance rates and then write (10) thrice with these squared values on its LHS. One can then invert the 3×3

linear system to get the coefficients σ_t^2, γ_t, and ω_t^2. From here, it is straightforward to get $\sigma_t = \sqrt{\sigma_t^2}$, $\omega_t = \sqrt{\omega_t^2}$, and $\rho_t = \frac{\gamma_t}{\sigma_t \omega_t}$.

When our assumptions are not necessarily holding, the quadratic function of k that one fits to 3 given IV quotes need not lie in the restricted class of quadratic functions described by (10). Consider an arbitrary quadratic function of moneyness k:

$$q(k) = c_0 + c_1 k + c_2 k^2, \quad k \in \mathbb{R},$$

where the constant coefficients c_0, c_1, and c_2 are real-valued. Our restricted class of quadratics imposes a single restriction on each of the three coefficients:

1. $c_0 > 0$
2. $c_2 > 0$
3. $\frac{c_1}{2\sqrt{c_0}\sqrt{c_2}} \in [-1, 1]$

The last condition can be interpreted as requiring that the implied correlation $\rho_t \in [-1, 1]$. Straightforward calculus shows that when the three restrictions above apply, the minimum of our quadratic function occurs at $k = -\frac{\sigma_t \rho_t}{\omega_t}$, i.e., the negative of the slope coefficient in a regression of $\ln S$ on $\ln I$. At this minimum, the implied variance rate $v_t^2(k)$ is positive if the three conditions are holding.

A rejection of any of these three restrictions can be regarded as either a failure of the (S, I) factor model or a failure of the options market maker. In the latter case, any of the three rejections leads to a factor-based arbitrage. Rejection of the first condition leads to vol trading. Rejection of the second condition leads to smile trading. Rejection of the third condition leads to skew trading.

To test this model when four or more IV's are given, one can do a linear regression at a fixed spot $S > 0$ and time $t \in [0, T]$, of the implied variance rates $v_t^2(k)$ on an intercept, on varying moneyness $k \equiv \ln(K/S)$, and on varying squared moneyness k^2. If the model works perfectly, then the R^2 from this linear regression should be 100%. Moreover, the above three conditions on the coefficients c_0, c_1, and c_2 must be always respected.

When three or more IV quotes are given by the market, a further test of the factor model is to see if the three coefficients produced by the quadratic fit or linear regression capture the realized variance of returns on the underlying, the realized covariation of percentages changes in stock price and any IV, and finally the realized variance of percentage changes in (all co-terminal) IV's.

3. Financial Interpretations of the Implied Variance Rate

In this section, we provide two financial interpretations of the implied variance rate. The first uses a dynamic trading strategy in a call option with a fixed strike price. The second uses a dynamic trading strategy in an always ATM call option.

3.1 *Fixed strike price*

Consider the gains that arise from a dynamic trading strategy that always holds N_t^c calls, delta-hedged with futures. This strategy is not self-financing, but a trivial extension of the portfolio can be forced to be self-financing by introducing a riskless asset, which has zero return by assumption. The position in the riskless asset is used to both self-finance and carry the gains from the calls and futures through time, that are not carried by the call position itself. Let $gN_t^cC_t(K)$ denote the gain at time $t \in [0,T]$ from always holding the N_t^c delta-hedged calls. From Itô's formula and financial considerations, we have $gN_t^cC_t(K) = N_t^cB_2(S_t, I_t(K), t)I_t(K)\omega_t dZ_t$, since the arbitrage-free gains from any dynamic trading strategy must be a $\mathbb{Q}$ local martingale under zero interest rates, and the contributions from W have been delta-hedged away. Now suppose we set N_t^c to the ratio of moneyness to cash vega, i.e.,

$$N_t^c \equiv \frac{k}{I_t(K)B_2(S_t, I_t(K), t)}.$$

Then we have

$$gN_t^cC_t(K) = \frac{k}{I_t(K)B_2(S_t, I_t(K), t)} \times B_2(S_t, I_t(K), t)I_t(K)\omega_t dZ_t = k\omega_t dZ_t.$$

Suppose that an investor supplements the above dynamic trading strategy by furthermore raising the exposure to futures by one dollar.

This is equivalent to always keeping one dollar invested in the stock and financing this dynamic share holding via borrowing and lending. Let V_t be the value of the combined dynamic trading strategies at time $t \in [0, T]$. Then the gain from the overall dynamic trading strategy is

$$gV_t = \frac{dS_t}{S_t} + gN_t^c C_t(K) = \sigma_t dW_t + k\omega_t dZ_t.$$

Now recall from (11) that

$$v_t^2(k)dt = (\sigma_t dW_t + k\omega_t dZ_t)^2. \tag{12}$$

Thus, the implied variance rate $v_t^2(k)$ captures the rate at which the quadratic variation of the portfolio value grows through time

$$v_t^2(k)dt = \left(\frac{dS_t}{S_t} + gN_t^c C_t(K)\right)^2, \tag{13}$$

where $N_t^c \equiv \frac{k}{I_t(K)B_2(S_t, I_t(K), t)}$, $t \in [0, T]$. It is interesting to note that S_t is also the value at time $t \in [0, T]$ of a fixed strike call since $S_t = C_t(0)$ under our zero dividends assumption.

3.2 *Floating strike price*

Suppose that the strike price of a holding of one call is allowed to move through time. Letting K_t denote the strike price of the call held at time $t \in [0, T]$, the value of the call holding at time $t \in [0, T]$ is

$$\begin{aligned} B(S_t, I_t(K_t), t; K_t, T) = {} & S_t N\left(\frac{\ln(K_t/S_t)}{I_t(K_t)\sqrt{T-t}} + \frac{I_t(K_t)\sqrt{T-t}}{2}\right) \\ & - K_t N\left(\frac{\ln(K_t/S_t)}{I_t(K_t)\sqrt{T-t}} \frac{I_t(K_t)\sqrt{T-t}}{2}\right). \end{aligned} \tag{14}$$

Although only one call is being held at each time $t \in [0, T]$, a dynamic trading strategy is needed to effect this holding as the strike moves through time. The cash vega of the unit holding of a call with a floating strike K_t is given by

$$I_t(K_t)B_2(S_t, I_t(K_t), t; K_t, T) = I_t(K_t)K_t\sqrt{T-t}N'\left(\frac{\ln(K_t/S_t)}{I_t(K_t)\sqrt{T-t}} - \frac{I_t(K_t)\sqrt{T-t}}{2}\right). \quad (15)$$

Now consider the cash value and cash vega when $K_t = S_t$, so that the one call being held at each time $t \in [0, T]$ is always ATM. Let $A_t \equiv A(S_t, I_t(S_t), t; S_t, T)$ be the simpler special case of call value when $K_t = S_t$

$$A_t = A(S_t, I_t(S_t), t; S_t, T) = S_t\left[N\left(\frac{I_t(S_t)\sqrt{T-t}}{2}\right) - N\left(-\frac{I_t(S_t)\sqrt{T-t}}{2}\right)\right]. \quad (16)$$

The cash vega of an always ATM ($K_t = S_t$) call also simplifies to

$$I_t(S_t)B_2(S_t, I_t(S_t), t; S_t, T) = I_t(S_t)S_t\sqrt{T-t}N' \times\left(-\frac{I_t(S_t)\sqrt{T-t}}{2}\right). \quad (17)$$

Consider the gains from always holding one ATM call which is also delta hedged

$$gA_t = A_2(S_t, I_t(S_t), t; S_t, T)I_t(S_t)\omega_t dZ_t, \quad t \in [0, T]. \quad (18)$$

If we change the scale of the holdings from one to the reciprocal of cash vega, then

$$\frac{gA_t}{A_2(S_t, I_t(S_t), t; S_t, T)I_t(S_t)} = \omega_t dZ_t, \quad t \in [0, T]. \quad (19)$$

Suppose we wish to financially interpret the implied variance rate $v_t^2(k)$ of an option with moneyness $k = \ln(K/S)$. Consider the gains that arise from keeping one dollar in stock and holding the ratio of moneyness k to ATM cash vega in always ATM calls. Thus, the implied variance rate $v_t^2(k)$ captures the rate at which the quadratic variation of this portfolio value grows through time

$$v_t^2(k)dt = \left(\frac{dS_t}{S_t} + k\frac{gA_t}{A_2(S_t, I_t(S_t), t; S_t, T)I_t(S_t)}\right)^2, \quad t \in [0, T]. \quad (20)$$

4. Approximation for Short Maturity Options

It is well known that in the Black model, the value of an ATM call is roughly proportional to its IV, especially at short maturities. As a result, the cash vega of an ATM call is well approximated by its cash value. Hence, the quantity $\frac{gA_t}{A_2(S_t,I_t(S_t),t;S_t,T)I_t(S_t)}$ in (20) can be approximated by the return $\frac{gA_t}{A_t}$ from always keeping one dollar in an always ATM call. In fact, when the always ATM call is always delta-hedged, the hedge portfolio return can be shown to be

$$\frac{gA_t}{A_t} = e^{-I_t^2(S_t)(T-t)/8}\omega_t dZ_t, \quad t \in [0,T]. \tag{21}$$

Suppose that the total ATM implied variance remaining, $I_t^2(S_t)$ $(T-t)$, is small, either because the ATM implied variance rate $I_t^2(S_t)$ is small, or the time to maturity, $T-t$, is small, or both. Then from (21), we have $\frac{gA_t}{A_t} \approx \omega_t dZ_t$, and hence from (20)

$$v_t^2(k)dt \approx \left(\frac{dS_t}{S_t} + k\frac{gA_t}{A_t}\right)^2, \quad t \in [0,T]. \tag{22}$$

In words, the implied variance rate at time $t \in [0,T]$ of an option with moneyness $k \equiv \ln(K/S_t)$ is approximately the rate at which the quadratic variation of a portfolio's value is growing at t, where the portfolio has k times as many dollars invested in always ATM calls as it has in the underlying stock. The approximation error approaches zero as the time to maturity decreases.

5. Empirical Tests of the Implied Variance Rate Formula

In this section, we use S&P 500 index options of various maturities to provide an empirical test of our results. The sample is from 1996 to 2017, comprising 5,537 trading days. For each of the 5,537 trading days and for each maturity, there were more than 3 strike prices so a cross sectional linear regression was run. Over the 5,537 trading days, we have a total of 73,097 cross-sectional linear regressions, about 13 maturities per day.

Using this data we express our findings using six figures (Figures 1–6) and three tables (Tables 1–3). Figures 1–3 show the

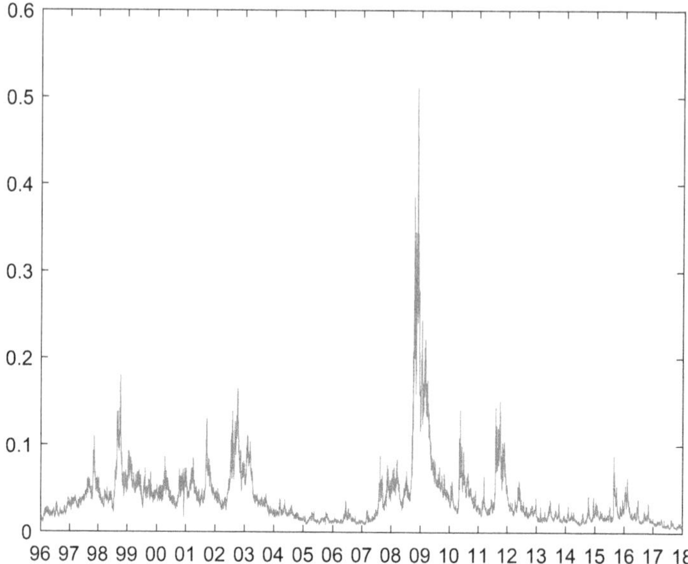

Figure 1: Time-series of σ^2. This figure plots the time-series of estimated σ^2 using S&P 500 index options with 30 to 90 days until expiration. The sample is from 1996 to 2017.

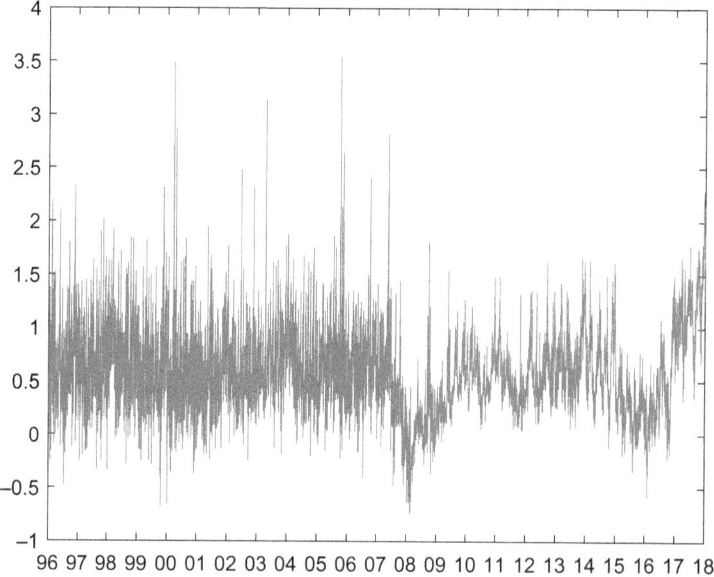

Figure 2: Time-series of ω^2. This figure plots the time-series of estimated ω^2 using S&P 500 index options with 30 to 90 days until expiration. The sample is from 1996 to 2017.

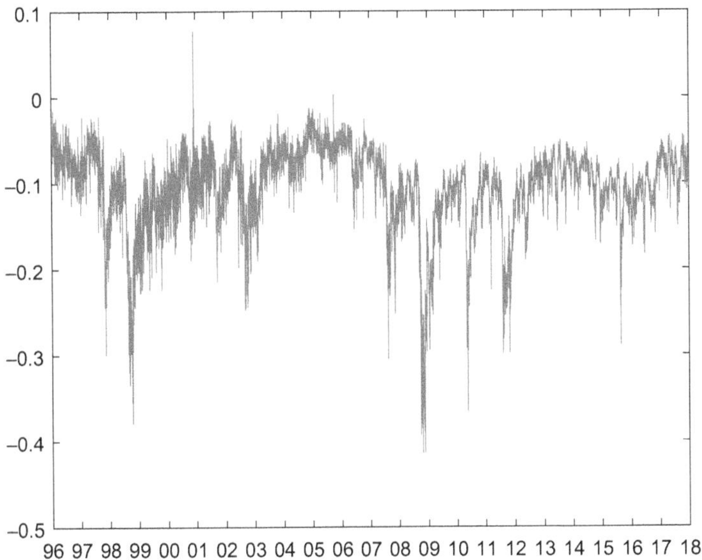

Figure 3: Time-series of γ. This figure plots the time-series of estimated γ using S&P 500 index options with 30 to 90 days until expiration. The sample is from 1996 to 2017.

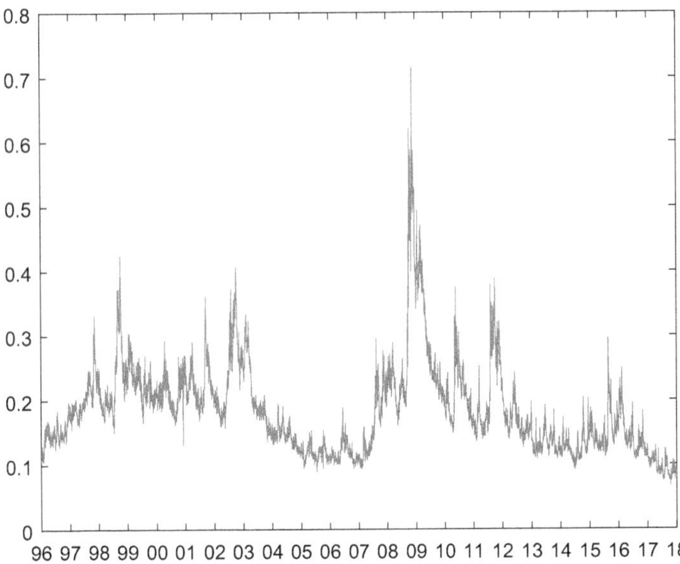

Figure 4: Time-series of σ. This figure plots the time-series of estimated σ using S&P 500 index options with 30 to 90 days until expiration. The sample is from 1996 to 2017.

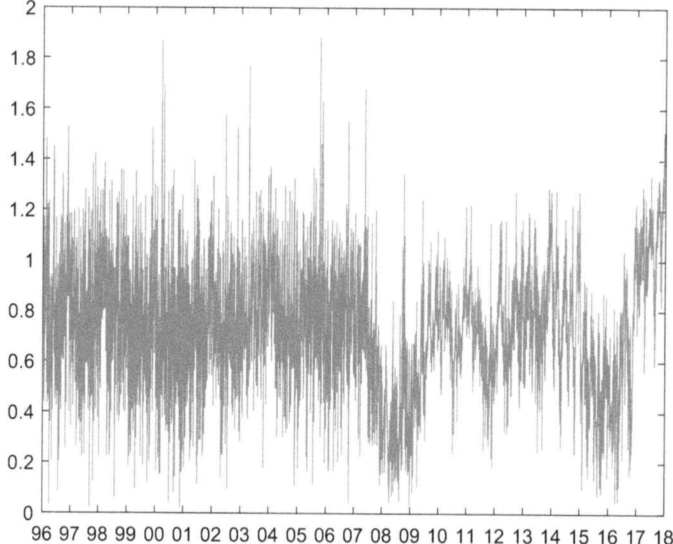

Figure 5: Time-series of ω. This figure plots the time-series of estimated ω using S&P 500 index options with 30 to 90 days until expiration. Days with negative estimated ω^2 are excluded, which is about 5.6% of the sample. The sample is from 1996 to 2017.

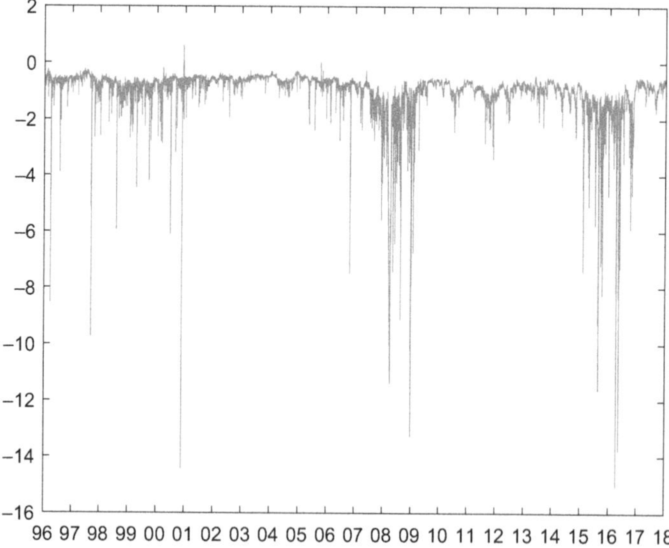

Figure 6: Time-series of ρ. This figure plots the time-series of implied ρ, $\rho = \frac{\gamma_t}{\sigma_t \omega_t}$, using S&P 500 index options with 30 to 90 days until expiration. The sample is from 1996 to 2017.

Table 1: Fitting the implied variance rate with a constant.

Percentage	Maturity	Intercept	R^2	Adj R^2	N
Panel A: Distribution of Regression Results					
1	9	0.007	0.000	0.000	7
2.5	11	0.009	0.000	0.000	9
25	51	0.023	0.000	0.000	17
50	136	0.036	0.000	0.000	25
75	319	0.053	0.000	0.000	37
97.5	785	0.125	0.000	0.000	76
99	912	0.160	0.000	0.000	88
Percentage	Maturity	Intercept	R^2	Adj R^2	N
Panel B: Median Regression Results for Each Maturity					
1m	18	0.020	0.000	0.000	26
3m	57	0.028	0.000	0.000	40
6m	128	0.035	0.000	0.000	20
9m	226	0.040	0.000	0.000	22
12m	316	0.042	0.000	0.000	24
2y	525	0.043	0.000	0.000	23
3y	851	0.047	0.000	0.000	36

Note: This table shows the daily regressions results of regressing the implied variance rate on a constant. The Black model predicts this fit would be perfect. The regressions are performed using co-terminal S&P 500 index options. Panel A shows the distribution of option maturity, coefficients, goodness-of-fit, and number of observations per maturity. Panel B shows the median coefficients, goodness-of-fit, and number of observations each maturity. The sample is from 1996 to 2017.

time series of the 3 slope coefficients in a linear regression on intercept, $2k$, and k^2. The intercept is always positive, as predicted by the model. Moreover, spikes in the intercept occur at known times of high volatility, suggesting the intercept is an alternative to VIX^2 as a forecast of the subsequent realized variance rate of returns on S&P 500. The slope coefficient on k^2 is positive on 94% of the observations, as predicted by the model. The 6% of the observations for which the slope coefficient on k^2 is negative are days and maturities for which the least squares fit is a frown. At such times, either

Table 2: Regressions of implied variance on moneyness.

Perecntage	Maturity (days)	Intercept	k	k^2	R^2	Adj R^2	N
Panel A: Distribution of Regression Results							
1	9	0.005	−0.598	−0.504	0.950	0.941	7
2.5	11	0.007	−0.455	−0.103	0.982	0.979	9
25	51	0.018	−0.203	0.044	0.998	0.998	17
50	136	0.029	−0.142	0.132	0.999	0.999	25
75	319	0.046	−0.099	0.486	1.000	0.999	37
97.5	785	0.122	−0.048	4.534	1.000	1.000	76
99	912	0.157	−0.040	7.280	1.000	1.000	88
Perecntage	Maturity (days)	Intercept	k	k^2	R^2	Adj R^2	N
Panel B: Median Regression Results for Each Maturity							
1m	18	0.016	−0.248	1.852	0.998	0.998	26
3m	57	0.022	−0.195	0.477	0.999	0.999	40
6m	128	0.028	−0.157	0.188	0.999	0.999	20
9m	226	0.034	−0.125	0.099	0.999	0.999	22
12m	316	0.035	−0.109	0.064	0.999	0.999	24
2y	525	0.037	−0.084	0.031	0.999	0.999	23
3y	851	0.039	−0.073	0.010	0.999	0.999	36

Note: This table shows the daily regressions results using specification as in equation (10). The regressions are performed using co-terminal S&P 500 index options. Panel A shows the distribution of option maturity, coefficients, goodness-of-fit, and number of observations per maturity. Panel B shows the median coefficients, goodness-of-fit, and number of observations each maturity. The sample is from 1996 to 2017.

Table 3: Frequency of ρ beyond the boundary.

	1m	3m	6m	9m	12m	2y	3y
Frequency of $\rho > 1$	0	0	0	0	0	0	0
Frequency of $\rho < -1$	0.145	0.248	0.375	0.498	0.592	0.699	0.914

Note: This table shows the frequency of the implied ρ larger than 1 or lower than −1, violating the boundary for correlation, for each maturity. The sample is from 1996 to 2017.

the factor model is unsupported or else a smile trade is available. Further empirical work on the profitability of such a smile trade is required. Figure 3 shows that the implied covariation rate is almost always negative. This means that the ATM slope of the quadratic function is almost always negative. Figures 4 and 5 show the time series of the stock index volatility and the IV volatility, respectively. Notice that our approach can be used to provide a forecast of realized short-term volatility using as few as three strike prices. In contrast, the well known VIX methodology is not considered to be accurate with only three strike prices. As a result, the VIX methodology is not used for currency options where at most 5 strike prices are liquid at each maturity. Figure 6 shows the time series of the estimated correlation coefficient. The estimated correlation coefficient is below -1 around 25% of the time. This is evidence of either factor model mis-specification or a signal that skew trading would be profitable. Further empirical work on the profitability of such a skew trade is required.

Table 1 shows the daily cross-sectional linear regression results of regressing the implied variance rate on just a constant. The Black model predicts that this fit would be perfect. The R^2 is by construction zero. The second table shows that the adjustment to the Black model that we propose leads to R^2 on the order of 95%. While we believe that an alternative specification of risk-neutral IV dynamics can produce an even higher R^2, the existence of an alternative dynamical specification which retains a probabilistic interpretation for the factor arbitrage-free implied variance rate remains open. Panel A in Tables 1 and 2 reports the cumulative distribution of variables of interest across all of the 73,097 cross sectional linear regressions for each day and for each maturity date. The variables including days until expiration, regression coefficients, R^2, and number of observations. Each column is independent, i.e., a 1% cumulative distribution in days until expiration probably does not correspond to a 1% cumulative distribution in σ^2 or a 1% cumulative distribution in the number of observations. Panel B in Tables 1 and 2 reports the median of the variables of interest within each maturity bucket. For example, 1m denotes all options with time to maturity of less than 1 month and 3m denotes all options with time to maturity of less than 3 months, but longer than 1 month.

Finally, Table 3 separates out the instances in which implied correlation is outside $[-1, 1]$ into maturity buckets. The incidence of apparent factor-based arbitrage based on $\rho_t < -1$ clearly increases with time to maturity. If the reason for the slope of ATM IV in k being too negative is the absence of jumps in S, then the maturity pattern should be the opposite of what we observe in Table 2. Nonetheless, the clear pattern in maturity suggests that an IV at some given strike and maturity can be used to anchor an IV at the same strike and a nearby maturity.

6. Summary and Further Research

When three or more IV's are known at a given maturity, we develop an IV curve $I_t(K), K > 0$, which has five properties:

(1) When exactly 3 IV's are given, $I_t(K), K > 0$ interpolates the three given implied volatilities.
(2) For $K > 0$, $k \equiv \ln(K/S)$, and fixed S, $v_t^2(k) \equiv I_t^2(K)$ is a simple explicit algebraic function of k.
(3) For $k \in \mathbb{R}$, $v_t^2(k)$ has a simple probabilistic interpretation.
(4) $I_t(K), K > 0$ is free of factor-based arbitrage.
(5) For $k \in \mathbb{R}$, $v_t^2(k)$ is testable, i.e., it can be rejected using data.

Empirical tests of the restricted quadratic function show good support for two of the three restrictions. The third restriction was not always supported since the implied correlation was below negative one about 25% of the time. It is unclear at this time whether the resulting skew trade would be profitable in these instances. Further theoretical analysis and empirical research is required.

https://doi.org/10.1142/9789811259142_0004

Chapter 4

Probability-Free Models in Option Pricing: Statistically Indistinguishable Dynamics and Historical vs Implied Volatility*

D. Brigo

Department of Mathematics, Imperial College, London

Abstract

We investigate whether it is possible to formulate option pricing and hedging models without using probability. We present a model that is consistent with two notions of volatility: a historical volatility consistent with statistical analysis, and an implied volatility consistent with options priced with the model. The latter will be also the quadratic variation of the model, a pathwise property. This first result, originally presented in [10,11], is then connected with the recent work of Armstrong *et al.* [1,2], where using rough paths theory it is shown that implied volatility is associated with a purely pathwise lift of the stock dynamics involving no probability and no semimartingale theory in particular, leading to option models without probability. Finally, an intermediate result by Bender *et al.* [5] is recalled. Using semimartingale theory, Bender *et al.* showed that one could obtain option prices based only on the semimartingale quadratic variation of the model, a pathwise property, and highlighted the difference between historical and implied volatility. All three works confirm the idea that while historical volatility is a statistical quantity, implied volatility is a pathwise one. This leads to a 20 years

*This chapter was presented at the conference *Options: 45 Years after the Publication of the Black–Scholes–Merton Model*, Jerusalem, 4–5 December 2018.

mini-anniversary of pathwise pricing through 1998, 2008 and 2018, which is rather fitting for a talk presented at the conference for the 45 years of the Black, Scholes and Merton (BSM) option pricing paradigm.

Keywords: Historical volatility, implied volatility, statistically indistinguishable models, option pricing, rough paths theory, pathwise finance, pathwise option pricing.

1. The Initial Question: Statistical Estimation and Valuation

In this chapter, we focus initially on the following question. Take two models S and Y of stock price dynamics under the objective (or statistical/historical/physical) probability measure $\mathbb{P}$. Fix a discrete time trading grid, starting from time 0 and up to a final time $T > 0$, with time step Δ. Δ can be as small as needed but it has to be fixed in advance, at time 0. We then consider pricing options on the stock, according to either model S or Y, via the continuous time theory of Black, Scholes and Merton (BSM) [7,19] and subsequent extensions, especially by Harrison *et al.* [16,17]. Our question is the following. Can we find situations where S and Y are statistically very close or even indistinguishable (under $\mathbb{P}$), having very close laws in the Δ grid, but where they imply very different option prices? Prices will be computed as expectations of discounted cash flows under the pricing (or risk-neutral/martingale) measure $\mathbb{Q}$. If we do find such situations, can we do this in a constructive way, rather than just proving they exist?

2. Indistinguishable Models Leading to Different Option Prices

To answer this question, we begin with two different models S and Y. We take S as the BSM model, and we construct a second model Y whose marginal laws are the same as S.

2.1 *Matching margins*

Start from the BSM model for the stock price S given by

$$dS_t = \mu S_t dt + \bar{\sigma} S_t dW_t,$$

(abbreviated BSM$(\mu, \bar{\sigma})$) with initial condition $S_0 = s_0$ under the objective measure $\mathbb{P}$. Here W is a Brownian motion under $\mathbb{P}$, while $s_0 > 0$, μ and $\bar{\sigma} > 0$ are constants.

We then look for a process Y,

$$dY = u(Y, \ldots)dt + \sigma_t(Y_t)dW_t,$$

with local volatility σ and with the same margins as S, namely $p_{S_t} = p_{Y_t}$ for all $t \in [0, T]$. Here for a random variable X we denote by p_X its probability density function. To find Y, invert the Fokker–Planck (FP) equation for Y and find the drift u such that the FP equation for the density of Y has solution equal to p_{S_t}, namely the lognormal density of the original S.

This was done in Brigo and Mercurio [10,11] using previous results on diffusions with laws on exponential families [8,9].

We obtain the following model for Y. To avoid singularities of our model coefficient u near $t = 0$, we start with a regularization in a small interval $[0, \epsilon)$ that has the same dynamics as S, and then we move to the different dynamics from time $[\epsilon, T]$. We obtain

$$\begin{aligned} d\bar{Y}_t &= \mu \bar{Y}_t\, dt + \bar{\sigma}\bar{Y}_t dW_t, \quad 0 \le t < \epsilon, \;\; \bar{Y}_0 = s_0, \\ Y_t &= \bar{Y}_t \quad \text{for } t \in [0, \epsilon), \\ dY_t &= u_t^{\sigma}(Y_t, s_0, 0)dt + \sigma_t(Y_t)dW_t, \quad Y_\epsilon = \bar{Y}_{\epsilon^-}, \;\; \epsilon \le t \le T, \qquad (1) \\ u_t^{\sigma}(x, y, \alpha) &:= \frac{1}{2}\frac{\partial(\sigma_t^2)}{\partial x}(x) + \frac{1}{2}\frac{(\sigma_t(x))^2}{x}\left[\frac{\mu}{\bar{\sigma}^2} - \frac{3}{2} - \frac{1}{\bar{\sigma}^2(t-\alpha)}\ln\frac{x}{y}\right] \\ &\quad + \frac{x}{2(t-\alpha)}\left[\ln\frac{x}{y} - \frac{\frac{\mu}{\bar{\sigma}^2} - \frac{1}{2}}{2 - \frac{1}{2\bar{\sigma}^2(t-\alpha)}}\right]. \end{aligned}$$

We have introduced $\bar{Y}$ to avoid singularities in the drift coefficient of the stochastic differential equation (SDE) (1) near $t = 0$.

The process Y, if the related SDE has a solution that is regular enough and admits densities, has the same marginal distribution as BSM$(\mu, \bar{\sigma})$: $p_{S_t} = p_{Y_t}$ for all t. We will show a fundamental example where everything works fine in Section 2.3.

2.2 *Matching the whole law on a* Δ *grid*

For our purposes of statistical indistinguishability, the above Y is not enough. A further fundamental property of the BSM$(\mu, \bar{\sigma})$ model is that its log-returns satisfy

$$\ln \frac{S_{t+\delta}}{S_t} \sim \mathcal{N}\left((\mu - \frac{1}{2}\bar{\sigma}^2)\delta,\ \bar{\sigma}^2\delta\right), \quad \delta > 0,\ t \in [0, T-\delta].$$

Alternative models such as our Y above do not share this property because identity of the marginal laws alone does not suffice to ensure it. We need equality of second order laws or of transition densities.

To tackle this issue, we restrict the set of dates for which the log-return property must hold true. Modify the definition of Y so that, given $\mathcal{T}^\Delta := \{0, \Delta, 2\Delta, \ldots, N\Delta\}$, $\Delta = T/N$, $\Delta > \epsilon$, we have

$$\ln \frac{Y_{i\Delta}}{Y_{j\Delta}} \sim \mathcal{N}\left(\left(\mu - \frac{1}{2}\bar{\sigma}^2\right)(i-j)\Delta,\ \bar{\sigma}^2(i-j)\Delta\right), \quad i > j. \qquad (2)$$

Limiting such key property to a finite set of times is not so dramatic. Indeed, only discrete time samples are observed in practice, so that once the time instants are fixed, our process Y cannot be distinguished statistically from the Black–Scholes process S.

The new definition of Y we propose now, to match log returns distributions in grids, is still based on our earlier Y. However, we use the earlier Y process locally in each time interval $[(i-1)\Delta, i\Delta)$. In such interval we define iteratively the drift u^σ as in the earlier Y but we translate back the time-dependence of a time amount $(i-1)\Delta$, thus locally restoring the dynamics of the original result for margins starting from time 0, and we replace Y_0 with the final value of Y in the previous interval. We obtain, in each interval $[i\Delta, (i+1)\Delta)$:

$$\begin{aligned}
d\bar{Y}_t &= \mu \bar{Y}_t dt + \bar{\sigma}\bar{Y}_t dW_t, \quad t \in [i\Delta, i\Delta+\epsilon),\ \bar{Y}_{i\Delta} = Y_{i\Delta^-} \\
Y_t &= \bar{Y}_t \quad \text{for } t \in [i\Delta, i\Delta+\epsilon), \\
dY_t &= u_t^\sigma(Y_t, Y_{\alpha(t)}, \alpha(t))dt + \sigma_t(Y_t)dW_t, \quad t \in [i\Delta+\epsilon, (i+1)\Delta), \\
&\qquad Y_{i\Delta+\epsilon} = \bar{Y}_{i\Delta+\epsilon^-},
\end{aligned} \qquad (3)$$

where $\bar{Y}_0 = Y_0 = s_0$, $u_t^\sigma(x,y,\alpha)$ was defined in the earlier Y and $\alpha(t) = i\Delta$ for $t \in [i\Delta,\ (i+1)\Delta)$.

It is clear that the transition densities of S and Y satisfy $p_{Y_{(i+1)\Delta}|Y_{i\Delta}}(x;y) = p_{S_{(i+1)\Delta}|S_{i\Delta}}(x;y)$ by construction.

Note also that the new process Y is not a Markov process in $[0,T]$. However, it is a Markov process in all time instants of $\mathcal{T}^\Delta$ (Δ-Markovianity).

Finally, note that now the two models S (BSM$(\mu,\bar{\sigma})$) and Y are *statistically indistinguishable* in $\mathcal{T}^\Delta$ since there they share the same finite-dimensional distributions. Any statistician who tried to estimate the two models from data could not find a way to distinguish them. Before turning to option prices implied by the two indistinguishable models, we need to show that we have not produced an empty theory so far. In other terms, we need to give concrete examples of σ for which our framework works rigorously. Such a fundamental case is addressed in Section 2.3.

2.3 A fundamental case: $\sigma_t(y) = \nu y$

We take now $\sigma(Y) = \nu Y$, so that also the volatility of Y is of BSM type, but with constant ν instead of $\bar{\sigma}$. In this case the equation for u specializes to

$$u_t^\nu(y, y_\alpha, \alpha) = y\left[\tfrac{1}{4}(\nu^2 - \bar{\sigma}^2) + \frac{\mu}{2}\left(\frac{\nu^2}{\bar{\sigma}^2} + 1\right)\right] + \frac{y}{2(t-\alpha)}\left(1 - \frac{\nu^2}{\bar{\sigma}^2}\right)\ln\frac{y}{y_\alpha},$$

and in this fundamental case one can show that the SDE for Y has a unique strong solution [10,11].

Moreover, the change of measure that replaces the drift u with rY is well defined and regular, so that it is possible to change probability measure from $\mathbb{P}$ to the equivalent pricing measure $\mathbb{Q}$ for the model Y.

This is precisely what we are interested in, since changing measure leads to some quite interesting developments. Before turning to the change of measure, a final remark concerning the regularization in $[0,\epsilon)$ is in order.

2.4 A technical link with the rough volatility literature

As Y has the same margins as S, it has to be positive like S, so that $Y_t > 0$. Then take $Z_t^\epsilon := \ln Y_t$:

$$
\begin{aligned}
Z_t^\epsilon &= Z_{j\Delta}^\epsilon + (\mu - \frac{1}{2}\bar{\sigma}^2)(t - j\Delta) \\
&+ \begin{cases} \bar{\sigma}(W_t - W_{j\Delta}) \qquad \text{for } t \in [j\Delta, j\Delta + \epsilon), \\ \left(\frac{t-j\Delta}{\epsilon}\right)^{\beta/2}\left[\bar{\sigma}(W_{j\Delta+\epsilon} - W_{j\Delta}) + \nu \int_{j\Delta+\epsilon}^{t}\left(\frac{u-j\Delta}{\epsilon}\right)^{-\beta/2} dW_u\right] \\ \text{for } t \in [j\Delta + \epsilon, (j+1)\epsilon). \end{cases}
\end{aligned} \tag{4}
$$

Here $\beta = 1 - \frac{\nu^2}{\bar{\sigma}^2}$. In [10] we show that we can take $\epsilon \to 0$ in the regularization, obtaining a limit Z

$$
Z_t = Z_{j\Delta} + \left(\mu - \frac{\bar{\sigma}^2}{2}\right)(t - j\Delta) + \nu \int_{j\Delta}^{t} \left[\frac{t - j\Delta}{u - j\Delta}\right]^{\frac{\beta}{2}} dW_u,
$$
$$
t \in [j\Delta, (j+1)\Delta).
$$

This process is well defined since the integral in the right-hand side exists finite almost surely even though its integrand diverges when $u \to j\Delta^+$. The above equation can be better compared to the Black and Scholes process when written in differential form:

$$
\begin{aligned}
dZ_t &= (\mu - \frac{1}{2}\bar{\sigma}^2)\, dt + \frac{\beta}{2}(t - j\Delta)^{\beta/2-1}\left(\int_{j\Delta}^{t} (u - j\Delta)^{-\beta/2} dW_u\right)\nu\, dt \\
&+ \nu\, dW_t \quad t \in [j\Delta, (j+1)\Delta).
\end{aligned}
$$

The central term in the right-hand side is needed to have returns equal to the Black and Scholes process even after changing the volatility coefficient from $\bar{\sigma}$ to ν. More precisely, the central term is the correction needed so that the exponential of Z will simultaneously have returns equal to those of BSM$(\mu, \bar{\sigma})$ and volatility coefficient equal to ν. Note that this term goes to zero for $\bar{\sigma} = \nu$. It is this term that makes our process non-Markov outside the trading time grid.

Finally, we point out that for all $\epsilon > 0$ there exists a probability measure $\mathbb{Q}^\epsilon$ equivalent to $\mathbb{P}$ and such that Z^ϵ is a Brownian motion under $\mathbb{Q}^{\epsilon}$. As noted in [4], informally taking the limit for $\epsilon \downarrow 0$ in such change of measure yields a "market price of risk" for the discrepancy between historical and implied volatilities. Such market price of risk has two distinguished properties that have been important in the rough volatility literature, see, for example, [3]: small time behaviour proportional to $t^{-\gamma}$ for some $0 < \gamma < 1$, and rougher trajectories than semimartingale ones.

2.5 *Arbitrarily different option prices under indistinguishable models*

We now consider option pricing based on the models S and Y. We will assume that interest rates r are deterministic and constant in time.

Recall our two indistinguishable models under the measure $\mathbb{P}$, and see what happens when we change measure to $\mathbb{Q}$:

$$dS_t = \mu S_t dt + \bar{\sigma} S_t dW_t^{\mathbb{P}} \ \Delta - \text{indistinguishable from}$$
$$dY_t = u_t^{\nu} dt + \nu \ Y_t \ dW_t^{\mathbb{P}},$$

but changing measure to $\mathbb{Q}$

$$dS_t = r S_t dt + \bar{\sigma} S_t dW_t^{\mathbb{Q}} \text{ very different from}$$
$$dY_t^{\nu} = r Y_t^{\nu} dt + \nu \ Y_t \ dW_t^{\mathbb{Q}}.$$

No arbitrage conditions are reflected in the fact that changing measure to $\mathbb{Q}$ enforces the drift r. If we now price a call option with the $\mathbb{Q}$ expectation of the discounted payoff we have

$$\mathbb{E}^{\mathbb{Q}}[e^{-rT}(S_T - K)^+] = \text{Black–Scholes}(\bar{\sigma}),\ \mathbb{E}^{\mathbb{Q}}[e^{-rT}(Y_T - K)^+] = \text{Black–Scholes}(\nu),$$

where the remaining inputs of the Black and Scholes formula, namely s_0, r, T are the same for both cases. Since the indistinguishability holds for every ν, we can take $\nu \downarrow 0$ and $\nu \uparrow +\infty$. This way we find the following.

Statistically indistinguishable stock price models in the Δ time grid imply option prices so different to span the whole no arbitrage interval $[(S_0 - Ke^{-rT})^+, S_0]$.

Perhaps surprisingly, they span a range that is not related to Δ. Since models are equivalent in a Δ grid, one might have expected that by tightening Δ one might have had option prices in a narrower range. This is not the case.

Our result shows that conjugating discrete and continuous time modeling (e.g., statistics and option pricing) has to be done carefully and is subject to important assumptions.

3. Reconciling Historical and Implied Volatility with a Single Dynamics

What if what we have seen is a way to account consistently for *historical* and *implied* volatility? Indeed, it is known that option prices trade independently of the underlying stock price, and we have been able to construct a stock price process Y^{ν} whose marginal distribution and transition density depend on the volatility coefficient $\bar{\sigma}$ (historical volatility), whereas the corresponding option price only depends on the volatility coefficient ν (implied volatility). As a consequence, we can provide a consistent theoretical framework justifying the differences between historical and implied volatility that are commonly observed in real markets.

4. Possible Explanation of Arbitrary Option Prices?

Since probability and statistics have proven to be deceptive when working in discrete time under $\mathbb{P}$, we try now to remove probability and statistics from valuation. We will achieve this by using ideas from rough paths theory. Rough paths theory has been initiated and developed by many researchers over the years, here we recall briefly first Föllmer [13], who introduced a form of Itô calculus without probability. A more general theory was introduced and developed in Lyons [18], Davie [12], Gubinelli [15] and Friz among others, see, for example, [14] and references therein. Applying ideas from rough paths theory, and from [12,14,15] in particular, in Armstrong *et al.* [1,2] we manage to re-interpret the Black–Scholes formula and option pricing in a purely pathwise sense.

After writing [1], we found out that there had been earlier attempts to build a pathwise theory of option pricing.

Bender *et al.* [5] had formulated option pricing, in the framework of semimartingale theory, relying only on the quadratic variation of price trajectories, which is a *pathwise property*. In our work [1,2], the analysis is brought one step further by abandoning the semimartingale setting. Using Davie's rough differential equations and *rough brackets* (see [14]) we abandon probability theory altogether. This entails the definition of Gubinelli derivatives, which in the classical Black and Scholes' framework are Gamma sensitivities of the options. Although ignored in the most classical formulas for portfolio dynamics, they play an active role in the convergence of the integrals describing portfolio processes, when such convergence is analysed pathwise as in [1,2]. We should also say that besides [5], there had been earlier attempts at a pathwise theory of option pricing. Such attempts are based on the above-mentioned non-probabilistic approach to Itô calculus by Föllmer [13] and are given in Bick and Willinger [6], see also the more recent work of Schied and Voloshchenko [20]. These approaches do not emphasize the role of Gamma as a Gubinelli derivative nor do they hold under the generality of rough path theory. Indeed, Föllmer calculus has the caveat that the integrals depend upon the discrete-time approximating sequence, which precludes obtaining important robustness results we illustrate in [1,2]. To bypass this problem, in [1,2], we use an augmented version of delta-hedging where one also invests in volatility swaps to hedge the second-order part of the pricing signal. This produces a robust trading strategy but at the cost of introducing assumptions on the price of volatility swaps to guarantee our strategy is self-financing. Furthermore, the above-mentioned pathwise formulations require paths that can be as rough as semimartingales but not rougher, namely paths of of finite p-variation for all $p > 2$. Using Rough Path Theory, we can accommodate paths of finite p-variation with $2 < p < 3$, thus showing that delta hedging can be extended to a broader class of price signals.

We now go back to the statistically indistinguishable models S and Y above, implying arbitrarily different option prices. We connect them to our discussion of pathwise properties. Since the results from [1,2,5] suggest that option pricing ultimately depends only on pathwise features of price trajectories, it is with the lenses of pathwise analysis that we can distinguish the $\mathbb{P}$ dynamics of S and of

Y, by looking at their quadratic variation. While probability and statistics could not distinguish between S and Y, the difference is instead captured by this aspect of price trajectories.

Paraphrasing:

- Probability and Statistics do not allow one to distinguish between S and Y in $\mathcal{T}^{\Delta}$.
- Prices of options written on S and Y are different, so that option prices allow one to distinguish between S and Y.
- One then conjectures that option prices cannot be properties of S and Y based on probability or statistics. With prices being traditionally associated with expectations of discounted cash flows, this seems initially counterintuitive.
- References [1,2] show that, in general, option prices can be derived based only on purely pathwise properties, without using probability theory anywhere and in a robust way, with paths that than be rougher than semimartingales. References [5,6,20] had obtained similar results earlier but within semimartingale theory or within paths with the same regularity as semimartingales.
- In particular, in models S and Y option prices are completely specified by probability-free pathwise properties of S and Y, confirming the above conjecture.

We now summarize how, in [1,2], we were able to give a probability-free, and more specifically semimartingale-free derivation of option pricing based on purely pathwise properties.

4.1 *Rough paths and option pricing*

We denote in general $X_{s,t} = X_t - X_s$. Recall the BSM$(\mu, \bar{\sigma})$ model

$$dS_t = S_t[\mu\, dt + \bar{\sigma}\, dW_t^{\mathbb{P}}],\;\; dB_t = rB_t\, dt, \quad 0 \le t \le T,$$

where we also included the risk-free bank account numeraire B. In the classic theory of SDEs, the above equation is a short form for an integral equation

$$S_t - S_0 = \int_0^t \mu S_u\, du + \int_0^t \bar{\sigma} S_u\, dW_u.$$

The last integral is an Ito stochastic integral. If one tries to re-formulate the above equation without probability, one will not be able to use stochastic integrals any more, and as a result one will need to define the integral $\int_0^t \bar{\sigma} S_u dW_u$ pathwise. To do this, one will need to add information on the price trajectory in the form of a lift. One needs to provide the input

$$\mathbb{S}_{s,t} = \int_s^t S_{s,u}\, dS_u.$$

This is really an input and is not defined a priori based only on properties of S: if the signal S has finite p-variation for $2 < p < 3$, as in case of paths in the Black–Scholes model, it is too rough to define the above intergral as a Stiltjes or Young integral. One needs therefore to add $\mathbb{S}$ as an input. To understand why this is important, we now explain how introducing $\mathbb{S}$ helps in defining integrals of the type $\int F(S_r)dS_r$. Consider $\int F(S_r)dS_r$ and try to write it as a Young integral. Take Taylor expansion $F(S_r) \approx F(S_u) + DF(S_u)S_{u,r}$. The Young integral can be seen as approximating $F(S_r)$, in each $[u,t] \in \pi$ with the zeroth-order term $F(S_u)$, where π is the partition for the discrete sums approximating the integral, and $|\pi|$ is the mesh size. Hence

$$\int_0^T F(S_r)dS_r = \lim_{|\pi|\to 0} \sum_{[u,t]\in\pi} \int_u^t F(S_u)dS_r = \lim_{|\pi|\to 0} \sum_{[u,t]\in\pi} F(S_u)S_{u,t}.$$

The limit is on *all partitions* whose mesh size tends to zero. If we cannot use a Young integral because S is too rough, we can try a first order expansion for $F(S)$ rather than a zeroth order one.

$$\begin{aligned}\int_0^T F(S_r)d\mathbf{S}_r &= \lim_{|\pi|\to 0} \sum_{[u,t]\in\pi} \int_u^t \left(F(S_u) + DF(S_u)S_{u,r}\right) dS_r \\ &= \lim_{|\pi|\to 0} \sum_{[u,t]\in\pi} (F(S_u)S_{u,t} + DF(S_u)\boxed{\mathbb{S}_{u,t}}). \end{aligned} \tag{5}$$

This intuition can be made rigorous with the relevant norms and metrics, see, for example, [14].

What attracted initially the interest of the author, prompting the initial work that later lead to the collaboration culminating in [1,2], is the fact that in a delta-hedging context, one can write the replication condition for a call option in a Black–Scholes type model as

$$\int_0^T \Delta(r, S_r)dS_r + \int_0^T \eta(r, S_r)dB_r = (S_T - K)^+ - V_0,$$

where V_0 is the option price at time 0 and Δ and η are the amounts of stock and cash in the self-financing replicating strategy. In particular, Δ is the sensitivity of the option price with respect to its underlying S. The above integral $\int_0^T \Delta(r, S_r)dS_r$ is an Ito integral. If one tries to re-write the replication condition using a purely pathwise integral, using rough integration as in [14], it is possible to do so by recalling that, according to (5),

$$\int_0^T \Delta(r, S_r)d\mathbf{S}_r = \lim_{|\pi|\to 0} \sum_{[u,t]\in\pi} (\Delta(u, S_u)S_{u,t} + D_S\Delta(u, S_u)\mathbb{S}_{u,t}).$$

In an option pricing setting, the term $D_S\Delta(u, S_u) =: \Gamma(u, S_u)$ turns out to be the second derivative of the option price with respect to its underlying term, the so called gamma of the option. Hence

$$\lim_{|\pi|\to 0} \sum_{[u,t]\in\pi} (\Delta(u, S_u)S_{u,t} + \Gamma(u, S_u)\mathbb{S}_{u,t}) + \int_0^T \eta(r, S_r)dB_r$$
$$= (S_T - K)^+ - V_0.$$

This immediately prompted the author to notice that gamma played an explicit role in the replication condition when the condition is expressed using purely pathwise integrals rather than Ito integrals. Traders have been always using gamma as a correction term, but the above limit shows a fundamental role for gamma already at the level of the replication condition. On the contrary, the Ito integral $\int_0^T \Delta(r, S_r)dS_r$ can be written as a limit where gamma does not appear. The author further proposed to interpet the lift $\mathbb{S}$ as related to a non-standard covariance swap. This is discussed further in [1,2] and will be expanded in future work.

Let us now go back to BSM and [1,2]. Before proceeding further, we need to explain that in [1,2] we do not use really full rough path theory. We presented above a sketch of how one makes sense of the BSM SDE for S in a purely pathwise way, but in effect we never use the full SDE. Indeed, we noted in the discussion above that only the quadratic variation of the SDE solution matters in determining the option price. Similarly, in the no-semimartingales pathwise case, we will not really need the pathwise analogous of the BSM SDE, but just a no-semimartingale analogous of the quadratic variation. More precisely, take S_t as a path of finite p variation with $2<p<3$ (Brownian motion has finite q variation for all $q>2$, so S is potentially rougher than BSM). Consider the lifted $\mathbf{S}_t := (S_t, \mathbb{S}_t)$, where $\mathbb{S}$ is our input for $\int S\, dS$. From a technical point of view in [1,2] we work with *reduced* rough paths, obtained from the pair $(S, \mathbb{S})$ by considering only the symmetric part of $\mathbb{S}$ (this distinction is essential in the multi-dimensional case, although here we are discussing the one-dimensional setting). This is equivalently described by the rough bracket defined in

$$[\mathbf{S}]_{u,t} = S_{u,t}S_{u,t} - 2\ \mathbb{S}_{u,t}.$$

We refer again to [14] for the details, and point out the early work of Föllmer [13] in this regard.

If $[\mathbf{S}]_{u,t}$ is regular enough to define a measure of $[u,t]$ with density $a(S_t)$ with $a(x)$ also regular, then the classic partial differential equation for the option price is defined entirely in terms of the *purely pathwise* bracket $[\mathbf{S}]$, involving no probability theory and no semimartingale theory in particular. It follows that the option price itself will not depend on the probabilistic setting but only on path properties.

The purely pathwise property $[\mathbf{S}]_{u,t}$ takes the place of implied volatility in determining the option price as a path property rather than a statistical property. The latter would be associated with historical volatility as a standard deviation (statistics).

5. Conclusions: 20 Years of Pathwise Pricing

The first result we reported in this chapter is the result of Brigo and Mercurio [10], where the process Y had simultaneously historical volatility $\bar{\sigma}$ as a statistical property and implied volatility ν as a pathwise property (quadratic variation). This is consistent with the later result of Bender, Sottinen and Valkeila [5] who note:

> [...] the covariance structure of the stock returns is not relevant for option pricing, but the quadratic variation is. So, one should not be surprised if the historical and implied volatilities do not agree: the former is an estimate of the variance and the latter is an estimate of the [semimartingale] quadratic variation.

This has been further generalized in Armstrong *et al.* [1,2] where historical volatility is a statistics of the variance too, while implied volatility is associated with a pathwise lift involving no semimartingale theory and no probability.

It is perhaps fitting that this 20 years anniversary of pathwise pricing, running through 1998, 2008 and 2018, is occurring at the conference on the 45th anniversary of the BSM option pricing theory, even though we should not forget earlier contributions like [6] and other recent contributions such as [20].

Acknowledgments

The author is grateful to Claudio Bellani for checking the draft of the chapter and for many helpful suggestions and to Mikko Pakkanen for referring him to the work of Bender, Sottinen and Valkeila. The author is further grateful to the organizers and participants of the conference "Options: 45 Years after the Publication of the Black–Scholes–Merton Model", held in Jerusalem on 4–5 December 2018, for their comments and suggestions.

References

[1] Armstrong, J., Bellani, C., Brigo, D., and Cass, T. (2018). Gamma-controlled pathwise hedging in generalised Black–Scholes models. https://arxiv.org/abs/1808.09378v1. Updated in April 2019 with the title "Option pricing models without probability", https://arxiv.org/abs/1808.09378v2.

[2] Armstrong, J., Bellani, C., Brigo, D., and Cass, T. (2021). Option pricing models without probability: A rough paths approach. *Mathematical Finance*, 2021, 1–28. https://doi.org/10.1111/mafi.12308.

[3] Bayer, C., Friz, P. and Gatheral, J. (2016). Pricing under rough volatility. *Quantitative Finance*, 16(6), 1–18.

[4] Bellani, C. (2018). *Connection Between the Result in Brigo Mercurio (2000) and Rough Volatility.* Internal note, Imperial College London.

[5] Bender, C., Sottinen, T., and Valkeila, E. (2008). Pricing by hedging and no-arbitrage beyond semimartingales. *Finance and Stochastics*, 12(4), 441–468.

[6] Bick, A. and Willinger, W. (1994). Dynamic spanning without probabilities. *Processes and their Applications*, 50(2), 349–374.

[7] Black, F. and Scholes, M. (1973). The pricing of options and corporate liabilities. *The Journal of Political Economy*, 81(3), 637–654.

[8] Brigo, D. (1997). On nonlinear SDEs whose densities evolve in a finite–dimensional family. In: *Stochastic Differential and Difference Equations, Progress in Systems and Control Theory*, Vol. 23, Birkhäuser, Boston, pp. 11–19.

[9] Brigo, D (2000). On SDEs with marginal laws evolving in finite-dimensional exponential families, *Statistics and Probability Letters*, 49, 127–134.

[10] Brigo, D. and Mercurio, F. (1998). Discrete time vs continuous time stock price dynamics and implications for option pricing, arXiv.org and SSRN.com.

[11] Brigo, D. and Mercurio, F. (2000). Option pricing impact of alternative continuous time dynamics for discretely observed stock prices. *Finance & Stochastics*, 4, 147–159.

[12] Davie, A.M. (2007). Differential equations driven by rough paths: An approach via discrete approximation. *Applied Mathematics Research eXpress (AMRX)*, 2, 40.

[13] Föllmer, H. (1981). Calcul d'Ito sans probabilités. *Séminaire de probabilités de Strasbourg* 15, 143–150.

[14] Friz, P. and Hairer, M. (2015). *A Course on Rough Paths*, Springer Verlag, Heidelberg.

[15] Gubinelli, M. (2004). Controlling rough paths. *Journal of Function Analytics*, 216, 86–140.

[16] Harrison, J.M. and Kreps, D.M. (1979). Martingales and arbitrage in multiperiod securities markets, *Journal of Economic Theory*, 20(3), 381–408.

[17] Harrison, J.M. and Pliska, S.R. (1981). Martingales and stochastic integrals in the theory of continuous trading, *Stochastic Processes and their Applications*, 11(3), 215–260.

[18] Lyons, T.J. (1998). Differential equations driven by rough. *Revista Matemática Iberoamericana*, 14(2), 215–310.

[19] Merton, R.C. (1973). Theory of rational option pricing. *Bell Journal of Economics and Management Science*, 4(1), 141–183.

[20] Schied, A. and Voloshchenko, I. (2016). Pathwise no-arbitrage in a class of delta hedging strategies. *Probability, Uncertainty and Quantitative Risk*, 1(1), 1–25.

https://doi.org/10.1142/9789811259142_0005

Chapter 5

VIX and Derivatives*

M. Brenner
Stern School of Business, New York University
mb4@stern.nyu.edu

1. Outline

- **Background**
- **The (short) History of VIX**
- **VIX Graphs**
- **VIX Research**
- **VIX Derivatives**
- **VIX Methodology**
- **VIX Settlement and manipulation**
- **XIV & February 5, 2018**
- **Ambiguity**

2. Background

2.1 *Brief history of derivatives markets*

- Pre 1970 — Commodities (Agric, Metals)
- Post 1970 — Financials (FX, Debt, Equities, Credit)

*This chapter was presented at The Black–Scholes–Merton Opium 45 Years later, Jerusalem, December 4–5, 2018.

2.2 *Size of markets (notional)-global*

- Exchange traded — 80 tr $ (Notional)
- Equities(ET) — 20–30 tr $ (Notional) (e.g., Korea 100% of spot)
- Over the counter — 630 tr $ (NOTIONAL)

2.3 *OTC derivative markets*

- Interest rate derivatives — 450 tr $
- Foreign exchange derivatives — 80 tr $
- Credit default swaps — 30 tr $
- Others (Commodities, equities, credit) — 70 tr $
- **Spot Glob**: Equity markets (40–50 tr), Bond markets (80–90 tr)
- VIX: F&O (ET; 15 tr $), Variance swaps (?)

3. History of VIX

1973 Options trade on CBOE, B-S-M Model Published

1974 Implied volatility is derived (Latane & Rendlman)

1983 Index options start trading, priced by B-S-M, options are quoted/traded by IV (OEX)

1986 A VOL Index (SIGMA) and derivatives on it proposed by Brenner and Galai, Published in the *Financial Analysts Journal* in 1989 & *Journal of Derivatives* (1993)

1987 OCT. 19 Market crash before the CRASH options on Equities priced with a "smile" due to stochastic volatility, jumps, "fat" tails, etc.
After the CRASH the "skew" was "born" (world wide)
Due to the observed negative correlation of S and σ Other models suggested (e.g., CEV)

1990 Demand for volume derivatives (variance swaps discussed by market players)

1993 CBOE launches VIX (averages of Implied Volatilities)

2003 A Goldman-Sachs methodology model free (not B-S-M), use our basic approach, a 30 day forecast based on 2 maturities

1990s	There is an OTC market in Variance Swaps (Dominated by GS)
2004	Futures on VIX Start Trading — Low Volume
2006	Options on VIX Start Trading — Large Volume
2006	ETFs on VIX are Introduced (Based on Futures)
2009	Futures on VSTOXX (Eurex)
2012	Options on VSTOXX (Eurex)
2015	iVX based on SSE50 ETF (Shanghai Stock Exchange)
2012–2017	Large Volumes in Options, Futures, ETFS (VIX, VSTOXX)
2018	February 5, Two ETNs are wiped out (XIV closes down) VIX derivatives volumes are down 30% (March–October 2018)[2]

4. Futures/Options on VIX (CBOE) (Figures 1–6)

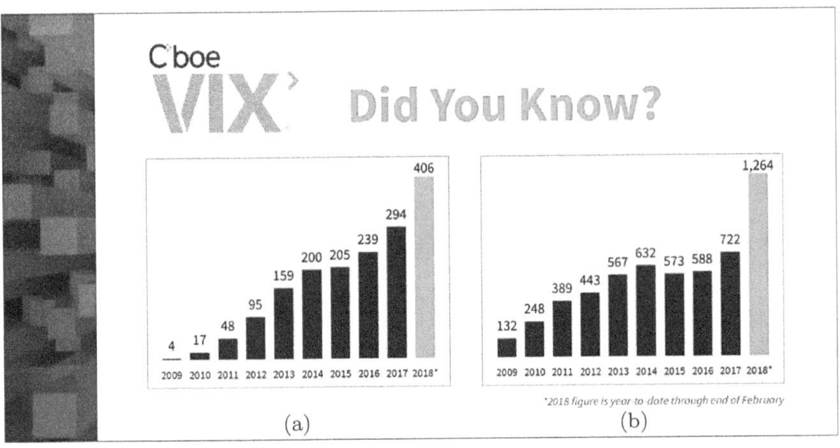

Figure 1: (a) VIX futures annual ADV (Contracts, in Thousands). (b) VIX options annual ADV (Contracts, in Thousands).

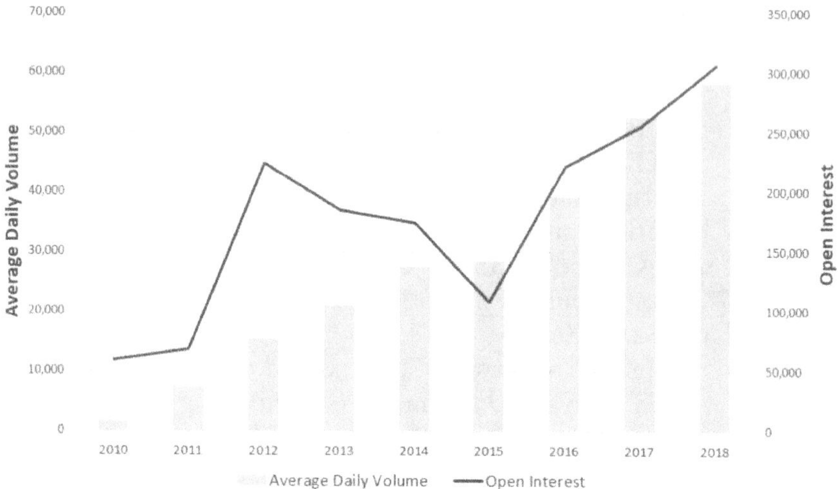

Figure 2: VSTOXX® volume & open interest (2010 to November 2018). *Source*: Eurex website. Futures only.

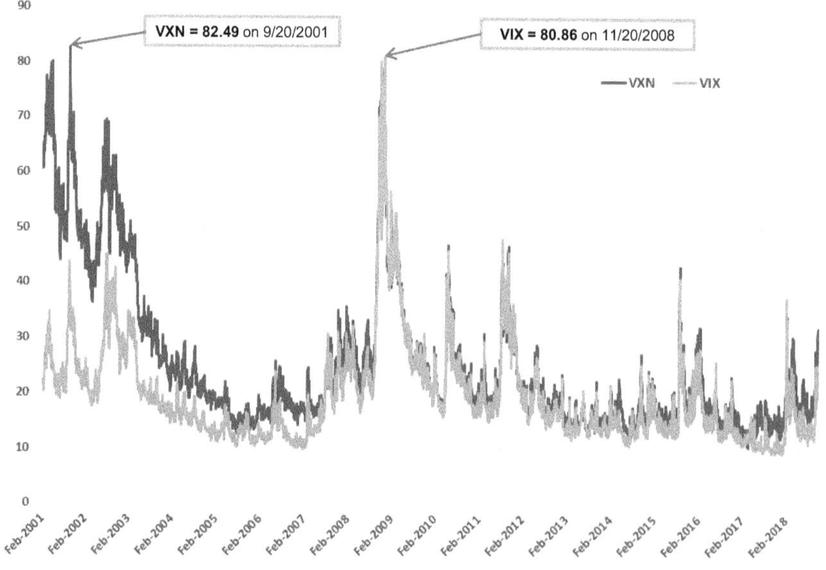

Figure 3: VIX and VXN (February 2001–November 2018).

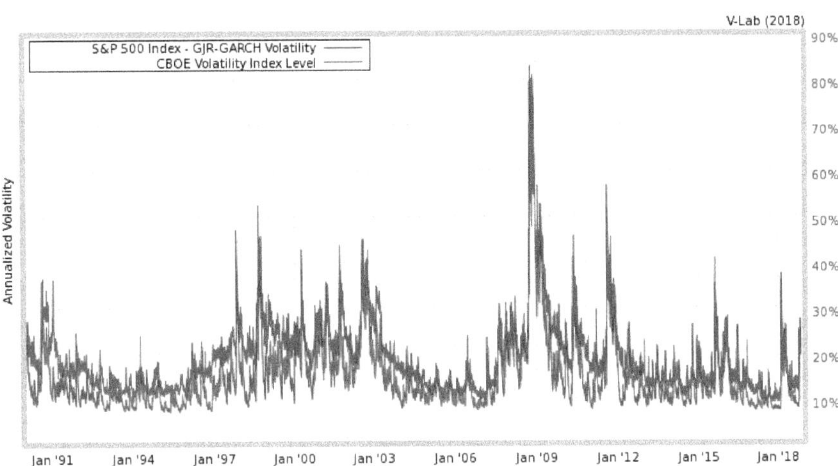

Figure 4: VIX vs GARCH volatility.

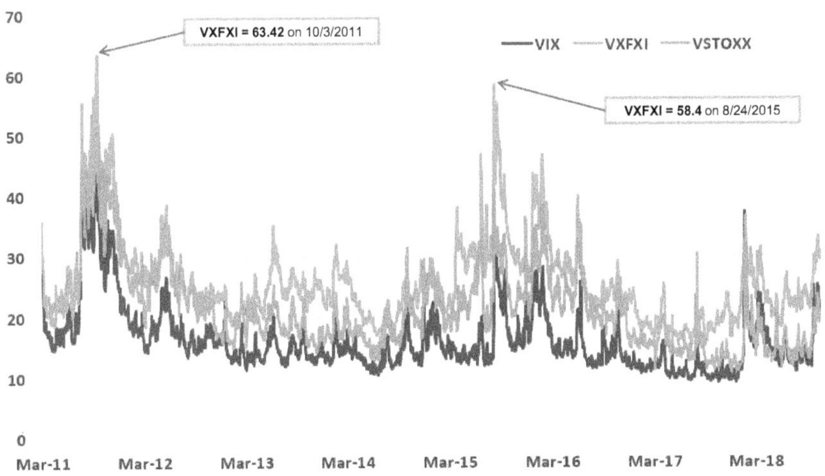

Figure 5: Volatility indexes in US (VIX), China (VXFXI), and Europe (VSTOXX).

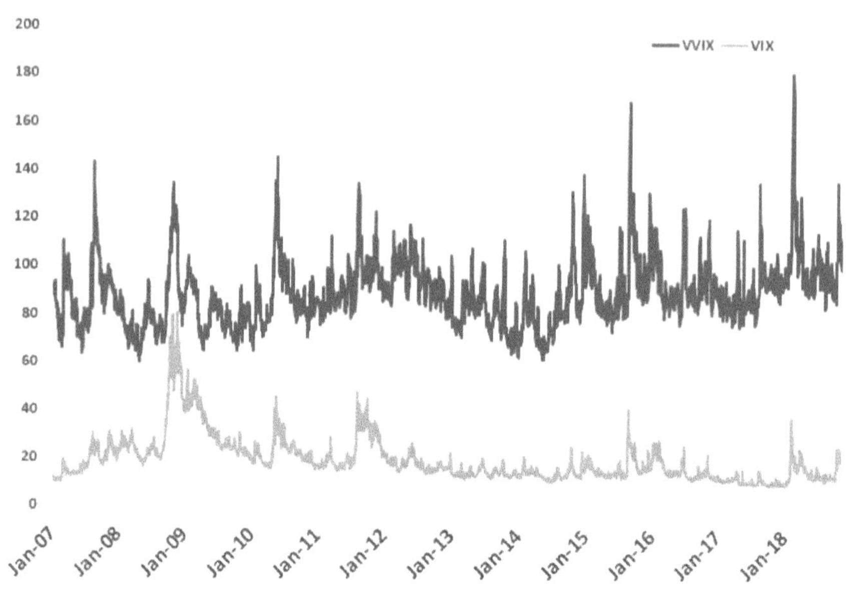

Figure 6: VIX and WIX.

5. VIX Research

In general, there are three strands of research related to VIX/VSTOXX:

(1) Using the index as a measure/proxy for market volatility in financial markets/real economy studies.
(2) Statistical and economic analysis of the index and it's relation to the realized variance and other parameters (e.g., trying to explain the variance premium (VP).
(3) Analyzing the VIX derivatives markets; futures, options, ETFs.

6. VIX Derivatives

Volatility Simple Regressions

$$\mathrm{RV} = a + b * \mathrm{HV} + c * \mathrm{VIX} + e$$

Using SPX & VIX data from January 1990 to November 2018

$$a = -0.507 \ (t = -0.56) \qquad b = 0.341 \ (t = 4.88)$$
$$c = 0.544(t = 6.55) \qquad R^2 = 60\%$$
$$\Delta\text{VIX} = a + b * \text{Returns} + e$$

Using daily SPX & VIX data from January 1990 to November 2018

$$a = 0.001(t = 2.16) \quad b = -4.15(t = -84.43) \quad R^2 = 50\%$$

7. VIX Methodology (in Brief)

- VIX is a 30 days IV index derived from S&P 500 index options using a weighted average of two near term maturities (today applied to many assets; e.g., oil, gold).
- VIX (model free GS): Using all OTM option prices weighted by the (inverse) square of the strike price (model "free").
- VXO (B-S-M methodology): CBOE: A weighted average IV of 8 ATM puts and calls of two near term options.
- A study by Carr and Wu (2006) shows a correlation of 98% between VIX and VXO.
- Brenner–Galai methodology: A strike and time weighted average of four ATM PRICES of call options. It is quasi "model free".

7.1 *VIX-Methodology (CBOE/GS)*

VIX is computed from the option quotes of all ATM & OTM Calls and Puts on the S&P (SPX) with a non-zero bid price using the following:

$$\sigma^2 = \frac{2}{T}\sum_i \frac{\Delta K_i}{K_i^2} e^{RT} Q(K_i) - \frac{1}{T}\left(\frac{F}{K_0} - 1\right)^2. \tag{1}$$

$Q(Ki)$ are option prices, F = futures price, T is 30, The volatility times 100 is the value of VIX(sq) level.

7.2 *VIX-Methodology (Brenner–Galai)*

$$C(T=30,K_1) = C_1^A(K_1)w + C_2^A(K_1)(1-w),$$

$$w = \frac{C^M(T=30,K_1) - C_2^M(K_1)}{C_1^M(K_1) - C_2^M(K_1)},$$

$$C^* = C(T=30,K_1)v + C(T=30,K_2)(1-v),$$

$$v = \frac{C^M(T=30,K=S) - C^M(T=30,K_2)}{C^M(T=30,K_1) - C^M(T=30,K_2)}.$$

VIX is obtained from converting C^* using B-S-M.

- Why volatility derivatives?
- Why volatility derivatives? Risk Management.
- Objective Hedging Volatility Risk (Vol of Vol).
- Dynamic Strategy (Delta Hedging) with plain vanilla options. (Cost unknown until end, high TC).
- Static Strategy derivatives on a volatility Index (Cost known, low TC).

VIX Derivatives (Observations)

- Options on VIX are among the three most active index options (call volume >> put volume).
- Futures & option on VIX; Big volumes big open interest.
- Bid-Ask spread wide by any measure (10–20% for ATM).
- Put-call ratio 0.6–0.8 (for SPX 1.2–1.4).
- Futures on realized variance; no volume.
- ETFs (VXX, others) trade on NASDAQ; large volume.
- Futures & options on VSTOXX (EUREX); large volume.
- Futures & options on iVX (SSE)???

VIX Derivatives (Pricing)

- Main issue: Pricing by no arbitrage, underlying is not traded (VIX options are European and cash settled).

- Futures: Replication of Var Swap is possible but not practical.
- Options: Same issue as VIX futures.
- How are the options priced? Of spot? Of futures?
- Does put-call-parity hold? Yes, *vis-a-vis* the futures.
- European markets; Options on VSTOXX futures, American options priced *vis-a-vis* the futures (Physical delivery).

8. VIX Settlement and Manipulation

Futures and options on VIX settle on the 3rd WED settlement index determind in opening auction of SPX options bids & offers can be placed/removed prices after settlement deviate from settlement study by Griffin and Shams (RFS 2017) evidence of attempted Manipulation in VIX:

(1) Large volume of SPX options on "S" day.
(2) Spikes in OTM (DOTM) options, more in puts.
(3) No spikes in spy (or OEX) options.

VSTOXX Different settlement, similar evidence.

9. February 5, 2018

- "Regulator Looks Into Alleged manipulation of VIX" (WSJ) February 5, 2018, what happened?
- XIV & SVXY short volatility "ETPs" lost 96% of NAV ($3.2 b) S&P 500 opening −0.8%, closing −4.1%.
- VIX 33% (+90%) February Fut 24% (+48%) March Fut 19.5 (+27%).
- The ETPs stop trading at 4:00 pm, Futures at 4:15.
- The ETPs bought 2.3 billion between 4:00 and 4:15 at higher prices (43% February Fut, 47% March Fut).
- Manipulation? How? 1. VIX Does not predict S&P2. February 5 is not an Expiration day.

10. Ambiguity (in Brief) (Figure 7)

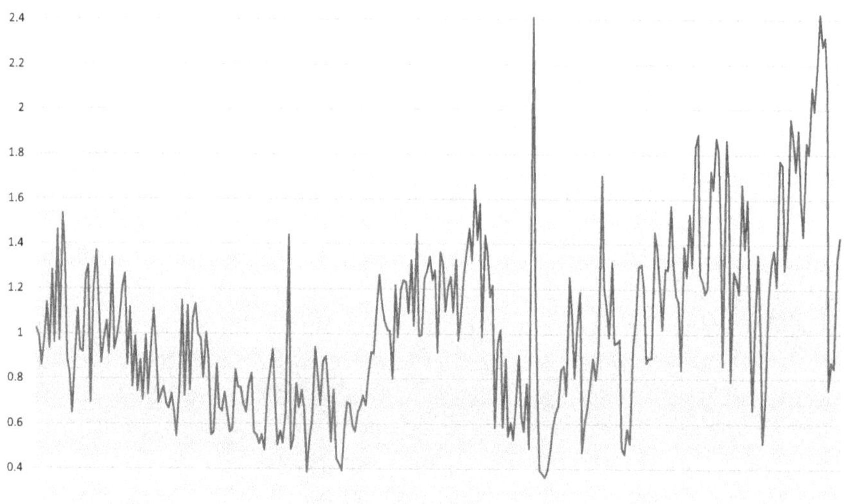

Figure 7: Ambiguity (June 30, 2018)

(1) What is Risk (known unknowns)?
Given probabilities with unknown outcomes.

(2) What is Ambiguity (unknown unknown)? (Knight's uncertainty). The Uncertainty of Probabilities that make up Risk.

(3) How is Ambiguity measured?
Ambiguity is measured by the "volatility" of the probabilities using real time market data.

https://doi.org/10.1142/9789811259142_0006

Chapter 6

Multivariate Fractional Brownian Motion and Generalizations of SABR Model

M. Musiela

OMI, University of Oxford,

Abstract

The SABR model is a generalization of the Constant Elasticity of Variance (CEV) model. It was introduced and analyzed by Hagan *et al.* [1]. Rapidly it has become the market standard for quoting cap and swaption volatilities thanks to the approximate formula for implied volatility which allowed real time risk management of large books of caps and swaptions. Later on it was also used in FX and equity markets.

The generalization introduces stochastic volatility to the CEV model. The volatility process is assumed to follow a geometric Brownian motion with zero drift, i.e., a martingale and no mean reversion. This assumption differs significantly from other models of stochastic volatility, where mean reversion is introduced.

In this chapter, another generalization of CEV and also of SABR is proposed. Namely, the Brownian motion defining the volatility process is replaced with a fractional Brownian motion. Such modification leads to the question of how one should define the dependence structure between the Brownian motion of the CEV model and the fractional Brownian motion of the new volatility process.

We link the choice to multivariate self-similarity property of stochastic drivers in the model.

Keywords: multivariate self-similarity, fractional Brownian motion, fractional SABR model

1. Introduction

SARB model is defined by the following dynamics

$$dX_t = X_t^{\beta} Y_t dW_t, \quad X_0 = x, \quad 0 \leq \beta \leq 1, \quad \alpha \geq 0,$$
$$dY_t = \alpha Y_t dZ_t, \quad Y_0 = \sigma, \quad d\langle W, Z\rangle_t = \rho dt, \quad |\rho| \leq 1,$$

where the vector process (W, Z) is a bivariate Brownian motion with the correlation ρ.

Many properties of SABR depend on its parameters. For instance, SABR reduces to CEV when the volatility of the volatility is equal to zero, i.e., when $\alpha = 0$. Another important property is linked to the level of β. If $\beta < \frac{1}{2}$ the process X hits 0 in finite time and the solution to the above equation may not be unique unless one specifies behavior at the boundary. For example, under the condition that when the process hits zero it stays there (it is absorbed at zero) the strong solution exists and is unique. Moreover, the strong solution exists and is unique when $\frac{1}{2} \leq \beta \leq 1$. The correlation ρ determines many properties of the above system. For instance, existence of moments of X, its uniform integrability, martingale vs local martingale property depend on it. Interested reader may consult Lyons and Musiela [2] for details.

There have been many attempts in the past to introduce fractional Brownian motion into financial models. Most of them, however, replaced the Brownian motion driving the asset dynamics, namely our process X, with a fractional Brownian motion. However, fractional Brownian motion is not a semimartingale and hence the standard stochastic calculus methodology breaks down. In fact one can show that such model specification leads to an arbitrage in the classical sense, see [3]. In our generalization, however, we replace the Brownian motion Z with a fractional Brownian motion. One could argue that there is no difference and we would face the same difficulties. This is because one needs to give sense to the equation for Y and to the bracket process $\langle \cdot, \cdot \rangle$. In this chapter, we address these issues.

We are not going to relay on the rough path theory to define the process Y. In our case there is no need to do it because the stochastic volatility of the SABR model can also be defined by the solution to the equation, namely, by

$$Y_t = \sigma \exp\left(\alpha Z_t - \frac{1}{2}\alpha^2 t\right).$$

This representation suggests a more general class of models, with the stochastic volatility process given by

$$Y_t = \sigma \exp\left(\alpha Z_t - \frac{1}{2}\alpha^2 \mathrm{Var} Z_t\right),$$

where the continuous bivariate process (W, Z) is Gaussian with zero mean and W is a Brownian motion. Define the covariance function of (W, Z) by

$$\Sigma(s,t) = \begin{pmatrix} s \wedge t & K(s,t) \\ K(s,t) & L(s,t) \end{pmatrix},$$

where $K(s,t) = EW_s Z_t$ and $L(s,t) = EZ_s Z_t$.

In order to define the bivariate Gaussian process (W, Z) one needs to choose the Gaussian process Z by choosing its covariance function $L(s,t)$ and to define the dependence structure between W and Z by choosing the function $K(s,t)$. The constraint is that the covariance function $\Sigma(s,t)$ is positive definite. The question is what arguments could be used to reduce the number of possible choices for the functions K and L.

2. Empirical Evidence

What empirical evidence one could use to motivate the choice of K?

Obviously, there will be an impact of the choice of the stochastic volatility process Y and of the dependence structure between the spot and its volatility on the movement of the spot. However, looking at the spot price movement alone may not be sufficient. The second source of information one could use is the joint evolution of the spot and of its stochastic volatility. The joint dynamics of X and Y determine the option prices.

We assume here that the option prices are quoted in terms of Black Scholes volatilities. It turns out that log-volatility behaves like a fractional Brownian motion with Hurst exponent H of the order

0.1 at any reasonable time scale, see [4]. Moreover, the at-the-money volatility skew is well approximated by a power function of time to expiry, see [5].

More precisely, if the implied Black Scholes volatility of an option as a function of log-moneyness k and time to expiration τ is denoted by

$$\sigma_{BS}(k, \tau),$$

the at-the-money (ATM) volatility skew is defined by

$$\psi(\tau) = \frac{\partial}{\partial k}\sigma_{BS}(k, \tau)\,|_{k=0}.$$

Empirical evidence suggests that for a large range of time to expiry

$$\psi(\tau) = C\tau^{-\alpha}, \quad 0 < \alpha < \frac{1}{2}.$$

Moreover, Fukasawa [6] shows that a model where log-volatility behaves like fractional Brownian Motion with Hurst exponent H generates ATM volatility skew of the form

$$\psi(\tau) = C\tau^{H-\frac{1}{2}}.$$

3. Fractional Brownian Motion

When the process Z is a fractional Brownian motion with Hurst exponent H the volatility process Y defined in the introduction takes the form

$$Y_t = \sigma \exp\left(\alpha Z_t - \frac{1}{2}\alpha^2 t^{2H}\right).$$

Let us recall that a fractional Brownian motion is a continuous zero mean Gaussian process with covariance function given by

$$EZ_s Z_t = \frac{1}{2}\left(|s|^{2H} + |t|^{2H} - |t-s|^{2H}\right), \quad s, \quad t > 0, \quad 0 < H < 1.$$

From now on we assume that the process Z is a fractional Brownian motion with Hurst exponent H.

In our model specification the process W is a Brownian motion and the process Z is a fractional Brownian Motion. The question remains how to specify the dependence structure between W and Z in order to define the bivariate Gaussian process (W, Z). The covariance function of the bivariate process (W, Z) is given by

$$\Sigma(s,t) = \begin{pmatrix} s \wedge t & K(s,t) \\ K(s,t) & \frac{1}{2}\left(|s|^{2H} + |t|^{2H} - |t-s|^{2H}\right) \end{pmatrix},$$

where $K(s,t) = EW_sZ_t$.

In order to define the dependence structure it is enough to choose the function $K(s,t)$. The only constraint is that the covariance function is $\Sigma(s,t)$ is positive definite. This is a rather week constraint and there are many possible choices one can make. For example, one can introduce another Brownian motion which is correlated with the one driving the asset dynamics and use it to define the process Z.

Indeed, it is well known that a fractional Brownian motion Z can be constructed with help of another Brownian motion, say, B. Interested reader can consult, for example, [7], for details.

We assume that the bivariate process (W, B) is a Brownian motion with correlation ρ or alternatively that $d\langle W, B\rangle_t = \rho dt$. One can define Z using B and Molchan–Golosov formula, namely,

$$Z_t = \int_0^t R(t,s)dB_s,$$

$$R(t,s) = c(H)F\left(\frac{1}{2} - H, H - \frac{1}{2}, \frac{1}{2} + H, \frac{s-t}{s}\right)(t-s)^{H-\frac{1}{2}},$$

$$c(H) = \sqrt{\frac{2H\Gamma\left(\frac{3}{2} - H\right)}{\Gamma\left(H + \frac{1}{2}\right)\Gamma(2-2H)}},$$

where F is Gauss hypergeometric function and Γ is the gamma function. It is easy to see that

$$K(s,t) = EW_sZ_t = \rho \int_0^{s\wedge t} R(t,u)du,$$

where $\rho = EW_1B_1$. Alternatively, one can define Z using Mandelbrot–Van Ness formula, where,

$$Z_t = \frac{1}{c_1(H)} \int_{-\infty}^{\infty} R_1(t,u)dB_u,$$

$$R_1(t,u) = ((t-u)^+)^{H-\frac{1}{2}} - ((-u)^+)^{H-\frac{1}{2}},$$

$$c_1(H) = \left(\int_0^{\infty} \left((1+u)^{H-\frac{1}{2}} - u^{H-\frac{1}{2}} \right)^2 du + \frac{1}{2H} \right)^{\frac{1}{2}},$$

Note that for this construction we define the Brownian motion B on the real line. In this case we have

$$K(s,t) = EW_sZ_t = \frac{\rho}{c_1(H)\left(H+\frac{1}{2}\right)} \begin{cases} t^{H+\frac{1}{2}} - (t-s)^{H+\frac{1}{2}} & 0<s<t \\ t^{H+\frac{1}{2}} & 0<t<s \end{cases}.$$

Note that because the process (W,Z) can be viewed as a linear transformation of the process (W,B), it is a bivariate Gaussian process and hence the matrix $\Sigma(s,t)$ is positive definite.

There are potentially other ways to define a fractional Brownian motion as a functional of the Brownian motion B each leading to a different specification of the dependence structure in the bivariate Gaussian process (W,Z). Moreover, one can define the process (W,Z) without reference to another Brownian motion. The question remains what arguments one can use to motivate the choice.

4. Self-Similarity

We are going to focus on the structural properties of the model that are desirable from the user perspective. Namely, on the self-similarity, and on the role it plays in financial modeling.

Perhaps the best example to use to explain the idea is to consider the classical Black Scholes model in which in order to derive the Black Scholes formula one simply calculates

$$E\left(\exp\left(\sigma W_T - \frac{1}{2}\sigma^2 T\right) - K\right)^+$$
$$= E\left(\exp\left(\sigma\sqrt{T}W_1 - \frac{1}{2}\sigma^2 T\right) - K\right)^+.$$

The above equality holds because the distributions of W_T and of $\sqrt{T}W_1$ coincide. This is obviously trivial from the mathematical perspective but important for the practitioners using such a model. Namely, the volatility parameter σ can be interpreted at different time scales. If σ represents the annual volatility, $T = 1$, the user can easily interpret it at any other time scale T.

In fact the Brownian motion W satisfies a much stronger self-similarity property, namely, the distributions of the processes $(W_{\lambda t}, t > 0)$ and $(\sqrt{\lambda}W_t, t > 0)$ coincide. This has obvious implications for the calculations of prices of path dependent options.

In the original SABR model a bivariate Brownian motion (W, Z) with correlation ρ is used to define the dynamics of the asset and of its volatility. Note that (W, Z) is self-similar in the following sense. The distributions of the processes $((W_{\lambda t}, Z_{\lambda t}), t > 0)$ and $((\lambda^{\frac{1}{2}} W_t, \lambda^{\frac{1}{2}} Z_t), t > 0)$ coincide.

In our generalization of the SABR model we proposed to replace the Brownian motion Z with a fractional Brownian motion. Note that the covariance function of the Gaussian process $(Z_{\lambda t}, t > 0)$ satisfies

$$\frac{1}{2}(|\lambda s|^{2H} + |\lambda t|^{2H} - |\lambda t - \lambda s|^{2H})$$
$$= \lambda^{2H}\frac{1}{2}(|s|^{2H} + |t|^{2H} - |t - s|^{2H}),$$

and hence it coincides with the covariance function of the process $(\lambda^H Z_t, t > 0)$. This means that the fractional Brownian motion is self-similar with the Hurst exponent H. Obviously, for the classical Brownian motion $H = \frac{1}{2}$.

So far we have constructed two bivariate Gaussian processes, one based on the Molchan–Golosov formula, and the other on Mandelbrot-Van Ness formula. Both lead to a bivariate Gaussian process (W, Z) in which the marginals are self-similar with Hurst exponents $\frac{1}{2}$ and H, respectively. What about the bivariate process (W, Z)?

In the next step we introduce the concept of multivariate fractional Brownian motion and of the multivariate self-similarity. In our setup we will only need these for bivariate processes.

We adapt the definitions from Amblard *et al.* [8].

Definition 1. A Multivariate fractional Brownian motion with parameter $H \in (0,1)^p$ is a p-dimensional continuous process satisfying the following three properties

- It is Gaussian,
- It is self-similar with vector parameter $H \in (0,1)^p$,
- It has stationary increments.

Here, self-similarity is understood as the joint self-similarity. More precisely, we use the following definition.

Definition 2. A multivariate process $(X(t) = (X_1(t), \ldots, X_p(t)))$, $t \in R$ is self-similar if there exists a vector $H = (H_1, \ldots, H_p) \in (0,1)^p$ such that for any $\lambda > 0$ the distributions of processes

$$((X_1(\lambda t), \ldots, X_p(\lambda t))), \quad t \in R),$$

and

$$(\lambda^{H_1} X_1(t), \ldots, \lambda^{H_p} X_p(t), \quad t \in R),$$

coincide. Vector H is the self-similarity parameter.

5. Covariance

Assume that the process (W, Z) is a bivariate fractional Brownian motion with parameter $\left(\frac{1}{2}, H\right)$. What is the the dependence structure between W and Z?

It turns out that the answer can be easily deduced from the general results of Amblard *et al.* [8], Coeurjolly *et al.* [9] and Lavancier *et al.* [10]. Indeed, they prove that there exist two constants $\delta \in [-1,1]$ and $\eta \in R$ such that for $0 < s < t$ we have

$$EW_sZ_t = \frac{1}{2}\left((\delta+\eta)\left|s\right|^{H+\frac{1}{2}} + (\delta-\eta)\left|t\right|^{H+\frac{1}{2}} - (\delta-\eta)\left|t-s\right|^{H+\frac{1}{2}}\right),$$

and for $0 < t < s$

$$EW_sZ_t = \frac{1}{2}\left((\delta+\eta)\left|s\right|^{H+\frac{1}{2}} + (\delta-\eta)\left|t\right|^{H+\frac{1}{2}} - (\delta+\eta)\left|t-s\right|^{H+\frac{1}{2}}\right),$$

where $\delta = EW_1Z_1$. In our case, when W is a Brownian motion, the above formulae can be simplified even further. For $0 < t < s$ we deduce, because of martingale property of W with respect to filtration $\mathcal{F}$ to which also Z is adapted and of bivariate self-similarity of (W, Z), that

$$EW_sZ_t = EZ_tE(W_s\,|\mathcal{F}_t) = EZ_tW_t = Et^H Z_1 t^{\frac{1}{2}} W_1 = t^{H+\frac{1}{2}} EW_1 Z_1$$
$$= \delta t^{H+\frac{1}{2}}.$$

It follows from the previous general expressions that

$$\eta = -\delta,$$

and consequently the dependence structure of the bivariate fractional Brownian motion (W, Z) is given by

$$EW_sZ_t = \delta \begin{cases} t^{H+\frac{1}{2}} - (t-s)^{H+\frac{1}{2}}, & 0 < s < t \\ t^{H+\frac{1}{2}}, & 0 < t < s \end{cases},$$

where

$$\delta = \frac{\rho}{c_1(H)\left(H+\frac{1}{2}\right)},$$

and

$$c_1(H) = \left(\int_0^\infty \left((1+u)^{H-\frac{1}{2}} - u^{H-\frac{1}{2}}\right)^2 du + \frac{1}{2H}\right)^{\frac{1}{2}}.$$

Remark 3. Note that when we use the Mandelbrot Van Ness formula to define the fractional Brownian motion Z, we define the bivariate Gaussian process (W, Z) which is a bivariate fractional Brownian motion with the vector parameter $\left(\frac{1}{2}, H\right)$.

Remark 4. One can also prove this directly, without making reference to the general results of Amblard *et al.* [8]. Indeed, we have

$$EW_{\lambda s}Z_{\lambda t} = \delta \begin{cases} (\lambda t)^{H+\frac{1}{2}} - (\lambda t - \lambda s)^{H+\frac{1}{2}}, & 0<s<t \\ (\lambda t)^{H+\frac{1}{2}}, & 0<t<s \end{cases},$$

$$= \lambda^{H+\frac{1}{2}}\delta \begin{cases} t^{H+\frac{1}{2}} - (t-s)^{H+\frac{1}{2}}, & 0<s<t \\ t^{H+\frac{1}{2}}, & 0<t<s \end{cases} = E\lambda^{\frac{1}{2}} W_s \lambda^H Z_t,$$

and hence the distributions of the processes

$$((W_{\lambda t}, Z_{\lambda t}), \quad t \in R),$$

and

$$\left(\lambda^{\frac{1}{2}} W_t, \lambda^H Z_t, \quad t \in R\right),$$

coincide. This means that the process (W, Z), where Z is given by the Mandelbrot Van Ness formula, is a bivariate fractional Brownian motion with the parameter $\left(\frac{1}{2}, H\right)$. One can consider the case when $t \in R$ or when $t > 0$.

6. Fractional SABR Model

The fractional SABR model is defined by the following expressions

$$\begin{aligned} dX_t &= X_t^{\beta} Y_t dW_t, X_0 = x, & 0 \leq \beta \leq 1, \ \alpha \geq 0, \\ Y_t &= \sigma \exp\left(\alpha Z_t - \frac{1}{2}\alpha^2 t^{2H}\right), & 0 < H < 1, \end{aligned}$$

where (W, Z) is a bivariate fractional Brownian motion with the vector parameter $\left(\frac{1}{2}, H\right)$. The above system can also be written as follows

$$dX_t = X_t^{\beta} dM_t, \quad X_0 = x,$$

where

$$M_t = \int_0^t Y_s \, dW_s.$$

Clearly, the equation for X remains the same as in the CEV model but the stochastic driver changes from W to the martingale M. Obviously, the properties of the model will be determined by the properties of the martingale M. Here we are focusing on scaling.

In order to study scaling properties in our model we indicate the dependence of the volatility process Y and of the martingale M on the model parameters by introducing the following notation

$$Y_t^{\alpha,\sigma} = \sigma \exp\left(\alpha Z_t - \frac{1}{2}\alpha^2 t^{2H}\right),$$

and

$$M_t^{\alpha,\sigma} = \int_0^t Y_s^{\alpha,\sigma} dW_s.$$

Note that self-similarity of Z implies equality of distributions of the following processes

$$(Y_{\lambda t}^{\alpha,\sigma}, \quad t > 0),$$

and

$$(Y_t^{\alpha\lambda^H,\sigma}, \quad t > 0).$$

Indeed

$$\begin{aligned} Y_{\lambda t}^{\alpha,\sigma} &= \sigma \exp\left(\alpha Z_{\lambda t} - \frac{1}{2}\alpha^2 (\lambda t)^{2H}\right) \underline{\underline{\mathcal{D}}} \\ &= \sigma \exp\left(\alpha \lambda^H Z_t - \frac{1}{2}\alpha^2 \lambda^{2H} t^{2H}\right) = Y_t^{\alpha\lambda^H,\sigma}, \end{aligned}$$

where the second equality means equal distributions.

For the martingale M, thanks to the joint self-similarity of (W, Z), we can deduce that the distributions of the processes

$$(M_{\lambda t}^{\alpha,\sigma}, \quad t > 0),$$

and

$$\left(M_t^{\alpha\lambda^H,\sigma\lambda^{\frac{1}{2}}}, \quad t > 0\right),$$

coincide. Indeed, we easily see that

$$\begin{aligned} M_{\lambda t}^{\alpha,\sigma} &= \int_0^{\lambda t} Y_s^{\alpha,\sigma} dW_s = \int_0^t Y_{\lambda u}^{\alpha,\sigma} dW_{\lambda u} \underline{\underline{\mathcal{D}}} \\ &= \int_0^t \sigma\lambda^{\frac{1}{2}} \exp\left(\alpha\lambda^H Z_u - \frac{1}{2}\alpha^2 \lambda^{2H} u^{2H}\right) dW_u \\ &= \int_0^t Y_u^{\alpha\lambda^H,\sigma\lambda^{\frac{1}{2}}} \\ dW_u &= M_t^{\alpha\lambda^H,\sigma\lambda^{\frac{1}{2}}}, \end{aligned}$$

where the third equality means equal distributions.

There are five parameters in our model, namely $\sigma, \alpha, \beta, \rho$ and H. The first two, σ and α represent volatility. From the above analysis we see that they scale differently. The volatility σ scales by $\lambda^{\frac{1}{2}}$ and the volatility of volatility α scales by λ^H. Parameters β and ρ determine shape of the smile and many mathematical properties of the model. The H parameter captures the ATM volatility skew.

In our next result we exploit the scaling. For this we introduce notation which indicates the dependence of the process X on the parameters α and σ, namely, $X^{\alpha,\sigma}$. It is easy to prove the following

Proposition 5. *Under the appropriate measurability and integrability conditions on the function G we have*

$$\mathrm{E}G(X_T^{\alpha,\sigma}) = \mathrm{E}G\left(X_1^{\alpha T^H,\sigma T^{\frac{1}{2}}}\right).$$

Proof. Recall that the equation for X written in terms of the martingale M has a unique strong solution. Therefore the solution can be written as follows

$$X_T^{\alpha,\sigma} = F\left(M_t^{\alpha,\sigma};\quad 0 \le t \le T\right),$$

for a certain functional F of path of $M^{\alpha,\sigma}$. Now using the bivariate self-similarity we get

$$\begin{aligned} \mathrm{E}G\left(X_T^{\alpha,\sigma}\right) &= \mathrm{E}G\left(F\left(M_t^{\alpha,\sigma};\quad 0 \le t \le T\right)\right) \\ &= \mathrm{E}G\left(F\left(M_t^{\alpha T^H,\sigma T^{\frac{1}{2}}};\quad 0 \le t \le 1\right)\right) = \mathrm{E}G\left(X_1^{\alpha T^H,\sigma T^{\frac{1}{2}}}\right). \end{aligned}$$

□

7. At-the-Money Volatility Skew

We are now going to estimate the at-the-money volatility skew implied by the fractional SABR model. Recall that, in the classical SABR model with $H = \frac{1}{2}$, when strike K is not too far from the forward x the implied volatility can be approximated by [1]).

$$\sigma_{BS}(k,1) = \sigma x^{\beta-1}\left(1 + \frac{1}{2}(1-\beta-\varrho\delta)k,\right.$$
$$\left.+\frac{1}{12}\left((1-\beta)^2 + \left(2-3\rho^2\right)\delta^2\right)k^2 + \cdots\right),$$

where for strike K and forward x

$$k = \log\frac{x}{K},$$

represents log-moneyness and

$$\delta = \frac{\alpha}{\sigma}x^{\beta-1}.$$

Therefore

$$\frac{\partial}{\partial k}\sigma_{\text{BS}}(k,1) = \sigma x^{\beta-1}\left(\frac{1}{2}(1-\beta-\rho\delta)\right.$$
$$\left.+\frac{1}{6}\left((1-\beta)^2 + \left(2-3\rho^2\right)\delta^2\right)k + \cdots\right),$$

and

$$\begin{aligned}\frac{\partial}{\partial k}\sigma_{\text{BS}}(k,1)\,|_{k=0} &= \sigma x^{\beta-1}\frac{1}{2}(1-\beta-\rho\delta),\\ &= Y_0X_0^{\beta-1}\frac{1}{2}(1-\beta-\rho)\frac{\alpha}{\sigma}X_0^{\beta-1}.\end{aligned}$$

For time to expiration τ using scaling we get

$$\begin{aligned}\frac{\partial}{\partial k}\sigma_{\text{BS}}(k,\tau)\,|_{k=0} &= Y_0X_0^{\beta-1}\frac{1}{2}(1-\beta) - \frac{1}{2}\rho\frac{\alpha\tau^{\frac{1}{2}}}{\sigma\tau^{\frac{1}{2}}}X_0^{\beta-1}\\ &= \frac{\partial}{\partial k}\sigma_{\text{BS}}(k,1),\end{aligned}$$

and hence the ATM volatility skew is flat in time to expiration.

In the fractional SABR, however, the volatility parameters α and σ scale differently in time to expiration. Using scaling of fractional SABR in

$$\frac{\partial}{\partial k}\sigma_{\text{BS}}(k,1)\,|_{k=0}\,,$$

we get

$$\frac{\partial}{\partial k}\sigma_{\rm BS}(k,\tau)\,|_{k=0} = Y_0 X_0^{\beta-1}\frac{1}{2}(1-\beta) - \frac{1}{2}\rho\frac{\alpha\tau^H}{\sigma\tau^{\frac{1}{2}}}X_0^{\beta-1}$$

$$= Y_0 X_0^{\beta-1}\frac{1}{2}(1-\beta) - \frac{1}{2}\rho\frac{\alpha}{\sigma}X_0^{\beta-1}\tau^{H-\frac{1}{2}}.$$

Note that $\sigma_{\rm BS}(k,1)$ corresponds to the implied volatility of the classical SABR for log-moneyness k and time to expiration 1 and not that of the fractional SABR. By applying scaling to this volatility we effectively assume that

$$\sigma_{\rm BS}(k,1) = \sigma_{\rm BS}^H(k,1),$$

where $\sigma_{BS}^H(k,1)$ denotes the implied volatility of the fractional SABR with Hurst exponent H and hence we assume that the at-the-money volatility skew for time to expiration 1 is flat in the Hurst exponent H. We are happy to make this assumption because our intention here is to explain the role of scaling and show consistency with known results. Alternatively, we could approximate $\frac{\partial}{\partial k}\sigma_{\rm BS}(k,\tau)\,|_{k=0}$ by a linear function of $\frac{\alpha}{\sigma}$ which leads to the same conclusion.

Recall that

$$dX_t = X_t^\beta Y_t\,dW_t = X_t X_t^{\beta-1} Y_t\,dW_t,$$

and hence $Y_0 X_0^{\beta-1}$, which approximates $X_t^{\beta-1}Y_t$ in the above expression, should be interpreted as an approximation to the short time lognormal volatility.

When $\beta \to 1$ we get

$$\frac{\partial}{\partial k}\sigma_{\rm BS}(k,\tau)\,|_{k=0} = -\frac{1}{2}\rho\sigma\tau^{H-\frac{1}{2}}.$$

We assume negative correlation $\rho < 0$.

For $\beta < 1$ we have

$$\frac{\partial}{\partial k}\sigma_{\rm BS}\,(k,\tau)\,|_{k=0} == Y_0 X_0^{\beta-1}\frac{1}{2}(1-\beta) - \frac{1}{2}\rho\frac{\alpha}{\sigma}X_0^{\beta-1}\tau^{H-\frac{1}{2}}.$$

For short time to expiration we recover the result of Fukasawa [6]. Moreover, scaling argument proves the power law behavior of the at-the-money volatility skew for any time to expiration.

This property is the main difference between the classical SABR with $H = \frac{1}{2}$, where the skew is flat, and the fractional SABR with $H < \frac{1}{2}$, where the skew obeys the power law with the negative exponent $H - \frac{1}{2}$.

References

[1] Hagan, P.S., Kumar, D., Lesniewski, A.S., and Woodward, D.E. (2002). Managing smile risk. *Wilmott*, September, 84–108.

[2] Lions, P.-L. and Musiela, M. (2007). Correlations and bounds for stochastic volatility models. *Ann. I. H. Poincare* — AN, 24, 1–16.

[3] Rogers, L.C.G. (1997). Arbitrage from fractional Brownian motion. *Mathematical Finance*, 7, 95–105.

[4] Gatheral, J., Jaisson, T., and Rosenbaum, M. (2018). Volatility is rough. *Quantitative Finance*, 18(6), 933–949.

[5] Bayer, C., Friz, P., and Gatheral, J. (2016). Pricing under rough volatility. *Quantitative Finance*, 16(6), 887–904.

[6] Fukasawa, M. (2017). Short-time at-the-money skew and rough fractional volatility. *Quantitative Finance*, 17(2), 189–198.

[7] Jost, C. (2006). *Transformation formulas for fractional Brownian motion. Stochastic Processes and their Applications*, 116(10), 1341–1357.

[8] Amblard, P.-O., Coeurjolly, J.-F., Lavancier, F., and Philippe, A. (2011). Basic properties of the multivariate fractional Brownian motion. *Bulletin de la Societe Mathematique de France*, Available: Arxiv 1007.0828.

[9] Coeurjolly, J.-F., Amblard, P.-O., and Achard, S. (2010). On multivariate fractional Brownian motion and multivariate fractional gaussian noise. *18th European Signal Processing Conference (EUSIPCO — 2010)*. Aalborg, Denmark.

[10] Lavancier, F., Philippe, A., and Surgailis, D. (2009). Covariance function of vector self-similar processes. *Statistics and Probability Letters*, 79(2009), 2415–2421.

[11] Amblard, P.-O. and Coeurjolly, J.-F. (2011). Identification of the multivariate fractional Brownian motion. *IEEE Transactions on Signal Processing*, 59, (11).

https://doi.org/10.1142/9789811259142_0007

Chapter 7

Buy Rough, Sell Smooth*

P. Glasserman[†] **and P. He**[‡]
Columbia Business School, New York, USA
[†]*pg20@columbia.edu*
[‡]*phe19@gsb.columbia.edu*

Abstract

Recent work has documented *roughness* in the time series of stock market volatility and investigated its implications for option pricing. We study a strategy for trading stocks based on measures of their implied and realized roughness. A strategy that goes long the roughest-volatility stocks and short the smoothest-volatility stocks earns statistically significant excess annual returns of 6% or more, depending on the time period and strategy details. The profitability of the strategy is not explained by standard factors. We compare alternative measures of roughness in volatility and find that the profitability of the strategy is greater when we sort stocks based on implied rather than realized roughness. We interpret the profitability of the strategy as compensation for near-term idiosyncratic event risk.

Keywords: Volatility, fractional Brownian motion, trading strategies, volatility skew.

---

*This chapter is derived from Glasserman, P. and He, P. (2020). Buy rough, sell smooth. *Quant. Finance*, 20(3): 363–378, DOI: 10.1080/14697688.2019.1675899. Reprinted by permission of Taylor & Francis Ltd.

1. Introduction

A recent line of research has found evidence that stock price volatility is *rough*, in the sense that the evolution of volatility is rougher than the paths of ordinary Brownian motion. The evidence for rough volatility comes from two sources: the time series behavior of realized volatility, and an empirical regularity of option-implied volatility at short maturities that turns out to be well explained by roughness. See Gatheral *et al.* [1], Bayer *et al.* [2], Fukasawa [3], Bennedsen *et al.* [4] and El Euch *et al.* [5] for background and further references.

Rough models of stochastic volatility replace an ordinary Brownian motion driving the dynamics of volatility with a *fractional* Brownian motion (fBM). The fBM family, indexed by a single parameter, includes ordinary Brownian motion and also processes with smoother and rougher paths. Empirical estimates here and in Gatheral *et al.* [1] and Bennedsen *et al.* [4] find parameter values smaller than 1/2 (the case of ordinary Brownian motion), corresponding to rougher paths. We refer to these estimates as measures of *realized* roughness.

By *implied* roughness, we mean estimates extracted from option prices. Implied volatilities from equity put options are ordinarily skewed, meaning that they are larger at lower strikes, particularly at short maturities. But the steepness of this skew typically falls quickly as the maturity extends — more quickly than predicted by most stochastic volatility models. Rough volatility models capture this feature. Stocks with greater realized roughness exhibit fast mean-reversion in volatility; stocks with greater implied roughness exhibit a fast decay in their implied-volatility skew.

The implications of these empirical regularities have received little attention beyond option markets. In this article, we seek to shed light on the possible sources and consequences of rough volatility by studying a trading strategy that trades stocks — not options — based on roughness in volatility. We sort stocks based on measures of realized or implied roughness and analyze a strategy that goes long the roughest quintile and short the smoothest quantile. When sorted on implied roughness, the strategy earns excess returns of 6% or more, after controlling for standard factors. The strategy is profitable in 13 out of the 17 years in our sample, including 2007, 2008, and 2009. The strategy based on realized roughness earns somewhat lower returns and is less robust to standard controls.

These results have several implications. First, they show that roughness matters for stock returns and is not just a feature of option markets. Second, they point to potential differences between implied and realized roughness, though in theory the two should coincide. Third, we will argue that the profitability of our implied rough-minus-smooth strategy reflects compensation for near-term idiosyncratic event risk. The fast decay in the implied volatility skew associated with implied roughness indicates near-term downside uncertainty that will be resolved quickly. We support this interpretation by examining the performance of our strategy near two types of events: our strategy earns higher returns near earnings announcements (which mainly resolve company-specific uncertainty) and lower returns near interest rate announcements by the Federal Reserve (which resolve market-wide uncertainty).

Efforts to date to model an underlying source of roughness have focused on market microstructure and the splitting of large orders, particularly El Euch *et al.* [6], Jusselin and Rosenbaum [7]. However, these models do not offer clear predictions on what types of stocks should exhibit greater roughness, which limits their application to our setting. Nevertheless, we investigate possible connections between roughness and market liquidity. We confirm a positive association between roughness and illiquidity (which may be seen as consistent with Jusselin and Rosenbaum [7]); but we also find that controlling for illiquidity reduces but does not eliminate the profitability of our implied strategy. Moreover, this strategy is limited to stocks with significant options trading, and these are generally larger and more liquid stocks. The profitability of our strategy therefore cannot be explained by an illiquidity premium.

Our results present an interesting contrast to the work of Xing *et al.* [8]. They find that a steep skew (corresponding to expensive puts at low strikes) forecasts negative earnings surprises, a finding we confirm in more recent data. This pattern supports a strategy of buying stocks with lower skews and selling stocks with steeper skews. One might expect stocks with a faster skew decay (greater implied roughness) to start with a steeper skew, in which case the strategy of Xing *et al.* [8] would lead to selling rough and buying smooth, just the opposite of the strategy we find profitable. Moreover, we find that roughness does not forecast earnings surprises, reinforcing the notion that the profitability of rough-minus-smooth reflects compensation for risk rather than cash flow predictability. Together these patterns indicate that the information in roughness is distinct from the skewness measure in Xing *et al.* [8].

Section 2 provides background on realized and implied roughness, and it explains the procedures we use to estimate both quantities. In Section 3, we evaluate the performance of strategies that buy the roughest quintile of stocks and short the smoothest quintile of stocks each month. We evaluate strategies using realized and implied measures of roughness, after controlling for standard factors. In Section 4, we control for additional factors through double sorts that hedge out other effects, including several measures of illiquidity and the levels of implied volatility and skewness. We find that returns on the implied strategy are robust to these controls. We also test robustness to these controls using Fama and MacBeth [9] time-series averages of cross-sectional regressions. In Section 5, we find that the performance of our strategy is enhanced when restricted to stocks with earnings announcements in the subsequent month and diminished near Federal Reserve announcements. We interpret these findings as evidence that rougher stocks (particularly as measured by implied roughness) are those facing near-term downside uncertainty.

2. Realized and Implied Roughness

2.1 *Realized roughness*

To discuss roughness, we first recall the definition of fractional Brownian motion; for additional background, see Mandelbrot and Van Ness [10] and Section 7.2 of Samorodnitsky and Taqqu [11]. A fractional Brownian motion with Hurst parameter $H \in (0,1)$ is a mean-zero Gaussian process $\{W_t^H, -\infty < t < \infty\}$ with stationary increments and covariance function given by

$$\mathbb{E}[W^H(t)W^H(s)] = \frac{1}{2}\left(|t|^{2H} + |s|^{2H} - |t-s|^{2H}\right). \tag{1}$$

The case $H = 1/2$ corresponds to ordinary Brownian motion. With $H \in (1/2, 1)$, fractional Brownian motion exhibits long-range dependence; processes with $H \in (0, 1/2)$ have paths that are rougher than those of ordinary Brownian motion, with small H indicating greater roughness.

As one indication of greater roughness, we have the following property of the moments of the increments of fractional Brownian motion. For any $t \in \mathbb{R}$, and $\Delta \geq 0$, and any $q > 0$,

$$\mathbb{E}[|W^H_{t+\Delta} - W^H_t|^q] = \mathbb{E}[|Z|^q]\Delta^{qH}, \quad Z \sim N(0, 1). \tag{2}$$

With smaller H, increments over a short interval Δ have larger moments.

As an example of a rough volatility model for an asset price $\{S_t, t \geq 0\}$, we could set

$$d \log S_t = \mu \, dt + \sigma_t \, dW_t \tag{3}$$

$$d \log \sigma_t = \nu \, dW^H_t; \tag{4}$$

this is a special case of a single-factor version of what Gatheral *et al.* [1] call the rough Bergomi model, after Bergomi [12]. More generally, the model specifies a mean-reverting log volatility process

$$d \log \sigma_t = -\kappa(\log \sigma_t - m) + \nu \, dW^H_t. \tag{5}$$

Here, μ, κ, m, and ν are constants, W is an ordinary Brownian motion, W^H is a fractional Brownian motion with $H \in (0, 1/2)$, and W and W^H may be correlated. The parameter H determines the roughness of the volatility process.

Empirical evidence for roughness in the time series of volatility can be found in Gatheral *et al.* [1], Bennedsen *et al.* [4], Livieri *et al.* [13], and later in this paper. Abi Jaber and El Euch [14] present an approximation method for rough volatility models that suggests a simple interpretation: rough volatility arises from mixing mean-reverting volatility processes with different speeds of mean reversion, driven by an ordinary Brownian motion, including components with arbitrarily fast mean reversion. The connection between roughness and fast mean reversion is also supported by the analysis of option prices in Garnier and Sølna [15]. Note that the relevant mean reversion here is in a stock's volatility and not in its price.

If we could observe $\log \sigma_t$ at times $t = 0, \Delta, 2\Delta, \ldots$ for some small $\Delta > 0$, we could estimate H by estimating

$$\mathbb{E}[|\log \sigma_{t+\Delta} - \log \sigma_t|^q] \tag{6}$$

for various values of $q > 0$, and then applying (2) to extract H. This is the method of Gatheral *et al.* (2018), which they apply more generally to estimate roughness, without necessarily assuming the specific model in (3)–(4) or (5).

In practice, σ_t cannot be observed and must be estimated, so we proceed as follows. Using trades from the Trade and Quote (TAQ) data, we apply the realized kernel method of Barndorff-Nielsen *et al.* [16] to estimate the daily integrated variance of returns; taking the square root yields our estimated daily volatility.[a] We obtained similar results using the realized variance of 5-minute returns, but the realized kernel method is designed to be less sensitive to microstructure noise.

The rest of the estimation procedure works with these daily volatilities, which we write as $\hat{\sigma}_d$, with d indexing days. We apply (6) with $q = 2$, estimating second moments over intervals of ℓ days, $\ell = 1, 2, \ldots, 10$. In each month, for each stock and each lag ℓ, we calculate

$$z_2(\ell) = \frac{1}{T - \ell} \sum_{d=1}^{T-\ell} (\log \hat{\sigma}_{d+\ell} - \log \hat{\sigma}_d)^2, \tag{7}$$

where T is the number of days in the month. Based on (2), we expect

$$z_2(\ell) \approx \nu^2 \ell^{2H}.$$

We therefore run a regression

$$\log z_2(\ell) = \beta_1 + \beta_2 \log \ell + \epsilon, \tag{8}$$

to estimate H as $\beta_2/2$. We also estimate the volatility of volatility ν by setting $\log \nu = \beta_1/2$. This procedure yields an estimate of H (and ν) for each stock in each month.

---

[a]We use the non-flat Parzen kernel as implemented in Kevin Sheppard's toolbox at https://www.kevinsheppard.com/MFE_Toolbox.

Gatheral *et al.* [1] estimate (7) and (8) for moments of several orders q and then run a regression of the slope in (8) against q. We find that using several moments rather than just $q = 2$ leads to very similar estimates of H.[b]

2.2 *Implied roughness*

By implied roughness we mean the value of H obtained by fitting option prices to a rough volatility model.

A conventional approach to evaluating an implied parameter would proceed as follows. Choose a specific model with some free parameters — in this case, a rough volatility model; find the parameters that bring the model's option prices closest to a set of market prices.

Applying this approach to extract H from option prices raises two issues. The first is a practical consideration: pricing options in rough volatility models requires Monte Carlo simulation, so inverting prices to evaluate H for hundreds of stocks and months is computationally daunting. The second issue is more fundamental: a misspecified model may lead to an incorrect value of H, even if the "true" volatility process in rough.

To circumvent these issues, we follow a simpler and more robust approach, based on the term structure of the at-the-money (ATM) skew. Write $\sigma_{BS}(k, \tau)$ for the Black–Scholes implied volatility of an option with time-to-maturity τ and log-moneyness $k = \log(K/S)$, where K is the option's strike price and S is the current level of the underlying. The ATM skew at maturity τ is given by

$$\phi(\tau) = \left| \frac{\partial \sigma_{BS}(k, \tau)}{\partial k} \right|_{k=0} \tag{9}$$

An empirical regularity of the ATM skew is that it flattens at longer maturities. This pattern is illustrated in Figure 1, which shows fitted implied volatilities for JPMorgan Chase on June 5, 2012, using

[b]In tests of alternative estimation methods on simulated data, for which we know H, we have found that the main source of error is the estimation of the daily integrated variances $\hat{\sigma}_d^2$ from intraday returns, rather than the estimation of H from the daily volatilities.

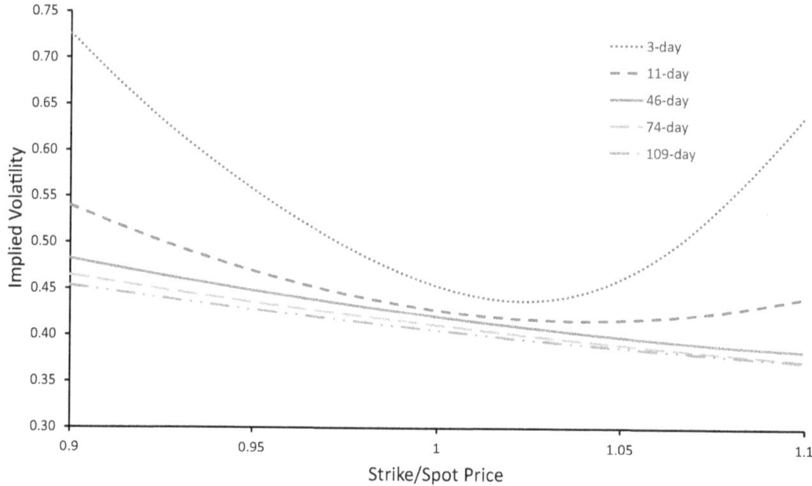

Figure 1: JPM implied volatilities on June 5, 2012. The curves show cubic spline fits at various maturities using raw data from OptionMetrics, plotted against the ratio of the put strike K to the spot price S. The ATM skew is the slope at $K/S = 1$. Its absolute value falls quickly as the maturity increases.

data from OptionMetrics. (We discuss the details of the fitting procedure below.) The horizontal axis shows the ratio of the strike price to the current stock price, so the ATM skew is the slope at a ratio of 1. The different curves correspond to different maturities. The slope is steepest (most negative) at the shortest maturity of three days and quickly flattens as we move to longer maturities.

The expansions of Fukasawa [17], Bayer *et al.* [2], El Euch *et al.* [5], and Forde and Zhang [18] characterize the rate of decay of the ATM skew for a very broad range of rough volatility models. These results (in particular as in Fukasawa [17]) show that the ATM skew admits an approximation of the form

$$\phi(\tau) \approx \text{constant} \times \tau^{H-1/2}, \quad \text{as } \tau \downarrow 0. \tag{10}$$

In other words, the ATM skew exhibits a power law decay at short maturities, with an exponent determined by H.

This idea is illustrated in Figure 2, which replicates similar figures in Gatheral *et al.* [1]. The horizontal axis records time-to-maturity τ, and the vertical axis records ATM skew $\phi(\tau)$. Each dot in the figure shows an estimate of $\phi(\tau)$, all calculated on September 15, 2005 (left panel) or June 20, 2013 (right panel), based on OptionMetrics data.

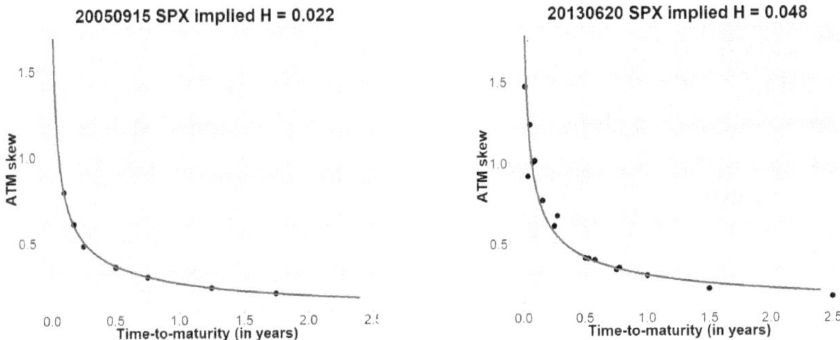

Figure 2: Term structure of the ATM skew for the S&P 500 index, as in similar figures in Gatheral *et al.* [1]. The charts plot the slope of the ATM skew against option maturity on Sep 15, 2005 (left) and Jun 20, 2013 (right), using OptionMetrics data.

The smooth curve in the figure shows a power law fit to the data, from which we estimate the exponent. In this example, the exponents are -0.48 (left) and -0.452 (right) corresponding to $H = 0.02$ and $H = 0.048$, respectively.

This is the approach we will use to calculate an option-implied value of H, after providing details of the calculation. The method is easy to use and readily lends itself to evaluating an implied H for hundreds of stocks, each day for nearly 20 years. The method is robust because it exploits the general property of rough volatility models in (9) rather than the detailed structure of a specific model.

Some may object to using the rate of decay of the ATM skew to extract an implied measure of roughness on the grounds that certain stochastic volatility models driven by ordinary Brownian motion may also be able to fit the term structure of ϕ. For example, Bergomi and Guyon [19] fit what appears to be a power law decay using a linear combination of two exponentials. Some might prefer to follow the more conventional approach with which we began this section, fitting a specific model to market prices and finding the value of H that fits best. But if the model fits option prices well, *that approach will lead to the same value of* H because if the model fits the data, then the market prices satisfy (10). Using (10) directly is simply a more efficient and more robust way of arriving at the implied H. Calling it implied roughness is also much simpler than calling it the rate of decay of the ATM skew (plus 1/2).

To carry out this approach, we proceed as follows. First, we merge CRSP and OptionMetrics data to link stock prices and option prices. Next, we filter out options following standard rules in the literature; these are detailed in the appendix. On each day for each stock, using only the filtered data, we use a cubic spline to fit implied volatility as a function of $\log(K/S)$. We take the derivative of the spline at $\log(K/S) = 0$ as the ATM skew $\phi(\tau)$. Then we run a regression

$$\log \phi(\tau) = c + (H - 1/2) \log \tau + \epsilon;$$

that is, we add 1/2 to the estimated slope in this regression to evaluate the implied H.

In addition to the realized measure discussed in Section 2.1 and the implied measure discussed here, we have tested a third measure — realized roughness of implied volatility, as in Livieri *et al.* [13]. In this approach, for each stock we take the ATM implied volatility, and we evaluate the realized roughness (following (7)–(8)) from the stock's time series of implied volatility. We have found that investment results based on this measure are very similar to those using realized roughness, so we do not discuss them further.

2.3 *Descriptive statistics of realized and implied roughness*

Our focus is on the cross-sectional relationship between roughness and stock returns, so in Table 1 we present summary statistics on the cross-sectional variation of implied and realized roughness. In each

Table 1: Monthly averages of cross-sectional summary statistics. The last column shows statistics for realized H estimated from the subset of stocks for which implied estimates are available.

	Implied H	Realized H	Realized H on Implied Universe
avg Mean	0.18	0.07	0.09
avg S.D.	0.21	0.10	0.10
avg 25th pctile	0.06	0.00	0.02
avg median	0.18	0.06	0.08
avg 75th pctile	0.30	0.14	0.15

month we calculate the mean, standard deviation and several quantiles (25%, 50%, 75%) of implied and realized roughness measures for all stocks; we then take the time-series average of these summary statistics and report them in the table.

As discussed in Section 2.2, we have values of implied roughness for only a subset of stock-month pairs. We refer to this subset as the "implied universe". In contrast, by the "full universe" we mean the larger set of stock-month pairs for which we have sufficient data to calculate a realized H and link TAQ, CRSP, and Compustat data. See the appendix for details on the filters applied.

In the last column of Table 1 we report summary statistics for realized roughness on the implied universe. The results in the table indicate that implied estimates of H are a bit larger than realized estimates and that this may be partly due to differences in the implied and realized universes, but the differences are small. Livieri *et al.* [13] find that values of realized H estimated from the time series of implied volatility are generally larger than values estimated from realized volatility, and they attribute the difference to a smoothing effect over an option's time to maturity. This effect may play some role in our estimates of implied H.

Table 2 reports time-series averages of cross-sectional means and standard deviations by industry, using industry classifications from Ken French's website.[c]

The estimates are very consistent across different sectors.

3. Sorted Portfolios

In this section, we test the performance of trading strategies that pick stocks based on realized or implied roughness. Each month, we sort stocks based on roughness (realized or implied) and group them into quintile portfolios. We evaluate the performance of a strategy that buys the roughest (smallest H) quintile and shorts the smoothest (largest H) quintile, holding these positions for one month. We calculate value-weighted returns in the month following the month in which portfolios are formed, and then repeat the procedure for the next month.

[c]http://mba.tuck.dartmouth.edu/pages/faculty/ken.french/data_library.html.

Table 2: Monthly averages of cross-sectional summary statistics by industry. The last two columns show statistics for realized H estimated from the subset of stocks for which implied estimates are available.

	Implied H		Realized H		Realized H on Imp. Univ.	
Industry	Avg Mean	Avg S.D.	Avg Mean	Avg S.D.	Avg Mean	Avg S.D.
Consumer NonDurables	0.18	0.23	0.07	0.10	0.08	0.10
Consumer Durables	0.17	0.19	0.07	0.10	0.09	0.09
Manufacturing	0.17	0.19	0.08	0.10	0.09	0.10
Energy	0.20	0.20	0.08	0.10	0.09	0.09
Chemicals	0.19	0.19	0.08	0.10	0.09	0.09
Business Equipment	0.18	0.21	0.08	0.10	0.09	0.10
Telecom	0.19	0.22	0.08	0.10	0.09	0.10
Utilities	0.17	0.22	0.08	0.10	0.10	0.09
Shops	0.18	0.20	0.07	0.10	0.08	0.10
Health	0.17	0.23	0.07	0.10	0.09	0.10
Finance	0.18	0.19	0.07	0.10	0.10	0.10
Other	0.17	0.21	0.07	0.10	0.09	0.10

In addition to calculating average returns, we calculate excess returns (alphas) relative to various factor models: a single-factor (CAPM) model using the overall return of the market, net of the risk-free rate; the three-factor Fama and French [20] model (with factors for the market, size, and book-to-market) augmented with a momentum factor, as in Carhart [21]; the five-factor model of Fama and French [22] (with factors for the market, size, book-to-market, earnings robustness, and investment conservativeness), again augmented with momentum.

We use stock prices from CRSP, factor returns from Ken French's website, and option implied volatilities from OptionMetrics. The OptionMetrics data starts in 1996, but we start from 2000 because much more data is available after 2000 than in the earlier years.

Table 3 shows results for stocks sorted on implied roughness. The columns show results for the quintile portfolios, sorted from smoothest (highest H) to roughest (lowest H). The last column shows results for the long-short strategy. The strategy earns an average monthly return of 0.49% (5.9% annually). Its alphas with respect to the various factor models range from 0.47% to 0.52% monthly, or 5.6% to 6.2% annually. The numbers in brackets are Newey and

Table 3: Performance of portfolios sorted on implied roughness. Alphas are monthly values in percent. Numbers in brackets are t-statistics.

	1 Smooth	2	3	4	5 Rough	5-1
Mean	0.22	0.39	0.37	0.33	0.71	0.49
Std. Dev.	4.82	4.76	4.69	5.08	5.26	2.63
CAPM Alpha	-0.28^{**}	-0.11	-0.13	-0.19	0.19	0.47^{**}
	[−2.51]	[−1.48]	[−1.39]	[−1.35]	[1.37]	[2.43]
FF-3-MOM Alpha	-0.33^{***}	-0.07	-0.07	-0.07	0.16	0.49^{***}
	[−2.88]	[−0.94]	[−0.94]	[−0.64]	[1.22]	[2.63]
FF-5-MOM Alpha	-0.29^{***}	-0.04	-0.04	0.03	0.24^{*}	0.52^{***}
	[−2.74]	[−0.58]	[−0.47]	[0.30]	[1.70]	[2.76]
Implied H	0.46	0.27	0.18	0.09	-0.11	
Size in billion \$	14.64	18.87	19.07	15.79	7.84	
Book-to-Market	0.48	0.44	0.42	0.41	0.43	
Number of stocks	153	152	153	152	152	
Portfolio persistence	61%	75%	76%	74%	63%	

West [23] t-statistics, and show that these excess returns are all statistically significant. Statistical significance at the 10%, 5% and 1% levels is indicated by *, **, and ***, respectively.

The lower half of Table 3 shows features of the quintile portfolios. By construction, the average implied H values decrease from left to right. The smoothest quintile has H close to the Brownian value of $1/2$, and the roughest quintile has a negative average H. A negative H is not meaningful as a Hurst parameter, but can certainly arise as an implied parameter through (10).

We see from Table 3 that the average book-to-market ratio is quite consistent across the quintiles, but size (measured by market cap) seems to be positively correlated with H, a point we will investigate further. The last row shows the percentage of stocks in each quintile that remain in the quintile from one month to the next.

Table 4 reports corresponding results using realized roughness. Panel A uses the full universe of CRSP stocks; Panel B limits the set of stocks used each month to the “implied universe”, meaning those that pass the filters we use for the implied roughness portfolios in Table 4.

Both panels of Table 4 show that stocks with rougher volatility (smaller realized H) tend to outperform stocks with smoother

Table 4: Performance of portfolios sorted on realized roughness. Alphas are monthly values in percent. Panel A shows results for all stocks and Panel B is limited to the stocks used in Table 3 for comparison.

	1 Smooth	2	3	4	5 Rough	5-1
PANEL A						
Mean	0.22	0.52	0.59	0.71	0.60	0.38
Std. Dev.	4.99	4.69	4.65	4.33	4.94	2.66
CAPM Alpha	-0.30^{***}	0.02	0.09	0.24^{**}	0.10	0.40^{**}
	[−3.08]	[0.18]	[1.20]	[2.45]	[0.71]	[2.03]
FF-3-MOM Alpha	-0.27^{***}	0.00	0.05	0.24^{***}	0.03	0.31
	[−2.97]	[0.00]	[0.61]	[2.71]	[0.22]	[1.56]
FF-5-MOM Alpha	-0.19^{**}	0.01	0.02	0.13	−0.01	0.17
	[−2.13]	[0.09]	[0.23]	[1.52]	[−0.10]	[0.97]
Realized H	0.23	0.12	0.06	0.01	−0.05	
Size in billion $	6.67	5.18	4.62	4.03	3.36	
Book-to-Market	0.69	0.67	0.64	0.65	0.70	
Number of stocks	611	613	614	614	614	
Portfolio persistence	79%	80%	80%	80%	80%	
PANEL B						
Mean	0.11	0.27	0.51	0.58	0.59	0.47
Std. Dev.	5.28	4.89	4.85	4.58	4.89	2.89
CAPM Alpha	-0.42^{***}	-0.24^{**}	0.00	0.10	0.09	0.51^{**}
	[−3.55]	[−2.16]	[0.01]	[0.94]	[0.71]	[2.51]
FF-3-MOM Alpha	-0.38^{***}	$-0.19*$	0.01	0.15	0.13	0.51^{***}
	[−3.49]	[−1.75]	[0.06]	[1.50]	[1.00]	[2.73]
FF-5-MOM Alpha	-0.25^{**}	−0.13	0.00	0.17	0.08	$0.33*$
	[−2.31]	[−1.19]	[−0.02]	[1.59]	[0.60]	[1.73]
Realized H	0.24	0.14	0.08	0.03	−0.04	
Size in billion $	18.38	16.37	15.31	13.69	12.18	
Book-to-Market	0.44	0.43	0.43	0.43	0.44	
Number of stocks	151	151	151	151	152	
Portfolio persistence	80%	82%	82%	82%	81%	

volatility (larger realized H). Comparing the last column of Table 4 (showing performance of the rough-minus-smooth long-short strategy), with the last column of Table 3, indicates that the effect is not quite as strong and not quite as statistically significant sorting on realized as sorting on implied roughness. Portfolio persistence is a bit greater using realized roughness, indicating that this strategy has somewhat lower turnover.

Comparing Panels A and B of Table 4, we find that sorting on realized roughness yields higher alphas when we limit the universe of stocks to those for which we can also calculate implied roughness. This is surprising because the stocks in the more limited universe are larger on average and have lower book-to-market ratios; smaller stocks and high book-to-market stocks generally have higher expected returns. We see a similar effect in Table 3, where controlling for the Fama-French factors improves performance.

It is worth noting that in both panels of Table 4 the highest returns are generally associated with the fourth quintile of realized H rather than the fifth quintile. The performance of the realized strategy could be substantially improved by buying the fourth quintile, rather than the fifth, and shorting the first. For consistency and to avoid data snooping, we work exclusively with the original long-fifth, short-first strategy; however, this may underestimate the efficacy of trading on realized roughness.

Tables 3 and 4 show average performance over the full period 2000–2016. To illustrate how performance varies over time, Figure 3 shows annual performance by year for the implied strategy. Remarkably, sorting on implied roughness, the rough-minus-smooth strategy is profitable in 13 out of the 17 years, including 2007–2009; indeed, 2008 was the strategy's best year. The strategy's only large significant

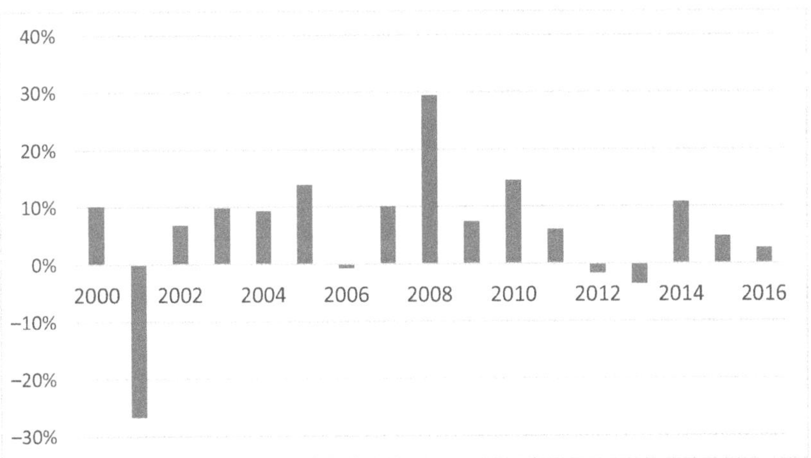

Figure 3: Annual performance of rough-minus-smooth strategy based on implied roughness.

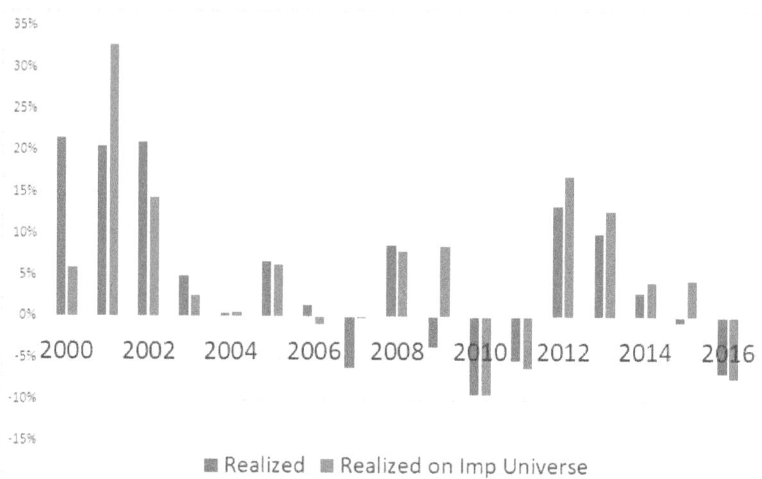

Figure 4: Annual performance of rough-minus-smooth strategy based on realized roughness, using all stocks or just the implied universe.

loss is in 2001, and the loss that year is almost entirely attributable to September, the month of the 9/11 attacks. We return to this point in Section 5.

Figure 4 shows annual performance of the strategy based on realized roughness. The figure shows performance of the realized strategy on the full universe and on the implied universe. Except in the early part of the sample, where the option data is more limited, the realized strategy generally performs similarly on the full and restricted sets of stocks. This confirms that the performance in Figure 3 is not attributable to the set of stocks included in the implied universe. Indeed, comparing Figures 3 and 4 shows that the realized and implied strategies have done well at different times, suggesting that combining the two signals could lead to even better performance. However from Table 4 we see that the realized strategy provides a smaller FF-5-MOM alpha than the implied strategy. We will see in Section 4 that the realized strategy is also less robust to controls for other factors.

The performance of the implied strategy in 2008 raises the question of whether sorting on roughness implicitly tilts the long-short portfolio to favor some industries over others. For example, a strategy that shorts bank stocks would have performed well in 2008. However, we saw in Table 2 that roughness estimates are similar across industries. Moreover, the average implied and realized H estimates for finance companies in particular are in the middle of the ranges across industries, indicating that a rough-minus-smooth strategy does not tend to favor or disfavor financial stocks.

4. Controlling for Other Factors

To better understand the performance of the rough-minus-smooth strategies, in this section we add controls for additional factors. We first discuss factors that might influence performance and then evaluate their impact using two methods — double sorts and Fama and MacBeth [9] regressions.

4.1 *Liquidity*

We observed previously that in Table 3 the average market cap across the five quintiles increases with H: rougher stocks tends to be smaller on average. This pattern suggests the possibility that roughness may reflect lower liquidity and therefore that a rough-minus-smooth strategy earns an illiquidity premium. This possibility is tempered by the fact that the stocks that pass the filters for calculating implied roughness are larger, on average, than those that do not. The question therefore requires a more systemic investigation.

A connection between realized roughness and liquidity was noted in an early version of Bennedsen *et al.* [4], but it was removed from subsequent versions of that paper. Bennedsen *et al.* [4] compare estimates of realized roughness with daily volume of trading in a stock.

In addition to trading volume, we consider the widely-used Amihud [24] illiquidity measure. The Amihud measure for a single stock in a single month sums the absolute values of the daily returns and divides the sum by the dollar volume for the month. Larger values of the Amihud measure are interpreted as indicating lower liquidity, whereas larger values of trading volume are associated with greater liquidity.

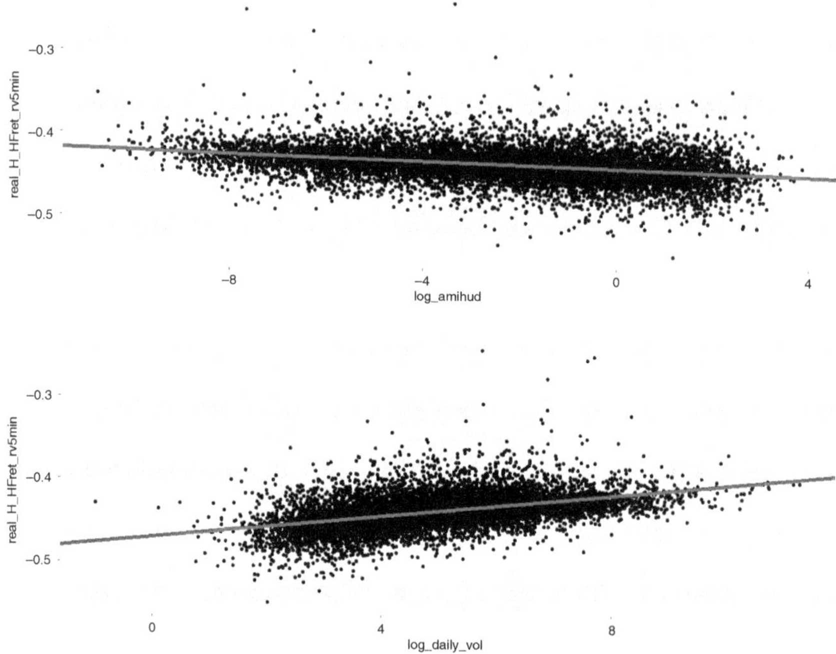

Figure 5: Realized roughness and liquidity. The figures plot realized roughness against the log of the Amihud illiquidity measure (top) and log daily volume (bottom). Each point shows a single stock in a single month.

Figures 5 and 6 compare, respectively, realized and implied estimates of H with the log of the Amihud measure and log daily volume. Each dot in the figure corresponds to a single stock in a single month. Consistent with the earlier version of Bennedsen *et al.* [24], we find a positive correlation (0.55) between realized H and log daily volume. Consistent with this pattern, we find a negative correlation (−0.46) between realized H and the log Amihud measure.

The results using implied roughness in Figure 6 are qualitatively similar but not as strong. The correlation between implied H and log daily volume is 0.28, and the correlation with the log Amihud measure is −0.40.

Beyond these empirical patterns, a potential link between roughness and liquidity is interesting because of efforts to explain realized roughness through market microstructure; see El Euch *et al.* [6] and Jusselin and Rosenbaum [7]. However, the explanations developed

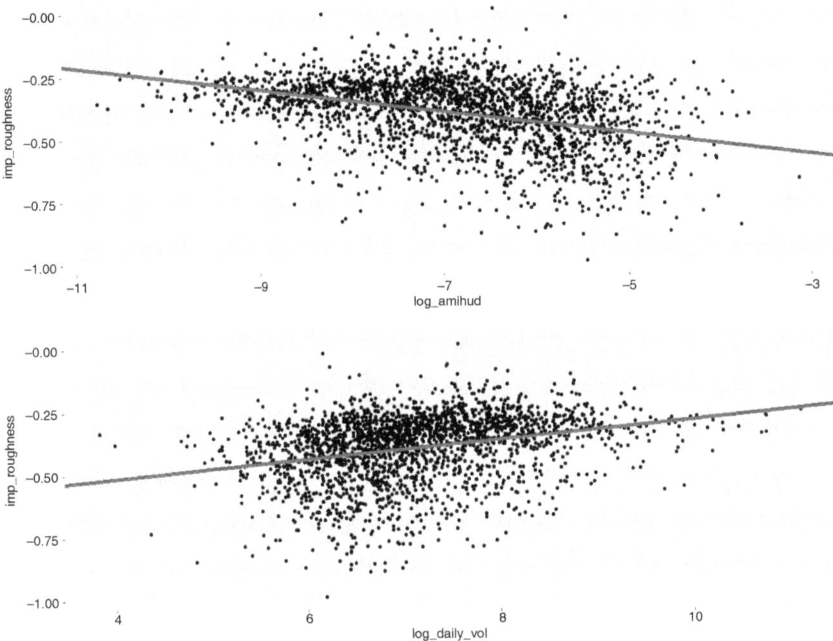

Figure 6: Implied roughness and liquidity. The figures plot implied roughness against the log of the Amihud illiquidity measure (top) and log daily volume (bottom). Each point shows a single stock in a single month.

to date are highly stylized, and they do not make clear predictions about whether greater roughness should be associated the more or less liquidity.[d]

4.2 *Implied volatility and skewness*

Implied roughness is a relatively complex feature of a stock's implied volatility surface, involving differences in implied volatilities across both strikes and maturities. To try to isolate the source of alpha in the implied rough-minus-smooth strategy, we will therefore control for more basic features — the level of the ATM implied volatility and the shape of implied volatility skew.

---

[d]According to Mathieu Rosenbaum (Personal communication), Jusselin and Rosenbaum [7] implies a longer transient price impact when H is smaller, which would be consistent with the correlations we find.

Several authors (particularly Conrad *et al.* [25] and Xing *et al.* [8]) have documented predictability in stock returns using measures of implied volatility and skewness. A fast decay in the ATM skew (low implied H) is potentially associated with high degree of near-term skewness or implied volatility. We therefore control for these factors.

As our measure of ATM implied volatility, we use the implied volatility for a one-month call with strike closest to the spot price as reported in implied volatility surface data set from OptionMetrics. We denote this by $\sigma_{1m}^{\text{Call}}(\frac{K}{S} = 1)$. Similar to Xing *et al.* [8], we use as our measure of implied volatility skew

$$\text{XZZ-skew} = \sigma_{1m}^{\text{Put}}\left(\frac{K}{S} = 0.9\right) - \sigma_{1m}^{\text{Call}}\left(\frac{K}{S} = 1\right), \tag{11}$$

the difference between the one-month implied volatility for a put with moneyness closest to 0.9 and the one-month implied volatility for a call with strike closest to the spot price.

Xing *et al.* [8] find that larger values of their skew measure predict lower stock returns in the cross section, a pattern that we find holds up as well using more recent data and a slightly different skew measure. Interestingly, this effect appears to run in the opposite direction of what we find using implied roughness. A smaller implied H indicates a faster decay of the ATM skew. If this indicates a higher initial value of the ATM skew, then the finding of Xing *et al.* [8] would suggest that stocks with smaller implied H have lower stock returns, yet we find exactly the opposite. This suggests that the performance of the rough-minus-smooth strategy is not explained by the XZZ-skew, a hypothesis we will check in the next sections.

4.3 *Double sorts*

To control for factors like liquidity or skewness that might influence the returns on our roughness quintile portfolios, in this section, we apply a standard double-sorting procedure.

Suppose, for example, that we want to control for illiquidity, using the Amihud measure. For each month, we proceed as follows. We sort stocks into deciles according to the Amihud measure. Within each of these illiquidity deciles, we sort stocks by roughness (realized or implied). We then take the roughest quintile from each of the illiquidity deciles — this is our rough portfolio. Similarly, we form our smooth portfolio by grouping all stocks that are in the smoothest quintile of any of the illiquidity deciles.

Under this construction, all levels of illiquidity are represented in the rough and smooth portfolios, so the performance of the rough-minus-smooth strategy should be unaffected by illiquidity: we have hedged out illiquidity. We sort into ten portfolios based on illiquidity in the first step in order to achieve a better balance of the conditioning factor between our controlled rough portfolio and smooth portfolio. The same procedure allows us to hedge out the effect of any other factor by first sorting on that factor.

We apply double sorts that condition on the following variables, one at a time:

- Average daily volume for each stock;
- The Amihud illiquidity measure;
- Turnover, measured as a stock's monthly trading volume divided by the average shares outstanding of that stock during the month;
- ATM implied volatility, as measured by the implied volatility for a 30-day option with strike closest to spot price;
- XZZ-skew, as defined in (11);
- Size (as measured by log market cap), book-to-market, and trailing 12-month return.

Table 5 shows the performance of the rough-minus-smooth strategy based on implied roughness after controlling for each of these factors through double sorts. The table shows average returns and alphas using either FF3-Mom or FF5-Mom factor models.

The first three rows of the table consider liquidity measures. Sorting first on average daily volume or the Amihud illiquidity measure reduces but does not eliminate the profitability of the strategy. Some reduction in performance is to be expected, given the correlation we documented in Section 4.1 between implied roughness and these measures. But the profitability of the strategy remains significant, particularly as measured by alpha relative to the Fama-French 5-factor with momentum, ranging from 3.1% to 5.4% per year, depending on the measure used, with t-statistics ranging from 2.0 to 3.0. Controlling for turnover actually increases the mean return of the strategy, with average monthly returns of 0.54%, and increases the t-statistics

Table 5: Performance of rough-minus-smooth portfolios using implied roughness, constructed through double sorts on various factors, for the period Jan 2000 through Jun 2016. Mean return and alphas are monthly values in percent. Numbers in brackets are t-statistics based on Newey-West standard errors.

Conditioning Variable	Mean Return	CAPM Alpha	FF3Mom Alpha	FF5Mom Alpha
Average Daily Volume	0.23*	0.21	0.23*	0.26**
	[1.84]	[1.60]	[1.81]	[2.01]
Average Daily Amihud	0.45***	0.46***	0.46***	0.40***
	[3.23]	[3.31]	[3.21]	[2.65]
Turnover	0.54***	0.53***	0.52***	0.45***
	[3.96]	[3.90]	[3.53]	[2.98]
XZZ Skew	0.46***	0.44**	0.49***	0.45***
	[2.79]	[2.54]	[2.96]	[2.61]
ATM Implied Volatility	0.59***	0.59***	0.59***	0.41**
	[3.54]	[3.51]	[3.32]	[2.28]
Size	0.41***	0.42***	0.46***	0.42***
	[3.24]	[3.31]	[3.53]	[3.16]
Book-to-Market	0.34**	0.32**	0.36**	0.35**
	[2.44]	[2.17]	[2.57]	[2.34]
12-Month Return	0.45***	0.43***	0.43***	0.48***
	[3.29]	[3.06]	[3.17]	[3.38]

to around 4.0. In short, liquidity by itself cannot account for the performance of the rough-minus-smooth strategy.

The next two rows of the table control for implied volatility and the ATM skew. Controlling for ATM implied volatility improves the average return and alphas to 7%, except for the FF5Mom alpha, which decreases a bit to 4.9% annually. Controlling for the XZZ-skew measure of Xing *et al.* [8] has only a small effect on the average return, alphas and t-statistics, and all alphas remain statistically significant. Thus, these well-known features of the implied volatility surface — the level of ATM volatility and skewness in implied volatility — cannot account for the performance of the rough-minus-smooth strategy.

The last three factors in the table serve as robustness checks. Sorting on size, book-to-market, and trailing returns may slightly reduce the performance of the strategy but does not eliminate — and may even strengthen — statistical significance.

Table 6 shows corresponding results based on realized roughness, using the full universe of stocks (Panel A) or the implied universe (Panel B). Here we find that controlling for liquidity (through average daily volume or the Amihud measure) removes the significance of returns and alphas of the rough-minus-smooth strategy. Controlling for size does as well in Panel A. These results suggest a strong association between realized roughness and illiquidity. In contrast, controlling for implied volatility and the ATM skew actually enhances the performance of the strategy. This further indicates that the effect of roughness, whether realized or implied, is not already reflected in the ATM volatility or the ATM skew.

4.4 *Fama–MacBeth Regressions*

To further investigate whether the performance of the rough-minus-smooth strategy is explained by other factors, we run regressions based on the specification

$$\mathrm{Ret}_{i,t} = b_{0t} + b_{1t} H_{i,t} + b'_{2t} \mathrm{CONTROLS}_{i,t-1} + e_{i,t}, \tag{12}$$

where $\mathrm{Ret}_{i,t}$ is the return of stock i in month t; $H_{i,t}$ is either realized or implied roughness of stock i in month t; $\mathrm{CONTROLS}_{i,t-1}$ is a vector of controls; and the $e_{i,t}$ are error terms. We estimate coefficients and their standard errors through Fama and MacBeth [9] regressions: in each month t, we run cross-sectional regressions to estimate b_{0t}, b_{1t}, and b_{2t}; we then take the time-series averages of these regression coefficients and use their time-series variation to estimate standard errors. Compared to the double sorts tested previously, these regressions have the advantage of allowing the simultaneous inclusion of multiple controls, but they have the disadvantage of imposing linearity on the relationship between returns and controls.

An alternative approach would be to run a panel regression to estimate (12) with no dependence on t in the coefficients. Since we are mainly interested in the cross-sectional relationship between roughness and returns, we would include month fixed-effects; and since monthly returns have very low autocorrelation, we would estimate standard errors clustered by month, following Petersen [26]. However, as also discussed in Petersen [26], Section 3, Fama–MacBeth standard

Table 6: Performance of rough-minus-smooth portfolios using realized roughness, constructed through double sorts on various factors, for the period Jan 2000 through Jun 2016. Mean return and alphas are monthly values in percent. Numbers in brackets are t-statistics based on Newey–West standard errors.

Conditioning Variable	Mean Return	CAPM Alpha	FF3Mom Alpha	FF5Mom Alpha
PANEL A: Full Universe				
Average Daily Volume	0.14	0.15	0.14	0.05
	[1.47]	[1.63]	[1.51]	[0.60]
Average Daily Amihud	0.12	0.17	0.12	−0.05
	[0.94]	[1.37]	[1.03]	[−0.45]
Turnover	0.38***	0.38**	0.33**	0.20
	[2.60]	[2.49]	[2.34]	[1.46]
XZZ Skew	0.54***	0.57***	0.53***	0.30*
	[3.10]	[3.22]	[3.36]	[1.95]
ATM Implied Volatility	0.54***	0.56***	0.59***	0.41**
	[2.81]	[2.92]	[3.17]	[2.15]
Size	0.12	0.18	0.13	−0.04
	[0.90]	[1.47]	[1.27]	[−0.37]
Book-to-Market	0.35***	0.38***	0.35***	0.20
	[2.63]	[2.90]	[2.73]	[1.55]
12-Month Return	0.51***	0.54***	0.50***	0.37**
	[3.06]	[3.12]	[3.19]	[2.34]
PANEL B: Implied Universe				
Average Daily Volume	0.22	0.25	0.21	0.08
	[1.43]	[1.64]	[1.48]	[0.56]
Average Daily Amihud	0.40*	0.47**	0.41**	0.22
	[1.94]	[2.31]	[2.40]	[1.35]
Turnover	0.60***	0.61***	0.63***	0.53***
	[3.13]	[3.09]	[3.38]	[2.79]
XZZ Skew	0.49**	0.53**	0.51***	0.27
	[2.41]	[2.51]	[2.88]	[1.54]
ATM Implied Volatility	0.62***	0.63***	0.62***	0.43*
	[2.81]	[2.77]	[2.88]	[1.95]
Size	0.49**	0.55***	0.53***	0.35**
	[2.41]	[2.70]	[3.13]	[2.10]
Book-to-Market	0.31*	0.34**	0.33**	0.14
	[1.83]	[2.05]	[2.05]	[0.88]
12-Month Return	0.55***	0.60***	0.57***	0.41**
	[2.96]	[3.08]	[3.47]	[2.47]

errors are more accurate than panel regressions with clustered standard errors under two conditions that are appropriate to our setting: (1) the main source of dependence in error terms comes from time effects (correlations in returns of different stocks in the same month); and (2) the number of time periods (201 months) is not very large compared with the number of stocks per month (up to 1108 stocks per month in the implied universe and 3577 per month for the full universe). The dependence in (1) is dealt with effectively by Fama–MacBeth regressions. The values in (2) would require the estimation of a very large covariance matrix between different stocks based on limited data in order to cluster by time. In light of these considerations, we use Fama–MacBeth regressions.

Table 7 shows the results. Panel A tests implied H; Panel B test realized H on the implied universe; and Panel C tests the realized H on the full universe of stocks. Each panel shows two regressions, one including only the corresponding roughness measure, and one including multiple controls. All explanatory variables have been standardized (cross-sectionally in each month) to make the coefficients comparable. Returns are in decimals, so a return of 5% is recorded as 0.05.

Panel A confirms the negative relationship between returns and implied H; including controls increases the magnitude and significance of the coefficient. Panel B shows that realized H has a significant relationship with returns when restricted to the implied universe, but this relationship is eliminated by the controls. In Panel C we find no significant relationship between realized H and returns on the full universe of stocks, with or without controls. Interestingly, our results confirm a strong negative relationship between returns and the skewness measure of Xing *et al.* [8], while also showing in Panel A that this control does not explain the effectiveness of implied roughness.

Our controls include return volatility and implied volatility, so the regressions in Table 7 also control for the volatility risk premium (Carr and Wu [27]) measured as the difference between implied and realized volatility. In particular, Panel A shows that the profitability of the implied strategy cannot be attributed to the volatility risk premium.

Table 7: Fama–MacBeth return regressions. Panel A, B, C each have two regression results, one with only one regressor (either implied or realized H) and the other including a complete set of controls. Panel A shows results for implied H. Panel B presents results for realized H on the implied universe. Panel C uses realized H and the unrestricted universe. Numbers in brackets are t-statistics based on Newey-West standard errors.

	Panel A		Panel B		Panel C	
Variable	Reg 1	Reg 2	Reg 3	Reg 4	Reg 5	Reg 6
Intercept	0.0043	0.0046	0.0043	0.0046	0.0088*	0.0078
	[0.83]	[0.91]	[0.83]	[0.90]	[1.66]	[1.49]
Implied H	−0.0010**	−0.0014***				
	[−2.04]	[−3.43]				
Realized H			−0.0015**	−0.0003	−0.0003	−0.0002
			[−2.10]	[−0.68]	[−0.51]	[−0.56]
XZZ Skew		−0.0034***		−0.0034***		−0.0036***
		[−5.30]		[−5.20]		[−6.56]
ATM volatilities		−0.0063***		−0.0062**		−0.0047**
		[−2.62]		[−2.56]		[−2.25]
Log Option Volume		−0.0033*		−0.0034*		−0.0015
		[−1.85]		[−1.91]		[−1.44]
Log Option Open Interest		0.0025		0.0024		−0.0012
		[1.58]		[1.53]		[−1.22]
Log Stock $ Volume		0.0044		0.0046		0.0006
		[1.38]		[1.45]		[0.25]
Log Stock Volume		0.0019		0.0018		0.0061***
		[1.06]		[1.03]		[3.58]
Turnover		−0.0019		−0.0020		−0.0027**
		[−1.47]		[−1.54]		[−2.51]
Book-to-Market		−0.0003		−0.0002		−0.0010
		[−0.29]		[−0.21]		[−0.36]
Log Size		−0.0095***		−0.0094***		−0.0079***
		[−2.89]		[−2.84]		[−3.01]
Past 6M Return		−0.0006		−0.0007		−0.0007
		[−0.49]		[−0.56]		[−0.59]
Past 12M Return		0.0010		0.0011		0.0010
		[0.93]		[0.98]		[1.01]
Past Return Volatility		−0.0024*		−0.0024		−0.0043***
		[−1.65]		[−1.63]		[−2.76]
Past Return Skew		−0.0005		−0.0004		−0.0002
		[−0.95]		[−0.88]		[−0.60]
Adj. R^2	0.29%	13.15%	0.46%	13.18%	0.14%	9.21%

5. Event Risk: Earnings Announcements and FOMC Meetings

In this section, we argue that cross-sectional differences in implied roughness of individual stocks reflect differences in near-term downside risk; we interpret the profitability of the rough-minus-smooth strategy as compensation for bearing this risk. We support this interpretation by considering the performance of the strategy around two types of events: company-specific earnings announcements, and interest rate announcements by the Federal Reserve's Open Markets Committee (FOMC). We present three pieces of evidence to support our argument. The strategy's profitability is greatest when restricted to stocks with earnings announcements in the subsequent month, when the potential for near-term idiosyncratic risk is high; roughness does not forecast earnings, suggesting that the strategy's profitability reflects compensation for risk rather superior selection of profitable companies; the strategy is not profitable in the lead-up to FOMC announcements — a period of elevated aggregate near-term risk rather than idiosyncratic near-term risk.

5.1 *Earnings announcements*

5.1.1 *Testing for earnings surprise predictability*

We begin by testing whether roughness predicts earnings surprises, as a possible explanation for the profitability of our strategy. Positive earnings surprises tend to be followed by stock price appreciation, so a signal that forecasts earnings surprises can serve as the basis for a profitable trading strategy. We will see, however, that this does not explain the profitability of the roughness signal.

We focus on the subset of data defined by

$$I^{ea} = \{(i,t)\colon \text{stock } i \text{ has an earnings announcement in month } t\},$$

using earnings announcement data from IBES. Letting I denote the full universe of stock-month pairs for which we have an implied roughness measure, $I \backslash I^{ea}$ denotes the subset that do not have an earnings announcement.

To measure earnings surprises, we use the standardized unexpected earnings (SUE) score from IBES. SUE measures the difference between a company's actual earnings and the mean forecast by analysts, normalized by the standard deviation of analyst forecasts in the previous quarter. To test for a relation between SUE and roughness, we use the Fama–MacBeth regression approach, meaning that we first run the following regression for every month t,

$$SUE_{i,t} = b_{0t} + b_{1t}H_{i,t-1} + e_{i,t}, \quad (i,t) \in I^{ea},$$

where $H_{i,t-1}$ denotes the implied roughness calculated for stock i in month $t-1$. We then average the b_{1t} over all months t and calculate standard errors adjusted for autocorrelation.

For comparison, we run the same analysis replacing implied roughness with the ATM skew in (11). Using data through 2005, Xing *et al.* [8] show that a greater ATM skew forecasts negative earnings surprises. In other words, before companies report disappointing earnings, low-strike puts become more expensive. Xing *et al.* [8] interpret this as evidence that investors with inside information trade on that information through options and that the stock market is slow to incorporate the information in option prices.

The left panel of Table 8 reports estimated coefficients and t-statistics for the two regressions. The bottom row confirms the finding of Xing *et al.* [8], with the benefit of more than ten years of additional data. The coefficient on the ATM skew is large, negative,

Table 8: Left panel shows coefficients and t-statistics in Fama–MacBeth regressions of standardized unexpected earnings (SUE) on implied roughness and ATM skew. Right panel shows the difference in average SUE in the top and bottom quintiles of stocks sorted by implied roughness or ATM skew. Numbers in brackets are t-statistics based on Newey–West standard errors.

FM Regression		Portfolio Sorting
Variable	Coeff.	Difference in SUE
Implied H	0.035	−0.087
	[0.155]	[−0.324]
ATM skew	−2.744***	−0.300***
	[−2.827]	[−3.277]

and statistically significant. In contrast, the coefficient on implied roughness is indistinguishable from zero. Implied roughness does not forecast earnings surprises, and the implied roughness signal is distinct from the information in the ATM skew.

The right panel of Table 8 further supports these conclusions. In this analysis, in each month t we limit ourselves to stocks with earnings announcements in month $t+1$. We sort these stocks into quintile portfolios based on roughness in month t. The table shows the difference in average SUE (in month $t+1$) between the highest and lowest roughness quintiles. The table shows the same comparison for stocks sorted on ATM skew in month t. We again see that a higher ATM skew forecasts negative earnings surprises whereas there is no relation between roughness and SUE. The profitability of the rough-minus-smooth strategy is not grounded in forecasting earnings.

5.1.2 *Strategy performance near earnings announcements*

Next we compare the performance of the rough-minus-smooth strategy when restricted to subsets of stocks based on the timing of earnings announcements. Specifically, we evaluate performance in three cases:

I^{ea}: sort stocks with announcements in month t based on roughness in month $t-1$;

$I \setminus I^{ea}$: sort stocks without announcements in month t based on roughness in month $t-1$;

$I^{ea,100}$: same as I^{ea} but only if at least 100 stocks in I have announcements in month t.

In all cases, portfolios are formed in month $t-1$ and returns are evaluated in month t.

Performance results under these restrictions are shown in the top panel of Table 9. Compared with the right-most column of Table 3, restricting attention to earnings-announcement stocks I^{ea} improves monthly alphas by roughly 40%, from around 0.50 to around 0.70. The estimated alphas are now only marginally significant, but this may be because the sample size (the number of stocks available each month) is now smaller. The results for $I^{ea,100}$ support this hypothesis: in months with at least 100 stocks available, the estimated monthly

Table 9: Top panel: Implied roughness strategy performance on stocks with earnings announcements in the next month (I^{ea}), in months with at least 100 candidate stocks ($I^{ea,100}$), and on stocks without earnings announcements $I \setminus I^{ea}$. Middle panel: Long-only performance on the same sets of stocks. Bottom panel: Long-only comparison of stocks with and without earnings announcements in the full universe of stock-month pairs. Numbers in brackets are t-statistics based on Newey-West standard errors.

	Mean Return	CAPM Alpha	FF3Mom Alpha	FF5Mom Alpha
Rough Minus Smooth (implied roughness universe)				
Earnings Announcement Stocks	0.71*	0.71*	0.70*	0.74*
(I^{ea})	[1.71]	[1.68]	[1.73]	[1.72]
EA Stocks — Threshold 100	1.00***	1.03***	1.07***	1.11***
($I^{ea,100}$)	[2.60]	[2.67]	[2.91]	[2.95]
No Earnings Announcement	0.30	0.28	0.29	0.29
($I \setminus I^{ea}$)	[1.41]	[1.23]	[1.25]	[1.22]
Long Only (implied roughness universe)				
Earnings Announcement Stocks	0.63*	0.12	0.14	0.20
(I^{ea})	[1.70]	[0.88]	[1.08]	[1.49]
EA Stocks — Threshold 100	0.47	−0.03	−0.01	0.09
($I^{ea,100}$)	[1.13]	[−0.28]	[−0.06]	[0.76]
No Earnings Announcement	0.29	−0.22***	−0.17***	−0.15**
($I \setminus I^{ea}$)	[0.81]	[−3.23]	[−2.69]	[−2.53]
Long Only (full universe)				
Earnings Announcement Stocks	0.77**	0.24**	0.21**	0.20**
(F^{ea})	[2.23]	[2.33]	[2.20]	[2.12]
No Earnings Announcement	0.38	−0.16***	−0.17***	−0.18***
($F \setminus F^{ea}$)	[1.12]	[−2.91]	[−2.79]	[−3.07]

alpha goes above 1.0 (an annual alpha of more than 12%) and is highly significant. (These results are not sensitive to the choice of 100 as threshold.) In contrast, when we exclude stocks with earnings announcements, the $I \setminus I^{ea}$ alphas are smaller than the alphas in Table 3 and not statistically significant.

Taken together, the results in the top panel of the table show that sorting on roughness is most effective when applied to stocks facing a near-term idiosyncratic risk in the form of an earnings surprise. We interpret this to mean that greater roughness signals greater near-term downside risk, and that this risk is compensated with a price discount and a subsequent higher average return.

The analysis in the top panel is necessarily restricted to the universe I of stock-month pairs for which implied roughness is available. As a benchmark, the second panel shows market returns and alphas for the restricted sets of stocks used in the top panel. The second panel treats each restricted set as a long-only portfolio. The bottom row shows that stocks without earnings announcements earn lower returns; but the main implication of the second panel is that the results in the top panel cannot be attributed to the restrictions in the definitions of I^{ea}, $I^{ea,100}$, and $I \setminus I^{ea}$. Moreover, the average implied H values in these three sets are nearly identical and all in 0.17–0.18.

This point is reinforced by the bottom panel. Here we drop the restriction to I and compare performance on the full universe of stocks with earnings announcements F^{ea} and without $F \setminus F^{ea}$. Stocks with earnings announcements earn higher returns than stocks without. Put differently, investors are compensated for bearing earnings announcement risk. Sorting on roughness identifies the stocks where this risk compensation is greatest.

These observations invite speculation on the implied strategy's losses in September 2001, which we mentioned in our discussion of Figure 3. Based on quintiles formed in August, the strategy would be long stocks facing near-term downside uncertainty. These stocks may have proved to be the most vulnerable to the disruptions and shock of the 9/11 attacks, leading the strategy to incur large losses.

5.2 *Strategy performance near FOMC announcements*

We now turn from considering individual corporate events to FOMC announcements, which are among the most important scheduled events for the aggregate market. Indeed, Lucca and Moench [28] find that the excess return of the stock market is mainly earned during the 24-hour window before the earnings announcement; in other periods the average excess return is not statistically different from zero.

If, as we have suggested, implied roughness ranks stocks on near-term idiosyncratic risk, then our strategy should not be expected to enhance returns in the lead-up to FOMC announcements.

Following Lucca and Moench [28], we consider announcements for the eight scheduled FOMC meetings each year. (Public announcements began in 1994, and our sample starts in 2000.) We define the pre-announcement period as the interval from the close of trading on day $d-2$ to the close on day d, where d denotes the FOMC announcement date. We compare the performance of our strategy when it is restricted to invest in (or outside of) the pre-announcement period.

Our strategy is based on monthly data, so these timing restrictions require some explanation. When we limit ourselves to investing in pre-announcement periods, we evaluate performance only in the eight months of the year with scheduled announcements. In each such month, we take the return for the month to be the return over the two days that make up the pre-announcement period. We can apply this restriction to stock-month pairs in the implied roughness universe, in which case we label it I^{preFOMC}, and we can apply the restriction to the full universe of stock-month pairs and label it F^{preFOMC}.

We label the opposite restrictions I^{nonFOMC} and F^{nonFOMC}. For the four months of each year without an FOMC announcement, the "nonFOMC" return is the just the ordinary monthly return. For the other eight months, the "nonFOMC" return is the return for the month excluding the two-day pre-announcement window.

The results are shown in Table 10, which has the same format as Table 9. The top panel compares the rough-minus-smooth strategy with the "preFOMC" and "nonFOMC" restrictions; the second panel shows long-only results with the same restrictions and limited to the universe of stock-month pairs for which we have implied roughness; the bottom panel shows long-only results when the restrictions are applied to the full universe of stock-month pairs.

The bottom panel is closest to the work of Lucca and Moench [28] and consistent with their conclusions: stocks earn higher returns during the pre-announcement period than at other times. The pattern is nearly identical in the middle panel, indicating that the I universe is representative of the full universe in its response to FOMC announcements.

Table 10: Top panel: Implied roughness strategy performance in the pre-announcement period (I^{preFOMC}) and outside the pre-announcement period (I^{nonFOMC}). Middle panel: Long-only performance of the implied universe I during the same time periods. Bottom panel: Long-only performance of the full universe during the same time periods.

	Mean Return	CAPM Alpha	FF3Mom Alpha	FF5Mom Alpha
Rough Minus Smooth (implied roughness universe)				
pre FOMC ann	0.09	0.11^{*}	0.08	0.11^{*}
(I^{preFOMC})	[1.53]	[1.72]	[1.40]	[1.78]
non pre-FOMC ann	0.43^{**}	0.40^{**}	0.42^{**}	0.43^{**}
(I^{nonFOMC})	[2.42]	[2.16]	[2.36]	[2.38]
Long Only (implied roughness universe)				
pre FOMC ann	0.41^{***}	0.27^{*}	0.33^{**}	0.32^{**}
(I^{preFOMC})	[3.20]	[1.92]	[2.24]	[2.12]
non pre-FOMC ann	0.12	-0.36^{***}	-0.35^{***}	-0.30^{***}
(I^{nonFOMC})	[0.34]	[−3.58]	[−3.25]	[−2.70]
Long Only (full universe)				
pre FOMC ann	0.41^{***}	0.26	0.37^{*}	0.36^{*}
(F^{preFOMC})	[2.59]	[1.38]	[1.81]	[1.76]
non pre-FOMC ann	0.26	-0.25^{**}	-0.29^{***}	-0.29^{***}
(F^{preFOMC})	[0.78]	[−2.49]	[−2.80]	[−2.66]

In the top panel, the results flip. Sorting on implied roughness is not profitable during the pre-announcement period, when all stocks are facing a high degree of near-term systematic risk. The rough-minus-smooth strategy earns its returns the rest of the year, away from the pre-announcement period.

Recall that implied roughness measures the rate of decay of the ATM skew. A larger ATM skew indicates greater concern for downside risk, so a projected rapid decay in the ATM skew suggests concerns for downside risk that will be resolved quickly. Taking the results of this section together with those of Section 5.1.2, we see that proximity to a company-specific event enhances the performance of our strategy whereas proximity to an aggregate event has the opposite effect. This pattern suggests that the near-term downside risk captured by implied roughness is idiosyncratic. Moreover, the profitability of the rough-minus-smooth strategy suggests that investors are compensated for bearing this particular type of risk.

Our investigation does not explain why this near-term idiosyncratic risk should earn a risk premium. But the puzzle is not specific to our setting. Leaving aside roughness, the bottom panel of Table 9 records a well-known phenomenon of stocks earning higher returns around earnings announcements. Sorting on implied roughness pushes this effect further.

6. Conclusions

We have investigated strategies for trading stocks based on measures of roughness in their volatility. We have compared long-short strategies based on realized roughness (calculated from high-frequency stock returns) and implied roughness (calculated from option prices). Both measures support a strategy of buying stocks with rougher volatilities and selling stocks with smoother volatilities; but sorting on implied roughness yields higher returns and is more robust to controlling for other factors. In particular, it is robust to controlling for illiquidity and the level of the ATM skew.

We have argued that implied roughness provides a measure of near-term idiosyncratic risk: a stock with greater implied roughness is one that the market perceives to have downside uncertainty that will be resolved quickly. On this interpretation, the profitability of our rough-minus-smooth strategy reflects compensation for bearing this risk. The performance of our strategy is enhanced near earnings announcements, when stocks face elevated idiosyncratic risk, and it is suppressed near FOMC announcements, when the dominant near-term risk is systematic.

Our work raises interesting questions for the rough volatility framework. Part of the appeal of this framework is that it simultaneously explains key features of realized volatility and the implied volatility surface extracted from option prices. Yet we find important differences in working with realized and implied measures of roughness. Estimating either measure of roughness from limited data presents significant difficulties, so it is unclear if the differences we observe present a challenge to the theoretical framework or simply call for better estimation methods.

Appendix: Filtering of Option Data

We apply some filtering rules when computing implied roughness to avoid using questionable data from illiquid options. We largely follow the rules in Xing *et al.* [8], which are quite standard in the empirical literature on options. We require the following features:

- Underlying stock volume for that day > 0;
- Underlying stock price for that day $>$ \$5;
- Implied volatility of the option $\geq 3\%$ and $\leq 200\%$;
- The option's open interest > 0;
- The option's volume can be 0 but has to be non-missing;
- The option has time to maturity $\tau \geq 5$ and $\tau \leq 365$ calendar days.

In addition, when estimating non-parametrically the ATM skew for each time-to-maturity τ, we set the minimal number of implied volatilities needed to measure the ATM skew for a particular time-to-maturity (for a particular stock on a particular day) at four.

When running a regression of the ATM skew term structure to estimate an implied H, we use the following filtering rules: The minimal number of ATM skews along the dimension of time-to-maturity (for a particular stock on a particular day) is three, meaning that there must be at least three points in the regression

$$\log \phi(\tau) = c + (H - 1/2) \log \tau + \epsilon.$$

For each day, we apply these filters to call and put options separately. If for a stock, both calls and puts pass the filtering rules on a given day, we use the average implied roughness $(H^{\text{call}} + H^{\text{put}})/2$ as the implied measure on that day; otherwise we use whichever type of option passes, and if neither passes the filters, we mark the value as NA for that stock on that day.

When forming monthly portfolios, we need to aggregate daily implied roughness measures into a monthly measure. We include a stock only if it has more than 15 non-NA daily implied roughness estimates for that month. (This is similar to what is used by Ang *et al.* [29]). Otherwise, we mark the implied measure for that stock and month as NA. These restrictions define our implied universe of stock-month pairs.

In estimating daily realized variance $\hat{\sigma}_d^2$ in Section 2.1, we use trade data only and we apply the data cleaning steps in Barndorff-Nielsen *et al.* [16].

References

[1] J. Gatheral, T. Jaisson, and M. Rosenbaum (2018). Volatility is rough. *Quantitative Finance*, 18(6): 933–949.
[2] C. Bayer, P. Friz, and J. Gatheral (2016). Pricing under rough volatility. *Quantitative Finance*, 16(6): 887–904.
[3] M. Fukasawa (2017). Short-time at-the-money skew and rough fractional volatility. *Quantitative Finance*, 17(2): 189–198.
[4] M. Bennedsen, A. Lunde, and M.S. Pakkanen (2016). Decoupling the short- and long-term behavior of stochastic volatility. *Working Paper*,
[5] O. El Euch, M. Fukasawa, J. Gatheral, and M. Rosenbaum (2018a). Short-term at-the-money asymptotics under stochastic volatility models. *arXiv preprint arXiv:1801.08675.*
[6] O. El Euch, M. Fukasawa, and M. Rosenbaum (2018b). The microstructural foundations of leverage effect and rough volatility. *Finance and Stochastics*, 22(2): 241–280.
[7] P. Jusselin and M. Rosenbaum (2018). No-arbitrage implies power-law market impact and rough volatility. *arXiv preprint arXiv:1805.07134.*
[8] Y. Xing, X. Zhang, and R. Zhao (2010). What does the individual option volatility smirk tell us about future equity returns. *Journal of Financial and Quantitative Analysis*, 45: 641–662.
[9] E.F. Fama and J.D. MacBeth (1973). Risk, return, and equilibrium: Empirical tests. *Journal of Political Economy*, 81(3): 607–636.
[10] B.B. Mandelbrot and J.W. Van Ness (1968). Fractional Brownian motions, fractional noises and applications. *SIAM Review*, 10(4): 422–437.
[11] G. Samorodnitsky and M. Taqqu (1994). *Non-Gaussian Stable Processes: Stochastic Models with Infinite Variance.* London: Chapman and Hall.
[12] L. Bergomi (2009). *Smile dynamics* iv.
[13] G. Livieri, S. Mouti, A. Pallavicini, and M. Rosenbaum (2018). Rough volatility: Evidence from option prices. *IISE Transactions*, pp. 1–21.
[14] E. Abi Jaber and O. El Euch (2018). Multi-factor approximation of rough volatility models. *arXiv preprint arXiv:1801.10359.*

[15] J. Garnier and K. Sølna (2018). Option pricing under fast-varying and rough stochastic volatility. *Annals of Finance*, 14(4): 489–516.
[16] O.E. Barndorff-Nielsen, P.R. Hansen, A. Lunde, and N. Shephard (2009). Realized kernels in practice: Trades and quotes. *Econometrics Journal*, 12(3): C1–C32.
[17] M. Fukasawa (2011). Asymptotic analysis for stochastic volatility: Martingale expansion. *Finance and Stochastics*, 15(4): 635–654.
[18] M. Forde and H. Zhang (2017). Asymptotics for rough stochastic volatility models. *SIAM Journal on Financial Mathematics*, 8(1): 114–145.
[19] L. Bergomi and J. Guyon (2012). Stochastic volatility's orderly smiles. *Risk*, 25(5):60.
[20] E.F. Fama and K.R. French (1993). Common risk factors in the returns on stocks and bonds. *Journal of Financial Economics*, 33(1): 3–56.
[21] M.M. Carhart (1997). On persistence in mutual fund performance. *The Journal of Finance*, 52 (1): 57–82.
[22] E.F. Fama and K.R. French (2015). A five-factor asset pricing model. *The Journal of Financial Economics*, 116(1):1–22.
[23] W.K. Newey and K.D. West (1987). A simple, positive semi-definite, heteroskedasticity and autocorrelation consistent covariance matrix. *Econometrica*, 55(3): 703–708.
[24] Y. Amihud (2002). Illiquidity and stock returns: Cross-section and time-series effects. *Journal of Financial Markets*, 5(1): 31–56.
[25] J. Conrad, R.F. Dittmar, and E. Ghysels (2013). Ex ante skewness and expected stock returns. *The Journal of Finance*, 68 (1): 85–124.
[26] M.A. Petersen (2009). Estimating standard errors in finance panel data sets: comparing approaches. *The Review of Financial Studies*, 22(1): 435–480.
[27] P. Carr and L. Wu (2008). Variance risk premiums. *The Review of Financial Studies*, 22(3):1311–1341.
[28] D.O. Lucca and E. Moench (2015). The pre-FOMC announcement drift. *The Journal of Finance*, LXX (1).
[29] A. Ang, R.J. Hodrick, Y. Xing, and X. Zhang (2006). The cross-section of volatility and expected returns. *The Journal of Finance*, 61(1): 259–299.

https://doi.org/10.1142/9789811259142_0008

Chapter 8

Volatility is Rough*

J. Gatheral[†,§], T. Jaisson[‡,¶], and M. Rosenbaum[‡,||]

[†] *Baruch College, The City University of New York, United States*

[‡] *Ecole Polytechnique, Paris, France*

[§] *jim.gatheral@baruch.cuny.edu*

[¶] *thibault.jaisson@polytechnique.edu*

[||] *mathieu.rosenbaum@polytechnique.edu*

Abstract

Estimating volatility from recent high frequency data, we revisit the question of the smoothness of the volatility process. Our main result is that log-volatility behaves essentially as a fractional Brownian motion with Hurst exponent H of order 0.1, at any reasonable time scale. This leads us to adopt the fractional stochastic volatility (FSV) model of Comte and Renault [21]. We call our model Rough FSV (RFSV) to underline that, in contrast to FSV, $H < 1/2$. We demonstrate that our RFSV model is remarkably consistent with financial time series data; one application is that it enables us to obtain improved forecasts of realized volatility. Furthermore, we find that although volatility is not a long memory process in the RFSV model, classical statistical procedures aiming at detecting volatility persistence tend to conclude the presence of long memory in data generated from it. This sheds light on why long memory of volatility has been widely accepted as a stylized fact.

---

*First version of the paper: 13 October 2014. This chapter is derived from Gatheral, J., Jaisson, T. and Rosenbaum, M. (2018). Volatility is rough. *Quant. Finance*, 18(6), 933–949. Reprinted by permission of Taylor & Francis Ltd.

Keywords: High frequency data, volatility smoothness, fractional Brownian motion, fractional Ornstein-Uhlenbeck, long memory, volatility persistence, volatility forecasting, option pricing, volatility surface.

1. Introduction

1.1 *Volatility modeling*

In the derivatives world, log-prices are often modeled as continuous semi-martingales. For a given asset with log-price Y_t, such a process takes the form

$$dY_t = \mu_t dt + \sigma_t dW_t,$$

where μ_t is a drift term and W_t is a one-dimensional Brownian motion. The term σ_t denotes the volatility process and is the most important ingredient of the model. In the Black–Scholes framework, the volatility function is either constant or a deterministic function of time. In Dupire's local volatility model, see [28], the local volatility $\sigma(Y_t, t)$ is a deterministic function of the underlying price and time, chosen to match observed European option prices exactly. Such a model is by definition time-inhomogeneous; its dynamics are highly unrealistic, typically generating future volatility surfaces (see Section 1.3) completely unlike those we observe. A corollary of this is that prices of exotic options under local volatility can be substantially off-market. On the other hand, in so-called stochastic volatility models, the volatility σ_t is modeled as a continuous Brownian semi-martingale. Notable amongst such stochastic volatility models are the Hull and White model [41], the Heston model [40], and the SABR model [39]. Whilst stochastic volatility dynamics are more realistic than local volatility dynamics, generated option prices are not consistent with observed European option prices. We refer to [33] and [46] for more detailed reviews of the different approaches to volatility modeling. More recent market practice is to use local-stochastic-volatility (LSV) models which both fit the market exactly and generate reasonable dynamics.

Consistent with our focus on derivatives, our goal in this work is to replicate features of the observed time series of volatility over time scales from one day to ten years say. Indeed, volatility modeling can probably only be relevant at time scales of order one day or more. Below this, at the sub-second time scale for example, it is not even clear what the meaning of volatility is (independently of a specific model). Nevertheless, in order to get accurate volatility measurements, we will rely on high frequency methods in our estimation procedures.

1.2 *Fractional volatility*

In terms of the smoothness of the volatility process, the preceding models offer two possibilities: very regular sample paths in the case of Black-Scholes, and volatility trajectories with regularity close to that of Brownian motion for the local and stochastic volatility models. Starting from the stylized fact that volatility is a long memory process, various authors have proposed models that allow for a wider range of regularity for the volatility. In a pioneering paper, Comte and Renault [21] proposed to model log-volatility using fractional Brownian motion (fBm for short), ensuring long memory by choosing the Hurst parameter $H > 1/2$. A large literature has subsequently developed around such fractional volatility models, for example [16,20,51].

The fBm $(W_t^H)_{t\in\mathbb{R}}$ with Hurst parameter $H \in (0,1)$, introduced in [43], is a centered self-similar Gaussian process with stationary increments satisfying for any $t \in \mathbb{R}$, $\Delta \geq 0$, $q > 0$:

$$\mathbb{E}[|W_{t+\Delta}^H - W_t^H|^q] = K_q \Delta^{qH}, \tag{1}$$

with K_q the moment of order q of the absolute value of a standard Gaussian variable. For $H = 1/2$, we retrieve the classical Brownian motion. The sample paths of W^H are Hölder-continuous with exponent r, for any $r < H$.[a] Finally, when $H > 1/2$, the increments of the fBm are positively correlated and exhibit long memory in the sense that

$$\sum_{k=0}^{+\infty} \mathrm{Cov}[W_1^H, W_k^H - W_{k-1}^H] = +\infty.$$

[a] Actually H corresponds to the regularity of the process in a more accurate way: in terms of Besov smoothness spaces, see Section 2.1.

Indeed, $\mathrm{Cov}[W_1^H, W_k^H - W_{k-1}^H]$ is of order k^{2H-2} as $k \to \infty$. Note that in the case of the fBm, there is a one to one correspondence between regularity and long memory through the Hurst parameter H.

As mentioned earlier, the long memory property of the volatility process has been widely accepted as a stylized fact since the seminal analyses of Ding, Granger and Engle [26], Andersen and Bollerslev [2] and Andersen *et al.* [4]. Initially, it appears that the term *long memory* referred to the slow decay of the autocorrelation function (of absolute returns for example), anything slower than exponential. Over time however, it seems that this term has acquired the more precise meaning that the autocorrelation function is not integrable, see [10], and even more precisely that it decays as a power-law with exponent less than 1. Much of the more recent literature, for example [9,15,17], assumes long memory in volatility in this more technical sense. Indeed, meaningful results can probably only be obtained under such a specification, since it is not possible to estimate the asymptotic behavior of the covariance function without assuming a specific form. Nevertheless, analyses such as that of Andersen *et al.* [4] use data that predate the advent of high-frequency electronic trading, and the evidence for long memory has never been sufficient to satisfy remaining doubters such as Mikosch and Stărică in [45]. To quote Rama Cont in [22]:

> ... the econometric debate on the short range or long range nature of dependence in volatility still goes on (and may probably never be resolved) ...

In the spirit of the above quote, in our view, the question as to whether the volatility time series exhibits long memory (in a technical sense) or not is not a very useful or fruitful one. Indeed we believe that in practice, the concept of long memory is too fragile to be applicable to an analysis involving ultra high frequency data (for example any seasonality may give rise to spurious long memory). Therefore we do not focus on long memory in this work. Still, we do show that the autocorrelation function of volatility does not behave as a power law, at least at usual time scales of observation. In particular, we are able to provide explicit expressions enabling us to analyze thoroughly the dependence structure of the volatility process.

1.3 *The shape of the implied volatility surface*

As is well-known, the implied volatility $\sigma_{\mathrm{BS}}(k, \tau)$ of an option (with log-moneyness k and time to expiration τ) is the value of the volatility parameter in the Black–Scholes formula required to match the market price of that option. Plotting implied volatility as a function of strike price and time to expiry generates the *volatility surface*, explored in detail in, for example, [33]. A typical such volatility surface generated from a "stochastic volatility inspired" (SVI) [34] fit to closing SPX option prices as of June 20, 2013[b] is shown in Figure 1. It is a stylized fact that, at least in equity markets, although the level and orientation of the volatility surface do change over time, the general overall shape of the volatility surface does not change, at least to a first approximation. This suggests that it is desirable to model volatility as a time-homogenous process, i.e. a process whose parameters are independent of price and time.

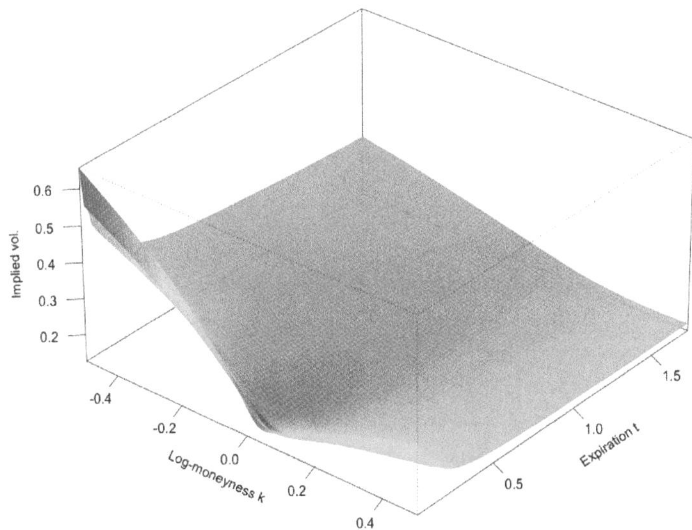

Figure 1: The S&P volatility surface as of June 20, 2013.

[b]Closing prices of SPX options for all available strikes and expirations as of June 20, 2013 were sourced from OptionMetrics (www.optionmetrics.com) via Wharton Research Data Services (WRDS).

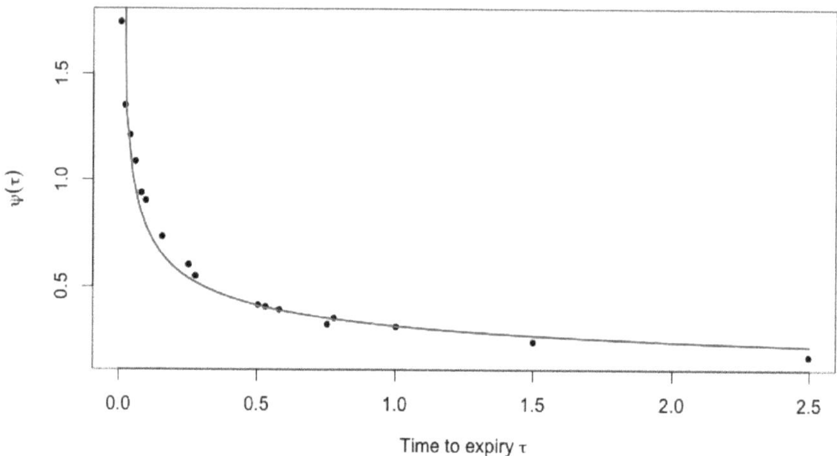

Figure 2: The black dots are non-parametric estimates of the S&P ATM volatility skews as of June 20, 2013; the red curve is the power-law fit $\psi(\tau) = A\,\tau^{-0.4}$.

However, conventional time-homogenous models of volatility such as the Hull and White, Heston, and SABR models do not fit the volatility surface. In particular, as shown in Figure 2, the observed term structure of at-the-money ($k = 0$) volatility skew

$$\psi(\tau) := \left|\frac{\partial}{\partial k}\sigma_{\text{BS}}(k,\tau)\right|_{k=0}$$

is well-approximated by a power-law function of time to expiry τ. In contrast, conventional stochastic volatility models generate a term structure of at-the-money (ATM) skew that is *constant* for small τ and behaves as a sum of decaying exponentials for larger τ.

In Section 3.3 of [32], as an example of the application of his martingale expansion, Fukasawa shows that a stochastic volatility model where the volatility is driven by fractional Brownian motion with Hurst exponent H generates an ATM volatility skew of the form $\psi(\tau) \sim \tau^{H-1/2}$, at least for small τ. This is interesting in and of itself in that it provides a counterexample to the widespread belief that the explosion of the volatility smile as $\tau \to 0$ (as clearly seen in Figures 1 and 2) implies the presence of jumps [14]. The main point here is that for a model of the sort analyzed by Fukasawa to generate a volatility surface with a reasonable shape, we would need to have a value of H close to zero. As we will see in Section 2, our empirical estimates of H from time series data are in fact very small.

The volatility model that we will specify in Section 3.1, driven by fBm with $H < 1/2$, therefore has the potential to be not only consistent with the empirically observed properties of the volatility time series but also consistent with the shape of the volatility surface. In this paper, we focus on the modeling of the volatility time series. A more detailed analysis of the consistency of our model with option prices is provided in [7].

1.4 *Main results and organization of the chapter*

In Section 2, we report our estimates of the smoothness of the log-volatility for selected assets. This smoothness parameter lies systematically between 0.08 and 0.2 (in the sense of Hölder regularity for example). Furthermore, we find that increments of the log-volatility are approximately normally distributed and that their moments enjoy a remarkable monofractal scaling property. This leads us to model the log of volatility using a fBm with Hurst parameter $H < 1/2$ in Section 3. Specifically we adopt the fractional stochastic volatility (FSV) model of Comte and Renault [21]. We call our model Rough FSV (RSFV) to underline that, in contrast to FSV, we take $H < 1/2$. We also show in the same section that the RFSV model is remarkably consistent with volatility time series data. The issue of volatility persistence is considered through the lens of the RFSV model in Section 4. Our main finding is that although the RFSV model does not have any long memory property, classical statistical procedures aiming at detecting volatility persistence tend to conclude the presence of long memory in data generated from it. This sheds new light on the supposed long memory in the volatility of financial data. In Section 5, we finally apply our model to volatility forecasting. In particular, we show that RFSV volatility forecasts outperform conventional AR and HAR volatility forecasts. Some proofs are relegated to the appendix.

2. Smoothness of the Volatility: Empirical Results

In this section, we report estimates of the smoothness of the volatility process for four assets:

- The DAX and Bund futures contracts, for which we estimate integrated variance directly from high frequency data using an estimator based on the model with uncertainty zones, see [49,50]. This model enables us to safely use all the ultra high frequency price data in order to perform our estimation, and thus to obtain accurate estimates over short time windows.

- The S&P and NASDAQ indices, for which we use precomputed realized variance estimates from the Oxford-Man Institute of Quantitative Finance Realized Library.[c]

2.1 *Estimating the smoothness of the volatility process*

Let us first pretend that we have access to discrete observations of the volatility process, on a time grid with mesh Δ on $[0,T]$: $\sigma_0, \sigma_\Delta, \ldots, \sigma_{k\Delta}, \ldots,$ $k \in \{0, \lfloor T/\Delta \rfloor\}$. Set $N = \lfloor T/\Delta \rfloor$, then for $q \geq 0$, we define

$$m(q,\Delta) = \frac{1}{N}\sum_{k=1}^{N} |\log(\sigma_{k\Delta}) - \log(\sigma_{(k-1)\Delta})|^q.$$

In the spirit of [53], our main assumption is that for some $s_q > 0$ and $b_q > 0$, as Δ tends to zero,

$$N^{qs_q} m(q,\Delta) \to b_q. \tag{2}$$

Under additional technical conditions, Equation (2) essentially says that the volatility process belongs to the Besov smoothness space $\mathcal{B}^{s_q}_{q,\infty}$ and does not belong to $\mathcal{B}^{s'_q}_{q,\infty}$, for $s'_q > s_q$, see [52]. Hence s_q can really be viewed as the regularity of the volatility when measured in l_q norm. In particular, functions in $\mathcal{B}^{s}_{q,\infty}$ for every $q > 0$ enjoy the Hölder property with parameter h for any $h < s$. For example, if $\log(\sigma_t)$ is a fBm with Hurst parameter H, then for any $q \geq 0$, Equation (2) holds in probability with $s_q = H$ and it can be shown that the sample paths of the process indeed belong to $\mathcal{B}^{H}_{q,\infty}$ almost surely. Assuming the increments of the log-volatility process are stationary

[c]http://realized.oxford-man.ox.ac.uk/data/download. The Oxford-Man Institute's Realized Library contains a selection of daily non-parametric estimates of volatility of financial assets, including realized variance (rv) and realized kernel (rk) estimates. A selection of such estimators is described and their performances compared in, for example, [35].

and that a law of large numbers can be applied, $m(q, \Delta)$ can also be seen as the empirical counterpart of

$$\mathbb{E}[|\log(\sigma_\Delta) - \log(\sigma_0)|^q].$$

Of course the volatility process is not directly observable, and an exact computation of $m(q, \Delta)$ is not possible in practice. We must therefore proxy spot volatility values by appropriate estimated values. Since the minimal Δ will be equal to one day in the sequel, we proxy the (true) spot volatility daily at a fixed given time of the day (11 am for example). Two daily spot volatility proxies will be considered:

- For our ultra high frequency intraday data (DAX future contracts and Bund future contracts,[d] 1248 days from May 13, 2010 to August 01, 2014[e]), we use the estimator of the integrated variance from 10 am to 11 am London time obtained from the model with uncertainty zones, see [49,50]. After renormalization, the resulting estimates of integrated variance over very short time intervals can be considered as good proxies for the unobservable spot variance. In particular, the one hour long window on which they are computed is small compared to the extra day time scales that will be of interest here.
- For the S&P and NASDAQ indices,[f] we proxy daily spot variances by daily realized variance estimates from the Oxford-Man Institute of Quantitative Finance Realized Library (3,540 trading days from January 3, 2000 to March 31, 2014). Since these estimates of integrated variance are for the whole trading day, we expect estimates of the smoothness of the volatility process to be biased upwards, integration being a regularizing operation. We compute the extent of this bias by simulation in Section 3.4 and more quantitatively in Appendix C.

[d]For every day, we only consider the future contract corresponding to the most liquid maturity.

[e]Data kindly provided by QuantHouse EUROPE/ASIA, http://www.quanthouse.com.

[f]And also the CAC40, Nikkei and FTSE indices in some specific parts of the paper.

In the following, we retain the notation $m(q, \Delta)$ with the understanding that we are only proxying the (true) spot volatility as explained above. We now proceed to estimate the smoothness parameter s_q for each q by computing the $m(q, \Delta)$ for different values of Δ and regressing $\log m(q, \Delta)$ against $\log \Delta$. Note that for a given Δ, several $m(q, \Delta)$ can be computed depending on the starting point. Our final measure of $m(q, \Delta)$ is the average of these values.

2.2 *DAX and Bund futures contracts*

DAX and Bund futures are amongst the most liquid assets in the world and moreover, the model with uncertainty zones used to estimate volatility is known to apply well to them, see [24]. So we can be confident in the reliability of our volatility proxy. Nevertheless, as an extra check, we will confirm the quality of our volatility proxy by Monte Carlo simulation in Section 3.4.

Plots of $\log m(q, \Delta)$ vs $\log \Delta$ for different values of q are displayed for the DAX in Figure 3, and for the Bund in Figure 4.

For both DAX and Bund, for a given q, the points essentially lie on a straight line. Under stationarity assumptions, this implies that

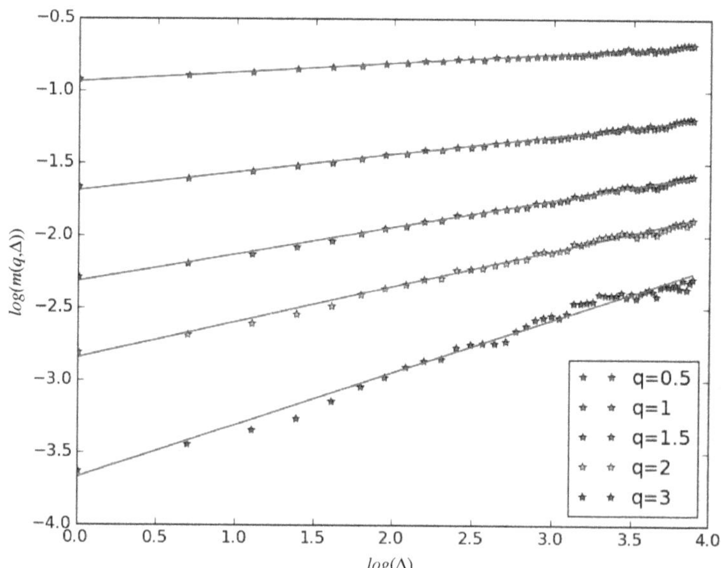

Figure 3: $\log m(q, \Delta)$ as a function of $\log \Delta$, DAX.

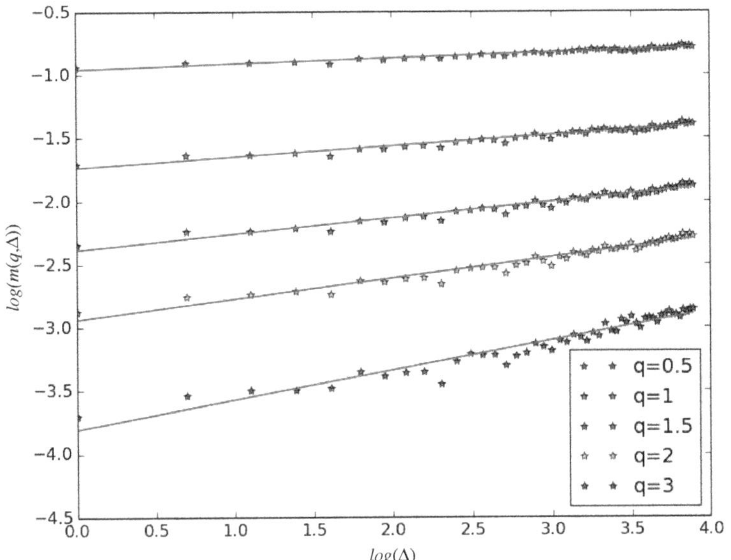

Figure 4: $\log m(q, \Delta)$ as a function of $\log \Delta$, Bund.

the log-volatility increments enjoy the following scaling property in expectation:

$$\mathbb{E}[|\log(\sigma_\Delta) - \log(\sigma_0)|^q] = b_q \Delta^{\zeta_q},$$

where $\zeta_q = q s_q > 0$ is the slope of the line associated to q. Moreover, the smoothness parameter s_q does not seem to depend on q. Indeed, plotting ζ_q against q, we obtain that $\zeta_q \sim H\, q$ with H equal to 0.125 for the DAX and to 0.082 for the Bund, see Figure 5.

We remark that the graphs for ζ_q are actually very slightly concave. However, we observe the same small concavity effect when we replace the log-volatility by simulations of a fBm with the same number of points. We conclude that this effect relates to finite sample size and is thus not significant.

2.3 *S&P and NASDAQ indices*

We report in Figures 6 and 7 similar results for the S&P and NASDAQ indices. The variance proxies used here are the precomputed 5-minute realized variance estimates for the whole trading day

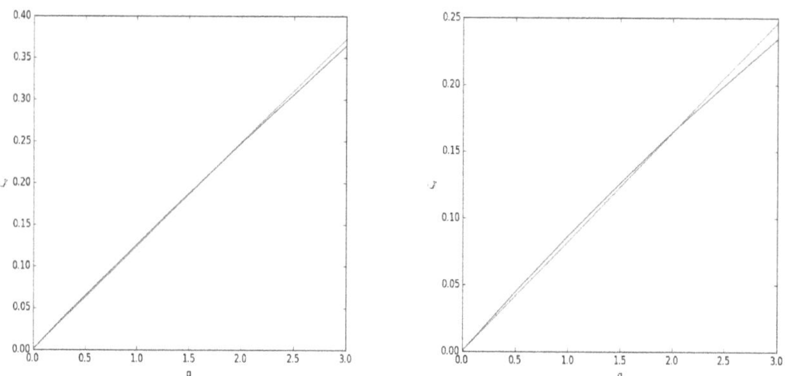

Figure 5: ζ_q (blue) and $0.125 \times q$ (green), DAX (left); ζ_q (blue) and $0.082 \times q$ (green), Bund (right).

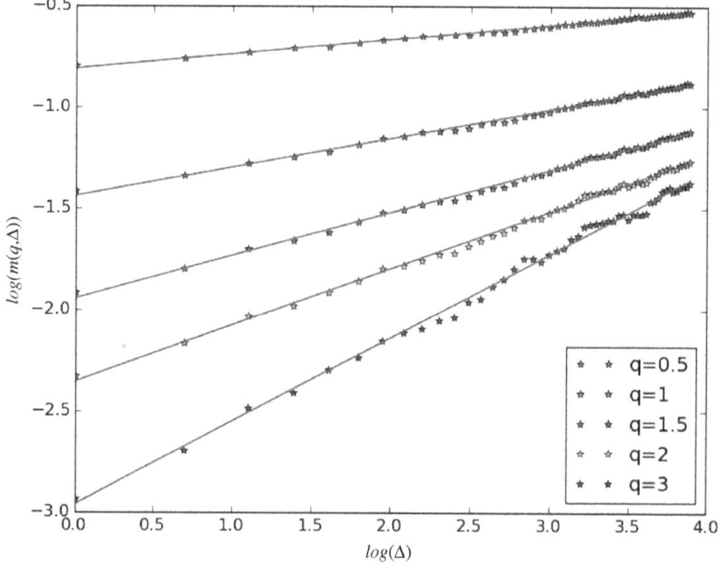

Figure 6: $\log m(q, \Delta)$ as a function of $\log \Delta$, S&P.

made publicly available by the Oxford-Man Institute of Quantitative Finance.

We observe the same scaling property for the S&P and NASDAQ indices as we observed for DAX and Bund futures and again, the s_q do not depend on q. However, the estimated smoothnesses are

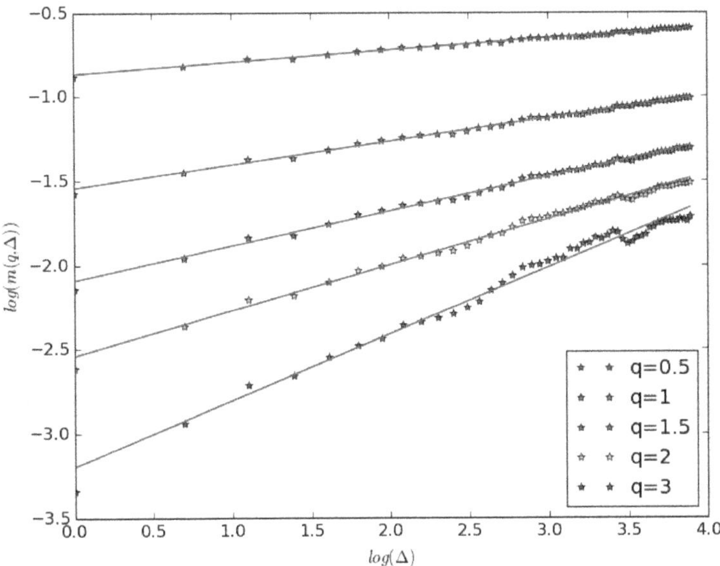

Figure 7: $\log m(q, \Delta)$ as a function of $\log(\Delta)$, NASDAQ.

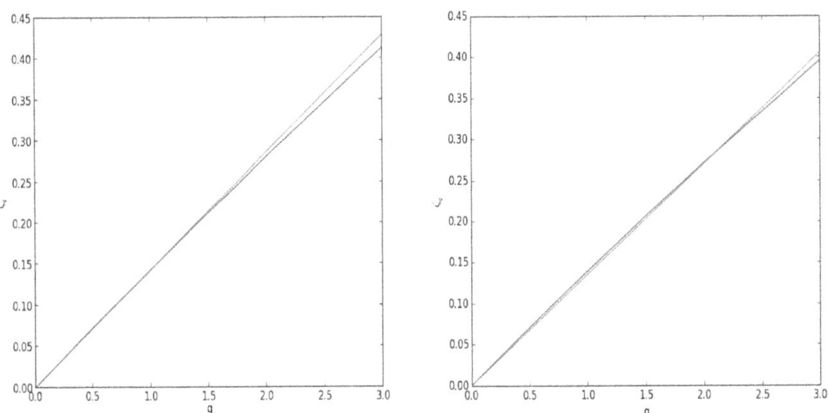

Figure 8: ζ_q (blue) and $0.142 \times q$ (green), S&P (left); ζ_q (blue) and $0.139 \times q$ (green), NASDAQ (right).

slightly higher here: $H = 0.142$ for the S&P and $H = 0.139$ for the NASDAQ, see Figure 8.

Once again, we do expect these smoothness estimates to be biased high because we are using whole-day realized variance estimates, as explained earlier in Section 2. Finally, we remark that as for DAX and Bund futures, the graphs for ζ_q are slightly concave.

2.4 *Other indices*

Repeating the analysis of Section 2.3 for each index in the Oxford-Man dataset, we find the $m(q, \Delta)$ present a universal scaling behavior. For each index and for $q = 0.5,\ 1,\ 1.5,\ 2,\ 3$, by doing a linear regression of $\log(m(q, \Delta))$ on $\log(\Delta)$ for $\Delta = 1, \ldots, 30$, we obtain estimates of ζ_q that we summarize in Table B.1 in the appendix.

2.5 *Distribution of the increments of the log-volatility*

Having established that all our underlying assets exhibit essentially the same scaling behavior,[g] we focus in the rest of the paper only on the S&P index, unless specified otherwise. That the distribution of increments of log-volatility is close to Gaussian is a well-established stylized fact reported for example in the journals [3] and [4] of Andersen *et al.* Looking now at the histograms of the increments of the log-volatility in Figure 9, with the fitted normal density superimposed in red, we see that, for any Δ, the empirical distribution of log-volatility increments is verified as being close to Gaussian. More impressive still is that rescaling the 1-day fit of the normal density by Δ^H generates (blue dashed) curves that are very close to the red fits of the normal density, consistent with the observed scaling.

The slight deviations from the Normal distribution observed in Figure 9 are again consistent with the computation of the empirical distribution of the increments of a fractional Brownian motion on a similar number of points.

2.6 *Does H vary over time?*

In order to check whether our estimations of H depends on the time interval, we split the Oxford-Man realized variance dataset into two halves and reestimate H for each half separately. The results are

[g] We have also verified that this scaling relationship holds for Crude Oil and Gold futures, with similar smoothness estimates.

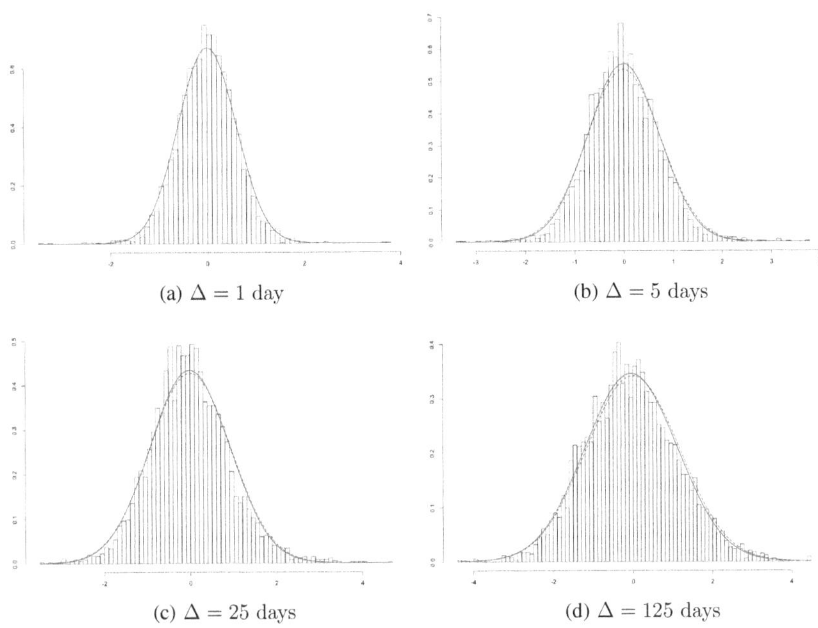

(a) $\Delta = 1$ day

(b) $\Delta = 5$ days

(c) $\Delta = 25$ days

(d) $\Delta = 125$ days

Figure 9: Histograms for various lags Δ of the (overlapping) increments $\log \sigma_{t+\Delta} - \log \sigma_t$ of the S&P log-volatility; normal fits in red; normal fit for $\Delta = 1$ day rescaled by Δ^H in blue.

presented in Table B.2 in the appendix. We note that although the estimated H all lie between 0.06 and 0.20, they seem to be higher in the second period which includes the financial crisis.

3. A Simple Model Compatible with the Empirical Scaling of the Volatility

In this section, we specify the RFSV model and demonstrate that it reproduces the empirical facts presented in Section 2.

3.1 *Specification of the RFSV model*

In the previous section, we showed that, empirically, the increments of the log-volatility of various assets enjoy a scaling property with constant smoothness parameter and that their distribution is close to Gaussian. This naturally suggests the simple model:

$$\log \sigma_{t+\Delta} - \log \sigma_t = \nu \left(W^H_{t+\Delta} - W^H_t \right), \tag{3}$$

where W^H is a fractional Brownian motion with Hurst parameter equal to the measured smoothness of the volatility and ν is a positive constant. We may of course write (3) under the form

$$\sigma_t = \sigma \exp(\nu W^H_t), \tag{4}$$

where σ is another positive constant.

However this model is not stationary, stationarity being desirable both for mathematical tractability and also to ensure reasonableness of the model at very large times. This leads us to impose stationarity by modeling the log-volatility as a fractional Ornstein–Uhlenbeck process with a very long reversion time scale.

A stationary fractional Ornstein–Uhlenbeck process (X_t) is defined as the stationary solution of the stochastic differential equation

$$dX_t = \nu \, dW^H_t - \alpha \, (X_t - m) dt,$$

where $m \in \mathbb{R}$ and ν and α are positive parameters, see [16]. As for usual Ornstein–Uhlenbeck processes, there is an explicit form for the solution which is given by

$$X_t = \nu \int_{-\infty}^{t} e^{-\alpha(t-s)} dW^H_t + m. \tag{5}$$

Here the stochastic integral with respect to fBm is simply a pathwise Riemann-Stieltjes integral, see again [16].

We thus arrive at the final specification of our RFSV model for the volatility on the time interval of interest $[0, T]$:

$$\sigma_t = \exp(X_t), \;\; t \in [0, T], \tag{6}$$

where (X_t) satisfies Equation (5) for some $\nu > 0$, $\alpha > 0$, $m \in \mathbb{R}$ and $H < 1/2$ the measured smoothness of the volatility. This model provides a very parsimonious description of the volatility process with only four parameters (and in practice only three, see below). Moreover, statistical inference methods for fractional Brownian motion and fractional Ornstein–Uhlenbeck process are well known, see [13,19,42].

Such a model is indeed stationary. However, if $\alpha \ll 1/T$, the log-volatility behaves locally (at time scales smaller than T) as a fBm. This observation is formalized in the following proposition.

Proposition 3.1. *Let W^H be a fBm and X^α defined by (5) for a given $\alpha > 0$. As α tends to zero,*

$$\mathbb{E}\Big[\sup_{t\in[0,T]} |X_t^\alpha - X_0^\alpha - \nu W_t^H|\Big] \to 0.$$

The proof is given in Appendix A.1.

Proposition 3.1 implies that in the RFSV model, if $\alpha \ll 1/T$, and we confine ourselves to the interval $[0, T]$, we can proceed as if the the log-volatility process were a fBm. Indeed, simply setting $\alpha = 0$ in (5) gives (at least formally) $X_t - X_s = \nu(W_t^H - W_s^H)$ and we immediately recover our simple non-stationary fBm model (3). Consequently, although the RFSV model is technically stationary, its ergodic behavior is of no interest for us; for example, estimation of the mean of the volatility is not possible in practice. Indeed, at any time scale of practical interest (from one day to several years), we see no evidence of ergodicity in the data, see Figure 13.

The following corollary implies that the (exact) scaling property of the fBm is approximately reproduced by the fractional Ornstein–Uhlenbeck process when α is small.

Corollary 3.1. *Let $q > 0$, $t > 0$, $\Delta > 0$. As α tends to zero, we have*

$$\mathbb{E}[|X_{t+\Delta}^\alpha - X_t^\alpha|^q] \to \nu^q\, K_q\, \Delta^{qH}.$$

The proof is given in Appendix A.2.

RFSV vs FSV

We recognize our RFSV model (6) as a particular case of the classical FSV model of Comte and Renault [21]. The key difference is that here we take $H < 1/2$ and $\alpha \ll 1/T$, whereas to accommodate the assumption of long memory, Comte and Renault have to choose $H > 1/2$. The analysis of Fukasawa referred to earlier in Section 1.3 implies in particular that if $H > 1/2$, the volatility skew function $\psi(\tau)$ is *increasing* in time to expiration τ (at least for small τ), which is obviously completely inconsistent with the approximately

$1/\sqrt{\tau}$ skew term structure that is observed. To generate a decreasing term structure of volatility skew for longer expirations, Comte and Renault are then forced to choose $\alpha \gg 1/T$. Consequently, for very short expirations ($\tau \ll 1/\alpha$), models of the Comte and Renault type with $H > 1/2$ still generate a term structure of volatility skew that is inconsistent with the observed one, as explained for example in Section 4 of [20].

In contrast, the choice $H < 1/2$ enables us to reproduce the observed smoothness and scaling of the volatility process and generate a term structure of volatility skew in agreement with the observed one. The choice $H < 1/2$ is also consistent with what is improperly called mean reversion by practitioners, which in fact corresponds to strong oscillations in the volatility process. Finally, taking α very small implies that the dynamics of our process is close to that of a fBm, see Proposition 3.1. This last point is particularly important. Indeed, recall that at the time scales we are interested in, the important feature we have in mind is really this fBm like-behavior of the log-volatility.

Finally, note that we could no doubt have considered other stationary models satisfying Proposition 3.1 and Corollary 3.1, where log-volatility behaves as a fBm at reasonable time scales; the choice of the fractional Ornstein–Uhlenbeck process is probably the simplest way to accommodate this local behavior together with the stationarity property.

3.2 *RFSV model autocovariance functions*

From Proposition 3.1 and Corollary 3.1, we easily deduce the following corollary, where $o(1)$ tends to zero as α tends to zero.

Corollary 3.2. *Let $q > 0$, $t > 0$, $\Delta > 0$. As α tends to zero,*

$$\mathrm{Cov}[X_t^\alpha, X_{t+\Delta}^\alpha] = \mathrm{Var}[X_t^\alpha] - \frac{1}{2}\nu^2\,\Delta^{2H} + o(1).$$

Consequently, in the RFSV model, for fixed t, the covariance between X_t and $X_{t+\Delta}$ is linear with respect to Δ^{2H}. This result is very well satisfied empirically. For example, in Figure 10, we see that for the S&P, the empirical autocovariance function of the log-volatility is indeed linear with respect to Δ^{2H}. Note in passing that at

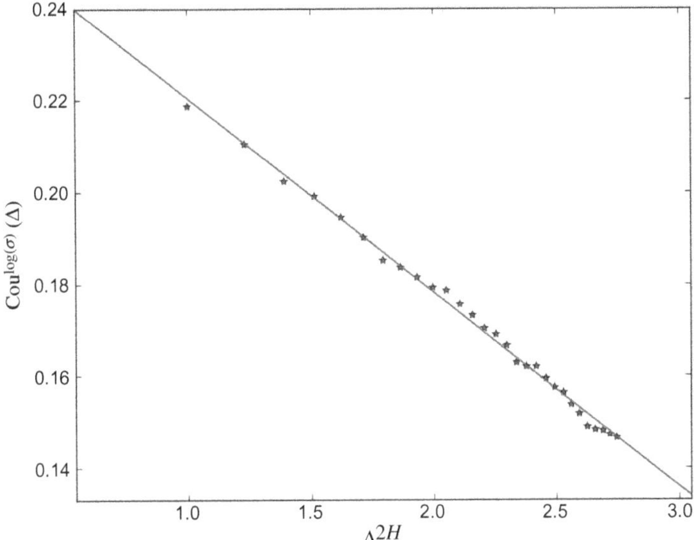

Figure 10: Autocovariance of the log-volatility as a function of Δ^{2H} for $H = 0.14$, S&P.

the time scales we consider, the term $\mathrm{Var}[X_t^\alpha]$ is higher than $\frac{1}{2}\nu^2\,\Delta^{2H}$ in the expression for $\mathrm{Cov}[X_t^\alpha, X_{t+\Delta}^\alpha]$.

Having computed the autocovariance function of the log-volatility, we now turn our attention to the volatility itself. We have

$$\mathbb{E}[\sigma_{t+\Delta}\sigma_t] = \mathbb{E}[e^{X_t^\alpha + X_{t+\Delta}^\alpha}],$$

with X^α defined by Equation (5). Since X^α is a Gaussian process, we deduce that

$$\mathbb{E}[\sigma_{t+\Delta}\sigma_t] = e^{\mathbb{E}[X_t^\alpha]+\mathbb{E}[X_{t+\Delta}^\alpha]+\mathrm{Var}[X_t^\alpha]/2+\mathrm{Var}[X_{t+\Delta}^\alpha]/2+\mathrm{Cov}[X_t^\alpha,X_{t+\Delta}^\alpha]}.$$

Applying Corollary 3.2, we obtain that when α is small, $\mathbb{E}[\sigma_{t+\Delta}\sigma_t]$ is approximately equal to

$$e^{2\mathbb{E}[X_t^\alpha]+2\mathrm{Var}[X_t^\alpha]}e^{-\nu^2\frac{\Delta^{2H}}{2}}. \tag{7}$$

It follows that in the RFSV model, $\log(\mathbb{E}[\sigma_{t+\Delta}\sigma_t])$ is also linear in Δ^{2H}. This property is again very well satisfied on data, as shown by Figure 11, where we plot the logarithm of the empirical counterpart of $\mathbb{E}[\sigma_{t+\Delta}\sigma_t]$ against Δ^{2H}, for the S&P with $H = 0.14$.

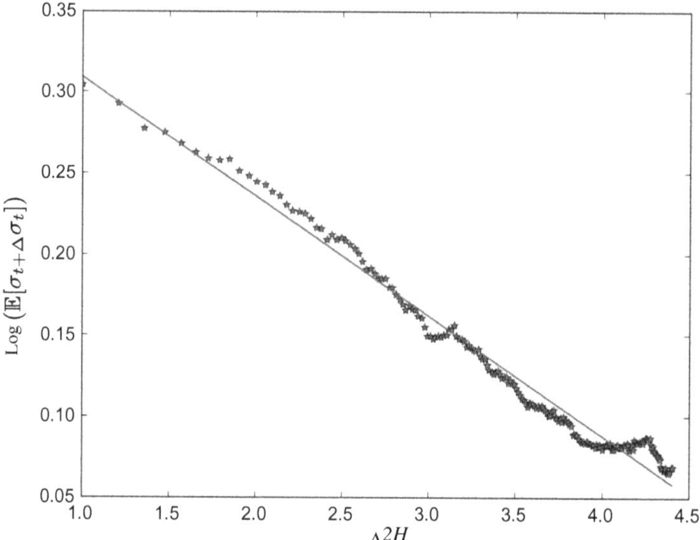

Figure 11: Empirical counterpart of $\log(\mathbb{E}[\sigma_{t+\Delta}\sigma_t])$ as a function of Δ^{2H}, S&P.

We note that putting Δ^{2H} on the x-axis of Figure 11 is really crucial in order to retrieve linearity. In particular, a corollary of (7) is that the autocovariance function of the volatility does not decay as a power law as widely believed; see Figure 12 where we show that a log–log plot of the autocovariance function does not yield a straight line.

3.3 *RFSV vs FSV again*

To further demonstrate the incompatibility of the classical long memory FSV model with volatility data, consider the quantity $m(2, \Delta)$. Recall that in the data (see Section 2) we observe the linear relationship $\log m(2, \Delta) \approx \zeta_2 \log \Delta + k$ for some constant k. Also, in both FSV and RFSV, we can consider

$$\begin{aligned} m(2, \Delta) &= \mathbb{E}\left[(X_{t+\Delta} - X_t)^2\right] \\ &= 2(\mathrm{Var}[X_t] - \mathrm{Cov}[X_t, X_{t+\Delta}]). \end{aligned}$$

In Figure 13, we plot $m(2, \Delta)$ with the parameters $H = 0.53$, corresponding to the FSV model parameter estimate of Chronopoulou

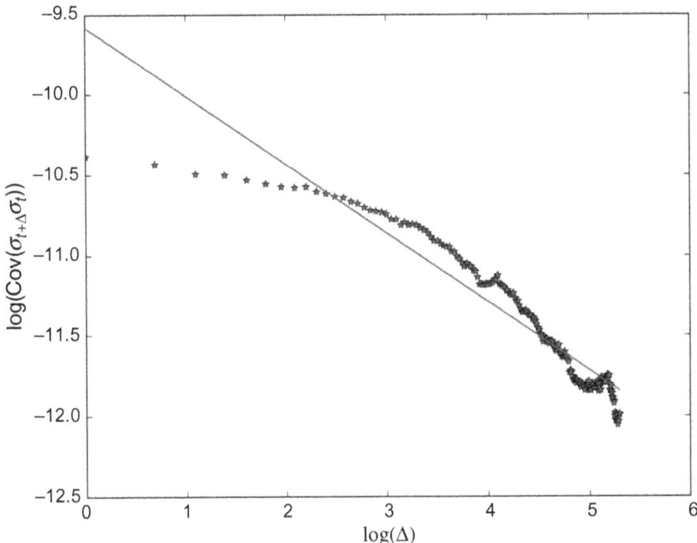

Figure 12: Empirical counterpart of $\log(\mathrm{Cov}[\sigma_{t+\Delta}, \sigma_t])$ as a function of $\log(\Delta)$, S&P.

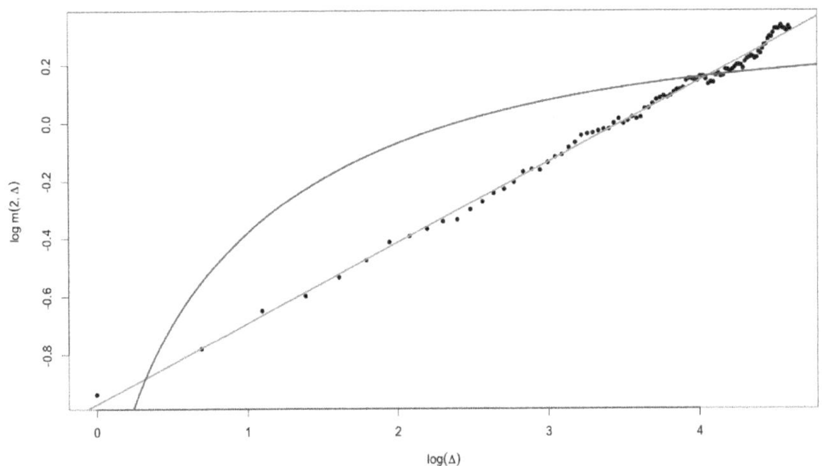

Figure 13: Long memory models such as the FSV model of Comte and Renault are not compatible with S&P volatility data. Black points are empirical estimates of $m(2, \Delta)$; the blue line is the FSV model with $\alpha = 0.5$ and $H = 0.53$; the orange line is the RFSV model with $\alpha = 0$ and $H = 0.14$.

and Viens in [18], and $\alpha = 0.5$ to ensure some visible decay of the volatility skew. The slope of $m(2, \Delta)$ in the FSV model for small lags is driven by the value of H; the lag at which $m(2, \Delta)$ begins to flatten and stationarity kicks in corresponds to a time scale of order $1/\alpha$. It is clear from the picture that to fit the data, we must have $\alpha \ll 1/T$ and the value of H must be set by the initial slope of the regression line, which as reported earlier in Section 2 is $\zeta_2 = 2 \times 0.14$.

3.4 *Simulation-based analysis of the RFSV model*

Our goal in this section is to show that in terms of smoothness measures, one obtains on simulated data from the RFSV model the same behaviors as those observed on empirical data. In particular, we would like to be able to quantify the positive bias associated with estimating H from whole-day realized variance data as in Section 2.3, relative to using data from a one-hour window as in Section 2.2.

We simulate the RFSV model for 2,000 days (chosen to be between the lengths of our two datasets). In order to account for the overnight effect, we simulate the volatility σ_t[h] and efficient price P_t[i] over the whole day. The parameters: $H = 0.14$, $\nu = 0.3$, $m = X_0 = -5$ and $\alpha = 5 \times 10^{-4}$, are chosen to be consistent with our empirical estimates from Section 2. To model microstructure effects such as the discreteness of the price grid, we consider that the observed price process is generated from P_t using the uncertainty zones model of [49] with tick value 5×10^{-4} and parameter $\eta = 0.25$.

Exactly as in Section 2, for each of the 2,000 days, we consider two volatility proxies obtained from the observed price and based on:

- The integrated variance estimator using the model with uncertainty zones over one hour windows, from 10 am to 11 am.
- The 5 minutes realized variance estimator, over eight hours windows (the trading day).

We now repeat our analysis of Section 2, generating graphs analogous to Figures 3, 4, 6 and 7 obtained on empirical data. Figure 14

[h]To simulate the fBm, we use a spectral method with 40,000,000 points (20,000 points per day). We then simulate X taking $X_{(n+1)\delta} - X_{n\delta} = \nu(W^H_{(n+1)\delta} - W^H_{n\delta}) + \alpha\delta(m - X_{n\delta})$ (with $\delta = 1/20000$).

[i]$P_{(n+1)\delta} - P_{n\delta} = P_{n\delta}\sigma_{n\delta}\sqrt{\delta}\,U_n$ where the U_n are iid standard Gaussian variables.

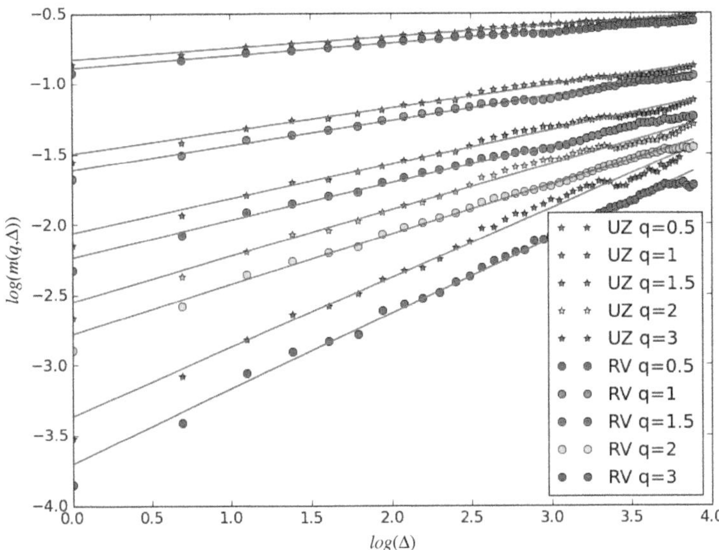

Figure 14: $\log(m(q,\Delta))$ as a function of $\log(\Delta)$, simulated data, with realized variance and uncertainty zones estimators.

compares smoothness measures obtained using the uncertainty zones estimator on one-hour windows with those obtained using the realized variance estimator on 8-hour windows.

When the uncertainty zones estimator is applied on a one-hour window (1/24 of a simulated day) as in Section 2.2, we estimate $H = 0.16$, which is close to the true value $H = 0.14$ used in the simulation. The results obtained with the realized variance estimator over daily eight-hour windows (1/3 of a simulated day) do exhibit the same scaling properties as those we see in the empirical data with a smoothness parameter that does not depend on q. However, the estimated H is biased slightly higher at around 0.18. As discussed in Section 2.1, this extra positive bias is no surprise and is due to the regularizing effect of the integral operator over the longer window. We note also that the estimated values of ν ("volatility of volatility" in some sense), obtained from the intercepts of the regressions, are lower with the longer time windows, again as expected. A detailed computation of the bias in the estimated H associated with the choice of window length in an analogous but more tractable model is presented in Appendix C.

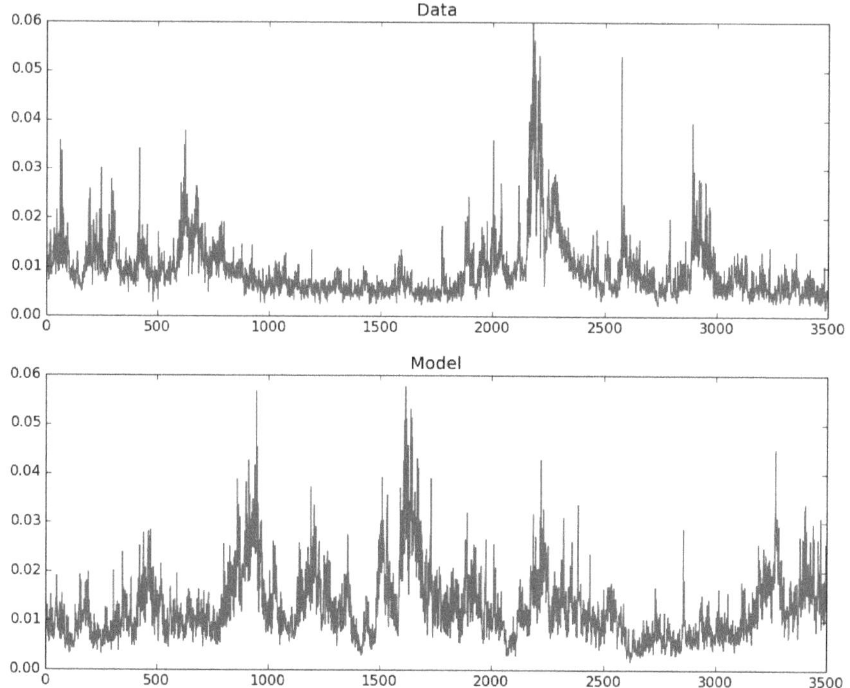

Figure 15: Volatility of the S&P (above) and generated by the model.

We end this section by presenting in Figure 15 a sample path of the model-generated volatility (spot volatility, directly from the simulation rather than estimated from the simulated price series) together with a graph of S&P volatility over 3,500 days.

A first reaction to Figure 15 is that the simulated and actual graphs look very alike. In particular, in both of them, persistent periods of high volatility alternate with low volatility periods. On closer inspection of the empirical volatility series, we observe that the sample path of the volatility on a restricted time window seems to exhibit the same kind of qualitative properties as those of the global sample path (for example periods of high and low activity). This fractal-type behavior of the volatility has been investigated both empirically and theoretically in, for example, [6,12,44].

At the visual level, we observe that this fractal-type behavior is also reproduced in our model, as we now explain. Denote by $L^{x,H}$ the law of the geometric fractional Brownian motion with Hurst exponent H and volatility x on $[0,1]$, that is $(e^{xW_t^H})_{t\in[0,1]}$. Then, when α is very small, the rescaled volatility process on $[0,\Delta]$: $(\sigma_{t\Delta}/\sigma_0)_{t\in[0,1]}$, has approximately the law $L^{\nu\Delta^H,H}$. Now remark that for H small, the function u^H increases very slowly. Thus, over a large range of observation scales Δ, the rescaled volatility processes on $[0,\Delta]$ have approximately the same law. For example, between an observation scale of one day and five years (1,250 open days), the coefficient x characterizing the law of the volatility process is "only" multiplied by $1250^{0.14}=2.7$. It follows that in the RFSV model, the volatility process over one day resembles the volatility process over a decade.

4. Spurious Long Memory of Volatility?

We revisit in this section the issue of long memory of volatility through the lens of our model. Recall that a stationary time series is said to exhibit long memory if the autocovariance function $\text{Cov}[\log(\sigma_t),\log(\sigma_{t+\Delta})]$ (or sometimes $\text{Cov}[\sigma_t,\sigma_{t+\Delta}]$) goes slowly to zero as $\Delta\to\infty$, and often even more precisely that it behaves as $\Delta^{-\gamma}$,[j] with $\gamma<1$ as $\Delta\to\infty$.

Thus, the classical approach to long memory is to consider a parametric class of models and to estimate within this class the parameter γ, typically based on empirical autocovariances, see [5] and Figure 12. As mentioned earlier in the introduction, the long memory of volatility is widely accepted as a stylized fact.

Specifically, in the RFSV model, we have from Corollary 3.2 that

$$\text{Cov}[\log(\sigma_t),\log(\sigma_{t+\Delta})]\approx A-B\Delta^{2H}$$

and from Equation (7) that

$$\text{Cov}[\sigma_t,\sigma_{t+\Delta}]\approx C\,e^{-B\Delta^{2H}}-D,$$

[j]Indeed the notion of empirical long memory does not make much sense outside the power law case; the empirical values of covariances at very large time scales are never measurable and thus one cannot conclude whether the series of covariances converges in general.

for some constants A, B, C and D. Moreover, we demonstrated in Figures 10 and 11 that these relations are consistent with the data. Thus the autocovariance function does not decay as a power law in the RFSV model nor does it appear to decay as a power law in the data.

Nevertheless, as an experiment, we can apply both to the data and to sample paths of the RFSV model some standard statistical procedures aimed at identifying long memory that have been used in the financial econometrics literature. Such procedures are of course designed to identify long memory under rather strict modeling assumptions. Consequently, spurious results may obviously then be obtained if the model underlying the estimation procedure is misspecified, which is the case with the RFSV model.[k]

With the same model parameters as in Section 3.4, we simulate our model over 3,500 days, which corresponds to the size of our dataset. Consider first the procedure in [4], where in the context of a fractional Gaussian noise (FGN) model with Hurst parameter $\hat{H}$, the authors test for long memory in the volatility by studying the scaling behavior of the quantity

$$V(\Delta) = \mathrm{Var}\left[\int_0^\Delta \sigma_s^2 \, ds\right]$$

with respect to Δ. In the FGN model, as $\Delta \to \infty$, the autocorrelation function $\rho(\Delta)$ behaves asymptotically as $\Delta^{2\hat{H}-2}$ and $V(\Delta)$ behaves asymptotically as $\Delta^{2\hat{H}}$ as $\Delta \to \infty$. Figure 16 presents the graph of the logarithm of the empirical counterpart of $V(\Delta)$ against the logarithm of Δ, on the S&P data and within our simulation framework.

We note from Figure 16 that both our simulated model and market data lead to very similar graphs, close to straight lines with slope 1.86, giving $\hat{H} = 0.93$.[l] Accordingly, in the setting of [4], we would deduce power law behavior of the autocorrelation function with exponent 0.14 and therefore long memory. Thus, if the data are generated

---

[k]Recall in particular that the RFSV model is only formally stationary.

[l]Note that there is no reason to expect that there should be any direct connection between $\hat{H}$ estimated for the FGN model and the H we estimated for the RFSV model.

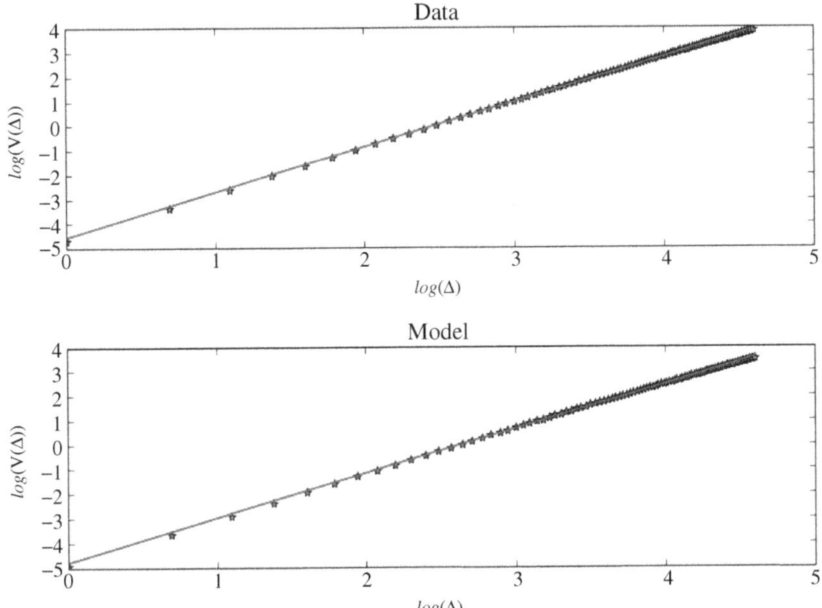

Figure 16: Empirical counterpart of $\log(V(\Delta))$ as a function of $\log(\Delta)$ on S&P (above) and simulation (below).

by a model like the RFSV model, one can easily be wrongly convinced that the volatility time series exhibits long memory.

In [5], in the context of an ARFIMA$(0, d, 0)$ model, the authors deduce long memory in the volatility by showing that the process ε_t obtained by fractional differentiation of the log-volatility $\varepsilon_t = (1 - L)^d \log(\sigma_t)$, with $d = 0.401$[m] (which is obtained by regression of the log-periodogram using the GPH estimator [36]) and L the lag operator, behaves as a white noise. To check for this, they compute the autocorrelation function of ε_t. We give in Figure 17 the autocorrelation functions of the logarithm of σ_t and ε_t, again both on the data and on the simulated path.

Once again, the data and the simulation generate very similar plots. We conclude that this procedure for estimating long memory

[m] It is shown in [36] that the autocorrelation functions of the ARFIMA$(0, d, 0)$ and the FGN model with Hurst parameter $\hat{H}$ have the same asymptotic behavior as $\Delta \to \infty$ if $d = \hat{H} - \frac{1}{2}$.

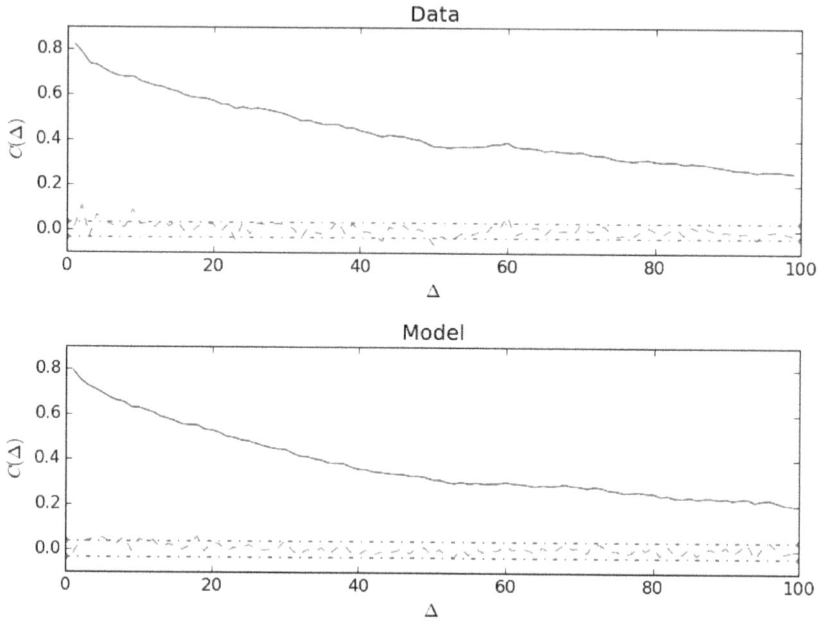

Figure 17: Autocorrelation functions of $\log(\sigma_t)$ (in blue) and ε_t (in green) and the Bartlett standard error bands (in red), for S&P data (above) and for simulated data (below).

is just as fragile as the first, and it is easy to wrongly deduce volatility long memory when applying it.

In conclusion, the RFSV model is yet another model in which classical estimation procedures identify spurious long memory; see [1,25,37,38] for various other such examples. Moreover, these procedures estimate the same long memory parameter from data generated from a suitably calibrated RFSV model as they estimate from empirical data. Once again, although the (near) non-stationarity of the RFSV model induces long swings in volatility, mirroring long-range dependence, it does not exhibit long memory in the classical power law sense.

5. Forecasting Using the RFSV Model

In this section, we present an application of our model: forecasting the log-volatility and the variance.

5.1 *Forecasting log-volatility*

The key formula on which our prediction method is based is the following one:

$$\mathbb{E}[W^H_{t+\Delta}|\mathcal{F}_t] = \frac{\cos(H\pi)}{\pi}\Delta^{H+1/2}\int_{-\infty}^{t}\frac{W^H_s}{(t-s+\Delta)(t-s)^{H+1/2}}ds,$$

where W^H is a fBm with $H < 1/2$ and $\mathcal{F}_t$ the filtration it generates, see Theorem 4.2 of [48]. By construction, over any reasonable time scale of interest, as formalized in Corollary 3.1, we may approximate the fractional Ornstein-Uhlenbeck volatility process in the RFSV model as $\log\sigma_t^2 \approx 2\nu\, W_t^H + C$, for some constants ν and C. Our prediction formula for log-variance then follows[n]:

$$\mathbb{E}\left[\log\sigma^2_{t+\Delta}|\mathcal{F}_t\right] = \frac{\cos(H\pi)}{\pi}\Delta^{H+1/2}\int_{-\infty}^{t}\frac{\log\sigma^2_s}{(t-s+\Delta)(t-s)^{H+1/2}}ds. \tag{8}$$

This formula, or rather its approximation through a Riemann sum (we assume in this section that the volatilities are perfectly observed, although they are in fact estimated), is used to forecast the log-volatility 1, 5 and 20 days ahead ($\Delta = 1,\ 5,\ 20$).

We now compare the predictive power of formula (8) with that of autoregressive (AR for short) and heterogeneous autoregressive (HAR for short) forecasts, in the spirit of [23].[o] Recall that for a given integer $p > 0$, the AR(p) and HAR predictors take the following form (where the index i runs over the series of daily volatility estimates):

- AR(p):

$$\widehat{\log(\sigma^2_{t+\Delta})} = K_0^\Delta + \sum_{i=0}^{p} C_i^\Delta \log(\sigma^2_{t-i}).$$

[n]The constants 2ν and C cancel when deriving the expression.

[o]Note that we do not consider GARCH models here since we have access to high frequency volatility estimates and not only to daily returns. Indeed, it is shown in [5] that forecasts based on the time series of realized variances outperform GARCH forecasts based on daily returns.

• HAR :

$$\widehat{\log(\sigma^2_{t+\Delta})} = K_0^\Delta + C_0^\Delta \log(\sigma_t^2) + C_5^\Delta \frac{1}{5}\sum_{i=0}^{4} \log(\sigma^2_{t-i})$$
$$+ C_{20}^\Delta \frac{1}{20}\sum_{i=0}^{19} \log(\sigma^2_{t-i}).$$

We estimate AR coefficients using the R `stats` library[p] on a rolling time window of 500 days. In the HAR case, we use standard linear regression to estimate the coefficients as explained in [23]. In the sequel, we consider $p = 5$ and $p = 10$ in the AR formula. Indeed, these parameters essentially give the best results for the horizons at which we wish to forecast the volatility (1, 5 and 20 days). For each day, we forecast volatility for five different indices.[q]

We then assess the quality of the various forecasts by computing the ratio P between the mean squared error of our predictor and the (approximate) variance of the log-variance:

$$P = \frac{\sum_{k=500}^{N-\Delta} \left(\log(\sigma^2_{k+\Delta}) - \widehat{\log(\sigma^2_{k+\Delta})}\right)^2}{\sum_{k=500}^{N-\Delta} \left(\log(\sigma^2_{k+\Delta}) - \mathbb{E}[\log(\sigma^2_{t+\Delta})]\right)^2},$$

where $\mathbb{E}[\log(\sigma^2_{t+\Delta})]$ denotes the empirical mean of the log-variance over the whole time period.

We note from Table 1 that the RFSV forecast consistently outperforms the AR and HAR forecasts, especially at longer horizons. Moreover, our forecasting method is more parsimonious since it only requires the parameter H to forecast the log-variance. Compare this with the AR and HAR methods, for which coefficients depend on the forecast time horizon and must be recomputed if this horizon changes.

[p]More precisely, we use the default Yule–Walker method.

[q]In addition to S&P and NASDAQ, we also investigate CAC40, FTSE and Nikkei, over the same time period as S&P and NASDAQ. For simplicity, the parameter H used in our predictor is computed only once for each asset, using the whole time period. This yields similar results to using a moving time window adapted in time.

Table 1: Ratio P for the AR, HAR and RFSV predictors.

	AR(5)	AR(10)	HAR(3)	RFSV
SPX2.rv $\Delta = 1$	0.317	0.318	0.314	**0.313**
SPX2.rv $\Delta = 5$	0.459	0.449	0.437	**0.426**
SPX2.rv $\Delta = 20$	0.764	0.694	0.656	**0.606**
FTSE2.rv $\Delta = 1$	0.230	0.229	0.225	**0.223**
FTSE2.rv $\Delta = 5$	0.357	0.344	0.337	**0.320**
FTSE2.rv $\Delta = 20$	0.651	0.571	0.541	**0.472**
N2252.rv $\Delta = 1$	0.357	0.358	0.351	**0.345**
N2252.rv $\Delta = 5$	0.553	0.533	0.513	**0.504**
N2252.rv $\Delta = 20$	0.875	0.795	0.746	**0.714**
GDAXI2.rv $\Delta = 1$	0.237	0.238	0.234	**0.231**
GDAXI2.rv $\Delta = 5$	0.372	0.362	0.350	**0.339**
GDAXI2.rv $\Delta = 20$	0.661	0.590	0.550	**0.498**
FCHI2.rv $\Delta = 1$	0.244	0.244	0.241	**0.238**
FCHI2.rv $\Delta = 5$	0.378	0.373	0.366	**0.350**
FCHI2.rv $\Delta = 20$	0.669	0.613	0.598	**0.522**

Remark that our predictor can be linked to that of [27], where the issue of the prediction of the log-volatility in the multifractal random walk model of [6] is tackled. In this model,

$$\mathbb{E}[\log(\sigma_{t+\Delta}^2)|\mathcal{F}_t] = \frac{1}{\pi}\sqrt{\Delta}\int_{-\infty}^{t} \frac{\log(\sigma_s^2)}{(t-s+\Delta)\sqrt{t-s}}ds,$$

which is the limit of our predictor when H tends to zero.

Note also that our prediction formula may be rewritten as

$$\mathbb{E}[\log(\sigma_{t+\Delta}^2)|\mathcal{F}_t] = \frac{\cos(H\pi)}{\pi}\int_0^{+\infty} \frac{\log(\sigma_{t-\Delta u}^2)}{(u+1)\,u^{H+1/2}}du.$$

For a given small $\varepsilon > 0$, let r be the smallest real number such that

$$\int_r^{+\infty} \frac{1}{(u+1)\,u^{H+1/2}}du \leq \varepsilon.$$

Then we have, with an error of order ε,

$$\mathbb{E}[\log(\sigma_{t+\Delta}^2)|\mathcal{F}_t] \approx \frac{\cos(H\pi)}{\pi}\int_0^{r} \frac{\log(\sigma_{t-\Delta u}^2)}{(u+1)\,u^{H+1/2}}du.$$

Consequently, the volatility process needs to be considered (roughly) down to time $t - \Delta r$ if one wants to forecast up to time Δ in the future. The relevant regression window is thus linear in the forecasting horizon. For example, for $r = 1$, $\varepsilon = 0.35$ which is not so unreasonable. In this case, as is well-known to practitioners, to predict log-volatility one week ahead, one should essentially look at the volatility over the last week. If trying to predict log-volatility one month ahead, one should look at the volatility over the last month.

5.2 *Variance prediction*

Recall that $\log \sigma_t^2 \approx 2\,\nu\, W_t^H + C$ for some constant C. In [48], it is shown that $W_{t+\Delta}^H$ is conditionally Gaussian with conditional variance

$$\mathrm{Var}[W_{t+\Delta}^H | \mathcal{F}_t] = c\,\Delta^{2H}$$

where

$$c = \frac{\Gamma(3/2 - H)}{\Gamma(H + 1/2)\,\Gamma(2 - 2H)}.$$

Thus, we obtain the following form for the RFSV predictor of the variance:

$$\widehat{\sigma_{t+\Delta}^2} = \exp\left(\widehat{\log \sigma_{t+\Delta}^2} + 2\,c\,\nu^2 \Delta^{2\,H}\right) \tag{9}$$

where $\widehat{\log(\sigma_{t+\Delta}^2})$ is the predictor from Section 5.1 and ν^2 is estimated as the exponential of the intercept in the linear regression of $\log(m(2, \Delta))$ on $\log(\Delta)$.

As previously, we compare in Table 2 the performances of the RFSV forecast with those of AR and HAR forecasts (constructed on variance rather than log-variance this time).

We find again that the RFSV forecast typically outperforms AR and HAR, although it is worth noting that the HAR forecast is already visibly superior to the AR forecast.

Since our working paper first appeared, much work has been done to estimate the roughness of volatility of other assets, notably by Bennedsen, Lunde and Pakkanen in [8]. In an analysis of E-mini S&P 500 futures data, at all timescales over 15 minutes, the out-of-sample forecasting performance of the estimator (9) is shown to be very

Table 2: Ratio P for the AR, HAR and RFSV predictors.

	AR(5)	AR(10)	HAR(3)	RFSV
SPX2.rv $\Delta = 1$	0.520	0.566	0.489	**0.475**
SPX2.rv $\Delta = 5$	0.750	0.745	0.723	**0.672**
SPX2.rv $\Delta = 20$	1.070	1.010	1.036	**0.903**
FTSE2.rv $\Delta = 1$	0.612	0.621	0.582	**0.567**
FTSE2.rv $\Delta = 5$	0.797	0.770	0.756	**0.707**
FTSE2.rv $\Delta = 20$	1.046	0.984	0.935	**0.874**
N2252.rv $\Delta = 1$	0.554	0.579	**0.504**	0.505
N2252.rv $\Delta = 5$	0.857	0.807	0.761	**0.729**
N2252.rv $\Delta = 20$	1.097	1.046	1.011	**0.964**
GDAXI2.rv $\Delta = 1$	0.439	0.448	0.399	**0.386**
GDAXI2.rv $\Delta = 5$	0.675	0.650	0.616	**0.566**
GDAXI2.rv $\Delta = 20$	0.931	0.850	0.816	**0.746**
FCHI2.rv $\Delta = 1$	0.533	0.542	0.470	**0.465**
FCHI2.rv $\Delta = 5$	0.705	0.707	0.691	**0.631**
FCHI2.rv $\Delta = 20$	0.982	0.952	0.912	**0.828**

similar to the performance of the other more highly parameterized estimators proposed. Interestingly, at daily and higher timescales, the simple estimator (9) is actually shown to outperform the more complicated estimators. It is also notable that rough volatility was confirmed for more than five thousand equities in [8]; we are not yet aware of any asset for which rough volatility has not been confirmed.

We emphasize that our point in this forecasting exercise is not to show that our rough volatility based approach is really superior to others. For example, we could have considered alternative competitors to the RFSV formula or refine the HAR procedure. We only wish to demonstrate that our forecast is probably at least as good as other predictors whilst being simpler, requiring only the estimation of H.

6. Conclusion

Using daily realized variance estimates as proxies for daily spot (squared) volatilities, we uncovered two startlingly simple regularities in the resulting time series. First we found that the distributions of increments of log-volatility are approximately Gaussian, consistent with many prior studies. Secondly, we established the monofractal scaling relationship

$$\mathbb{E}\left[|\log(\sigma_\Delta) - \log(\sigma_0)|^q\right] = K_q\, \nu^q\, \Delta^{q\,H}, \tag{10}$$

where H can be seen as a measure of smoothness characteristic of the underlying volatility process; typically, $0.06 < H < 0.2$. The simple scaling relationship (10) naturally suggests that log-volatility may be modeled using fractional Brownian motion.

The resulting Rough Fractional Stochastic Volatility (RFSV) model turns out to be formally almost identical to the FSV model of Comte and Renault [21], with one major difference: In the FSV model, $H > 1/2$ to ensure long memory whereas in the RFSV model $H < 1/2$, typically, $H \approx 0.1$. Moreover, in the FSV model, the mean reversion coefficient α has to be large compared to $1/T$ to ensure a decaying volatility skew; in the RFSV model, the volatility skew decays naturally just like the observed volatility skew, $\alpha \ll 1/T$ and indeed for time scales of practical interest, we may proceed as if α were exactly zero.

We further showed that applying standard test procedures to volatility time series simulated with the RFSV model would lead us to erroneously deduce the presence of long memory, with parameters similar to those found in prior studies. Despite that volatility in the RFSV model (or in the data) is not a long memory process, we can therefore explain why long memory of volatility is widely accepted as a stylized fact.

Thus the RFSV model is able to replicate the stylized facts of the time series, i.e. *Volatility is rough.* More precisely, we have shown that within a specific class of models (which we strongly argue to be relevant), empirical daily realized variance values are much more likely to be sampled from a rough volatility process than from a smooth process. Whether or not instantaneous variance is rough cannot of course be determined ultimately since instantaneous variance is latent and not observable; as mentioned in the introduction, it is not even clear that such an object exists independently of a specific model.

It is of course plausible that other models are compatible with many of our observations. In fact, there are probably many ways to design a process so that most of our empirical results are reproduced (for example estimation errors when estimating volatility can be quite significant for some models, leading to downward biases in the measurement of the smoothness). However, what we show here is that we cannot find any evidence against the RFSV model. In statistical terms, the null hypothesis that the data generating process of the volatility is a RFSV model cannot be rejected based on our analysis. Even more, it is likely that the RFSV model is simpler, more parsimonious and more tractable than any other such model. In particular we do not address the question of volatility jumps. Neither do we insist that there are no jumps in volatility. Rather, one of the main messages of our work is that our model is able to replicate the stylized facts of the time series without having to appeal to jumps, see [11] for another example where a continuous process can mimic the properties obtained from data generated by a process with jumps.

As an application of the RFSV model, we showed how to forecast volatility at various time scales, at least as well as when using Fulvio Corsi's impressive HAR estimator, but with only one parameter — H!

We focus in this work on the statistical properties of the RFSV model. In [7], the authors explore the implications of the RFSV model (written under the physical measure $\mathbb{P}$) for option pricing (under the pricing measure $\mathbb{Q}$). In particular, following Mandelbrot and Van Ness, the fBm that appears in the definition (6) of the RFSV model may be represented as a fractional integral of a standard Brownian motion as follows [43]:

$$W_t^H = \int_0^t \frac{dW_s}{(t-s)^\gamma} + \int_{-\infty}^0 \left[\frac{1}{(t-s)^\gamma} - \frac{1}{(-s)^\gamma}\right] dW_s, \tag{11}$$

with $\gamma = \frac{1}{2} - H$. The observed anticorrelation between price moves and volatility moves may then be modeled naturally by anticorrelating the Brownian motion W that drives the volatility process with the Brownian motion driving the price process. As already proved by Fukasawa [32], such a model with a small H reproduces the observed decay of at-the-money volatility skew with respect to time to expiry, asymptotically for short times. It is shown that an appropriate extension of Fukasawa's model, consistent with the RFSV model, fits the entire implied volatility surface remarkably well. In particular, this model accurately reproduces the extreme short dated smiles, with no jumps. Moreover, despite that it would seem from (11) that knowledge of the entire path $\{W_s : s < t\}$ of the Brownian motion would be required, it turns out that the statistics of this path necessary for option pricing are traded and thus easily observed. Remarkably, Heston-type formulas can also be obtained in the rough volatility framework, see [30,31].

Finally, note that there are microstructural foundations to rough volatility models. Indeed, it is explained in [29] how rough volatility emerges as the scaling limit of a Hawkes process based description of the order flow in the context of high frequency trading and metaorder splitting.

Acknowledgments

We are very grateful to the referees of *Econometrica*, the *Journal of the American Statistical Association*, the *Journal of Business and Economic Statistics*, and *Quantitative Finance* whose careful reading and valuable comments have helped us improve substantially our presentation of this work. We also thank Masaaki Fukasawa for several interesting discussions.

Appendix A Proofs

A.1 *Proof of Proposition* 3.1

Starting from Equation (5) and applying integration by parts, we get

$$X_t^\alpha = \nu W_t^H - \int_{-\infty}^t \nu\alpha e^{-\alpha(t-s)} W_s^H ds + m.$$

Therefore,

$$(X_t^\alpha - X_0^\alpha) - \nu W_t^H = -\int_0^t \nu\alpha e^{-\alpha(t-s)} W_s^H ds$$
$$-\int_{-\infty}^0 \nu\alpha(e^{-\alpha(t-s)} - e^{\alpha s}) W_s^H ds.$$

Consequently,

$$\sup_{t\in[0,T]} |(X_t^\alpha - X_0^\alpha) - \nu W_t^H| \leq \nu\alpha T\hat{W}_T^H + \int_{-\infty}^0 \nu\alpha(e^{\alpha s} - e^{-\alpha(T-s)})\hat{W}_s^H ds,$$

where $\hat{W}_t^H = \sup_{s\in[0,t]} |W_s^H|$. Using the maximum inequality of [47], we get

$$\mathbb{E}\big[\sup_{t\in[0,T]} |(X_t^\alpha - X_0^\alpha) - \nu W_t^H|\big]$$
$$\leq c\left(\nu\alpha T T^H + \int_{-\infty}^0 \nu\alpha(T\alpha e^{\alpha s})|s|^H ds\right),$$

with c some constant. The term on the right hand side is easily seen to go to zero as α tends to zero.

A.2 *Proof of Corollary* 3.1

We first recall Equation (2.2) in [16] which writes:

$$\mathrm{Cov}[X_{t+\Delta}^\alpha, X_t^\alpha] = K \int_{\mathbb{R}} e^{i\Delta x} \frac{|x|^{1-2H}}{\alpha^2 + x^2} dx,$$

with $K = \nu^2\Gamma(2H+1)\sin(\pi H)/(2\pi)$.[r] Now remark that

$$\mathbb{E}[(X_{t+\Delta}^\alpha - X_t^\alpha)^2] = 2\mathrm{Var}[X_t^\alpha] - 2\mathrm{Cov}[X_{t+\Delta}^\alpha, X_t^\alpha].$$

Therefore,

$$\mathbb{E}[(X_{t+\Delta}^\alpha - X_t^\alpha)^2] = 2K \int_{\mathbb{R}} (1 - e^{i\Delta x}) \frac{|x|^{1-2H}}{\alpha^2 + x^2} dx.$$

This implies that for fixed Δ, $\mathbb{E}[|X_{t+\Delta}^\alpha - X_t^\alpha|^2]$ is uniformly bounded by

$$2K \int_{\mathbb{R}} (1 - e^{i\Delta x}) \frac{|x|^{1-2H}}{x^2} dx.$$

[r]This covariance is real because it is the Fourier transform of an even function.

Moreover, $X^\alpha_{t+\Delta} - X^\alpha_t$ is a Gaussian random variable and thus for every q, its moment of order $(q+1)$ is uniformly bounded (in α) so that the family $|X^\alpha_{t+\Delta} - X^\alpha_t|^q$ is uniformly integrable. Therefore, since by Proposition 3.1,

$$|X^\alpha_{t+\Delta} - X^\alpha_t|^q \to \nu^q |W^H_{t+\Delta} - W^H_t|^q, \text{ in law,}$$

we get the convergence of the sequence of expectations.

Appendix B Estimations of *H*

B.1 *On different indices*

Table B.1: Estimates of ζ_q for all indices in the Oxford-Man dataset.

Index	$\zeta_{0.5}/0.5$	ζ_1	$\zeta_{1.5}/1.5$	$\zeta_2/2$	$\zeta_3/3$
SPX2.rv	0.128	0.126	0.125	0.124	0.124
FTSE2.rv	0.132	0.132	0.132	0.131	0.127
N2252.rv	0.131	0.131	0.132	0.132	0.133
GDAXI2.rv	0.141	0.139	0.138	0.136	0.132
RUT2.rv	0.117	0.115	0.113	0.111	0.108
AORD2.rv	0.072	0.073	0.074	0.075	0.077
DJI2.rv	0.117	0.116	0.115	0.114	0.113
IXIC2.rv	0.131	0.133	0.134	0.135	0.137
FCHI2.rv	0.143	0.143	0.142	0.141	0.138
HSI2.rv	0.079	0.079	0.079	0.080	0.082
KS11.rv	0.133	0.133	0.134	0.134	0.132
AEX.rv	0.145	0.147	0.149	0.149	0.149
SSMI.rv	0.149	0.153	0.156	0.158	0.158
IBEX2.rv	0.138	0.138	0.137	0.136	0.133
NSEI.rv	0.119	0.117	0.114	0.111	0.102
MXX.rv	0.077	0.077	0.076	0.075	0.071
BVSP.rv	0.118	0.118	0.119	0.120	0.120
GSPTSE.rv	0.106	0.104	0.103	0.102	0.101
STOXX50E.rv	0.139	0.135	0.130	0.123	0.101
FTSTI.rv	0.111	0.112	0.113	0.113	0.112
FTSEMIB.rv	0.130	0.132	0.133	0.134	0.134

B.2 *On different time intervals*[s]

Table B.2: Estimates of H over two different time intervals for all indices in the Oxford-Man dataset.

Index	H (first half)	H (second half)
SPX2.rk	0.115	0.158
FTSE2.rk	0.140	0.156
N2252.rk	0.083	0.134
GDAXI2.rk	0.154	0.168
RUT2.rk	0.098	0.149
AORD2.rk	0.059	0.114
DJI2.rk	0.123	0.151
IXIC2.rk	0.094	0.156
FCHI2.rk	0.140	0.146
HSI2.rk	0.072	0.129
KS11.rk	0.109	0.147
AEX.rk	0.168	0.151
SSMI.rk	0.206	0.183
IBEX2.rk	0.122	0.149
NSEI.rk	0.112	0.124
MXX.rk	0.068	0.118
BVSP.rk	0.074	0.134
GSPTSE.rk	0.075	0.147
STOXX50E.rk	0.138	0.132
FTSTI.rk	0.080	0.171
FTSEMIB.rk	0.133	0.140

Appendix C The Effect of Smoothing

Although we are really interested in the model

$$\log \sigma_{t+\Delta} - \log \sigma_t = \nu \left(W^H_{t+\Delta} - W^H_t \right),$$

[s]Note that we used realized kernel rather than realized variance estimates to generate Table B.2. Results obtained using different estimators are almost indistinguishable.

consider the more tractable (fractional Stein and Stein or fSS) model:

$$v_{t+\Delta} - v_t = \alpha \left(W^H_{t+\Delta} - W^H_t \right),$$

where $v_t = \sigma^2$. We cannot observe v_t but suppose we can proxy it by the average

$$\hat{v}^\delta_t = \frac{1}{\delta} \int_0^\delta v_u \, du.$$

We would, for example, like to estimate $m(2,\Delta) = \mathbb{E}\left[(v_{t+\Delta} - v_t)^2\right]$. However, we need to proxy spot variance with integrated variance so instead we have the estimate

$$\begin{aligned}
m^\delta(2,\Delta) &= \mathbb{E}\left[(\hat{v}^\delta_{t+\Delta} - \hat{v}^\delta_t)^2\right] \\
&= \frac{1}{\delta^2}\, \mathbb{E}\left[\left(\int_0^\delta (v_{u+\Delta} - v_u)\, du\right)^2\right] \\
&= \frac{\alpha^2}{\delta^2} \int_0^\delta \int_0^\delta \mathbb{E}\left[(W^H_{u+\Delta} - W^H_u)\,(W^H_{s+\Delta} - W^H_s)\right] du\, ds \\
&= \int_0^\delta \int_0^\delta \left(|u - s + \Delta|^{2H} - |u - s|^{2H}\right) du\, ds, \qquad \text{(C.1)}
\end{aligned}$$

where the last step uses that:

$$\mathbb{E}\left[W^H_u\, W^H_s\right] = \frac{1}{2}\left(u^{2H} + s^{2H} - |u - s|^{2H}\right),$$

and the symmetry of the integral.

We assume that the length δ of the smoothing window is less than one day so $\Delta > \delta$. Then easy computations give

$$\begin{aligned}
&\int_0^\delta \int_0^\delta |u - s + \Delta|^{2H}\, du\, ds \\
&\quad = \frac{1}{2H+1}\,\frac{1}{2H+2}\left((\Delta+\delta)^{2H+2} - 2\,\Delta^{2H+2} + (\Delta-\delta)^{2H+2}\right)
\end{aligned}$$

and

$$\int_0^\delta \int_0^\delta |u - s|^{2H}\, du\, ds = \frac{2}{2H+1}\,\frac{1}{2H+2}\,\delta^{2H+2}.$$

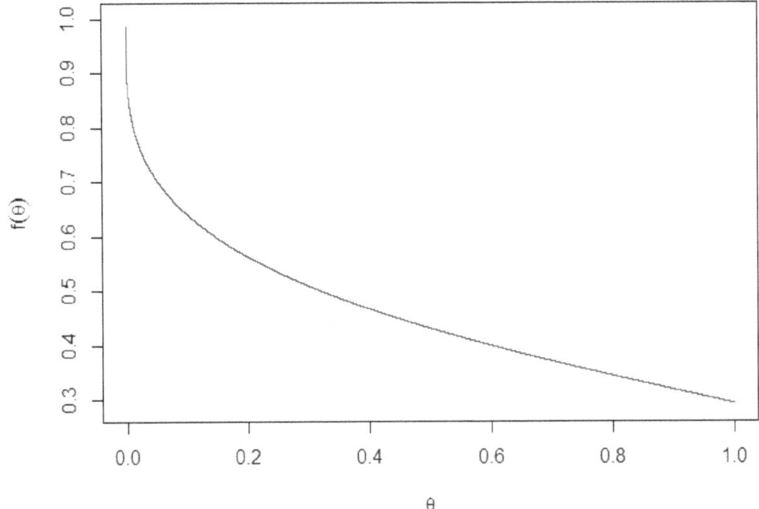

Figure C.1: $f(\theta)$ vs $\theta = \delta/\Delta$ with $H = 0.14$.

Substituting back into (C.1) gives

$$\begin{aligned} m^\delta(2,\Delta) &= \alpha^2\,\Delta^{2\,H}\,\frac{1}{2\,H+1}\,\frac{1}{2\,H+2}\,\frac{1}{\theta^2} \\ &\quad\times\left((1+\theta)^{2\,H+2} - 2 - 2\,\theta^{2\,H+2} + (1-\theta)^{2\,H+2}\right) \\ &=: \alpha^2\,\Delta^{2\,H}\,f(\theta). \end{aligned}$$

where $\theta = \delta/\Delta$.

Figure C.1 shows the effect of smoothing on the estimated variance in the fSS model. Keeping δ fixed, as Δ increases, $f(\theta) = f(\delta/\Delta)$ increases towards one. Thus, in a linear regression of $\log m^\delta(2,\Delta)$ against $\log\Delta$, we will obtain a higher effective H (from the higher slope) and a lower effective ("volatility of volatility") α, exactly as we observed in the RSFV model simulations in Section 3.4.

Numerical example

In the simulation of the RSFV model in Section 3.4, we have $H = 0.14$, $\delta_1 = 1/24$ for the UZ estimate and $\delta_2 = 1/3$ for the RV estimate. We now reproduce a fSS analogue of the RFSV simulation plots of $m(2,\Delta)$ in Figure 14. Specifically, for each $\Delta \in \{1, 2, ..., 100\}$, with

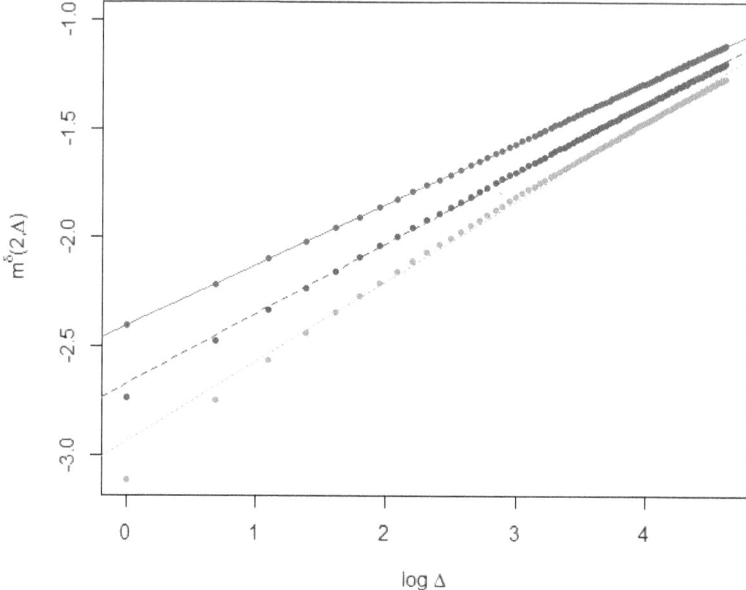

Figure C.2: Analogue of Figure 14 in the fSS model: The blue solid line is the true $m(2,\Delta)$; the red long-dashed line is the UZ estimate $m^{\delta_1}(2,\Delta)$; the orange short-dashed line is the RV estimate $m^{\delta_2}(2,\Delta)$.

Table C.1: Estimated model parameters from the regressions shown in Figure C.2.

Estimate	Est. α	Est. H
Exact ($\delta = 0$)	0.300	0.140
UZ ($\delta = 1/24$)	0.263	0.161
RV ($\delta = 1/3$)	0.230	0.184

$\alpha = 0.3$ and $\delta = \delta_1$ or $\delta = \delta_2$, we compute the $m^\delta(2,\Delta)$ and regress $\log m^\delta(2,\Delta)$ against $\log \Delta$. The regressions are shown in Figure C.2 and results tabulated in Table C.1.

In Figure C.2 and Table C.1, we observe similar qualitative and quantitative biases from our fSS model simulation as we observe in our simulation of the RSFV model with equivalent parameters in Section 3.4.

Acknowledgment

Thibault Jaisson gratefully acknowledges financial support from the chair "Risques Financiers" of the Risk Foundation and the chair "Marchés en Mutation" of the French Banking Federation.

Mathieu Rosenbaum gratefully acknowledges financial support from the ERC 679836 STAQAMOF.

References

[1] T.G. Andersen and T. Bollerslev (1997). Heterogeneous information arrivals and return volatility dynamics: Uncovering the long-run in high frequency returns. *The Journal of Finance*, 52(3), 975–1005.

[2] T.G. Andersen and T. Bollerslev (1997). Intraday periodicity and volatility persistence in financial markets. *Journal of Empirical Finance*, 4(2), 115–158.

[3] T.G. Andersen, T. Bollerslev, F.X. Diebold, and H. Ebens (2001). The distribution of realized stock return volatility. *Journal of Financial Economics*, 61(1), 43–76.

[4] T.G. Andersen, T. Bollerslev, F.X. Diebold, and P. Labys (2001). The distribution of realized exchange rate volatility. *Journal of the American Statistical Association*, 96(453), 42–55.

[5] T.G. Andersen, T. Bollerslev, F.X. Diebold, and P. Labys (2003). Modeling and forecasting realized volatility. *Econometrica*, 71(2), 579–625.

[6] E. Bacry and J.F. Muzy (2003). Log-infinitely divisible multifractal processes. *Communications in Mathematical Physics*, 236(3), 449–475.

[7] C. Bayer, P. Friz, and J. Gatheral (2016). Pricing under rough volatility. *Quantitative Finance*, 16(6), 887–904.

[8] M. Bennedsen, A. Lunde, and M.S. Pakkanen (2016). Decoupling the short- and long-term behavior of stochastic volatility. *Available at SSRN 2846756.*

[9] S.R. Bentes and M.M. da Cruz (2011). Is stock market volatility persistent? A fractionally integrated approach.

[10] J. Beran (1994). *Statistics for Long-memory Processes*, Volume 61. CRC Press.

[11] B.M. Bibby, I.M. Skovgaard, M. Sørensen, *et al.* (2005). Diffusion-type models with given marginal distribution and autocorrelation function. *Bernoulli*, 11(2), 191–220.

[12] J.-P. Bouchaud and M. Potters (2003). *Theory of Financial Risk and Derivative Pricing: From Statistical Physics to Risk Management.* Cambridge University Press.

[13] A. Brouste and S.M. Iacus (2013). Parameter estimation for the discretely observed fractional Ornstein–Uhlenbeck process and the Yuima R package. *Computational Statistics*, 28(4), 1529–1547.

[14] P. Carr and L. Wu (2003). What type of process underlies options? A simple robust test. *Journal of Finance*, 58(6), 2581–2610.

[15] Z. Chen, R.T. Daigler, and A.M. Parhizgari (2006). Persistence of volatility in futures markets. *Journal of Futures Markets*, 26(6), 571–594.

[16] P. Cheridito, H. Kawaguchi, and M. Maejima (2003). Fractional Ornstein–Uhlenbeck processes. *Electron. J. Probab*, 8(3), 14.

[17] A. Chronopoulou (2011). Parameter estimation and calibration for long-memory stochastic volatility models.In F. G. Viens, M. C. Mariani, and I. Florescu, editors, *Handbook of Modeling High-Frequency Data in Finance*, pp. 219–231. John Wiley & Sons.

[18] A. Chronopoulou and F.G. Viens (2012). Estimation and pricing under long-memory stochastic volatility. *Annals of Finance*, 8(2-3), 379–403.

[19] J.-F. Coeurjolly (2001). Estimating the parameters of a fractional Brownian motion by discrete variations of its sample paths. *Statistical Inference for Stochastic Processes*, 4(2), 199–227.

[20] F. Comte, L. Coutin, and É. Renault (2012). Affine fractional stochastic volatility models. *Annals of Finance*, 8(2-3), 337–378.

[21] F. Comte and E. Renault (1998). Long memory in continuous-time stochastic volatility models. *Mathematical Finance*, 8(4), 291–323.

[22] R. Cont (2007). Volatility clustering in financial markets: Empirical facts and agent-based models. In G. Teyssière and A. P. Kirman, editors, *Long Memory in Economics*, pp. 289–309. Berlin, Heidelberg: Springer.

[23] F. Corsi (2009). A simple approximate long-memory model of realized volatility. *Journal of Financial Econometrics*, 7(2), 174–196.

[24] K. Dayri and M. Rosenbaum (2015). Large tick assets: Implicit spread and optimal tick size. *Microstructure and Liquidity*, 1(1), 155003.

[25] F.X. Diebold and A. Inoue (2001). Long memory and regime switching. *Journal of Econometrics*, 105(1), 131–159.

[26] Z. Ding, C.W. Granger, and R.F. Engle (1993). A long memory property of stock market returns and a new model. *Journal of Empirical Finance*, 1(1), 83–106.

[27] J. Duchon, R. Robert, and V. Vargas (2012). Forecasting volatility with the multifractal random walk model. *Mathematical Finance*, 22(1), 83–108.

[28] B. Dupire.Pricing with a smile (1994). *Risk Magazine*, 7(1), 18–20.

[29] O. El Euch, M. Fukasawa, and M. Rosenbaum (2016). The microstructural foundations of leverage effect and rough volatility. *arXiv preprint arXiv:1609.05177*

[30] O. El Euch and M. Rosenbaum (2016). The characteristic function of rough heston models. *arXiv preprint arXiv:1609.02108.*

[31] O. El Euch and M. Rosenbaum (2017). Perfect hedging in rough heston models. *arXiv preprint arXiv:1703.05049.*

[32] M. Fukasawa (2011). Asymptotic analysis for stochastic volatility: Martingale expansion. *Finance and Stochastics*, 15(4), 635–654.

[33] J. Gatheral (2006). *The Volatility Surface: A Practitioner's Guide*, volume 357. John Wiley & Sons.

[34] J. Gatheral and A. Jacquier (2014). Arbitrage-free SVI volatility surfaces. *Quantitative Finance*, 14(1), 59–71.

[35] J. Gatheral and R.C. Oomen (2010). Zero-intelligence realized variance estimation. *Finance and Stochastics*, 14(2), 249–283.

[36] J. Geweke and S. Porter-Hudak (1983). The estimation and application of long memory time series models. *Journal of Time Series Analysis*, 4(4), 221–238.

[37] C.W. Granger and N. Hyung (2004). Occasional structural breaks and long memory with an application to the S&P 500 absolute stock returns. *Journal of Empirical Finance*, 11(3), 399–421.

[38] C.W. Granger and T. Teräsvirta (1999). A simple nonlinear time series model with misleading linear properties. *Economics Letters*, 62(2), 161–165.

[39] P.S. Hagan, D. Kumar, A.S. Lesniewski, and D.E. Woodward (2002). Managing smile risk. *Wilmott Magazine*, pp. 84–108.

[40] S.L. Heston (1993). A closed-form solution for options with stochastic volatility with applications to bond and currency options. *Review of Financial Studies*, 6(2), 327–343.

[41] J. Hull and A. White (1993). One-factor interest-rate models and the valuation of interest-rate derivative securities. *Journal of Financial and Quantitative Analysis*, 28(2), 235–254.

[42] J. Istas and G. Lang (1997). Quadratic variations and estimation of the local Hölder index of a Gaussian process. *Annales de l'IHP Probabilités et Statistiques*, 33(4), 407–436.

[43] B.B. Mandelbrot and J.W. Van Ness (1968). Fractional Brownian motions, fractional noises and applications. *SIAM Review*, 10(4), 422–437.

[44] R.N. Mantegna and H.E. Stanley (2000). *Introduction to Econophysics: Correlations and Complexity in Finance*. Cambridge University Press.

[45] T. Mikosch and C. Stărică (2000). Is it really long memory we see in financial returns. In P. Embrechts, editor, *Extremes and Integrated Risk Management*, pp. 149–168. Risk Books.
[46] M. Musiela and M. Rutkowski (2006). *Martingale methods in financial modelling*, Volume 36. Springer.
[47] A. Novikov and E. Valkeila (1999). On some maximal inequalities for fractional Brownian motions. *Statistics & Probability Letters*, 44(1), 47–54.
[48] C.J. Nuzman and V.H. Poor (2000). Linear estimation of self-similar processes via Lamperti's transformation. *Journal of Applied Probability*, 37(2), 429–452.
[49] C.Y. Robert and M. Rosenbaum (2011). A new approach for the dynamics of ultra-high-frequency data: The model with uncertainty zones. *Journal of Financial Econometrics*, 9(2), 344–366.
[50] C.Y. Robert and M. Rosenbaum (2012). Volatility and covariation estimation when microstructure noise and trading times are endogenous. *Mathematical Finance*, 22(1), 133–164.
[51] M. Rosenbaum. Estimation of the volatility persistence in a discretely observed diffusion model (2008). *Stochastic Processes and their Applications*, 118(8), 1434–1462.
[52] M. Rosenbaum (2009). First order p-variations and Besov spaces. *Statistics & Probability Letters*, 79(1), 55–62.
[53] M. Rosenbaum (2011). A new microstructure noise index. *Quantitative Finance*, 11(6), 883–899.

https://doi.org/10.1142/9789811259142_0009

Chapter 9

Things We Think We Know

L.C.G. Rogers

Statistical Laboratory, University of Cambridge
Cambridge, United Kingdom

lcgr1@cam.ac.uk

Abstract

A model is useless if it cannot be taken to data, so it makes sense to begin modeling by looking at the data. Simple exploratory techniques can quickly reveal stylized facts of the data, and may suggest modeling hypotheses, but it is important to be cautious before jumping to conclusions, and to keep an open mind about other possibilities. This chapter considers some examples related to asset returns.

Keywords: Rough volatility, high frequency data, multiscale volatility.

1. Models of Asset Returns

If S_t denotes the price of an asset at time t, then the celebrated Black–Scholes–Merton model proposes that S evolves as

$$dS_t = S_t(\sigma dW_t + \mu dt), \tag{1}$$

where W is a standard Brownian motion, and $\sigma > 0$, μ are constants. Crucially for derivative pricing, when we work in the pricing measure we have that μ is equal to the riskless rate r, an observation which goes back at least to Merton and Samuelson [4]. The Black–Scholes–Merton model has a number of strengths:

(S1) it is simple and tractable;
(S2) there is only one unknown parameter, σ;

(S3) it generalizes naturally to many dimensions; and
(S4) passing from continuous time to discrete time and back is easy and natural.

Property **(S1)** allows many closed-form options prices to be obtained, and makes numerical computations easier. Property **(S2)** is the basis of the entire technology of implied volatility. Property **(S3)** is achieved if we let the vector of log-prices of many assets be a Brownian motion with constant drift and covariance. For property **(S4)**, the discrete-time analogue of the Black–Scholes–Merton model is a random walk, and passing back to continuous time is in effect just Donsker's theorem. This is important because any numerical computation has to be done with finite statespace and finite time set. Set against these strengths are some folklore weaknesses, notably:

(W1) volatility is not constant;
(W2) returns[a] are not Gaussian.

We see the first of these from the plot of any asset returns; for example, Figure 1 shows the plot of returns on IBM stock. The right-hand panel is a diagnostic plot of the cumulative sum of squared returns.

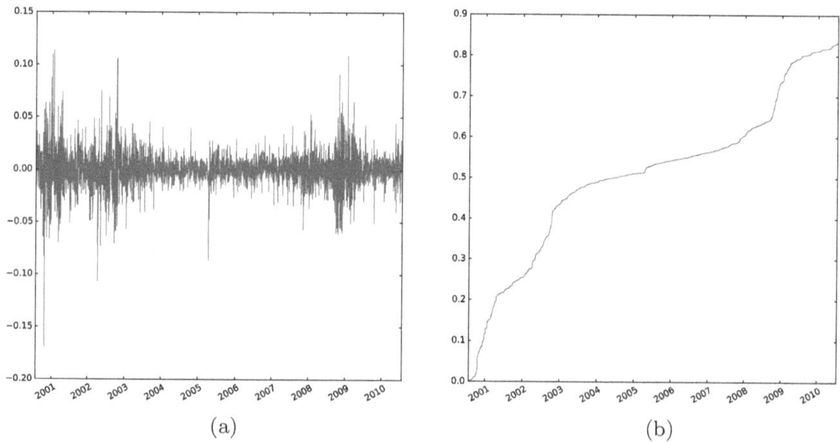

Figure 1: (a) IBM returns and (b) Cumsum of squared IBM returns.

[a]We shall speak of *returns* instead of the longer but more precise *log returns*.

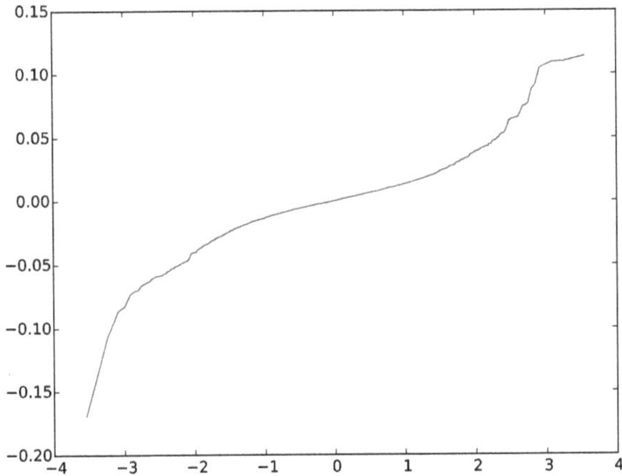

Figure 2: *q-q* plot of IBM returns.

If returns were IID, then this plot would be a straight line, but it plainly is not.

To show that log returns are not Gaussian, we commonly do a *q-q* plot, Figure 2. If returns were IID Gaussian, this plot would be a straight line, which visually appears not to be the case. But we need to be cautious — we already *know* from Figure 1 that returns are not IID, so *a fortiori* they are not IID Gaussian — Figure 2 tells us nothing useful. Attempts to model assets as log-Lévy processes relax the Gaussian assumption of the Black–Scholes–Merton model, but retain the obviously wrong assumption of IID returns.

2. Alternative Asset Models

The Black–Scholes–Merton model is an excellent first choice, but we see that it is not the whole story, so we need to consider other modeling directions. Sadly, there is no consensus about what the next modeling family should be. Among widely-studied choices, we could list:

(1) log-Lévy models (which we know do not fit the data);
(2) stochastic volatility models such as Heston, Bates, etc.;
(3) local volatility models, popularized by Dupire and others;
(4) rough volatility models, promoted by Gatheral and co-workers;

(5) regime switching models, as considered by Elliott and others;
(6) GARCH models, the favourite of econometricians.

Before investing too much intellectual capital in any particular alternative class of models, it is well worth considering to what extent the strengths **(S3)** and **(S4)** of the Black–Scholes–Merton model survive: if we lose **(S3)** then the alternative class can only deal with one asset at a time, and if we lose **(S4)** then numerics or interpretation will be problematic. The econometricians' favourite, GARCH, fails spectacularly on both counts. But the purpose of this chapter is not to survey and argue the strengths and weaknesses of various alternative asset models, rather the purpose is to draw attention to the need for care in exploration of data; and to illustrate this, we now concentrate on the fourth model in the list above, rough volatility models. This topic is relatively recent, but has been received so enthusiastically that it now has its very own website https://sites.google.com/site/roughvol/home, and the seminal paper [2] of Gatheral *et al.* [2], boldly declares in its title that "Volatility is rough". Let us inspect the evidence for this claim.

3. Rough Volatility

The empirical evidence for rough volatility is based on daily estimates of realized variance made available via the website of the Oxford Man Institute https://www.oxford-man.ox.ac.uk/research/realized-library/. The reader should visit for more detail on the methodologies used to calculate these estimates from high-frequencey data; suffice it to say that various procedures are used, and produce quite similar estimates. Letting $\hat{\sigma}_t$ denote the estimate on day t of the annualized volatility of the asset, what Gatheral *et al.* calculate in [2] is the quantity

$$m(q,\Delta) \equiv N^{-1} \sum_{t=1}^{N} |\log \hat{\sigma}_{t+\Delta} - \log \hat{\sigma}_t|^q, \tag{2}$$

for a range of values $q = 0.5, 1.0, 1.5, 2.0, 2.5, 3.0$ and lags $\Delta \in \{1, \ldots, 50\}$. Their remarkable finding is that apparently

$$m(q,\Delta) \propto \Delta^{\alpha q}, \tag{3}$$

for some α which is not the same for all the indices considered in [2], but is generally in the range $[0.07, 0.20]$. This is remarkable, because for any diffusion-based model we would expect that (for short lags at least) $\alpha = 0.5$, from the Brownian scaling. This surprising finding is the basis of the claim that volatility is rough. Moreover, the increments of $\log \hat{\sigma}_t$ appear to have Gaussian distributions. The plots in Figure 3 show these findings. In the top left panel is the daily estimates of volatility, in the top right panel is the cumulative sum of squared changes in volatility, in the bottom left panel are q-q plots of the increments in $\log \hat{\sigma}$ over six different time lags, and in the bottom right panel we have the plots of $\log m(q, \Delta)$ against $\log \Delta$ for six different values of q, with best-fit lines superimposed. The slopes of the best-fit lines are proportional to q, which leads Gatheral *et al.* [2] to propose that $X_t \equiv \log \hat{\sigma}_t$ is a fractional Brownian motion (fBM):

$$X_{t+\Delta} - X_t \sim N(0, v\Delta^{2\alpha}), \tag{4}$$

for some $v > 0$. Fractional Brownian motion has long memory, which is a contentious property; as Gatheral *et al.* state in their paper, "The evidence for long memory has never been sufficient to satisfy remaining doubters such as Mikosch and Starica [3]". One of the main points made in [3] is that when we calculate the ACF of a time series, the interpretation of what we see presumes that the series is stationary,[b] and departures from this assumption tend to produce the appearance of long-range dependence. In this instance, it may not be an issue; from the top right panel of Figure 3 we see the cumulative sum of squared differences growing linearly, so this at least is consistent with stationarity.

The fBM model certainly appears to fit the data well, but there are two main objections to it, which are the same objection, considered operationally and theoretically:

(1) the model is highly non-Markovian; in order to predict the future of X, we need to know the *entire* history;
(2) what *economic* story could we tell that would result in a model where we need to know the *entire* history in order to predict the future?

---

[b]... just as the q-q plot requires the data to be IID ....

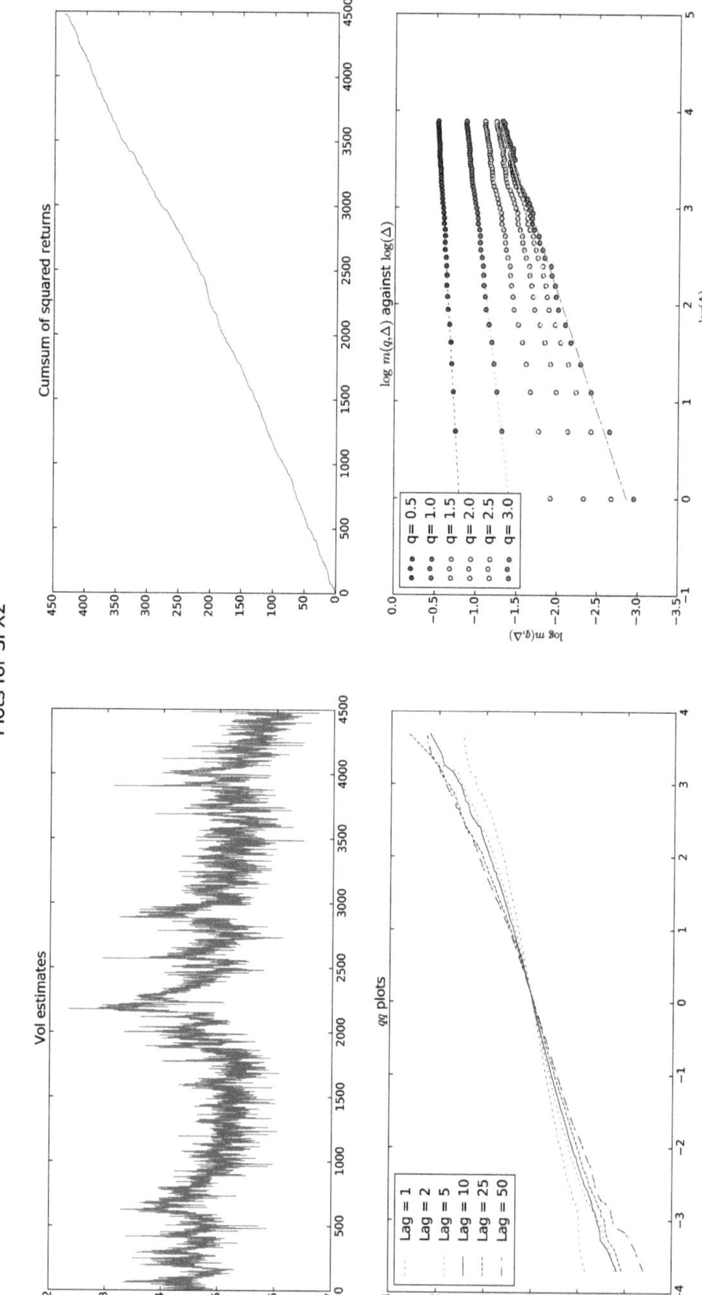

Figure 3: Daily volatility estimates of the S&P500.

In any case, since the value of α varies from one index to another, there is clearly no universal law applicable to all assets. *What could we do that would be better?*

4. A Simpler Alternative to Rough Volatility

When we look again at the top left panel in Figure 3, we see a plot which fluctuates strongly on small time scales, but on longer time scales the level seems to be changing. If the level did not change, we could try to model the data as an Ornstein–Uhlenbeck (OU) process with strong mean reversion and high volatility; as the level appears to be changing, we could try an energetic OU process mean-reverting to a slower one:

$$dY_t = \sigma_Y \, dW_t' - \beta \, Y_t \, dt, \tag{5}$$

$$dX_t = \sigma_X \, dW_t + \lambda \, (Y_t - X_t) \, dt. \tag{6}$$

We refer to this model as OU-OU. Figure 4 is the analogue of Figure 3 for data generated by the model (5),(6) with parameter values $\sigma_X^2 = 20$, $\sigma_Y^2 = 0.625$, $\lambda = 210$ and $\beta = 2.5$. The qualitative behavior is very similar. Moreover, the model is a bivariate diffusion, with linear dynamics and a joint Gaussian distribution, so it really is very nice to work with. It is an example of a multi-scale model of the kind analysed by Papanicolaou, Fouque, Sircar and others; see [1] for a consolidated account of this theme.

So we have two models, the rough volatility model and the OU-OU which both seem to explain the observed data well; is there any way to choose between them? Figure 5 shows the bottom right-hand panel of Figure 4 with a longer range of values for Δ. The linear fits are shown as dashed lines, and the true values (which we know because we know the model which generated the data) are shown as solid curves. There is close agreement *in the original range of Δ values*, but as we move to much shorter timescales large differences emerge. So this tells us that if we are to distinguish between the rough volatility story and the OU–OU story, we need to look at these shorter time scales.

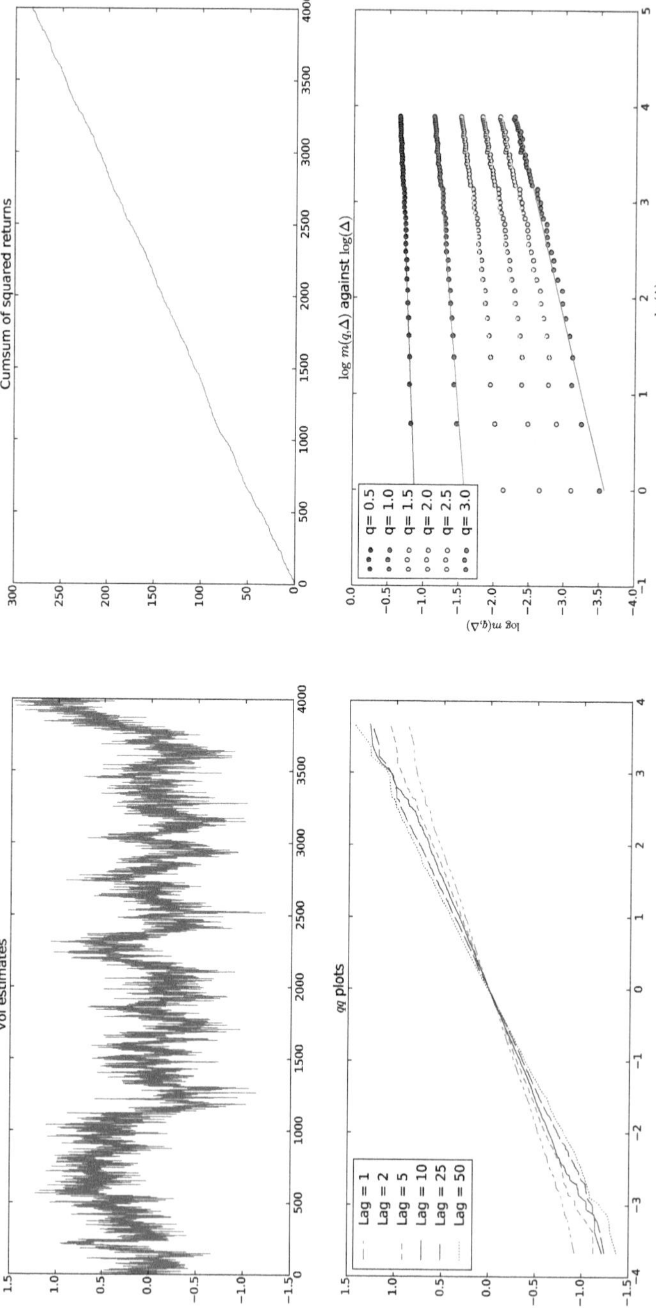

Figure 4: Plots for the FIX2000.

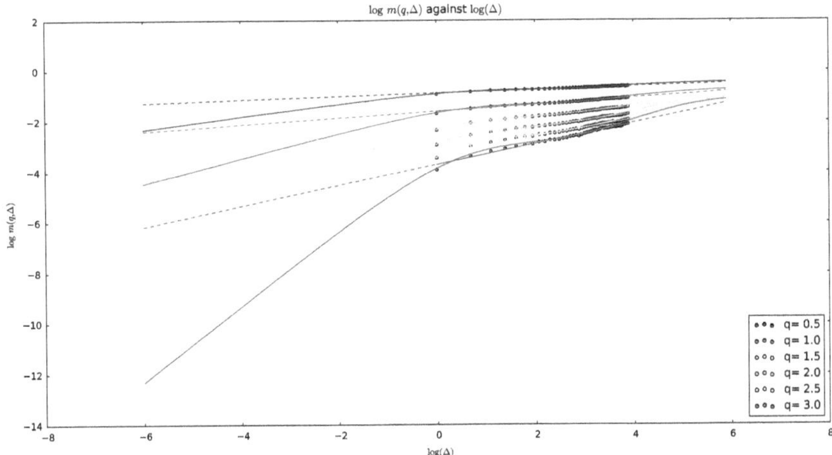

Figure 5: Plot for the FIX2000.

5. High-Frequency Data

The estimates presented on the Oxford Man website are derived from high frequency data, but that data is not made available. So here we have to be content with something smaller scale, but which is nevertheless indicative. This is based on seven days of WTI futures tick data. Firstly we extract the times at which the mid-price has moved by one tick, which excludes events where the mid-price moves by half a tick, usually caused by the volume at the best bid or best ask momentarily falling to zero. Then we exclude market closed times. Finally we count for each minute the number of one-tick moves which happened in that minute. This gives us for each minute an estimate of the speed of the market; in a diffusion model, the variance σ^2 measures the speed, and in a discrete point process model (which is what we have in high-frequency data) it is the rate of the point process which measures the speed. The number of events in a given interval estimates the rate, so is a suitable proxy for variance in this context. Figure 6 shows what we get; once again, the apparent linearity in the bottom right panel is striking.

Zooming in on the data panel, we see Figure 7. The most striking feature is the extreme variability, with the numbers of events in consecutive minutes often differing by an order of magnitude. In view of this, one may wonder whether a model with continuous paths holds

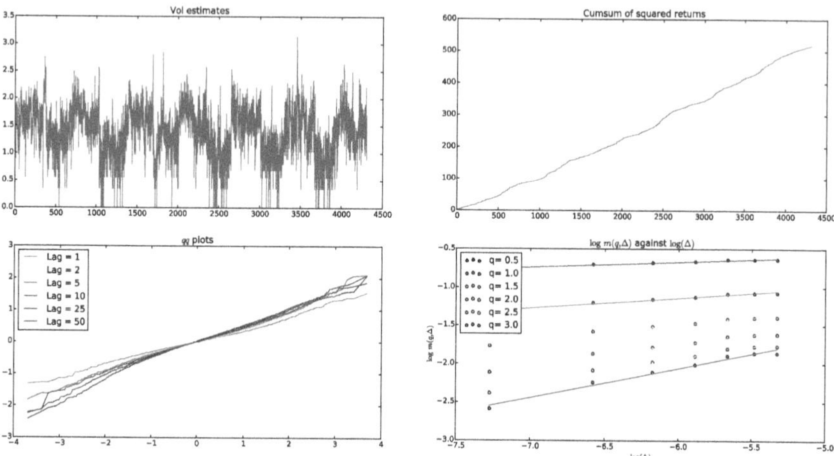

Figure 6: Plot for WTI high frequency data.

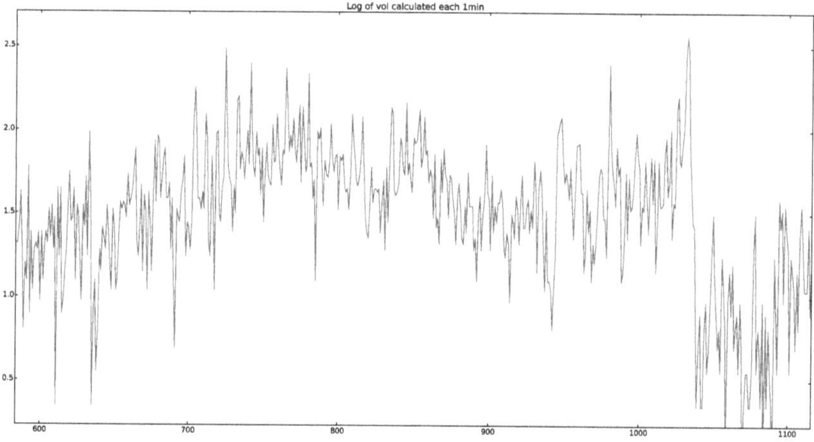

Figure 7: Close-up of WTI high frequency data.

at such time scales; a scatter plot reveals Figure 8, and presented in this form it is hard to feel confident that there really is a continuous trajectory here. Maybe what we are seeing is some more regular process plus additive IID noise? To try to understand this possibility, we formed estimates of α for the raw data shown in Figure 7, and then for the MA(2) and MA(3) of these. Intriguingly, for the raw data we get estimates in the range found by Gatheral *et al.*, but for an MA(3)

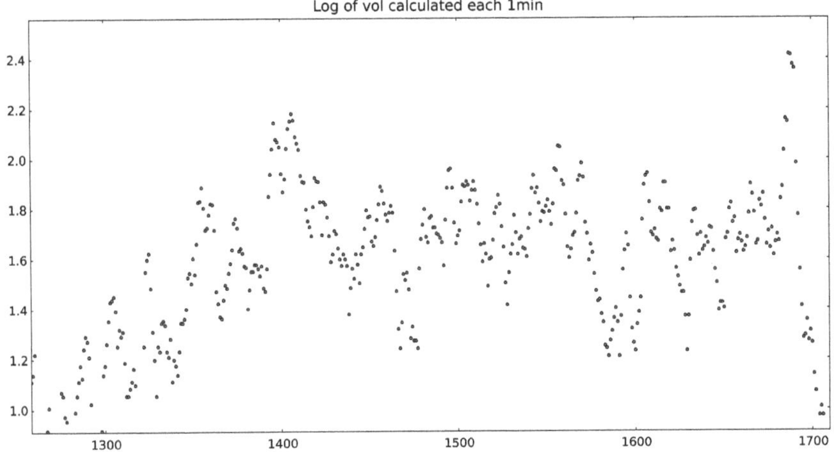

Figure 8: Close-up of WTI high frequency data.

we find the estimates much closer to the limiting value 0.5 we would obtain from a diffusion model!

q	raw	MA(2)	MA(3)
0.5	0.137	0.327	0.482
1.0	0.132	0.319	0.468
1.5	0.130	0.316	0.460
2.0	0.129	0.314	0.455
2.5	0.128	0.313	0.450
3.0	0.128	0.313	0.446

6. Conclusions

What we have seen in this chapter is that the notion that volatility is rough, that is, governed by a fractional Brownian motion, is *not* an incontrovertible established fact; simpler models explain the observations just as well. Neither makes much sense at very high frequency, but at this sort of timescale any estimates will be noisy. However, if we are concerned to model volatility because we want to calculate option prices, then the timescales we care about are days, weeks or months, not minutes, so a model that explains the data well on those timescales is valuable. The OU–OU model proposed here works on those timescales, and moreover is much easier to work with, being a bivariate Gaussian diffusion, amenable to the multiscale option pricing techniques explained in Fouque *et al.* [1].

References

[1] Fouque, J.-P., Papanicolaou, G., Sircar, R., and Sølna, K. (2011). *Multiscale Stochastic Volatility for Equity, Interest Rate, and Credit Derivatives.* Cambridge University Press.

[2] Gatheral, J., Jaisson, T., and Rosenbaum, M. (2018). Volatility is rough. *Quantitative Finance*, 18(6), 933–949.

[3] Mikosch, T. and Starica, C. (2000). Is it really long memory we see in financial returns. *Extremes and Integrated Risk Management*, *12*, 149–168.

[4] Samuelson, P. and Merton, R.C. (1969). A complete model of warrant pricing that maximizes utility. *IMR; Industrial Management Review*, 10(2), 17–46.

https://doi.org/10.1142/9789811259142_0010

Chapter 10

Cumulant Formulas for Implied Volatility

R. Lee

Department of Mathematics, University of Chicago

rogerlee@math.uchicago.edu

1. Implied Volatility and its Importance

- Black–Scholes–Merton pricing function C^{BS}. Input: volatilty σ (annualized standard deviation of returns, in percentage points), and output: option price C (in dollars).
- This relationship is 1-to-1. So instead of quoting C, we can quote the σ that produces C. Irrespective of empirical validity of BSM.
- Allows for comparison of option prices across different strikes, expiries, observation dates, and underlyings. Can be interpreted as a forward-looking expectation of variability of underlying.
- Meta-theorem: Instead of approximating option prices directly, better to use C^{BS}(implied volatility approximation), even though (or because!) implied volatility approx is a compound approximation.

2. Relate Implied Volatility Skew to Underlying Distribution

- How does implied volatility **level** relate to **variance**?
- How does implied volatility **skew slope** relate to **skewness**?
- How does implied volatility **curvature** relate to **kurtosis**?

3. Notations

- All prices expressed as forward or futures prices.
- Underlying stock or index S.
- Log strike $k = \log(K/S_0)$.
  So $k = 0$ is the ATM, $k > 0$ are OTM calls, $k < 0$ are OTM puts.
- Implied volatility IV,
  Implied variance IV^2,
  The volatility skew for a fixed expiry is $IV(k)$ for $-\infty < k < \infty$.
- How does IV relate to risk-neutral distribution of S_T or its return

$$R := \log(S_T/S_0).$$

4. Exact Relationship: Distribution $\longleftrightarrow$ Implied Volatilities

How to obtain probability distribution of S_T from implied volatilities?

- Plug implied volatilities into C^{BS}, to obtain option prices $C(K)$.
- Differentiate $C(K)$ twice wrt K to obtain density function.

How to obtain implied volatilities from probability distribution of S_T?

- Integrate payoff $(S-K)^+ \times$ density of S_T to get $C(K)$ or: Integrate payoff *transform* $\times$ *CF* of $\log S_T$ to get $C(K)$.
- From $C(K)$ invert C^{BS} function, to get implied volatilities.

However,

- We may not have a full probability distribution. We may have only the moments.

- We may not have a full volatility skew. We may have only a few features: level, slope, convexity.

5. Moments

For a random variable X

- The nth **moment** is $\mathbb{E}X^n$.
  Example: $n = 1$. The first moment of X is its mean.
- The nth **central moment** is $\mathbb{E}(X - \mathbb{E}X)^n$
  Example: $n = 2$. The second central moment of X is its **variance**

$$\operatorname{var}(X) = \mathbb{E}(X - \mathbb{E}X)^2 = \mathbb{E}(X^2) - (\mathbb{E}X)^2$$

  and its square root is the standard deviation $\operatorname{std}(X)$.
- The nth **standardized moment** is

$$\mathbb{E}Z^n \quad \text{where } Z := \frac{X - \mathbb{E}X}{\operatorname{std}(X)}.$$

  Example: $n = 3$. The 3rd standardized moment of X is its **skewness**.
  Example: $n = 4$. The 4th standardized moment of X is its **kurtosis**.

6. Cumulants

For a random variable X that has a finite moment generating function

$$M(z) := \mathbb{E}e^{zX},$$

in some open interval around 0, the nth cumulant is nth derivative

$$\kappa_n := L^{(n)}(0),$$

of $L := \log M$, the cumulant generating function (CGF).

- The first cumulant is the **mean**: $\kappa_1 = \mathbb{E}X$.
- The second cumulant is the **variance**: $\kappa_2 = \mathbb{E}(X - \mathbb{E}X)^2$.
- The third standardized cumulant is the **skewness**

$$\kappa_3/\kappa_2^{3/2} = \frac{\mathbb{E}(X - \mathbb{E}X)^3}{(\operatorname{var} X)^{3/2}}.$$

- The fourth standardized cumulant is the **excess kurtosis**

$$\kappa_4/\kappa_2^2 = \frac{\mathbb{E}(X - \mathbb{E}X)^4}{(\operatorname{var} X)^2} - 3.$$

7. Skewness and Kurtosis

- Think of a distribution with negative (positive) skewness as having a fatter left (right) tail.
- Write **skewness** or **skew** for $\kappa_3/\kappa_2^{3/2}$.
- Kurtosis $= \mathbb{E}Z^4 = \operatorname{var}(Z^2) + (\mathbb{E}Z^2)^2 = \operatorname{var}(Z^2) + 1$, where $Z = \frac{X - \mathbb{E}X}{\operatorname{std} X}$, so kurtosis measures how much the squared standardized **deviation** Z^2 itself **deviates** around its mean of 1. Financial interpretation: "volatility of volatility".
- Normal distribution has kurtosis 3. Write **kurt** for **excess kurtosis** $= \kappa_4/\kappa_2^2 =$ **kurtosis** $- 3$.

8. How do Skewness/Kurtosis Relate to Implied Volatilty?

Let $R := \log(S_T/S_0)$

- Backus–Foresi–Wu (1997,2004):

$$IV(k)\sqrt{T} \approx \operatorname{std}(R)\Big(1 - \frac{\operatorname{skewness}(R)}{6} d_1(k) + \frac{\operatorname{kurt}(R)}{24}(d_1^2(k) - 1)\Big)$$

$$\approx \kappa_2^{1/2}\Big(1 - \frac{\kappa_3/\kappa_2^{3/2}}{6} d_1(k) + \frac{\kappa_4/\kappa_2^2}{24}(d_1^2(k) - 1)\Big).$$

The three terms give level, slope, and convexity. Specifically:

implied volatility skew slope $\approx$ skewness/6,

where slope is of dimensionless volatality wrt log-strike.
- The $-d_1$ is the standardized log-strike

$$-d_1(k, T) = \frac{k}{\operatorname{std}(R)} - \frac{\operatorname{std}(R)}{2},$$

e.g., the $-d_1 = 1$ strike is ≈ 1 standard deviation above ATM.

9. BFW Approach

- Gram–Charlier approximation of general standardized density in terms of its cumulants and normal density

$$f_R(x) \approx \phi(x) - \frac{\text{skewness}(R)}{6}\phi'''(x) + \frac{\text{kurt}(R)}{24}\phi''''(x).$$

- Price options using approximate density. Convert to implied volatilities.
- But no error estimates.

10. Our Approach

- Specify an asymptotic regime.
- Prove rigorous O error estimates.
- Obtain refined results.
- Provide intuition.

11. Cumulant Expansion for Implied Volatility

Skewness formula for implied volatility

$$\boxed{IV(k)\sqrt{T} = \text{std} + \frac{\text{skew} \times \text{var}}{4} + \frac{\text{skew}}{6}k + \cdots}$$

Comments

- IV slope agrees with BFW: volatality skew slope = skewness/6.
- IV level differs from BFW. Here $\frac{\text{skew}\times\text{var}}{4}$ instead of $-\frac{\text{skew}\times\text{var}}{12}$.

12. Five Moments

- Suppose you believe that five shape features suffice to parameterize the implied volatility skew: ATM level, ATM slope, ATM curvature, left-hand wing slope, right-hand wing slope.

- For instance, the five parameters in Gatheral's SVI function

$$IV^2(k) = a + b\Big(\rho(k-m) + \sqrt{(k-m)^2+\sigma^2}\Big),$$

can be mapped explicitly into these five shape features.
- Then asymptotically **five moments** (or moment indices) of the underlying distribution map explicitly into these five shape features, and hence into a description of the full volatility skew.

13. The Book of Five Moments

Five moments: Std, skew, kurt of $\log S_T$. Moment indices ($\pm$) of S_T

$$\begin{aligned}
\text{ATM level} &\longleftrightarrow \text{std} + \frac{\text{skew} \times \text{var}}{4} \\
\text{ATM slope} &\longleftrightarrow \frac{\text{skew}}{6} \\
\text{ATM convexity} &\longleftrightarrow \frac{\text{kurt}}{24\ \text{std}} \\
\text{Right-hand wing slope of } IV^2T &\longleftrightarrow \psi(p^*) \\
\text{Left-hand wing slope of } IV^2T &\longleftrightarrow \psi(q^*),
\end{aligned}$$

where

$$p^* := \sup\{p : \mathbb{E}S_T^{1+p} < \infty\}, \qquad q^* := \sup\{q : \mathbb{E}S_T^{-q} < \infty\},$$

and

$$\psi(x) := 2(\sqrt{x+1} - \sqrt{x})^2 = 2 + 4x - 4\sqrt{x^2+x}.$$

14. Moment Formula

The last two relationships are by moment formula (2004).

Intuition: write $C^{bs}(k, \cdot)$ as function of dimensionless implied volatility.

$$C^{bs}(k, \sqrt{\beta k}) = \Phi(-\sqrt{f_1(\beta)k}) - e^k \Phi(-\sqrt{f_2(\beta)k}),$$
$$\sim \frac{1}{\sqrt{2\pi}}\left(\frac{e^{-f_1(\beta)k/2}}{\sqrt{f_1(\beta)k}} - \frac{e^k e^{-f_2(\beta)k/2}}{\sqrt{f_2(\beta)k}}\right) = \frac{e^{-f_1(\beta)k/2}}{B\sqrt{k}},$$

where

$$f_{1,2}(y) := f_{+,-}(y) := \left(\frac{1}{\sqrt{y}} \pm \frac{\sqrt{y}}{2}\right)^2.$$

On the other hand, $C(k) = O(e^{-kp})$ for all p with $\mathbb{E}S_T^{1+p} < \infty$. So

$$C(k) \approx e^{-kp^*}.$$

Matching C^{bs} and C decay rates,

$$p^* = f_1(\beta)/2 \quad \text{or} \quad \beta = \psi(p^*).$$

15. Implied Volatility: BFW vs Refined vs Exact (Figure 1)

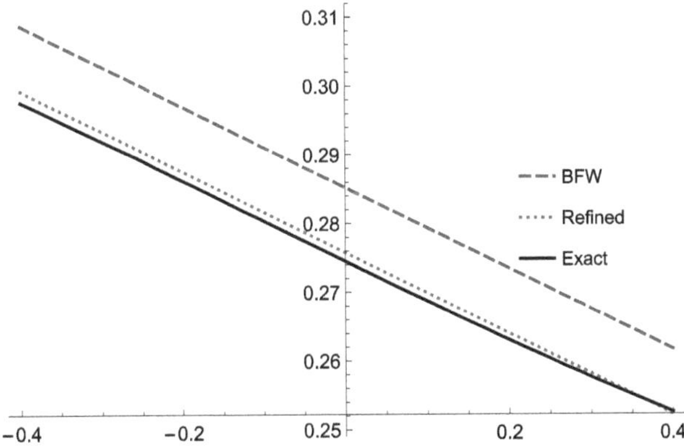

Figure 1: Comparison of exact implied volatility and two approximations $T = 1.0$, diffusive volatality $\sigma = 0.2$, jump rate $\lambda = 1$, jump size $c = -0.2$.

16. Intuition: Jump–Diffusion Dynamics

- For intuition take the simplest special case of a jump–diffusion.
- Drive S with Brownian W, independent Poisson(λ) process N.

Let jumps (in log) of size c arrive randomly at rate λ.

Let $\sigma > 0$. In other words, $S_t = S_0 \exp(X_t)$ where

$$dX_t = -a\ dt + \sigma\ dW_t + c\ dN_t,$$

where $a := \lambda(e^c - 1) + \sigma^2/2$ makes S driftless.

- Now consider a family of such processes indexed by ε, such that

$$\lambda = \varepsilon/T \quad \text{and} \quad c = O(\varepsilon^{1/4}) \text{ as } \varepsilon \to 0.$$

- Interpretation of $\varepsilon = \lambda T$: expected number of jumps in $[0, T]$.
- Consider the $\varepsilon \to 0$ asymptotics of **small jump size, intensity**.

17. Option Price Approximation

Following Merton, price the call by conditioning on how many jumps occur in $[0, T]$.

$$\begin{aligned} C = &\ \mathbb{P}(\texttt{0 jumps}) \times \mathbb{E}[(S_T - K)^+ | \texttt{0 jumps}] \\ &+ \mathbb{P}(\texttt{1 jump}) \times \mathbb{E}[(S_T - K)^+ | \texttt{1 jump}] \\ &+ \mathbb{P}(\texttt{2+ jumps}) \times \mathbb{E}[(S_T - K)^+ | \texttt{2+ jumps}] \quad \longleftarrow \text{negligible} \\ = &\ e^{-\varepsilon} C^{BS}(S_0 e^{-\varepsilon(e^c - 1)}) + e^{-\varepsilon} \varepsilon C^{BS}(S_0 e^{-\varepsilon(e^c - 1) + c}) + O(\varepsilon^2). \\ = &\ C^{BS}(S_0) + \varepsilon \Big(\frac{1}{2} S_0^2 (e^c - 1)^2 C^{BS}_{SS}(S_0) + \frac{1}{6} S_0^3 (e^c - 1)^3 C^{BS}_{SSS}(S_0) \Big) \\ &+ O(\varepsilon^2), \end{aligned}$$

by third-order (**delta-gamma-speed**) Taylor expansion around S_0.

18. Implied Volatility Approximation

So implied volatility has asymptotics

$$\mathrm{IV} = \sigma + \varepsilon IV_1 + O(\varepsilon^2),$$

where price perturbation **divided by vega** gives the volatality perturbation:

$$\begin{aligned}\varepsilon \mathrm{IV}_1 &= \varepsilon \frac{\frac{1}{2}S_0^2(e^c-1)^2 C_{SS}^{BS}(S_0) + \frac{1}{6}S_0^3(e^c-1)^3 C_{SSS}^{BS}(S_0)}{C_\sigma^{BS}(S_0)} \\ &= \frac{\lambda}{2\sigma}(e^c-1)^2 + \frac{\lambda}{6\sigma^3}(e^c-1)^3\Big(\frac{\log(K/S_0)}{T} - \frac{3}{2}\sigma^2\Big),\end{aligned}$$

using the Black–Scholes–Merton vega, gamma, and speed

$$C_\sigma^{BS} = S\sqrt{T}N'(d_1) \quad C_{SS}^{BS} = \frac{N'(d_1)}{S\sigma\sqrt{T}}$$

$$C_{SSS}^{BS} = \Big(-\frac{\log(S/K)}{\sigma^2 T} - \frac{3}{2}\Big)\frac{C_{SS}^{BS}}{S},$$

Confirmation: **Skewness** $\approx \frac{\lambda T(e^c-1)^3}{\sigma^3 T^{3/2}} = 6\times$ **Skew**.

The extra term not in BFW is the $-3/2$.

It comes from differentiating gamma

$$\frac{e^{-d_1^2/2}}{S\sigma\sqrt{T}},$$

thus combining $\boxed{-1/2}$ from $-d_1$ and the $\boxed{-1}$ exponent from S^{-1}.

Both of which are due to **log**-normality of BSM.

19. Conclusions

- Implied volatility level, slope, curvature linked to cumulants: variance, skewness, kurtosis.
- Refine BFW in a near-Gaussian regime.
- Intuition: order-3 Taylor (Delta-Gamma-Speed) approximation.

https://doi.org/10.1142/9789811259142_0011

Chapter 11

Implied Volatility Asymptotics: Black–Scholes and Beyond

P. Tankov

CREST-ENSAE, Institut Polytechnique de Paris, avenue Henry Le Chatelier 91120 Palaiseau, France

peter.tankov@ensae.fr

1. Introduction

After 1973, Black–Scholes formula quickly became a universal benchmark for option pricing, and implied volatility a universal measure of magnitude of option premium. The implied volatility is defined as the value of volatility to be used in the Black–Scholes formula to obtain either the market quote of the option price (market implied volatility) or the price of the option computed in an alternative model (model implied volatility). The implied volatility depends on the strike and the exercise date of the option, and exhibits a convex shape as function of strike, which is referred to as the *implied volatility smile* (see Figure 1, right graph), whereas the slope of the implied volatility curve is referred to as the *implied volatility skew*. The phenomenon of implied volatility smile is documented well before 1987 crash (see Figure 1, left graph). Quoting from [8], *The actual prices on listed options tend to differ in certain systematic ways from the values given by the formula. Options that are way out of the money tend to be overpriced, and options that are way into the money tend to be underpriced.* Rubinstein [29] writes: *Black–Scholes option pricing*

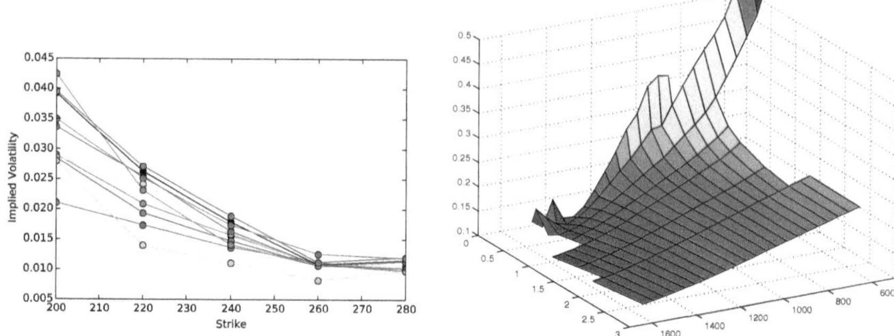

Figure 1: Left: IV smiles of IBM options with 1 year to expiry, observed in June 1975 and Right: Implied volatility of the S&P index on a typical day. CBOE. *Source*: Ref. [23].

formula is often reported to produce model values which differ in systematic ways from market prices, and compares five alternative models which were developed to address this bias. At the same time, the skew of index options appears to have strongly increased after 1987 (see Figure 2, top graph), and the publication activity on alternative implied volatility models really started in earnest after this date (see Figure 2, bottom graph).

The implied volatility is a measure of option premium which keeps to the minimum the influence of time to maturity, strike price or asset value. Analyzing alternative models in terms of their volatility surface allows to evaluate their suitability as option pricing models and devise efficient calibration algorithms. A number of properties of implied volatility surfaces which are invariant within asset classes (stylized facts) may be established. The following properties concern mostly equity and index options.

- As function of strike, the IV is downward sloping (skew).
- The ATM skew is more pronounced for short maturities, often with a power-law blow-up as $T \to 0$.
- The IV away from the money blows up as $T \to 0$.
- The IV smile flattens for options far from maturity.
- The IV surface exhibits stochastic behavior as function of time.

The stylized facts often concern the behavior of implied volatility in extreme strike/maturity regimes

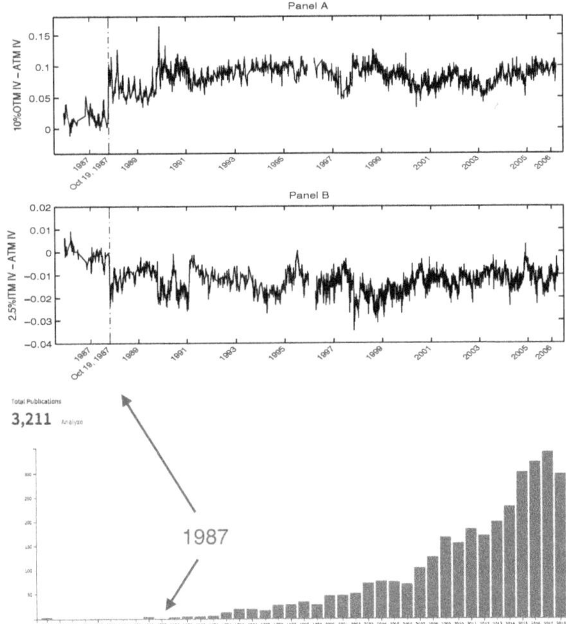

Figure 2: Top: implied volatility skew of S&P 500 options with one month to maturity and Bottom: number of published articles including the terms "implied volatility" per year. Web of Science.
Source: Ref. [6].

- Options close to expiry: $T \to 0$.
- Options far from expiry: $T \to \infty$.
- Large/small strikes: $K \to \infty/K \to 0$.
- ATM skew and convexity as $T \to 0$.
- Mixed regimes: strike is renormalized to obtain non-trivial behavior as $T \to 0$ or $T \to \infty$ (e.g., delta quotation in FX markets) (see [15]).

Computing the implied volatility by numerical inversion of BS formula in these regimes may be difficult due to singularity. The asymptotic formulas remove the singularity and provide more explicit expressions. On the other hand, in alternative models, asymptotic formulas allow to access the limiting implied volatility directly, to check the stylized facts and (possibly) design efficient pre-calibration algorithms. In this chapter, we review the asymptotic formulas for implied volatility in three regimes: the small-maturity regime (Section 2), the large-maturity regime (Section 3) and the large/small strike regime (Section 4).

Notation. Throughout the chapter, we use the simplified Black–Scholes formula obtained by introducing the log-strike $k = \log \frac{Ke^{-rT}}{Se^{-qT}}$ and normalizing the price by Se^{-qT}. Here r denotes the interest rate and q the dividend yield.

$$c^{BS}(k,T,\sigma) = N\left(\frac{-k+\frac{\sigma^2 T}{2}}{\sigma\sqrt{T}}\right) - e^k N\left(\frac{-k-\frac{\sigma^2 T}{2}}{\sigma\sqrt{T}}\right),$$

where N is the standard normal distribution function. Sometimes we shall also need the two-argument version, depending on the total integrated variance:

$$c^{BS}(k,v) = N\left(\frac{-k+\frac{v}{2}}{\sqrt{v}}\right) - e^k N\left(\frac{-k-\frac{v}{2}}{\sqrt{v}}\right).$$

The implied volatility of option with time to expiry T and log-strike k will be denoted by $I(T,k)$ and defined by

$$c^{BS}(k,T,I(T,k)) = c(k,T), \tag{1}$$

where $c(k,T)$ is the (renormalized) call option price given by the market or by an alternative model, in which case we write

$$c(k,T) := \mathbb{E}^{\mathbb{Q}}[(e^{X_T} - e^k)^+],$$

where

$$X_T = \log \frac{S_T}{S} - (r-q)T,$$

denotes the log price of the asset corrected for the interest and the dividends.

2. Implied Volatility Close to Maturity

2.1 *Approximate inversion of the Black–Scholes formula*

Assume that in the pricing model in question

(i) The discounted ex-divided price e^{X_t} has a constant expectation under the measure $\mathbb{Q}$;
(ii) The price process is continuous at $T = 0$.

These properties may fail in strict local martingale models, or in models where the asset price jumps immediately up or down following a coin toss, but clearly these are not restrictive assumptions which hold it most reasonable models. Then, by the dominated convergence theorem we may deduce that the option price satisfies

$$\lim_{T\downarrow 0} c(k,T) = 1 - e^k + \lim_{T\downarrow 0} \mathbb{E}[(e^k - e^{X_T})^+] = (1-e^k)^+.$$

Since the Black–Scholes price $c^{BS}(k,v)$ is a strictly increasing function of v, satisfying $\lim_{v\to 0} c^{BS}(k,v) = (1-e^k)^+$, we conclude that in such models

$$\lim_{T\to 0} TI^2(T,k) = 0. \tag{2}$$

The approximate computation of the implied volatility is based on the following key formula: for $x \to -\infty$,

$$N(x) \sim \frac{n(x)}{|x|},$$

where n is the standard normal density and the sign $\sim$ means that the ratio of the two quantities tends to 1. In the limit $v \to 0$, for $k \neq 0$ fixed, we then get,

$$c^{BS}(k,v) \sim \frac{v^{\frac{3}{2}}}{k^2} Sn\left(\frac{-k+\frac{v}{2}}{\sqrt{v}}\right).$$

Taking the logarithm and multiplying by v, then,

$$\lim_{v\downarrow 0} v \log c^{BS}(k,v) = -\frac{k^2}{2}.$$

In view of (2), we conclude that the implied volatility satisfies

$$I^2(T,k) \sim -\frac{1}{2}\frac{k^2}{T\log c(k,T)}, \quad \text{as } T \to 0. \tag{3}$$

At the money ($k = 0$) the behavior is different: here we have

$$I(T,0) \sim c(0,T)\sqrt{\frac{2\pi}{T}}, \quad T \to 0,$$

whenever (2) is satisfied.

2.2 *ATM skew*

An important characteristic of an option pricing model is the behavior of the at-the-money (ATM) implied volatility skew, or the slope of the implied volatility. Differentiating the Black–Scholes formula, we see that the implied volatility skew satisfies

$$\begin{aligned}\partial_k I(T,k) &= \frac{\partial_k c(k,T) - \partial_k c^{BS}(k,T,I(T,k))}{\partial_I c^{BS}(k,T,I(T,k))} \\ &= \frac{\mathbb{P}^{BS}[S_T \geq K] - \mathbb{P}[S_T \geq K]}{e^{-k} n(d_1)\sqrt{T}},\end{aligned}$$

where under $\mathbb{P}^{BS}$, S_T is the asset price in the BS model with volatility $I(T,k)$. Substituting $k = 0$, we obtain the formula for ATMF skew:

$$\partial_k I(T)_{ATMF} = \frac{\mathbb{P}^{BS}[X_T \geq 0] - \mathbb{P}[X_T \geq 0]}{n\left(\frac{I(T)\sqrt{T}}{2}\right)\sqrt{T}}.$$

As $T \to 0$, under the conditions stated in the beginning of this section, we get

$$\partial_k I(T)|_{ATMF} = \frac{\sqrt{2\pi}}{\sqrt{T}} \left\{\mathbb{P}^{BS}[X_T \geq 0] - \mathbb{P}[X_T \geq 0]\right\} \left\{1 + O(I^2(T,0)T)\right\}.$$

As a side remark, observe that according to this formula the ATM skew cannot expode faster than at the rate $\frac{\sqrt{2\pi}}{\sqrt{T}}$, in agreement with [22].

The ATM skew thus arises as a measure of *asymmetry of the stock price distribution function around the money*, compared to the asymmetry of the Black–Scholes model. Similarly, the ATM convexity measures the difference of the stock price *density* around the money compared to the Black–Scholes model.

2.3 *Diffusion models*

Local volatility and diffusion stochastic volatility models models are close to Black–Scholes as $T \to 0$. In these models ATM skew converges to a constant value as $T \to 0$, which not consistent with the observed behavior of option prices, see Figure 3, left graph.

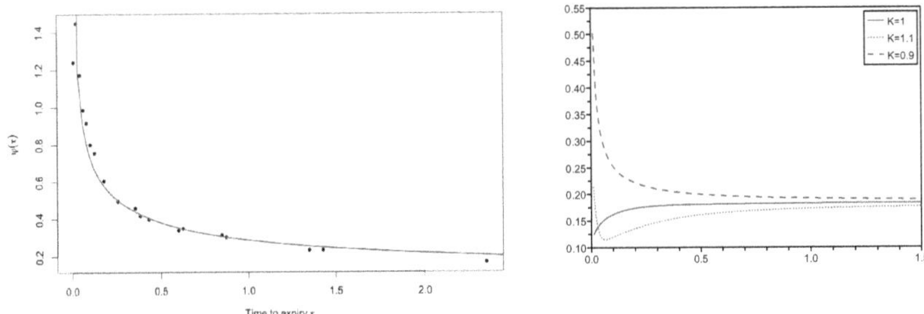

Figure 3: Left: ATM skew of S&P options on 8/14/13 and Right: Behavior of implied volatility as function of time to maturity in Merton's jump diffusion model.
Source: Ref. [3].

The limiting smile in these models also exists and can be computed using singular heat kernel expansions or large deviations, see [7,16,19] and for stochastic volatility models [13,24] among many others.

2.4 *Jump-diffusion and Lévy models*

Models where the log-price X is a *jump diffusion/Lévy process* have been proposed as solution to the *short-term smile blow-up* problem. Such models have been shown to exhibit *model-independent* OTM smile explosion [2,10,28,31]. For example let X be a Lévy process with Lévy measure ν under $\mathbb{Q}$. Then, for $k > 0$, the small time probability distribution of X satisfies

$$\mathbb{P}[X_T \geq k] \sim T\nu([k,\infty)) \quad \text{as } T \to 0,$$

and similarly, the OTM call price, under sufficient integrability conditions satisfies

$$c(k,T) = \mathbb{E}^{\mathbb{Q}}[(e^{X_T} - e^k)^+] \sim T\int_k^\infty (e^x - e^k)\nu(dx).$$

Substituting this asymptotic into (3), we get the model-independent smile explosion formula:

$$I^2(T,k) \sim \frac{1}{2}\frac{k^2}{T\log\frac{1}{T}}.$$

In the ATM case, the behavior is, once again, different and the jumps do not contribute to the smile [2,12,26,31]:

$$\lim_{t\to 0} I(t,0) = \begin{cases} \sigma & \text{if diffusion component} \\ 0 & \text{in pure jump models} \end{cases}.$$

Figure 3, right graph, illustrates the ATM and OTM implied volatility behavior in Merton's jump diffusion model.

2.5 *Universal parametrization of k_t and the limiting smile*

Fixed k results are of limited use for model calibration since the market implied volatility does not tend to zero or infinity. Very short-term options are commonly quoted in FX markets, but their strike is not fixed. Instead, the FX markets use delta quotation, which implies that the strikes of short-maturity quoted options are closer to the money than those of longer-maturity ones (see Figure 4).

This suggests that to explain short-maturity smile behavior while avoiding the smile explosion phenomenon in jump-diffusion models, one must find a *time-dependent strike* $k_t \neq 0$ such that

$$\lim_{t\to 0} k_t = 0 \quad \text{and} \quad \exists \lim_{t\to 0} I(t,k_t).$$

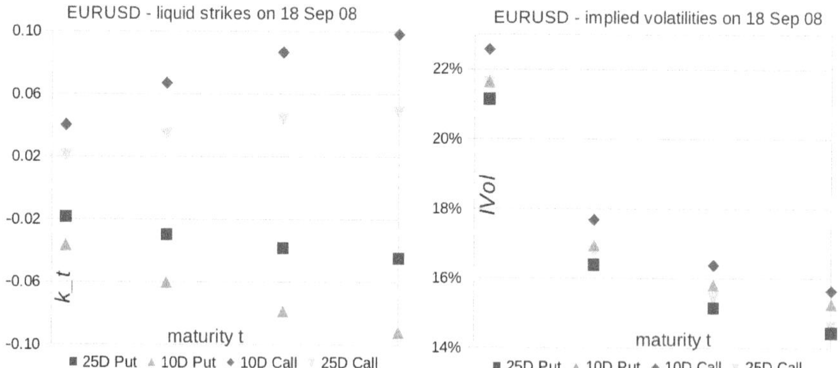

Figure 4: Left: Quoted log-strikes; and corresponding Right: Implied volatilities for FX options.

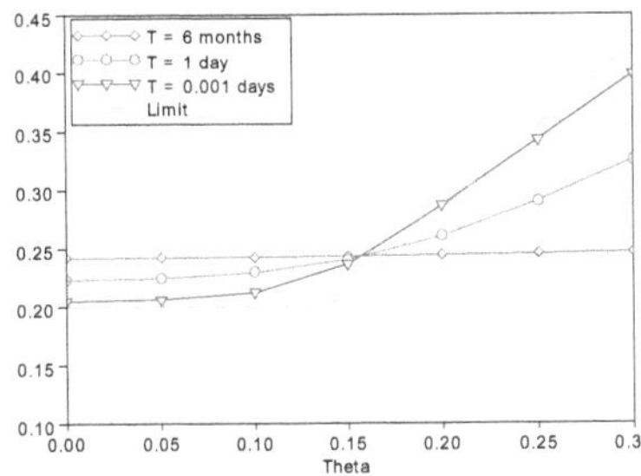

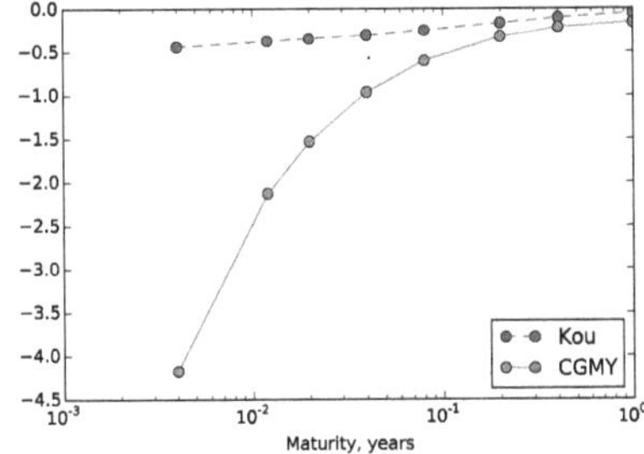

Figure 5: Left: Convergence to the U-shaped limiting smile in the CGMY model with non-zero diffusion component and Right: Behavior of ATM skew in Lévy models as function of time.

Such a universal parameterization was developed in [25]. These authors introduce a model-free parametrization of the log-strike (which is different from but similar to delta quoting convention), under which there exists a well defined limiting smile in jump-diffusion and Lévy models:

$$k_t = \theta\sqrt{t\log(1/t)} \quad \theta \in \mathbb{R}\setminus\{0\}.$$

Let $I(t, k_t)$ be the implied volatility in the model where X is a Lévy process. Then, $\lim_{t\to 0} k_t = 0$ and $I_0(\theta) = \lim_{t\to 0} I(t, k_t)$ satisfies

$$I_0(\theta) = \max\left\{\frac{-\theta}{\sqrt{1-(\alpha_- - 1)^+}}, \sigma, \frac{\theta}{\sqrt{1-(\alpha_+ - 1)^+}}\right\}, \qquad \theta \in \mathbb{R}\backslash\{0\}.$$

Here $\alpha_\pm$ is the Blumenthal–Getoor index of positive/negative jumps of X. Figure 5, left graph illustrates the convergence to the U-shaped limiting smile in the CGMY model with non-zero diffusion component. The convergence to the limiting smile is admittedly very slow, nevertheless the time-dependent parameterization of the strike may be useful to avoid explosive smiles even relatively far from the limit.

2.6 *ATM skew in jump-diffusion/Lévy models*

The skew behavior in jump-diffusion or Lévy-based models depends on the structure of the small jumps and the presence of the diffusion component. When X is a *finite intensity jump-diffusion* with dynamics

$$X_t = bt + \sigma W_t + \sum_{i=1}^{N_t} Y_i,$$

the diffusion component dominates in small time and jumps only contribute to the skew by modifying the drift of the process compared to its Black–Scholes value. As a result, the skew converges to a non-zero limit, which, as we have seen, is not compatible with the skews observed in the market. Since the probability of having a jump before time T is of order of T, the exercise probability has the following form.

$$\mathbb{P}[X_T \geq 0] = \mathbb{P}[bT + \sigma W_T \geq 0] + O(T).$$

Substituting this into the ATM skew formula and applying L'Hopital's rule then gives,

$$\begin{aligned}\lim_{T\downarrow 0} \partial_k I(T,k)|_{ATMF} &= \sqrt{2\pi} \lim_{T\downarrow 0} \frac{\mathbb{P}[\sigma W_T - \frac{\sigma^2}{2}T \geq 0] - \mathbb{P}[bT + \sigma W_T \geq 0]}{\sqrt{T}} \\ &= \sqrt{2\pi} \lim_{T\downarrow 0} \frac{\mathbb{P}[Z \geq \frac{\sigma}{2}\sqrt{T}] - \mathbb{P}[Z \geq -\frac{b}{\sigma}\sqrt{T}]}{\sqrt{T}} \\ &= -\frac{b}{\sigma} - \frac{\sigma}{2}.\end{aligned}$$

For pure jump processes, the skew has an explosive behavior. The rate of explosion is strongest for finite-variation processes. In this case, $\mathbb{P}[X_T \geq 0] \to \mathbf{1}_{b>0}$ (see [30, Theorem 43.20]), so that

$$\partial_k I(T,k)|_{\text{ATMF}} \sim -\sqrt{\pi/2}\text{sgn}\,(b_0)T^{-1/2}, \quad T \to 0.$$

This is the fastest rate of skew explosion compatible with an arbitrage-free model.

The most interesting case is that of infinite variation pure jump Lévy processes, which allow to obtain various rates of skew explosion between 0 and $\frac{1}{2}$. For example, in the well known CGMY model [9], the jump measure has a singularity at zero of type $\frac{C}{|x|^{1+Y}}$. For $Y > 1$, this is an infinite variation Lévy process, and the ATMF implied volatility skew explores at rate $T^{1/2-1/Y}$ (see [11],[17]).

2.7 *Rough volatility models*

Recently, the *rough stochastic volatility* models have become popular. In these models, the trajectories are continuous but the volatility is driven by the fractional Brownian motion with Hurst index $H < \frac{1}{2}$ or a similar process. In these models, similarly to the CGMY process, a power-law behavior of the short-term ATM skew is observed (see [1,14]).

$$\partial_k I(T,k)|_{\mathrm{ATMF}} \sim CT^{H-1/2}.$$

3. Implied Volatility Far from Maturity

We start once again with a rough *a priori* estimate of the behavior of implied volatility. Assume that in the pricing model in question

(i) The (discounted ex-dividend) asset price has constant expectation under $\mathbb{Q}$;
(ii) The price process converges to 0 a.s. as $T \to \infty$ (this is not such a strong assumption since a positive martingale always converges).

By the dominated convergence the option price then satisfies

$$\lim_{T\to\infty} c(k,T) = 1 - \lim_{T\downarrow 0} \mathbb{E}[e^k \wedge e^{X_T}] = 1.$$

Since the Black–Scholes price $c^{BS}(k,v)$ is a strictly increasing function of v, satisfying $\lim_{v\to\infty} c^{BS}(k,v) = 1$, we conclude that in such models

$$\lim_{T\to\infty} TI^2(T,k) = \infty. \tag{4}$$

For convenience, rewrite the BS formula as follows.

$$c^{BS}(k,v) = 1 - N\left(\frac{k - v/2}{\sqrt{v}}\right) - e^k N\left(\frac{-k - v/2}{\sqrt{v}}\right).$$

Using the asymptotics for N, we then get, as $v \to \infty$,

$$1 - c^{BS}(k,v) \sim \frac{4}{\sqrt{v}} n\left(\frac{k - v/2}{\sqrt{v}}\right).$$

so that

$$\lim \left\{ \log(1 - c^{BS}(k, v)) + \frac{v}{8} \right\} = 0,$$

and in view of (4) we conclude that the implied volatility satisfies the following asymptotic formula:

$$\begin{aligned} \lim_{T\to\infty} I^2(T,k) &= -\lim_{T\to\infty} \frac{8}{T} \log(1 - c(k,T)) \\ &= -\lim_{T\to\infty} \frac{8}{T} \log \mathbb{E}\left[e^{X_T} \wedge e^k\right]. \end{aligned}$$

In addition in view of the following simple inequality,

$$(y \wedge 1)(1 \wedge e^k) < y \wedge e^k \leq (y \wedge 1)(1 \vee e^k),$$

we conclude that the above limit does not depend on k:

$$\lim_{T\to\infty} I^2(T,k) = -\lim_{T\to\infty} \frac{8}{T} \log(1-c(0,T)) = -\lim_{T\to\infty} \frac{8}{T} \log \mathbb{E}\left[e^{X_T} \wedge 1\right].$$

We conclude that smile flattens at large maturities in all arbitrage-free models (see [27,32]).

3.1 *Lévy processes and Cramer's theorem*

The exact limiting implied volatility far from maturity may be computed using large deviations techniques. Here we once again consider the example of Lévy processes where the arguments are particularly simple. Let X be a Lévy process such that $\mathbb{E}[e^{uX_T}] = e^{T\psi(u)}$. First, start with a simple estimate.

$$\mathbb{P}[X_T \geq 0] \leq \mathbb{E}\left[e^{X_T} \wedge 1\right] = \mathbb{E}\left[e^{X_T} \wedge 1\right] \leq \min_{p\in[0,1]} \mathbb{E}[e^{pX_T}] = e^{T \min_{p\in[0,1]} \psi(p)}.$$

By Cramer's theorem of large deviations, the lower bound has a similar limit in log-scale:

$$\lim_{T\to\infty} \frac{1}{T} \log \mathbb{P}[X_T \geq 0] = -\Lambda^*(0) = \inf_{p\in\mathbb{R}} \psi(p),$$

but u is convex, and since X is a martingale, $\psi'(0) \leq 0$ and $\psi'(1) \geq 0$, so that the infimum can be taken over $[0,1]$, and the two limits are

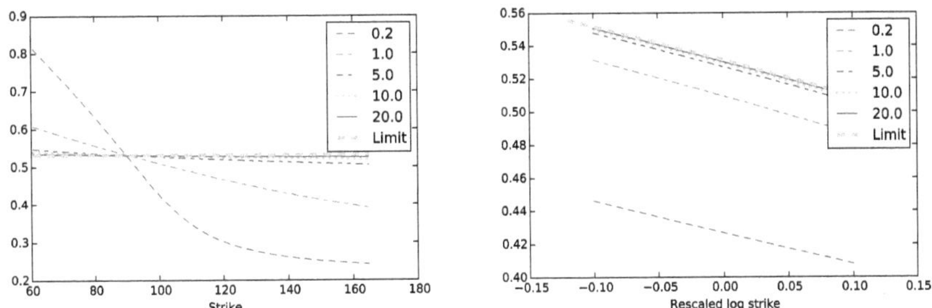

Figure 6: Convergence of the implied volatility to the large-maturity limit in Kou's jump diffusion model. Left: Original strike. Right: Rescaled log-strike.

actually the same. It follows that,

$$\lim_{T\to\infty} I^2(T,k) = -8 \min_{p\in[0,1]} \psi(p).$$

The convergence of the implied volatility to this limit is illustrated in Figure 6, left graph, in Kou's jump-diffusion model. Contrary to the small maturity asymptotics, here the convergence is acually quite fast, already for 5-year options the smile is almost completely flat.

3.2 *Renormalizing the smile*

To obtain a non-trivial limiting smile in Lévy models as $T \to \infty$, consider a renormalized log-strike proportional to T. Following the same argument as above,

$$\mathbb{P}[X_T \geq kT] \leq \mathbb{E}[e^{X_T-kT} \wedge 1] \leq e^{T\min_{p\in[0,1]}(\psi(p)-pk)},$$

and Cramer's theorem gives

$$\lim_{T\to\infty} \frac{1}{T} \log \mathbb{P}[X_T \geq kT] = -\Lambda^*(k) = \inf_{p\in\mathbb{R}} (\psi(p) - pk),$$

provided that $k \geq \mathbb{E}[X_1] = \psi(0)$. If, in addition, $\psi'(1) \geq k$, then the infimum in the right-hand side may be taken over the interval $[0,1]$. In conclusion, for $k \in [\psi'(0), \psi'(1)]$, in Lévy models,

$$\lim_{T\to\infty} \frac{1}{T} \log(1-c(kT,T)) = \lim_{T\to\infty} \frac{1}{T} \log \mathbb{E}[e^{X_T} \wedge e^{kT}] = k + \min_{p\in\mathbb{R}}(\psi(p)-pk).$$

Applying this formula in the Black–Scholes model with volatility σ, we get:

$$\lim_{T\to\infty}\frac{1}{T}\log(1-c^{BS}(kT,T,\sigma)) = k + \min_{p\in[0,1]}(\frac{\sigma^2}{2}(p^2-p)-pk)$$
$$= k - \frac{(\sigma^2/2+k)^2}{2\sigma^2}.$$

Comparing the two formulas, we see that the limiting implied volatility $\bar{I}(k) = \lim_{T\to\infty} I(Tk,T)$ must solve the following equation:

$$\frac{(\bar{I}^2(k)/2+k)^2}{2\bar{I}^2(k)} = -\min_{p\in[0,1]}(\psi(p)-pk) := L(k),$$

which means that

$$\bar{I}(k) = \sqrt{2}(\sqrt{L(k)}+\sqrt{L(k)-k}).$$

This formula may be extended to all strikes using similar arguments. See [20], for an extension to affine jump-diffusions. Figure 6, right graph illustrates the convergence of the renormalized implied volatility to the limiting smile in Kou's jump-diffusion model.

4. Extreme Strikes

In this section, we review the asymptotic formulas for the smile for a fixed time, T, which we take equal to 1 without loss of generality, in the limit of large and small strikes. To simplify the notation, we omit the time argument of option prices and implied volatilities. To begin, consider the large strike limit, and make the following assumption

- The asset price satisfies

$$\mathbb{E}^{\mathbb{Q}}[S_1^{1+p}] < \infty$$

  for some $p > 0$.

Under this assumption, it is easy to check that the call price decays exponentially with log strike:

$$c(k,T) = O(e^{-pk}), \quad k\to\infty.$$

On the other hand, for $\beta \in (0,2)$, the Black–Scholes price satisfies

$$c^{BS}(k,\sigma=\sqrt{\beta k}) = N\left(\frac{-1+\frac{\beta}{2}}{\sqrt{\beta}}\sqrt{k}\right) - e^k N\left(\frac{-1-\frac{\beta}{2}}{\sqrt{\beta}}\sqrt{k}\right)$$
$$\sim \frac{\beta^{3/2}\sqrt{k}}{1-\frac{\beta^2}{4}} n\left(\frac{-1+\frac{\beta}{2}}{\sqrt{\beta}}\sqrt{k}\right).$$

This means that for k sufficiently large, the implied volatility $I(k)$ satisfies $I(k) \le \sqrt{\beta^* k}$, where $\beta^* \in (0,2)$ is the solution of the equation

$$(1-\beta/2)^2 = 2p\beta.$$

With this *a priori* estimate of implied volatility, we can now deduce the following asymptotics of the call option price:

$$-\frac{1}{k}\log c(k) \sim \frac{1}{2}\left(-\frac{\sqrt{k}}{I(k)} + \frac{I(k)}{2\sqrt{k}}\right)^2, \quad k \to \infty,$$

from which it can be easily deduced that

$$\frac{I(k)}{\sqrt{k}} \sim \sqrt{2}\left(\sqrt{1-\frac{\log c(k)}{k}} - \sqrt{-\frac{\log c(k)}{k}}\right), \quad k \to \infty.$$

A similar formula holds for the left tail: assuming that $\mathbb{E}^Q[S_1^{-p}] < \infty$ for some $p > 0$, we get that

$$\frac{I(k)}{\sqrt{-k}} \sim \sqrt{2}\left(\sqrt{1+\frac{\log p(k)}{k}} - \sqrt{\frac{\log p(k)}{k}}\right), \quad k \to -\infty.$$

If X is a Lévy process with exponential tail decay: $\mathbb{P}[X \le k] \sim e^{\lambda k}$ then

$$\frac{I(k)}{\sqrt{-k}} \sim \sqrt{2}\left(\sqrt{\lambda+1} - \sqrt{\lambda}\right).$$

This asymptotic behavior is illustrated in Figure 7 in the context of Kou's model. See [4,5,18,21] for more information on strike asymptotics.

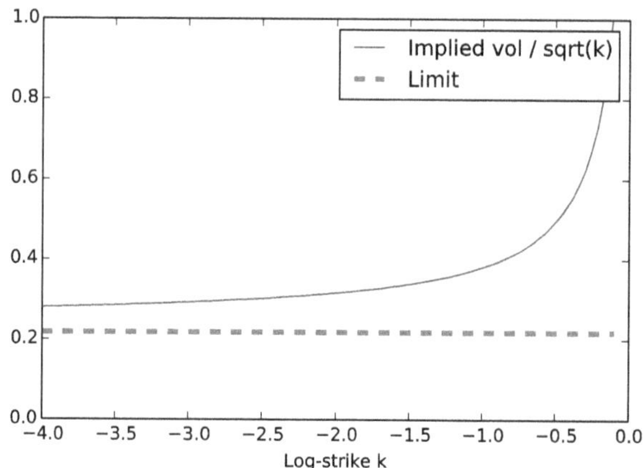

Figure 7: Convergence of the implied volatility for low strikes in Kou's model.

5. Conclusion

In conclusion, the Black–Scholes formula is a very rich mathematical object and in the last 10–15 years, many beautiful papers used fine features of this formula to obtain asymptotic expressions for implied volatility in alternative models. Sometimes (for example in the long-maturity case) these asymptotics lead to fast calibration algorithms; most of the time they are not precise enough but are still useful to improve our understanding of the models.

References

[1] Alòs, E., León, J.A., and Vives, J. (2007). On the short-time behavior of the implied volatility for jump-diffusion models with stochastic volatility. *Finance and Stochastics*, 11(4) 571–589.

[2] Andersen, L. and Lipton, A. (2013). Asymptotics for exponential Lévy processes and their volatility smile: Survey and new results. *International Journal of Theoretical and Applied Finance*, 16(01), 1350001.

[3] Bayer, C., Friz, P., and Gatheral, J. (2016). Pricing under rough volatility. *Quantitative Finance*, 16(6), 887–904.

[4] Benaim, S. and Friz, P. (2009). Regular variation and smile asymptotics. *Mathematical Finance*, 19(1), 1–12.

[5] Benaim, S. and Friz, P. (2008). Smile asymptotics II: Models with known moment generating functions. *Journal of Applied Probability*, 45(1), 16–32.

[6] Benzoni, L., Collin-Dufresne, P., and Goldstein, R.S. (2011). Explaining asset pricing puzzles associated with the 1987 market crash. *Journal of Financial Economics*, 101(3), 552–573.

[7] Berestycki, H., Busca, J., and Florent, I. (2002). Asymptotics and calibration of local volatility models. *Quantitative Finance* 2(1), 61–69.

[8] Black, F. (1975). Fact and fantasy in the use of options. *Financial Analysts Journal*, 31(4), 36–72.

[9] Carr, P., Geman, H., Madan, D.B., and Yor, M. (2002). The fine structure of asset returns: An empirical investigation. *The Journal of Business*, 75(2), 305–332.

[10] Figueroa-López, J.E. and Forde, M. (2012). The small-maturity smile for exponential Lévy models. *SIAM Journal on Financial Mathematics*, 3(1), 33–65.

[11] Figueroa-López, J.E. and Ólafsson, S. (2016). Short-term asymptotics for the implied volatility skew under a stochastic volatility model with Lévy jumps. *Finance and Stochastics*, 20(4), 973–1020.

[12] Figueroa-López, J.E., Gong, R., and Houdré, C. (2016). High-order short-time expansions for ATM option prices of exponential Lévy models. *Mathematical Finance*, 26(3), 516–557.

[13] Forde, M. and Jacquier, A. (2009). Small-time asymptotics for implied volatility under the Heston model. *International Journal of Theoretical and Applied Finance*, 12(06), 861–876.

[14] Fukasawa, M. (2011). Asymptotic analysis for stochastic volatility: Martingale expansion. *Finance and Stochastics*, 15(4), 635–654.

[15] Gao, K. and Lee, R.W. (2014). Asymptotics of implied volatility to arbitrary order. *Finance and Stochastics*, 18(2), 349–392.

[16] Gatheral, J., Hsu, E.P., Laurence, P., Ouyang, C., and Wang, T.-H. (2012). Asymptotics of implied volatility in local volatility models. *Mathematical Finance: An International Journal of Mathematics, Statistics and Financial Economics*, 22(4), 591–620.

[17] Gerhold, S., Gülüm, I.C., and Pinter, A. Small-maturity asymptotics for the at-the-money implied volatility slope in Lévy models. *Applied Mathematical Finance*, 23(2), 135–157.

[18] Gulisashvili, A. (2010). Asymptotic formulas with error estimates for call pricing functions and the implied volatility at extreme strikes. *SIAM Journal on Financial Mathematics*, 1(1), 609–641.

[19] Henry-Labordère, P. (2008). Analysis, Geometry, and Modeling in Finance: Advanced Methods in Option Pricing. Chapman and Hall/CRC.

[20] Jacquier, A., Keller-Ressel, M., and Mijatović, A. (2013). Large deviations and stochastic volatility with jumps: Asymptotic implied volatility for affine models. *Stochastics an International Journal of Probability and Stochastic Processes*, 85(2), 321–345.

[21] Lee, R.W. (2004). The moment formula for implied volatility at extreme strikes. *Mathematical Finance: An International Journal of Mathematics, Statistics and Financial Economics*, 14(3), 469–480.
[22] Lee, R.W. (2005). Implied volatility: Statics, dynamics, and probabilistic interpretation. In *Recent Advances in Applied Probability*, Springer, Boston, MA, pp. 241–268.
[23] MacBeth, J.D. and Merville, L.J. (1979). An empirical examination of the Black–Scholes call option pricing model. *The Journal of Finance*, 34(5), 1173–1186.
[24] Medvedev, A. and Scaillet, O. (2006). Approximation and calibration of short-term implied volatilities under jump-diffusion stochastic volatility. *The Review of Financial Studies*, 20(2), 427–459.
[25] Mijatović, A. and Tankov, P. (2016). A new look at short-term implied volatility in asset price models with jumps. *Mathematical Finance*, 26(1), 149–183.
[26] Muhle-Karbe, J. and Nutz, M. (2011). Small-time asymptotics of option prices and first absolute moments. *Journal of Applied Probability*, 48(4), 1003–1020.
[27] Rogers, L.C.G. and Tehranchi, M.R. (2010). Can the implied volatility surface move by parallel shifts? *Finance and Stochastics*, 14(2), 235–248.
[28] Roper, M. and Rutkowski, M. (2009). On the relationship between the call price surface and the implied volatility surface close to expiry. *International Journal of Theoretical and Applied Finance*, 12(04), 427–441.
[29] Rubinstein, M. (1985). Nonparametric tests of alternative option pricing models. *The Journal of Finance*, 40(2), 455–480.
[30] Sato, K.-I. (1999). *Lévy Processes and Infinitely Divisible Distributions*. Cambridge University Press.
[31] Tankov, P. (2011). Pricing and hedging in exponential Lévy models: review of recent results. In *Paris-Princeton Lectures on Mathematical Finance*, Springer, Berlin, Heidelberg, pp. 319–359.
[32] Tehranchi, M.R. (2009). Asymptotics of implied volatility far from maturity. *Journal of Applied Probability*, 46(3), 629–650.

https://doi.org/10.1142/9789811259142_0012

Chapter 12

The Smile of Stochastic Volatility Models*

J. Guyon

Bloomberg L.P., Quantitative Research,
Columbia University,
Department of Mathematics, NYU,
Courant Institute of Mathematical Sciences, NYU

jguyon2@bloomberg.net
jg3601@columbia.edu
julien.guyon@nyu.edu

1. Outline

- Motivation.
- Expansion of the smile at order 2 in volatility of volatility ("vol of vol").
- Short maturities and long maturities.
- First example: A family of Heston-like models.
- Second example: The two-factor Bergomi model.
- Numerical experiments.
- Rederiving the link between skew and skewness of log-returns.
- Conclusion.

---

*Based on joint work with Lorenzo Bergomi [28], partially published in Risk (May 2012).

2. Motivation

- Consider the following general dynamics for a diffusive stochastic volatility model:

$$dX_t = -\frac{1}{2}\xi_t^t dt + \sqrt{\xi_t^t} dW_t^1, \quad X_0 = x,$$
$$d\xi_t^u = \lambda(t, u, \xi_t^{\cdot}) \cdot dW_t, \quad \xi_0^u = y^u. \tag{1}$$

- $X_t = \ln S_t$.
- $\xi_t^{\cdot} \equiv (\xi_t^u, t \leq u)$: instantaneous forward variance curve from t onwards. ξ^u = driftless process under any risk-neutral measure [1,2]; initial value y^u read on market prices of variance swap (VS) contracts: $\xi_0^u = \frac{d}{du}\left(\hat{\sigma}_u^2 u\right)$, where $\hat{\sigma}_u$ is the implied variance swap volatility for maturity u.
- $\lambda = (\lambda_1, \ldots, \lambda_d)$: volatility of forward instantaneous variances.
- $W = \left(W^1, \ldots, W^d\right)$ = a d-dimensional Brownian motion. W^1 drives the spot dynamics.
- No dividend. Zero rates and repos (for the sake of simplicity).
- **No closed-form formula** available **for the price of vanilla options** in Model (1).
- Our goal: find a **general approximation of the smile which does not depend on a particular specification of the model**, i.e., on a particular choice of λ.
- $\Rightarrow$ We will derive **general asymptotic expansion of the smile, for small vol of vol, at second order**.
- Scaling factor ε: $\lambda \to \varepsilon\lambda$. X and ξ then depend on ε: $X \to X^\varepsilon$ and $\xi \to \xi^\varepsilon$.
- Two important assumptions: **no local volatility component**, and λ **does not depend on the asset value**.

Other approaches include:

- Vol of vol/correlation expansions in some particular cases of "first generation" stochastic volatility models see, for example, such as the Heston model [3], see, for example, [4,6,31].
- Short-term smile asymptotics for more or less general dynamics of the underlying, and for a more or less large range of strikes: [7–15,29,30].
- Rapid variation of volatility: [16].
- Slow variation of volatility: [17,18].

- Small variation of the underlying or the volatility: [5,15,18–20].
- Large time-to-maturity: [21].
- An analysis of the smile in general (local) stochastic volatility models, possibly including jumps in the asset price, is also conducted in Lipton [22].

- It is well known that the smile produced by stochastic volatility models is generated by the covariance of forward variances with themselves and spot.
- Our goal: **pinpoint exactly** which functionals of these covariances determine the vanilla smile.
- Important to ensure, while varying ε, that implied volatilities of some specific payoffs are unchanged, so that the overall volatility level is not altered in the model.
- In our framework, **variance swap volatilities are unchanged** as ε is varied.

3. Expansion of the Price of a Vanilla Option

- Consider the vanilla option delivering $g(X_T^\varepsilon)$ at time T.
- Price $P^\varepsilon\left(t, X_t^\varepsilon, \xi_t^{\cdot,\varepsilon}\right)$. We write $P^\varepsilon(t,x,y)$: **the variable** $y :=$ $(y^u, t \le u \le T)$ **is a curve.**
- P^ε solves the PDE $(\partial_t + L^\varepsilon) P^\varepsilon = 0$ with terminal condition $P^\varepsilon(T,x,y) = g(x)$, where $L^\varepsilon = L_0 + \varepsilon L_1 + \varepsilon^2 L_2$ with

$$L_0 = -\frac{1}{2} y^t \partial_x + \frac{1}{2} y^t \partial_x^2,$$

$$L_1 = \int_t^T du\ \mu(t,u,y)\ \partial^2_{xy^u},$$

$$L_2 = \frac{1}{2}\int_t^T du \int_t^T du'\ \nu(t,u,u',y)\ \partial^2_{y^u y^{u'}},$$

$$\mu(t,u,y) = \sqrt{y^t}\lambda_1(t,u,y) = \frac{\mathbb{E}\left[dX_t d\xi_t^u | \xi_t = y\right]}{dt} = \frac{\mathbb{E}\left[\frac{dS_t}{S_t} d\xi_t^u | \xi_t = y\right]}{dt},$$

$$\nu(t,u,u',y) = \sum_{i=1}^d \lambda_i(t,u,y)\lambda_i(t,u',y) = \frac{\mathbb{E}\left[d\xi_t^u d\xi_t^{u'} | \xi_t = y\right]}{dt}.$$

3.1 *The Perturbation Equations*

- Assume that $P^\varepsilon = P_0 + \varepsilon P_1 + \varepsilon^2 P_2 + \varepsilon^3 P_3 + \cdots$

$$\begin{aligned}0 &= \left(\partial_t + L_0 + \varepsilon L_1 + \varepsilon^2 L_2\right)\left(P_0 + \varepsilon P_1 + \varepsilon^2 P_2 + \varepsilon^3 P_3 + \cdots\right)\\ &= \left(\partial_t + L_0\right) P_0 + \varepsilon\left(\left(\partial_t + L_0\right) P_1 + L_1 P_0\right)\\ &\quad + \varepsilon^2\left(\left(\partial_t + L_0\right) P_2 + L_1 P_1 + L_2 P_0\right)\\ &\quad + \varepsilon^3\left(\left(\partial_t + L_0\right) P_3 + L_1 P_2 + L_2 P_1\right) + \cdots\end{aligned}$$

- $\Rightarrow$ The leading term P_0 and the correction terms $P_1, P_2, P_3, \ldots$ are solutions to the PDEs:

$$\begin{aligned}\left(\partial_t + L_0\right) P_0 = 0, &\quad P_0(T, x, y) = g(x)\\ \left(\partial_t + L_0\right) P_1 + L_1 P_0 = 0, &\quad P_1(T, x, y) = 0\\ \left(\partial_t + L_0\right) P_n + L_1 P_{n-1} + L_2 P_{n-2} = 0, &\quad P_n(T, x, y) = 0, \quad \forall n \geq 2\end{aligned}$$

- L_0 = infinitesimal generator associated to X^0, the unperturbed diffusion for which $\varepsilon = 0$. L_0 = standard **one-dimensional Black–Scholes operator** with deterministic volatility $\sqrt{y^t}$ at time t.
- Each P_n = solution to the traditional **one-dimensional** diffusion equation **with a source term** $H_n = L_1 P_{n-1} + L_2 P_{n-2}$:

$$\left(\partial_t + L_0\right) P_n + H_n = 0.$$

- Feynmann–Kac theorem $\Rightarrow$

$$\begin{aligned}P_0(t, x, y) &= \mathbb{E}\left[g\left(X_T^{0,t,x}\right)\right],\\ P_n(t, x, y) &= \mathbb{E}\left[\int_t^T H_n(s, X_s^{0,t,x}, y) ds\right], \quad \forall n \geq 1,\end{aligned}$$

where $X^{0,t,x}$ is the unperturbed process where $\varepsilon = 0$, starting at log-spot x at time t:

$$dX_s^{0,t,x} = -\frac{1}{2} y^s ds + \sqrt{y^s} dW_s^1, \quad X_t^{0,t,x} = x.$$

3.2 *The price at order* 0

- P_0 is the **Black–Scholes** price with time-dependent volatility $\sqrt{y^t}$:

$$P_0(t,x,y) = \mathbb{E}\left[g\left(x + \int_t^T \sqrt{y^s}dW_s^1 - \frac{1}{2}\int_t^T y^s ds\right)\right]$$
$$= P_{BS}\left(x, \int_t^T y^s ds\right),$$

where

$$P_{BS}(x,v) = \mathbb{E}\left[g\left(x + \sqrt{v}G - \frac{1}{2}v\right)\right], \quad G \sim \mathcal{N}(0,1). \tag{2}$$

- $v = \int_t^T y^s ds$ is the total variance of X^0 integrated from t to T.
- $P_0(t,x,y)$ depends on the curve $y \equiv (y^s, t \leq s \leq T)$ only through v.
- P_{BS} is solution to the **Black–Scholes PDE** [28].

$$\partial_v P_{BS} = \frac{1}{2}\left(\partial_x^2 - \partial_x\right) P_{BS}, \quad P_{BS}(x,0) = g(x). \tag{3}$$

Links the vega and gamma of a vanilla option in the unperturbed state.

A crucial observation:

- Because L_0 incorporates no local volatility, L_0 and ∂_x commute so

$$\left(\partial_t + L_0\right)\partial_x^p P_0 = \partial_x^p\left(\partial_t + L_0\right)P_0 = 0.$$

- $\Rightarrow \partial_x^p P_{BS}\left(X_t^0, \int_t^T y^s ds\right) \equiv \partial_x^p P_0(t, X_t^0, y)$ is a martingale for all integer p.
- Equation (3) then shows that **for all integers** m, n, $\partial_v^m \partial_x^n P_{BS}\left(X_t^0, \int_t^T y^s ds\right)$ **is a martingale.**
- This is crucial in the computations of P_1 and P_2.

3.3 *The price at order* 1

- Let us define the **integrated spot-variance covariance** function $C_t^{X\xi}(y)$:

$$C_t^{X\xi}(y) = \int_t^T ds \int_s^T du\ \mu(s,u,y)$$
$$= \int_t^T ds \int_s^T du \frac{\mathbb{E}\left[\frac{dS_s}{S_s} d\xi_s^u | \xi_s = y\right]}{ds}.$$

- We then have

$$P_1(t,x,y)$$
$$= \mathbb{E}\left[\int_t^T L_1 P_0(s, X_s^{0,t,x}, y) ds\right]$$
$$= \mathbb{E}\left[\int_t^T ds \int_s^T du\ \mu(s,u,y)\ \partial_{y^u}\left(\partial_x P_{BS}\left(X_s^{0,t,x}, \int_s^T y^r\, dr\right)\right)\right]$$
$$= \mathbb{E}\left[\int_t^T ds \int_s^T du\ \mu(s,u,y)\ \partial_{xv}^2 P_{BS}\left(X_s^{0,t,x}, \int_s^T y^r\, dr\right)\right]$$
$$= \int_t^T ds \int_s^T du\ \mu(s,u,y) \mathbb{E}\left[\partial_{xv}^2 P_{BS}\left(X_s^{0,t,x}, \int_s^T y^r\, dr\right)\right]$$
$$= C_t^{X\xi}(y)\ \partial_{xv}^2 P_{BS}\left(x, \int_t^T y^r\, dr\right).$$

3.4 *The price at order* 2

A similar result holds for the second order correction:

$$P_2 = P_2^{L_2 P_0} + P_2^{L_1 P_1}$$

$$P_2^{L_2 P_0}(t,x,y) = \frac{1}{2} C_t^{\xi\xi}(y)\ \partial_v^2 P_{BS}\left(x, \int_t^T y^r\, dr\right)$$

$$P_2^{L_1 P_1} = P_{2,0}^{L_1 P_1} + P_{2,1}^{L_1 P_1}$$

$$P_{2,0}^{L_1 P_1}(t,x,y) = \frac{1}{2} C_t^{X\xi}(y)^2\ \partial_x^2 \partial_v^2 P_{BS}\left(x, \int_t^T y^r\, dr\right)$$

$$P_{2,0}^{L_1P_1}(t,x,y) = C_t^{\mu}(y)\ \partial_x^2\partial_v P_{BS}\left(x, \int_t^T y^r dr\right)$$

$$C_t^{\xi\xi}(y) = \int_t^T ds \int_s^T du \int_s^T du'\ \nu(s,u,u',y)$$

$$= \int_t^T ds \int_s^T du \int_s^T du'\ \frac{\mathbb{E}\left[d\xi_s^u d\xi_s^{u'} | \xi_s = y\right]}{ds}$$

$$C_t^{\mu}(y) = \int_t^T ds \int_s^T du\ \mu(s,u,y)\ \partial_{y^u}\left(C_s^{X\xi}(y)\right)$$

$C_t^{\xi\xi}(y)$: **integrated variance-variance covariance** function. Alòs, Gatheral, and Radoičić [26] have recently derived a similar (but slightly different) expansion, to any order.

3.5 *Expansion of the implied volatility*

- We write $C^{X\xi} = C_0^{X\xi}(y)$, $C^{\xi\xi} = C_0^{\xi\xi}(y)$ and $C^{\mu} = C_0^{\mu}(y)$.
- **In the general diffusive stochastic volatility model (1), at second order in the vol of vol ε, the implied volatility for maturity T and strike K is quadratic in $L = \ln\left(\frac{K}{S_0}\right)$:**

$$\widehat{\sigma}^{\varepsilon}(T,K) \ = \ \widehat{\sigma}_T^{\text{ATM}} + \mathcal{S}_T \ln\left(\frac{K}{S_0}\right) + \mathcal{C}_T \ln^2\left(\frac{K}{S_0}\right) + O(\varepsilon^3). \quad (4)$$

- Coefficients are

$$\widehat{\sigma}_T^{\text{ATM}} \ = \ \hat{\sigma}_T^{\text{VS}}\left[1 + \frac{\varepsilon}{4v}C^{X\xi} + \frac{\varepsilon^2}{32v^3}\left(12\left(C^{X\xi}\right)^2 - v\,(v+4)\,C^{\xi\xi} + 4v\,(v-4)\,C^{\mu}\right)\right]$$

$$\mathcal{S}_T = \hat{\sigma}_T^{\text{VS}}\left[\frac{\varepsilon}{2v^2}C^{X\xi} + \frac{\varepsilon^2}{8v^3}\left(4C^{\mu}v - 3\left(C^{X\xi}\right)^2\right)\right]$$

$$\mathcal{C}_T \ = \ \hat{\sigma}_T^{\text{VS}}\frac{\varepsilon^2}{8v^4}\left(4C^{\mu}v + C^{\xi\xi}v - 6\left(C^{X\xi}\right)^2\right).$$

- $v = \int_0^T \xi_0^s ds$ and $\hat{\sigma}_T^{\text{VS}} = \sqrt{\frac{v}{T}}$, the VS implied volatility for maturity T.

3.6 *Comments*

ATM implied volatility:

$$\widehat{\sigma}_T^{\mathrm{ATM}} = \hat{\sigma}_T^{\mathrm{VS}} \left[1 + \frac{\varepsilon}{4v} C^{X\xi} \right.$$
$$\left. + \frac{\varepsilon^2}{32v^3} \left(12 \left(C^{X\xi} \right)^2 - v\,(v+4)\, C^{\xi\xi} + 4v(v-4)C^{\mu} \right) \right].$$

- ATM implied volatility = variance swap volatility + spread. At first order, spread $= \frac{C^{X\xi}}{4\sqrt{vT}}\varepsilon$.
- Typically, on the equity market, $C^{X\xi} < 0$: ATM implied volatility lies below the variance swap volatility.
- When spot returns and forward variances are uncorrelated, $C^{X\xi} = C^{\mu} = 0$ so that

$$\widehat{\sigma}_T^{\mathrm{ATM}} = \hat{\sigma}_T^{\mathrm{VS}} \left(1 - \frac{\varepsilon^2}{32v^3} v\,(v+4)\, C^{\xi\xi} \right).$$

  Because $C^{\xi\xi} \geq 0$, ATM implied volatility lies again below variance swap volatility. The higher the volatility of variances, the smaller the ATM implied volatility.

ATM skew: $\mathcal{S}_T = \hat{\sigma}_T^{\mathrm{VS}} \left[\frac{\varepsilon}{2v^2} C^{X\xi} + \frac{\varepsilon^2}{8v^3} \left(4C^{\mu} v - 3\left(C^{X\xi} \right)^2 \right) \right].$

- ATM skew $\mathcal{S}_T$ is of order ε. It has the sign of $C^{X\xi}$. $\mathcal{S}_T$ vanishes when spot returns and forward variances are uncorrelated, even at second order. ATM skew is produced only by the spot-variance correlation.
- Link ATM vol-VS vol-ATM skew:

$$\widehat{\sigma}_T^{\mathrm{ATM}} = \hat{\sigma}_T^{\mathrm{VS}} + \frac{\left(\hat{\sigma}_T^{\mathrm{VS}} \right)^2 T}{2} \mathcal{S}_T.$$

- At first order in ε, ATM skew has same sign as the difference between ATM implied volatility and variance swap volatility.

ATM convexity: $\mathcal{C}_T = \hat{\sigma}_T^{\mathrm{VS}} \frac{\varepsilon^2}{8v^4} \left(4C^{\mu} v + C^{\xi\xi} v - 6\left(C^{X\xi} \right)^2 \right)$

- Curvature $\mathcal{C}_T$ is of order ε^2.
- Not only does it involve variance/variance covariance: spot/variance covariance (squared) contributes as well.
- If spot and variances are uncorrelated, $\mathcal{C}_T = \frac{C^{\xi\xi}}{8v^{5/2}\sqrt{T}} \varepsilon^2 \geq 0$.

3.7 *Another derivation which stays at the level of operators*

- Recall that the price P^ε of the vanilla option is solution to $(\partial_t + L_t^\varepsilon)\, P^\varepsilon = 0$ with $L_t^\varepsilon = L_{0,t} + \varepsilon L_{1,t} + \varepsilon^2 L_{2,t}$, and terminal condition $P^\varepsilon(T, x, y) = g(x)$.
- Price can be expressed in terms of the semigroup $(U_{st}^\varepsilon, 0 \leq s \leq t \leq T)$ attached to the family of differential operators L_t^ε: $P^\varepsilon(t, \cdot) = U_{tT}^\varepsilon g$.
- The semigroup is defined by

$$U_{st}^\varepsilon = \lim_{n\to\infty} \left(1 - \delta t L_{t_0}^\varepsilon\right)\left(1 - \delta t L_{t_1}^\varepsilon\right)\cdots\left(1 - \delta t L_{t_{n-1}}^\varepsilon\right), \quad \delta t = \frac{t-s}{n},$$
$$t_i = s + i\delta t.$$

- It satisfies $U_{rt}^\varepsilon = U_{rs}^\varepsilon U_{st}^\varepsilon$ for $0 \leq r \leq s \leq t \leq T$, hence the notation $:\!\exp\left(\int_s^t L_\tau^\varepsilon d\tau\right)\!:$, where :: denotes time ordering:
- **We can directly expand U_{st}^ε in powers of ε.** Usual time-dependent perturbation technique in quantum mechanics. U_{st}^0 is called the free propagator.
- Consider the general situation where a differential operator L_t is perturbed by another operator H_t: $L_t^\varepsilon = L_t + \varepsilon H_t$
- From the definition of the semigroup, $U_{st}^\varepsilon = U_{st}^{(0)} + \varepsilon U_{st}^{(1)} + \varepsilon^2 U_{st}^{(2)} + \cdots$ with

$$U_{st}^{(1)} = \int_s^t d\tau\ U_{s\tau}^0 H_\tau U_{\tau t}^0,$$
$$U_{st}^{(2)} = \int_s^t d\tau_1 \int_{\tau_1}^t d\tau_2\ U_{s\tau_1}^0 H_{\tau_1} U_{\tau_1\tau_2}^0 H_{t_2} U_{\tau_2 t}^0.$$

- $\Rightarrow P^\varepsilon = P_0 + \varepsilon P_1 + \varepsilon^2 P_2 + \cdots$, with

$$P_1 = \int_t^T d\tau\ U_{t\tau}^0 L_{1,\tau} U_{\tau T}^0 g,$$
$$P_2 = \int_t^T d\tau\ U_{t\tau}^0 L_{2,\tau} U_{\tau T}^0 g + \int_t^T d\tau_1 \int_{\tau_1}^T d\tau_2\ U_{t\tau_1}^0 L_{1,\tau_1} U_{\tau_1\tau_2}^0 L_{1,\tau_2} U_{\tau_2 T}^0 g.$$

- We recover the expressions of P_1 and P_2.

4. Short Maturity: Structural Dependencies

- Assume $d\xi_t^t = \cdots dt + \varepsilon(\xi_t^t)^\varphi dB_t$;
- Let ρ_{SV} be the correlation between S_t and instantaneous variance $V_t = \xi_t^t$;
- Heston: $\varphi = \frac{1}{2}$, $\rho_{SV} = \rho$;
  Bergomi: $\varphi = 1$, $\rho_{SV} = \alpha_\theta\left((1-\theta)\rho_{SX} + \theta\rho_{SY}\right)$;
- Then for short maturities

$$\mathcal{S}_0 \simeq \frac{\varepsilon}{4}\rho\left(\widehat{\sigma}^{\text{ATM}}\right)^{2\varphi-2}. \tag{5}$$

$$\mathcal{C}_0 \simeq \varepsilon^2\left(\left(\frac{1}{12}\varphi - \frac{7}{48}\right)\rho^2 + \frac{1}{24}\right)\left(\widehat{\sigma}^{\text{ATM}}\right)^{4\varphi-5}. \tag{6}$$

- $\Rightarrow$ Short-term ATM skew does not depend on short-term ATM vol iff $\varphi = 1$ (observed in equity markets).
- $\Rightarrow$ Short-term ATM convexity does not depend on short-term ATM vol iff $\varphi = \frac{5}{4}$. And $(\forall\rho_{SV},\ \mathcal{C}_0 \geq 0) \iff \varphi \geq \frac{5}{4}$.

5. Long-term Asymptotics of Implied Volatility

- Assume the term-structure of variance swaps volatilities is flat: $\xi_0^t \equiv \xi$.
- Assume that for large $u-t$, $\mu(t,u,y) \propto (u-t)^{-\alpha}$, $\alpha > 0$.
  Then at higher order in ε, for long maturities,

$$\mathcal{S}_T \propto T^{-\alpha} \quad \text{if } \alpha < 1,$$

$$\mathcal{S}_T \propto T^{-1} \quad \text{if } \alpha > 1.$$

  α is exactly a signature of the long-time decay of the spot/variance covariance function.
- Assume that for large $u-t$ and $u'-t$, $\nu(t,u,u',y) \propto (u-t)^{-\beta}$ $(u'-t)^{-\beta}$, $\beta > 0$.
  Also assume that spots and volatilities are uncorrelated ($\mu \equiv 0$).
  Then at higher order in ε, for long maturities,

$$\mathcal{C}_T \propto T^{-2\beta} \quad \text{if } \beta < 1,$$

$$\mathcal{C}_T \propto T^{-2} \quad \text{if } \beta > 1.$$

- Exponential decay $\leftrightarrow \beta > 1$.

6. First Example: A Heston-like Model

$$dX_t = -\frac{1}{2}V_t dt + \sqrt{V_t} dW_t^1, \qquad X_0 = x$$

$$dV_t = -k\left(V_t - V_\infty\right)dt + \lambda\left(V_t\right)^\varphi\left(\rho dW_t^1 + \sqrt{1-\rho^2}dW_t^2\right), \quad V_0 = V. \tag{7}$$

- The instantaneous forward variance reads

$$\xi_t^u = \mathbb{E}\left[V_u | V_t\right] = V_\infty + \left(V_t - V_\infty\right)e^{-k(u-t)},$$

  and its dynamics is:

$$d\xi_t^u = \lambda e^{-k(u-t)}\left(\xi_t^t\right)^\varphi\left(\rho dW_t^1 + \sqrt{1-\rho^2}dW_t^2\right).$$

- The initial term-structure of instantaneous forward variances is

$$y^u \equiv \xi_0^u = v_\infty + \left(v - v_\infty\right)e^{-ku}.$$

- Like **in all classic "first generation" stochastic volatility models, this term-structure is determined by the model parameters**, and the current value of the instantaneous volatility.
- The volatility $\lambda(t, u, y)$ of instantaneous forward variances depends on the instantaneous forward variance curve $y = (y^s, t \leq s \leq T)$ only through the instantaneous spot variance y^t:

$$\lambda_1(t, u, y) = \rho\left(y^t\right)^\varphi e^{-k(u-t)},$$
$$\lambda_2(t, u, y) = \sqrt{1-\rho^2}\left(y^t\right)^\varphi e^{-k(u-t)}.$$

- As a consequence,

$$C^{X\xi} = \frac{\rho}{k}\int_0^T ds (y^s)^{\varphi+\frac{1}{2}}\left(1 - e^{-k(T-s)}\right),$$

$$C^{\xi\xi} = \sum_{i=1}^{2}\int_0^T ds\left(\int_s^T du\,\lambda_i(s, u, y)\right)^2$$
$$= \frac{1}{k^2}\int_0^T ds (y^s)^{2\varphi}\left(1 - e^{-k(T-s)}\right)^2,$$

$$C^{\mu} = \left(\varphi + \frac{1}{2}\right) \frac{\rho^2}{k} \int_0^T ds (y^s)^{\varphi+\frac{1}{2}} \int_s^T du (y^u)^{\varphi-\frac{1}{2}} e^{-k(u-s)} \times \left(1 - e^{-k(T-u)}\right).$$

- This coincides with Equations (3.7) to (3.10) in Lewis (2000), where $J^{(1)} = C^{X\xi}$, $J^{(3)} = \frac{1}{2}C^{\xi\xi}$, and $J^{(4)} = C^{\mu}$.

7. Second Example: The Bergomi Model

$$dX_t = -\frac{1}{2}\xi_t^t dt + \sqrt{\xi_t^t} dW_t^S,$$

$$d\xi_t^u = \xi_t^u \alpha_\theta \omega \left((1-\theta) e^{-k_X(u-t)} dW_t^X + \theta e^{-k_Y(u-t)} dW_t^Y\right) = \lambda(t, u, \xi_t^\cdot) \cdot dW_t,$$

$d\langle W^S, W^X\rangle_t = \rho_{SX} dt$, $d\langle W^S, W^Y\rangle_t = \rho_{SY} dt$, $d\langle W^X, W^Y\rangle_t = \rho_{XY} dt$.

- The normalizing factor

$$\alpha_\theta = \left((1-\theta)^2 + 2\rho_{XY}\theta(1-\theta) + \theta^2\right)^{-1/2}$$

is such that the very-short term variance $\xi_t^{t,\omega}$ has log-normal volatility ω.

- We pick $k_X > k_Y$, θ is a parameter which mixes the short-term factor W^X and the long-term factor W^Y.

- After a Cholesky transform, this can be restated using independent Brownian motions W^1, W^2 and W^3 as follows:

$$W^S = W^1,$$

$$W^X = \rho_{SX} W^1 + \sqrt{1-\rho_{SX}^2} W^2,$$

$$W^Y = \rho_{SY} W^1 + \chi_{XY}\sqrt{1-\rho_{SY}^2} W^2 + \sqrt{\left(1-\chi_{XY}^2\right)\left(1-\rho_{SY}^2\right)} W^3,$$

where $\chi_{XY} = \frac{\rho_{XY} - \rho_{SX}\rho_{SY}}{\sqrt{1-\rho_{SX}^2}\sqrt{1-\rho_{SY}^2}}$.

- ρ_{SX}, ρ_{SY} and ρ_{XY} define a correlation matrix $\Longleftrightarrow \chi_{XY} \in [-1,1]$.
- The volatility of variance $\lambda = (\lambda_1, \lambda_2, \lambda_3)$ reads

$$\lambda_1(t,u,y) = y^u \alpha_\theta \left((1-\theta)\, \rho_{SX} e^{-k_X(u-t)} + \theta \rho_{SY} e^{-k_Y(u-t)} \right),$$

$$\lambda_2(t,u,y) = y^u \alpha_\theta \left((1-\theta) \sqrt{1-\rho_{SX}^2}\, e^{-k_X(u-t)} \right.$$
$$\left. + \theta \chi_{XY} \sqrt{1-\rho_{SY}^2}\, e^{-k_Y(u-t)} \right),$$

$$\lambda_3(t,u,y) = y^u \alpha_\theta \theta \sqrt{\left(1-\chi_{XY}^2\right)\left(1-\rho_{SY}^2\right)} e^{-k_Y(u-t)}.$$

8. Numerical Experiments

We pick the Bergomi model with a flat initial term structure of variance swap prices (see Figure 1) and

θ	k_X	k_Y	ρ_{SX}	ρ_{SY}	ρ_{XY}	χ_{XY}	ξ
0.25	8	0.35	−0.8	−0.48	0	−0.73	$(0.2)^2$

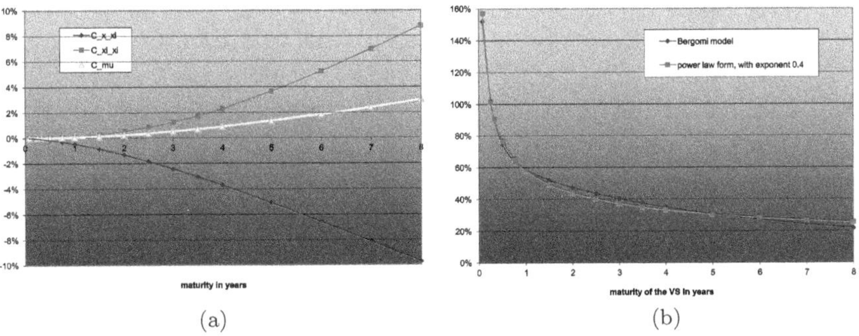

(a) (b)

Figure 1: (a) Integrated covariance functions in the Bergomi model, $\omega = 400\%$ and (b) instantaneous volatility of VS volatility at inception, $\omega = 400\%$.

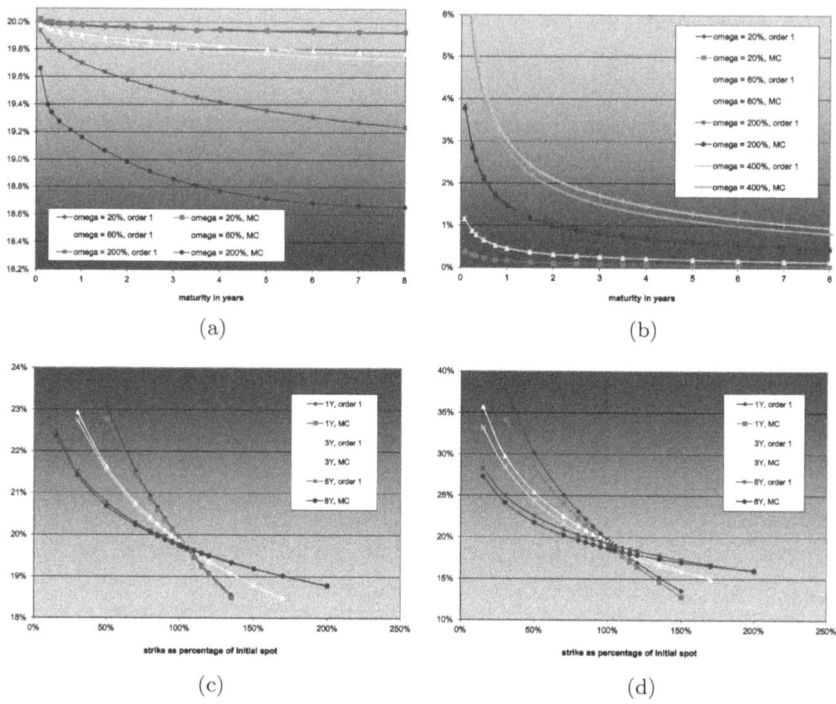

Figure 2: (a) ATM implied volatility; (b) ATM skew; (c) smile, $\omega = 60\%$ and (d) smile, $\omega = 200\%$.

8.1 *First order*

- **ATM skew very sharply estimated by the first order expansion**, even for large values of the volatility of variance ω (see Figure 2).
- **ATM volatility well captured by the expansion at first order in ω only for small values of** ω (say, up to 60%).
- True ATM implied volatilities are below their first order approximates $\Rightarrow$ ATM volatility is a very concave function of ω, around $\omega = 0$. In view of the expression for $\widehat{\sigma}_T^{\mathrm{ATM}}$, this means that, for the set of parameters picked,

$$12C^{X\xi 2} - C^{\xi\xi}v\,(v+4) + 4C^{\mu}v\,(v-4) \leq 0.$$

- **Global shape of smile well captured by first order expansion:** the true implied volatility for strike K is indeed approximately affine in $\ln(K/S_0)$.
- But level of smile well captured only for small values of ω.

8.2 *Second order*

We first consider the situation when spot returns and forward variances are uncorrelated. In this case, the ATM skew vanishes, and so does its expansion at second order in ω. We pick

θ	k_X	k_Y	ρ_{SX}	ρ_{SY}	ρ_{XY}	ξ
0.25	8	0.35	0	0	0	$(0.2)^2$

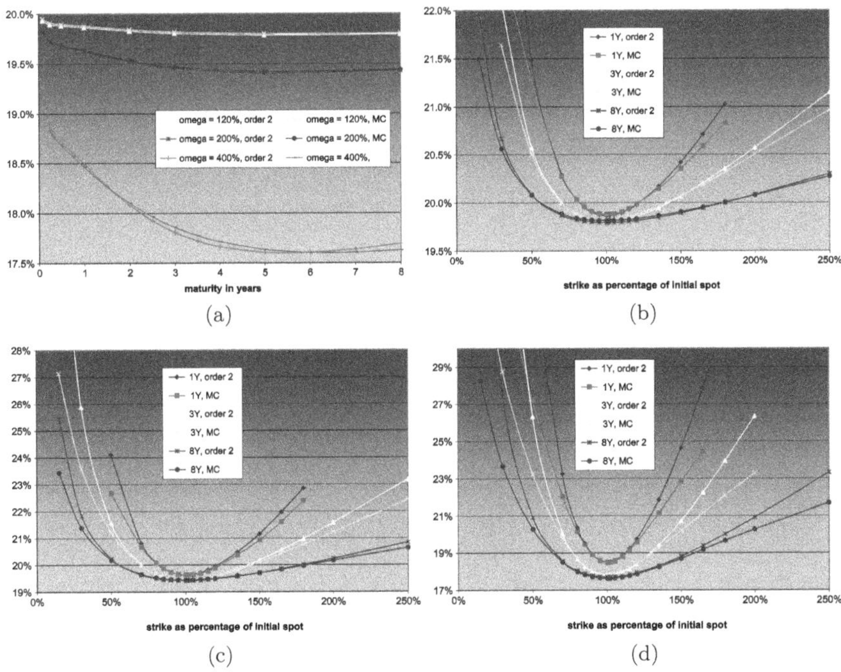

Figure 3: (a) At-the-money implied volatility; (b) smile, $\omega = 120\%$; (c) smile, $\omega = 200\%$ and (d) smile, $\omega = 400\%$.

- **ATM implied volatility very sharply estimated by the second order expansion**, even up to $\omega = 400\%$ and to long maturities. For $T = 15$ years, estimate is less than 15 bps above true ATM volatility (see Figure 3).
- Looking at the whole smile: second order expansion of the implied volatility is excellent around the money, but becomes too large for strikes far from the money.
- Not surprising: No arbitrage $\Rightarrow$ for very small and very large strikes, $\widehat{\sigma}(T,K)^2$ grows at most linearly with $\ln(K/S_0)$ (see [18]), whereas second order estimate for $\widehat{\sigma}(T,K)^2$ grows like $\ln^4(K/S_0)$, see (4). Remainder $O(\omega^3) = R(\omega,T,K)$ is large for large K, for finite ω.
- Nevertheless, even for $\omega = 400\%$, a maturity of 8 years and an out-the-money strike of 250%, the error is only 1.5 point of volatility.

Finally on Figure 4, we numerically check the accuracy of the second order expansion of the smile in the general case of correlated spot returns and variances. Going to second order in ε improves accuracy.

9. Rederiving the Link Between Skew and Skewness of Log-Returns

- Remember $\mathcal{S}_T = \frac{C^{X\xi}}{2v^{3/2}\sqrt{T}}\varepsilon + O\left(\varepsilon^2\right)$.
- Let us now compute the skewness s_T of log-returns:

$$s_T = \frac{\mathbb{E}\left[\mathcal{X}_T^3\right]}{\mathbb{E}\left[\mathcal{X}_T^2\right]^{3/2}}, \qquad \mathcal{X}_T = X_T - \mathbb{E}\left[X_T\right] = \int_0^T \sqrt{\xi_t^{t,\varepsilon}}\,dW_t^1.$$

- We have $\mathbb{E}\left[\mathcal{X}_T^2\right] = \int_0^T \xi_0^t dt + O(\varepsilon)$ and $\mathbb{E}\left[\mathcal{X}_T^3\right] = 3\varepsilon C^{X\xi} + O\left(\varepsilon^2\right)$.
- At first order in the vol of vol, the skewness of (the distribution of) $\ln\left(S_T/S_0\right)$ is thus

$$s_T = \frac{3\varepsilon C^{X\xi}}{\left(\int_0^T \xi_0^t dt\right)^{3/2}}.$$

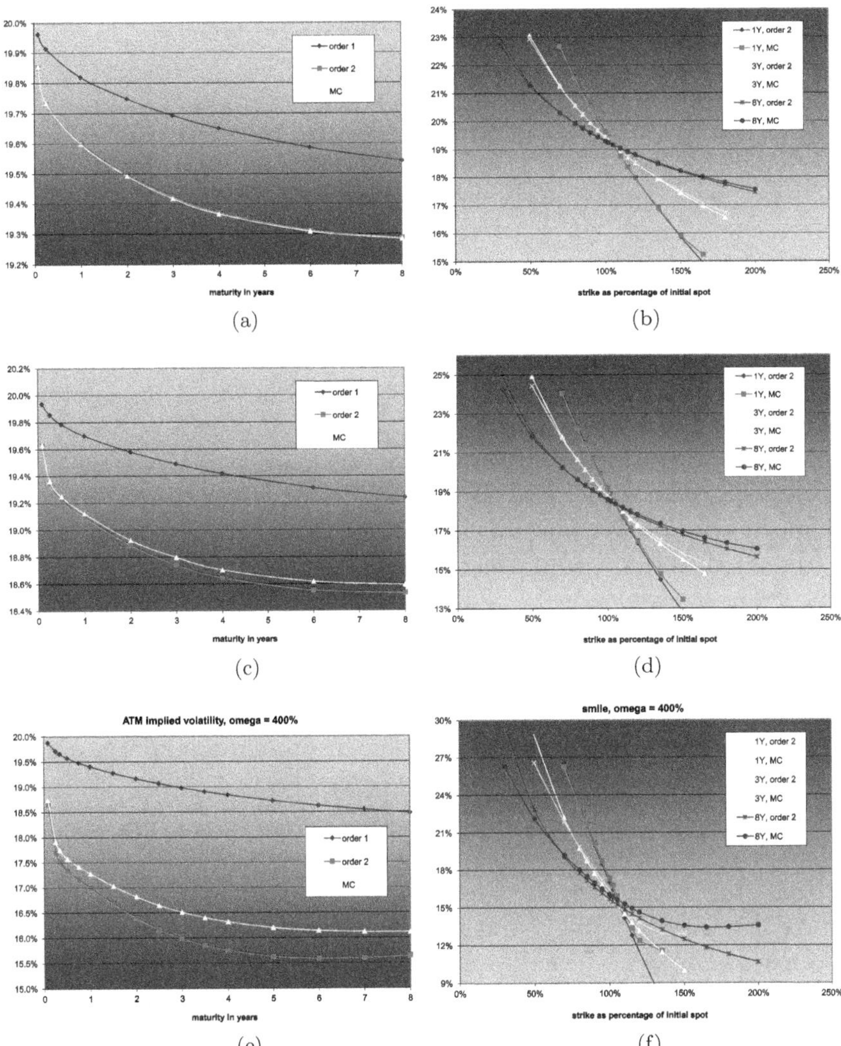

Figure 4: (a) ATM implied volatility, $\omega = 120\%$; (b) smile, $\omega = 120\%$; (c) ATM implied volatility, $\omega = 200\%$; (d) smile, $\omega = 200\%$; (e) ATM implied volatility, $\omega = 400\%$ and (f) smile, $\omega = 400\%$.

- The ATM skew $\mathcal{S}_T$ simply reads

$$\mathcal{S}_T = \frac{s_T}{6\sqrt{T}} + O(\varepsilon^2),$$

(see [23–25]).
- This links $C^{X\xi}$ to the skewness of $\ln S_T$.

10. Conclusion

- We provide an expansion at order two in volatility of volatility for **general stochastic volatility models** based on a forward variance formulation.
- VS volatilities for all maturities are unchanged as ε is varied.
- At order two in ε, **the smile is exactly quadratic in log-moneyness** and **depends on only three model-dependent dimensionless quantities**:
  - $C^{X\xi}$, the **integrated spot/variance covariance function**,
  - $C^{\xi\xi}$, the **integrated variance/variance covariance function**,
  - C^{μ}, akin to an **integrated spot-skew covariance function** which, like $C^{x\xi}$, depends only on instantaneous spot/variance covariances.
- We shed light on the significance of $C^{X\xi}$ by rederiving a simple link between the ATM skew and the skewness of $\ln S_T$.
- From our general expression we derive the short-maturity limits of ATM volatility, skew, curvature: we give **structural dependencies of the ATM skew and curvature on ATM volatility**.
- We also link the **long-term decay of the ATM skew and curvature** to the **decay of spot/variance and variance/variance covariance functions**.
- Numerical experiments in the case of a two-factor version of the Bergomi model show good agreement of the order one expression for the ATM skew, and of the order two expression for the ATM volatility, even for large values of the volatility of short-dated variance (around 400%) that are typical of implied levels of equity indices.

11. Risk Magazine, May 2012

CUTTING EDGE. DERIVATIVES PRICING

Stochastic volatility's orderly smiles

Lorenzo Bergomi and Julien Guyon derive an expansion of the volatility surface of general stochastic volatility models at second order in volatility of volatility that is accurate for a wide range of strikes. They characterise the shape of stochastic volatility smiles in terms of three effective quantities that compactly summarise the joint dynamics of spot and volatilities in the model

Stochastic volatility models generate an implied volatility surface as well as its associated dynamics. While Monte Carlo simulation is always an option, a fast and accurate approximation of the volatility surface is a useful implement for assessing any given model. In this article, we obtain such an approximation at second order in the volatility of volatility for a general class of stochastic volatility models.

Using this approximation, we derive some structural properties of stochastic volatility smiles: we highlight the dependence of the level of short-term at-the-money (ATM) skew and curvature on the short-term ATM volatility, and we also link the decay of ATM skew and curvature for long maturities to the decay of the spot/volatility and volatility/volatility covariance functions. We finally provide

variance covariance is thus modelled through λ_1. We assume that the asset pays no dividends and for the sake of simplicity take zero rates and repos.

Forward variances ξ^u are driftless. Their initial value can be calibrated on market prices of variance swap (VS) contracts: $\xi_0^u = d/du(\hat{\sigma}_u^2 u)$, where $\hat{\sigma}_u$ is the implied VS volatility for maturity u. Alternatively, the ξ_0^u can be chosen so as to recover market prices of other instruments, such as ATM vanilla options for all maturities. Second-generation stochastic volatility models, such as the Bergomi model (2005), in which the dynamics of the ξ^u is directly modelled, are naturally expressed in the form of equation (1). By contrast, first-generation stochastic volatility models, such as the Heston (1993) or the double-lognormal model (Gatheral, 2008), are built on an autonomous dynamics for the instantaneous variance $V_t = \xi_t^t$. This imposes structural constraints on the shape of the initial variance curve ξ_0^u. Still, first-generation models can be cast as forward variance models and our analysis applies to them as well (see the example of the Heston model below).

For a general model (1), the pricing equation for European-style payouts is not analytically solvable. While many different approximations have been proposed for specific first-generation models, the general case of forward variance models has not been considered in the literature. In this article, we derive an approximation of the smile produced by the generic model (1) at second order in the volatility of volatility. To this end, we introduce a scaling factor ε for the volatilities of instantaneous forward variances: $\lambda \to \varepsilon\lambda$. Expanding at order two in ε is thus exactly equivalent to expanding at order two in λ. Our derivation relies on the property that in model (1) the volatility of S_t incorporates no local volatility component, and that λ does not depend on S_t. Mixed local/stochastic volatility models lie outside our scope, and the stochastic volatility must be an autonomous process.

While it is obvious that the smile produced by stochastic volatility models is generated by the covariance of forward variances with themselves and S_t, our aim in this article is to pinpoint which functionals of these covariances determine the vanilla smile. We also demonstrate that the accuracy of a second-order expansion is practically adequate whenever far out-of-the-money strikes are not considered.

In this respect, it is important to ensure that implied volatilities of some specific payouts are unchanged, so that the overall volatility

References

[1] Dupire, B. (1993). *Arbitrage Pricing with Stochastic Volatility*, preprint.

[2] Bergomi, L. (2005). *Smile Dynamics 2*, Risk Magazine, October.

[3] Heston, S. (1993). A closed-form solution for options with stochastic volatility with applications to bond and currency options, *The Review of Financial Studies*, 6(2), 327–343.

[4] Antonelli, F. and Scarlatti, S. (2009). Pricing options under stochastic volatility: A power series approach, *Finance and Stochastics*, 13, 269–303.

[5] Benhamou, E., Gobet, E., and Miri, M. (2009). Smart expansion and fast calibration for jump diffusion, *Finance and Stochastics*, 13, 563–589.

[6] Lewis, A. (2009). *Option Valuation Under Stochastic Volatility*, Finance Press.
[7] Alòs, E., León, J.A., and Vives, J. (2007). On the short-time behavior of the implied volatility for jump-diffusion models with stochastic volatility, 11, 571–589.
[8] Berestycki, H., Busca, J., and Florent, I. (2004). Computing the Implied volatility in Stochastic Volatility Models, *Communications on Pure and Applied Mathematics*, 57(10), 1352–1373.
[9] El Euch, O., Fukasawa, M., Gatheral, J., and Rosenbaum, M. (2019). Short-term at-the-money asymptotics under stochastic volatility models. *SIAM Journal of Financial Mathematics*, 10(2), 491–511.
[10] Forde, M., Jacquier, A., and Lee, R. (2012). The small-time smile and term structure of implied volatility under the Heston model. *SIAM Journal of Financial Mathematics*, 3(1), 690–708.
[11] Friz, P., Gerhold, S., and Pinter, A. (2018). Option pricing in the moderate deviations regime. *Mathematical Finance*, 28(3), 962–988.
[12] Hagan, P., Kumar, D., Lesniewski, A., and Woodward, D. (2002). *Managing Smile Risk*, Wilmott Magazine, September, 84–108.
[13] Medvedev, A. and Scaillet, O. (2007). Approximation and calibration of short-term implied volatilities under jump-diffusion stochastic volatility, *Review of Financial Studies*, 20(2), 427–459.
[14] Osajima, Y. (2006). *Asymptotic Expansion Formula of Implied Volatility for Dynamic SABR Model and FX Hybrid Model*, UTMS 2006-29, The University of Tokyo.
[15] Pagliarani, S. and Pascucci, A. (2017). The exact Taylor formula of the implied volatility, *Finance and Stochastics*, 21, 661–718.
[16] Fouque, J.-P., Papanicolaou G., and Sircar, K.R. (2000). *Derivatives in Financial Markets with Stochastic Volatility*, Cambridge University Press.
[17] Sircar, K.R. and Papanicolaou, G. (1999). Stochastic volatility, smile and asymptotics. *Applied Mathematical Finance*, 6, 107–145.
[18] Lee, R. (2001). Implied and local volatilities under stochastic volatility, *International Journal of Theoretical and Applied Finance*, 4(1), 45–89. Lee, R. (2004). The moment formula for implied volatility at extreme strikes, *Mathematical Finance*, 14(3), 469–480.
[19] Benhamou, E., Gobet, E., and Miri, M. (2010). Closed forms for European options in a local volatility model, 13(4), 603–634.
[20] Bompis, R. and Gobet, E. (2018). Analytical approximations of local-Heston volatility model and error analysis. *Mathematical Finance*, 28(3), 920–961.
[21] Forde, M. and Jacquier, A. (2011). The large-maturity smile for the Heston model. *Finance and Stochastics*, 15(4), 755–780.

[22] Lipton, A. (2002). *The Vol Smile Problem*, Risk Magazine, February, 61–65.

[23] Backus, D., Foresi, S., Li K., and Wu L. (1997). *Accounting for Biases in Black–Scholes*, Working Paper.

[24] Jarrow, R. and Rudd, A. (1982). Approximate option valuation for arbitrary stochastic processes, *Journal of Financial Economics*, 10, 347–369.

[25] Corrado, C. and Su, T. (1996). Skewness and kurtosis in S&P 500 index returns implied by option prices, *The Journal of Financial Research*, 19(2), 175–192.

[26] Alòs, E., Gatheral, J., and Radoičić, R. (2020). Exponentiation of conditional expectations under stochastic volatility, *Quantitative Finance*, 20(1), 13–27.

[27] Bergomi, L. and Guyon, J. (2012). *Stochastic Volatility's Orderly Smiles*, Risk magazine, May.

[28] Black, F. and Scholes, M. (1973). The pricing of options and corporate liabilities, *The Journal of Political Economy*, 81(3), 637–654.

[29] Henry-Labordère, P. (2005). *A General Asymptotic Implied Volatility for Stochastic Volatility Models*, SSRN Preprint.

[30] Henry-Labordère, P. (2008). *Analysis, Geometry, and Modeling in Finance: Advanced Methods in Option Pricing*, Chapman & Hall, CRC Financial Mathematics.

[31] Benhamou, E., Gobet, E., and Miri, M. (2010). Time dependent Heston model. *SIAM Journal of Finance Mathematics*, 1, 289–325.

https://doi.org/10.1142/9789811259142_0013

Chapter 13

A Neural Network Approach to Understanding Implied Volatility Movements*

J. Cao, J. Chen, and J. Hull

Joseph L. Rotman School of Management
University of Toronto

Abstract

We employ neural networks to understand volatility surface movements. We first use daily data on options on the S&P 500 index to derive a relationship between the expected change in implied volatility and three variables: the return on the index, the moneyness of the option, and the remaining life of the option. This model provides an improvement of 10.72% compared with a simpler analytic model. We then enhance the model with an additional feature: the level of the VIX index prior to the change being observed. This produces a further improvement of 62.12% and shows that the expected response of the volatility surface to movements in the index is quite different in high and low volatility environments.

Keywords: Options, implied volatility movements, neural networks, deep learning.

*This chapter is derived from Cao, J., Chen, J. and Hull, J. (2020). A neural network approach to understanding implied volatility movements. *Quant. Finance*, 20(9): 1–9. Doi:10.1080/14697688.2020.1750679. Reprinted by permission of Taylor & Francis Ltd.

1. Introduction

It is well established that there is a negative relationship between an equity's volatility and its price. Black [1], Christie [2], Cheung and Ng [3] and Duffee [4] demonstrate this using linear regressions of return on subsequent changes in volatility for individual stocks and stock portfolios. Other authors have documented that the negative relationship extends to implied volatilities as well as physical volatilities. Cont and da Fonseca [5], for example, who carried out a principal components analysis of volatility surface movements, find that shifts in the level of implied volatilities are negatively correlated with the return on the underlying asset. Poulsen *et al.* [6] find that for both U.S. and European markets the correlation between returns and at-the-money implied volatilities is highly negative, about −0.85.

The reason for the negative relationship has been the subject of much research. Black [1] suggested a leverage argument. As the equity price moves up (down), leverage decreases (increases) and as a result volatility decreases (increases). In the alternative volatility feedback effect hypothesis, the causality is the other way round. When there is an increase (decrease) in volatility, the required rate of return increases (decreases) causing the stock price to decline (increase). The two competing explanations have been explored by a number of authors including French *et al.* [7], Campbell and Hentschel [8], Bekaert and Wu [9], Bollerslev *et al.* [10], Hens and Steude [11], and Hasanhodzic and Lo [12]. On balance, the empirical evidence appears to favor the volatility feedback effect. For example, the negative relationship seems to hold even when the equity is issued by a company that has very little debt in its capital structure.

Changes in equity prices do not lead to all implied volatilities changing by the same amount. In this paper we use machine learning to produce a model of the dependence of the volatility surface on return for an equity index. We first use a three-feature neural network model to explore the relationship between the change in the implied volatility of an option on the S&P 500 index and:

(a) the daily return of the index;
(b) the moneyness of the option; and
(c) the option's time to maturity.

We will refer to this as the "three-feature model". We then add a market sentiment indicator, the VIX index, to create a more elaborate model, which we will refer to as the "four-feature model". Our results are based on about two million daily observations on call options on the S&P 500 between 2010 and 2017 from OptionMetrics.

Our measure of moneyness is the delta calculated from the practitioner Black–Scholes model. The practitioner Black–Scholes model is a model where the volatility parameter in the Black–Scholes formula is replaced by the implied volatility. The practitioner delta for a European option on an index is therefore

$$\delta_{\mathrm{BS}} = e^{-qT} N\left(\frac{\ln(S/K) + (r - q + \sigma_{\mathrm{imp}}^2/2)T}{\sigma_{\mathrm{imp}}\sqrt{T}}\right)$$

where N is the cumulative standard normal distribution function, S is the index level, K is the strike price, T is the time to maturity, r is the risk-free rate, q is the dividend yield and σ_{imp} is the implied volatility of the option.[a]

The practitioner Black–Scholes delta is a measure of moneyness widely used by practitioners. Indeed, practitioners often define at-the-money call options as options where $\delta_{\mathrm{BS}} = 0.5$ and at-the-money put options as options where $\delta_{\mathrm{BS}} = -0.5$. For call options, δ_{BS} is close to zero for deep out-of-the-money options and close to 1.0 for deep-in-the-money options. For put options, δ_{BS} is close to zero for deep out-of-the-money options and close to -1.0 for deep-in-the-money options.

Developing an empirical model for the relationship between volatility surface movements and equity returns is important for a number of reasons. It can be used to test the extent to which a particular stochastic volatility model is consistent with market data. This can be done by determining numerically the relationship between volatility surface movements and the features listed above for the stochastic volatility model under consideration and then comparing it with the empirically determined relationship. An empirical model has the potential to provide useful information for a trader who has

[a]The practitioner gamma and vega are defined similarly by setting the volatility parameter equal to the implied volatility of the option under consideration.

to quote implied volatilities in a market where equity prices are moving fast. It can also be used to estimate a minimum variance delta for hedging. This is a hedge ratio that takes account of expected volatility changes as well as the change in the underlying asset price. The minimum variance delta is

$$\delta_{\mathrm{BS}} + \upsilon_{\mathrm{BS}} \frac{\partial \sigma_{\mathrm{imp}}}{\partial S}$$

where υ_{BS} is the practitioner vega and $\partial \sigma_{\mathrm{imp}} / \partial S$ is estimated from empirical results.

Other research which uses machine learning for modeling volatility changes is Nian *et al.* [13]. This focuses on minimum variance delta estimates and shows that machine learning can lead to hedging improvements. Our research is more general. We are concerned with understanding movements in the whole volatility surface.

Our objective is to use machine learning tools to estimate the function Fin the relationship

$$E(\Delta \sigma_{\mathrm{imp}}) = F\left(\frac{\Delta S}{S}, \delta_{\mathrm{BS}}, T, V\right)$$

where E denotes expected value, σ_{imp} is an option's implied volatility, S is the S&P 500 index, δ_{BS} is the option's moneyness measure just mentioned, T is the option's time to maturity, and V is the level of the VIX index (observed immediately prior to the changes in the implied volatility and the index). Our research provides an application of multi-layer neural networks in finance.[b] As explained below, a multi-layer neural network is a useful tool for estimating complex nonlinear functions when a large amount of data is available.

Hull and White [14] in considering minimum variance delta estimates propose the following analytic model:

$$E(\Delta \sigma_{\mathrm{imp}}) = \frac{\Delta S}{S} \frac{a + b\delta_{\mathrm{BS}} + c\delta_{\mathrm{BS}}^2}{\sqrt{T}}$$

where a, b, and c are parameters. In this model the expected change in the implied volatility is linearly dependent on the return on the index,

[b]Tests of the use of artificial neural networks for option pricing are provided by Hutchison *et al.* (1994) and Cucklin and Das (2017).

inversely proportional to the square root of the time to maturity and quadratic in the practitioner Black–Scholes delta. The parameters a, b, and c are estimated from data. This model was found to produce results that compared favorably with more elaborate stochastic volatility models, and we use it as a benchmark. We find that a three-feature neural network model produces a 10.72% improvement over this model. Adding the VIX index as a fourth feature produces a further improvement of 62.12%.

The organization of the paper is as follows. Section 2 describes the nature of neural networks. Section 3 explains the data and how it was used. Section 4 explains the way algorithms were implemented. Section 5 presents the results for the three-feature model. Section 6 examines the extra explanatory power of the VIX index and conclusions are in Section 7.

2. Neural Networks

Artificial neural networks (ANNs) are at the very core of deep learning. They were first introduced by McCulloch and Pitts [15] who presented a simplified model of how the neurons in a human brain can perform computations. In recent years, improvements in computer processing speed and the large volumes of data that are being generated in many spheres have led to renewed interest in ANNs.

Traditionally, finance and economics have used linear models or models involving simple transformations of linear functions. ANNs enable nonlinear functions involving many parameters to be estimated from large data sets. The structure of an ANN is shown in Figure 1. There are a number of inputs, referred to as features and one or more outputs, referred to as targets. In our first application, there are three features: index return, moneyness (as measured by the Black–Scholes delta), and time to maturity. There is one target, the change in the implied volatility. We then add an additional market sentiment indicator, the VIX index, as a feature.

The inputs form the input layer and the outputs form the output layer. The calculations necessary to determine the output layer from the input layer involve one or more hidden layers. Each hidden layer has a number of nodes at which values are calculated. In Figure 1,

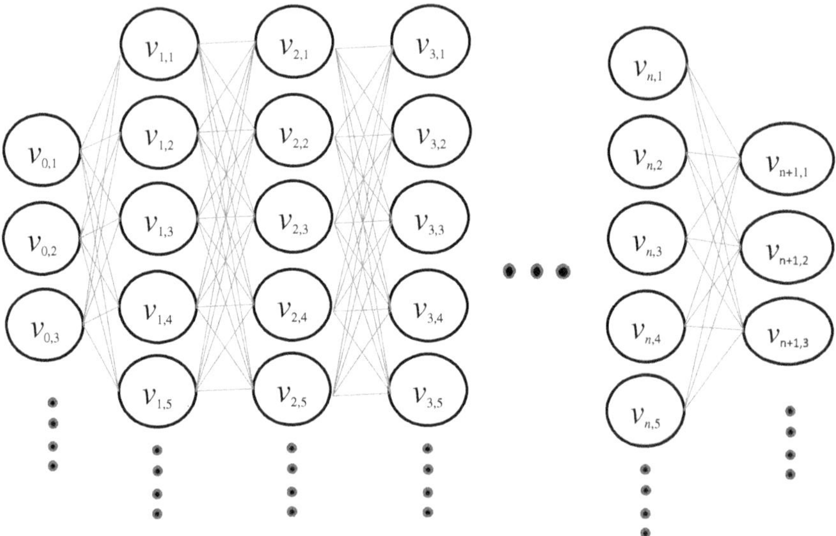

Figure 1: The structure of an artificial neural network. The $v_{0,j}$ are the inputs and the $v_{n+1,j}$ are the outputs.

there are n hidden layers, an input layer, and an output layer. The left-most layer is the input layer and contains the values of the input variables (or features). The right-most layer is the output layer and contains the output variables (or targets).

Instead of developing a model to estimate the outputs directly from the inputs we specify functions relating the values at the nodes comprising one layer to values at the nodes comprising the previous layer. The first function is used to transform the values of the features in the input layer to the values at the nodes in the first layer. Further functions are used to transform the values at the nodes in layer i to values at the nodes in layer $i+1$ $(1 \leq i \leq n-1)$. A final function is used to transform the values at the nodes in layer n to the target values in the output layer. These functions are referred to as activation functions. ANNs that have multiple hidden layers are referred to as deep neural networks. See Hull [16] for more details.

The Universal Approximation Theorem, derived by Hornik [17], states that an ANN with a single hidden layer can approximate any function arbitrarily closely. However, a very large number of nodes may be required and in some situations it may be more practical to use multiple layers so that there are fewer nodes overall.[c]

Suppose that there are m_0 features, m_i nodes in hidden layer i $(1 \leq i \leq n)$, and m_{n+1} targets. We will refer to the input layer as layer 0 and the output layer as layer $n+1$. Define $v_{i,j}$ as the value at the jth node of layer i $(0 \leq i \leq n+1,\ 1 \leq j \leq m_i)$. The variable $v_{0,j} = x_j$ is the value of the jth feature and $v_{n+1,j}$ is the estimate of the jth target given by the model.

The formula for calculating the $v_{i,j}$ $(1 \leq i \leq n+1$ and $1 \leq j \leq m_i)$ can be written

$$v_{i,j} = f_i\left(b_{i,j} + \sum_{k=1}^{m_{i-1}} w_{i-1,k,j} v_{i-1,k}\right) \tag{1}$$

In this formula f_i defines the activation function used to calculate values at the nodes of layer i $(1 \leq i \leq n+1)$. The $b_{i,j}$ and $w_{i,k,j}$ are parameters of the model. Specifically, $w_{i,k,j}$ is the weight assigned to the value at the kth node of layer i when the value at jth node of layer $i+1$ is being calculated and $b_{i,j}$ is a constant, known as the bias, which is added to the weighted value computed for the jth node of layer i.

The number of parameters in Equation (1) can be quite large. For example if there are F features, H hidden layers, M nodes in each hidden layer, and T targets there are

$$(F+1)M + M(M+1)(H-1) + (M+1)T$$

parameters in total. We used three hidden layers and 80 nodes per hidden layer. The number of parameters in the three and four feature models were therefore 13,361 and 13,441, respectively. The huge number of parameters compared with traditional models naturally leads to overfitting concerns. As we discuss later these concerns are addressed by dividing the data into a training set, validation set, and test set and choosing an appropriate stopping rule for the algorithm.

The weights and biases are chosen to minimize an objective function that captures the difference between the estimated target values for the training set and the actual values. Our application involves

[c]See Telgarsky (2016) for a discussion of this.

only one target (the change in implied volatility) and our objective function is the mean squared error between the estimated target and the actual target across all the options used for training.

The minimization is accomplished using a steepest descent algorithm. Initial values are assigned to the weights and biases. An iterative procedure is then carried out to improve the objective function by changing these parameters. On each iteration a partial derivative of the objective function is calculated with respect to each of the parameters. Each parameter is then reduced by the product of its partial derivative and a constant, referred to as the learning rate. The iterations are referred to as epochs.

For large data sets and models involving many parameters this procedure is made computationally feasible by a technique known as backpropagation. This was proposed by Rummelhart *et al.* [18] and involves working back through the layers calculating the required partial derivatives using the chain rule.

The vanilla gradient descent algorithm described above can sometimes be slow. To speed up the learning process, several variations have been developed. For example,

- *Mini-batch stochastic gradient descent.* This algorithm randomly splits the training data into small mini-batches. Instead of using the whole training data to calculate gradient, it updates model parameters based on the gradient calculated from a single batch with each of the mini-batches being used in turn. Because the algorithm estimates the gradient using a small sample of the training data, it is less computationally expensive and often leads to much faster learning.
- *Gradient descent with momentum.* This algorithm calculates gradient as an exponentially decaying moving average of past gradients. This approach helps to build up parameter update "velocity" in any direction that has a consistent gradient.
- *Gradient descent with adaptive learning rates.* A learning rate that is too small will result in many epochs being required to reach a reasonable result. A learning rate that is too high may lead to oscillations and a poor result. Different model parameters may benefit from different learning rates at different stages of training. Because choosing proper learning rates can be difficult, many algorithms try to automate the process. For example, RMSProp (Root

Mean Squared Propagation) and Adam (Adaptive Moment Estimation) are both popular adaptive learning rate algorithms that adjust learning rate at each iteration for each model parameter.

In this chapter, we use a mini-batch size of 512 and implement Adam methods with the parameters suggested in Kingma and Ba [19].[d]

In practice, the algorithms we have described are not used to fully minimize the loss function. This would be computationally quite time consuming. Also the nature of the algorithms and the large number of parameters used are such that as training increases more of the idiosyncrasies of the training data tend to be reflected in the model. A stopping rule is therefore specified both for computational efficiency and to avoid overfitting. We describe the stopping rule we used in Section 4.

3. Data

We used S&P 500 call options data from OptionMetrics between January 2010 and December 2017. The data for each option on each day includes the strike price, time to maturity, index level, and implied volatility, as well as hedge parameters such as delta, gamma, vega, and theta derived from the practitioner Black–Scholes model.

The data was filtered in a number of ways. We only retained options where the information provided was complete. Options with remaining lives less than 14 days were removed from the data set. Options for which the practitioner Black–Scholes delta was less than 0.05 or greater than 0.95 were removed from the data set. The data was then sorted to produce observations for the same option on two successive trading days. This resulted in about 2.07 million observations on daily volatility changes for 53,653 call options.

The three features we used in the first stage of this research are the S&P 500 daily change, time-to-maturity, and the practitioner Black–Scholes delta. There is one target, the implied volatility change. In the second stage we added the VIX index as a feature. A summary of

[d]Initial value of weights can also affect convergence speed. In our training, we apply the Glorot uniform initializer suggested by Glorot and Bengio (2010).

Table 1: Summary statistics of features and target.

	S&P 500 Daily Change (%)	Time-to-Maturity	Delta	VIX	Implied Volatility Change (%)
Mean	0.05	0.81	0.63	15.89	−0.06
Std	0.87	0.97	0.29	5.41	1.12
Min	−6.66	0.06	0.05	9.14	−45.30
Median	0.05	0.34	0.72	14.42	−0.01
Max	4.74	4.38	0.95	48.00	36.85

statistical properties of the features and target variables is provided in Table 1.

To apply the neural network technique, we randomly divided the data into a training set, a validation set, and test set, with a 7:2:1 ratio. We used the training set and the validation set to train and fine-tune the neural network model, and then evaluated the model performance with the test set. All results presented are those for the test set.

4. Model Selection Criteria

Key elements of a neural network model are the activation function, the number of layers and the number of nodes per layer. The activation functions f_i in equation (1) for $i \leq n$ are designed to distinguish between positive and negative signals. We considered four different activation functions that have been suggested in the literature: the sigmoid, the rectified linear unit (relu), the leaky relu, and the exponential linear unit. The functional forms are shown in Table 2. They all have attractive properties for backpropagation algorithms. For $i = n + 1$ the activation function is $f(x) = x$ so that a linear function relates values at the nodes on the final hidden layer to the target. (This is usual practice when a continuous variable is being estimated.) We present results for a model with three hidden layers and 80 nodes per layer. We found models with sigmoid activation functions generally perform better (lower mean squared errors) and we will therefore only present results from using the sigmoid activation function.

Table 2: Alternative activation functions. The value used for a in the leaky relu and exponential linear unit activation functions was 0.03.

Sigmoid	$f(x) = \dfrac{1}{1+e^{-x}}$
Relu	$f(x) = \max(x, 0)$
Leaky relu	$f(x) = \begin{cases} x & x \geq 0 \\ ax & x < 0 \end{cases}$
Exponential linear unit	$f(x) = \begin{cases} x & x \geq 0 \\ a(e^x - 1) & x < 0 \end{cases}$

To avoid overfitting, we experimented with a number of different early stopping rules. A common approach involves stopping when the mean square error for the validation set starts to trend up. For our data this happened only after a very large number of epochs if at all, a result which may be indicative of local overfitting.[e] In the end, we decided to use the smoothness of the predicted change in the volatility surface as our criterion. We manually inspected a three-dimensional plot of the volatility surface change as the number of epochs was increased and stopped when this was no longer smooth. This led to earlier stopping than that would be indicated by other rules. In both of the three-factor models and four-factor model we stopped after 4,000 epochs. The choice of the stopping rule did not affect the general shape of the volatility surface movements, but it did affect the smoothness of the results.

5. Results for Three-Feature Model

Hull and White [14] propose a simple analytic model for determining volatility surface movements. Their model is

$$E(\Delta\sigma_{\text{imp}}) = \frac{\Delta S}{S} \frac{a + b\delta_{\text{BS}} + c\delta_{\text{BS}}^2}{\sqrt{T}} \tag{2}$$

This model involves three parameters, a, b, and c, which can be estimated using linear regression. The best fit parameters for our data

[e]See for example Lawrence and Giles (2000).

Table 3: Parameters estimated for the analytic model in Equation (2) using training set and validation data sets: January 2010–December 2017. Time is measured in years and the implied volatility change is measured in decimal form.

Parameter	Value	t-statistic
a	−0.2329	−165.3
b	0.4176	66.5
c	−0.4892	−84.5

Table 4: Percentage gain of three-feature model over analytic model in Equation (2) for different index returns and different times to maturity.

Time to Maturity	Index Return				All
	<−1%	−1%–0	0–1%	>1%	
0–6 m	28.39	y3.65	1.07	26.13	11.48
6 m–1 yr	20.56	−1.42	−2.29	14.13	5.14
1 yr–2 yr	13.49	1.62	−1.69	15.94	4.52
>2 yr	11.12	2.02	3.23	7.54	4.23
All	26.76	3.28	0.98	25.09	10.72

are shown in Table 3. We use the model as a benchmark. Similar to Hull and White [14], we define the Gain from using Model A rather than Model B as

$$\text{Gain} = 1 - \frac{SSE[\text{Model A}]}{SSE[\text{Model B}]} \tag{3}$$

where SSE denotes sum of squared errors.

The gain from using the three-feature machine learning model rather than the analytic model was 10.72%. The mean squared error for the test set was 0.0000984 (with implied volatilities measured as decimals). To investigate the sources of the gain we calculated the gain given by the three-feature model for a number of different subsets of the data. Our results are summarized in Table 4. This shows that the gain is greatest for (a) situations when the index return is higher than +1% or lower than −1% and (b) short maturity options.

Table 5: Expected daily changes in volatility given by the analytic model in Equation (2) for options with different moneyness and time to maturity. Volatility is measured in basis points per year. Moneyness is measured by the practitioner Black–Scholes delta. The table considers scenarios where the daily return on the index is (a) −1.25%, (b) +1.25%.

Index Return = −1.25%					Index Return = +1.25%				
B-S	Time to Maturity				B-S	Time to Maturity			
Delta	3 m	6 m	1 yr	1.5 yr	Delta	3 m	6 m	1 yr	1.5 yr
0.1	49	35	25	20	0.1	−49	−35	−25	−20
0.3	38	27	19	15	0.3	−38	−27	−19	−15
0.5	37	26	18	15	0.5	−37	−26	−18	−15
0.7	45	32	23	18	0.7	−45	−32	−23	−18
0.9	63	45	32	26	0.9	−63	−45	−32	−26

Table 6: Expected daily volatility changes given by three-feature model for options with different moneyness and time to maturity. Volatility is measured in basis points per year. Moneyness is measured by the practitioner Black–Scholes delta. The table considers scenarios where the daily return on the index is (a) −1.25%, (b) +1.25%.

Index Return = −1.25%					Index Return = +1.25%				
B-S	Time to Maturity				B-S	Time to Maturity			
Delta	3 m	6 m	1 yr	1.5 yr	Delta	3 m	6 m	1 yr	1.5 yr
0.1	33	23	16	6	0.1	−54	−42	−36	−28
0.3	18	14	10	8	0.3	−41	−32	−25	−25
0.5	17	14	8	6	0.5	−39	−32	−24	−23
0.7	20	16	9	9	0.7	−43	−36	−25	−20
0.9	29	21	9	8	0.9	−62	−43	−26	−14

Tables 5 and 6 show the volatility changes predicted by the analytic model in Equation (2) and the three-feature model for index returns of −1.25% and +1.25%. Plots of the volatility surface changes are in Figure 2. As might be expected, the results from the two models are similar. The volatility surface moves up when the return is negative and moves down when the return is positive. The change decreases as the time to maturity increases and is greatest for low-delta and high-delta options.

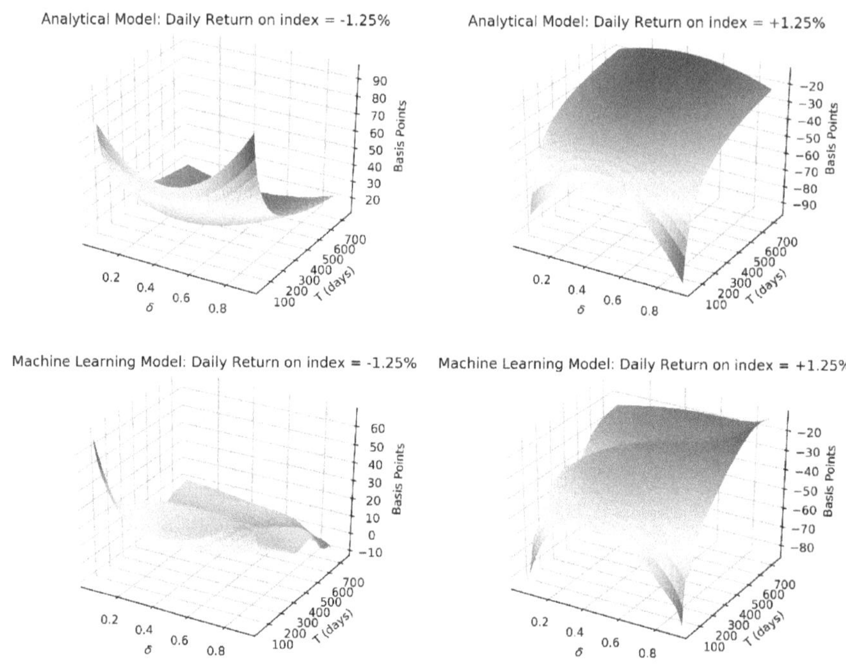

Figure 2: Expected change in implied volatility for analytical and machine learning 3-feature model.

The analytic model in Equation (1) is linear in the return. The impact of a gain of $X\%$ on a particular option's implied volatility is equal and opposite to that of a gain of $-X\%$. The same is not true for the three-feature neural network model. The reduction in implied volatilities arising from a daily return of 1.25% is on average about twice as great the increase in implied volatilities arising from a daily return of -1.25%. The change in the implied volatility predicted by the analytic model is too high for large negative returns and too low for large positive returns. This nonlinearity suggests that the gamma, as well as the delta of a portfolio, may be affected by volatility uncertainty.

6. Results for Four-Feature Model

The four-feature model is designed to test whether the behavior of the volatility surface in high volatility environments is different from

Table 7: Percentage gain of four-feature model over three-feature model for different index returns and different times to maturity.

	Index Return				
VIX Index	$< -1\%$	-1%–0%	0%–1%	>1%	All
<=13%	85.00	52.26	53.69	89.23	55.23
13%–19%	67.73	51.34	46.64	70.17	53.41
>=19%	80.01	72.09	69.69	86.02	78.78
All	77.01	55.49	53.41	80.80	62.12

that in low volatility environments. The fourth feature is the value of the VIX index on the day before the index return and volatility change are observed. With a mean squared error of 0.0000372 for the test set, the four-feature model produces a gain of 62.12% over the three-feature model. Table 7 shows the gain as a function of the VIX index and the index return. It shows that the gain is greatest for high and low values of the index return and high and low values of the VIX.

Table 8 shows the expected changes in the volatility given by the four-feature model when the index return is +1.25% and −1.25%, and the VIX has values of 13% and 16%. Figure 3 shows corresponding charts. It is interesting to note that, when the VIX is low (13%) and there is a big increase in the index (+1.25%), all points on the volatility surface increase. This is quite different behavior from the average shown in Table 6. As with most of our other results, this one is most marked for high delta short maturity options. Table 6 shows that the expected change in the implied volatility of a three-month option with a delta of 0.9 is −62 basis points when the index return is +1.25%. Conditional on a low VIX index of 13% this change is 84 basis points, over 146 basis points greater. Presumably a high index return in a low volatility environment is seen as signal of high future volatilities.

Our results show that the VIX index and the return on the index interact in a way that makes the basic Hull–White three-parameter model at best an incomplete description of volatility surface movements. We illustrate this in Table 9 which shows the Hull–White parameters for different ranges of the index return and the VIX index. The parameters a can be viewed as an indicator

Table 8: Expected daily volatility changes given by four-feature model for options with different moneyness and time to maturity. Volatility is measured in basis points per year. Moneyness is measured by the practitioner Black–Scholes delta. The table considers scenarios where the daily return on the index is −1.25% and +1.25%, and the VIX index is 13%, 16%.

Index Return = −1.25%; VIX = 13%

B-S Delta	Time to Maturity 3 m	6 m	1 yr	1.5 yr
0.1	41	25	12	5
0.3	21	14	9	5
0.5	16	8	3	2
0.7	15	6	1	1
0.9	13	−1	−10	−11

Index Return = +1.25%; VIX = 13%

B-S Delta	Time to Maturity 3 m	6 m	1 yr	1.5 yr
0.1	4	1	0	1
0.3	16	11	6	5
0.5	26	18	12	8
0.7	37	25	16	12
0.9	84	62	45	35

Index Return = −1.25%; VIX = 16%

B-S Delta	Time to Maturity 3 m	6 m	1 yr	1.5 yr
0.1	41	30	20	14
0.3	36	28	20	15
0.5	34	26	20	16
0.7	34	25	21	18
0.9	46	32	28	29

Index Return = +1.25%; VIX = 16%

B-S Delta	Time to Maturity 3 m	6 m	1 yr	1.5 yr
0.1	−88	−58	−33	−24
0.3	−76	−49	−27	−19
0.5	−72	−47	−27	−19
0.7	−88	−59	−37	−27
0.9	−188	−114	−59	−38

of the size of volatility surface movements for low delta options. A negative value of a indicates that positive returns lead to negative volatility surface movements and vice versa. It can be seen that for returns less than −1%, a is approximately the same regardless of the VIX index. For returns greater than −1%, the values of a indicate that the magnitude of the low-delta volatility movements increases as VIX increases. For values of the VIX less than 19, the magnitude of low-delta volatility surface movements decreases as the index return increases. When VIX is low and the return is highly positive, a is positive indicating the volatility surface moves in the opposite direction to that normally expected for a positive return. This is consistent with our ANN result mentioned above.

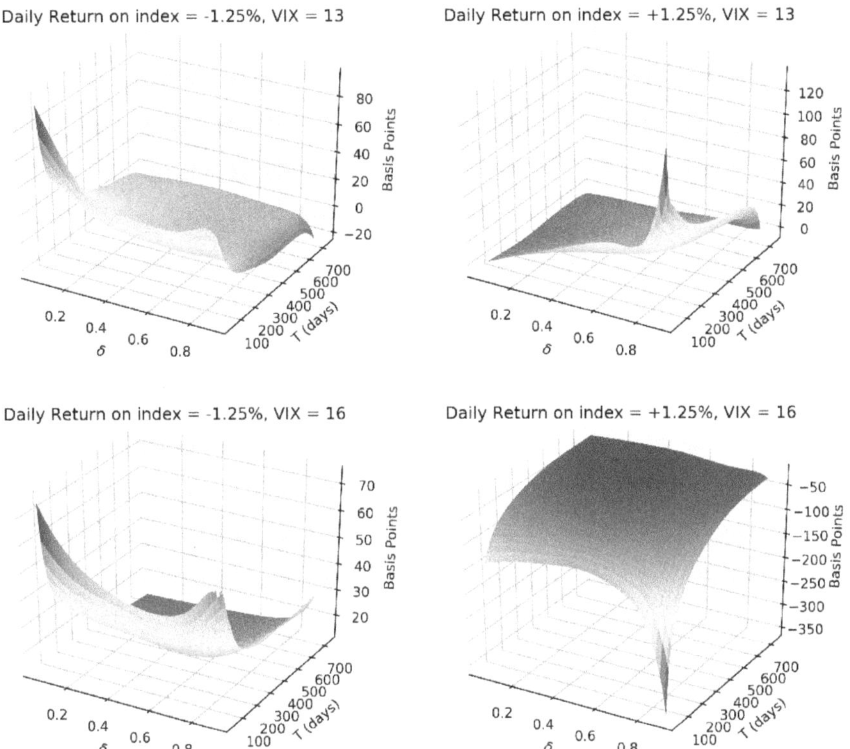

Figure 3: Expected change of implied volatility surface for 4-feature machine learning model.

The parameter b can be interpreted as the slope of the implied volatility as a function of delta for low delta options. It can be seen that this slope is always positive and tends to increase as the VIX index increases and the index return increases. The parameter c measures the extent the curvature of the relationship between implied volatility and delta (see Figures 2 and 3). As in the case of the low-delta slope, this is greatest in situations where the VIX index is high and the index return is high.

As mentioned earlier, one application of this research is to minimum variance delta hedging. The Hull–White model sets the minimum variance delta as

$$\delta_{\mathrm{BS}} + \frac{v_{\mathrm{BS}}}{S\sqrt{T}}(a + b\delta_{\mathrm{BS}} + c\delta_{\mathrm{BS}}^2)$$

Table 9: Regression parameters under different market scenarios. Time is measured in years and the implied volatility change is measured in decimal form.

	VIX ≤ 13			$13 <$ VIX < 19			VIX ≥ 19		
Index Return	a	b	c	a	b	c	a	b	c
$\leq -1\%$	−0.269	0.297	−0.357	−0.228	0.233	−0.137	−0.280	0.476	−0.508
$-1\% \pm 1\%$	−0.133	0.297	−0.282	−0.208	0.407	−0.394	−0.291	0.556	−0.631
$\geq +1\%$	0.008	0.370	−0.357	−0.191	0.466	−0.540	−0.277	0.737	−1.033
All	−0.156	0.275	−0.278	−0.208	0.358	−0.343	−0.274	0.572	−0.730

where $\delta_{\rm BS}$ and $v_{\rm BS}$ are the delta and vega parameters calculated from the practitioner Black–Scholes model, S is the index level, and T is the time to maturity. It is clear from our research that the current level of the VIX, which is not included in the Hull–White model, has a bearing on volatility movements and therefore on the minimum variance delta. A potential simple improvement on the Hull–White model is to use the final row in Table 9 to adjust the a, b, and c parameters according to the level of the VIX index. For example, for an option with a delta of 0.5, the table indicates that the delta adjustment when the VIX is greater than 19 is 48% higher than when the VIX is in the 13–19 range, and this is 30% greater than when the VIX is less than 13.

7. Conclusions

Machine learning is usually used as a prediction tool. The values of features observed prior to time t are used to predict target values at or after time t. In this chapter, we show how machine learning can be used to explore a nonlinear relationship between variables. We consider the relationship between the change in the S&P 500 index and the contemporaneous change in the implied volatility of an option on the index as a function of option's maturity and its moneyness. Our results are generally supportive of the negative correlation between the implied volatilities and asset returns that has been documented in the literature and is discussed in the introduction. However, we do find one notable exception. When volatilities are low and the index return is particularly high there is a tendency for volatilities to increase.

The use of a three feature neural network model refines the expected volatility change estimates produced by Hull and White [14]. The difference between the two models is most marked for high-delta short-maturity options and when extreme positive or negative returns are observed. The Hull–White model tends to understate the impact of large positive returns and overstate the impact of large negative returns.

Volatility surface movements depend on the initial level of volatility. We demonstrated this by including the level of the VIX index on Day $t-1$ as a feature to determine expected volatility surface changes between Day $t-1$ and Day t. It is normally the case that the whole volatility surface moves up when the index declines and moves down when the index increases. As mentioned, we have shown that this is not necessarily what happens when there is a large positive return in the index. When the large positive return occurs in an environment where volatilities were (prior to the return being observed) low, the movement in the volatility surface is the opposite of that normally associated with a positive return. For example, when the VIX is 13% and a +1.25% index return occurs, the expected changes in implied volatilities are mostly positive. When the VIX is a more normal 16% the expected changes are highly negative. The changes are most marked for high-delta short-maturity options.

This research assumed a stationary model. When we tested the model on the most recent 10% of the data it performed slightly less well than on a test set which was randomly chosen from our complete data set. A possible area for further research is to extend our model to one where the time sequence of the data is taken into account. This could be done using a recurrent neural network where Equation (1) is modified so that $v_{i,j}$ depends on the previous day's estimates as well as on the current day's values at the immediately preceding nodes. The long short-term memory approach of Hochreiter and Schmidhuber [20] could also be used.

Another possible extension of our research would be to train a model on the errors in an analytic model such as Hull and White [14] rather than on the movements in the volatility surface itself. This is analogous to a widely used machine learning method known as gradient boosting where there are a sequence of predictors each one trying to correct the errors of the previous one.

Acknowledgments

We would like to thank Peter Christoffersen who, before his untimely death in mid-2018, provided the inspiration for this paper. We also thank the Rotman Financial Innovation Hub (FinHub) and the Global Risk Institute in Financial Services for support.

References

[1] Black, F. (1976). Studies of stock price volatility changes, *Proceedings of the Business and Economics Section of the American Statistical Association*, 177–181.

[2] Christie, A. (1982). The stochastic behavior of common stock variances: Value, leverage, and interest rate effects, *Journal of Financial Economics*, 10, 407–432.

[3] Cheung, Y.-W. and Ng, L. (1992). Stock price dynamics and firm size: An empirical investigation, *Journal of Finance*, 47, 1985–1997.

[4] Duffee, G. (1995). Stock returns and volatility: A firm level analysis, *Journal of Financial Economics*, 37, 399–420.

[5] Cont, R. and da Fonseca, J. (2002). Dynamics of implied volatility surfaces, *Quantum Finance*, 2, 45–60.

[6] Poulsen, R., Schenk-Hoppé, K.R., and Ewald, C.-O. (2009). Risk minimization in stochastic volatility models: Model risk and empirical performance, *Quantum Finance*, 9, 693–704.

[7] French, K.R., Schwert, G.W., and Stambaugh, R.F. (1987). Expected stock returns and volatility, *Journal of Financial Economics*, 19, 3–29.

[8] Campbell, J.Y. and Hentschel, L. (1992). No news is good news: An asymmetric model of changing volatility in stock returns, *Journal of Financial Economics*, 31, 281–331.

[9] Bekaert, G. and Wu, G. (2000). Asymmetric volatility and risk in equity markets, *The Review of Financial Studies*, 13, 1–42.

[10] Bollerslev, T., Litvinova, J., and Tauchen, G. (2006). Leverage and volatility feedback effects in high-frequency data, *Journal of Financial Econometrics*, 4, 353–384.

[11] Hens, T. and Steude, S.C. (2009). The leverage effect without leverage, *Finance Research Letters*, 6, 83–94.

[12] Hasanhodzic, J. and Lo, A. (2013). Black's leverage effect is not due to leverage, Working Paper, MIT.

[13] Nian, K., Coleman, T.F., and Li, Y. (2018). Learning minimum variance discrete hedging directly from the market, *Quantum Finance*, 18, 1115–1128.

[14] Hull, J. and White, A. (2017). Optimal delta hedging for options, *Journal of Banking Finance*, 82, 180–190.

[15] McCulloch, W. and Pitts, W. (1943). A logical calculus of ideas in nervous activity, *Bulletin of Mathematical Biophysics*, 5, 115–133.

[16] Hull, J., *Machine Learning in Business: An Introduction to the World of Data Science*, www-2.rotman.utoronto.ca/~hull/mlbook.

[17] Hornik, K. (1991). Approximation capabilities of multilayer feedforward networks, *Neural Networks*, 4, 251–257.

[18] Rummelhart, G., Hinton, G., and Williams, R. (1986). Learning internal representations by error propagation, *Nature*, 323, 533–536.

[19] Kingma, D.P. and Ba, L.J. (2017). Adam: A method for stochastic optimization, *3rd International Conference on Learning Representations, ICLR 2015*. Available online at https://arxiv.org/pdf/1412.6980.pdf. Last accessed January 8, 2019.

[20] Hochreiter S. and Schmidhuber, J. (1997). Long short-term memory, *Neural Computation*, 9(8), 1735–1780.

[21] Culkin, R. and Das, S.R. (2017). Machine learning in finance: The case of deep learning for option pricing, *Journal of Investment Management*, 15, 92–100.

[22] Glorot, X. and Bengio, Y. (2010). Understanding the difficulty of training deep feed forward neural networks. Available online at http://proceedings.mlr.press/v9/glorot10a/glorot10a.pdf. Last accessed January 8, 2019.

[23] Hutchison, J.M., Lo, A.W., and Poggio, T. (1994). A nonparametric approach to pricing and hedging derivative securities via learning networks, *Journal of Finance*, 49, 851–889.

[24] Lawrence, S. and Giles, C.L. (2000). Overfitting and neural networks: Conjugate gradient and backpropagation, *Proceedings of International Joint Conference on Neural Networks, Como, Italy, IEEE Computer Society*, Los Alamitos, CA, 114–119.

[25] Telgarsky, M. (2016). Benefits of depth in neural networks, *JMLR: Workshop and Conference Proceedings*, 49, 1–23.

https://doi.org/10.1142/9789811259142_0014

Chapter 14

Modeling Volatility Risk in Equity Options Market: A Statistical Approach

D. Dobi[*,‡] **and M. Avellaneda**[*,†,§]

[*]*Courant Institute of Mathematical Sciences, 251 Mercer Street, New York*

[†]*Finance Concepts SARL, 49-51 Avenue Victor-Hugo, Paris, France*

[‡]*doris.dobi@gmail.com*

[§]*Deceased*

Abstract

This chapter provides a cross-sectional analysis of US option markets based on implied volatility data from August 2004 to August 2013. We analyse the implied volatility surface (IVS) for each security in the OptionMetrics database. We use implied volatility data across 13 deltas and four expiration dates. Employing methods from principal component analysis (PCA), and results from random matrix theory (RMT), we identify the significant eigenvalues of the correlation matrix of implied volatilities and conclude that, usually, three principal components suffice to reproduce the IVS. In this way we reduce dimensionality of the options market without loosing meaningful information. From this analysis we classify equities into those carrying mostly "systemic" risk and into those carrying mostly "idiosyncratic" risk.

Based on the PCA results, we formulate a model which can be used to describe the dynamics of the *joint statistics* of the IVS of all US options, yet is compact and computationally feasible. Using 9 volatility points to represents each IVS, the model offers significant dimension reduction for each asset as well as for all assets in aggregate.

We conclude with a PCA study of the correlation matrix of the entire cross-section equities and options market.[a] We find that the the number of significant factors driving the US equities and options market are as follow:

1. Equities in SPX: **15** significant factors (account for 55% of variance, out of an initial 440 variables).
2. Equities and options with underlying in SPX: **84** significant factors (account for 55% of variance, out of an initial 4400 variables).
3. Equities in OptionMetrics: **20** significant factors (account for 24% of variance, out of an initial 3,141 variables).
4. All equities and options with underlying asset in OptionMetrics: **108** significant factors (account for 50% of variance, out of an initial 31,410 variables).

Keywords: Implied volatility surface, principal component, principal component analysis, random matric theory, options market, correlation matrix, systemic risk, idiosyncratic risk, computationally feasible, dimension reduction, significant factors, spectrum, convexity, MP-threshold, signal, noise, significant, empirical density.

1. Introduction

There have been many studies which seek to classify the "number of factors" needed to econometrically model the market [3,4,6,10]. Principal component analysis of correlation matrices shows that around 15 components can be used to capture the vast majority of systemic movement in the equity market. These 15 factors account for 55% of the variation in returns. This represents dramatic dimensional reduction, and is the analogue for equities of Litterman and Scheinkman [10] who find that 82% of the variation in returns of all Treasury bond correlations can be explained in terms of only three factors (or principal components).

On the other hand, not as much work has been done on classifying factors underlying option returns. Avellaneda and Cont [1], Carmona and Nadtochiy [5], Cont and Fonseca [6], Dupire [7], and Schweizer and Wissel [12] are among some of the researchers who delve into this topic. Cont and Fonseca [6] find that the variance in returns of the correlation matrix of implied volatility of DAX options can be explained by roughly three principal components.

[a] As made available by the OptionMetrics database.

In this chapter, we show that the implied volatility surface (IVS) of most equity option contracts can be described using four principal components, and usually three components suffice. We suggest that the size of the leading eigenvalue can be used to characterize the type of risk intrinsic to options on a specific underlying asset. Furthermore, we propose a parsimonious framework which can be used to reproduce the IVS of any option.

In order to better understand the volatility of option positions, we classify options into those that carry mostly systemic risk and into those that carry mostly idiosyncratic risk. Systemic risk gives an indication of exposure to or vulnerability to aggregate market risk. Idiosyncratic risk, on the other hand, measures underlying-asset-specific risk, or the risk tied with the specific nature of the underlying and uncorrelated to overall-market risk. Idiosyncratic risk can be thought of as corresponding to corporate events, such as takeovers, company-specific news releases, earnings, and so forth. Small cap companies, new issues, and thinly traded companies usually carry idiosyncratic risk, whereas large caps, blue chips and broadly traded stocks are more indicative of systemic risk.

We propose to analyse the volatility risk of options by studying the fluctuations of the IVS. Due to the fact that there are many available strikes and expiration dates for a given option contract, the option market is considerably larger than the equities market. Original data on the options market is 130 times bigger than that of the equities market.[b]

We characterize the significant part of the spectrum[c] of IVS fluctuations using principal component analysis (PCA) and results from random matrix theory (RMT). We standardize the data by looking as the correlation matrix of implied volatility returns. Studying the distribution of the resulting eigenvalues allows us to classify an asset according to the type of risk it carries. We find that the leading eigenvalue of the correlation matrix plays a critical role in our classification scheme.

We propose various dimensionality-reducing models for replicating the IVS. We refer to these models as pivot models to indicate

[b]As made available by the OptionMetrics database. In our statistical analysis we use 52 of these 130 points to generate the original IVS; see below.

[c]Defined here as the set of all eigenvalues.

the use of a few implied volatility returns (the pivots) in generating the entire IVS via linear interpolation. We keep in mind certain constraints any such model must adhere to; the most crucial being efficiency in the number of pivots used. In particular, our pivot model must reduce dimensionality, and abide by limitations in computing power and resources.

To measure the quality of each model, we test how well each pivot scheme preserves the spectrum of the original correlation matrix. In addition, we also compare how well the replicated data preserves original risk classification. Both of these tests are used to determine how well the interpolated IVS replicates the original IVS.

Our work shows that if we use 9-pivots to generate the IVS, we get excellent results while offering very significant dimensionality reduction of over 14 times the original data size. This 9 pivot model provides a firm basis for a risk-management system for portfolios of options. Based on these results, we perform a PCA of the correlation matrix of the entire equities and equity options market. The dimensionality reduction gained from the 9 pivot model makes large PCA computations feasible on the market as a whole.

We conclude by determining the number of significant components in the entire options and equity markets. In order to accomplish this, we employ the Marchenko–Pastur distribution and the Tracy–Widom law from RMT [3,4,9,13]. Results are given in the last section.

2. Principal Component Analysis of the Correlation Matrix of the Implied Volatility Surfaces

Consider the IVS for SPX given in Figure 1, clearly the implied volatility surface is not constant in neither strike (K) nor maturity (T). Furthermore, the (IVS) fluctuates; it is precisely this feature of the IVS that is crucial in managing the risk of a portfolio of options (see Figure 2).

We use empirical results as a stepping stone for better understanding the behavior of implied volatility. We begin by extracting the first four principal components of the correlation matrix of the IVS for SPX where we couple the implied volatility with the underlying asset.

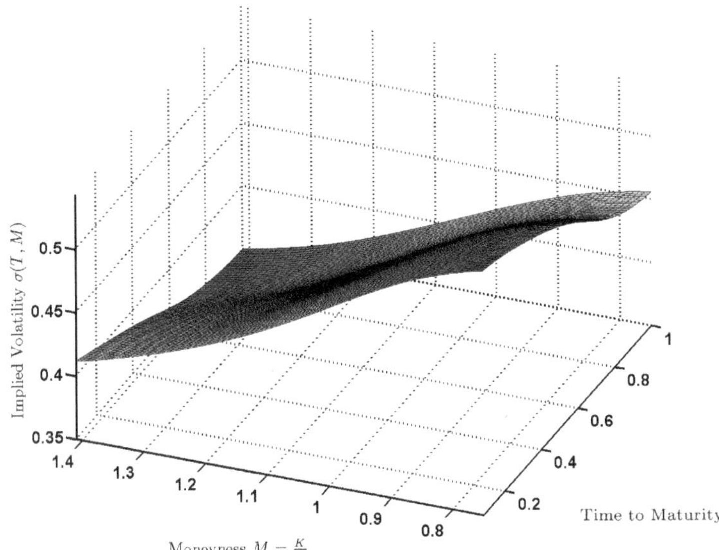

Figure 1: Implied volatility surface for SPX using call options, December 12, 2008.

There are 130 available[d] implied volatilities across each of the 10 maturities $\in \{30, 60, 91, 122, 152, 182, 273, 365, 547, 730\}$ and each of the 13 deltas $\in \{20, 25, \ldots, 75, 80\}$. For our analysis, we use a subset of 52 of these 130 points: the implied volatility return[e] across each of the 4 maturities $\in \{30, 60, 91, 182\}$ and across all 13 available deltas $\in \{20, 25, \ldots, 75, 80\}$.[f] This choice is somewhat arbitrary and is made to reduce computation while preserving available information. Figure 3 depicts this selection. The data matrix on which the correlation matrix is computed is constructed as follows: our first variable (i.e., the first column) is the underlying stock returns and each subsequent variable (i.e., each subsequent column) is one of the 52 implied volatility returns.[g]

[d]Via OptionMetrics.

[e]We use log-returns in order to standardize and compare across different implied volatilities.

[f]In percentage terms, as these are hedge deltas.

[g]As a reminder, the implied volatility returns are computed for a specific call option contract for each given day in our sample.

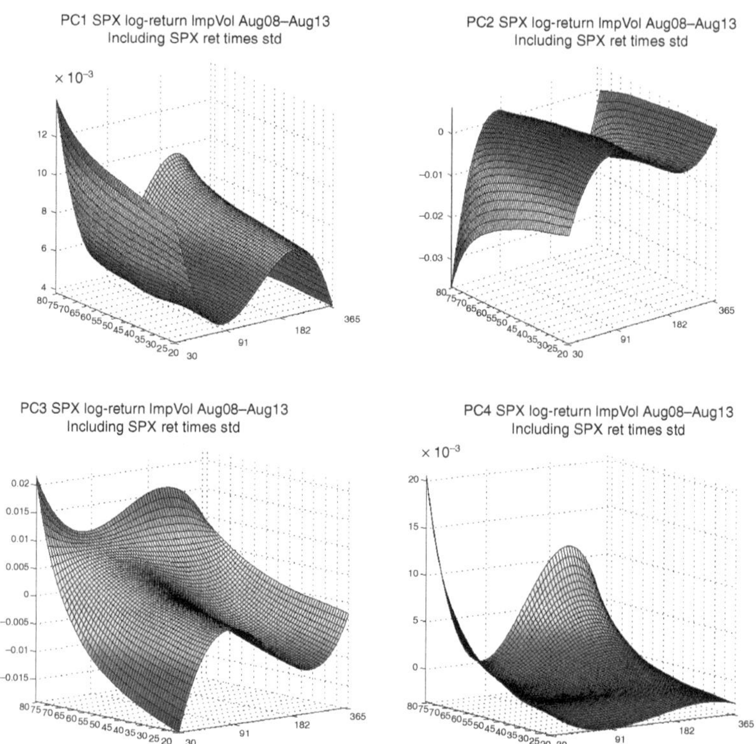

Figure 2: Results based on PCA decomposition of the correlation matrix of log-returns of SPX coupled with the log-returns of the implied volatilities for SPX call options. Displayed are the first four principal components which account for roughly 94%, 3%, 2%, and 7% of the variation of the implied volatility surface for SPX respectively. The z-axis represents implied volatility, and $30, 91, 182, 365$ represent the time to expiry. Time period dates from August 31, 2008 until August 31, 2013.

From the principal components we seek to determine how the IVS changes in time. For example, we see that the first principal component usually explains about 90% of the variation in the IVS, and is usually "flat": this tells us that around 90% of the change in the shape of the IVS is due to a parallel shift of the entire surface.

The second and third components are either flat and very similar to the first component, or they exhibit time-skew and/or delta-skew, in which case the remaining change in the shape of the surface is attributed to skew. The fourth component exhibits a convexity-effect and usually has very little explanatory power for how the surface varies, but is nonetheless included for completeness. See the appendix

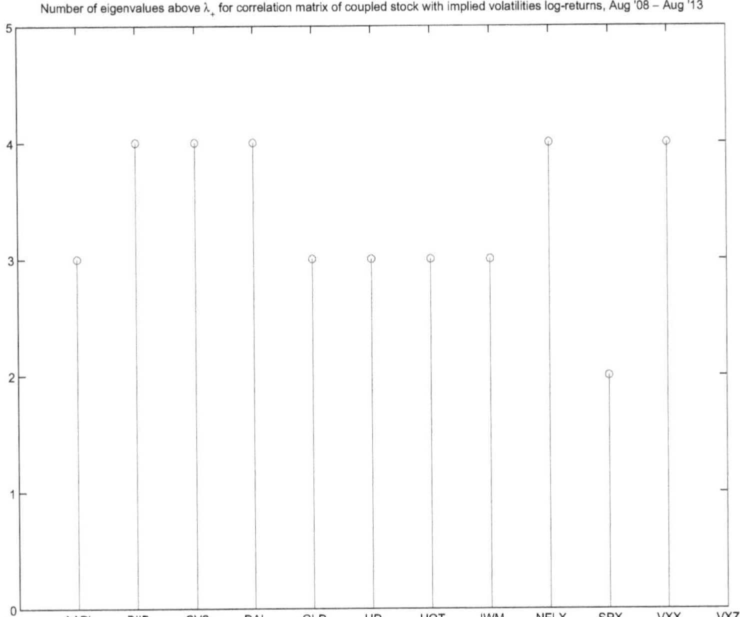

Figure 3: Results indicate that around three or four of the top eigenvalues are usually significant as determined by exceeding the MP-threshold λ_+. By projecting along these corresponding eigenvectors we may distinguish signal from noise in the correlation matrix.

for some additional examples of top principal component surfaces for various major underlying assets.

3. Implied Volatility Surfaces and Random Matrix Theory

Let X denote an $M \times N$ random matrix whose entries are i.i.d. with mean 0 and variance $\sigma^2 < \infty$. Denote the correlation matrix and the spectrum (viewed as random variables) by:

$$Y_N = \frac{1}{N} X X' \quad \text{and} \quad \{\lambda_1, \lambda_2, \ldots, \lambda_m\}.$$

Consider the density of states (DOS):

$$d\mu_M(A) := \frac{1}{M} \#\{\lambda_j \in A\}, A \subset \mathbb{R}.$$

We will make use of

Proposition 1 (Marchenko–Pastur (MP) distribution). *Assume* $M, N \to \infty$ *s.t.* $\frac{M}{N} \to \Lambda \in (0, \infty)$. *Then* $d\mu_M \to d\mu_\Lambda$ *in distribution, where* $d\mu_\Lambda$ *is the MP distribution with parameter* Λ. *It is the probability measure on* $[0, \infty]$, *given by the density*

$$d\mu_\Lambda(x) := \frac{1}{2\pi x \Lambda}\sqrt{(\lambda_+ - x)(x - \lambda_-)}\mathbb{1}_{[\lambda_-, \lambda_+]}.$$

With an additional point mass of $(1 - \frac{1}{\Lambda})$ *at* 0 *for* $\Lambda > 1$.

We define the *MP-threshold* to be the upper bound λ_+: $(1 + \sqrt{\frac{N}{T}})^2$. From our analysis, $N = 53$ for the number of variables we use (1 for the underlying asset, and 52 implied volatility returns), and $T =$ max (asset creation date, August 2004). We normalize variance across each implied volatility series to 1.

We observe that the vast majority of the variation in the IVS is explained by the first three or four principal components (Figures 4 and 5). An application of RMT in the style of Bouchaud and Potters [2] confirms these results.

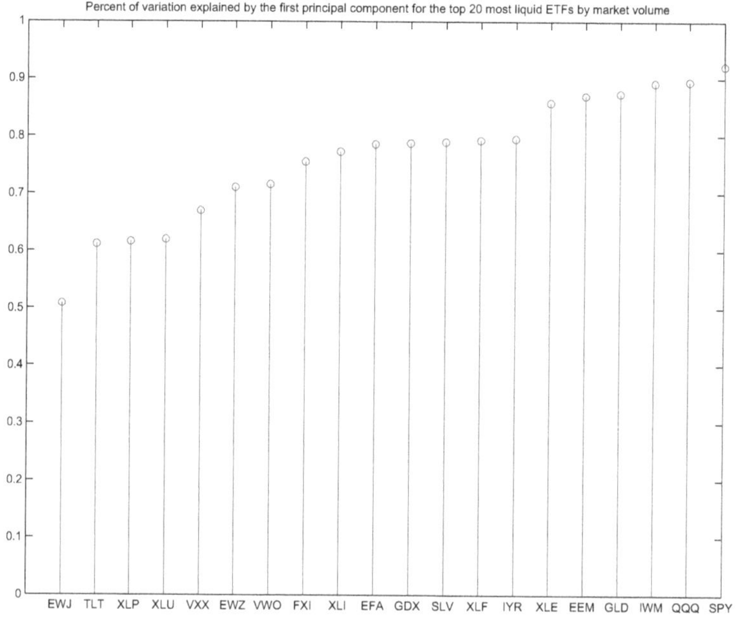

Figure 4: Percent of variation explained by the first component for the 20 most liquid ETFs listed. Data from August 2004 (or creation of asset) until August 2013 in order of increasing systemic risk.

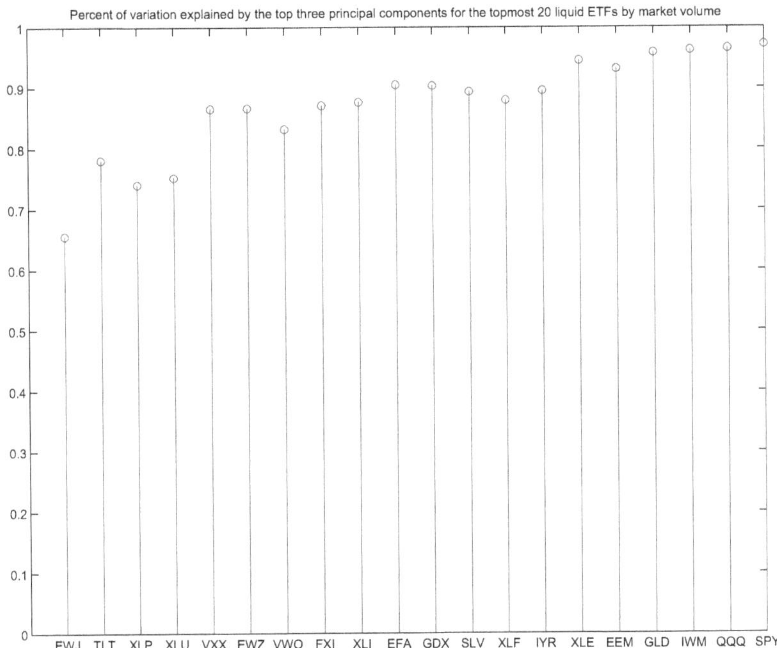

Figure 5: Percent of variation explained by the first three components for the 20 most liquid ETFs. Data from August 2004 (or creation of asset) until August 2013.

All eigenvalues greater than the MP-threshold λ_+ will be referred to as *significant*. These eigenvalues give us information about the true correlation matrix of the market[h] and hence are useful in separating signal from noise. In our study, we find that across all IVSs[i] studied usually three or four of the eigenvalues and their corresponding eigenvectors lie above of their corresponding MP upper bound.

As further support that we can use the MP distribution as an indicator of where to separate noise from signal, i.e., that the underlying assumptions of the MP-distribution hold for our empirical data, we perform the following experiment:

1. For each option in OptionMetrics we generate a random matrix R with the same underlying distribution as the empirical data by permuting the time-series for each of the 53-variables.

[h]Please refer to the Bouchaud and Potters [3] for a more detailed description.
[i]As made available by the OptionsMetrics database.

2. We compute the correlation matrix C of R, and compute the spectrum of C.
3. We compute the empirical CDF $F_n(x) := \frac{1}{n}\sum_{i=1}^{n}(\mathbf{1}_{X_i \leq x})$ where X_i represents the ith eigenvalue. For us, $n = 53$.
4. Using the Kolmogorv–Smirnov test, we calculate the test statistic

$$D_n = \sqrt{n}\sup_x |F_n(x) - \mathrm{CMP}(x)|,$$

where $\mathrm{CMP}(x)$ the cumulative MP distribution.

Using this framework, we test the null hypothesis that the empirical data is generated from the corresponding MP-distribution. We find that for 98% of the option contracts in OptionMetrics we cannot reject the null hypothesis at the 1% significance level. In addition, we find that for 100% of the option contracts with an underlying in SPX we cannot reject the null hypothesis at the 1% significance level. Thus, we can apply MP to matrices with the same underlying distribution as our empirical data. Below we include the number of eigenvalues exceeding the MP-threshold for various major underlying assets.

4. Classification of Optionable Stocks into "Systemic" and "Idiosyncratic"

In Figure 6, we display the percent of variation explained by the first principal component for the top 20 most liquid ETFs, where liquidity is measured as average daily volume traded. The percent variation explained by the first three components is given in Figure 7 for these same ETFs. We can see that for the majority of these ETFs the percent explained by the first three eigenvectors is above 90. The first eigenvalue is also shown, and it usually accounts for between 70% and 90% of variation.

In addition, we determine the number of eigenvalues (before normalization) which exceed the MP threshold in Figure 8. We display the results below. From this analysis, we find that the majority of the ETFs have around three or four eigenvalues which exceed the MP threshold; again confirming that the topmost three eigenvalues can be used to separate signal from noise in the correlation matrix.

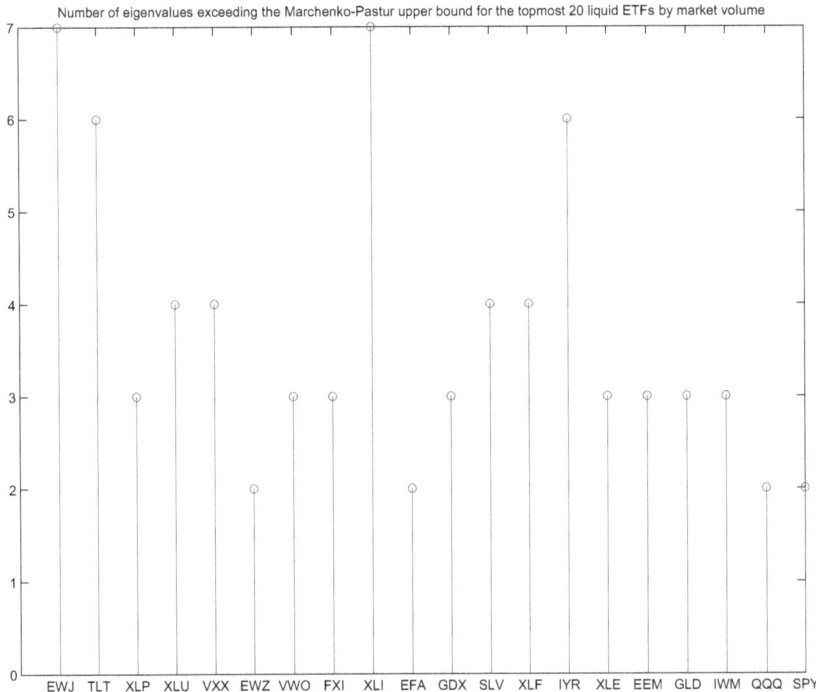

Figure 6: Number of eigenvalues exceeding the MP upper limit of the spectrum for the 20 most liquid ETFs.

We've proposed using the magnitude of the leading eigenvalue as an indicator of the equity's exposure to systemic risk. The higher the principal eigenvalue, the stronger the *level effect* in describing the movement of the IVS. This effect can be interpreted as a roughly equal change across all volatility products, indicating systemic risk. On the other side, the magnitude of the second and third eigenvalues indicates idiosyncratic risk. These eigenvalues capture non-uniform movements in the IVS, i.e., the "volatility" of skew in the IVS.

It is interesting to see whether the eigenvalues are correlated to other properties of the stocks such as average daily volume traded,[j] to the daily volatility of the stock, or to the correlation of the individual stock to the index itself (i.e., the market index). We present the results of these inquiries for the constituents of S&P 500 in Table 1.

[j]All data is computed from August 2004 to August 2013 on a daily basis.

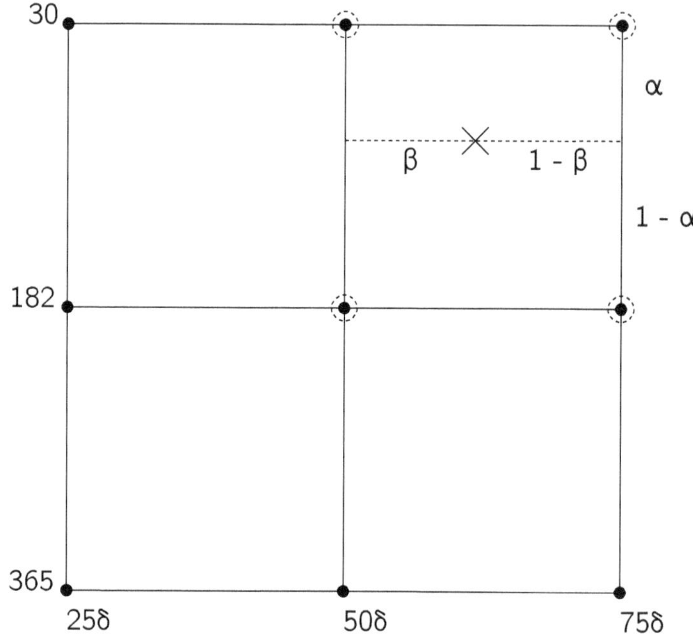

Figure 7: Example schema of linear interpolation amongst the pivots via projection onto δ-space and time-to-expiration-space. In this schema we use 9 pivots, and the point we wish to replicate is denoted by an X.

Table 1: Correlation Matrix of the constituents of the S&P 500.

EV1	EV2	EV3	EV4	# > MP	Volatility	Corr. to Matrix	Volume
1.00	−0.77	−0.85	−0.94	−0.89	0.26	0.15	0.33
−0.77	1.00	0.72	0.74	0.62	−0.15	−0.25	−0.17
−0.85	0.72	1.00	0.81	0.72	−0.29	−0.17	−0.25
−0.94	0.74	0.81	1.00	0.88	−0.22	−0.16	−0.24
−0.89	0.62	0.72	0.88	1.00	−0.23	−0.00	−0.26
0.26	−0.15	−0.29	−0.22	−0.23	1.00	−0.00	0.04
0.15	−0.25	−0.17	−0.16	−0.00	−0.00	1.00	−0.03
0.33	−0.17	−0.25	−0.24	−0.26	0.04	−0.03	1.00

From the correlations matrix we see that there is a strong negative correlation between the first eigenvalue with the second and the third eigenvalues, and a very strong negative correlation with the fourth eigenvalue. These results can be explained by the fact that the sum of

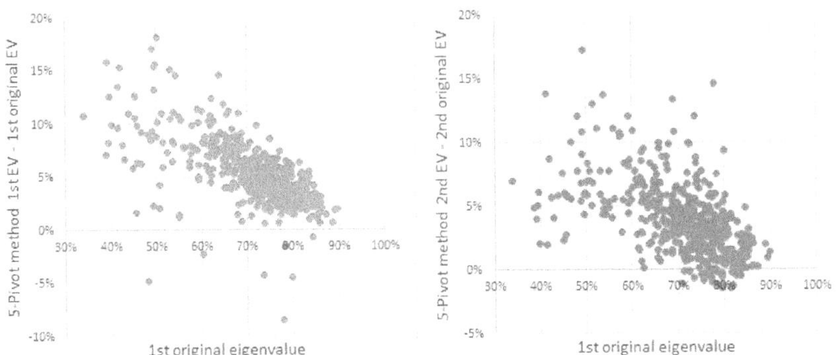

Figure 8: Difference between the top two eigenvalues of the 5 pivot model and those of the original spectra. The x-axis is the list of all constituents of SPX in increasing order of their first eigenvalue as computed from the original data using all 52 implied volatility returns.

the eigenvalues must be 1[k]; so the higher the leading eigenvalue, the lower the remaining eigenvalues. Better yet, the results can also be explained in terms of idiosyncratic risk; the higher the leading eigenvalue the less idiosyncratic risk, and hence the lower the remaining eigenvalues.

We compare the correlation of each eigenvalue with the underlying stock's correlation to the market we see that there is a small positive correlation with the leading eigenvalue, and negative correlations with the remaining eigenvalues. This ties in with our interpretation above; *the higher the principal eigenvalue the less idiosyncratic risk the underlying stock carries, and the more it behaves like the overall market.*

The opposite conclusion holds for the remaining eigenvalues, especially the second, which gives a stronger indication of idiosyncratic risk (skew fluctuations). Furthermore, in part due to the positive correlation to the market, we expect to see that stocks with less idiosyncratic risk and more systemic risk move more on average as they are more influenced by economic or "macro" news (and speculation) on a daily basis. This conclusion is also reflected by our correlation matrix, which shows positive correlation of volatility to

[k]We normalize each eigenvalue by dividing by the sum of all eigenvalues, which are all positive since the correlation matrix is positive definite.

the first eigenvalue, and negative correlation of volatility to the latter eigenvalues.

Let's now take a look at the top 15 underlying constituents in S&P 500 whose options market exhibit the highest leading eigenvalue, as well as the bottom 15 underlying constituents whose options market exhibits the lowest leading eigenvalue, and see how our story of idiosyncratic systemic risk fits in (Table 2).

The leading eigenvalue explains more of the variation in the IVS for the top 15 stocks than for the bottom 15. Options on Goldman Sachs (GS) for example, have leading eigenvalue with explanatory power as much as over three times that of options on Kinder Morgan (KMI). Another observation which is readily apparent is that the bottom 15 names are small-cap growth stocks or newly-formed companies. The opposite observation holds for the top 15 names: they are large, widely recognized, popular in the media, and well-established companies. This observation further supports our claim that idiosyncratic risk in negatively correlated to the principal eigenvalue. The bottom 15 underlying stocks carry a lot of idiosyncratic risk which is intimately connected to the specific nature of their business. The top 15 underlying assets are much more dependent on the

Table 2: Top 15 underlying constituents and bottom 15 underlying constituents by first eigenvalue.

Bottom 15 Constituents	EV1	Top 15 Constituents	EV1
KMI	0.27272	GS	0.87176
POM	0.31406	JPM	0.87092
WEC	0.34958	BAC	0.85115
PNW	0.35611	SLB	0.84669
HCBK	0.35995	CAT	0.84219
NLSN	0.36338	AAPL	0.84126
TE	0.36342	XOM	0.84109
NU	0.3667	NOV	0.83737
BMS	0.37675	CME	0.83639
XEL	0.3828	MA	0.8358
WIN	0.38664	MS	0.83471
RSG	0.39779	APA	0.83081
FTR	0.40043	GOOG	0.83011
MKC	0.40475	HIG	0.8301
XYL	0.40596	HES	0.82965

state of the overall market and carry less idiosyncratic risk and more systemic risk.

Furthermore, we have that the top 15 underlying stocks above have an average correlation to the market of 63% (overall average is 60%), an average daily volatility of 2.8% (overall average is 2.3%), an average number of eigenvalues exceeding MP-threshold of 3 (overall average is 4.3), and an average daily trading volume of three times that of the market. On the other hand, the bottom 15 underlying stocks above have an average correlation to the market of 47% (overall average is 60 percent), an average daily volatility of 1.5% (overall average is 2.3%), an average number of eigenvalues exceeding MP-threshold of 7.3 (overall average is 4.3), and an average daily trading volume of three times less than that of the market. In Tables 3 and 4 we display the relevant information for all available remaining assets.[1]

We now show the results for the average values of the variables discussed across all remaining assets, and those for the top and bottom 1% (which amounts to around 33 assets each).

For each option contract in OptionMetrics with available data (about 3800 underlying assets in total) we compute the PC surfaces as well as the corresponding spectrum of the correlation matrix across 52 implied volatilities. We use tools from PCA as well as RMT to determine which part of the spectrum is significant. It turns out that we rarely need more than three or four of the leading components in

Table 3: Correlation matrix of all remaining remaining assets (around 3300).

EV1	EV2	EV3	EV4	# EVs > MP	Vol.	Corr.	Daily Volume
1.00	−0.64	−0.83	−0.89	−0.83	0.01	−0.03	0.07
−0.64	1.00	0.59	0.47	0.29	0.03	−0.15	−0.06
−0.83	0.59	1.00	0.71	0.64	0.05	0.02	−0.06
−0.89	0.47	0.71	1.00	0.78	−0.018	−0.01	−0.06
−0.83	0.29	0.64	0.78	1.00	0.01	0.20	−0.05
0.01	0.03	0.05	−0.01	0.01	1.00	−0.12	−0.02
−0.03	−0.15	0.02	−0.01	0.20	−0.12	1.00	0.07
0.07	−0.06	−0.06	−0.06	−0.05	−0.02	0.07	1.00

Note: Corr. refers to the correlation with the market index.

[1]Column headers use same shorthand notation as in Table 2.

Table 4: Average values across all remaining assets (around 3300) and those of the bottom and top 1%.

	EV1	EV2	EV3	EV4	# EVs > MP	Vol.	Corr.	Volume
Top 1%	0.921	0.031	0.017	0.012	1.617	0.030	0.208	168M
Bottom 1%	0.322	0.166	0.114	0.074	7.30	0.023	0.159	.65M
Mrkt Avg.	0.590	0.115	0.077	0.042	5.08	0.031	0.278	4.5M

order capture most of the change in the IVS. We also determine that the leading eigenvalue is an important indicator of the type of risk an option contract carries.

Similarly to the equity case, we classify option contracts into two classes: those carrying mostly systemic risk, and those carrying mostly idiosyncratic risk. Systemic risk increases with the first eigenvalue, while idiosyncratic risk decreases with the first eigenvalue, and increases with the second and third eigenvalues. The magnitude of the leading eigenvalue gives the percent of variation explained by the first principal component surface. We find that the first principal component surface is usually flat, and hence represents a parallel shift of the IVS. The larger the first eigenvalue, the greater the contribution of the parallel shift to the change of the IVS. This parallel shift is reflected in a roughly equal change across all implied volatility points.

On the other side of this picture we have idiosyncratic risk. The higher the second and third eigenvalues, the more the variation of the IVS is due to skew. In this case, we have unequal changes across the implied volatility points, thus reflecting unequal expectations of future asset prices in the options market.

5. First Dimensional Reduction: The Pivot Method

Options are forward-looking in time, so the idiosyncratic or systemic components of the underlying stock affect the option market via a forward-looking expectation of future news about the underlying asset. This is where the distinction between idiosyncratic or systemic component plays a significant role. If we are faced with options on a market-index like SPY or QQQ, or a similar broad-market ETF, the leading eigenvalue is usually very large. We are dealing with systemic risk, and must risk-manage accordingly. If we are faced with a sector-specific asset or a very opaque and less popular one, we are faced with more idiosyncratic risk which is pertinent to the nature of the business itself, the second and third eigenvalues have higher magnitude, and this is the risk we face when trading its options.

So far, we have constructed our IVS and determined the principal components by using the 52 implied volatility points determined by expiration $\in \{30, 91, 182, 365\}$ and $\delta \in \{20, 25, \ldots, 75, 80\}$. In the next few sections, we examine to what extent we can further reduce the number of implied volatility points in modeling the change of the IVS. We refer to each individual implied volatility return as a *pivot*. We analyse how many pivots are necessary to capture the movement of the surface while keeping in mind that a large reduction in dimensionality is desirable due to the decrease in computation it provides.

Pivots are specific implied volatility returns which we use to generate all other implied volatilities via time and delta projections and linear interpolation as demonstrated in Figure 9. For example, the implied volatility return corresponding to a 25-delta and 182-day expiration option could constitute a pivot. In chapter one we used the 52 pivots to model our principal component surface. We can model the first few principal components of the surface via 52 pivots

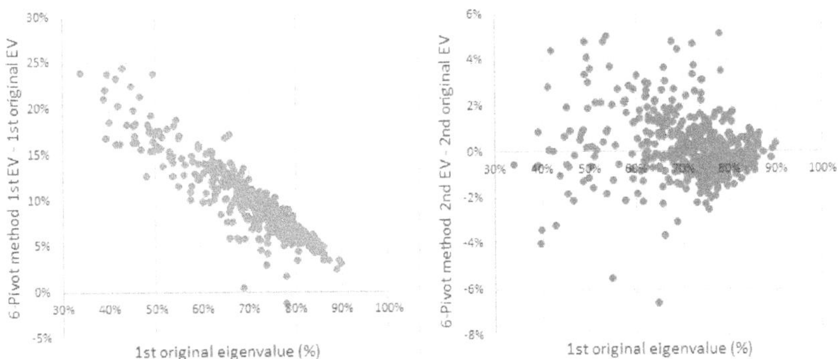

Figure 9: Difference between the top two eigenvalues of the 6 pivot model and those of the original spectra. The x-axis is the list of all constituents of SPX in increasing order of their first eigenvalue as computed from the original data using all 52 implied volatility returns.

as we've already done so, but we seek to reduce the number of pivots used (i.e., reduce dimensionality) and still preserve the original structure of the 52-pivot IVS.

From our analysis we find that in times of crises and very high volatility, such as October 2008 (Lehman Brothers bankruptcy), May 2010 (2010 Flash Crash), and November 2011 (US federal government credit-rating downgrades), the leading eigenvalue tends to increase, reflecting the temporary increase in systemic risk associated with the option's market, i.e., every underlying asset begins to behave more like the market index. From a risk-management perspective, and in the framework of our pivot model, the implications of these results are that in high-volatility periods, we would need less pivots to model the dynamics of the IVS. Another way to see this is that since the leading eigenvalue captures the average correlation among all implied volatilities, and since our dynamic analysis shows systematic increase in the first eigenvalue during high-volatility periods, this indicates an overall increase in the average correlation among all implied volatilities of the options market, hence less pivots are necessary for interpolation.

We analyse 2 pivot, 4 pivot, 5 pivot, 6 pivot, 7 pivot, 9 pivot and 12 pivot models in terms of how well they preserve the spectrum of the correlation matrix of the original data. The pivots used for each model are summarized in Table 5.

Any of the above pivot methods provides a great reduction in the number of implied volatilities we have to use to generate our IVS. Once we have the pivots, we obtain any other point in the IVS by:

1. Locating the grid the point is located in.
2. Interpolating amongst the pivots delineating this grid.

In order to interpolate amongst the pivots, we project onto delta-space and time-to-expiration-space. So that if we let α be the projection along the time-to-maturity axis and β the projection along the δ axis, and we seek the value of the implied volatility return $\mathrm{iv}_{\mathrm{ret}}$ at time t for some δ and k, $\mathrm{iv}_{\mathrm{ret}}(t, \delta, k)$, then we obtain this via interpolation by projecting onto the nearest delta and the nearest time-to-expiration axis available:

$$\begin{aligned}\mathrm{iv}_{\mathrm{ret}}(t, \delta, k) &= \beta(\alpha \mathrm{iv}_{\mathrm{ret}}(t, \delta_+, k_+) + (1-\alpha)\mathrm{iv}_{\mathrm{ret}}(t, \delta_+, k_-)) \\ &\quad + (1-\beta)(\alpha \mathrm{iv}_{\mathrm{ret}}(t, \delta_-, k_+) + (1-\alpha)\mathrm{iv}_{\mathrm{ret}}(t, \delta_-, k_-)),\end{aligned}$$

Table 5: Implied volatilities used as pivots for each model.

	2 Pivots	4 Pivots	5 Pivots	6 Pivots	7 Pivot	9 Pivots	12 Pivots
25δ 30				YES	YES	YES	YES
50δ 30	YES	YES	YES			YES	YES
75δ 30				YES	YES	YES	YES
25δ 91				YES	YES		YES
50δ 91					YES		YES
75δ 91				YES	YES		YES
25δ 182		YES	YES			YES	YES
50δ 182			YES			YES	YES
75δ 182		YES	YES			YES	YES
25δ 365				YES	YES	YES	YES
50δ 365	YES	YES	YES			YES	YES
75δ 365				YES	YES	YES	YES

Note: The right-hand side indicates the implied volatility used, e.g., 25δ 365 refers to a 25δ option expiring in 365 days. Each pivot model has a YES indicating that it uses the pivot in that row.

where $\alpha = \frac{k-k_-}{k_+-k_-}$ and $\beta = \frac{\delta-\delta_-}{\delta_+-\delta_-}$. Here $\delta_+ \geq \delta \geq \delta_-$ and $k_+ \geq k \geq k_-$ and the interpolation is done with pivots available in the specified model. In addition, for any other pivots (δ_1, k_1) we have $\delta_1 \geq \delta_+$ or $\delta_1 \leq \delta_-$, likewise $k_1 \geq k_+$ or $k_1 \leq k_-$. In other words, (δ_+, δ_-) gives the "tightest" delta pivot enclosure and (k_+, k_-) gives the "tightest" time-to-expiration pivot enclosure. If $\delta \geq 75$ then we simply interpolate via projection in time-to-expiration along the $\delta = 75$ axis. Likewise for $\delta \leq 25$.

We interpolate the original return data matrix for each constituent of SPX using each of the pivot models as shown in Table 5. For each model, we use the interpolated data matrix to generate its corresponding correlation matrix, and then perform a PCA on this correlation matrix which generates the spectrum as well. We compare the spectrum of the interpolated data correlation matrix with that of the original correlation matrix. We use the degree of agreement between the two spectra as a measure of the success of the model. We repeat this procedure for the topmost 20 liquid ETFs as well.

The graphs that follow display the difference between the top two eigenvalues generated by the pivot models (the difference for the remaining eigenvalues goes to zero) and the original eigenvalues for each constituent of SPX. As expected, the difference diminishes as the number of pivots increases, i.e., more pivots give better agreement with the original spectra.

For each constituent of SPX, in terms of replicating the top 2 eigenvalues of the correlation matrix, there is little difference between the 4 pivot model and the 5 pivot model. The 6 pivot model performs better than both and is comparable to the 7 pivot model, but slightly outperforms it. The 9 pivot model does better than any of the previous models. The 12 pivot model performs best of all (please refer to Figures 10–14).[m]

It is important to note that since the constituent stocks are ordered by increasing original leading eigenvalue, and all differences tend to zero, the number of pivots used in our model is less important for options which carry more systemic risk and more important for those which carry more idiosyncratic risk. Otherwise said, a model with many pivots becomes necessary for modeling the IVS of those options carrying mainly idiosyncratic risk.

In addition to studying how well a model preserves those eigenvalues exceeding the MP-threshold (i.e., the critical eigenvalues), it is interesting to see how well it preserves the original distribution of stocks across different risk-classes. We classify the different risk-classes as follows[n]:

- **Very Idiosyncratic:** first eigenvalue is more than two standard deviations less than the mean.
- **Idiosyncratic:** first eigenvalue is between one and two standard deviations less than the mean.
- **Somewhat Idiosyncratic:** first eigenvalue is between zero and one standard deviations less than the mean.
- **Somewhat Systemic:** first eigenvalue is between zero and one standard deviations more than the mean.

[m]The same results hold for the twenty most liquid ETFs: the 2 pivot model is insufficient, the 4 pivot model and the 5 pivot model are very similar, and are both surpassed by the 6 pivot model. The 6 pivot model is almost indistinguishable from the 7 pivot model. The 9 pivot model does better yet. The 12 pivot model does best of all and is in very good agreement with the original spectra.

[n]We use mean to refer to the average value of all constituent eigenvalues, and standard deviation to refer to the standard deviation of all constituent eigenvalues.

- **Systemic:** first eigenvalue is between one and two standard deviations more than the mean.
- **Very Systemic:** first eigenvalue is more than two standard deviations more than the mean.

We analyse how the distribution across these risk-classes changes with each model for the constituents of the S&P 500. The original distribution across the six different risk classes is computed using all 52 implied volatility returns (Figures 10–12).

From Figure 13, we see that the vast majority of options whose underlying is a constituent of the S&P 500 carry slight systemic risk, the next largest risk class is made up of those options with slight idiosyncratic risk. We perform the same analysis for each pivot model described in Table 5, and display the results in Figure 14. We compare how well each model preserves the initial distribution by overlaying the original distribution on top of each model distribution. We find that the distributions produced by the 4 pivot and the 5 pivot model produce very similar results, and both underestimate the original distribution more than the 6 pivot model. The 7 pivot model actually underestimates the original distribution more than the 6 pivot model.

From Figure 14, we see that the 2 pivot model does a very bad job of preserving the original distribution across the various risk classes; it places most options under the systemic-risk class. The 6 pivot

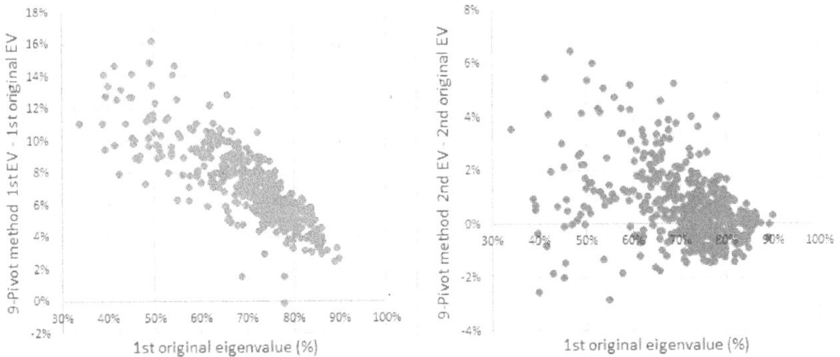

Figure 10: Difference between the top two eigenvalues of the 9 pivot model and those of the original spectra. The x-axis is the list of all constituents of SPX in increasing order of their first eigenvalue as computed from the original data using all 52 implied volatility returns.

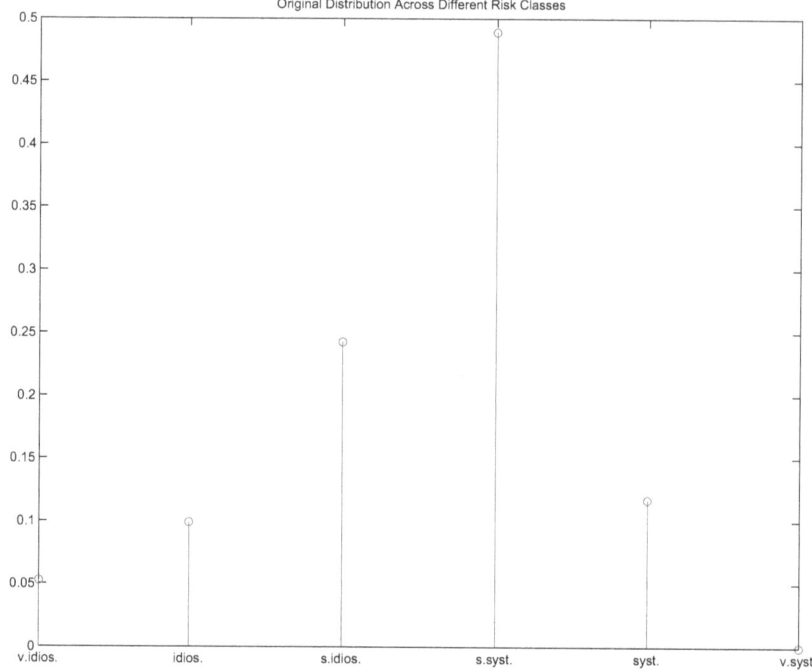

Figure 11: Original distribution across the various risk-classes using all 52 pivots for options on the constituents of S&P 500.

model performs considerably better than the 2 pivot model, but still deviates considerably from the original distribution. The 9 pivot and the 12 pivot models are very comparable, and both do a good job of replicating the original distribution.

As previously mentioned, during high-volatile periods, there is an overall increase in systemic risk, and thus an overall increase in the first eigenvalue. From this section, we see that the discrepancy of any of the pivot models decreases with the first eigenvalue (Figures 10–12). Hence any one of these models will perform even better during such periods when risk-management become even more crucial. In light of these results, *we recommend the 9 pivot model for simulating fluctuations in the IVS. We have seen that the 9 pivot and 12 pivot models are very comparable, yet the 9 pivot model has the benefit of an additional 33% dimensionality reduction.*

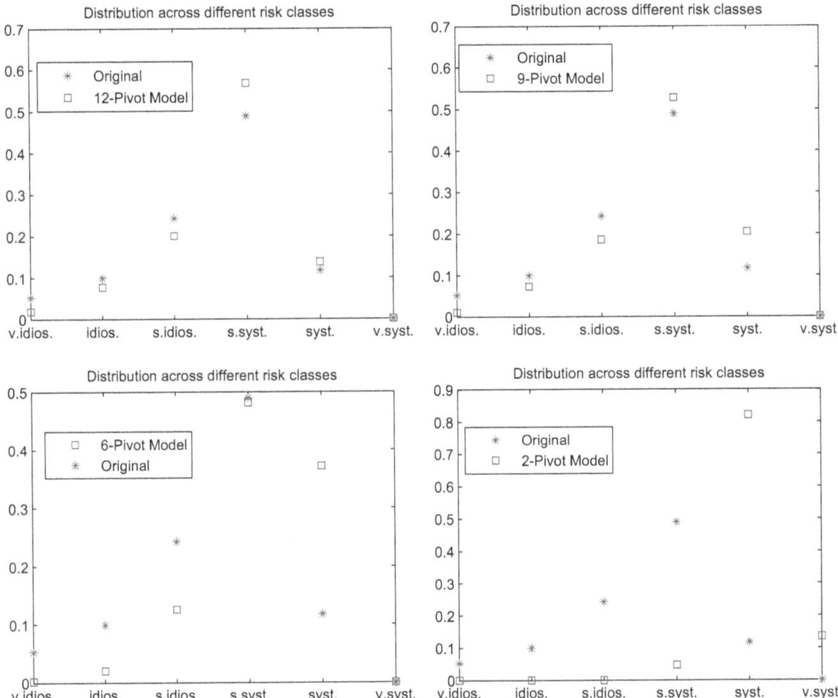

Figure 12: Original distribution across the various risk-classes using all 52 pivots for options on the constituents of S&P 500 vs the distribution produced by each model indicated.

6. Second Dimensional Reduction: Cross-Sectional Analysis of Correlations via RMT

Based on the 9 pivot model, we perform PCA on the correlation matrix of all equity returns and implied volatility returns of the US options market. In other words, for each of 3,141[o] options in OptionMetrics, we collect the historical data for the 9 implied volatilities used as pivots in our 9 pivot model, and organize them into a large data matrix of 31,410 ($= 3141 * (1 + 9)$, 1 for the underlying asset returns and 9 for the corresponding implied volatility returns) columns.

[o]We only use those underlying assets with at least 500 days of available data.

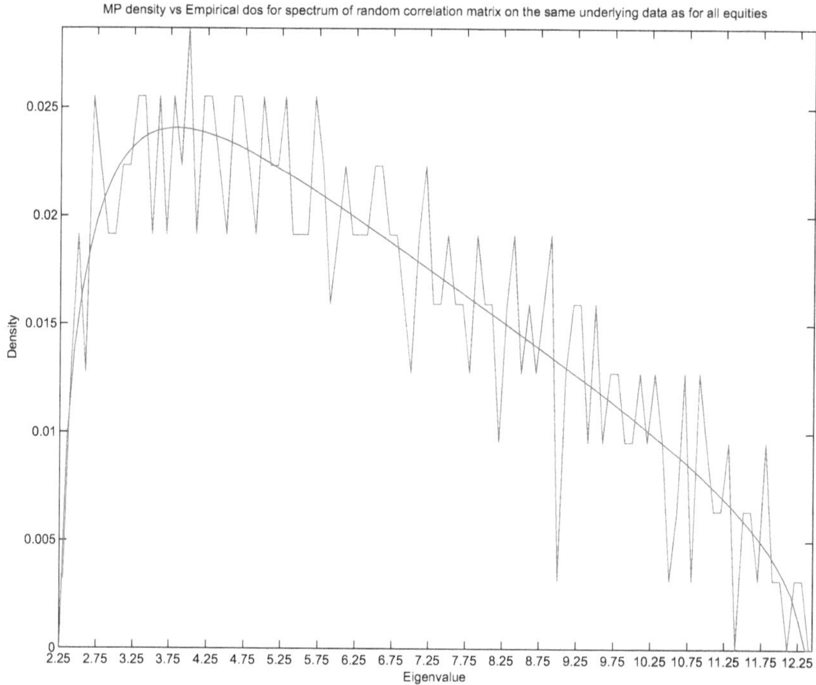

Figure 13: Empirical density of all eigenvalues of correlation matrix of randomly permuted time-series on all original equities data (blue line) vs MP distribution (red). For both distributions there is a point mass of weight 84% at zero. 3,141 variable used each over 500 observations. We find that we cannot reject the null hypothesis that the two distributions are the same based on Kolmogorov–Smirnov 2-series test at the 1% significance level.

The time period we use dates from August 31, 2004 until August 31, 2013. We make the restriction that each name and each contract should have at least 500 days of data. Using this data we perform different experiments involving the 3,141 equities as well as the constituents of the S&P 500 (to be able to compare with Bouchaud and Potters [3]).

We begin our analysis with the underlying constituents of S&P 500. We first examine the equities market as determined by these constituents, without the implied volatilities (like Bouchaud and Potters [3]). In this case, we find that 16 of the eigenvalues (out of the initial 440) are greater than the MP upper bound $\lambda_+ = 2.15$,

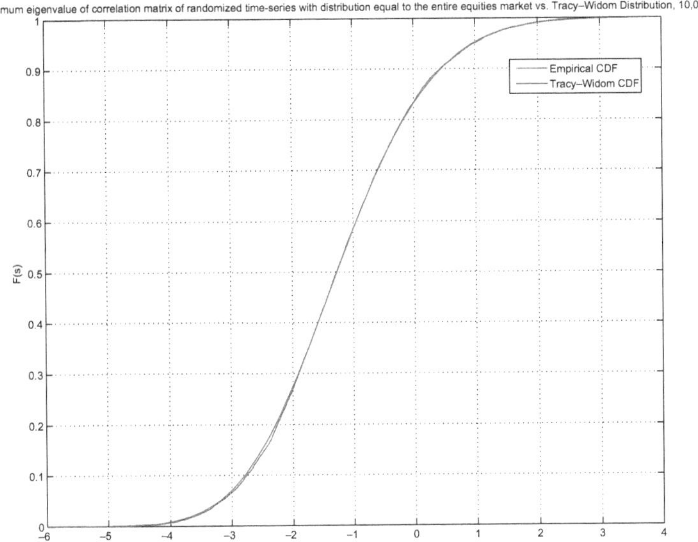

Figure 14: Cumulative density of maximum eigenvalue of randomly permuted time-series on original data of all equities vs TW. We find that we cannot reject the null hypothesis that the two distributions are the same based on Kolmogorov–Smirnov one-series test at the 1% significance level. We use 500 observations and 3,141 variables. Overall 10,000 simulations were performed and the corresponding eigenvalue in each case was computed.

and they account for roughly 55% of the variation in the overall surface.

The boundary between significant and insignificant nodes is not easy to determine in practice. With the goal of better distinguishing fluctuations in the spectrum, we recall the Tracy–Widom (TW) law as we apply it to our analysis. Using the same set-up as in the MP case, the TW Law states:

Proposition 2 (Tracy–Widom Law). *The distribution of the largest eigenvalue,* $\lambda_{\max}$, *of a random correlation matrix is given by*

$$Pr(T\lambda_{\max} < \mu_{TN} + s\sigma_{TN}) = F_1(s),$$

with

$$\mu_{TN} = (\sqrt{T - 0.5} + \sqrt{N - 0.5})^2,$$

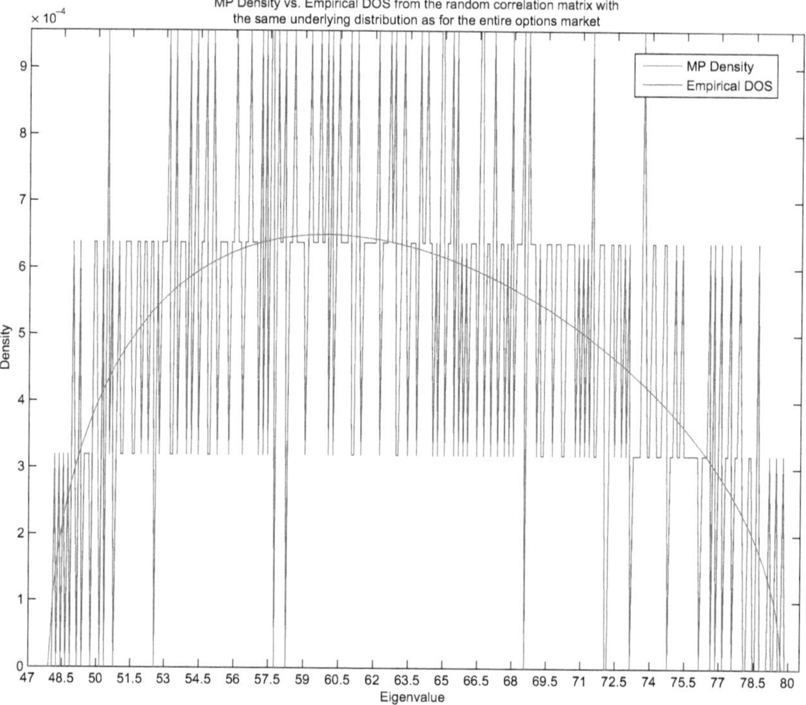

Figure 15: Empirical density of all eigenvalues of correlation matrix of randomly permuted time-series on entire options data vs MP distribution: $\lambda_+ = 79.67$ and $\lambda_- = 47.97$. For both distributions there is a point mass of weight 98.41% at zero. 31,410 variable used each over 500 observations.

and

$$\sigma_{TN} = (\sqrt{T - 0.5} + \sqrt{N - 0.5})\left(\frac{1}{\sqrt{T - 0.5}} + \frac{1}{\sqrt{N - 0.5}}\right)^{\frac{1}{3}}.$$

TW holds for specific β-ensembles: Gaussian Orthogonal Ensemble: $\beta = 1$, Gaussian Unitrary Ensemble: $\beta = 2$, and Gaussian Symplectic Ensemble: $\beta = 4$. We use $\beta = 1$. $F_1(s)$ is stated in terms of the Painleve II differential equation, and other equivalent formulations. We leave that part of the theory out as it is not directly relevant.[p]

[p]We use the $s \to F_1(s)$ table from Michael's Prahofer's website: http://www-m5.ma.tum.de/KPZ. In Figure 15 we plot the CDF $F_1(s)$. For a more thorough

Tracy–Widom holds only for specific distributions of the underlying data. In particular, it has been shown [2] that fat-tails can massively increase the maximum eigenvalue in the theoretical limiting spectrum of the random matrix. It would be of interest to know how applicable both MP and TW are when we consider a random matrix with the same underlying distribution as our original data.

In order to test the applicability of TW and MP in calibrating and testing the eigenvalues of our empirical correlation matrices, we take the original data, and for each variable (i.e., for each implied volatility return or underlying asset return) we permute its time series independently of the time-series of any other variable. We then test how the results compare to those predicted by MP and TW (Figure 16). We perform this randomization experiment for each of four markets: equities as determined by the constituents of the S&P 500, options with underlying in the S&P 500, all assets available in OptionMetrics, and all options with an underlying asset in OptionMetrics. We display the results for the latter two markets below.[q]

We present the results on the same inquiries as above for the options market with underlying a constituent of S&P 500. We find that the number of eigenvalues which exceed the MP threshold $\lambda_+ = 6.12$ is 84, and these eigenvalues account for 55 percent of the variation. It is interesting to note that the more insignificant eigenvectors are distributed according to the maximum entropy distribution (i.e., standard Gaussian in this case), whereas the corresponding top eigenvectors deviate from this distribution indicating more structure. We show this for options on stocks in S&P 500, but the same phenomena holds for the equities market on S&P 500, the overall equities market, and the overall options market.

We present results for the equities market as a whole as determined by available data in OptionMetrics, and for those assets with at least 500 days of data. This amounts to 3,141 variables and 500 observations. We find that the number of eigenvalues which exceed the MP threshold $\lambda_+ = 12.30$ is 20, and these eigenvalues account for

treatment of this theory please refer to *Topics in Random Matrix Theory*, by Terence Tao [6].

[q]The results for the former two markets are similar to those of the latter two, but we omit them for the sake of brevity.

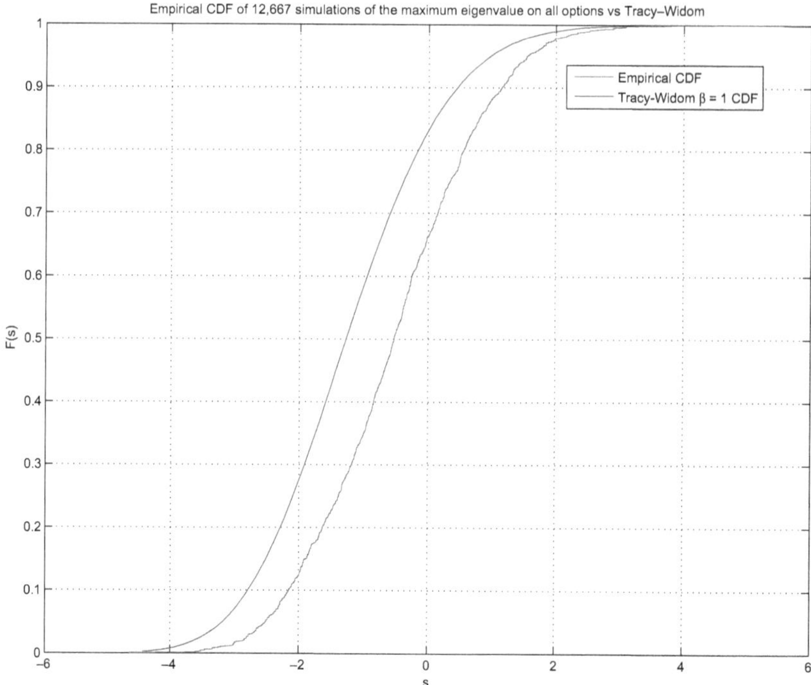

Figure 16: CDF of largest eigenvalue of the correlation matrix of time-series permuted data on the entire options market vs TW $\beta = 1$ CDF. We use 500 observations and 31,410 variables. Overall 12,667 simulations were performed and the corresponding maximum eigenvalue in each case was computed. Note that in this case the discrepancy between the theoretical and the empirical distribution is greater than for the other markets, but this does not in anyway alter our conclusion that we may approximate the largest eigenvalue of a random correlation matrix with the same underlying distribution as our empirical data via TW. This is because we care about large values of s (as demonstrated in the tables that follow), and the two distributions converge for $s > 3$.

24% of the variation. Eighty five percent of the maximum eigenvalues of 10,000 randomized simulations lie below $\lambda_+ = 12.29$, and all maximum eigenvalues lie in the range $(11.94, 12.53)$. For this market, we use 2026 observations and 3,140 variables.

We now present results on the same inquiries as above for the options market as a whole as determined by available data in OptionMetrics, and for those assets with at least 500 days of data. This amounts to 31,410 variables and 500 observations. The number of

Table 6: Significance of eigenvalues in the entire equities market a la TW.

Top 25 Eigenvalues	s-value	$F_1(s)$
$\lambda_1 = 328.25$	5076	1
$\lambda_5 = 23.58$	181	1
$\lambda_{10} = 16.22$	63	1
$\lambda_{15} = 14.22$	31	1
$\lambda_{20} = 12.42$	2.18	0.9924
$\lambda_{21} = 12.18$	−1.64	0.38
$\lambda_{22} = 11.89$	−6.39	3.22e-07
$\lambda_{23} = 11.81$	−7.59	7.65e-11
$\lambda_{24} = 11.67$	−9.93	7.36e-22
$\lambda_{25} = 11.52$	−12.26	1.49e-38

Notes:
- 3,141 assets and 500 days used.
- All together 3,141 eigenvalues were estimated.
- Corresponding theoretical value for $\lambda_+ = 12.295$ (via TW).
- 20 eigenvalues exceed λ_+ and account for 24% of variation.
- All twenty are deemed significant by TW.

eigenvalues which exceed the MP threshold $\lambda_+ = 79.67$ is 108, and these eigenvalues account for 50% of the variation. About 70% of all maximum eigenvalues for each of 12,667 randomized simulations lie below λ_+, and all maximum eigenvalues lie in the range $(78.98, 80.32)$. For this market we use 500 observations and 31,410 variables.

The results above further allow us to conclude that we may apply the Marchenko–Pastur distribution and the TW law in order to determine the significant eigenvalues is our original correlation matrix. Tables 6 and 7 shows the significant eigenvalues for the entire equity and options market.

To summarize, we have determined that we may reduce dimension greatly in each of the four markets considered. Specifically markets on the underlying assets are determined by 15 and by 20 factors out of the original 440 and 3,141 variables used (refer to appendix). The options markets on these underlying assets are determined by a comparable number of factors: 84 and 108 out of an original 4,400 and 31,410 variable respectively.

Finally, we compare the correlation of the residuals of all assets in OptionMetrics and its corresponding MP distribution. We have

Table 7: Significance of eigenvalues in the entire options market a la TW.

Top 110 Eigenvalues	s-value	$F_1(s)$
$\lambda_1 = 3742$	24843	1
$\lambda_5 = 209.27$	879.14	1
$\lambda_{10} = 143.5$	433.04	1
$\lambda_{20} = 118.19$	261.32	1
$\lambda_{40} = 102.62$	155.74	1
$\lambda_{50} = 97.40$	120.35	1
$\lambda_{70} = 90.48$	73.35	1
$\lambda_{90} = 84.56$	33.21	1
$\lambda_{107} = 80.21$	3.70	0.9996
$\lambda_{108} = 80.04$	2.60	0.996
$\lambda_{109} = 79.65$	−0.10	0.80
$\lambda_{110} = 79.41$	−1.71	0.35

Notes:
- 31,410 assets and 500 days used.
- All together 31,410 eigenvalues were estimated.
- Corresponding theoretical value for $\lambda_+ = 79.672$ (via TW).
- 108 eigenvalues exceed λ_+ and account for 50% of variation.
- All 108 are deemed significant by Tracy–Widdom.

determined that this market consists of 20 significant factors. Hence, we perform a multi-linear regression of the original data matrix on these 20 factors, determine the matrix of residuals, and compute the correlation of the residuals matrix. Since we wish to consider all information as co-movements of variables regardless of their variance, and in order to apply Marchenko–Pastur, we normalize the correlation of the residuals matrix so that each column has variance equal to 1. Then we compute the spectrum of the correlation of residuals and plot the corresponding density of states (dos). The result can be seen in Figure 17.

7. Conclusion

"Idiosyncratic" assets have more activity on higher-order modes, whereas "systemic" assets' IVSs are driven primarily by the first mode. During times of high-volatility and general market turmoil, the leading eigenvalue increases and the number of eigenvalues exceeding the MP threshold decreases. Specifically, the magnitude of the leading eigenvalue and the number of eigenvalues exceeding the

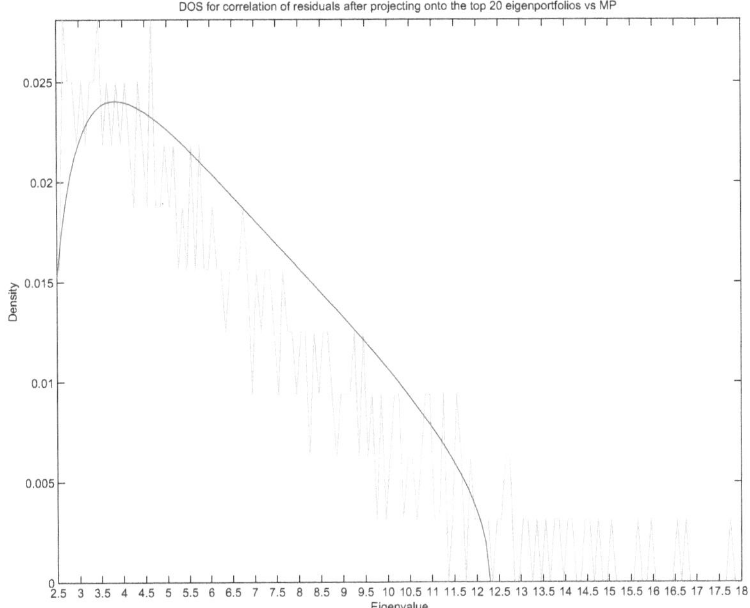

Figure 17: Spectrum of correlations of residuals after projecting onto the top 20 eigenportfolios for all assets in OptionMetrics. Point mass of weight 84% for both distributions. We project onto the first 20 eigenportfolios (accounts for 24% of var.). Twenty eigenvalues lie outside of $\lambda_+ = 12.30$ and are deemed significant by TW. We cannot reject the null hypothesis that the two densities are the same based on Kolmogorov–Smirnov test at the 5% significance level.

MP threshold are strongly negatively correlated. This phenomenon indicates higher systemic risk for all options during high-volatility periods.

We formulate various pivot models which we use to reduce the number of variables needed to model the IVS. Of the seven pivot models formulated, we test each model by comparing how well it preserves the original spectrum. We also test how well it preserves the distribution across various types of risk faced by options whose underlying stock is a constituent of the S&P 500 (Figures 18–20).

Our results from this section indicate that the 6 pivot model, the 9 pivot model, and the 12 pivot model are acceptable in terms of how well they replicate the original statistics. Naturally, we find that the 12 pivot model is best, followed by the 9 pivot model, and last the 6 pivot model. In terms of overall efficacy, we recommend and use the 9 pivot model.

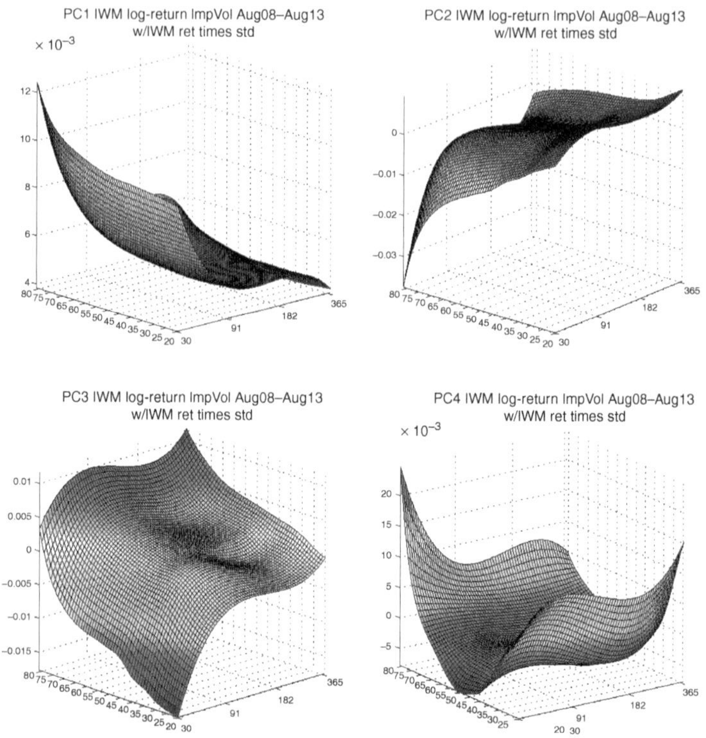

Figure 18: Results based on PCA decomposition of the correlation matrix of the log-returns of IWM coupled with the implied volatilities log-returns for IWM options. Displayed are the first four principal components which account for roughly 88, 4, 2, and 1% of the variation of the implied volatility surface for IWM, respectively. Time period dates from August 31, 2008 until August 31, 2013.

We conclude by performing a PCA of the entire equities and options market as made available by OptionMetrics using a 9 pivot description of the IVSs. We begin with the markets as determined by constituents of S&P 500 and their options. To better distinguish signal from noise in these markets in their entirety, in addition to PCA and MP, we also employ the TW Law in order to determine the significant part of the spectrum.

We first test the applicability of both MP and TW by considering random matrixes with the same underlying distribution as our empirical data. We find that the results from using such random matrixes are in excellent agreement with those predicted by both MP and by TW. In particular, the underlying distribution of our empirical data forms an ensemble class on which Tracy–Widom applies, thus ruling

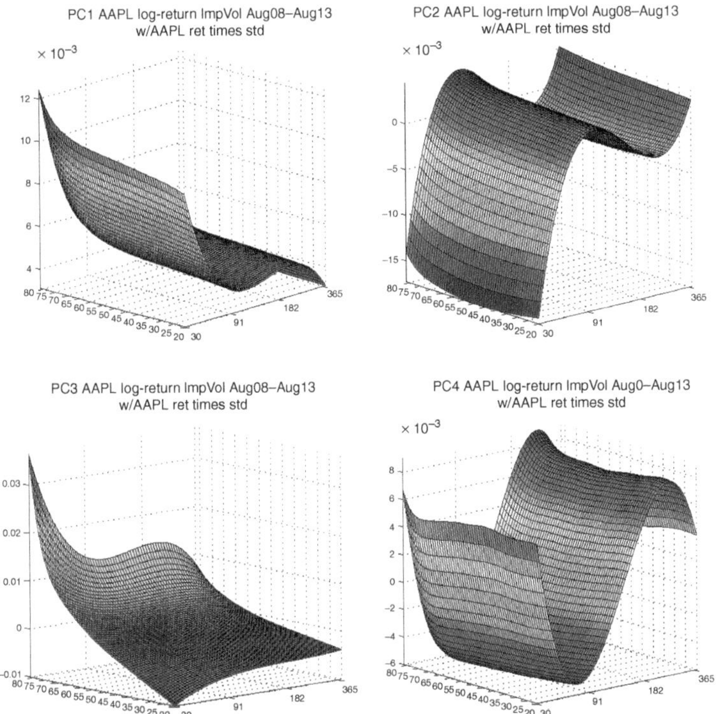

Figure 19: Results based on PCA decomposition of the correlation matrix of the log-returns of AAPL coupled with the implied volatilities log-returns for AAPl options. Displayed are the first four principal components which account for roughly 86, 7, 2, and 1% of the variation of the implied volatility surface for AAPL, respectively. Time period dates from August 31, 2008 until August 31, 2013.

out "fat-tail" effects [2]. Utilizing all of the aforementioned tools, we classify the number of significant factors driving the US equities and options market as follows:

1. Equities in SPX: **15** significant factors (account for 55% of variance, 440 total number of eigenvalues estimated).
2. Equities and options with underlying in SPX: **84** significant factors (account for 55% of variance, 4,400 total number of eigenvalues estimated).
3. Equities in OptionMetrics: **20** significant factors (account for 24% of variance, 3,141 total number of eigenvalues estimated).
4. All equities and options with underlying asset in OptionMetrics: **108** significant factors (account for 50% of variance, 3,1410 total number of eigenvalues estimated).

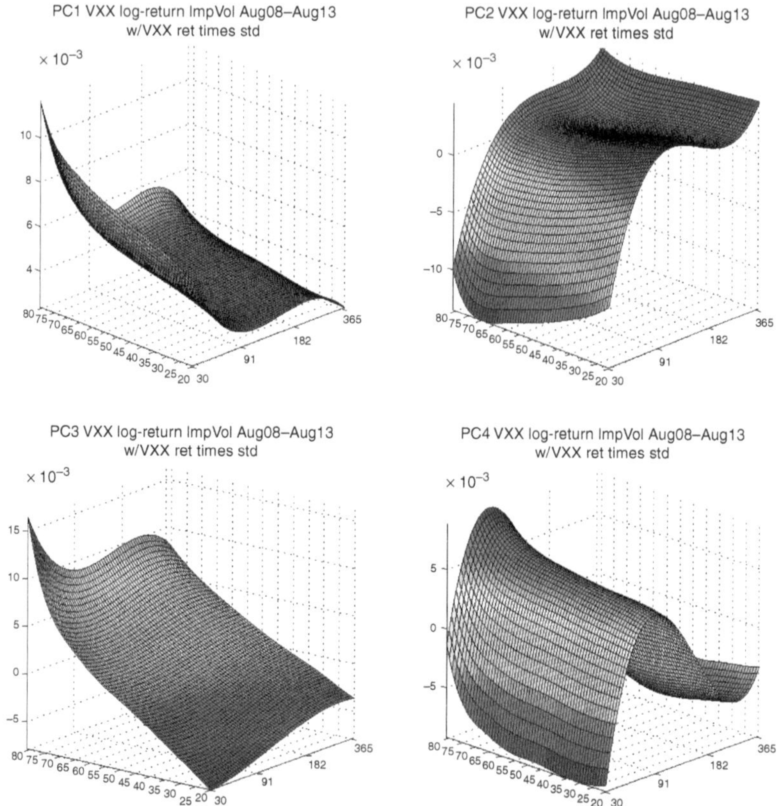

Figure 20: Results based on PCA decomposition of the correlation matrix of the log-returns of VXX coupled with the implied volatilities log-returns for VXX options. Displayed are the first four principal components which account for roughly 66, 15, 5, and 4% of the variation of the implied volatility surface for VXX, respectively. We find that the latter eigenvectors carry more explanatory power for this volatility product when compared to the instruments above. Volatility products require more eigenvalues and corresponding principal components to account for variation. Usually the top 4 eigenvalues still account for at least 90% of variation. The surfaces indicate mainly a "flat" effect. Time period dates from August 31, 2008 until August 31, 2013.

Results 1 and 3 are in agreement with those of Bouchaud and Potters [3]. Results 2 and 4 provide us with very large dimension reduction in the option-market space (84 significant factors from 4,400, and 108 significant factors from 31,410 respectively).

A. Appendix

For the sake of conciseness we do not include code nor all of our results. All code and databases of results are ready upon request.

We made the assertion that the first eigenvalue λ_1 of a correlation matrix can be used as an approximation for the average correlation $\langle\rho\rangle$, we give the proof below. Let C be the correlation matrix, and V the matrix of eigenvectors in the spectral decomposition of C. We can write:

$$\begin{aligned}\lambda_1 = V^{(1)T}CV^1 &= \sum_{i=1}^{N}(V_i^1)^2 + \sum_{i\neq j} V_i^1 V_j^1 \rho_{ij} = 1 + \sum_{i\neq j} V_i^1 V_j^1 \rho_{ij} \\ &= 1 + \sum_{i\neq j} V_i^1 V_j^1 \frac{\sum_{i\neq j} V_i^1 V_j^1 \rho_{ij}}{\sum_{i\neq j} V_i^1 V_j^1}.\end{aligned}$$

Rearranging gives,

$$\frac{\lambda_1 - 1}{\sum_{i\neq j} V_i^1 V_j^1} = \frac{\sum_{i\neq j} V_i^1 V_j^1 \rho_{ij}}{\sum_{i\neq j} V_i^1 V_j^1}$$

$\therefore$ Since $V_i^1 \approx \frac{1}{\sqrt{N}}$ then $\sum_{i\neq j} V_i^1 V_j^1 \approx N\frac{N-1}{N} = N - 1$

hence, $\frac{\lambda_1 - 1}{N-1} \approx \rho$, so that, $\rho \approx \frac{\lambda_1}{N}$.

References

[1] Avellaneda, M. and Cont, R. (2002). Special issue on volatility modeling. *Quantitative Finance*, 2(1), 6–7.

[2] Biroli, G., Bouchaud, J-P., and Potters, M. (2009). On the top eigenvalue of heavy-tailed random matrices. http://arxiv.org/abs/cond-mat/0609070.

[3] Bouchaud, J-P. and Potters, M. (2009). Financial application of random matrix theory: A short review. *Finance and Stochastics*, 5(1), 3–32.

[4] Bouchaud, J-P., Laloux, L., and Potters, M. (2005). Financial applications of random matrix theory: Old laces and new pieces. *APPB*, 36(9), 2767–2784.

[5] Carmona, R. and Nadtochiy, S. (2008). Local volatility dynamic models. *Finance and Stochastics*, 13, pp. 1–48.

[6] Clewlow, L., Hodges, S.D., and Skiadopoulos, G. (2004). The Dynamics of Smiles. Quantitative Methods in Finance, Athens: Typothito Dardanos, pp. 119–153.
[7] Cont, R. and Fonseca, J. (2002). Dynamics of implied volatility surfaces. *Quantitative Finance*, 2, 45–60.
[8] Dupire, B. (1994). *Pricing With a Smile*. Risk, 7(1), 18–20.
[9] Plerou, V. *et al.* (1999). Universal and nonuniversal properties of cross correlations in financial time series. *Physical Review Letters*, 83(7), 1471–1474.
[10] Laloux, *et al.* (2000). Random matrix theory and financial correlations. *International Journal of Theoretical and Applied Finance*, 3(3), 391–397.
[11] Litterman, R. and Scheinkman, J. (1991). Common factors affecting bond returns. *The Journal of Fixed Income*, 1, 62–74.
[12] Lopez-Alonso, J.M. and Alda, J. (2007). Correlations in finance: A statistical approach. *Noise in Complex Systems and Stochastic Dynamics II.*
[13] Rebonato (2006). Forward-rate volatilities and the swaption matrix: why neither time-homogeneity nor time-dependence will do. *International Journal of Theoretical and Applied Finance*, 9(5), 705–746.
[14] Rebonato R. and Joshi, M. (2002). A joint empirical and theoretical investigation of the modes of deformation of swaption matrices: implications for model choice. *International Journal of Theoretical and Applied Finance*, 5(7), 667–694.
[15] Joshi, M. and Rebonato, R. (2006). A stochastic-volatility, displaced-diffusion extension of the LIBOR Market Model. *Quantitative Finance*, 3(6), 458–469.
[16] Rebonato, R., McKay, K. and White, R., (2009). The SABR/LIBOR Market Model: Pricing, calibration and hedging for complex interest-rate derivatives. John Wiley & Sons.
[17] Schweizer, M. and Wissel, J. (2008). Arbitrage-free market models for option prices: The multi-strike case. *Finance and Stochastics*, 12(4), 469–505.
[18] Skiadopoulos, G., Hodges, S., and Clewlow, L. (2000), The dynamics of the SP 500 implied volatility surface. *Review of Derivatives Research*, 3(1), 263–282.
[19] Tao, T. (2012). *Topics in Random Matrix Theory* (Vol. 132). American Mathematical Soc.
[20] Zhao, B. and Hodges, S.D. (2013). Parametric modeling of implied smile functions: A generalized SVI model. *Review of Derivatives Research*, 16(1), 53–77.

https://doi.org/10.1142/9789811259142_0015

Chapter 15

A General Theory of Option Pricing

D. Gershon

School of Business Administration,
The Hebrew University of Jerusalem

David.Gershon@mail.huji.ac.il

Abstract

We present a generic formalism for option pricing which does not require specifying the stochastic process of the underlying asset price, undergoing a Markovian stochastic behavior. We first derive a consistency condition that the risk neutral density function to maturity must satisfy in order to guarantee no arbitrage. As an example, we show that when the underlying asset price undergoes a continuous stochastic process with deterministic time dependent standard deviation the formalism produces the Black–Scholes–Merton pricing formula. We provide data from the market to prove that the price of European options is independent of the term structure of the volatility prior to maturity. Based on this observation we offer a method to calculate the density function to maturity that satisfies the consistency condition we derived. In the general case the price of European options depends only on the moments of the price return of the underlying asset. When the underlying asset undergoes a continuous time process then only moments up to second order contribute to the European option price. In this case any set of option prices on three strikes with the same maturity contains the information to determine the whole volatility smile for this maturity. Using a great amount of data from the option markets we show that our formalism generates European option prices that match the markets prices very accurately in all asset classes: currencies, equities, interest rates and commodities. Finally, using bootstrapping method with market data of the whole term structure we determine the probability transfer density function from inception to maturity, thus allowing the calculation of path dependent options. Comparison of the results of the model to the market shows a very high level of accuracy.

Keywords: Option pricing, probability density function, volatility smile, exotic options, continuous time finance.

1. Introduction

Since the invention of the celebrated Black–Scholes–Merton (BSM) [1] option pricing formula, all option pricing methods were based on determining first a specific stochastic process for the underlying asset, typically either single Brownian motion (e.g., BSM, Black and Derman [2], local volatility by Dupire [3] and Derman and Kani [4], the SABR model by Hagan, Kumar, Lesniewski, and Woodward [5]) or a multiple correlated Brownian motions processes (e.g., Heston [6], BGM model by Brace, Gatarek and Musiela [7], Local stochastic volatility by Lipton (2002)) or as fractional Brownian motion known as rough volatility by El Euch, Gatheral and Rosenbaum [8].

There are two problems with this approach. In 45 years of research none of these models generate the volatility smile as observed in the market in all asset classes. Moreover, there is no economic way to choose which model should describe the price of financial assets.

In this chapter, we approach option pricing in a fundamental way. We do not specify the stochastic process in this chapter at all. Rather than this, we only assume that there are some two unknown correlated stochastic processes which form the underlying asset vector X_t. We can denote $X_t = (u_t, v_t)$, $u_t = \log s_t$ where s_t is the underlying asset price at time t. (Note that in some stochastic volatility models v_t is referred to as the stochastic volatility of the underlying asset). We first approach v_t without further specification and show that in the integration that yields the option price it can be "averaged out", ending with the option price as a function of u_t only. This is not surprising given the theorem of Gyongy [9] that the density function of a multi-Brownian motion processes can be mapped to a density function of a single Brownian motion. As a mean to calculate the option price with expiry T easily, way we can choose v_t^2 to be the expected time averaged variance of u_t over $(t, T]$. This simplifies the integral further.

We show that we can calculate the price of European options with expiry time T without knowing the dynamics (diffusion) of the stochastic process from time t to $t + \delta t$. Instead, need to know the probability density function from inception to time t for $0 \leq t \leq T$ When we assume that X_t is a continuous time process (i.e., no jumps) then because of the well-known Dynkin theorem, it turns out that the European option price depends on four stochastic quantities denoted by $(\nu_t; \lambda_t; \eta_t; \rho_t)$ which are the representation of the expectation at time t of the rate of the infinitesimal changes of the moments of the vector (u_t, v_t) up to second order.

We then prove in the chapter by data from the options market a fundamental property of volatility smiles: The same volatility smile at expiry T can appear in the market with totally different volatility smiles at expiry time $t < T$. In other words, the volatility smile is not a result of a unique stochastic process of the underlying asset and a spectrum of different processes, which yield different volatility smiles at time $t < T$ can yield the same volatility smile at time T. This property is usually referred to as saying that the volatility smile is "term structure independent". In particular, the volatility smile can be a result of time-homogenous density function. Therefore, without loss of generality we calculate the option price using time homogeneous density function. In this case, one of the four quantities (ν_t) diminishes and $\lambda_t, \eta_t, \rho_t$ are time independent. Thus, it turns out that in the most general time continuous process the European option price depends on three time-independent quantities $\Sigma_0 = (\lambda_0, \eta_0, \rho_0)$. In the case that λ_0, η_0, ρ_0 are three constants, knowing these three constants determine option prices for any strike at expiry T. In simple words, if we know very accurately from the market the option price of three strikes at expiry T we can determine the whole volatility smile uniquely.

Hence without knowing the specific stochastic process X_t we are able to express the European option price for a given expiry T as a function of three quantities λ_0, η_0, ρ_0 that correspond only to this expiry. These quantities are stochastic. Hence, when we take the option price of three strikes at expiry T we can only get their current value for expiry T and obtain the current volatility smile for expiry T.

Writing the option price as a time and spot integral with a time-homogeneous density function yields a consistency condition that the density function has to obey, given the three quantities Σ_0. In the chapter, we show how to solve the density function numerically for a given expiry T. Hence the density function g that satisfies the consistency condition is a function of T and Σ_0, $g = g(s_0, s, T, \Sigma_0)$, where s_0, Σ_0 represents the current market conditions. We demonstrate a numerical procedure to solve the density function given option prices of three strikes at maturity T. The quantities λ_0, η_0, ρ_0 are obtained in this procedure because they serve as a "calibration" to ensure that the density function generates the three given option prices.

$\lambda_0, \eta_0, \rho_0$ are implied from prices of options in the market and may change frequently. $g = g(s_0, s, T, \Sigma_0)$ can be calculated in advance for any T and Σ_0.

While by construction we can refer to λ_0, η_0, ρ_0 symbolically as representing the "volatility" of the underlying asset, the correlation of the "volatility" with the underlying asset price and the "volatility of the volatility", in reality they can be mapped to any conventional three market quantities. For example, in the currency options market they can be mapped numerically to the ATM volatility, 25 delta risk reversals and 25 delta butterfly. In the interest rates options market they can be mapped to the collars, strangles and at the At the Money forward volatility.

The advantage of our approach is that in order to calculate the European price for expiry time T we do not need to know the stochastic process of the underlying asset. In the simple case when the volatility (or process v_t) is deterministic and time dependent we obtain the BSM option price.

After we show how to calculate the density function, we show that this approach delivers accurate volatility smiles of options in all asset classes (currencies, equities, interest rates, commodities) by comparing to the market data. This further demonstrates our claim that the volatility smile is a result of the same principle in all kind of European options.

While in theory for any expiry T and a set of λ_0, η_0, ρ_0 we need to calculate the density function $g(s_0, s, T, \Sigma_0)$, in reality we can map the function g to a smooth function and store a few parameters to represent $g(s_0, s, T, \Sigma_0)$ quite accurately.

In the next step, the approach to calculate the density function for maturity T as a function of three parameters Σ_0 is used further to derive the dynamics or diffusion process of the underlying asset. Toward the end of the chapter we describe the methodology to include the term structure of European options observed in the market in order to obtain the probability transfer density function, known also as the conditional probability. Again, the conditional probability is obtained without the need to pre-specify the stochastic process of the price of the underlying asset. First we divide the time interval T to small time increments δt and using our market data we compute the volatility smiles for each expiry $t = i\delta t$ for $i = 1, \ldots, T/\delta t$. Then, at any given spot and time t we use the same type of density function but for expiry time $T = t + \delta t$, i.e., $g(s_t, s_{t+\delta t}, \delta t, \Sigma_t(s_t, \delta t))$.

From the volatility smile at time t and the volatility smile at time $t + \delta t$ we can calculate the three quantities $\Sigma_t(s_t, \delta t)$ for each s at time t. this allows us to calculate the transition probability from s_t to $s_{t+\delta t}$.

To prove consistency of this method, we show that when we use this formalism for the transition probability and apply it for different term structures but with the same market data for expiry T, we receive the same volatility smile at maturity T.

After solving for the three-dimensional field $\Sigma_t(s_t, \delta t)$ for any $0 < s_t$ and $0 \leq t < T$, one can calculate the dynamics of the transition of the underlying asset and use it for calculating path dependent Exotic options. To show that this formalism generates accurately the prices of path dependent Exotic options as seen in the market we compare the results of the method to the relatively liquid American barrier and binary options in the currency exotic options markets and the results of this formalism are quite close to the market prices.

The chapter is organized as follows. In Section 2, we derive the formalism for European options pricing. In Section 3, we provide market data analysis to prove that European option volatility smile is independent of the term structure. This allows us to focus first on the time homogeneous density function. In Section 4, we present the consistency condition that the density function to maturity has to satisfy and solve for it so we obtain the volatility smile for the maturity. In Section 5, we show how to obtain the probability transfer density function when the term structure of volatility is given. This allows the calculation of path dependent options. In Section 6, we compare our methodology to the market. We show that the volatility smile generated is accurate in all asset classes and more over that the calculation of path dependent options is very close to the market prices. Section 7, concludes.

2. Integral Representation for European Option Pricing

2.1 *General formalism*

Consider a (vector) Markov process **X** in a filtered space $(\Omega, \{\mathcal{F}_t\})$ on the state-space $(\mathbb{X}\mathcal{X})$ with the transition semigroup $(P_t)_{t\geq 0}$

$$X = (\Omega, \{\mathcal{F}_t\colon t \geq 0\}, (\mathrm{X}_t\colon \mathrm{t} \geq 0\}, \{P_t\colon t \geq 0\}, \{\mathbf{P}^{\mathrm{x}}\colon x \in \mathbb{X}\}, \quad (1)$$

on which an $\mathcal{F}_t$-measurable random variable X_t in the measurable state-space $(\mathbb{X}\mathcal{X})$ is defined for every $t \geq 0$ and $\mathbf{P}^x$ is the law of the process when it starts at x. We shall follow the notations of Rogers and Williams (2000). We assume that $\mathbb{X} =$ (some set of) $\mathcal{R}^d$.

For a bounded measurable analytic function $f : (\mathbb{R}^+ \times \mathbb{X}) \to \mathbb{X} \to \mathbb{R}$ we define $\mathbf{P}_s(t)$ so that

$$E[f(t+s, X_{t+s})|X_t = x] = \int f(t+s, y)\, P_s(t, x, dy) \equiv \mathbf{P}_s\, f(t, x)$$
$$\text{for any } s, t \geq 0. \quad (2)$$

We denote by $\mathcal{G}$ the (infinitesimal) generator of $(P_t)_{t\geq 0}$

$$\mathcal{G}f(t, x) \equiv \lim_{h\to 0} \frac{\mathbf{P_h}\, f(t, x) - f(t, x)}{h}. \quad (3)$$

We consider only functions f in the domain $\mathcal{D}(\mathcal{G})$ of the generator for which the limit exists. The intricate technical issues regarding the limit are covered by Ethier and Kurtz (2009).

Since the transition semi-group satisfies $\mathbf{P}_{s+t} = \mathbf{P}_s\mathbf{P}_t = \mathbf{P}_t\mathbf{P}_s$ for any $s, t \geq 0$ it follows that

$$\mathcal{G}\mathbf{P}_t f = \mathbf{P}_t \mathcal{G} f \quad \text{for } f \in \mathcal{D}(\mathcal{G}). \quad (4)$$

Thus

$$\boldsymbol{P}_T f(0, x) - f(0, x) = \int_0^T \mathbf{P_t}\mathcal{G} f(0, x) dt = \int_0^T \mathcal{G}\boldsymbol{P}_\mathbf{t} f(0, x) dt, \quad (5)$$

which is Dynkin's formula. Equation (5) can be written as

$$E[f(T,X_T)|X_0=x]-f(0,x)=E\left[\int_0^T \mathcal{G}f(t,X_t)dt|X_0=x\right]. \quad (6)$$

Since the function f is analytic we use the Tailor expansion, which we express with the multi-index α

$$f(t,x+\xi)=f(t,x)+\sum\nolimits_{\alpha>0}\xi^\alpha D^\alpha f(t,x)/\alpha! \quad \alpha\equiv(\alpha_1,\ldots,\alpha_d), \quad (7)$$

where

$$\xi^\alpha=\prod_{i=1}^d \xi_i^{\alpha_i};\ \alpha!=\prod_{i=1}^d(\alpha_i)!. \quad (8)$$

Hence for $f\in\mathcal{D}(\mathcal{G})$

$$\mathcal{G}f(t,x)=\frac{\partial f}{\partial t}(t,x)+\lim\nolimits_{h\to 0}\sum\nolimits_{\alpha>0}\frac{E[(X_{t+h}-x)^\alpha|X_t=x]}{h} \times D^\alpha f(t,x)/\alpha! \quad (9)$$

provided that the limits exist for all α. Now we define

$$\omega^\alpha(t,x)=\lim\nolimits_{h\to 0}\frac{E[(X_{t+h}-x)^\alpha|X_t=x]}{h}/\alpha!, \quad (10)$$

and provided that the interchange of summation and taking the limit is justified, then we obtain

$$\begin{aligned}&E[f(T,X_T)|X_0=x]-f(0,x)\\&=\int_0^T P_t(0,x,dy)\left[\frac{\partial f}{\partial t}(t,y)\sum\nolimits_{\alpha>0}\omega^\alpha(t,y)D^\alpha f(t,y)\right]dt\\&=\int_0^T \mathbf{P_t}\left[\frac{\partial f}{\partial t}(0,x)+\sum\nolimits_{\alpha>0}\omega^\alpha(0,x)D^\alpha f(0,x)\right]dt. \quad (11)\end{aligned}$$

Continuous time process: According to Dynkin theorem (e.g., Roger and Williams III.13.3), if X is a continuous time Markov process then the generator $\mathcal{G}$ is a second order differential operator for all infinitely differential functions of compact support C_k^∞ in the domain $\mathcal{D}(\mathcal{G})$. This means that for a continuous process

$$\omega^\alpha = 0 \quad \text{for } \alpha \equiv \alpha_1 + \cdots + \alpha_d > 2. \tag{12}$$

Let us denote the process X_t as

$$X_t \equiv (u_t, v_t). \tag{13}$$

Equation (11) is then

$$\begin{aligned} &E[f(T, u_T, v_T)|u_0 = u, v_0 = v] - f(0, u, v) \\ &= \int_0^T \mathbf{P_t} \times \left[\frac{\partial f}{\partial t}(0, u, v) + \sum\nolimits_{\alpha>0} \omega^\alpha(0, u, v) D^\alpha f(0, u, v)\right] dt \end{aligned} \tag{14}$$

In Equation (14) the expectation is over two stochastic variables u and v. In the next step we want to express the expectation of the function f as expectation of one stochastic variable u where the expectation over v is an implicit function of u. The purpose of this step is to reduce the dimensionality of the problem.

Using the tower property of conditional expectation, for any test function $\tilde{f}$ we have

$$\begin{aligned} \mathbf{P_t}\, \tilde{f}(0, u, v) &= E[\tilde{f}(u_t, v_t|u_0 = u, v_0 = v] \\ &= E[E(\tilde{f}(u_t, v_t|u_t)|u_0 = u, v_0 = v]. \end{aligned} \tag{15}$$

Provided that $v \to \tilde{f}(u, v)$ is continuous and strictly monotone for each u then there exists some $v_t^*(u|u_0, v_0)$ such that

$$\begin{aligned} E[E(\tilde{f}(u_t, v_t|u_t)|u_0 = u, v_0 = v] &= E[E(\tilde{f}(u_t, v_t^*(u_t, u_0, v_0)|u_0 \\ &= u, v_0 = v]. \end{aligned} \tag{16}$$

Applying conditional expectation on Equation (14) $v_t^*(u)$ is defined so that

$$\begin{aligned} &E_{V_t}\left[\frac{\partial f}{\partial t}(t, u_t, v_t) + \sum\nolimits_{\alpha>0} \omega^\alpha(t, u_t, v_t) D^\alpha f(t, u_t, v_t)|u_t = u\right] \\ &= \frac{\partial f}{\partial t}(t, u, v_t^*(u)) + \sum\nolimits_{\alpha>0} \omega^\alpha(t, u_t, v_t^*(u)) D^\alpha f(t, u_t, v_t^*(u)) \end{aligned} \tag{17}$$

where $D^{\alpha} f(t, u_t, v_t^*) \equiv D^{\alpha} f(t, u_t, v_t)|_{V_t} = V_t^*$. Therefore

$$E[f(T, u_T, V_T)|u_0 = u, v_0 = v] - f(0, u, v) = E\left[\int_0^T \left(\frac{\partial f}{\partial t}(t, u_t, v_t^*)\right.\right.$$

$$\left.\left. + \sum_{\alpha>0} \omega^{\alpha}(t, u_t, v_t^*) D^{\alpha} f(t, u_t, v_t^*)\right] dt\right]. \quad (18)$$

Let us now choose f to be the price of a European (call or Put) option with strike K and maturity T. We denote the underlying asset price at time $t \geq 0$ by S_t. We define

$$u_t \equiv \log s_t. \quad (19)$$

The formalism above is general. We will define the stochastic variable v_t momentarily.

2.2 *No-arbitrage condition*

Now we introduce the no-arbitrage condition. We define the following market $\mathcal{M}$:

$\mathcal{M}$ = {The underlying asset, European call and put options with maturity time T and every strike K, a bond with maturity time T}.

Using the fundamental theorem of asset pricing [10], the market admits no arbitrage opportunity if and only if there exists at least one risk neutral probability measure such that for every strike K

$$\begin{aligned} f(0, u, v, T, K) &= e^{-r_{0T}T} E[f(T, u_T, v_T, T, K,)] \\ &= e^{-r_{0T}T} E[(\pm(S_T - K))^+ | u_0 = u,\ v_0 = v], \quad (20) \end{aligned}$$

where E is the expectation in the risk neutral measure, $\pm$ corresponds to Call and Put options. r_{0T} is the risk free rate to maturity

$$r_{0T} T \equiv \int_0^T r_t \, dt, \quad (21)$$

where r_t is the instantaneous risk free interest rate.

Alternatively, using

$$f(t,u,v) = E[e^{-r_rT(T-t)}(\pm(S_T - K))^+|u_t = u,\ v_t = v], \quad (22)$$

we define the quantity $h(t,u,v)$ which is a martingale

$$h(t,u,v) = e^{-r_0 t} f(t,u,v) = e^{-r_0 T T} E[(\pm(S_T - K))^+|u_t = u, \\ v_t = v]. \quad (23)$$

Thus,

$$\begin{aligned} h(0,u,v) &= f(0,u,v) = E[h(T,u_T,v_T|u_0 = u, v_0 = v] \\ &= e^{-r_{0T}T} P_T f(T,u,v) \\ &= e^{-r_{0T}T}\bigg(f(0,u,v) + E\bigg[\int_0^T \bigg[\frac{\partial f}{\partial t}(t,u,v) \\ &\quad + \sum\nolimits_{\alpha>0} \omega^\alpha(t,u,v) D^\alpha f(t,u,v)\bigg] dt\bigg]\bigg) \end{aligned} \quad (24)$$

Hence Equation (18) can be rewritten as

$$f(0,u,v)(e^{r_{0T}T} - 1) = \bigg[\int_0^T \bigg(\frac{\partial f}{\partial t}(t,u_t,v_t^*)\bigg) + \sum_{\alpha>0} \omega^\alpha \\ \times (t,u_t,v_t^*) D^\alpha f(t,u_t,v_t^*))dt \,|\, u_0 = u, v_0 = v\bigg]. \quad (25)$$

The advantage of Equation (25) is the fact that the option price is obtained with the probability density function from inception to time t and does not involve the probability density transfer from time t to $t + \delta t$.

The most natural variable for v_t is the time average volatility to maturity.

Denote $\omega^{2,0}(t,x) = \lim_{h\to 0} \frac{E[(X_{t+h}-x)^2|X_t=x]}{h}/2$ from Equation (10), and assuming that for any t the limit exists for any x in $\mathbb{X}$, then for a fixed option maturity time $T > 0$ we define the second variable v_t by

$$v_t^2 \equiv E\bigg[\int_t^T \omega^{2,0}(t')dt'|\mathcal{F}_t\bigg]\bigg/(T-t) \quad \text{for } 0 \le t \le T, \quad (26)$$

which is the stochastic process that corresponds to the "average" forward volatility of the asset price until maturity, at time t.

Before we show how to calculate the volatility smile with this approach let us observe some examples.

2.3 *Using the density function to calculate the integrals*

Let us now denote the risk neutral probability density function from s_1 at time t_1 to s_2 at time t_2 as $g^{t_1,t_2}(s_1, s_2) \equiv g(s_2, t_2|s_1, t_1)$ and for simplicity we define $g^t(S) \equiv g^{t_0,t}(S_0, S)$. We also denote

$$\sigma_t = \sigma_t(S_t, S_0, \sigma_0) \equiv v_t^*(u|u_0, v_0). \tag{27}$$

For simplicity we omit the subscript $_{\text{call/put}}$ in the European option price $f_{\text{call/put}}(s_t, K, T-t)$ for a strike K and expiry T.

Equation (25) can be rewritten as

$$\begin{aligned} f(s_0, K, T)(e^{rT} - 1) = \int_0^{\mathrm{T}} \mathrm{d}t \int_0^{\infty} \mathrm{d}s\ g^t(s)\,[\partial_t f(s, \sigma_t(s, s_0), K, T-t) \\ + \sum_{2 \geq n+m > 0} \mathrm{s}^n \omega_t^{n,m}(s, \sigma_t(s, s_0))_s^n \partial_{\sigma_t}^m \\ \times f(s, \sigma_t(s, s_0) K, T-t)] \end{aligned} \tag{28}$$

with

$$f_{\text{call/put}}(s, K, T-t) = e^{-\int_t^T r_t dt} \int_0^{\infty} ds_T (\pm(s_T - K))^+ g^{\mathrm{t,T}} g(s, s_T) \tag{29}$$

and in $\omega_t^{n,m} n$ and m correspond to the derivatives by s and σ, respectively.

For simplicity we omit the dependency of σ_t on s_t, s_0, σ_0. Notice that the dependency on σ_t in the density function can be absorbed into the dependency of s_t. If s_t undergoes a continuous time process then $n + m < 3$.

Claim 1: $\omega_t^{1,0} = r_t - q_t$.

Proof: Let us define q_t as the instantaneous dividend (carry) rate and q is defined at $t_0 = 0$ by

$$q \equiv \int_0^T q_t dt/T. \tag{30}$$

A European call option with strike $K = 0$ must satisfy for all $0 \leq t \leq T$

$$f(s_t, \sigma_t, K = 0,\ T - t) = se^{-\int_t^T q_{t'} dt'}. \tag{31}$$

When plugging Equation (31) into the integral in Equation (28) we obtain

$$\int_0^T dt \int_0^\infty ds\, g^t(s)\,[\partial_t + s\,\omega_t{}^{1,0}\partial_s]se^{-\int_t^T q_{t'}dt'} = \int_0^T dt \int_0^\infty ds\, g^t(s)$$

$$s(\omega_t{}^{1,0} + q_t)e^{-\int_t^T q_{t'}dt'} = s_0 e^{-qT} \int_0^T dt(\omega_t{}^{1,0} + q_t)\, e^{\int_0^t r_{t'}dt'}, \tag{32}$$

where in Equation (32) we used the property of the risk neutral density function $g(s,t)$

$$\int_0^\infty ds\, g^t(s)s = s_0 e^{\int_0^t (r_{t'} - q_{t'})dt'}. \tag{33}$$

Hence

$$\begin{aligned} f(s_0, K = 0, T)(e^{rT} - 1) &= s_0 e^{-qT}(e^{rT} - 1) \\ &= s_0 e^{-qT} \int_0^T dt(\omega_t^{1,0} + q_t)\, e^{\int_0^t r_{t'}dt'}, \end{aligned} \tag{34}$$

or

$$e^{\int_0^T r_t dt} - 1 = \int_0^T dt(\omega_t{}^{1,0} + q_t)\, e^{\int_0^t r_{t'}dt'}. \tag{35}$$

Therefore $\omega_t{}^{1,0} = r_t - q_t$. □

Hence in the continuous time process Equation (25) can be written as

$$f(s_0, 0, K)(e^{rT} - 1)$$
$$= \int_0^T dt \int_0^\infty dsg^t(s)\,[\partial_t f(s, \sigma_t, K, T - t)$$
$$+s(\mathbf{r}_t - q_t)\partial_s f(s, \sigma_t, K, T - t) + \nu_t(s, \sigma_t)\partial_\sigma f(s, \sigma_t, K, T - t)$$
$$+ s^2\lambda_t(s, \sigma_t)\partial^2_{ss} f(s, \sigma_t, K, T - t) + \eta_t(s, \sigma_t)\partial^2_{\sigma\sigma} f(s, \sigma_t, K, T - t)$$
$$+s\rho_t(s, \sigma_t)\partial^2_{\sigma s} f(s, \sigma_t, K, T - t)], \tag{36}$$

where

$$\omega_t^{0,1} = \nu_t; \quad \omega_t^{2,0} = 2\lambda_t; \quad \omega_t^{0,2} = 2\eta_t; \quad \omega_t^{1,1} = \rho_t. \tag{37}$$

and $\sigma_t = \sigma_t$ (s). From the definition in Equation (37) $2\lambda_t$ is the variance of $\log(s_t)$, $2\eta_t$ is the variance of σ_t and ρ_t is the covariance of $\log(s_t)$ and σ_t.

Equation (36) is a general equation for option pricing and includes *all* the continuous time pricing models.

2.4 *The PDE of the density function to maturity*

Equation (36) for Call options becomes

$$f(s_0, K, T)(e^{rT} - 1) = (1 - e^{-rT}) \int_0^\infty ds_T g^T(s_T)(s_T - K)^+$$
$$= \int_0^T dt \int_0^\infty \mathrm{ds} \int_{\mathrm{K}}^\infty ds_T(s_T - K)g^t(s)[\partial_t + s_{(r_t - q_t)}\partial_s$$
$$+ \nu_t(s, \sigma_t)\partial_\sigma + s^2\lambda_t(s, \sigma_t)\partial^2_{\mathrm{ss}} + \eta_t(s, \sigma_t)\partial^2_{\sigma\sigma} + s\rho_t(s,\ \sigma_t)\partial^2_{\sigma \mathrm{s}}]$$
$$\times \left(e^{-\int_{\mathrm{t}}^{\mathrm{T}} \mathrm{r}_{t'} dt'} \mathrm{g}^{t,\mathrm{T}}(s, S_T, \sigma_t)\right). \tag{38}$$

After rearranging terms Equation (38) to can be written as

$$(1 - e^{-rT}) \int_{\mathrm{K}}^\infty ds_T(s_T - K)g^T(s_T) = \int_{\mathrm{K}}^\infty ds_T(s_T - K) \int_0^T dte^{-\int_{\mathrm{t}}^{\mathrm{T}} r_{t'}\mathrm{dt}'}$$
$$\int_0^\infty dsg^t(s)[\partial_t + r_t + s(r_t - q_t)\partial_s + \nu_t(s, \sigma_t)\partial_\sigma + s^2\lambda_t(s, \sigma_t)\partial^2_{\mathrm{ss}}$$
$$+\eta_t(s, \sigma_t)\partial^2_{\sigma\sigma} + s\rho_t(s, \sigma_t)\partial^2_{\sigma \mathrm{s}}]g^{t,\mathrm{T}}(s, S_T, \sigma_t). \tag{39}$$

Since for any Markov process the Chapman–Kolmogorov equation is satisfied, hence for any $0 < t < T$

$$\int_0^\infty dsg^t(s)g^{t,T}(s, S_T, \sigma_t) = g^T(s_T). \tag{40}$$

Using the fact that $\int\limits_0^T dtr_t e^{-\int\limits_t^T r_{t'}dt'} = (1 - e^{-rT})$, Equation (40) is satisfied when the function $g^{t,T}(s, S_T, \sigma_t)$ obeys the following PDE:

$$\begin{aligned}[]&[\partial_t + r_t + s(r_t - q_t)\partial_s + \nu_t(\mathrm{s}, \sigma_t)\partial_\sigma + s^2\lambda_t(s, \sigma_t)\partial^2_{\mathrm{ss}} + \eta_t(s, \sigma_t)\partial^2_{\sigma\sigma} \\ &\quad + s\rho_t(s, \sigma_t)\partial^2_{\sigma s}]\ g^{t,T}(s, S_T, \sigma_t) = r_t g^{t,T}(s, S_T, \sigma_t).\end{aligned} \tag{41}$$

Or

$$\begin{aligned}[]&[\partial_t + s(r_t - q_t)\partial_s + \nu_t(s, \sigma_t)\partial_\sigma + s^2\lambda_t(s, \sigma_t)\partial^2_{\mathrm{ss}} + \eta_t(s, \sigma_t)\partial^2_{\sigma\sigma} \\ &\quad + s\rho_t(s, \sigma_t)\partial^2_{\sigma \mathrm{s}}]g^{t,T}(s, S_T, \sigma_t) = 0.\end{aligned} \tag{42}$$

Using $t = 0$ hence the general form for the vanilla smile in continuous time process is dictated by

$$\begin{aligned}[]&[\partial_t + s_0(r_0 - q_0)\partial_s + \nu_0\partial_\sigma + s_0^2\lambda_0\partial^2_{\mathrm{ss}} + \eta_0\partial^2_{\sigma\sigma} + s_0\rho_0\partial^2_{\sigma\mathrm{s}}]g^T \\ &\quad \times (t, s, S_T, \sigma(s))\,|_{t=0, s=s_0, \sigma=\sigma_0} = 0.\end{aligned} \tag{43}$$

Equation (43) is a general PDE for all continuous time models. It shows that $g^T(s_T)$ depends on the same constants $\nu_0, \lambda_0, \eta_0, \rho_0$ for all s_T.

Changing variables to $\tau = T - t$, $y = S_T/s$, Equation (43) can be rewritten as

$$\begin{aligned}[]&[-\partial\tau - y(2\lambda_0 + r_0 - q_0)\partial_y + \nu_0\partial_\sigma + y^2\lambda_0\partial^2_{\mathrm{yy}} + \eta_0\partial^2_{\sigma\sigma} - y\rho_0\partial^2_{\sigma\mathrm{y}}] \\ &\quad \times g^\tau(y, \sigma) = 0\end{aligned} \tag{44}$$

2.5 *An Example: Deterministic time dependent volatility yields the BSM model*

In the specific case where the underlying assets undergoes a continuous time process with a deterministic time dependent volatility then we can show that Equation (42) produces the BSM formula for European options.

Consider the case that v_t^2 in Equation (26) is deterministic and time dependent. In Equation (16) $v_t^*(u|u_0, v_0) = v_t$. Let us define $\omega_t^{2,0}(t) \equiv \theta_t^2$ of Equation (10) and therefore in Equation (26)

$$\sigma_t^2(T-t) = \int_t^T \theta_{t'}^2 dt';\ \omega_t^{0,1} = \partial_t\,\sigma_t = (\sigma_t - \theta_t^2/\sigma_t)/2(T-t);$$
$$\times\,\omega_t{}^{1,1} = \omega_t^{0,2} = 0. \tag{45}$$

Equation (42) for Call options with deterministic σ_t is

$$[\partial_t + s(r_t - q_t)\partial_s + \partial_t\,\sigma_t\partial_\sigma + \frac{1}{2}\,s^2\theta_t^2\partial_{\text{ss}}^2]g^{t,T}(s, S_T, \sigma_t) = 0. \tag{46}$$

When we plug $\partial_t\,\sigma_t$ of Equation (45) into Equation (46), the solution for Equation (46) is the log-normal density function

$$\mathrm{g}^{t,T}(s, S_T, \sigma_t) = \frac{1}{s_T\sqrt{2\pi\int_t^T\theta_t^2 dt}}e^{-d_{tT}^2/2} = \frac{1}{\sigma_t s_T\,\sqrt{2\pi(T-t)}}e^{-d_{tT}^2/2}. \tag{47}$$

With

$$d_{tT} = \left(\log\frac{s_T}{s} - \int_t^T (r_t - q_t)dt\right)/\sigma_t\sqrt{T-t} + \sigma_t\sqrt{T-t}/2. \tag{48}$$

Plugging $t = 0$ in Equation (47) and using the definition in Equation (29) we obtain the Black–Scholes–Merton price with the volatility σ_{0T}, *i.e.*, $f\ (s_0, K, T) = \text{BSM}\ (s_0, \sigma_{0T}, r_{0T}, q_{0T}, T)$.

The option price for time dependent non-stochastic volatility depends only on σ_{0T} and is independent of σ_{0t} for $t < T$. Hence, we can equivalently solve Equation (46) with a constant $\sigma_t = \sigma_{0T}$ for all $0 \le t \le T$, or $0 = \partial_t\sigma_t$.

The fact that the option price depends only on the volatility until maturity means that the price of European options is independent of the specific term structure of volatility and rates before the maturity.

3. Evidence that the Volatility Smile is Independent of the Term Structure

Before we proceed with calculating the option price we would like to show a clear proof that in financial markets the volatility smile for a given maturity is not an outcome of a specific term structure of the volatility. The same volatility smile for maturity T can appear in the option markets with very different volatility smiles for maturities earlier than T. In other words, when one looks at a given volatility smile for expiry T there is no mapping to the term structure of the volatility for maturities shorten than T. This means that in order to calculate the volatility smile for a given maturity T one does not need to know the specific term structure of volatility for maturities $t < T$.

3.1 *The methodology*

In order to investigate this point we gathered the daily close rates of the OTC volatility smile from the period January 2, 2010 to December 31, 2019 in the currency market and gold where the data is available and accurate. We looked at several currency pairs which have the same trading conventions including: EUR/USD, EUR/JPY, GBP/USD, AUD/USD, EUR/TYR, XAU/USD (Euro, Japanese Yen, British pound, Australian Dollar, Turkish Dollar, Gold).

Since we need to normalize the strikes by the spot rate it is easy to use the FX market where the smile is quoted with the BS implied volatility and the strikes are quoted in Delta. In other word in the FX market the option price is quoted as BSM(s, σ_{implied}, K, T) and the strike is represented by Delta where

$$\text{Delta}_{\text{call}}[f(s_0, K, T)] = N(d_1); \quad \text{Delta}_{\text{put}}[f(s_0, K, T)] = 1 - N(d_1). \tag{49}$$

In the FX market the volatility smile is represented by five strikes which correspond to:

At the money volatility σ_{ATM} which corresponds to the strike for which the delta of the call and the delta of the put options are opposite; the strike that corresponds to $\text{Delta}_{\text{call}} = 25\%$; the strike that corresponds to $\text{Delta}_{\text{put}} = -25\%$; the strike that corresponds to $\text{Delta}_{\text{call}} = 10\%$; the strike that corresponds to $\text{Delta}_{\text{put}} = -10\%$. These five points on the volatility smile are quite liquid and the bid-ask spreads is quite small.

Hence each volatility smile is a set of five volatilities

$$\text{VolSmile} \equiv \{\sigma_{\text{ATM}}, \sigma_{\text{call}}(25\text{D}), \sigma_{\text{put}}(25\text{D}), \sigma_{\text{call}}(10\text{D}), \sigma_{\text{put}}(25\text{D})\}. \tag{50}$$

We collected the daily volatility smile for expiries 1 month, 2 month, 3 month, 6 month and 1 year. For a given date and currency pair we look at the volatility smiles for five expiries. We refer to the set of five volatility smiles from 1 month to 1 year as the **term structure** of volatility.

First we looked for 1 year volatility smiles that appear twice or more in the data set regardless of the currency pair. This gives dates and currency pairs. Then for each 1 year smile that appears twice or more we looked at volatility smiles for the expiries 1 month, 2 month, 3 month and 6 month and compare the sets. In other words if

$$\begin{aligned} \text{VS} &= \text{VS(date 1, ccy 1, expiry 1 year)} \\ &= \text{VS(date 2, ccy 2, expiry 1 year)} \end{aligned}$$

then we compare the smiles in the other expiries, i.e.,

$$\begin{aligned} \text{VS} = \text{VS(date 1, ccy 1, expiry } i < 1 \text{ year) compare to} \\ \text{VS(date 2, ccy 2, expiry } i < 1 \text{ year)} \end{aligned}$$

3.2 *The results of our analysis*

We found 1,303 cases where exactly the same volatility smile appeared twice or more in non-consecutive days.

In 94% of the cases the volatility smiles for previous expiries were very different. The only times they were not different were when a similar term structure traded two consecutive days.

All together we found in 67% of the cases the volatility smile of 1 year was same for the same currency pair at two different dates (at least 1 week apart) and in 33% of the cases the same 1 year volatility smile traded with different currency pairs (always at different dates). In all these cases the rest the term structure for maturities 6,3,2,1 months are significantly different. For example in one term structure σ_{ATM}'s are ascending and in the other they are descending. In some cases in the first expiries $\sigma_{\text{call}}(25\text{ D}) \gg \sigma_{\text{put}}(25\text{ D})$ and in the other $\sigma_{\text{call}}(25\text{ D}) \ll \sigma_{\text{put}}(25\text{ D})$.

3.3 *Conclusions*

The same 1 year volatility smile appeared with different currencies at different dates but usually with different term structure.

In Table 1, we show three examples.

Table 1 proves that we do not need to know the term structure in order to calculate the volatility smile for expiry T. In particular we

Table 1: Examples for different volatility surfaces with the same volatility smile at maturity.

Currency Pair:		**EUR/USD**				
Dates:	8-Dec-16	16-Jan-15				
1 Year Smile	ATM	25D Call	25D Put	10D Call	10D Put	
		10.66	9.9	12.29	9.88	14.22
	Date	1 m	2 m	3 m	6 m	1 y
ATM	8-Dec-16	9.00	9.51	9.73	10.84	10.66
	16-Jan-15	13.14	12.38	12.01	11.21	10.66
25D call	8-Dec-16	8.80	9.16	9.33	9.34	9.9
	16-Jan-15	12.28	11.52	11.17	10.435	9.9
25D put	8-Dec-16	9.72	10.44	10.87	12.57	12.28
	16-Jan-15	14.54	13.82	13.54	12.77	12.28
Currency Pair:		**GBP/USD**				
Dates:	Dec 1 2014		Sep 9 2014			
1 Year Smile	ATM	2SD Call	25D Put	10D Call	10D Put	
		7.87	7.57	8.86	7.79	10.21
	Date	1 m	2 m	3 m	6 m	1 y
ATM	Dec 1 2014	6.32	6.6	6.77	7.58	7.87
	Sep 9 2014	10.94	9.2	8.67	8	7.87

(*Continued*)

Table 1: (*Continued*)

Currency Pair:		**GBP/USD**				
25D call	Dec 1 2014	6.06	6.32	6.47	7.26	7.57
	Sep 9 2014	10.17	8.52	8.06	7.58	7.57
25D put	Dec 1 2014	6.92	7.23	7.S3	8.48	8.86
	Sep 9 2014	12.44	10.S2	9.91	9.06	8.86
Aug 6 2015	AUD/USD		July 20 2012		EUR/USD	
			Sep 9 2014			
1 Year Smile		ATM	25D Call	25D Put	10D Call	10D Put
		11.66	11.04	13.1	11.18	14.98
	Date	1 m	2 m	3 m	6 m	1 y
ATM	Jan 23 2017	11.93	11.99	11.88	11.64	11.66
	July 29 2010	9.24	9.68	9.89	10.65	11.66
25D call	Jan 23 2017	11.55	11.56	11.42	11.11	11.04
	July 29 2010	9.19	9.46	9.62	10.16	11.04
25D put	Jan 23 2017	12.61	12.81	12.83	12.82	13.1
	July 29 2010	9.63	10.26	10.61	11.75	13.1

can choose a fully consistent term structure and use it to solve for the option price. For example, we can calculate the volatility smile for a time homogeneous density function.

4. Calculating the Price of European Options

4.1 *Homogeneous density function*

The conclusion from Section 2 is that since the volatility smile in independent of the term structure there exist time independent functions $\{\omega_t^{n,m}\}$ that can be used in Equation (36).

In order to calculate the option price in Equation (36) one needs to know the density functions $g^t(s)$ and $g^{t,T}(s, s_T)$ for all $t \in [0, T]$. The volatility smile for expiry T is obtained from $g^T(s_T)$. Since the volatility smile is independent of the term structure, without loss of generality we can use a **time homogeneous** density function which satisfies Equation (51)

$$g^{t_1,t_2}(s_1, s_2) = g^{t_2-t_1}(s_1, s_2) \quad \text{for all } 0 \le t_1 < t_2 \le T, \tag{51}$$

which means that for a given h

$$\frac{\partial}{\partial t} g^{t,t+h}(s_1, s_2) = 0 \quad \text{for all } 0 \le t \le T. \tag{52}$$

From the convolution Equation (40) and the condition of Equation (51), $g^T(s_T)$ defines uniquely $g^{t_1,t_2}(s_1, s_2)$ for all $0 \le t_1 < t_2 \le T$.

It is important to clarify that we use a homogenous probability density function for mathematical comfort only, since the result of the integral should not depend on $g^t(s)$ for $t < T$ provided that $g^t(s)$ and $g^{t,T}(s, s_T)$ preserve all probability consistency conditions for every s_1, s_2 and $t \in [0, T]$. In Section 4, we demonstrate how to use bootstrapping from the Vanilla term structure to calculate the conditional probability density function $g^{t_1,t_2}(s_1, s_2)$ for $0 < t_1 < t_2 \le T$.

In the continuous time process, by definition from Equations (10) and (34) the probability density function can be written for $h \to 0$ as

$$g^{t,t+h}(s_1, s_2) = g^{t,t+h}(s_1, s_2, t, \nu_t, \lambda_t\, \eta_t, \rho_t). \tag{53}$$

Since for time homogeneous density function $g^{t,t+h}(s_1, s_2)$ is independent of t, therefore by definition, for time homogeneous density function the functions $\nu_t, \lambda_t, \eta_t, \rho_t$ are independent of t.

Claim 2: When the density function is time homogeneous them $\lambda_t = \sigma_t^2/2$ and $\nu_t = 0$.

Proof: Consider the continuous time process in Equation (36). From the definition in Equation (10), (18) and (26) for $t = T$

$$2\lambda_T = \omega^{2,0}(T) = lim_{t\to 0}\, \mathrm{E} \int_{T-t}^{T} \omega^{2,0}(t')dt'|F_{T-t}]/t = \sigma_T^2(s), \tag{54}$$

where the limit in Equation (54) exists because we assume that $\omega^{2,0}$ has a finite limit.

Thus from Equations (52) and (54) we obtain $\lambda_t = \sigma_t^2/2$ for $0 \leq t \leq T$.

Now we define the Martingale

$$M_t(T) = E\left[\int_0^T \omega^{2,0}(t')^2 dt' | \mathcal{F}_t\right] = (T-t)\sigma_t^2 + \int_0^t \omega^{2,0}(t')^2 dt'. \tag{55}$$

Therefore, applying the Ito formula

$$d(\sigma_t) = d(\sigma_t^2)/2\sigma_t = \frac{dM_t(T)}{(T-t)2\sigma_t} - \frac{\omega^{2,0}(t)^2 - \sigma_t^2}{(T-t)2\sigma_t} dt. \tag{56}$$

Using

$$\omega^{2,0}(t)^2 = \sigma_t^2 \quad \text{for all } 0 < t \leq T. \tag{57}$$

Hence

$$\nu_t = E[\lim_{h\to 0}(M_{t+h}(T) - M_t(T))/h]/(T-t)2\sigma_t.$$

In time homogeneous density function ν_t is time independent, i.e., $\nu_t = \nu(s_t\sigma_t)$. However, since $M_t(T)$ is time independent, we can write

$$M_t(T) = \mathrm{E}\left[\int_0^T \omega^{2,0}(t')^2\, dt' | \mathcal{F}_t\right] = M(s_0, \sigma_0, s_t, \sigma_t).$$

Since we have in the denominator $(T-t)$, if follows that if ν_t is time independent then $\nu_t = 0$. □

Going forward we omit the subscript t from η_t, ρ_t and λ_t and let us now write $\lambda = 1/2\sigma_t^2$. Equation (36) becomes

$$\begin{aligned} &f(s_0, 0, K)(e^{rT} - 1) \\ &= \int_0^T dt \int_0^\infty dsg^t(s)[\partial_t f(s, \sigma_t, K, T-t) \\ &\quad + s(r_t - q_t)\partial_s f(s, \sigma_t, K, T-t)\frac{1}{2}s^2\sigma_t^2\partial_{\mathrm{ss}}^2 f(s, \sigma_t, K, T-t) \\ &\quad + \eta\partial_{\sigma\sigma}^2 f(s, \sigma_t, K, T-t)\rho s\partial_{\sigma\mathrm{s}}^2 f(s, \sigma_t, K, T-t)]. \end{aligned} \tag{58}$$

Corollary. The price of a European option when the underlying asset price undergoes a continuous time process must satisfy Equation (58) where the density function is time homogeneous, $\eta(s, \sigma_t)$ and $\rho = \rho(s, \sigma_t)$.

Finally, let us define $\sigma_t = \sigma_0 \zeta_t$. As we saw in claim 1, in the specific case that σ_t is deterministic and is independent of s then $\zeta_t = 1$. In the general case $\zeta_t = \zeta_t(s)$; and we can write Equation (58) as

$$\begin{aligned} f(s_0, 0, K)(e^{rT} - 1) \\ = \int_0^T dt \int_0^\infty ds g^t(s)[\partial_t f(s, \sigma_0\zeta_t, K, T-t), \\ + s(r_t - q_t)\partial_s f(s, \sigma_0\zeta_t, K, T-t) \\ + \frac{1}{2}s^2\sigma_0^2\zeta_t^2\partial_{\mathrm{ss}}^2 f(s, \sigma_0\zeta_t, K, T-t) + \frac{1}{\sigma_0^2}\eta\partial_{\zeta\zeta}^2 f(s, \sigma_0\zeta_t, K, T-t) \\ + \frac{1}{\sigma_0}\rho s\partial_{\zeta s}^2 f(s, \sigma_0\zeta_t, K, T-t)]. \end{aligned} \tag{59}$$

In the simplest case the functions η, ρ are independent of s and σ and Equation (59) has three constants which we denote σ_0, η_0 and ρ_0.

4.2 *The consistency condition for $g^T(s)$*

Before we show a useful method to calculate $g^{t_1,t_2}(s_1, s_2)$ from $g^T(s_T)$ for a "smooth" time homogeneous density function in Section 3.3, let us describe how we obtain the time homogeneous density function $g(s_T, T)$.

First, we define the operator Θ that generates $g^{t_1,t_2}(s_1, s_2)$ from the density function $g^T(s_T)$ as

$$\Theta^{t_1,t_2}(s_1, s_2)g^T = g^{t_1,t_2}(s_1, s_2). \tag{60}$$

We now define

$$\begin{aligned} L(s_0, K, T) \equiv \int_0^T dt \int_0^\infty ds g^t(s)(\partial_t f(s, t, \sigma_t, K, T) \\ + \sum_{2 \geq n+m > 0} s^n \omega^{n,m} \partial_s^n \partial_{\sigma_t}^m f(s, \sigma_t(s)t)) \end{aligned}$$

$$= \int_0^T dt \int_0^\infty ds\Theta^{0,t}(s_0 s)g^T(\partial_t f(s,t,\sigma_t,K,T) + \sum_{2\geq n+m>0} s^n \omega^{n,m} \partial_s^n \partial_{\sigma_t}^m f(s,\sigma_t(s),t)), \tag{61}$$

where

$$f(s,t,\sigma_t,K,T) = e^{-\int_t^T r_t dt} \int_0^\infty ds_T(\pm(s_T - K))^+ \Theta^{t,T}(s,s_T)g^T. \tag{62}$$

In the integral of Equation (61) we need to express the density function in Equation (62) in terms of $\sigma_t(s)$ so we can derive by σ. The function $\sigma_t(s)$ is obtained by solving Equation (63).

$$\int_0^\infty ds_T(s_T - K)^+ \Theta^{t,T}(s,s_T)g^T = \int_0^\infty ds_T(s_T - K)^+ \frac{1}{\sigma_t(s)s_T\sqrt{2\pi(T-t)}} e^{-(\log \frac{s_T}{s} - (T-t)(r_{tT} - q_{tT}) + \sigma_t(s)^2(T-t)/2)^2/(2\sigma_t(s)^2(T-t))}. \tag{63}$$

Notice that $\sigma_t(s)$ is effectively the implied BSM volatility for the given density function. This allows us to derive $f(s,t,\sigma_t(s),K)$ by σ_t in Equation (61) and calculate the integral $L\ (s_0,K,T)$ in for a given density function $g^T(s)$.

Finally, Equation (26) can be written as

$$e^{rT} f(s_0,K,T) = f(s_0,K,T) + \mathcal{L}(s_0,K,T). \tag{64}$$

Using $g^T(s) = e^{rT} \left. \frac{\partial^2 f(s_0,K,T)}{\partial K^2} \right|_{K=s}$ we obtain the **consistency condition** for $g^T(s)$:

$$g^T(s) = \frac{\partial^2}{\partial K^2}(f(s_0,K,T) + L(s_0,K,T)) \mid_{K=s}. \tag{65}$$

4.3 *Calculating $g^T(s)$ by iteration for the continues time process*

Suppose we are given option prices f_1, f_2, f_3 for 3 strikes K_1, K_2, K_3 respectively, with maturity T, so that

$$f_i = f(s_0,T,K_i). \tag{66}$$

The density function $g^T(s)$ can be obtained numerically by iteration as follows.

We start with a first guess for $g^T(s)$, for example the log normal density function in (47).

- We now discretize the time to maturity T to N equal time intervals (for N large enough) and denote these times t_i, $i = 0, \ldots, N$.
- From the first guess for $g^T(s)$, we calculate the density function $g^{t_i}(s) = g^{t_0,t_i}(s_0, s)$ and the density function $g^{t_i,T}(s, s_T)$ for all $0 < i < N$ using the operator of Equation (60) for time homogeneous density function in a method we explain momentarily in Section 3.3.
- Using these density functions for all t_i we now calculate the integral of Equation (61) for the strikes K_1, K_1, K_3 expressed with the three unknown values of σ_0, η_0 and ρ_0.
- With the given option prices f_i we now determine the values of σ_0, η_0 and ρ_0 so that Equation (66) is satisfied for the three strikes. The values that satisfy Equation (66) are denote by $\sigma_{0,0}, \eta_{0,0}, \rho_{0,0}$ of the first guess of $g^T(s)$.
- Next, we calculate the integral for a large set of strikes $\{K_j\}$ using the calculated values of $\sigma_{0,0}, \eta_{0,0}, \rho_{0,0}$. Applying Equation (65), we obtain a new density function $g^T(s_T)$.
- We now use the new $g^T(s_T)$ and recalculate integrals for the strikes K_1, K_1, K_3 and using Equation (66) we obtain the new σ_0, η_0 and ρ_0 for the first iteration which we denote $\sigma_{0,1}, \eta_{0,1}, \rho_{0,1}$. Repeating the calculation for a large set of strikes $\{K_j\}$ we obtain from Equation (65) a new $g^T(s_T)$.
- We continue the iteration process of recalculating $g^T(s_T)$ and we stop after m steps when $g^T(s_T)$ converges, meaning that after m iterations $g^T(s_T)$ changes by less than some predetermined value ε for every s_T. (Alternatively the convergence condition can be phrased such that the maximal change of option prices of all the strikes that determine $g^T(s_T)$ in Equation (65) is less than a predetermined value ε.) The converged density function $g_G^T(s_T) = g_G^T\,(\frac{s}{s_0}, \sigma_{0,m}, \eta_{0,m}\, \rho_{0,m})$ is the density function to maturity. Set σ_0, η_0 and ρ_0 as $\sigma_{0,m}, \eta_{0,m}, \rho_{0,m}$ respectively, then

$$g_G^T(s) = g_G^T\left(\frac{s}{s_0}\sigma_0,\ \eta_0, \rho_0\right) = g_G^T\left(\frac{s}{s_0}\,\Sigma^T\right), \tag{67}$$

where $\Sigma^T \equiv (\sigma_0, \eta_0,\ \rho_0)$. Hence using given option prices of three strikes with maturity T we can calculate the whole volatility smile for maturity T. Σ^T depends on the market conditions at every given moment, it varies between different maturities and assets and it has different representations in different assets. At a given time t the European option price for maturity T is

$$f = f(s_t, \Sigma_t^T K, T-t, r_t q_t). \tag{68}$$

4.4 A Numerical method to calculate $g^{t_1,t_2(s_1,s_2)}$ from $g^T(s_T)$ for time homogeneous density function

In the following, we propose a numerical method to calculate the density function $g^{t_1,t_2}(s_1, s_2)$ for $t_1 < t_2 \leq T$. First, let us demonstrate how to calculate $g^{t/2}$(s) when $g^t(s)$ is given.

We denote the cumulative distribution function of $g^t(s)$ by $G^t(s) = \int_0^s ds_1 g^t(s_1)$. Let us denote $G^t(s) = \tilde{G}^t(\log s/s_0)$. Assuming that $\tilde{G}^t$ is a continuous and strictly monotonic function, we now define the one to one mapping

$$\tilde{G}^t(\log s/s_0) \equiv N(X_t), \tag{69}$$

where $N(X_t)$ is the cumulative Normal distribution function. Hence $X_t(\log s)$ is normally distributed. Since the mapping is one to one then

$$X_t = N^{-1}\tilde{G}^t(\log s/s_0). \tag{70}$$

Now define the function $V_t(X_t)$ which is strictly positive since the mapping is between two distribution functions

$$V_t(X_t) = \frac{d\log\ s(X_t)}{dX_t}. \tag{71}$$

Hence

$$\log s(X_t) = \int_{-\infty}^{X_t} V_t(x)dx \quad -\infty < X_t < \infty. \tag{72}$$

Given the function $\log s(X_t)$, the call option price for strike K and maturity t is

$$f(s_0, K, t)_{\text{Call}} = e^{-\int_0^t r_{t'}dt'} \int_{-\infty}^{\infty} dx(\mathrm{e}^{\log s_t(x)} - K)^+ n(x), \tag{73}$$

where $n(x)$ is the standard normal density function of x. Using the property that

$$g^t(s) = \int ds_1 g^{t/2}(s_1) g^{t/2,t}(s_1, s) = \int ds_1 g^{t/2}(s_1) g^{t/2}(s_1, s), \quad (74)$$

we can write Equation (73) as

$$f(s_0, K, t)_{\text{Call}} = e^{-\int_0^t \mathrm{r}_{t'} dt'} \int_{-\infty}^{\infty} dx \int_{-\infty}^{\infty} dy$$

$$n(x) n(y - x)(e^{\log \mathrm{S_t(y)}} - \mathrm{K})^+ = e^{-\int_0^t \mathrm{r}_{t'} dt'} \int_{-\infty}^{\infty} dx$$

$$\int_{-\infty}^{\infty} dy n(x) n(y)(e^{\log \mathrm{S_t}(x+y)} - K)^+, \quad (75)$$

and

$$\log \mathrm{S_t}(x + y) = \int_{-\infty}^{x+y} V_{t/2}(\mathrm{z}) dz. \quad (76)$$

We find the function $V_{t/2}(X_t)$ by requiring that for many different strikes $\{K_i\}$ the option prices obtained with the expressions (75), (76) will be the same as the option prices obtained directly from $g^t(\mathrm{s})$ Let us select M points for z, z_m which span the integration area in Equation (76). Once we know $V_{t/2}(z_m)$ for all the z_m we can interpolate between the $z_m's$ Hence we are solving for M values $V_{t/2}(z_m)$.

We define for each one of the strikes K_i

$$f_i \equiv f(s_0, K_i, t); \; \tilde{f}_i \equiv e^{-r_t t} \int_{-\infty}^{\infty} dx \int_{-\infty}^{\infty} dy \, n(x) n(y)$$

$$\times (e^{\int_{-\infty}^{x+y} V_{t/2}(z) dz} - K_i)^+. \quad (77)$$

The M values of $V_{t/2}(z_m)$ are obtained by optimization over all strikes $\{K_i\}$

$$\{V_{t/2}(z_m)\} \text{ such that } \min \sum_{(\{K_i\})} (f_i - \tilde{f}_i)^2. \quad (78)$$

We now start with $g^T(s)$ and calculate $g^{T/2}(s)$, $g^{T/4}(s), \ldots,$ $g^{T/2^N}(s)$ for N as large as required. Denote $t_1 = T/2^N$ we can define $g^{T/2^N}(s)$ as the **kernel** density function. The rest of the $g^{t_i}(s)$ are obtained by using convolutions with the kernel density function.

5. Obtaining the Conditional Probability Transfer Density by Bootstrapping the European Options Term Structure

In this section, we demonstrate how to use the term structure of European option prices in order to calculate the probability transfer density function. In other words, if we are given option prices for some strikes $\{K_{1i}\}$ with maturity T_1 and some option prices for some strikes $\{K_{2i}\}$ with maturity T_2, we can calculate the conditional probability $g(s_1 T_1 \to s_2,\, T_2)$.

First, using the option prices for $\{K_{1i}\}$, we calculate the density function for T_1 $g_G(s_{T_1}/s_0, \gamma_{10}, \eta_{10}, \rho_{10}, T_1)$, and using the option prices for $\{K_{2i}\}$, we calculate the density function for T_2 $g_G(s_{T_2}/s_0, \gamma_{20}, \eta_{20}, \rho_{20}, T_2)$. The density function $g(s_1, T_1 \to s_2,\, T_2)$ satisfies

$$g(s_1 T_1 \to s_2, T_2) = g_G\left(\frac{s_2}{s_1}, \gamma_0(s_1), \eta_0(s_1), \rho_0(s_1), T_2 - T_1\right). \quad (79)$$

Being associated with variance and covariance, the functions $\gamma_0(s_1), \eta_0(s_1), \rho_0(s_1)$ need to satisfy some conditions. Since $\gamma_0(s_1), \eta_0(s_1)$ are variances, they have to be strictly positive. We expect them to have one minimum and the values at very large and very small s should be higher than at the current underlying asset price s_0. Hence $\gamma_0(s_1)$, $\eta_0(s_1)$ are positive with a smile shape. $\rho_0(s_1)$ is a covariance, and we expect it to be monotonically increasing since with large moves of the underlying asset, we expect its covariance to align with the direction of the move. In other words, with a large move of the underlying asset, its standard deviation grows, and the correlation is high and positive. With a large move down, again the standard deviation grows, and the correlation is high in absolute value but negative.

We use Equation (87) to calculate the functions $\gamma_0(s_1), \eta_0(s_1)$ and $\rho_0(s_1)$.

$$P(K, T_2, s_0) = df_1 \int ds_1 g(s_0, 0 \to s_1, t_1)) P(K, T_2 - T_1, s_1), \quad (80)$$

where $g(s_0, 0 \to s_1, T_1)$ is derived from the smile at T_1, df_1 is the discount factor from time zero to time t_1, and

$$P(K, T_2 - T_1, s_1) = P(K, T_2 T_1, s_1 \gamma_0(s_1) \eta_0(s_1), \rho_0(s_1)). \quad (81)$$

The functions $\gamma_0(s_1), \eta_0(s_1), \rho_0(s_1)$ should satisfy Equations (80) and (81) for all strikes K subject to the condition (regularization) that the functions $\gamma_0(s_1), \eta_0(s_1)$ are strictly positive with one minimum and the function $\rho_0(s_1)$ is monotonically increasing.

The numerical procedure to obtain $\gamma_0(s_1), \eta_0(s_1), \rho_0(s_1)$ is detailed in our chapter [11].

Once the functions $\gamma_0(s_1), \eta_0(s_1), \rho_0(s_1)$ are obtained, the conditional density function is obtained from Equation (79). In order to calculate exotic options, we need to repeat the calculation for all $0 < t_i,\ t_{i+1} \leq T$ for small time increments. Using $\gamma_0(s_1, t_i, t_{i+1}), \eta_0(s_1, t_\mathrm{i}, t_{\mathrm{i}+1}), \rho_0(s_1, t_i, t_{i+1})$ we obtain

$$g(s_1, t_i \to s_2, t_{i+1}) = g_G\left(\frac{s_2}{s_1}, \gamma_0(s_1, t_\mathrm{i}, t_{\mathrm{i}+1}), \eta_0(s_1, t_\mathrm{i}, t_{\mathrm{i}+1}),\right.$$
$$\left. \times\, \rho_0(s_1, t_\mathrm{i}, t_{\mathrm{i}+1}) t_{i+1} - t_i\right). \tag{82}$$

6. Empirical Evidence from the Option Markets

In the previous section, we showed that in the continuous time model, three parameters γ, η and ρ determine the whole smile for the expiry T. In this section, we want to compare the model to the various Vanilla European option markets. For each asset class (currencies, equities, interest rates and commodities) and every expiry we need to find three numbers that provide the closest fit to the market. Then, we can see if using the fit the model generate prices that are within the bid/ask spread in the market and typically closest to the middle between the bid and the ask prices (mid-market).

6.1 *Representations of* Σ^T *in different asset classes*

In all liquid options market there are liquid traded option strategies that provide live representations to the three quantities of Σ^T.

In currencies the three quantities are ATM delta neutral volatility, 25 delta risk reversals and 25 delta butterflies. In commodities these three quantities are ATM forward volatility, 25 delta risk reversals and 25 delta Butterflies. In rates these are the ATM Forward volatility, PP basis points collars and PP basis points strangles, where PP depends on the current forward rate (e.g., 50 basis points). In equities these are ATM spot or ATM forward volatility, $X\%$ vs (100-X)% spot collars and strangles where X depends on the volatility of the stock/index (e.g., 90% vs 110% collars and strangles).

6.2 *Methodology*

We consider European Vanilla options in all asset classes. In currencies the OTC Vanilla options are European. In interest rates the OTC swaptions (options on swaps) are European. In equities we look at exchange traded options. We either look at European options on indices or at stock options of companies that never pay dividend and so the options trade as European. In commodities we look at exchange traded options where the underlying is the futures on the underlying asset so we can treat them as European options.

In order to examine the accuracy of the model we do the following:

For a given asset, we take option prices of call and put options of all the strikes for a given expiry t_i. We then look for four parameters that simultaneously provide the best fit to the prices. The four parameters are the forward rate for the expiry $F(t_i)$ and γ_{t_i}, η_{t_i} and ρ_{t_i}. In general we try to fit to mid-market but when we are given both bid and ask prices the fit has a high weight on being within the bid/ask spread. Also we assign a higher weight to accuracy near the forward rate than at very high and low strikes where the liquidity of the prices in the market is much smaller.

Finally, we did two tests. The first is with mid-market rates of year end. These rates are used to determine the P/L of trading books are so are considered especially accurate. Our data is from December 31, 2015. We took a very large sample of liquid assets. The second test is with intraday prices of some exchange traded assets.

6.3 *Year-end rates: Comparing the model to the most accurate mid-market*

Currencies: We look at nine currency pairs which represent the whole spectrum from the liquidity and interest perspectives: EUR/USD; USD/JPY; EUR/JPY; EUR/GBP; EUR/CHF; GBP/USD; EUR/CHF; USD/KRW; EUR/PLN. The data we have is ATM volatility, the volatility of 25 Delta call, 25 Delta put,

Table 2: Accuracy of the model in 1 year expiration for currencies.

	Strike	10d Put	25d Put	ATM	25d Call	10d Call
EUR/USD	Model	12.447	11.238	10.100	9.513	9.555
	Market	12.438	11.238	10.100	9.513	9.563
USD/JPY	Model	11.480	9.838	9.050	9.563	11.048
	Market	11.500	9.838	9.050	9.563	11.050
USD/GBP	Model	14.236	12.213	10.425	9.588	9.655
	Market	14.350	12.213	10.425	9.588	9.650
EUR/JPY	Model	13.867	11.800	10.300	10.000	10.657
	Market	13.925	11.800	10.300	10.000	10.625
EUR/GBP	Model	11.376	10.650	10.525	11.250	12.526
	Market	11.350	10.650	10.525	11.250	12.500
EUR/CHF	Model	12.110	9.475	7.700	7.425	8.410
	Market	12.150	9.475	7.700	7.425	8.360
USD/KRW	Model	10.475	10.450	11.300	13.250	15.365
	Market	10.400	10.450	11.300	13.250	15.390
EUR/PLN	Model	7.031	6.775	7.150	8.425	10.036

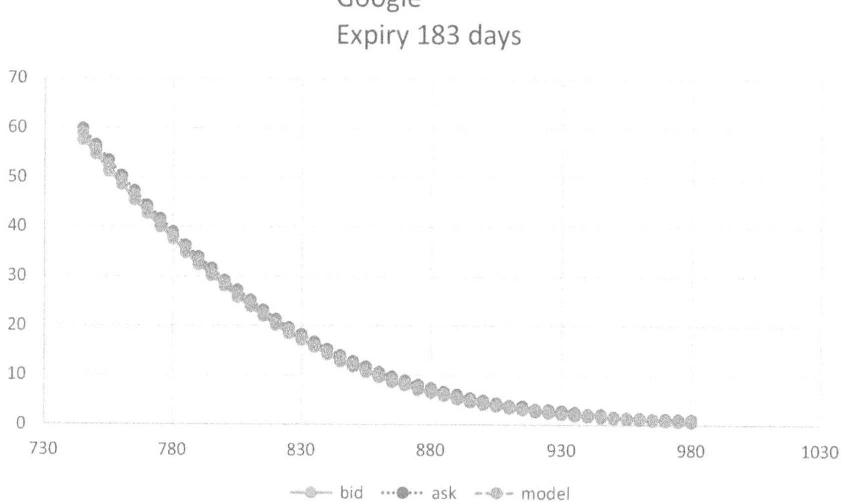

Figure 1: Accuracy of the model in Google options expiration 6 months.

10 Delta call, 10 Delta put. We use the ATM volatility and the volatility of the 25 Delta call and put as the three inputs (see Table 2). We

Table 3: Accuracy of the model in 5 year × 5 year interest rates swaptions.

		Forward Rate															
USD	Strike	0.709%	1.209%	1.709%	1.959%	2.209%	2.459%	2.584%	2.709%	2.834%	2.959%	3.209%	3.459%	3.709%	4.209%	4.709%	5.709%
	Market	62.17	49.35	41.93	39.13	36.79	34.76	33.85	32.99	32.23	31.51	30.23	29.21	28.29	27.05	26.37	26.11
	Model	62.01	49.02	45.51	38.99	36.61	34.64	33.62	32.74	32.21	31.32	30.13	29.02	28.11	27.21	26.51	27.01
EUR	Strike			0.694%	0.944%	1.194%	1.444%	1.569%	1.694%	1.819%	1.944%	2.194%	2.444%	2.694%	3.194%	3.694%	4.694%
	Market			63.44	49.52	45.56	43.96	42.57	41.34	40.25	38.4	35.66	33.77	32.42	30.68	26.37	26.11
	Model			62.92	49.03	45.23	44.01	42.29	41.28	40.21	38.53	35.59	33.81	32.49	29.77	26.42	25.99
JPY	Strike							0.431%	0.681%	0.931%	1.181%	1.431%	1.681%	2.181%	2.681%		
	Market							61.66	55.82	53.37	52.26	51.73	51.48	51.34	51.39		
	Model							61.13	56.01	53.76	52.47	51.55	51.33	51.42	51.79		

calculate the 10 Delta call and put volatilities in the model and compare them to the market data of 10 Delta calls and puts from the broker.

Equities: We look at call options on Google stock and the S&P indicex with maturities from about 1 month to 2 years (see Figures 1 and 2).

Commodities: We consider Brent and Gold call option prices with maturities up to 3 years for Brent and 1 year for gold; see Figures 3 and 4.

Interest rates: We look at OTC prices of the most liquid swaptions in EUR, USD, JPY and CHF with maturities from one year to 10 years when the underlying swap is five years (1Y5Y; 2Y5Y; 5Y5Y; 10Y5Y) (see Table 3). The broker provides log-normal volatilities. In the case of EUR, the brokers provide both the regular and the shifted volatility. In the case of CHF, the brokers provide only the shifted volatility.

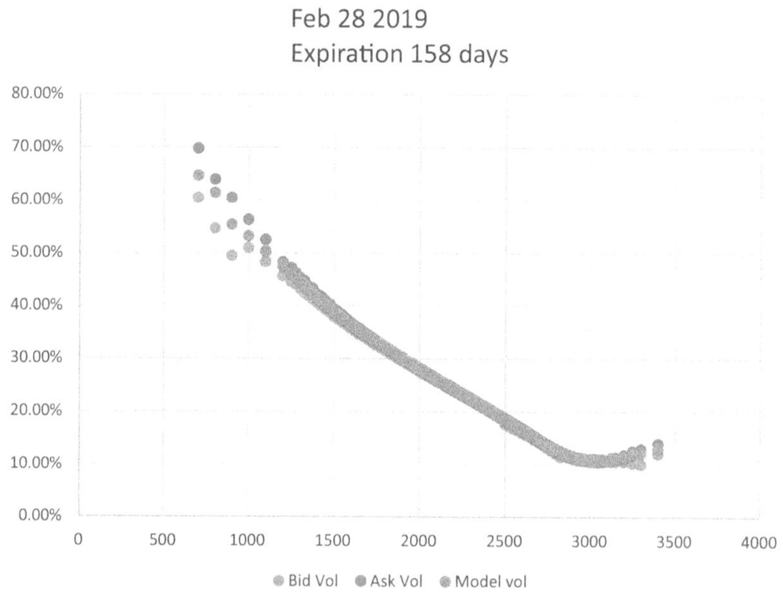

Figure 2: Accuracy of the model in intraday rates SPX index.

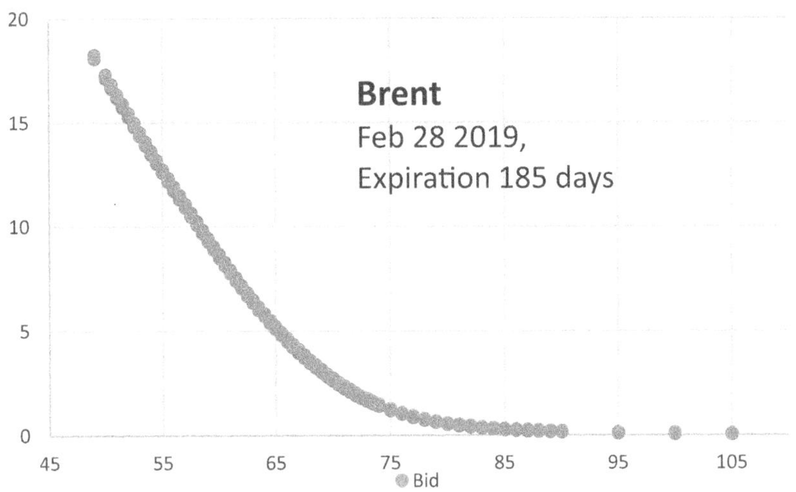

Figure 3: Accuracy of the model in intraday rates Brent options.

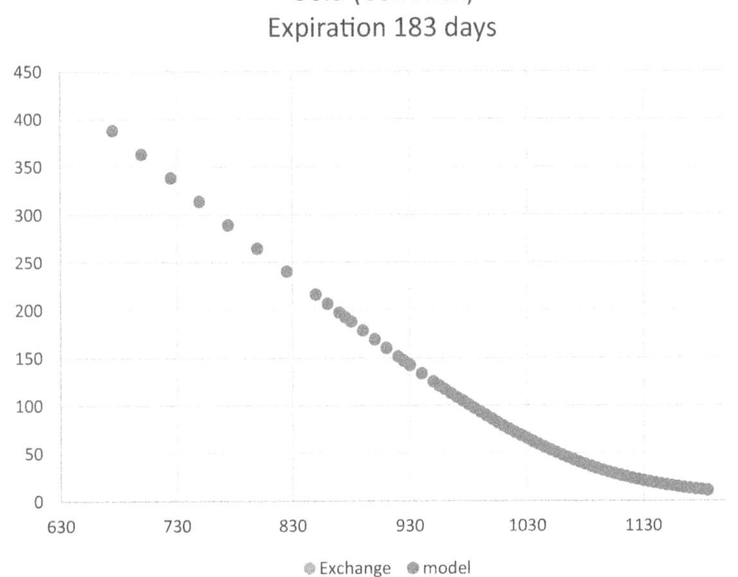

Figure 4: Accuracy of the model in Gold options with expiry 6 month.

Table 4: Calculating the volatility smile at expiry T using the bootstrapping method with different term structures. As can be see the volatility smile from the three different term structures are very close.

	6 Month Vanilla Smile Using Different Term Structures											
		Term Structure 1				Term Structure 2				Term Structure 3		
	Tenor	ATM	25d RR	25d Fly		ATM	25d RR	25d Fly		ATM	25d RR	25d Fly
	1w	12.00%	2.000%	0.250%		8.00%	1.000%	0.150%		10.00%	2.000%	0.250%
	zlu	11.73%	2.00%	0.25%		8.27%	1.13%	0.16%		10.00%	2.000%	0.250%
	3ra	11.00%	2.00%	0.25%		8.96%	1.48%	0.20%		10.00%	2.000%	0.250%
	6M	10.00%	2.000%	0.250%		10.00%	2.000%	0.250%		10.00%	2.000%	0.250%
Strikes	0.900	0.940	0.980	1.020	1.060	1.100	1.140	1.18C	1.220	1.260	1.30C	1.340
TS 1	10.81%	1.11%	9.51%	9.09%	9.32%	9.96%	10.74%	11.62%	12.56%	13.56%	14.68%	15.92%
TS 2	10.81%	10.10%	9.53%	9.10%	9.34%	9.97%	10.69%	11.63%	12.55%	13.61%	14.69%	15.92%
TS 3	10.80%	10.11%	9.52%	9.13%	9.33%	10.01%	10.72%	11.63%	12.56%	13.54%	14.71%	15.94%
Market	10.85%	10.15%	9.55%	9.13%	9.31%	9.95%	10.73%	11.60%	12.54%	13.58%	14.74%	15.98%

As can be seen from Tables 2–4, it is fair to say that the model universally matches the vanilla market in all asset classes. Our conclusion is that all European vanilla options obey the same model.

Intra-day rates: To examine our option pricing method during the real time trading hours where live bids and offers are quoted, we

Table 5: Examples of prices of exotic options from the interbank broker market compared to the price obtained from the model. Three types of exotic options are examined: Double no touch, one touch and barrier options.

Double No Touch						
Date	ccy	Spot	Expiry	Range	Market	Model
13-Nov-15	EURUSD	1.079	2M	1.040–1.1200	21	20.6
22-Mar-16	USDJPY	113.35	2M	108.00–115.00	29	28.1
22-Mar-16	USDJPY	111.4	2M	109.50–115.00	17.75	16.9
23-Mar-16	EURUSD	1.1215	2M	1.0750–1.1450	24.75	24.6
9-Nov-15	EURUSD	1.074	3M	1.0250–1.1150	18.5	18.3
11-Nov-15	EURUSD	1.0755	3M	1.050–1.15	19.75	20.1
1-Feb-16	EURUSD	1.0835	3M	1.030–1.1300	12.25	12.1
25-Feb-16	USDJPY	112.05	3M	106.00–118.00	35	33.75
1-Mar-16	EURUSD	1.086	3M	1.055-1.1150	6.75	6.4
5-Feb-16	EURUSD	1.1195	4M	1.060–1.1400	8.25	7.9
17-Mar-16	USDJPY	112.5	4M	106.00–115.00	17.5	16.9
23-Mar-16	USDJPY	112.3	5M	104–115.50	25.25	24.9
9-Feb-16	USDJPY	115.3	6M	110–120	10.5	10.3
24-Feb-16	USDJPY	111.85	6M	102.5–114.5	9.9	9.9
9-Nov-15	EURUSD	1.077	9M	1.000–1.1500	20	19.6
6-Nov-15	EURUSD	1.0875	1Y	0.97–1.19	35.5	35.7
25-Feb-15	EURUSD	1.105	1Y	1.0300–1.1700	9.5	9.4
29-Feb-16	EURUSD	1.092	1Y	1.000–1.1800	20.25	20.1
1-Mar-16	EURUSD	1.087	1Y	1.000–1.1800	21.25	21
2-Mar-16	EURUSD	1.0855	1Y	0.9600–1.2000	40.25	39.9
17-Mar-16	EURUSD	1.122	1Y	1.0200–1.1750	14	14.1
5-Apr-16	EURUSD	1.1395	1Y	1.000–1.2000	24	24
5-Apr-16	USDJPY	110.5	1Y	100.00–120.00	37.75	37

One Touch							
Date	Ccy	Spot	Expiry	Barrier	BS	Market	Model
6-Nov-15	USDJPY	121.8	11 DAYS	125	4.6	7.5	7.6
8-Feb-16	EURUSD	1.117	42 DAYS	1.06	14.3	13.25	13.1
14-Apr-16	USDJPY	109.15	49 DAYS	107.4	68	62.25	61.9
10-Feb-16	EURUSD	1.1295	SM	1.000	7	9.75	9.6

(*Continued*)

Table 5: (*Continued*)

Barriers									
Date	Ccy	Spot	Expiry	Strike		Barrier	Call/Put	Market	Model
11-Nov-15	EURUSD	1.075	2M	1.0325	KO	1.0975	EUR P	0.455	0.46
10-Nov-15	EURUSD	1.0745	3M	1.03	RKO	0.97	EUR P	0.2d	0.24
2-Mar-16	EURUSD	1.0845	3M	1.13	KO	1.0525	EUR C	0.655	0.66
10-Nov-15	USDJPY	123.2	4M	116	KO	127.5	USD P	0.38	0.37
2-Mar-16	EURUSD	1.086	4M	1.05	RKO	1	EUR P	0.16	0.16
7-Dec-15	EURUSD	1.0885	6M	1.035	KO	1.12	EUR P	0.78	0.77
7-Dec-15	EURUSD	1.084	6M	1.04	Kl	1.04	EUR C	1.42	1.41
2-Feb-16	EURUSD	1.0905	6M	1.07	RKO	1.0J	EUR P	0.24	0.23
5-Feb-16	EURUSD	1.12	6M	1.04	KO	1.15	EUR P	0.465	0.47
8-Feb-16	EURUSD	1.1125	6M	1.18	KO	1.075	EUR C	0.83	0.84
24-Feb-16	USDJPY	111.75	6M	107	Kl	107	USD C	1.9	1.89
14-Apr-16	USDJPY	109.2	6M	103	KO	115	USD P	1.21	1.19
16-Nov-15	EURUSD	1.072	8M	1.15	KO	1.05	EUR C	0.615	0.63
8-Feb-16	EURUSD	1.1145	9M	1.02	Kl	1.02	EUR C	0.965	0.95
17 Mar-16	USDJPY	112.15	10M	124	KO	105	USD C	0.48	0.48
5-Feb-16	EURUSD	1.1125	315 DAYS	1.01	KI	1.01	EUR C	1.015	1.011
8-Dec-15	EURUSD	1.0865	1Y	1.16	Kl	1.16	EUR P	1.29	1.31
9-Feb-16	USDJPY	115.2	1Y	115.2	KO	130	USD C	0.46	0.46
9-Feb-16	USDJPY	115.2	1Y	130	KO	111	USD C	0.46	0.47
10 Feb-16	EURUSD	1.1295	1Y	1.05	KO	1.16	EUR P	0.81	0.8
1-Mar-16	EURUSD	1.087	1Y	1.05	RKO	0.95	EUR P	0.34	0.35
2-Mar-16	EURUSD	1.0875	1Y	1.21	KO	J	EUR C	1.165	1.18
3-Mar-16	USDJPY	113.95	1Y	100	Kl	1Z0	USD P	0.34	0.32
5-Apr-16	USDJPY	110.95	1Y	100	RKO	90	USD P	0.21	0.23
11 Apr-16	EURUSD	1.141	1Y	1.15	Kl	1.05	EUR C	0.5	0.47
14-Apr-16	EURUSD	1.137	1Y	1.075	KO	1.18	EUR P	1.2d	1.23

provide some additional examples on Brent, FTSE index, Google and options on futures on GBP interest rates.

We used live bid/ask prices of options on Brent taken during the middle of the trading day on February 2, 2018 and examine the first seven expiry dates.

The second example is options on the FTSE index during the middle of the trading day on February 2, 2018 and examine the first eight expiry dates.

The third example is options on Google which trade as European options since Google by declaration does not pay dividends. We used option prices quoted during the middle of the trading day on May 10, 2018 and examined the first fourteen expiry dates.

In all the examples the model is within the bid/ask spread for all strikes.

These examples with different barriers, maturities and strikes of four kinds of options help us to verify that the transfer density we developed in the previous section is indeed the transfer density in the options market; see Table 5.

7. Conclusions

In this chapter, we presented a general formalism for pricing options by calculating the density function to maturity and the conditional density function without pre-assuming the underlying asset stochastic process. The only information about the behavior of the underlying asset that is required in order to determine the option price is the set of moments $\omega^{n,m}$ in the risk neutral measure. In the most general case, the moments can be functions of the underlying asset and the standard deviation of the underlying asset, $\omega^{n,m} = \omega^{n,m}(s\sigma_t)$ since we can use a time homogeneous density function. However, when we use continuous time process then we need to know only $\omega^{1,1}\omega^{0,2}, \omega^{2,0}$. These quantities are implied from option prices. The process to obtain the density function and the volatility smile is numerical but generates very accurate results compared to the market data. This three-parameter model very accurately replicates option prices in all asset classes. In addition, we suggest a method to obtain the probability density transfer function from the term structure of the European Vanilla options that allows the calculation of path dependent options. This numerical process requires a lot of calculations and in return it generates accurate results vs the market. These calculations can be done in advance though. Finally, we presented a procedure to obtain the conditional probability density function using the term structure of the vanilla options. This allows for the calculation of path dependent options.

Acknowledgments

I am deeply grateful to Chris Rogers for many very helpful discussions. I am also thankful to Alex Lipton for his insightful comments and to Peter Carr for useful advices.

References

[1] Black, F. and Scholes, M. (1973). The pricing of options and corporate liabilities. *Journal of Political Economy*, 81(3), 637–654. doi:10.1086/260062.

[2] Black, F., Derman, E., and Toy, W. (1990). A one-factor model of interest rates and its application to treasury bond options. *Financial Analysts Journal*, 24–32.

[3] Dupire, B. (1994). Pricing with a smile. *Risk*, 7(1), 18–20. http://www.risk.net/data/risk/pdf/technical/2007/risk20_0707_technical_volatility.pdf

[4] Derman, E. and Kani, I. (1994). Riding on a smile. *Risk*, 7(2), 139–145, 32–39. (PDF). *Risk*. Retrieved 2007-06-01.

[5] Hagan, P., Kumar, D., Lesniewski, A., and Woodward, D. (2002). Managing smile risk, *Wilmott Magazine*, September, 84–108.

[6] Heston, S. (1993). A closed-form solution for options with stochastic volatility with applications to bond and currency options. *Review of Financial Studies*, 6, 327–343; Empirical performance of alternative option pricing models 2049 (PDF). *Journal of Finance*, 47(4), 1259–1282.

[7] Brace, A., Gatarek, D., and Musiela, M. (1997). The market model of interest rate dynamics, *Mathematical Finance*, 7(2), 127–154.

[8] El Euch, O., Gatheral, J, and Rosenbaum, M. (2017). Roughening Heston. *Risk*, 84–89.

[9] Gyongy, I. (1986). Mimicking the one-dimensional marginal distributions of processes having an Itˆo di_erential. *Probability Theory and Related Fields*, 71(4), 501.

[10] Delbaen, F. and Schachermayer, W. (1994). A general version of the fundamental theorem of asset pricing. *Mathematical Annuals*, 300, 463–520.

[11] Gershon, D. (2017). *A Universal Model for Pricing all Options*, SSRN.

[12] Carr, P., Wu, L., and Yuzhao, Z. (2018). *Vol, Skew, and Smile Trading*, NYU Working Paper.

[13] Gershon, D. (2018). Model independent volatility smile with empirical confirmations, SSRN.

https://doi.org/10.1142/9789811259142_0016

Chapter 16

Old Problems, Classical Methods, New Solutions*

A. Lipton

Abu Dhabi Investment Authority, Abu Dhabi, United Arab Emirates

The Jerusalem School of Business Administration, The Hebrew University of Jerusalem, Jerusalem, Israel

Connection Science and Engineering, Massachusetts Institute of Technology, Cambridge, MA, USA

alexlipt@mit.edu

Abstract

We use a powerful extension of the classical method of heat potentials, recently developed by the present author and his collaborators, to solve several significant problems of financial mathematics. We consider the following problems in detail: (a) calibrating the default boundary in the structural default framework to a constant default intensity, (b) calculating default probability for a representative bank in the mean-field framework, (c) finding the hitting time probability density of an Ornstein–Uhlenbeck process. Several other problems, including pricing American put options and finding optimal mean-reverting trading strategies, are mentioned in passing. Besides, two nonfinancial applications — the supercooled Stefan problem and the integrate-and-fire neuroscience problem — are briefly discussed as well.

---

*This chapter is derived from Lipton, A (2020). Old problems, classical methods, new solutions. *International Journal of Theoretical and Applied Finance*, 23(4): 2050024.

1. Introduction

The method of heat potentials (MHP) is a highly robust and versatile approach frequently exploited in mathematical physics; see, e.g., [24,48,50,51] among others. It is essential in numerous vital fields, such as thermal engineering, nuclear engineering, and material science. However, it is not particularly well-known in mathematical finance, even though the first meaningful use in this context was described by the present author almost twenty years ago. The specific application was to pricing barrier options with curvilinear barriers; see [31], Section 12.2.3.

In this document, we demonstrate how a powerful extension of the classical MHP, recently developed by the present author and his collaborators, can be used to solve seemingly unrelated problems of applied mathematics in general and financial mathematics in particular; see [35–39]. Specifically, we use the extended method of heat potentials (EMHP) for (a) calibrating the default boundary for a structural default model with constant default intensity, (b) finding a semi-analytical solution of the mean-field problem for a system of interacting banks, (c) developing a semi-analytical description for the hitting time density for an Ornstein–Uhlenbeck process. Besides, we demonstrate the efficacy of the EMHP by considering two non-financial applications: (a) the supercooled Stefan problem, (b) the integrate-and-fire model in neuroscience.

We note in passing that, in addition to the problems discussed in this document, the EMHP has been successfully used for pricing American put options and for finding optimal strategies for mean-reverting spread trading; see [36,37].

We emphasize that in most cases, the EMHP beats all other known approaches to the problem in question, and in some instances, for example, for the boundary calibration problem, it is the only one that can be used effectively.

The chapter is organized as follows. In Section 2, we present the mathematical preliminaries regarding the classical MHP and describe its useful extensions and generalizations, which we call the EMHP. In Section 3, we examine the structural default problem. In Section 4, we study the mean-field banking system in the structural default framework and analyze its stability and resilience. In Section 5, we describe the EMHP approach to calculating the hitting time probability distribution for an Ornstein–Uhlenbeck process. The EMHP turns to be a powerful and versatile tool, which solves this complicated problem in its entirety. In Sections 6 and 7, we consider two non-financial applications of the EMHP — the supercooled Stefan problem and the integrate-and-fire neuron excitation model. We draw our conclusions in Section 8.

2. Mathematical Preliminaries

In this section, we describe the classical MHP and its beneficial extensions proposed by the author and his collaborators. The MHP is uniquely well-suited to solving rather challenging problems occurring routinely in applied mathematics in general, and in financial engineering in particular. In a nutshell, this method allows one to reduce a complicated partial differential equation of the parabolic type with a time-dependent boundary to a much simpler Volterra integral equation.

2.1 *The method of heat potentials*

Consider a standard heat equation in a one-sided domain with a moving boundary $b^{>}(t)$:

$$\frac{\partial}{\partial t}E^{>}(t,x) = \frac{1}{2}\frac{\partial^2}{\partial x^2}E^{>}(t,x), \quad b^{>}(t) \leq x < \infty,$$

$$E^{>}(0,x) = \varepsilon^{>}(x), \quad E^{>}(t, b^{>}(t)) = e^{>}(t), \quad E(t, x \to \infty) \to 0. \tag{1}$$

Here and below, we use the superscript $>$ ($<$) to emphasize the fact that we are interested in the computational domain limited by the boundary from below (above).Without loss of generality, we can assume that $\varepsilon > (x) = 0$; the case of a nonzero initial condition can be solved by splitting:

$$E^{>} = E(t,x) + F^{>}(t,x), \tag{2}$$

$$E(t,x) = \textstyle\int_{b(t)}^{\infty} H(t, x-y)\,\varepsilon^{>}(y)\,dy, \tag{3}$$

where $H(t,x)$ is the standard heat kernl,

$$H(t,x)=\frac{e^{-\frac{x^2}{2t}}}{\sqrt{2\pi t}}. \tag{4}$$

Thus, we can restrict ourselves to the case of zero initial condition:

$$\begin{gathered}\frac{\partial}{\partial t}F^{>}(t,x)=\frac{1}{2}\frac{\partial^2}{\partial x^2}F^{>}(t,x),\quad b^{>}(t)\leq x<\infty,\\ F^{>}(0,x)=0,\quad F^{>}(t,b^{>}(t))=f^{>}(t),\quad F(t,x\to\infty)\to 0,\end{gathered} \tag{5}$$

where

$$f^{>}(t)=e^{>}(t)-E(t,b(t)). \tag{6}$$

The MHP allows one to represent $F^{>}(t,x)$ in the form

$$F^{>}(t,x)=\int_0^t\frac{(x-b^{>}(t'))\exp\left(-\frac{(x-b^{>}(t'))^2}{2(t-t')}\right)\nu^{>}(t')}{\sqrt{2\pi(t-t')^3}}dt', \tag{7}$$

where $\nu^{>}(t)$ solves the Volterra equation of the second kind:

$$\nu^{>}(t')+\int_0^t\frac{\Theta^{>}(t,t')\,\Xi^{>}(t,t')\,\nu^{>}(t')}{\sqrt{2\pi(t-t')}}dt'=f^{>}(t), \tag{8}$$

and

$$\begin{gathered}\Theta^{<}(t,t')=\frac{b^{>}(t)-b^{>}(t')}{(t-t')},\quad \Xi^{>}(t,t')=e^{-\frac{(t-t')\Theta^{>2}(t,t')}{2}},\\ \Theta^{>}(t,t)=\frac{db^{>}(t)}{dt},\quad \Xi^{>}(t,t)=1.\end{gathered} \tag{9}$$

Similarly, the solution to the problem

$$\frac{\partial}{\partial t}F^{<}(t,x)=\frac{1}{2}\frac{\partial^2}{\partial x^2}F^{<}(t,x),\ \infty<x\leq b^{<}(t),$$
$$F^{<}(0,x)=0,\quad F^{<}(t,x\to-\infty)\to 0,\quad F^{<}(t,b(t))=f^{<}(t),\tag{10}$$

has the form

$$F^{<}(t,x)=\int_0^t\frac{(x-b^{<}(t'))\exp\left(-\frac{(x-b^{<}(t'))^2}{2(t-t')}\right)\nu^{<}(t')}{\sqrt{2\pi(t-t')^3}}dt',\tag{11}$$

where

$$-\nu^{<}(t')+\int_0^t\frac{\Theta^{<}(t,t')\,\Xi^{<}(t,t')\,\nu^{<}(t')}{\sqrt{2\pi(t-t')}}dt'=f^{<}(t),\tag{12}$$

Finally, the solution to the two-sided problem

$$\frac{\partial}{\partial t}F^{><}(t,x)=\frac{1}{2}\frac{\partial^2}{\partial x^2}F^{><}(t,x),\quad b^{>}(t)\leq\ x\leq b^{<}(t),$$
$$F^{><}(0,x)=0,\ F^{><}\left(t,b^{<}(t)\right)=f^{<}(t),\ F^{><}\left(t,b^{>}(t)\right)=f^{>}(t),\tag{13}$$

has the form

$$F^{><}(t,x)=\int_0^t\frac{(x-b^{>}(t'))\exp\left(-\frac{(x-b^{>}(t'))^2}{2(t-t')}\right)\nu^{>}(t')}{\sqrt{2\pi(t-t')^3}}dt'$$
$$+\int_0^t\frac{(x-b^{<}(t'))\exp\left(-\frac{(x-b^{<}(t'))^2}{2(t-t')}\right)\nu^{<}(t')}{\sqrt{2\pi(t-t')^3}}dt',\tag{14}$$

$$\nu^{>}(t') + \int_0^t \frac{\Theta^{>>}(t,t')\,\Xi^{>>}(t,t')\,\nu^{>}(t')}{\sqrt{2\pi(t-t')}}dt'$$

$$+ \int_0^t \frac{\Theta^{><}(t,t')\,\Xi^{><}(t,t')\,\nu^{<}(t')}{\sqrt{2\pi(t-t')}}dt' = f^{>}(t),$$

$$-\nu^{<}(t') + \int_0^t \frac{\Theta^{<>}(t,t')\,\Xi^{<>}(t,t')\,\nu^{>}(t')}{\sqrt{2\pi(t-t')}}dt'$$

$$+ \int_0^t \frac{\Theta^{<<}(t,t')\,\Xi^{<<}(t,t')\,\nu^{<}(t')}{\sqrt{2\pi(t-t')}}dt' = f^{<}(t), \quad (15)$$

where

$$\Theta^{>>}(t,t') = \frac{b^{>}(t) - b^{>}(t')}{(t-t')}, \quad \Theta^{><}(t,t') = \frac{b^{>}(t) - b^{<}(t')}{(t-t')}, \text{ etc.} \quad (16)$$

2.2 *Extensions*

While Equations (7) and (8) provide an elegant solution to problem (2), in many instances we are interested in the behavior of this solution on the boundary itself. For instance, in numerous problems of mathematical finance, some of which are described below, what we need to know is the function

$$g^{>}(t) = \frac{1}{2}\frac{\partial}{\partial x}F^{>}(t, b^{>}(t)), \quad (17)$$

which represent the outflow of probability from the computational domain. This function can be calculated in two ways.

On the one hand, we can integrate the heat equation and get

$$\frac{d}{dt}\int_{b^{>}(t)}^{\infty} F^{>}(t,x)\,dx = \int_{b^{>}(t)}^{\infty} \frac{\partial}{\partial t}F^{>}(t,x)\,dx = \frac{1}{2}\int_{b^{>}(t)}^{\infty} \frac{\partial^2}{\partial x^2}F^{>}(t,x)\,dx$$

$$= -\frac{1}{2}\frac{\partial}{\partial x}F^{>}(t, b^{>}(t)) = -g^{>}(t). \quad (18)$$

Equation (7) yields

$$\int_{b^{>}(t)}^{\infty} F^{>}(t,x)\,dx = \int_0^t \frac{\Xi^{>}(t,t')\,\nu^{>}(t')}{\sqrt{2\pi(t-t')}}dt', \quad (19)$$

so that

$$g^{>}(t) = -\frac{d}{dt}\int_0^t \frac{\Xi^{>}(t,t')\,\nu^{>}(t')}{\sqrt{2\pi(t-t')}}dt'. \tag{20}$$

On the other hand, a useful formula derived by the present author and his collaborators; see [35–37,39], gives an alternative expression for $g^{>}(t)$:

$$g^{>}(t) = -\left(\frac{1}{\sqrt{2\pi t}} + \frac{db^{>}(t)}{dt}\right)\nu^{>}(t) - \frac{1}{2}\int_0^t \frac{\left(\Phi^{>}(t,t') + \Theta^{>2}(t,t')\,\Xi^{>}(t,t')\,\nu^{>}(t')\right)}{\sqrt{2\pi(t-t')}}dt', \tag{21}$$

where

$$\Phi^{>}\left(t,t'\right) = \frac{\left(\nu^{>}(t) - \Xi^{>}(t,t')\,\nu^{>}(t')\right)}{(t-t')},\quad \Phi^{>}(t,t) = \frac{d\nu^{>}(t)}{dt} + \frac{1}{2}\left(\frac{db^{>}(t)}{dt}\right)^2\nu^{>}(t). \tag{22}$$

On the surface, Equations (20),(21) look very different. However, a useful Lemma proven in [39], allows one to connect the two.

Lemma: *Let* $\Psi(t,t')$ *be a differentiable function, such that* $\Psi(t,t) = 1$. *Then*

$$\frac{d}{dt}\int_0^t \frac{\Psi(t,t')\,\nu(t')}{\sqrt{2\pi(t-t')}}dt' = \frac{\nu(t)}{\sqrt{2\pi t}} + \frac{1}{2}\int_0^t \frac{\nu(t) - \left(\Psi(t,t') - 2(t-t')\,\Psi_t(t,t')\right)\nu(t')}{\sqrt{2\pi(t-t')^3}}dt', \tag{23}$$

Alternatively,

$$\frac{d}{dt}\int_0^t \frac{\Psi(t,t')\,\nu(t')}{\sqrt{2\pi(t-t')}}dt' = \int_0^t \frac{\frac{\partial}{\partial t'}\left(\left(\Psi(t,t') - 2(t-t')\,\Psi_t(t,t')\right)\nu(t')\right)}{\sqrt{2\pi(t-t')}}dt'. \tag{24}$$

We emphasize that Equation (21) is easier to use than Equation (20) in most situations because it does not involve differentiation. However, if the cumulative outflow $G^{>}(t) = \int_0^t g^{>}(t')\,dt'$

is of interest, the latter equation can be more efficient, since it can be rewritten as follows:

$$G^{>}(t) = -\int_0^t \frac{\Xi^{>}(t,t')\,\nu^{>}(t')}{\sqrt{2\pi(t-t')}}dt'. \tag{25}$$

We can calculate $g^{<}(t)$ and $g^{><}(t)$ by the same token. It is important to understand that both Equations (21) and (20) can be used in the one-sided case, however, in the case when two boundaries are present, we can *only* use Equation (21) because this equation allows calculating $g^{>}$ and $g^{<}$ individually while Equation (20) calculates the difference $g^{>} - g^{<}$.

2.3 *Generalizations*

If the MHP were applicable only to the standard Wiener process, it would be advantageous, if somewhat narrow in scope. Fortunately, it can be applied to a general diffusion satisfying the so-called Cherkasov's condition, which guarantees that it can be transformed into the standard Wiener process. Such diffusions are studied in [9], [46], and [5]. The applications of Cherkasov's condition in financial mathematics are discussed in [31], Section 4.2, and [34], Chapter 9.

Consider a diffusion governed by

$$d\tilde{x}_{\tilde{t}} = \delta\left(\tilde{t},\tilde{x}_{\tilde{t}}\right)d\tilde{t} + \sigma\left(\tilde{t},\tilde{x}_{\tilde{t}}\right)dW_{\tilde{t}}, \quad \tilde{x}_0 = \tilde{z}, \tag{26}$$

We wish to calculate boundary-related quantities, such as the distribution of the hitting time of a given time-dependent barrier $b\left(\tilde{t}\right)$:

$$\tilde{s} = \inf\left\{\tilde{t} : \tilde{x}_{\tilde{t}} = \tilde{b}(\tilde{t})\right\}, \quad \tilde{z} \neq \tilde{b}(0). \tag{27}$$

To this end, we introduce

$$\begin{aligned} \beta\left(\tilde{t},\tilde{x}\right) &= \sigma\left(\tilde{t},\tilde{x}\right)\int^{\tilde{x}} \frac{1}{\sigma\left(\tilde{t},y\right)}dy, \\ \gamma\left(\tilde{t},\tilde{x}\right) &= 2\delta\left(\tilde{t},\tilde{x}\right) - \sigma\left(\tilde{t},\tilde{x}\right)\sigma_{\tilde{x}}\left(\tilde{t},\tilde{x}\right) - 2\sigma\left(\tilde{t},\tilde{x}\right)\int^{\tilde{x}} \frac{\sigma_{\tilde{t}}\left(\tilde{t},y\right)}{\sigma^2\left(\tilde{t},y\right)}dy, \end{aligned} \tag{28}$$

where the lower limit of integration is chosen as convenient. Define

$$P\left(\tilde{t},\tilde{x}\right)=\begin{vmatrix}\beta\left(\tilde{t},\tilde{x}\right) & \gamma\left(\tilde{t},\tilde{x}\right)\\ \beta_{\tilde{x}}\left(\tilde{t},\tilde{x}\right) & \gamma_{\tilde{x}}\left(\tilde{t},\tilde{x}\right)\end{vmatrix},$$

$$Q\left(\tilde{t},\tilde{x}\right)=\begin{vmatrix}\sigma\left(\tilde{t},\tilde{x}\right) & \gamma\left(\tilde{t},\tilde{x}\right)\\ \sigma_{\tilde{x}}\left(\tilde{t},\tilde{x}\right) & \gamma_{\tilde{x}}\left(\tilde{t},\tilde{x}\right)\end{vmatrix}, \tag{29}$$

$$R\left(\tilde{t},\tilde{x}\right)=\begin{vmatrix}\sigma\left(\tilde{t},\tilde{x}\right) & \beta\left(\tilde{t},\tilde{x}\right) & \gamma\left(\tilde{t},\tilde{x}\right)\\ \sigma_{\tilde{x}}\left(\tilde{t},\tilde{x}\right) & \beta_{\tilde{x}}\left(\tilde{t},\tilde{x}\right) & \gamma_{\tilde{x}}\left(\tilde{t},\tilde{x}\right)\\ \sigma_{\tilde{x}\tilde{x}}\left(\tilde{t},\tilde{x}\right) & \beta_{\tilde{x}\tilde{x}}\left(\tilde{t},\tilde{x}\right) & \gamma_{\tilde{x}\tilde{x}}\left(\tilde{t},\tilde{x}\right)\end{vmatrix},$$

and assume that Cherkasov's condition is satisfied, so that

$$R\left(\tilde{t},\tilde{x}\right)\equiv 0. \tag{30}$$

Then we can transform $\tilde{x}$ into the standard Wiener process via the following mapping

$$t=t(\tilde{t},\tilde{x})=\int_0^{\tilde{t}}\Phi^2(u,\tilde{x})du,$$

$$x=x(\tilde{t},\tilde{x})=\Phi(\tilde{t},\tilde{x})\frac{\beta\left(\tilde{t},\tilde{x}\right)}{\sigma\left(\tilde{t},\tilde{x}\right)}+\frac{1}{2}\int_0^{\tilde{t}}\Phi(u,\tilde{x})\frac{P\left(u,\tilde{x}\right)}{\sigma\left(u,\tilde{x}\right)}du, \tag{31}$$

where

$$\Phi(\tilde{t},\tilde{x})=\exp\left[-\frac{1}{2}\int_0^{t}\frac{Q\left(u,\tilde{x}\right)}{\sigma\left(u,\tilde{x}\right)}du\right]. \tag{32}$$

In particular, the initial condition becomes

$$z=\frac{\beta\left(0,\tilde{z}\right)}{\sigma\left(0,\tilde{z}\right)}. \tag{33}$$

The corresponding transition probability density transforms as follows

$$\tilde{p}(\tilde{t},\tilde{x};\tilde{z})=\left|\frac{\partial x(\tilde{t},\tilde{x})}{\partial\tilde{x}}\right|p(t,x;z). \tag{34}$$

Moreover, the boundary transforms to

$$\tilde{b}(\tilde{t}) \to b(t) = \Phi(\tilde{t}, \tilde{b}(\tilde{t}))\frac{\beta\left(\tilde{t}, \tilde{b}(\tilde{t})\right)}{\sigma\left(\tilde{t}, \tilde{b}(\tilde{t})\right)} + \frac{1}{2}\int^{\tilde{t}} \Phi(u, \tilde{b}(\tilde{t}))\frac{P\left(u, \tilde{b}(\tilde{t})\right)}{\sigma\left(u, \tilde{b}(\tilde{t})\right)}du. \tag{35}$$

Since the MHP is specifically designed for dealing with curvilinear boundaries, we get a solvable problem. A powerful application of the above approach is demonstrated in Section 5, where the hitting time probability distribution for an Ornstein–Uhlenbeck process is studied.

2.4 *Numerics*

There are numerous well-known approaches to solving Volterra equations; see, [30], among many others. We choose the most straightforward approach and show how to solve the following archetypal Volterra equation with weak singularity numerically:

$$\nu(t) + \int_0^t \frac{K(t,t')}{\sqrt{t-t'}}\nu(t')\,dt' = f(t), \tag{36}$$

where $K(t,t')$ is a non-singular kernel. We write

$$\int_0^t \frac{K(t,t')\nu\,(t')}{\sqrt{t-t'}}dt' = -2\int_0^t K(t,t')\nu\left(t'\right)\,d\sqrt{t-t'}. \tag{37}$$

We wish to map this equation to a grid $0 = t_0 < t_1 < \cdots < t_N = T$. To this end, we introduce the following notation:

$$f_k = f(t_k), \quad \nu_k = \nu\left(t_k\right), \quad K_{k,l} = K(t_k, t_l), \quad \Delta_{k,l} = t_k - t_l. \tag{38}$$

Then, the right hand side of Equation (37) can be approximated by the trapezoidal rule as

$$f_k = \nu_k + \sum_{l=1}^{k}\left(K_{k,l}\nu_l + K_{k,l-1}\nu_{l-1}\right)\Pi_{k,l} = 0, \tag{39}$$

where

$$\Pi_{k,l} = \frac{\Delta_{l,l-1}}{\left(\sqrt{\Delta_{k,l-1}} + \sqrt{\Delta_{k,l}}\right)}, \tag{40}$$

so that

$$\nu_k = \frac{\left(f_k - K_{k,k-1}\nu_{k-1} - \sum_{l=1}^{k-1}\left(K_{k,l}\nu_l + K_{k,l-1}\nu_{l-1}\right)\Pi_{k,l}\right)}{\left(1 + K_{k,k}\sqrt{\Delta_{k,k-1}}\right)}. \tag{41}$$

Thus, ν_k can be found by induction starting with $\nu_0 = f_0$.

Equation (41) is the blueprint for all the subsequent numerical calculations.

3. The Structural Default Model

3.1 *Preliminaries*

The original, and straightforward, structural default model was introduced by Merton, [41], who assumed that default could happen only at debt maturity. His model was extended by Black and Cox, [4], who considered the default, which can happen at any time by introducing flat default boundary representing debt covenants. Numerous authors expanded their model including [3,18,19], who considered a curvilinear boundary whose shape can be calibrated to the market default probability. One of the major unsolved issues with the above model was articulated by Hyer *et al.*, [19], who pointed out that, unless the shape of the default boundary is very carefully chosen, the probability of short-term default is too low. This issue was addressed by several authors, including [13,17,32], who proposed to introduce jumps and or uncertainty to increase this probability. We show below that it is possible to calibrate the default boundary in such a way that constant default intensity can be matched. We emphasize that the direct problem — calculating the default probability given the boundary — is linear (albeit relatively involved), while the inverse problem — finding the boundary given the default probability — is nonlinear (and hence even more involved). Additional details are given in [37].

3.2 *Formulation*

We wish to find the boundary for a structural default model corresponding to a constant default intensity η. We denote the corresponding default probability by

$$\pi(t) = 1 - e^{-\eta t}. \tag{42}$$

The introduce time τ, such that default is impossible for $t < \tau$. Thus the default boundary starts at $t = \tau$. The idea is to calculate the corresponding boundary $b(t;\tau,\eta)$, provided it exists, and then let $\tau \to 0$.

It is clear that at time $t = \tau - 0$, the transition probability is

$$p(\tau, x) = H(\tau, x), \tag{43}$$

where H is the heat kernel:

$$H(\tau, x) = \frac{e^{-\frac{x^2}{2\tau}}}{\sqrt{2\pi\tau}}. \tag{44}$$

At time $t = \tau$, the first possibility of default occurs. For $t > \tau$ the transition probability satisfies the following Fokker–Planck problem

$$\begin{gathered}\frac{\partial}{\partial t}p(t,x) = \frac{1}{2}\frac{\partial^2}{\partial x^2}p(t,x), \quad b(t) \le x < \infty, \\ p(\tau, x) = H(\tau, x), \quad p(t, b(t)) = 0, \quad p(t, x \to \infty) \to 0. \end{gathered} \tag{45}$$

The default probability density $g(t)$ is given by

$$g(t) = \frac{1}{2}\frac{\partial}{\partial x}p(t, b(t)). \tag{46}$$

Alternatively,

$$\pi(t) = 1 - \int_{b(t)}^{\infty} p(t,x)\,dx, \quad g(t) = \frac{d\pi(t)}{dt}. \tag{47}$$

3.3 *Governing system of integral equations*

We split p as follows:

$$p(t,x) = q(t,x) + r(t,x), \tag{48}$$

where

$$\frac{\partial}{\partial t}q(t,x) = \frac{1}{2}\frac{\partial^2}{\partial x^2}q(t,x), \ -\infty < x < \infty,$$
$$q(\tau,x) = H(\tau,x)\Theta(x-b(\tau)), \ q(t,x\to-\infty)\to 0, \ q(t,x\to\infty)\to 0, \tag{49}$$

$$\frac{\partial}{\partial t}r(t,x) = \frac{1}{2}\frac{\partial^2}{\partial x^2}r(t,x), \ b(t) \le x < \infty,$$
$$r(\tau,x) = 0, \ r(t,b(t)) = -q(t,b(t)), \ r(t,x\to\infty)\to 0. \tag{50}$$

and $\Theta(x)$ is the Heaviside function. Solving Equation (49) as a convolution of heat kernel with the initial condition, we get

$$q(t,x) = \frac{e^{-\frac{x^2}{2t}}}{\sqrt{2\pi t}}N\left(\frac{\frac{ux}{t}-b(\tau)}{\sqrt{u}}\right), \tag{51}$$

where $u = (t-\tau)\tau/t$; see [37]. Thus

$$g(t) = \frac{1}{2}\frac{\partial}{\partial x}r(t,b(t)) - \frac{H(t,b(t))}{2t}\left(b(t)N\left(\frac{\frac{ub(t)}{t}-b(\tau)}{\sqrt{u}}\right)\right.$$
$$\left.-uH\left(u,\frac{ub(t)}{t}-b(\tau)\right)\right). \tag{52}$$

Accordingly, in view the discussion in Section 2.2, we need to solve the following system of integral equations:

$$\nu(t) + \int_\tau^t \frac{\Theta(t,t')\Xi(t,t')\nu(t')}{\sqrt{2\pi(t-t')}}dt' + H(t,b(t))N\left(\frac{ub(t)-tb(\tau)}{t\sqrt{u}}\right) = 0,$$

$$\eta e^{-\eta t} + \left(\frac{1}{\sqrt{2\pi t}} + \frac{db(t)}{dt}\right)\nu(t) + \frac{1}{2}\int_\tau^t \frac{\Phi(t,t') + \Theta^2(t,t')\Xi(t,t')\nu(t')}{\sqrt{2\pi(t-t')}}dt' \tag{53}$$

$$+\frac{H(t,b(t))}{2t}\left(b(t)N\left(\frac{\frac{ub(t)}{t}-b(\tau)}{\sqrt{u}}\right) - uH\left(u,\frac{ub(t)}{t}-b(\tau)\right)\right) = 0.$$

Alternatively, we can rewrite Equations (53) in integrated form

$$
\begin{aligned}
&\nu(t)+\int_{\tau}^{t}\frac{\Theta(t,t')\,\Xi(t,t')\,\nu(t')}{\sqrt{2\pi(t-t')}}dt'+H(t,b(t))\,N\left(\frac{ub(t)-tb(\tau)}{t\sqrt{u}}\right)=0,\\
&1-e^{-\eta t}+\int_{\tau}^{t}\frac{\Xi(t,t')\,\nu(t')}{\sqrt{2\pi(t-t')}}dt'-N\left(\frac{b(t)}{\sqrt{t}}\right)-N\left(\frac{\sqrt{t}b(\tau)}{\sqrt{u(u+t)}}\right)\\
&\qquad+BVN\left(\frac{\sqrt{t}b(\tau)}{\sqrt{u(u+t)}},\frac{b(t)}{\sqrt{t}};\sqrt{\frac{u}{u+t}}\right)=0,
\end{aligned}
\tag{54}
$$

where $BVN(.,.;.)$ is the bivariate normal distribution.

We postpone the discussion of the corresponding numerics until the next Section, where a more general case is considered.

3.4 *The choice of b_τ*

Recall that the default probability has the form

$$
\pi(t)=1-e^{-\eta t}. \tag{55}
$$

The barrier has to start at $\tau=\hat{\tau}$, $\hat{\tau}\to 0$, and there should be no barrier before that. We wish to find $b(\hat{\tau})$ such that

$$
\pi(\hat{\tau})=1-\int_{b(\hat{\tau})}^{\infty}\frac{\exp\left(-\frac{x^2}{2\hat{\tau}}\right)}{\sqrt{2\pi\hat{\tau}}}dx=1-N\left(-\frac{b(\hat{\tau})}{\sqrt{\hat{\tau}}}\right)=1-e^{-\eta\hat{\tau}}. \tag{56}
$$

Thus,

$$
N\left(-\frac{b(\hat{\tau})}{\sqrt{\hat{\tau}}}\right)=e^{-\eta\hat{\tau}}, \tag{57}
$$

and

$$
b(\hat{\tau})=-\sqrt{\hat{\tau}}N^{-1}\left(e^{-\eta\hat{\tau}}\right). \tag{58}
$$

Now,

$$N^{-1}(y) \underset{y\to 1}{\sim} \sqrt{2f(\eta)}, \tag{59}$$

where

$$\eta = -\ln\left(2\sqrt{\pi}(1-y)\right), \quad f(\eta) = \eta - \frac{\ln\eta}{2} + \frac{\ln\eta - 2}{4\eta} + \frac{(\ln\eta)^2 - 6\ln\eta + 14}{16\eta^2}, \tag{60}$$

so that

$$b(\hat{\tau}) = -\sqrt{2\hat{\tau} f\left(-\ln\left(2\sqrt{\pi}\left(1-e^{-\eta\hat{\tau}}\right)\right)\right)} \approx -\sqrt{2\hat{\tau}\ln\left(\frac{1}{2\sqrt{\pi}\eta\hat{\tau}}\right)}. \tag{61}$$

3.5 *Default boundaries*

Default boundaries calibrated to several representative values of η are shown in Figure 1.

We show that solutions of Equations (53) and (54) coincide modulo numerical error in Figure 2.

3.6 *Main conjecture*

Conjecture: *For a given time interval $I^{(T)} = [0, T]$, there exists a parameter interval $I^{(\eta)}(T) = [0, \eta^*(T)]$, such that for any $\eta \in I^{(\eta)}(T)$, the default boundary $b(t)$ can be calibrated to the default intensity η. We can construct the corresponding boundary as follows:*

$$b(t;\eta) = \lim\nolimits_{\tau\to 0} b(t;\tau,\eta), \quad 0 < t \leq T, \tag{62}$$

where $b(t;\tau,\eta)$ is found by solving either Equations (53) or (54).

We illustrate our conjecture in Figure 3.

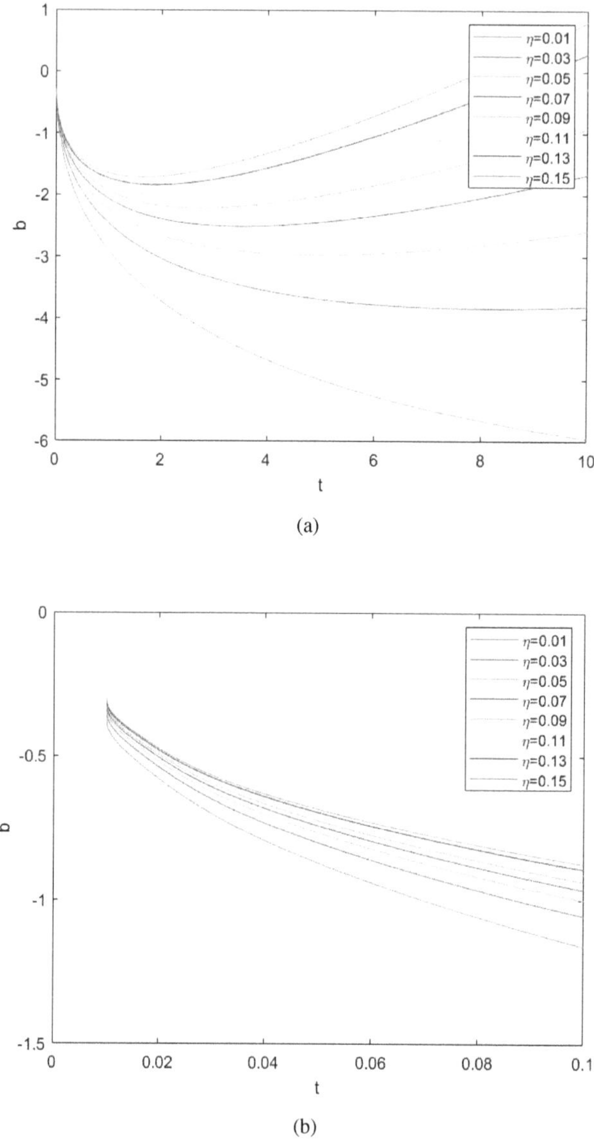

Figure 1: In Figures 1(a)–(b), we show the default boundaries for several representative values of the default intensity η. We choose $\tau = 0.01$. In Figure 1(a), we choose $0.01 < t < 10.0$ to capture their overall behavior; In Figure 1(b), we choose $0.01 < t < 0.1$ so that small features can be shown.

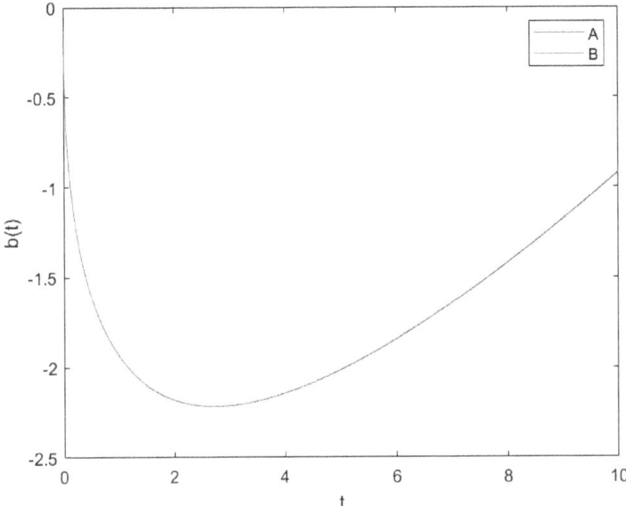

Figure 2: In this figure, we choose the default intensity $\eta = 0.09$ and show that boundaries calculated by solving Equations (53) and (54) coincide modulo numerical errors.

4. Mean-Field Banking System

4.1 *Preliminaries*

No bank is an island — they operate as a group. Tangible links between banks manifest themselves via interbank loans; intangible links are manifold — overall sentiment, ease of doing business, and others. Hence, to build a meaningful structural default model for a bank, one needs to take into account this bank's interactions with all the banks whom it lends to or borrows from. Eisenberg and Noe developed a Merton-like model of the bank default (default can happen only at maturity) in the seminal paper [12]. The present author extended the Eisenberg–Noe model to the Black–Cox setting (default can happen at any time before maturity provided that debt covenants are violated); see [33]. Lipton's work was subsequently generalized in [21,22]. Recently, several authors considered the interconnected banking system in the mean-field framework and studied a representative bank; see [16,20,25,42,43] among many others. In this section, we also use the mean-field approach. Additional details are given in [39].

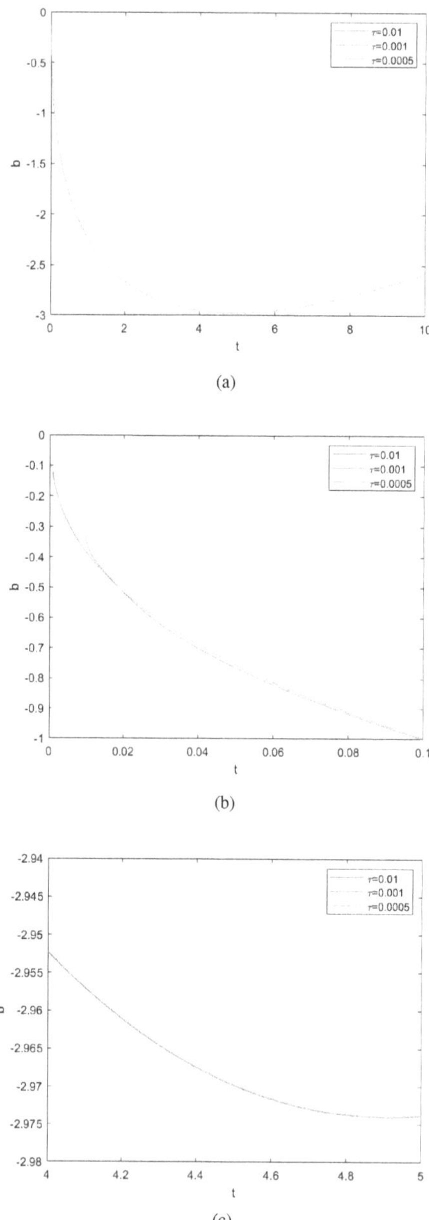

Figure 3: In this figure, we choose the default intensity $\eta = 0.05$ and illustrate our main conjecture numerically by constructing three boundaries corresponding to $\tau = 0.01$, 0.001, and 0.0005, respectively. It is clear that after a short initial period, these boundaries begin overlapping.

4.2 *Interconnected banking system*

We follow [33] and assume that the dynamics of bank i's total external assets is governed by

$$\frac{dA_t^i}{A_t^i} = \mu_i \, dt + \sigma_i \, dW_t^i, \tag{63}$$

where W^i are independent standard Brownian motions for $1 \leq i \leq n$, and the liabilities, both external L_i and mutual L_{ij}, are constant.

Bank i is assumed to default when its assets fall below a certain threshold determined by its liabilities, namely at time $\tau_i = \inf\{t : A_t^i \leq \Lambda_t^i\}$, where Λ^i is a default boundary which we now work out. At time $t = 0$,

$$\Lambda_0^i = R_i \left(L_i + \textstyle\sum_{j \neq i} L_{ij} \right) - \textstyle\sum_{j \neq i} L_{ji}, \tag{64}$$

where R_i is the recovery rate of bank i. If bank k defaults at time t, the default boundary of bank i jumps by $\Delta\Lambda_t^i = (1 - R_i R_k) L_{ki}$.

The distance to default $Y_t^i = \log(A_t^i / \Lambda_t^i)/\sigma$ has the following dynamics:

$$Y_t^i = Y_0^i + (\mu - \sigma^2/2)t + W_t^i - \frac{1}{\sigma} \log \left(1 + \frac{\gamma}{N} \textstyle\sum_{k \neq i} (1 - R^2) \frac{1}{\Lambda_0} \mathbf{1}_{\{\tau_k \leq t\}} \right), \tag{65}$$

or, approximately,

$$Y_t^i = Y_t^0 + (\mu - \sigma^2/2)t + W_t^i - \frac{\gamma(1 - R^2)}{\sigma \Lambda_0} L_t^N, \tag{66}$$

where

$$L_t^N = \frac{1}{N} \sum_k \mathbf{1}_{\{\tau_k \leq t\}}. \tag{67}$$

In the limit for $N \to \infty$, all Y_t^i have the same dynamics:

$$\begin{aligned} Y_t &= Y_0 + W_t - \alpha L_t, \\ L_t &= \mathbb{P}(\tau \leq t), \quad \tau = \inf\{t \in [0, T] : Y_t \leq 0\}, \end{aligned} \tag{68}$$

where $\alpha = \gamma(1 - R^2) / \sigma \Lambda_0$ characterizes the strength of interbank interactions. Thus, we are dealing with a mean-field problem — the behavior of a representative bank depends on the behavior of all other banks, and all of them have the same dynamics. Hence, the problem in question is nonlinear.

We follow [39] and write the increasing process L as

$$\alpha L_t = -\int_0^t \mu(t')\,dt' = -M(t), \tag{69}$$

for some negative μ, so that p satisfies

$$\begin{gathered}\frac{\partial}{\partial t}p(t,x;z) = -\mu(t)\frac{\partial}{\partial x}p(t,x;z) + \frac{1}{2}\frac{\partial^2}{\partial x^2}p(t,x;z),\ 0 \le x < \infty,\\ p(0,x;z) = \delta_z(x),\ p(t,0;z) = 0,\ p(t,x\to\infty)\to 0.\end{gathered} \tag{70}$$

As we already know,

$$g(t;z) \equiv \frac{dL_t}{dt} = \frac{1}{2}p_x(t,0;z), \tag{71}$$

so that Equations (70) can be written in the self-consistent form

$$\begin{gathered}\frac{\partial}{\partial t}p(t,x;z) = \frac{\alpha}{2}\frac{\partial}{\partial x}p(t,0;z)\frac{\partial}{\partial x}p(t,x;z) + \frac{1}{2}\frac{\partial^2}{\partial x^2}p(t,x;z),\ 0 \le x < \infty,\\ p(0,x;z) = \delta_z(x),\ p(t,0;z) = 0,\ p(t,x\to\infty)\to 0.\end{gathered} \tag{72}$$

The change of variables $(t,x) \to (t,y) = (t, x - M(t))$ yields the familiar initial-boundary-value problem (IBVP):

$$\begin{gathered}\frac{\partial}{\partial t}p(t,y) = \frac{1}{2}p_{yy}(t,y),\quad 0 \le y < \infty,\\ p(0,y) = \delta_z(y),\quad p(t,-M(t)) = 0,\quad p(t,y\to\infty)\to 0.\end{gathered} \tag{73}$$

As before, we split p in two parts

$$p(t,y) = H(t,y) + r(t,y), \tag{74}$$

where $H(t,y)$ is the standard heat kernel, while r is the solution of the following problem:

$$\begin{gathered}\frac{\partial}{\partial t}r(t,y) = \frac{1}{2}\frac{\partial^2}{\partial y^2}r(t,y),\quad 0 \le y < \infty,\\ r(0,y) = 0,\ r(t,-M(t)) = -\frac{\exp\left(-\frac{(M(t)+z)^2}{2t}\right)}{\sqrt{2\pi t}},\\ r(t,y\to\infty)\to 0.\end{gathered} \tag{75}$$

4.3 Governing system of integral equations

Using our standard approach, we obtain the following system of non-linear Volterra integral equations

$$\nu(t) + \int_0^t \frac{\Theta(t,t')\,\Xi(t,t')\,\nu(t')}{\sqrt{2\pi(t-t')}}dt' + H(t, t\Theta(t,0) - z) = 0,$$

$$\mu(t) + \left(\frac{1}{\sqrt{2\pi t}} + \alpha\mu(t)\right)\nu(t) + \frac{1}{2}\int_0^t \frac{\Phi(t,t') + \Theta^2(t,t')\,\Xi(t,t')\,\nu(t')}{\sqrt{2\pi(t-t')}}dt'$$
$$+\frac{(t\Theta(t,0) - z)\,H(t, t\Theta(t,0) - z)}{2t} = 0, \tag{76}$$

where

$$\Theta(t,t') = \frac{\alpha\int_{t'}^{t}\mu(t'')\,dt''}{(t-t')},\quad \Xi(t,t') = e^{-\dfrac{(t-t')\,\Theta^2(t,t')}{2}},$$

$$\Phi(t,t') = \frac{(\nu(t) - \Xi(t,t')\,\nu(t'))}{(t-t')},$$

$$\Theta(t,t) = \alpha\mu(t),\ \Xi(t,t) = 1,\ \Phi(t,t) = \nu'(t) + \frac{1}{2}\alpha^2\mu^2(t)\,\nu(t).$$

4.4 Numerical solution

In the spirit of Equation (39), we get the following approximation for Equations (76) for $k > 0$:

$$\nu_k + \frac{1}{\sqrt{2\pi}}\sum_{l=1}^{k}\left(P_{k,l}^{(1)}\nu_l + P_{k,l-1}^{(1)}\nu_{l-1}\right)\Pi_{k,l} + \vartheta_k = 0,$$

$$\mu_k + \left(\frac{1}{\sqrt{2\pi\Delta_{k,0}}} + \alpha\mu_k\right)\nu_k + \frac{1}{2\sqrt{2\pi}}\sum_{l=1}^{k}(\Phi_{k,l}$$
$$+\Phi_{k,l-1} + P_{k,l}^{(2)}\nu_l + P_{k,l-1}^{(2)}\nu_{l-1}\Big)\,\Pi_{k,l} + \iota_k = 0. \tag{77}$$

Here and below we use the following notation

$$\Theta_{k,l} = \alpha \frac{\sum_{i=l+1}^{k} (\mu_i + \mu_{i-1}) \Delta_{i,i-1}}{2\Delta_{k,l}}, \ P_{k,l}^{(i)} = \Theta_{k,l}^{i} e^{-\frac{\Delta_{k,l}\Theta_{k,l}^{2}}{2}},$$

$$Q_{k,l} = P_{k,l}^{(2)} - \frac{P_{k,l}^{(0)}}{\Delta_{k,l}}, \quad \Phi_{k,l} = \frac{\nu_k - P_{k,l}^{(0)}\nu_{k-1}}{\Delta_{k,l}}, \quad k > l,$$

$$\Theta_{k,k} = \ \alpha\mu_k, \ P_{k,k}^{(i)} = \alpha^i \mu_k^i, \ Q_{k,k} \text{ undefined}, \ \Phi_{k,k} = \frac{\nu_k - \nu_{k-1}}{\Delta_{k,k-1}}$$

$$+ \frac{1}{2}\alpha^2 \mu_k^2 \nu_k,$$

$$\vartheta_k = H\left(\Delta_{k,0}, \Delta_{k,0}\Theta_{k,0} - z\right), \quad \iota_k = \frac{\left(\Delta_{k,0}\Theta_{k,0} - z\right)\vartheta_k}{2\Delta_{k,0}}, \ k > 0. \tag{78}$$

For $k = 0$ we have:

$$(\nu_0, \mu_0) = (0, 0).$$

For $k = 1$ we have:

$$\nu_1 = -\frac{H\left(\Delta_{1,0}, \frac{\Delta_{1,0}\alpha\mu_1}{2} - z\right)}{\left(1 + \sqrt{\frac{\Delta_{1,0}}{2\pi}}\alpha\mu_1\right)},$$

$$\mu_1 - \left(\frac{\left(\frac{1}{\sqrt{2\pi\Delta_{1,0}}} + \alpha\mu_1 + \frac{\alpha^2\mu_1^2}{2\sqrt{2\pi\Delta_{1,0}}}\right)}{\left(1 + \sqrt{\frac{\Delta_{1,0}}{2\pi}}\alpha\mu_1\right)} - \frac{\left(\frac{\Delta_{1,0}\alpha\mu_1}{2} - z\right)}{2\Delta_{1,0}} \right)$$

$$\times H\left(\Delta_{1,0}, \frac{\Delta_{1,0}\alpha\mu_1}{2} - z\right) = 0, \tag{79}$$

where the nonlinear equation for μ_1 has to be solved by the Newton–Raphson method.

For $k > 1$ we have

$$\left(1+\sqrt{\frac{\Delta_{k,k-1}}{2\pi}}\alpha\mu_k\right)\nu_k+\sqrt{\frac{\Delta_{k,k-1}}{2\pi}}P^{(1)}_{k,k-1}\nu_{k-1}$$
$$+\frac{1}{\sqrt{2\pi}}\sum_{l=1}^{k-1}\left(P^{(1)}_{k,l}\nu_l+P^{(1)}_{k,l-1}\nu_{l-1}\right)\Pi_{k,l}+\vartheta_k=0,$$
$$\mu_k+\left(\frac{1}{\sqrt{2\pi\Delta_{k,0}}}+\alpha\mu_k+\frac{\alpha^2\mu_k^2}{2\sqrt{2\pi\Delta_{k,k-1}}}\right.$$
$$\left.+\frac{1}{2\sqrt{2\pi}}\sum_{l=1}^{k-1}\frac{(\Delta_{k,l}+\Delta_{k,l-1})\Pi_{k,l}}{\Delta_{k,l}\Delta_{k,l-1}}\right)\nu_k\frac{1}{2}\sqrt{\frac{\Delta_{k,k-1}}{2\pi}}Q_{k,k-1}\nu_{k-1}$$
$$+\frac{1}{2\sqrt{2\pi}}\sum_{l=1}^{k-1}(Q_{k,l}\nu_l+Q_{k,l-1}\nu_{l-1})\Pi_{k,l}+\iota_k=0. \tag{80}$$

Assuming that $(\nu_1,\mu_1),\ldots,(\nu_{k-1},\mu_{k-1})$ are known, we can express ν_k in terms of μ_k:

$$\nu_k=-\frac{\left(\sqrt{\frac{\Delta_{k,k-1}}{2\pi}}P^{(1)}_{k,k-1}\nu_{k-1}+\frac{1}{\sqrt{2\pi}}\sum_{l=1}^{k-1}\left(P^{(1)}_{k,l}\nu_l+P^{(1)}_{k,l-1}\nu_{l-1}\right)\Pi_{k,l}+\vartheta_k\right)}{\left(1+\sqrt{\frac{\Delta_{k,k-1}}{2\pi}}\alpha\mu_k\right)}, \tag{81}$$

and obtain a nonlinear equation for μ_k:

$$\mu_k-\frac{\left(\frac{1}{\sqrt{2\pi\Delta_{k,0}}}+\alpha\mu_k+\frac{\alpha^2\mu_k^2}{2\sqrt{2\pi\Delta_{k,k-1}}}+\frac{1}{2\sqrt{2\pi}}\sum_{l=1}^{k-1}\frac{(\Delta_{k,l}+\Delta_{k,l-1})\Pi_{k,l}}{\Delta_{k,l}\Delta_{k,l-1}}\right)}{\left(1+\sqrt{\frac{\Delta_{k,k-1}}{2\pi}}\alpha\mu_k\right)}$$
$$\times\left(\sqrt{\frac{\Delta_{k,k-1}}{2\pi}}P^{(1)}_{k,k-1}\nu_{k-1}+\frac{1}{\sqrt{2\pi}}\sum_{l=1}^{k-1}\left(P^{(1)}_{k,l}\nu_l+P^{(1)}_{k,l-1}\nu_{l-1}\right)\Pi_{k,l}+\vartheta_k\right)$$
$$+\frac{(Q_{k,k-1}\Delta_{k,k-1}-1)\nu_{k-1}}{2\sqrt{2\pi\Delta_{k,k-1}}}+\frac{1}{2\sqrt{2\pi}}\sum_{l=1}^{k-1}(Q_{k,l}\nu_l+Q_{k,l-1}\nu_{l-1})\Pi_{k,l}+\iota_k=0, \tag{82}$$

which again is solved by the Newton–Raphson method.

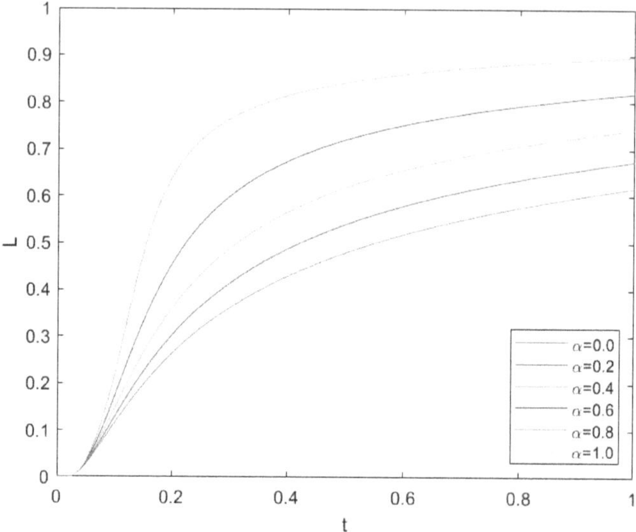

Figure 4: In this figure, we demonstrate the loss probability for the initial position $z = 0.5$ and several representative values of α, which characterizes the strength of interbank interactions.

In Figure 4, we show cumulative loss probability for several representative values of α.

A striking feature of this figure is the "phase transition" occurring at $\alpha \approx 1.0$, when default after a finite time becomes inevitable. By contrast, for $\alpha = 0$, the default probability reaches unity only asymptotically when $t \to \infty$.

We notice that for $\alpha = 0$, $\mu(t)$, $\nu(t)$ can be calculated analytically. For benchmarking purposes, we compare numerical and analytical results in Figures 5(a) and 5(b). As usual, the efficiency of the Newton-Raphson method, which is illustrated in Figure 5(c) is nothing short of miraculous.

In Figure 6, we represent shifted probability density surfaces $p(t, x - z; z)$ for representative values of α used in Figure 4.

The shift is made in order to make the connection with Section 3 more transparent; after this shift all the processes start at 0 and the boundaries are given by $b = -0.5$.

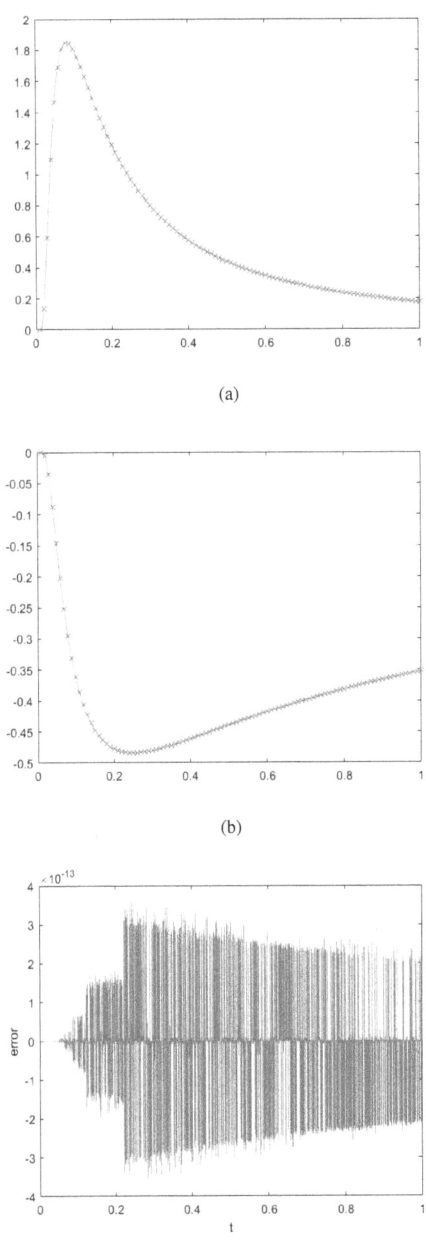

Figure 5: In Figures 5(a)–(b), we choose $z = 0.5$, $\alpha = 0$, and we show $\mu(t)$ and $\nu(t)$ calculated numerically and analytically. In Figure 5(c), we choose $z = 0.5$, $\alpha = 0.6$, and we show the error generated by the Newton–Raphson method.

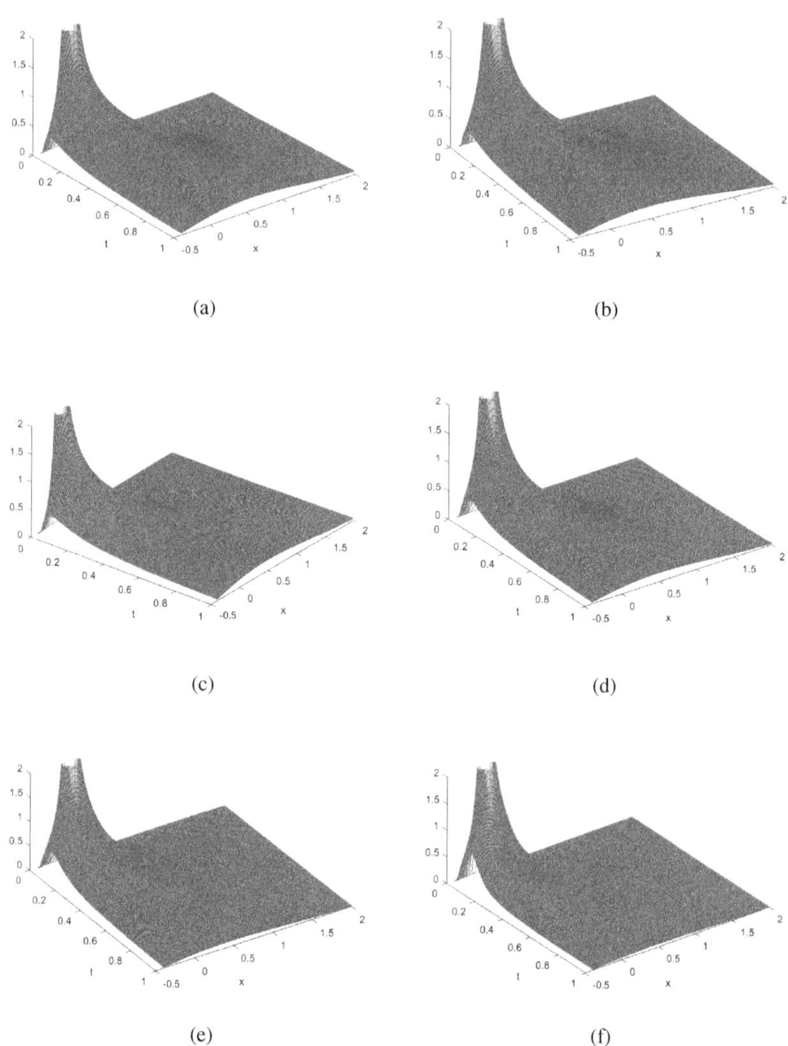

Figure 6: In Figures 6(a)–(f) we show the probability density function $p(t, x - z; z)$. We shift the domain down by $-z$ in order to make comparison with the structural default model considered in Section 3 more transparent. In Figures 6(a) and (b) we show analytical and numerical results for $\alpha = 0$. In Figures 6(c)–(f) we show numerical results for $\alpha = 0.2, 0.4, 0.6, 0.8$, respectively.

5. Hitting Time Probability Distribution for an Ornstein–Uhlenbeck Process

5.1 *Preliminaries*

In a seminal paper, Fortet developed an original approach to calculating probability distribution of the hitting time for a diffusion process, [14]. Fortet's equation can be viewed as a variant of the Einstein–Smoluchowski equation, [11,49]. A general overview can be found in [6,7].

Numerous attempts to find an analytical result for the Ornstein–Uhlenbeck (OU) process have been made since 1998 when Leblanc and Scaillet first derived an analytical formula, which contained a mistake, [26]. Two years later, Leblanc *et al.* published a correction on the paper [27]; unfortunately, the correction was erroneous as well, as was shown by [15].

Several authors used the Laplace transform to find a formal semi-analytical solution, [1,29,47].

In this section, we use the EMHP to calculate the distribution of the hitting time for an OU process. Our approach is semi-analytical and can handle both constant and time-dependent parameters. It is worth noting that the latter case cannot be solved using the Laplace transform method. Additional information can be found in [36].

5.2 *Main equations*

To calculate the density $g(t,z)$ of the hitting time probability distribution, we need to solve the following forward problem

$$\frac{\partial}{\partial t}p(t,x;z) = p(t,x;z) + x\frac{\partial}{\partial x}p(t,x;z) + \frac{1}{2}\frac{\partial^2}{\partial x^2}p(t,x;z),$$
$$p(0,x;z) = \delta_z(x), \quad p(t,b(t);z) = 0, \quad p(t,x;z\to\infty)\to 0. \tag{83}$$

This distribution is given by

$$g(t,z) = \frac{1}{2}\frac{\partial}{\partial x}p(t,b;z). \tag{84}$$

5.3 *Particular case, b = 0*

Before solving the general problem via the EMHP, let us consider a particular case of $b = 0$. Green's function for the OU process in question has the form

$$G(t,x;z) = e^t H\left(\eta(t), e^t x - z\right), \tag{85}$$

where

$$\eta(t) = \frac{e^{2t} - 1}{2} = e^t \sinh(t). \tag{86}$$

Since $b = 0$, the method of images works, so that

$$\begin{aligned} p(t,x;z) &= e^t H\left(\eta(t), e^t x - z\right) - e^t H\left(\eta(t), e^t x + z\right), \\ g(t) &= \frac{1}{2}\frac{\partial}{\partial x} p(t,0) = \frac{z e^{2t} H(\eta(t), -z)}{\eta(t)}, \\ G(t) &= \int_0^t g(t')\,dt' = 2N\left(-\frac{z}{\sqrt{\eta(t)}}\right). \end{aligned} \tag{87}$$

This result is useful for benchmarking purposes.

5.4 *General case*

To be concrete, consider the case $z > b(0)$. We wish to transform the IBVP (83) into the standard IBVP for a heat equation with a moving boundary. To this end, we introduce new independent and dependent variables as follows:

$$\begin{aligned} q(\tau,\xi) &= e^{-t} p(t,x), \quad \tau = \eta(t), \quad \xi = e^t x, \\ p(t,x) &= \sqrt{1+2\tau}\, q(\tau,\xi), \quad t = \ln\left(\sqrt{1+2\tau}\right), \quad x = \frac{\xi}{\sqrt{1+2\tau}}, \end{aligned} \tag{88}$$

and get the IBVP of the form

$$\begin{aligned} &\frac{\partial}{\partial \tau} q(\tau,\xi) = \frac{1}{2}\frac{\partial^2}{\partial \xi^2} q(\tau,\xi), \qquad \beta(\tau) \le \xi < \infty, \\ &q(0,\xi) = \delta_z(\xi), \quad q(\tau,\beta(\tau)) = 0, \quad q(\tau,\xi\to\infty) \to 0. \end{aligned} \tag{89}$$

Here

$$\beta(\tau) = \sqrt{1+2\tau}\tilde{b}(\ln(\sqrt{1+2\tau})). \tag{90}$$

5.5 *The governing system of integral equations*

The corresponding system of Volterra integral equations has the form

$$\begin{aligned}
&\nu(\tau) + \int_0^\tau \frac{\Theta(\tau,\tau')\,\Xi(\tau,\tau')\,\nu(\tau')}{\sqrt{2\pi(\tau-\tau')}}d\tau' + H(\tau,\beta(\tau)-z) = 0,\\
&\mu(\tau) + \left(\frac{1}{\sqrt{2\pi\tau}} + \beta'(\tau)\right)\nu(\tau)\\
&\quad + \frac{1}{2}\int_0^\tau \frac{\Phi(\tau,\tau') + \Theta^2(\tau,\tau')\,\Xi(\tau,\tau')\,\nu(\tau')}{\sqrt{2\pi(\tau-\tau')}}d\tau'\\
&\quad + \frac{(\beta(\tau)-z)\,H(\tau,\beta(\tau)-z)}{2\tau} = 0,
\end{aligned} \tag{91}$$

where

$$\mu(\tau) = (1+2\tau)\,g\left(\ln\left(\sqrt{1+2\tau}\right)\right). \tag{92}$$

This system is linear, so that $\mu(\tau)$ is expressed in terms of $\nu(\tau)$ directly and there is no need to use the Newton–Raphson method.

5.6 *Flat boundary*

Assuming that the boundary is flat, we can simplify Equation (91) somewhat. We notice that

$$\frac{\beta(\tau)-\beta(\tau')}{\tau-\tau'} = \frac{2b}{\sqrt{1+2\tau}+\sqrt{1+2\tau'}}, \tag{93}$$

introduce

$$\theta = \sqrt{1+2\tau}-1, \quad \theta' = \sqrt{1+2\tau'}-1, \quad 0 \le \theta' \le \theta < \infty, \tag{94}$$

and write the first Equation (91) in the form

$$\nu(\theta) + \frac{2b}{\sqrt{\pi}} \int_0^\theta \frac{\exp\left(-\frac{b^2(\theta-\theta')}{(2+\theta+\theta')}\right)(1+\theta')\,\nu(\theta')}{\sqrt{(2+\theta+\theta')^3(\theta-\theta')}} d\theta'$$

$$+ \frac{e^{-\frac{((1+\theta)b-z)^2}{((1+\theta)^2-1)}}}{\sqrt{\pi\left((1+\theta)^2-1\right)}} = 0. \tag{95}$$

Provided that $\nu(\theta)$ is known, we can represent $g(t)$ is the form

$$g(t) = -\frac{\left(e^t b - z\right)\exp\left(-\frac{\left(e^t b - z\right)^2}{(e^{2t}-1)} + 2t\right)}{\sqrt{\pi\,(e^{2t}-1)^3}} - \left(e^t b + \frac{e^{2t}}{\sqrt{\pi\,(e^{2t}-1)}}\right)\nu(t)$$

$$+ \frac{1}{\sqrt{\pi}} e^{2t} \int_0^\theta \frac{\left(\left(1 - 2b^2\frac{(\theta-\theta')}{(2+\theta+\theta')}\right)\exp\left(-b^2\frac{(\theta-\theta')}{(2+\theta+\theta')}\right)\nu(\theta') - \nu(\theta)\right)(1+\theta')}{\sqrt{(2+\theta+\theta')^3(\theta-\theta')^3}} d\theta'. \tag{96}$$

It is worth noting that the analytical solution is available in two cases: (A) when $b=0$ the solution can be found by using the method of images, (B) when $b(t) = Ae^{-t} + Be^{t}$ the boundary transforms into the linear boundary $2B\tau + A + B$, which can be treated by the method of images as well.

We show the probability density function (pdf) and the cumulative density function (cdf) for the hitting time in Figure 7. It is interesting to note that the undulation of the boundary causes considerable variations in the pdfs, which are naturally less pronounced for the corresponding cdfs.

5.7 *Abel integral equation*

Consider Equation (95), which we got for the standard OU process. For small values of θ, this equation can be approximated by an Abel

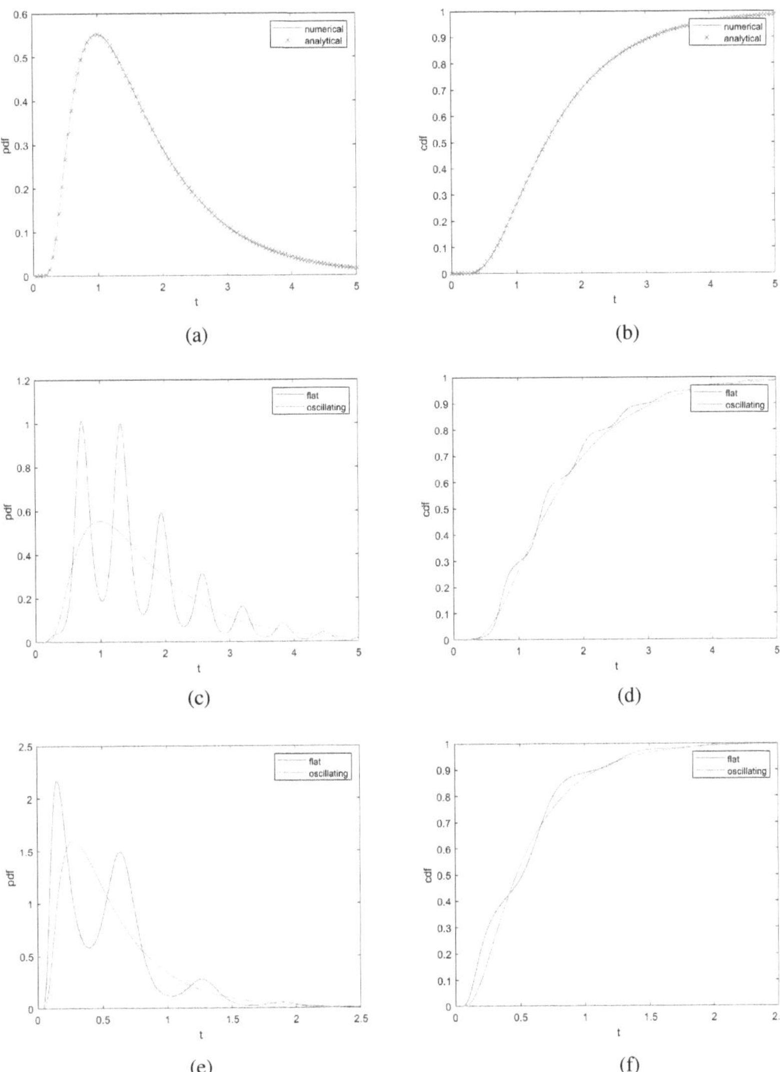

Figure 7: In Figures 7(a)–(f), we show the pdf and cdf for the hitting time probability distribution. In Figures 7(a), (b) $z = 2$, $b(t) = 0$, so that both numerical and analytical expressions are available. These expressions are in perfect agreement. In Figures 7(c), (d) $z = 2$, $b(t) = 0$ and $b(t) = 0.2\sin(10.0t)$. In Figures 7(e), (f) $z = 2$, $b(t) = 1.0$ and $b(t) = 1.0 + 0.2\sin(10.0t)$. Variations in the pdf caused by the barrier undulations are astonishingly profound.

integral equation of the second kind.

$$\nu(\theta) + \frac{b}{\sqrt{2\pi}} \int_0^\theta \frac{1}{\sqrt{\theta - \theta'}} \nu(\theta')\, d\theta' + H(\theta, b - z) = 0. \tag{97}$$

This equation can be solved analytically using direct–inverse Laplace transforms. The direct Laplace transform yields

$$\bar{\nu}(\Lambda) + b\frac{\bar{\nu}(\Lambda)}{\sqrt{2\Lambda}} + \frac{e^{-\sqrt{2\Lambda}(z-b)}}{\sqrt{2\Lambda}} = 0. \tag{98}$$

Then, $\bar{\nu}(\Lambda)$ can be expressed as

$$\bar{\nu}(\Lambda) = -\frac{e^{-\sqrt{2\Lambda}(z-b)}}{\sqrt{2\Lambda} + b}. \tag{99}$$

Taking the inverse Laplace transform, we get the final expression for $\nu(\theta)$

$$\nu(\theta) = be^{\frac{b^2}{2}\theta + b(z-b)} N\left(-\frac{b\theta + z - b}{\sqrt{\theta}}\right) - \frac{\exp\left(-\frac{(b-z)^2}{2\theta}\right)}{\sqrt{2\pi\theta}}. \tag{100}$$

Alternatively, one can represent an analytical solution of an Abel equation

$$y(t) + \xi \int_0^t \frac{y(s)ds}{\sqrt{t-s}} = f(t). \tag{101}$$

in the form

$$y(t) = F(t) + \pi\xi^2 \int_0^t \exp[\pi\xi^2(t-s)] F(s)\, ds, \tag{102}$$

where

$$F(t) = f(t) - \xi \int_0^t \frac{f(s)\, ds}{\sqrt{t-s}}, \tag{103}$$

see [45].

Abel equations naturally arise in many financial mathematics situations, mainly, when fractional differentiation is involved, see, e.g., [2].

6. The Supercooled Stefan Problem

In Sections 6 and 7, we deal with relatively rare instances when financial mathematics results can be successfully used in the broader applied mathematics context rather than the other way around.

The Stefan problem is of great theoretical and practical interest, see, e.g., [10,23,48] and references therein. The classical Stefan problem studies the evolving boundary between the two phases of the same medium, such as ice and water. Thus, this problem boils down to solving the heat equation with a free boundary, which is determined by a matching condition. The main equations for the supercooled Stefan problem, are very similar to the mean-field banking equations:

$$\begin{gathered}\frac{\partial}{\partial t}p\left(t,x\right)=\frac{1}{2}\frac{\partial^{2}}{\partial x^{2}}p\left(t,x\right),\quad b\left(t\right)\leq x<\infty,\\ p\left(0,x\right)=\delta_{z}\left(x\right),\quad p\left(t,b\left(t\right)\right)=0,\quad p\left(t,X\rightarrow\infty\right)\rightarrow0,\end{gathered}\tag{104}$$

where p is the negative temperature profile, and b is the liquid-solid boundary. The location of the boundary is determined by the matching condition

$$\frac{d}{dt}b\left(t\right)=\frac{\alpha}{2}\frac{\partial}{\partial x}p\left(t,x\right).\tag{105}$$

As usual, we represent p as $p=H+r$, where r solves the following IBVP

$$\begin{gathered}\frac{\partial}{\partial t}r\left(t,x\right)=\frac{1}{2}\frac{\partial^{2}}{\partial x^{2}}r\left(t,x\right),\ b\left(t\right)\leq x<\infty,\\ r\left(0,x\right)=0,\ r\left(t,b\left(t\right)\right)=-H\left(t,b\left(t\right)-z\right),\ r\left(t,X\rightarrow\infty\right)\rightarrow0,\end{gathered}\tag{106}$$

By using Equation (20) we get the following system of coupled Volterra equations:

$$\begin{gathered}\nu\left(t'\right)+\int_{0}^{t}\frac{\Theta\left(t,t'\right)\Xi\left(t,t'\right)\nu\left(t'\right)}{\sqrt{2\pi\left(t-t'\right)}}dt'+H\left(t,b\left(t\right)-z\right)=0,\\ b\left(t\right)+\frac{\alpha}{2}\int_{0}^{t}\frac{\Xi\left(t,t'\right)\nu\left(t'\right)}{\sqrt{2\pi\left(t-t'\right)}}dt'=0.\end{gathered}\tag{107}$$

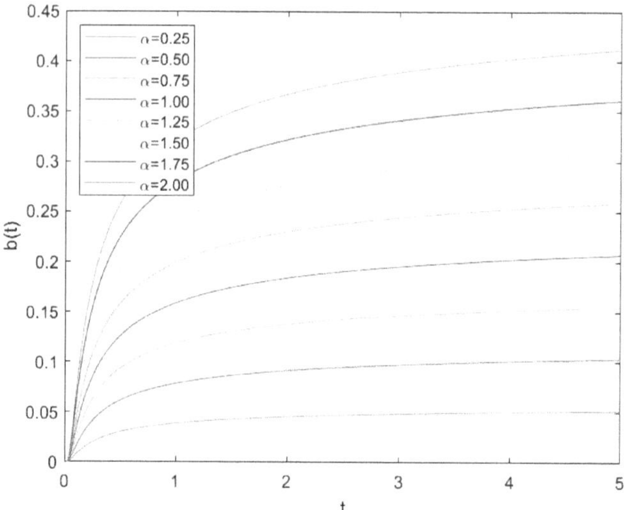

Figure 8: In this figure, we show the solid–liquid boundaries $b(t)$ for several representative values of α.

where

$$\Theta\left(t,t'\right)=\frac{b\left(t\right)-b\left(t'\right)}{\left(t-t'\right)},\quad \Xi\left(t,t'\right)=e^{-\frac{\left(t-t'\right)\Theta^{2}\left(t,t'\right)}{2}},$$

$$\Theta\left(t,t\right)=\frac{db\left(t\right)}{dt},\quad \Xi\left(t,t\right)=1. \tag{108}$$

System of integral equations (107) is very similar to system (54) and can be solved by the same token.

In Figure 8, we show $b\left(t\right)$ for several representative values of α.

7. The Integrate-and-Fire Neuron Excitation Model

7.1 *Governing equations*

We briefly describe the famous integrate-and-fire model in neuroscience, see, e.g., [8,28,44] . The integrate-and-fire model is a mathematical description of the properties of specific cells (spiking neurons) in the nervous system generating sharp electrical potentials across their cell membrane. These spikes last roughly one millisecond. Spiking neurons are a significant signaling unit of the nervous system as a whole, so that understanding their operation is of great theoretical and practical importance.

The neuron excitation problem has the form:

$$\begin{aligned} \frac{\partial}{\partial t}p(t,x) &= \frac{\partial}{\partial x}\left((x-\mu(t))\,p(t,x)\right) + \frac{1}{2}\frac{\partial^2}{\partial x^2}p(t,x) + \lambda(t)\,\delta_{X_0}(x), \\ & -\infty < x \le 0, \\ p(0,x) &= p_0(x),\ p(t,-\infty)=0,\ p(t,0)=0, \\ X_0 < 0,\ \lambda(t) &= -\frac{1}{2}\frac{\partial}{\partial x}p(t,0),\ \mu(t) = m_0 + m_1\lambda(t), \end{aligned} \tag{109}$$

where $p(t,x) > 0$ is the probability density of finding neurons at a voltage x. Without loss of generality, we choose

$$p_0(x) = \delta_\xi(x), \quad \xi < 0. \tag{110}$$

Equation (109) preserve probability in the sense that

$$\frac{d}{dt}\int_{-\infty}^{0} p(t,x)\,dx = 0. \tag{111}$$

Indeed, integration of the main equation yields:

$$\begin{aligned} \frac{d}{dt}\int_{-\infty}^{0} p(t,x)\,dx &= \int_{-\infty}^{0} \frac{\partial}{\partial t}p(t,x)\,dx \\ = \int_{-\infty}^{0}\left(\frac{\partial}{\partial x}\left((x-\mu(t))\,p(t,x)\right) + \frac{1}{2}\frac{\partial^2}{\partial x^2}p(t,x) + \lambda(t)\,\delta_{X_0}(x)\right)dx & \\ &= \frac{1}{2}\frac{\partial}{\partial x}p(t,0) + \lambda(t) = 0. \end{aligned} \tag{112}$$

7.2 The stationary problem

Because the integrate-and-fire equations are probability-preserving, there exists a stationary solution, which solves the time-independent

Fokker–Planck problem:

$$0 = \frac{\partial}{\partial x}\left((x-\mu)\,p(x)\right) + \frac{1}{2}\frac{\partial^2}{\partial x^2}p(x) + \lambda\delta_{X_0}(x),$$

$$p(-\infty) = 0, \qquad p(0) = 0, \quad -\infty < x \leq 0, \tag{113}$$

$$\lambda = -\frac{1}{2}\frac{\partial}{\partial x}p(0), \qquad \mu = m_0 + m_1\lambda.$$

We represent $p(x)$ in the form

$$p(x) = p^{<}(x)\left(1 - \Theta(x - X_0)\right) + p^{>}(x)\,\Theta(x - X_0), \tag{114}$$

where $\Theta(.)$ is the Heaviside function, and notice that

$$p^{<}(X_0) = p^{>}(X_0) \equiv \nu,$$

$$\frac{1}{2}\left(\frac{\partial}{\partial x}p^{>}(X_0) - \frac{\partial}{\partial x}p^{<}(X_0)\right) = -\lambda, \tag{115}$$

where ν, λ are unknown constants, which have to be determined as part of the solution. In view of the boundary conditions, it is clear that

$$(x-\mu)\,p^{>}(x) + \frac{1}{2}\frac{\partial}{\partial x}p^{>}(x) = c^{>} \equiv -\lambda,$$

$$(x-\mu)\,p^{<}(x) + \frac{1}{2}\frac{\partial}{\partial x}p^{<}(x) = c^{<} \equiv 0. \tag{116}$$

Moreover, since p is continuous at $x = X_0$ the second matching condition (115) is satisfied automatically.

The method of separation of variables yields

$$p^{<}(x) = \nu e^{(X_0-\mu)^2-(x-\mu)^2}. \tag{117}$$

while the method of variation of constants yields

$$p^{>}(x) = 2\lambda\left(e^{\mu^2-(x-\mu)^2}D(-\mu) - D(x-\mu)\right), \tag{118}$$

where $D(.)$ is Dawson's integral,

$$D(x) = e^{-x^2}\int_0^x e^{y^2}dy. \tag{119}$$

Thus,

$$\nu = 2\lambda\left(e^{\mu^2-(X_0-\mu)^2}D\left(-\mu\right) - D\left(X_0-\mu\right)\right), \tag{120}$$

and

$$p^{<}\left(x\right) = 2\lambda\left(e^{\mu^2}D\left(-\mu\right) - e^{(X_0-\mu)^2}D\left(X_0-\mu\right)\right)e^{-(x-\mu)^2}. \tag{121}$$

At the same time, in the stationary case, the probability density $p\left(x\right)$ has to integrate to unity:

$$\int_{-\infty}^{0} p\left(x\right)dx = \int_{-\infty}^{X_0} p^{<}\left(x\right)dx + \int_{X_0}^{0} p^{>}\left(x\right)dx = 1, \tag{122}$$

which is a nonlinear equation for λ, because both μ and ν are known functions of λ. Once this equation is solved numerically, the entire profile is determined. It is worth noting that the integral $\int_{-\infty}^{X_0} p^{<}\left(x\right)dx$ can be computed analytically:

$$\begin{aligned}\int_{-\infty}^{X_0} p^{<}\left(x\right)dx &= \nu\int_{-\infty}^{X_0} e^{(X_0-\mu)^2-(x-\mu)^2}dx \\ &= \sqrt{\pi}\nu e^{(X_0-\mu)^2}N\left(\sqrt{2}\left(X_0-\mu\right)\right),\end{aligned} \tag{123}$$

while the second integral $\int_{X_0}^{0} p^{>}\left(x\right)dx$ can be split into two parts, the first of which can be computed analytically, and the second one has to be computed numerically:

$$\begin{aligned}&\int_{X_0}^{0} 2\lambda\left(e^{-x(x-2\mu)}D\left(-\mu\right) - D\left(x-\mu\right)\right)dx \\ &= 2\lambda\left(\sqrt{\pi}e^{\mu^2}\left(N\left(-\sqrt{2}\mu\right) - N\left(\sqrt{2}\left(X_0-\mu\right)\right)\right)D\left(-\mu\right)\right. \\ &\quad \left. - \int_{X_0-\mu}^{-\mu} D\left(x\right)dx\right).\end{aligned} \tag{124}$$

Thus, the corresponding nonlinear equation for λ can be written as

$$\begin{aligned}&\sqrt{\pi}(e^{\mu^2}N(-\sqrt{2}\mu)D(-\mu) - e^{(X_0-\mu)^2}N(\sqrt{2}(X_0-\mu))D(X_0-\mu)) \\ &- \int_{X_0-\mu}^{-\mu} D(x)dx - \frac{1}{2\lambda} = 0.\end{aligned} \tag{125}$$

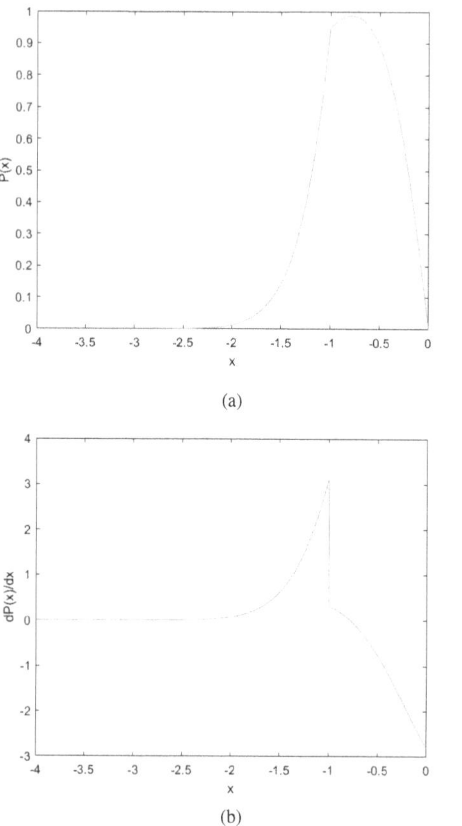

Figure 9: In Figures (a)–(b) we show the stationary distribution $p(x)$ and its derivative $dp(x)/dx$ for the following parameter values: $X_0 = -1$, $m_0 = 0.5$, $m_1 = 0.1$. The corresponding value of λ, which is computed as part of the solution, is 1.4002.

We show the stationary profile $p(x)$ and its derivative $dp(x)/dx$ in Figure 9. As expected, $dp(x)/dx$ jump down at $x = X_0$.

7.3 *The nonstationary problem*

First, we use the following transformation of variables:

$$t = t, y = x - M(t), \ M(0) = 0, \ \frac{\partial}{\partial t} = \frac{\partial}{\partial t} - M'(t)\frac{\partial}{\partial y}, \ \frac{\partial}{\partial x} = \frac{\partial}{\partial y}, \tag{126}$$

and get the following IBVP:

$$\begin{aligned}
\frac{\partial}{\partial t}p(t,y) &= \frac{\partial}{\partial y}\left(\left(y+M'(t)+M(t)-\mu(t)\right)p(t,y)\right) \\
&\quad +\frac{1}{2}\frac{\partial^2}{\partial y^2}p(t,y)+\lambda(t)\,\delta_{X_0-M(t)}(x), \\
&\quad \times\infty<y\leq -M(t), \\
p(0,y) &= \delta_{\xi}(y),\ p(t,-\infty)=0,\ p(t,-M(t))=0, \\
\lambda(t) &= -\frac{1}{2}\frac{\partial}{\partial y}p(t,-M(t)),\ \mu(t)=m_0+m_1\lambda(t). \quad (127)
\end{aligned}$$

Thus, by choosing M in such a way that

$$M'(t)+M(t)-\mu(t)=0, \qquad M(0)=0, \quad (128)$$

or, explicitly,

$$M(t)=\textstyle\int_0^t e^{-(t-t')}\mu(t')\,dt', \quad (129)$$

we get the IBVP for the standard Ornstein–Uhlenbeck process:

$$\begin{aligned}
\frac{\partial}{\partial t}p(t,y) &= \frac{\partial}{\partial y}\left(yp(t,y)\right)+\frac{1}{2}\frac{\partial^2}{\partial y^2}p(t,y)+\lambda(t)\,\delta_{X_0-M(t)}(x), \\
&\quad \times\infty<y\leq -M(t), \\
p(0,y) &= \delta_{\xi}(y),\ p(t,-\infty)=0,\ p(t,-M(t))=0, \\
\lambda(t) &= -\frac{1}{2}\frac{\partial}{\partial y}p(t,-M(t)),\ \mu(t)=m_0+m_1\lambda(t). \quad (130)
\end{aligned}$$

As usual, we split $p(t,x)$ as follows:

$$p(t,x)=e^t H\left(\eta(t),e^t y-\xi\right)+r(t,x), \quad (131)$$

where the first term solves the governing equation and satisfies the initial, but not the boundary conditions, while $r(t,x)$ solves the following IBVP:

$$\begin{aligned}
\frac{\partial}{\partial t} r(t,y) &= \frac{\partial}{\partial y}(yr(t,y)) + \frac{1}{2}\frac{\partial^2}{\partial y^2} r(t,y) + \lambda(t)\,\delta_{X_0 - M(t)}(x), \\
&\quad \times \infty < y \leq -M(t), \\
r(0,y) &= 0,\ r(t,-\infty) = 0,\ r(t,-M(t)) = \chi_0(t), \\
\lambda(t) &= -\frac{1}{2}\frac{\partial}{\partial y} r(t,-M(t)) + \chi_1(t),\ \mu(t) = m_0 + m_1\lambda(t),
\end{aligned} \tag{132}$$

where

$$\begin{aligned}
\chi_0(t) &= -e^t H\left(\eta(t), e^t M(t) + \xi\right), \\
\chi_1(t) &= -\frac{e^{2t}\left(e^t M(t) + \xi\right)}{2\eta(t)} H\left(\eta(t), e^t M(t) + \xi\right).
\end{aligned} \tag{133}$$

We apply the familiar change of variables (88) and get the following IBVP for $q(\tau,\theta) = e^{-t} r(t,y)$:

$$\begin{aligned}
\frac{\partial}{\partial \tau} q(\tau,\theta) &= \frac{1}{2}\frac{\partial^2}{\partial \theta^2} q(t,\theta) + \varkappa(\tau)\,\delta_{X_0 - M(t)}(x),\ \infty < \theta \leq \Gamma(\tau), \\
q(0,\theta) &= 0,\ q(\tau,-\infty) = 0,\ q(\tau,\Gamma(\tau)) = \varrho_0(\tau), \\
\varkappa(\tau) &= -\frac{(1+2\tau)}{2}\frac{\partial}{\partial \theta} q(\tau,\Gamma(\tau)) + \varrho_1(\tau),
\end{aligned} \tag{134}$$

where

$$\begin{aligned}
\Gamma_0(\tau) &= \sqrt{1+2\tau}\left(X_0 - M\left(\ln\left(\sqrt{1+2\tau}\right)\right)\right), \\
\Gamma(\tau) &= -\sqrt{1+2\tau}\, M\left(\ln\left(\sqrt{1+2\tau}\right)\right), \\
\varrho_0(\tau) &= -H(\tau, \Gamma(\tau) - \xi), \\
\varrho_1(\tau) &= \frac{(\Gamma(\tau) - \xi)}{2\tau} H(\eta(t), \Gamma(\tau) - \xi).
\end{aligned} \tag{135}$$

Denoting $q(\tau, \Gamma_0(\tau))$ by $\nu(\tau)$, we can split the IBVP (134) into two IBVPs:

$$\begin{gathered}\frac{\partial}{\partial \tau} q^{>}(\tau, \theta)=\frac{1}{2} \frac{\partial^2}{\partial \theta^2} q^{>}(t, \theta), \ \Gamma_0(\tau) \leq \theta \leq \Gamma(\tau), \\ q^{>}(0, \theta)=0, \ q(\tau, \Gamma_0(\tau))=\nu(\tau), \ q(\tau, \Gamma(\tau))=\varrho_0(\tau),\end{gathered} \tag{136}$$

$$\begin{gathered}\frac{\partial}{\partial \tau} q^{<}(\tau, \theta)=\frac{1}{2} \frac{\partial^2}{\partial \theta^2} q^{<}(t, \theta), \quad \infty<\theta \leq \Gamma_0(\tau), \\ q^{<}(0, \theta)=0, \ q(\tau, \theta \rightarrow-\infty) \rightarrow 0, \ q(\tau, \Gamma_0(\tau))=\nu(\tau),\end{gathered} \tag{137}$$

and a matching condition:

$$\begin{aligned} & \frac{\partial}{\partial \theta} q^{<}(t, \Gamma_0(\tau))-\frac{\partial}{\partial \theta} q^{>}(t, \Gamma_0(\tau)) \\ & \quad=2\left(-\frac{(1+2 \tau)}{2} \frac{\partial}{\partial \theta} q^{>}(\tau, \Gamma(\tau))+\varrho_1(\tau)\right) .\end{aligned} \tag{138}$$

We can now use results from Section 2 to reduce these equations to a very efficient (but highly nonlinear) system of Volterra integral equations. An analysis of the corresponding system will be presented elsewhere.

8. Conclusions

In this document, we have described an analytical framework for solving several relevant and exciting problems of financial engineering. We have shown that the EMHP is a powerful tool for reducing partial differential equations to integral equations of Volterra type. Due to their unique nature, these equations are relatively easy to solve. In some cases, we can solve these equations analytically by judiciously using the Laplace transform. In other cases, we can solve them numerically by constricting highly accurate numerical quadratures. We have demonstrated that the EMHP has numerous applications in mathematical finance and far beyond its confines.

Acknowledgment

The author gratefully acknowledges valuable discussions with his Investimizer colleagues Marsha Lipton and Marcos Lopez de Prado. The contents of this paper were presented at a conference at the Hebrew University of Jerusalem in December 2018. Exemplary efforts of the organizers, David Gershon and Mathieu Rosenbaum, are much appreciated. Some of the ideas described here were developed jointly with Vadim Kaushansky and Christoph Reisinger.

References

[1] Alili, L., Patie, P., and Pedersen, J.L. (2005). Representations of the first hitting time density of an Ornstein–Uhlenbeck process, *Stochastic Models*, 21(4), 967–980.

[2] Andersen, L. and Lipton, A. (2013). Asymptotics for exponential Lévy processes and their volatility smile: survey and new results, *International Journal of Theoretical and Applied Finance*, 16 (1) 1350001 (98 pages).

[3] Avellaneda, M. and Zhu, J. (2001). Distance to default, *Risk*, 14(12), 125–129.

[4] Black, F. and Cox, J. C. (1976). Valuing corporate securities: Some effects of bond indenture provisions, *Journal of Finance*, 31(2), 351–367.

[5] Bluman, G. W. (1980). On the transformation of diffusion processes into the Wiener process, *SIAM Journal of Applied Mathematics*, 39(2), 238–247.

[6] Borodin, A. N. and Salminen, P. (2012). *Handbook of Brownian Motion: Facts and Formulae* (Birkhäuser, Basel).

[7] Breiman, L. (1967). First exit times from a square root boundary. In *Fifth Berkeley Symposium*, Vol. 2, pp. 9–16 (Berkeley).

[8] Carrillo, J., González, M., Gualdani, M., and Schonbek, M. (2013). Classical solutions for a nonlinear Fokker–Planck equation arising in computational neuroscience, *Communications in Partial Differential Equations*, 38(3), 385–409.

[9] Cherkasov, I. D. (1957). On the transformation of the diffusion process to a Wiener process, *Theory of Probability and its Applications*, 2(3), 373–377.

[10] Delarue, F., Nadtochiy, S., and Shkolnikov, M. (2017). Global solutions to the supercooled Stefan problem with blow-ups: Regularity and uniqueness. *ArXiv* preprint.

[11] Einstein, A. (1905). Über die von der molekularkinetischen theorie der wärme geforderte bewegung von in ruhenden flüssigkeiten suspendierten teilchen, *Annals of Physics*, 322(8), 549–560.
[12] Eisenberg, L. and Noe, T. H. (2001). Systemic risk in financial systems, *Management Science*, 47(2), 236–249.
[13] Finkelstein, V. and Lardy, J. P. (2001) Assessing default probabilities from equity markets: Simple closed-form solution. Presented at the *ICBI Global Derivatives Conference*, Juan les Pins.
[14] Fortet, R. (1943) Les fonctions aleatoires du type de Markoff associées a certaines équations linéaires aux dérivées partielles du type parabolique, *Journal of Mathematics and its Pure Applications*, 22, 177–243.
[15] Göing-Jaeschke, A. and Yor, M. (2003). A clarification note about hitting times densities for Ornstein–Uhlenbeck processes, *Finance Stoch.*, 7(3), 413–415.
[16] Hambly, B., Ledger, S., and Sojmark, A. (2018). A McKean–Vlasov equation with positive feedback and blow-ups. ArXiv:1801.07703.
[17] Hilberink. B. and Rogers, L. C. G. (2002) Optimal capital structure and endogenous default, *Finance and Stochastics*, 6, 237–263.
[18] Hull, J. and White, A. (2001). Valuing credit default swaps, II, *Journal of Derivatives*, 8(3), 12–22.
[19] Hyer, T., Lipton, A., Pugachevsky, D., and Qui, S. (1998). A hidden-variable model for risky bonds. Bankers Trust Working Paper.
[20] Ichiba, T., Ludkovski, M., and Sarantsev, A. (2018). Dynamic contagion in a banking system with births and defaults. ArXiv:1807.09897.
[21] Itkin, A. and Lipton, A. (2015). Efficient solution of structural default models with correlated jumps and mutual obligations, *International Journal of Computer Mathematics*, 92(12), 2380–2405.
[22] Itkin, A. and Lipton, A. (2017). Structural default model with mutual obligations, *Review of Derivatives Research*, 20,15–46.
[23] Kamenomostskaja, S. L. (1961). On Stefan's problem, *Matematicheskii Sbornik (Novaya Seriya)* 53 (95), 489–514.
[24] Kartashov, E. (2001). Analytical Methods in the Theory of Heat Conduction of Solids. Vysshaya Shkola, Moscow 706.
[25] Kaushansky, V. and Reisinger, C. (2019). Simulation of particle systems interacting through hitting times, *Discrete & Continuous Dynamical Systems* — B, 24 (10), 5481-5502.
[26] Leblanc, B. and Scaillet, O. (1998). Path dependent options on yields in the affine term structure model, *Finance Stochastic*, 2(4), 349–367.
[27] Leblanc, B., Renault, O., and Scaillet, O. (2000) A correction note on the first passage time of an Ornstein–Uhlenbeck process to a boundary, *Finance Stochastic*, 4(1), 109–111.

[28] Lewis, T. J. and Rinzel, J. (2003). Dynamics of spiking neurons connected by both inhibitory and electrical coupling, *Journal of Computational Neuroscience*, 14(3), 283–309.
[29] Linetsky, V. (2004) Computing hitting time densities for CIR and OU diffusions: Applications to mean-reverting models, *Journal of Computational Finance*, 7, 1–22.
[30] Linz, P. (1985) Analytical and Numerical Methods for Volterra Equations (SIAM, Philadelphia, Pennsylvania, USA).
[31] Lipton, A. (2001). *Mathematical Methods for Foreign Exchange: A Financial Engineer's Approach.* World Scientific, Singapore.
[32] Lipton, A. (2002). Assets with Jumps, *Risk*, 15 (9), 149–153.
[33] Lipton, A. (2016). Modern monetary circuit theory, stability of interconnected banking network, and balance sheet optimization for individual banks, *International Journal of Theoretical and Applied Finance*, 19(6), 1650034 (57 pages).
[34] Lipton, A. (2018). *Financial Engineering: Selected Works of Alexander Lipton.* World Scientific, Singapore.
[35] Lipton, A. and Kaushansky, V. (2018). On the first hitting time density of an Ornstein–Uhlenbeck process. ArXiv:1810.02390.
[36] Lipton, A. and Kaushansky, V. (2020). On the first hitting time density for a reducible diffusion process. *Quantitative Finance.* Doi: 10.1080/14697688.2020.1713394
[37] Lipton, A. and Kaushansky, V. (2020). Physics and derivatives: On three important problems in mathematical finance, *The Journal of Derivatives*, 27, to appear.
[38] Lipton, A. and Lopez De Prado, M. (2020). A closed-form solution for optimal mean-reverting trading strategies. SSRN:3534445. https://papers.ssrn.com/sol3/papers.cfm?abstract_id=3534445.
[39] Lipton, A., Kaushansky, V., and Reisinger, C. (2019). Semi-analytical solution of a McKean–Vlasov equation with feedback through hitting a boundary, *European Journal of Applied Mathematics.* Doi:10.1017/S0956792519000342.
[40] Lopez De Prado, M. (2018). *Advances in Financial Machine Learning.* John Wiley Sons, Hoboken, New Jersey, USA.
[41] Merton, R. (1974). On the pricing of corporate debt: The risk structure of interest rates, *Journal of Finance* 29, 449–470.
[42] Nadtochiy, S. and Shkolnikov, M. (2017). Particle systems with singular interaction through hitting times: Application in systemic risk modeling. arXiv preprint.
[43] Nadtochiy, S. and Shkolnikov, M. (2018). Mean field systems on networks, with singular interaction through hitting times. ArXiv preprint.

[44] Ostojic, S., Brunel, N., and Hakim, V. (2009). Synchronization properties of networks of electrically coupled neurons in the presence of noise and heterogeneities, *Journal of Computational Neuroscience*, 26, no. 3, 369–392.
[45] Polyanin, A. D. and Manzhirov, A. V. (1998). *Handbook of Integral Equations*, CRC Press, Boca Raton, FL.
[46] Ricciardi, L. M. (1976). On the transformation of diffusion processes into the Wiener process, *Journal of Mathematics and its Analytical Applications*, 54(1), 185–199.
[47] Ricciardi, L. M. and Sato, S. (1988). First-passage-time density and moments of the Ornstein–Uhlenbeck process, *Journal of Applied Probabilities*, 25(1), 43–57.
[48] Rubinstein, L. (1971). The Stefan Problem. Vol. 27 of Translations of Mathematical Monographs, *American Mathematical Society,* Providence, Rhode Island, USA.
[49] Von Smoluchowski, M. (1906). Zur kinetischen theorie der brownschen molekularbewegung und der suspensionen, *Annals of Physics*, 326(14), 756–780.
[50] Tikhonov, A. N. and Samarskii, A. A. (1963). *Equations of Mathematical Physics.* Dover Publications, New York. English translation.
[51] Watson, N. A. (2012). Introduction to Heat Potential Theory. Number 182 in Mathematical Surveys and Monographs. *American Mathematical Society*, Providence, Rhode Island, USA.

https://doi.org/10.1142/9789811259142_0017

Chapter 17

25 Years of Local Volatility and Beyond

B. Dupire

Head of Quantitative Research, Bloomberg L.P.

bdupire@bloomberg.net

1. Outline

- Local Volatility Model (LVM)
- Forward Equations: A Simpler Derivation of the BSM PDE
- Function Itô Calculus: A Framework for Path Dependence
    - BSM/LVM PDE for Path-Dependent Options
    - Volatility Risk Management for Path-Dependent Options
    - A Risk Scale to Compare Options

2. Local Volatility Model

Black–Scholes–Merton (BSM model): Perhaps the most successful and most used model in economics. It lead to many extensions.

BSM '73 $$\frac{dS_t}{S_t} = \mu_t dt + \sigma dW_t$$

Constant volatility

Merton '73 $$\frac{dS_t}{S_t} = \mu_t dt + \sigma(t) dW_t$$

Simplest extension that can be calibrated to the term structure of volatility.

LVM D. '93 $\frac{dS_t}{S_t} = \mu_t dt + \sigma(S_t, t) dW_t$

Simplest extension that can be calibrated to the implied volatility surface.

2.1 *Barrier option prices*

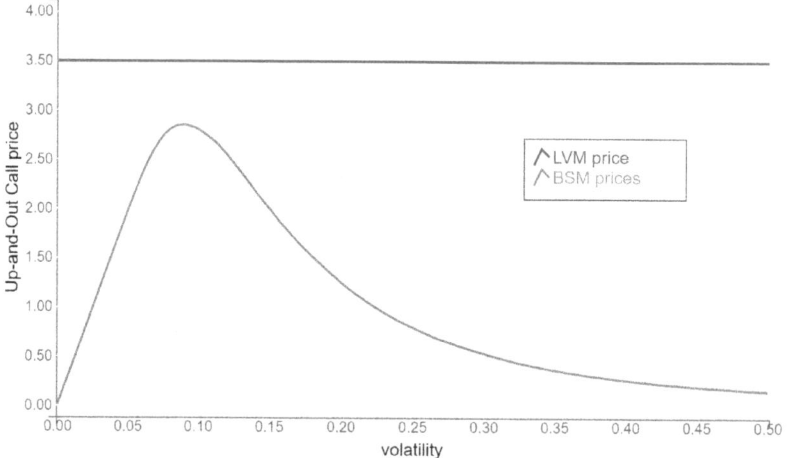

Figure 1: Prices for Up-and-Out call.

Up-and-out call benefits from high volatility at the strike and low volatility at the barrier. In a market with negative skew, the LVM price can be higher than the BSM (flat skew) price for that option for **any** level of the volatility parameter (see Figure 1).

2.2 *Link European options/path-dependent (exotic) options*

- The Local Volatility function $\sigma(S, t)$ is equivalent to the price of all European options.

- LVM is **one** way to price path dependent options.
- It establishes a link between European and exotic prices.

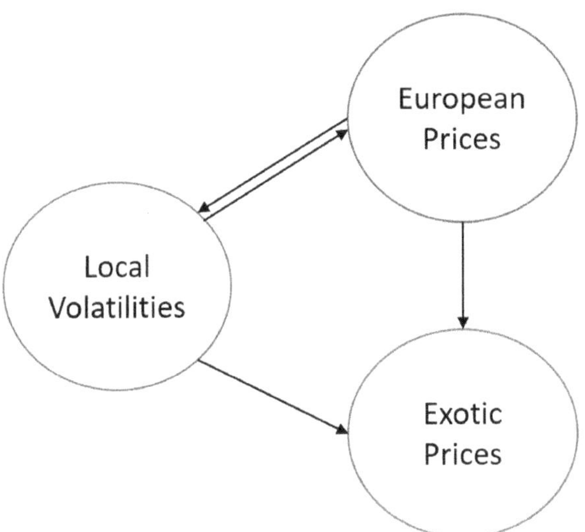

2.3 *One simple model that fits market smiles*

We know that a model with $\frac{dS}{S} = \mu_t dt + \sigma(S,t)dW$ would generate smiles.

Questions:

- Can we find $\sigma(S,t)$ that fits market smiles?
- If yes, is the solution unique?
- If yes, can it be computed explicitly?

Answers:

- Yes, we can find it
- Yes, it is unique
- Yes, it is explicit

2.4 *The risk-neutral solution*

In general there is an infinite number of processes that can fit the market, but only one that is a risk-neutral process and a 1D Markov diffusion (see Figure 2).

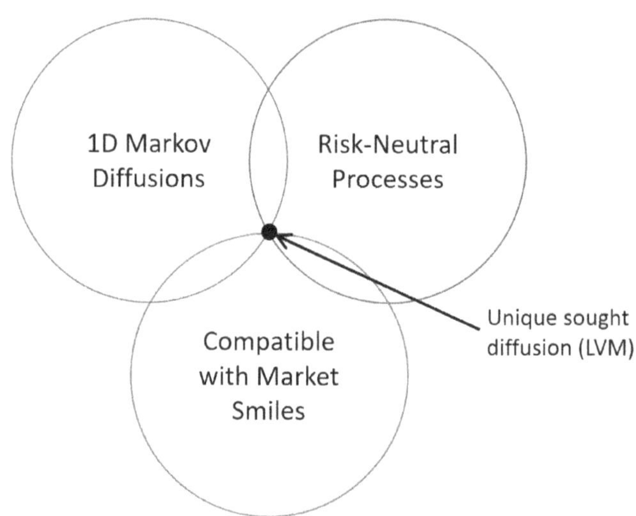

Figure 2: Conditions on processes.

2.5 *Implied and local volatility surfaces (see Figure 3)*

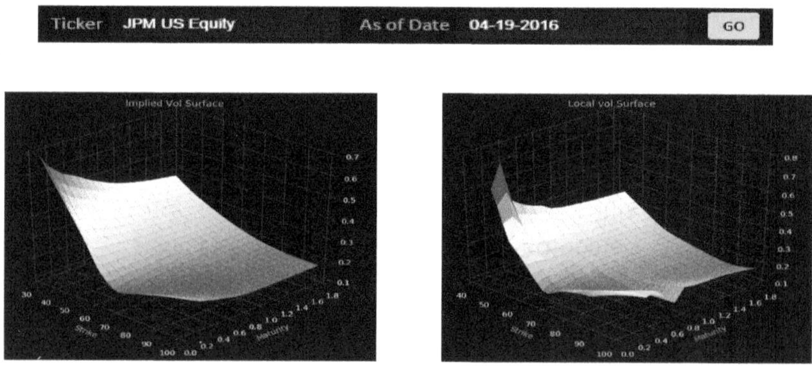

Figure 3: (a) Implied volatility surface and (b) local volatility surface.

2.6 *Forward equation*

Define $C(S, t, K, T)$ as the price of time t for spot price S of European Call option $C_{K,T}$ of strike K and maturity T.

In the absence of carry (no interest rates, no dividends):

- BWD equation: price of one option C_{K_0,T_0} for different (S,t)

$$\frac{\partial C}{\partial t} = -\frac{1}{2}\sigma^2(S,t)S^2\frac{\partial^2 C}{\partial S^2}.$$

- FWD equation: price of all options $C_{K,T}$ for a given (S_0, t_0)

$$\frac{\partial C}{\partial T} = \frac{1}{2}\sigma^2(K,T)K^2\frac{\partial^2 C}{\partial K^2}.$$

- Advantage of FWD equation:
    - If local volatilities known, fast computation of implied volatility surface.
    - If current implied volatility surface known, extraction of local volatilities:

$$\sigma(K,T) = \sqrt{\frac{2}{K^2}\frac{\partial C}{\partial T} / \frac{\partial^2 C}{\partial K^2}}.$$

3. Forward Equations: A Simpler Derivation of the BSM PDE

3.1 *Local volatility model forward equation*

$$\frac{dS}{S} = \mu_t dt + \sigma(S,t)dW \quad \text{we assume no carry.}$$

Applying Itô's Lemma to $f(S)$: $df = f'(S)dS + \frac{1}{2}\sigma^2(S,t)S^2 f'(S)dt$

Thus, as $f'(S)dS$ is costless, the marginal cost at T of extending the maturity of the f payoff is:

$$\frac{1}{2}\sigma^2(S_T,T)S_T^2 f''(S_T) \quad \text{(no need of Itô anymore now)}$$

For $f(S) = (S-K)^+$:

$$\frac{1}{2}\sigma^2(S_T,T)S_T^2\delta_K(S_T) = \frac{1}{2}\sigma^2(K,T)K^2\delta_K(S_T)$$

Expressing the cost at 0:

$$\frac{\partial C}{\partial T} = \frac{1}{2}\sigma^2(K,T)K^2\frac{\partial^2 C}{\partial K^2} \quad \text{from Breeden–Litzenberger.}$$

3.2 A simpler proof of Black–Scholes–Merton PDE

Computing the cost of extending the maturity of an option gives a forward equation, which is another way to compute the same option price.

It provides another proof of the BSM result

- without hedging argument
- without arbitrage argument
- without change of measure
- without local time/Tanaka formula

simply using Itô's Lemma and basic accounting.

3.3 The Beauty of Forward Equations

The marginal cost at T of extending the maturity is

$$\frac{1}{2}\sigma^2(S_T,T)S_T^2 f''(S_T).$$

Its price at time 0 is

$$\frac{1}{2}\int_0^\infty \sigma^2(S_T,T)S_T^2 f''(S_T)\text{Price}_0(\delta_{S_T})dS_T.$$

For the Call payoff, two nice surprises:

1. The integral reduces to $\frac{1}{2}\sigma^2(K,T)K^2\text{Price}_0(\delta_K)$

2. The value at 0 of $\delta_K(S_T)$ can be expressed in terms of derivatives of

$$C\text{: Price}_0(\delta_K(S_T)) = \frac{\partial^2 C}{\partial K^2}.$$

Eventually it gives

$$\frac{\partial C}{\partial T} = \frac{1}{2}\sigma^2(K,T)K^2\frac{\partial^2 C}{\partial K^2}.$$

3.4 *Another Beauty of Forward Equations*

More good surprises in the presence of carry:

- Interest rates r (if constant or function of time) lead to a constant term in the money, which can be expressed as a first derivative with respect to K.
- Dividend yield or foreign rate q for a currency option (if constant or function of time) lead to Calls themselves.
- So the forward equation is a forward PDE, which allows for fast computation

$$\frac{\partial C}{\partial T} = \frac{\sigma^2(K,T)}{2} K^2 \frac{\partial^2 C}{\partial K^2} - (r-q)K\frac{\partial C}{\partial K} - qC.$$

- When interest rates or dividend yields are a function of S, it requires an integral and we obtain a PIDE instead of a PDE.

3.5 *Stochastic Volatility*

From "Unified Theory of Volatility" (D. '96):

- A stochastic volatility model

$$\frac{dS}{S} = \mu_t dt + \sigma_t dW,$$

is calibrated to the market if and only if

$$\mathbb{E}[\sigma_T^2 | S_T = K] = \sigma_{\text{loc}}^2(K,T).$$

- Gives a forward PDE (if no carry)

$$\frac{\partial C}{\partial T} = \frac{1}{2}\mathbb{E}[\sigma_T^2 | S_T = K] K^2 \frac{\partial^2 C}{\partial K^2}.$$

- Local variance can be locked in

3.6 *Stochastic local volatility*

As a consequence, a model

$$\frac{dS}{S} = \mu_t dt + l(S,t)\alpha_t dW_t$$
$$d\alpha_t = \cdots \quad \text{(quite general)},$$

is calibrated to the market if and only if

$$l(S,t) = \frac{\sigma_{\text{loc}}(S,t)}{\sqrt{\mathbb{E}[\alpha_t^2 | S_t = S]}}.$$

It is common to first specify the dynamics of α_t and then compute the leverage function $l(S,t)$.

3.7 *Summary of local volatility model properties*

Σ_0 is the initial volatility surface.

- $\sigma(S,t)$ calibrated to $\Sigma_0 \Longleftrightarrow \sigma =$ local volatility.
- σ_t calibrated to $\Sigma_0 \Longleftrightarrow \mathbb{E}[\sigma_T^2 | S_T = K] = \sigma_{\text{loc}}^2(K,T)$.
- Implied volatility $\hat{\sigma}_{K,T}$ deterministic function of (S,t) (if no jumps) $\Longleftrightarrow$ model is LVM.
- Extracts the notion of FWD volatility. More precisely, the Local Variance (square of local volatility) is the Conditional Instantaneous Forward Variance.
- The Local Variance plays the role of Instantaneous Forward Rate in fixed income, and it can be locked in by trading options of different strikes and maturities.

3.8 *Path-dependent (or exotic) options*

A few questions in the case of exotic options:

- Is it possible to define Greeks (sensitivities) for exotic options?
- Does the BSM/LVM pricing PDE hold for exotic options?
- Can an exotic option be hedged with European options?
- Can exotic and European options be compared on a risk scale?

These questions are answered by the Functional Itô Calculus.

4. Functional Itô Calculus: A Framework for Path Dependence

4.1 *Review of Itô calculus (see Figure 4)*

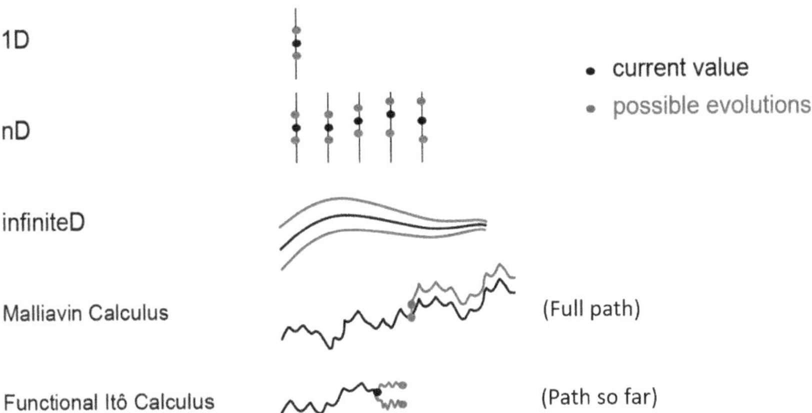

Figure 4: Differentiation in several settings.

4.2 *Functional derivatives*

x_t is the value at t. $X_t = \{x_s, s \in [0,t]\}$ is the path over $[0,t]$.
$f(X_t) \in \mathbb{R}$ is the value of the functional f at path X_t

Two Operators:

X_t X_t^h (Bump, h) $X_{t,\delta t}$ (Flat extension, δt)

Space derivative

$$\Delta_x f(X_t) \equiv \lim_{h \to 0} \frac{f(X_t^h) - f(X_t)}{h}$$

Time derivative

$$\Delta_t f(X_t) \equiv \lim_{\delta t \to 0} \frac{f(X_{t,\delta t}) - f(X_t)}{\delta t}$$

4.3 *Examples of functionals and their derivatives*

f	x_t	$\int_0^T x_u du$	$E_t\left[\int_0^T x_u du\right]$	$\int_0^t a_u dx_u$	QV_t
$\Delta_x f$	1	0	$T-t$	a_{t^-}	$2(x_t - x_{t^-})$
$\Delta_t f$	0	x_t	0	0	0

$$\text{If } f(X_t) = h(x_t, t), \text{ then } \begin{cases} \Delta_x f = \frac{\partial h}{\partial x} \\ \Delta_t f = \frac{\partial h}{\partial t} \end{cases}$$

Notice that Δ_x and Δ_t do not always commute.

For instance, for $f(X_t) = \int_0^t x_u du$

$$\Delta_x(\Delta_t f(X_t)) = \Delta_x(x_t) = 1,$$
$$\Delta_t(\Delta_x f(X_t)) = \Delta_t(0) = 0.$$

4.4 *Results and applications*

- Functional versions of Itô formula, Feynman–Kač and BSM PDE.
- Super-replication (refinement of Kramkov optional decomposition).
- Lie Bracket of price and time functional derivatives.
- Characterisation of attainable claims.
- Decomposition of volatility risk.

4.4.1 *BSM/LVM PDE for path-dependent options*

BSM PDE for Path-dependent Options

PPDE generalizes Black–Scholes–Merton PDE to path-dependent options and path-dependent dynamics.

If $g(Y_T)$ is the payoff of a path-dependent option, Then

$$f(X_t) = \mathbb{E}[e^{-\int_t^T r(Y_u)du} g(Y_T) | Y_t = X_t],$$

(if smooth) satisfies

$$\Delta_t f(X_t) + \frac{1}{2} b(X_t)^2 \Delta_{xx} f(X_t) + r(X_t)(\Delta_x f(X_t) x_t - f(X_t)) = 0$$

The Γ-Θ trade-off for European options also holds for path-dependent options, even with infinite number of state variables. The PPDE has the same shape as PDE but the derivatives are now functional derivatives.

4.4.2 *Volatility risk management for path-dependent options*

Volatility risk management in local volatility model

- LVM is complete and provides perfect replication of even path-dependent options via dynamic trading of the underlying
- But we want to hedge against the model, for instance, if the instantaneous volatility at later times does not follow the local volatility $\sigma(S,t)$
- It can be achieved via perturbative analysis that gives the sensitivity $m(x,t)$ of an exotic option to a bump in Local Variance at (x,t)

$$m(x,t) = \frac{1}{2}\varphi(x,t)\mathbb{E}[\Delta_{xx}f(X_t)|x_t = x],$$

where $\varphi(x,t)$ is the Risk-Neutral density of $x_t = x$.

Hedging an exotic option with a portfolio of European options

- It provides a portfolio of European options that behaves as the exotic option for any small move of the local volatility or implied volatility surface

$$PF \equiv \int_0^T \int_0^\infty \alpha(K,T')C_{K,T'}\,dK\,dT'.$$

- The coefficients of the portfolio of European options that have the same sensitivities are given as the source term of a PDE

$$\alpha(K,T) = -\left(\frac{\partial h(K,T)}{\partial t} + \frac{1}{2}\frac{\partial^2\left(v_0(K,T)h(K,T)\right)}{\partial x^2}\right),$$

with

$$h(x,t) = \mathbb{E}[\Delta_{xx}f(X_t)|x_t = x].$$

- It gives a decomposition of the volatility risk by strike and maturity.

Asian option hedge

Coefficients $\alpha(K, T)$ of the portfolio of European options with the same volatility sensitivities in the Bachelier model (see Figure 5)

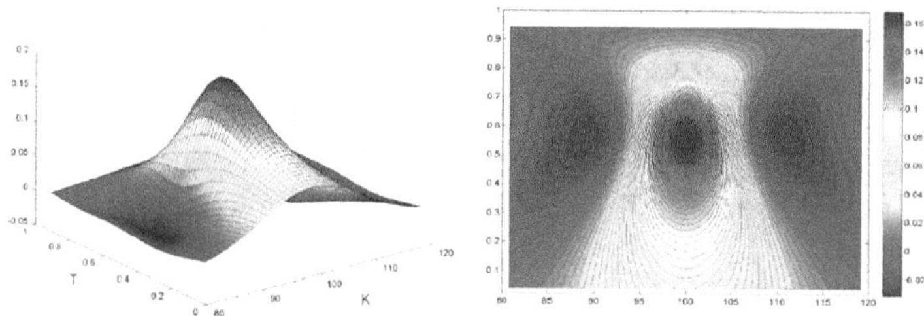

Figure 5: Portfolio coefficients of the hedge of an Asian option.

Forward start option hedge

Forward start option payoff: $f(X_{T_2}) = (x_{T_2} - x_{T_1})^+$

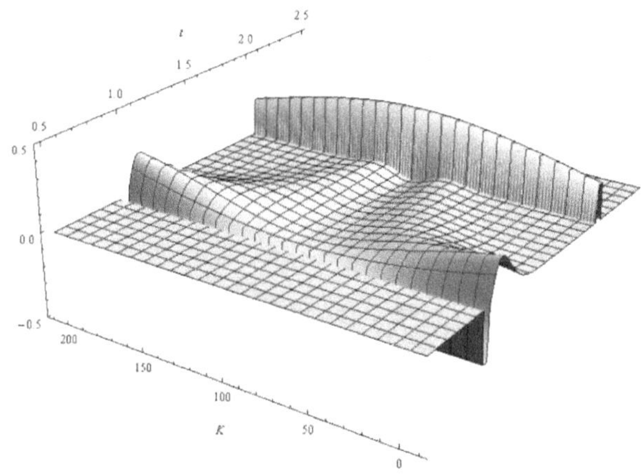

4.4.3 *A risk scale to compare options*

Computing risk as well

It is not enough to compute the price. Risk has to be estimated as well.

Two examples of Barrier options (see Figure 6):

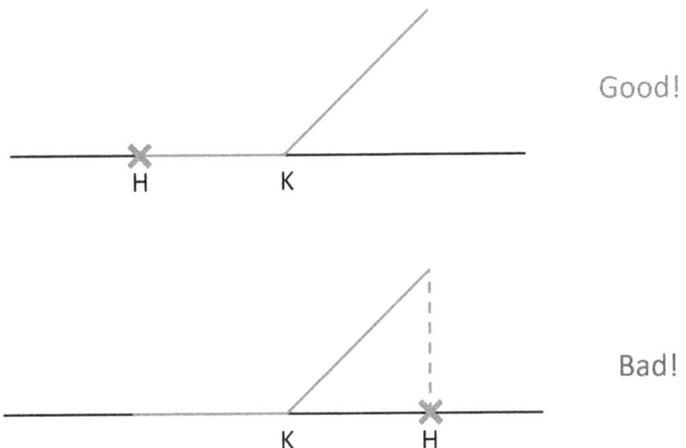

Figure 6: (a) Down-and-Out-Call (b) up-and-Out Call.

A measure of risk

- Delta hedge removes the first order risk.
- Leaves exposed to the second order risk.
- It is magnified by the (functional) Gamma.

Variance of the replication error in BSM with hedge every δt (Define $f(X_t)$ the same way as above)

$$\frac{1}{2}\sigma^4 \delta t\, \mathbb{E}\left[\int_0^T \Delta_{xx}^2 f(X_t) x_t^4 dt\right].$$

- Gives a risk scale.
- Optimal hedge by projection.

Risk scale
Taking the standard deviation of the replication error as a measure of risk, one can compare various options (see Tables 1 and 2)

Table 1: Summary of residual risk values for ATM exotic options $T = 1$.

	Price	std Risk (Δ)	Std Risk (Δ+ Vanillas PF)	Std RiskΔ/(Price X) / Std Risk Δ (Call)(/PriceCall)	Std RiskΔ + Vanillas PF(/Price X) / Std RiskΔ(Call)(/PriceCall)	$\mathbb{H}^2_\Gamma$
Call	7.98	0.68 (8.5%)	0 (0 %)	1	0	1
Asian	4.61	0.47 (10.2%)	0.08 (1.7%)	0.69 (1.20)	0.12 (0.20)	0.97
DOC ($H = 80$)	7.81	0.63 (8.1%)	0.16 (2.1 %)	0.93 (0.95)	0.24 (0.24)	0.93
UOC ($H = 140$)	6.16	1.66 (27.0%)	0.87 (14.1%)	2.44 (3.16)	1.28 (1.66)	0.73
UOC ($H = 120$)	1.46	1.13 (77.5%)	0.82 (56.0%)	1.67 (9.10)	1.20 (6.58)	0.48
UIC ($H = 120$)	6.52	1.34 (20.6%)	0.82 (12.6%)	1.97 (2.41)	1.21 (1.47)	0.63
OT ($H = 120$)	0.32	0.07 (21.6%)	0.04 (13.3%)	0.10 (2.57)	0.06 (1.48)	0.58

Table 2: Ranking of ATM exotic options $T = 1$ from the safest to the riskiest (A = absolute, R = relative).

Rank	Δ (A)	Δ (R)	Δ+ Vanillas PF (A)	Δ+ Vanillas PF (R)
1	Asian (0.47)	DOC (8.1%)	Call (0)	Call (0%)
2	DOC (0.63)	Call (8.5%)	Asian (0.08)	Asian (1.7%)
3	Call (0.68)	Asian (10.2%)	DOC (0.16)	DOC (2.7%)
4	UIC (1.66)	UIC (20.6%)	UIC (0.82)	UIC (12.6%)
5	UOC ($H = 120$)(1.13)	One-Touch (21.6%)	UOC ($H = 120$)(0.82)	One-Touch (13.3%)
6	UOC ($H = 140$)(1.34)	UOC ($H = 140$)(27.0%)	UOC ($H = 140$)(0.87)	UOC ($H = 140$)(14.1%)
7	OT different scale	UOC ($H = 120$)(77.5%)	OT different scale	UOC ($H = 120$)(56.0%)

5. Conclusion

- LVM is the simplest extension of BSM calibrated to the implied volatility surface.
- We present a simple derivation of the forward PDE.

In addition, thanks to the Functional Itô Calculus,

- Greeks for path-dependent options can be defined and computed.
- The BSM/LVM PDE can be extended to path dependent options.
- Volatility Risk Management can be achieved.
- Volatility risk can be computed and exotic options can be compared on a risk scale.

References

[1] Black, F. and Scholes M. (1973). The pricing of options and corporate liabilities. *Journal of Political Economy*, 81, 637–654.
[2] Carr, P. (2004). Derivatives pricing: The classic collection. *Risk Books*.
[3] Dupire, B. (1994). Pricing with a smile. *Risk Magazine*, 7, 18–20.
[4] Dupire, B. (1996). A unified theory of volatility. *Paribas*, Working Paper (Republished in [2]).
[5] Dupire, B. (2019). Functional Itô calculus. Republished in *Quantitative Finance*, 5, 721–729.
[6] Merton, R. (1973). The theory of rational option pricing. *Bell Journal of Economics and Management Science*, 4, 141–183.

https://doi.org/10.1142/9789811259142_0018

Chapter 18

Swap Rate à la Stock: Bermudan Swaptions Made Easy*

D. Gatarek[†,§] **and J. Jabłecki**[‡,¶]

[†]*Systems Research Institute, Polish Academy of Sciences, Poland*

[‡]*University of Warsaw and National Bank of Poland, Poland*

[§]*dariusz.gatarek@ibspan.waw.pl*

[¶]*juliusz.jablecki@nbp.pl*

Abstract

We show how Markovian projection together with some clever parameter freezing can be used to reduce a full-fledged local volatility interest rate model — such as Cheyette [1] — to a "minimal" form in which the swap rate evolves essentially like a dividend-paying stock. Using a number of numerical examples we compare such a minimal "poor man's" model to a full-fledged Cheyette local volatility model and the market benchmark Hull–White one-factor model. Numerical tests demonstrate that the "poor man's" model is in fact sufficient to price Bermudan interest rate swaptions. The main practical implication of this finding is that — once local volatility, dividend and short rate parameters are properly stripped from the volatility surface and interest rate curve — one can readily use the widely popular equity derivatives software for pricing exotic interest rate options such as Bermudans.

Keywords: Local volatility, Cheyette model, Bermudan options.

---

*This chapter is derived from Gatarek, D. and Jabłecki, J. (2020). Swap rate à la stock: Bermudan swaptions made easy. *Wilmott*, (109):44–51. https://doi.org.10.1002.wilm.10874. Reprinted by permission of Wiley.

1. Introduction and Motivation

Pricing interest rate derivatives — especially of the more exotic type — is often seen as more complicated than pricing derivatives on equity or commodity underlyings. After all, the latter deal with "tangible", self-contained assets. In contrast, in interest rate derivatives the underlyings are often not even, strictly speaking, proper assets (one cannot "buy" or "sell" an interest rate), and exist only as different bits of a general collection — i.e. the term structure or yield curve — making the conceptual challenge and computational effort considerably greater. This is perhaps most clearly seen in the case of products with path dependence or early exercise features, such as American or Bermudan options.

While a standard European option gives the right — but no obligation — to purchase a given underlying instrument at expiration for a pre-agreed price, American options allow buyers to exercise their right at any time before expiration. Similarly, Bermudans offer the possibility to exercise on any one of a specified set of dates before maturity. For a typical equity underlying, an American-style option gives the owner the right — but no obligation — to buy the underlying at a pre-agreed price at any time before expiration. Although there is no analytical solution for the price of an American equity option, the multiple-exercise feature can in fact be accurately and efficiently handled through Least Squares Monte Carlo or finite difference schemes, and can be shown to depend on the dividend yield and its relation to the short rate (Figure 1).

Contrast this with the problem of pricing a Bermudan swaption giving the right to enter into one of several fixed-for-floating interest rate swaps, each of which is observed on a different exercise date and, technically, each is driven by a different forward process. Here, we no longer have an option on a single underlying, but rather a complicated best-of chooser option granting the holder the right to choose among several European options on swap rates with different fixing dates. Moreover, what determines the value of the early exercise premium is no longer the interdependence between the short rate and dividend yield but rather the mean reversion or correlation between the underlying forward swap rates (Figure 2).

Building again on the chooser option analogy, if the correlation among the payoffs is high, the option to exercise early is clearly not

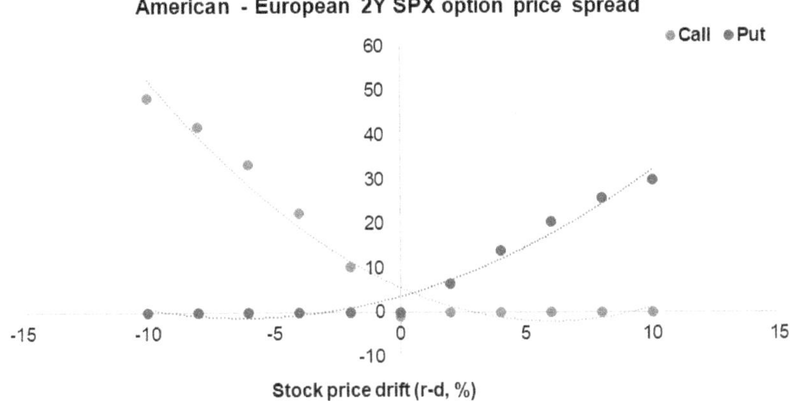

Figure 1: The sensitivity of European and American options on S&P 500 to short rate and dividend.

Note: 2Y SPX options, local volatility model calibrated to market data as of April 27, 2018; ATM = 2678.81.

so valuable. Conversely, if correlation is low or negative, then high payoffs on the early options are likely to be followed by low payoffs on the later ones and vice versa so having the Bermudan exercise right improves the chances of making money in more scenarios. Unfortunately, accounting properly for the correlation among different swap rates requires a formal no-arbitrage model for the joint evolution of the entire term structure of interest rates. Or so it would seem at least ....

In this note, we argue that a full-fledged term structure model is actually not necessary to price Bermudan swaptions. Instead, we show how a cleverly chosen set of approximations leads to an equity-like local volatility process for the swap rate, driven by its own "short rate" and "dividend yield" — both implied from the term structure of interest rates. The equity-like process effectively "synthesizes" the information on volatility and correlation contained in the core swap rates, spanned by a given Bermudan swaption. As a result, the latter can be priced as any American-style option on a dividend paying stock, using standard equity derivatives software. While not exactly arbitrage free and limited in application to swap rate derivatives, such equity-like model can be seen as a "poor man's" approach that delivers very accurate approximations of Bermudan swaption prices

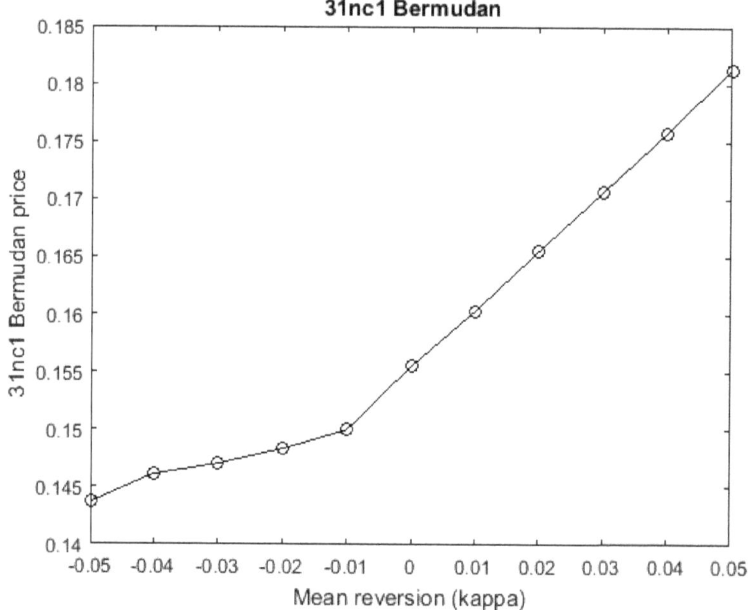

Figure 2: Sensitivity of a 30Y Bermudan swaption price to short rate mean reversion speed.

Note: Market benchmark model of Hull & White $dr(t) = (\theta(t) - \kappa(t)r(t))\,dt + \sigma(t)dW(t)$ calibrated to the **same** set of co-terminal swaptions each time with different κ.

Source: US Data as October 5, 2016.

at a considerably lower computational cost and effort than full term structure models.

2. Notation and Modeling Framework

As usual with interest rate instruments, we start by introducing a uniformly spaced tenor structure:

$$0 = T_0 < T_1 < \cdots < T_N, \tag{1}$$

with $T_n = \delta n$. Typically, $\delta = 0.25$ — for quarterly payments — or $\delta = 0.5$ for semiannual ones. Let $P(t, T)$ be the time t price of a zero coupon discount bond paying 1 for sure at T. A **fixed-for-floating interest rate swap** (IRS) with unit notional, fixed rate (coupon) K, and a specified tenor structure $\mathcal{T} = \{T_n\}_{n=\alpha+1}^{\beta}$ is a contract whereby two parties exchange differently indexed cashflows over a pre-agreed time span. Specifically, on each date $T_n \in \mathcal{T}$, the fixed leg pays δK, whereas the floating leg pays the LIBOR rate given by:

$$\frac{1 - P(T_{n-1}, T_n)}{\delta P(T_{n-1}, T_n)} \times \delta, \tag{2}$$

when the fixed leg is paid, the IRS is called a "payer", conversely the swap is called a "receiver". The **forward swap rate** $S_{\alpha,\beta}(t)$ corresponding to the tenor structure $\mathcal{T}$ is the rate in the fixed leg that sets it equal to the floating leg and hence makes the net present value of the transaction equal zero:

$$S_{\alpha,\beta}(t) \equiv \frac{P(t, T_\alpha) - P(t, T_\beta)}{\sum_{n=\alpha+1}^{\beta} P(t, T_n)\delta}. \tag{3}$$

The portfolio of zero-coupon bonds in the denominator of (3) is the so called annuity factor, for which we will often use a continuous-time definition, writing $N_{\alpha,\beta}(t) \equiv \int_{T_\alpha}^{T_\beta} P(t, u)du$ along with

$$S_{\alpha,\beta}(t) = \frac{P(t, T_\alpha) - P(t, T_\beta)}{N_{\alpha,\beta}(t)}. \tag{4}$$

A **European payer (receiver) swaption** with strike K, maturity T_α and tenor $T_\beta - T_\alpha$ (henceforth referred to also as $T_\alpha \times (T_\beta - T_\alpha)$, or T_α-into-$(T_\beta - T_\alpha)$) is simply an option that gives the holder the right to enter at T_α into a payer (receiver) swap which matures at T_β and entitles to pay (receive) fixed rate K in exchange for floating LIBOR rate on the tenor dates $\mathcal{T}$. Thus, the price of a European payer swaption with unit notional at T_α is given by

$$N_{\alpha,\beta}(T_\alpha)\,(S_{\alpha,\beta}(T_\alpha) - K)^+, \tag{5}$$

where $x^+ = \max(x, 0)$. Finally, a **Bermudan receiver (payer) swaption** is an option to enter at any time T_i, $i \in \{\alpha, \alpha+1, ..., \beta-1\}$, into a swap which terminates at T_β and gives the holder the right to receive (pay) a pre-determined fixed rate K in exchange for floating Libor. The period up to T_α is called the lockout or no-call period, and hence a Bermudan swaption with final exercise date $T_{\beta-1}$ and first exercise T_α is often called "T_β no-call T_α", or "$T_\beta$ncT_α". For example, a 11nc1 swaption with annually spaced exercise dates can be exercised at the beginning of any year, starting from year 1. By exercising the option, the holder enters a swap starting at the time of exercise (i.e. years 1, 2, 3, ..., 10) and ending at year 11.

By convention, European swaption prices are often expressed in terms of their Black implied volatilities, i.e. log-normal volatilities that plugged into the Black swaption price formula yield the market price. More recently, reflecting the popular recognition that interest rates in advanced economies can indeed go below zero, the Bachelier model has become the standard quotation mechanism.

Like most options markets, the swaption market exhibits a pronounced implied volatility skew — apparent in both Black and Bachelier conventions (Figure 3). This dependence of implied volatility on swaption strike is not consistent with the constant volatility assumption underlying both Bachelier and Black approaches, calling for a more refined treatment.

One of the most popular approaches for handling smiles — at least in equity and FX setting — has long been the so called local volatility model developed by Derman and Kani [2] and Dupire [3] and later extended in multiple directions (see e.g. [4–8]; cf. also Gatheral [9] for

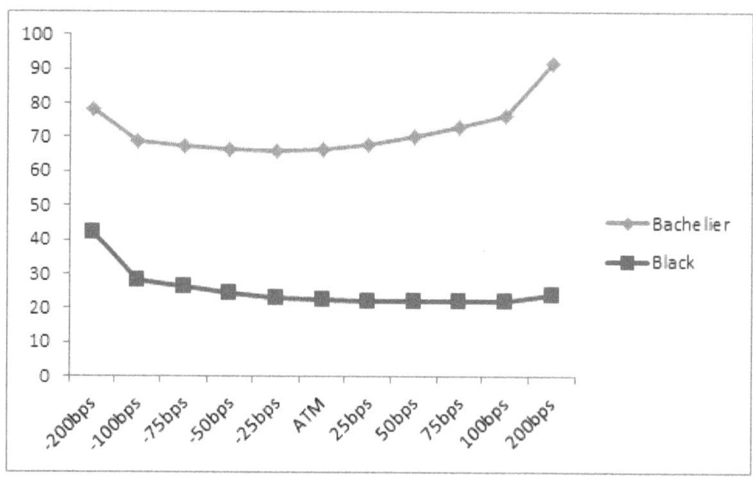

Figure 3: Black and Bachelier implied volatilities for 1×10 USD swaption (in bp; as of April 27, 2018).

a practical overview of volatility modeling). These models proposed a small departure from the Black–Scholes world by postulating that the instantaneous volatility of the underlying instrument be a deterministic function of its spot price and time. Such framework retained the completeness of the Black–Scholes approach thus allowing the option to be perfectly replicated by dynamically trading the underlying. Perhaps more importantly, Dupire showed, the local volatility function could be derived in a non-parametric way from quoted vanilla option prices, which by construction ensured a perfect fit to the market smile and hence allowed to price exotics consistently with vanilla options. Dupire's famous local volatility equation featured — as one of the inputs — a partial derivative of option price with respect to expiration (a "calendar spread"). While not problematic for equity underlyings, the derivative of option price with respect to maturity is not properly defined for interest rate underlyings,[1] which proved to be a major hurdle in applying the local volatility approach in the interest rate space. In a recent contribution, however, we have tried to present a unified approach to local volatility modeling, one that encompasses all asset classes, and applies equally to interest rate underlyings. We present the thrust of the argument for completeness, adapting it to the case at hand.

As a first step, we need to introduce a new spot process, S, defined as the value of a forward swap rate (3), with fixed termination date T, rolling with time t into successive fixing dates (for convenience, we opt for continuous notation):

$$S(t) \equiv \frac{1 - P(t,T)}{\int_t^T P(t,s)ds}, \quad t < T. \tag{6}$$

We do not need to specify formally the dynamics of $S(t)$, other than by saying that is an Ito process with diffusion $\sigma(t)$ satisfying the usual regularity conditions. The instantaneous forward rate $f(t,T)$

[1]Indeed, there is typically only a single option on a given interest rate product — e.g. there is only one option on an interest rate swap initiating in, say, 5 years and maturing in 15 years, namely the 5y-into-10y swaption. A swaption on the fixed-tenor 10-year swap with a different maturity, say, 1 year, will be written on a different underlying, driven by a different forward process.

with maturity T contracted at t is defined by

$$f(t,T) \equiv -\frac{\partial \ln P(t,T)}{\partial T} \iff P(t,T) = \exp\left(-\int_t^T f(t,s)ds\right), \tag{7}$$

while the instantaneous spot rate $r(t)$ — i.e. the short rate — capturing the locally risk-free return from a continuously compounded money market account $B(t) \equiv \exp\left\{\int_0^t r(s)ds\right\}$ can be formalized as

$$r(t) \equiv f(t,t). \tag{8}$$

We also let $N(t) = \int_t^T P(t,s)ds$ and for notational convenience denote $Q(t) = \int_t^T P(0,s)ds$ and $D(t) = \frac{N(t)}{B(t)}$. We may now rewrite (5) in our new notation, expressing the time zero value of an option with strike K and maturity t on a swap terminating at T as

$$C(t,K) = \mathbb{E}^{\mathbb{Q}}\left[(S(t)-K)^+ D(t)\right]. \tag{9}$$

Note that since $S(\cdot)$ is now defined as a spot process, $C(t,K)$ is properly defined as a function of maturity time t. We can apply Tanaka's formula to the payoff to get

$$d(S(t)-K)^+ = 1_{\{S(t)>K\}}dS(t) + \frac{1}{2}\delta(S(t)-K)d\left\langle S(t)\right\rangle_t. \tag{10}$$

Thus, after some algebra,

$$\begin{aligned} d\left(D(t)(S(t)-K)^+\right) &= \frac{1}{2}D(t)\delta(S(t)-K)\sigma^2(t)dt \\ &\quad + 1_{\{S(t)>K\}}\left(d\left(D(t)S(t)\right) - KdD(t)\right). \end{aligned}$$

Taking expected value of both sides ultimately yields (see Gatarek and Jabłecki [10] for details of the proof)

$$\begin{aligned} \frac{\partial C(t,K)}{\partial t} &= \frac{1}{2}\frac{\partial^2 C(t,K)}{\partial K^2}\mathbb{E}^t\left[\sigma^2(t)|S(t)=K\right] \\ &\quad - \int_K^\infty \frac{\partial^2 C(t,x)}{\partial x^2}\left\{\mathbb{E}^t\left[\left.\frac{r(t)}{N(t)}\right| S(t)=x\right]\right. \\ &\quad \left.+ K\mathbb{E}^t\left[\left.\frac{1}{N(t)}\right| S(t)=x\right]\right\}dx, \end{aligned} \tag{11}$$

where $\mathbb{E}^t[\cdot]$ is the expectation under t-forward measure defined for any ξ by

$$\mathbb{E}^t(\xi) \equiv \frac{\mathbb{E}^{\mathbb{Q}}[D(t)\xi]}{\mathbb{E}^{\mathbb{Q}}[D(t)]}. \tag{12}$$

The result above is clearly unwieldy because of the conditional expectations in the integrand. Hence, Gatarek and Jabłecki [10] propose to "localize" the respective the drift and diffusion terms in processes S and D by introducing a term structure model, borrowed from Cheyette [1], in which yields and all derivable quantities — such as swap rates — are driven by a single state variable. This then makes it possible to extract the local volatility function $\mathbb{E}^t\left[\sigma^2(t)|S(t)=K\right]$ directly from market prices, map it onto the short rate volatility in the Cheyette model, and price swaptions in a local volatility framework through Monte Carlo or finite differences. Here, we consider a somewhat different approach which at the cost of some rigour and formalism delivers a substantial improvement in simplicity and intuitive appeal.

3. Swap Rate à la Stock

The main idea is to naively "localize" the expressions under expectations in (11) through a clever approximation, thus circumventing the need for the introduction of a formal yield curve model. To achieve this, we resort to a standard practice of freezing the yield curve, as done by Brace *et al.* [11]. This is a fairly standard technique, often used by practitioners and academics alike (see e.g. [12–14] for some recent examples). Concretely, we assume that

$$P(t,T) \approx \frac{P(0,T)}{P(0,t)}. \tag{13}$$

The approximation in (13) is actually not as restrictive as it might seem. To verify this, we regress the 1-year ahead 9-year zero coupon bond price $P(t+1,t+10)$ and the 5-year ahead 5-year zero coupon bond price $P(t+5,t+10)$ against their time t "frozen" forecasts calculated as $P(t,t+10)/P(t,t+1)$ and $P(t,t+10)/P(t,t+5)$ respectively. We use US Treasury yield curve data for the period June 1961

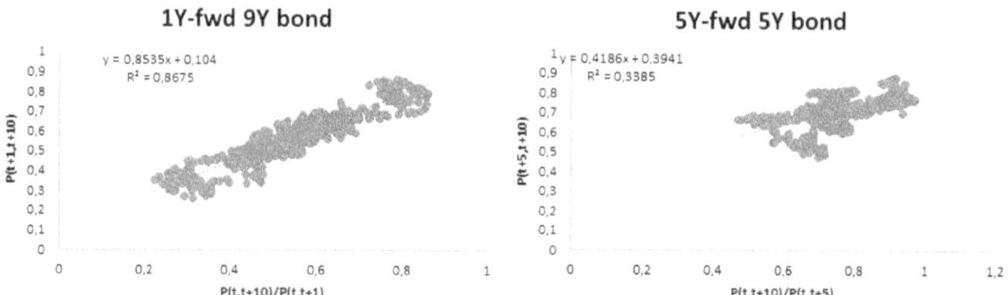

Figure 4: Regression fit of the 1-year forward 9-year zero coupon bond price and the 5-year forward 5-year zero coupon bond price against their time t "frozen" forecasts.

through March 2018. In both cases the fit is reasonably good (with correlation 93% and 58% and RMSE of 10% and 13% of the bond price), although clearly deteriorates somewhat as we move further out in time (Figure 4).

It follows from (13) that

$$P(0,t)\int_t^T P(t,s)ds \approx \int_t^T P(0,s)ds, \tag{14}$$

so that

$$\frac{r(t)}{N(t)} = \frac{r(t)S(t)}{1-P(t,T)} \approx \frac{f(0,t)P(0,t)}{P(0,t)-P(0,T)}S(t) \tag{15}$$

and

$$\frac{1}{N(t)} \approx \frac{P(0,t)}{Q(t)}. \tag{16}$$

Set $p(t) \equiv \frac{f(0,t)P(0,t)}{P(0,t)-P(0,T)}$ and $q(t) \equiv -\frac{Q'(t)}{Q(t)}$. Under these approximations, the integrand in Equation (11) simplifies greatly and we obtain

$$\frac{\partial C(t,K)}{\partial t} - \frac{1}{2}\frac{\partial^2 C(t,K)}{\partial K^2}\sigma^2(t,K) \approx K\frac{\partial C(t,K)}{\partial K}$$
$$(p(t)-q(t)) - p(t)C(t,K). \tag{17}$$

Differentiating both sides of (17) yields the Fokker–Planck equation

$$\frac{\partial C^3(t,K)}{\partial t \partial K^2} - \frac{1}{2}\frac{\partial^2}{\partial K^2}\left(\frac{\partial^2 C(t,K)}{\partial K^2}\sigma^2(t,K)\right)$$
$$= -\frac{\partial}{\partial K}\left(\frac{\partial^2 C(t,K)}{\partial K^2}\{p(t) - Kq(t)\}\right) + \frac{\partial^2 C(t,K)}{\partial K^2}q(t,K). \tag{18}$$

Now, it can be shown that the unique solution to (18) is the transition density generated by the following diffusion

$$d\widetilde{S} = \sigma\left(t, \widetilde{S}(t)\right) d\widetilde{W}(t) + \widetilde{S}(t)\left(q\left(t\right) - p(t)\right) dt, \tag{19}$$

The process $\widetilde{S}(t)$ is quite interesting: its instantaneous volatility is given by the local volatility function of the rolling swap rate (6) and its drift is driven by the spread $q(t) - p(t)$. Note that this is very similar to the situation we encounter in the equity world where the risk neutral drift of a share of stock features the risk-free rate and the stock's dividend yield. Thus, we have effectively constructed equity-like dynamics for the swap rate process $\widetilde{S}(t)$ with its own "short rate" $q(t)$ and "dividend yield" $p(t)$ (Figure 5).

Building on this analogy further, we consider a new discount process $Q(t)$ with dynamics

$$dQ(t) = -Q(t)q(t)dt, \tag{20}$$

which follows directly from (16), since

$$q(t) = \frac{P(0,t)}{Q(t)} = -\frac{dQ(t)}{dt}\frac{1}{Q(t)}.$$

Using the Feynman–Kac theorem we can express the solution of the PDE in (17) as the expected value of the underlying function's terminal payoff. The payoff itself is a function of our equity-like process whose drift and diffusion coefficients are implicitly defined as the coefficients of the PDE. Thus, the time zero price of an option $\widetilde{C}$ on $\widetilde{S}$ with maturity t and strike K is given by

$$\mathbb{E}\left[Q(t)\left(\widetilde{S}(t) - K\right)^+\right] \tag{21}$$

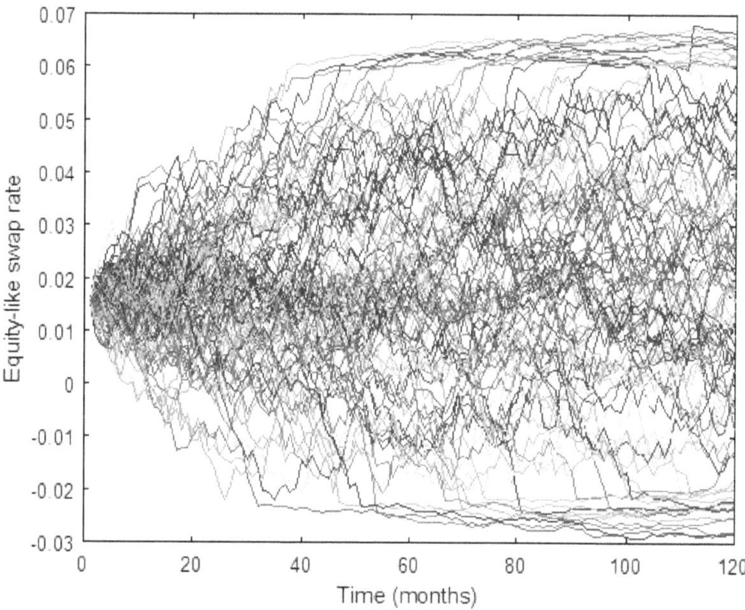

Figure 5: Sample paths of the equity-like swap rate $\widetilde{S}(t)$.

Note: Paths generated under the assumption that $T = 11$ years and $\sigma\left(t, \widetilde{S}(t)\right)$ is flat at at 0.009.

and needs to satisfy the general PDE

$$\begin{aligned} &\frac{\partial \widetilde{C}(t,K)}{\partial t} - \frac{1}{2}\frac{\partial^2 \widetilde{C}(t,K)}{\partial K^2}\sigma^2(t,K) \\ &\quad = K\frac{\partial \widetilde{C}(t,K)}{\partial K}\left(p(t) - q(t)\right) - p(t)\widetilde{C}(t,K) \end{aligned} \tag{22}$$

which itself is an approximation of the general equation (11). Hence, we conclude that

$$\begin{aligned} \widetilde{C}(t,K) &= \mathbb{E}\left[Q(t)\left(\widetilde{S}(t) - K\right)^+\right] = Q(t)\mathbb{E}\left[\left(\widetilde{S}(t) - K\right)^+\right] \\ &\approx \mathbb{E}\left[D(t)\left(S(t) - K\right)^+\right] = C(t,K), \end{aligned} \tag{23}$$

or equivalently, that $\mathbb{E}\big[Q(t)(\widetilde{S}(t) - K)^+\big] \approx \mathbb{E}^t\left[Q(t)\,(S(t) - K)^+\right]$. The above conclusion can greatly simplify the process of pricing swaptions, reducing it to the calculation of a risk-neutral expectation of $\widetilde{S}(t)$, with no need for a full-fledged term structure model or an estimation of the swap level. In fact, (23) can be handled using a classic equity option Monte Carlo or finite difference prices which should make it particularly useful for practitioners. Naturally, swaption price derived using (23) is just an approximation of swaption price derived using a full term structure model (such as Cheyette), but it turns out to be a very accurate one. We demonstrate this point in numerical examples below.

4. Bermudan Swaption Pricing

Ultimately, the proof of the pudding is in the eating. Thus, we now test our equity-like swap rate model on a sample Bermudan swaption structure, using different numerical techniques, and comparing the results against the full local volatility Cheyette model and the standard Hull-White model. Recall that, given a tenor structure $\mathcal{T} = \{T_n\}_{n=\alpha}^{\beta}$, the price of "$T_\beta$ no-call T_α" Bermudan receiver swaption $\mathbf{RBS}_{\alpha,\beta}(t,K)$ has time t value given by

$$\mathbf{RBS}_{\alpha,\beta}(t,K) = \sup_{\tau\in\mathcal{T}} \mathbb{E}\left((K - S_{\tau,\beta}(\tau))^+ D(\tau)\right). \tag{24}$$

But we already know from (23) that $\mathbb{E}\left[Q(t)(K - \widetilde{S}(t))^+\right] \approx \mathbb{E}\left[D(t)\,(K - S(t))^+\right]$ which suggests that

$$\mathbf{RBS}_{\alpha,\beta}(t,K) \approx \sup_{\tau\in\mathcal{T}} \mathbb{E}\left((K - \widetilde{S}_{\tau,\beta}(\tau))^+ Q(\tau)\right) = \widetilde{\mathbf{RBS}}_{\alpha,\beta}(t,K). \tag{25}$$

Concretely, we now set $T_\alpha = 1$ and $T_\beta = 11$ for a 11nc1 Bermudan swaption which we price using USD interest rate curve and volatility data as of October 5, 2016. As a first step, we extract the local volatility surface from the quoted prices of co-terminal swaptions

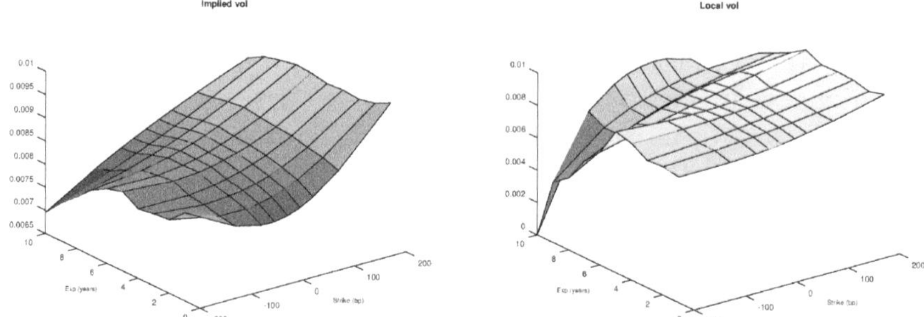

Figure 6: Co-terminal normal implied volatility surface and corresponding stripped local volatility surface.

Note: Terminal swap maturity is fixed at 11 years; data as of October 5, 2016.

$1 \times 10, 2 \times 9, 3 \times 8, \ldots, 10 \times 1$ using the rearranged PDE (17)[2]:

$$\sigma(t,K)^2 \approx 2\frac{\partial_t C(t,K) - (q(t) - p(t))\, K\partial_K C(t,K) + p(t)C(t,K)}{\partial^2_{KK} C(t,K)}. \tag{26}$$

Figure 6 shows the implied volatility surface of co-terminal swaptions with terminal fixed at 11 years and the corresponding local volatility, while Figure 7 shows the generic risk-free rate and dividend yield. Note how the two are related and rise in tandem as t approaches the final maturity.

To estimate $\widetilde{\mathbf{RBS}}_{\alpha,\beta}(t,K)$ we use two numerical techniques: least squares Monte Carlo (LSMC) and the Crank–Nicholson finite difference scheme (CN). For the LSMC we choose simply the underlying "swap rate" along with its second and third powers, and a constant, in the continuation value regression. The Monte Carlo uses 12 time steps per year and 20,000 paths and the entire routine is repeated 100 times which allows for the calculation of the approximate simulation standard error. The CN scheme uses the following mesh parameters:

$$S_{\text{ini}} = 0.0163, \quad S_0 = 0, \quad S_{\max} = 2S_0$$

[2]To be precise, we convert swaption prices into Bachelier implied volatilities and then perform the stripping, which seems to produce much more stable results.

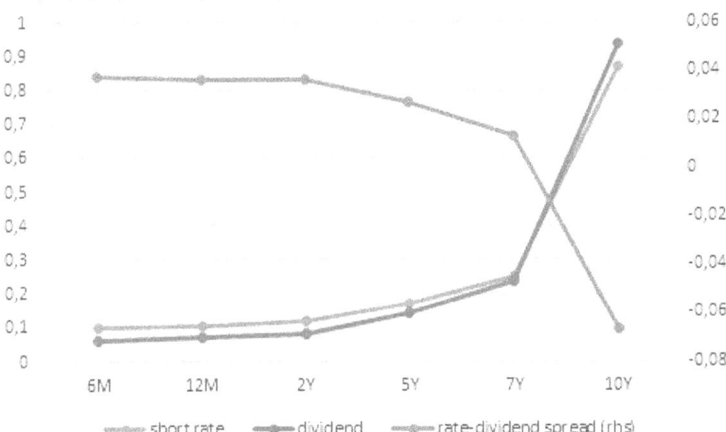

Figure 7: Stripped "risk-free" rate and "dividend" yield of the equity-like swap rate process (19).
Note: $p(t) = \frac{f(0,t)P(0,t)}{P(0,t)-P(0,T)}$ and $q(t) = \frac{P(0,t)}{\int_t^T P(0,s)ds}$, $T = 11$. Values stripped from yield curve data as of October 5, 2016.

$$dS = 0.0001 \implies M = 326$$
$$dt = 0.02 \implies N = 50$$

We benchmark results against the market standard Hull-White one-factor model implemented in a tree-based approach as well as local volatility Cheyette model with mean reversion parameter $\kappa = 0.1\%$ simulated using LSMC.

The results for a range of strikes are shown in Figure 8. The prices produced by the four models are generally closely aligned, but what is particularly important is how close the minimal model — with an evolution of only a single process — is to the Cheyette model which features a fully fledged, no-arbitrage term structure dynamics. The minimal model lends itself to a straightforward implementation via a finite difference scheme which guarantees faster convergence as compared to the Cheyette Monte Carlo implementation. Figure 9 shows convergence profiles for the Crank–Nicholson scheme under different grid set-ups. As for standard equity options, convergence of the finite difference method for the minimal model is very fast in terms of both δt and δS — in fact all price estimates are within 0.04% of the number obtained using highest grid resolution.

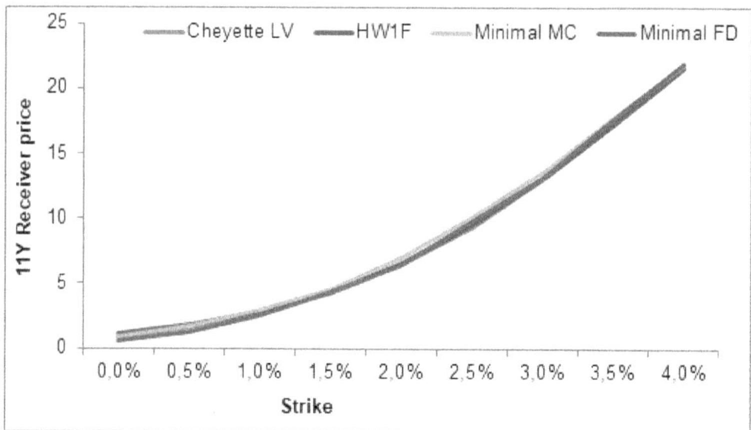

Figure 8: Prices and Monte Carlo standard errors (where appropriate) of a 11nc1 Bermudan receiver swaption with 100 notional.

Note: "MC" stands for Least Squares Monte Carlo; "FD" denotes Crank–Nicholson finite difference scheme. The models are all calibrated to the same set of co-terminal swaptions: $1 \times 10, 2 \times 9, 3 \times 8, \ldots, 10 \times 1$ using USD market data as of October 5, 2016; local volatility surface used is given in Figure 6.

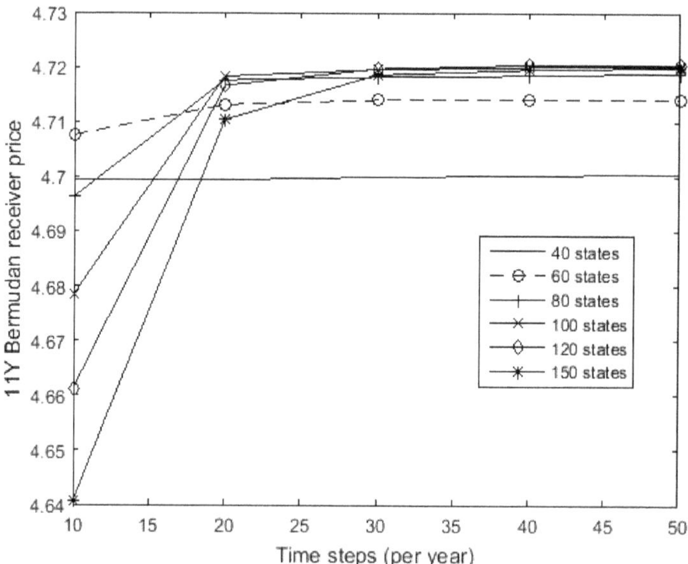

Figure 9: Convergence profiles for a finite difference implementation of the equity-like "minimal model" (11Y Bermudan swaption, ATM = 0.0163).

5. Discussion

We have presented above a simple trick that allows us to price Bermudan swaptions essentially as if they were options on a dividend paying stock. The practical significance of this contribution is that, while the approach is not strictly arbitrage free and unfortunately can be directly applied only to swap rate derivatives, it offers a potentially attractive solution especially in cases when the development of a fully-fledged interest rate model is too time or resource consuming. Perhaps the most attractive feature of the model is that it makes it possible to transpose some of the well-established rules of thumb from the world of equities to interest rate space. While this is still a work in progress, we show below a stylized example demonstrating how the exercise premium in a Bermudan swaption is linked to the spread between the implied "short rate" and "dividend", which in turn can be linked to the observed yield curve shapes. Specifically, we consider 5 yield curve regimes and a benchmark case of a flat term structure shown in Figure 10.

For each of the scenarios we price an 11Y Bermudan receiver swaption and the corresponding 1×10 European swaption. As shown in Figure 11, the difference between the two — i.e. the exercise

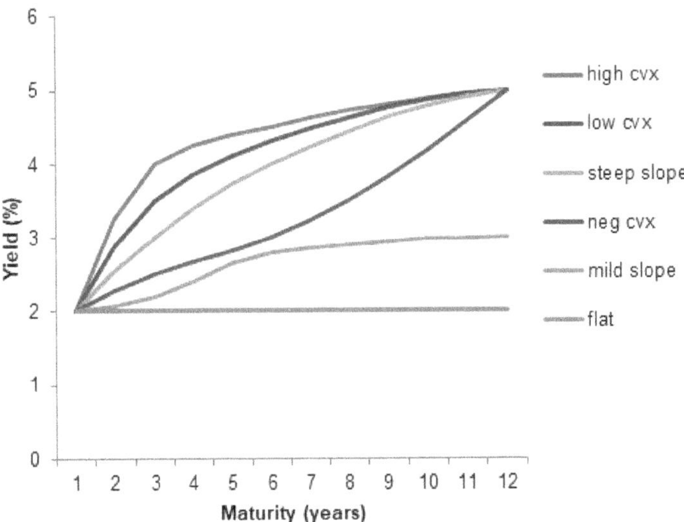

Figure 10: Stylized yield curve shapes scenarios.

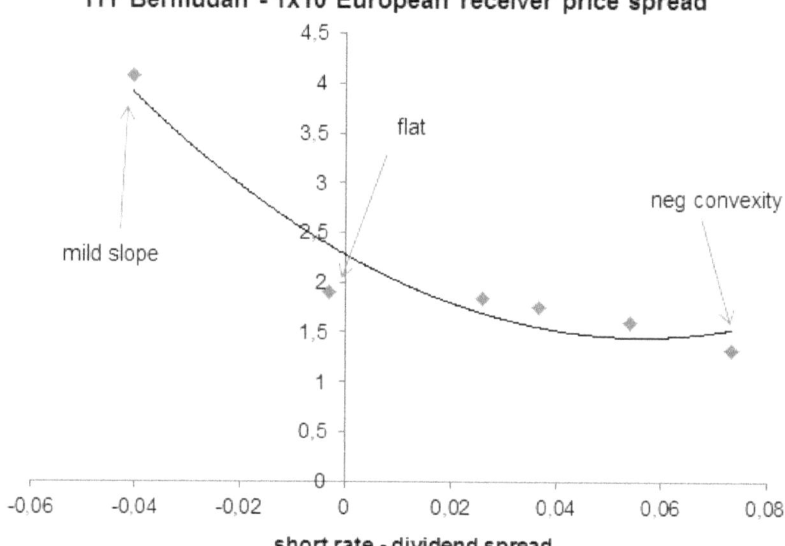

Figure 11: 11Y Bermudan — 1×10 European receiver swaption price spread (exercise premium).

Note: Short rate and dividend rates calculated as averages over the tenor structure.

premium — varies with the rolling swap rate drift, captured by the short rate-dividend spread implied by each yield curve scenario. Thus, our model provides an interesting analogy to the case of equities (Figure 1), and may lead to useful rules of thumb for gauging the size of exercise premium depending on the specific yield curve view.

From a theoretical standpoint, we hope to have countered the widely held belief that the pricing of Bermudan swaptions requires a formal term structure model. This may be counterintuitive. After all, it is well known that what determines the value of the early exercise premium in a Bermudan structure is the correlation between the underlying forward swap rates — which at first glance does not appear to be captured by our equity-like swap rate model. In fact, however, information about rate correlations and volatilities is captured by the local volatility and, to a lesser extent also, the "short rate" $q(t)$ and "dividend" $p(t)$. To see this, consider the forward swap rates into which our "T_β no-call T_α" Bermudan receiver allows exercising: $S_{\alpha,\beta}(t), S_{\alpha+1,\beta}(t), ..., S_{\beta-1,\beta}(t)$. Suppose we were to use a proper multi-factor yield curve model (say, LMM) so that the swap rates would evolve according to the following Ito processes:

$$\begin{aligned} dS_{\alpha,\beta}(t) &= \mu_{\alpha}(t)dt + \sigma_{\alpha}dW_{\alpha}(t) \\ dS_{\alpha+1,\beta}(t) &= \mu_{\alpha+1}(t)dt + \sigma_{\alpha+1}dW_{\alpha+1}(t) \\ &\dots \\ dS_{\beta-1,\beta}(t) &= \mu_{\beta-1}(t)dt + \sigma_{\beta-1}dW_{\beta-1}(t) \end{aligned}$$

with $dW_i dW_j = \rho_{ij}(t)dt$. Then, as shown by Rebonato, the terminal correlation $\mathrm{corr}(S_{i,\beta}(T_i), S_{j,\beta}(T_j))$ — which is the key value driver for our Bermudan – could be roughly approximated by

$$\frac{\int_0^{T_i} \sigma_i(t)\sigma_j(t)\rho_{i,j}(t)dt}{\sqrt{\int_0^{T_i} \sigma_i^2(t)dt}\sqrt{\int_0^{T_j} \sigma_j^2(t)dt}}. \tag{27}$$

Now, (27) clearly depends not only on $\rho_{i,j}(t)$ but it is also driven by the instantaneous volatilities $\sigma_i(t), \sigma_j(t)$. The latter, however, are picked up by the local volatility function of our equity-like swap rate, as $\sigma(t, K)$ is determined from the implied volatilities of the forward swap rates $S_{\alpha,\beta}(t), S_{\alpha+1,\beta}(t), ..., S_{\beta-1,\beta}(t)$.

References

[1] Cheyette, O. (1992). Term structure dynamics and mortgage valuation, *The Journal of Fixed Income*, 1(4), 28–41.
[2] Derman, E. and Kani, I. (1994). Riding on a Smile, *Risk*, 7(2), 277–284.
[3] Dupire, B. (1994). Pricing with a smile. *Risk*, 7(1), 18–20.
[4] Carr, P. and Madan, D. (1998). Towards a theory of volatility trading, *Volatility: New Estimation Techniques for Pricing Derivatives*, (29), 417–427.
[5] Carr, P., Geman, H., Madan, D., and Yor, M. (2004). From local volatility to local Lévy models, *Quantitative Finance*, 4(5), 581–588.
[6] Carmona, R. and Nadtochiy, S. (2009). Local volatility dynamic models, *Finance and Stochastics*, 13(1), 1–48.
[7] Coleman, T.F., Li, Y., and Verma, A. (1999). Reconstructing the unknown local volatility function, *Journal of Computational Finance*, 2(3), 77–102.

[8] Durrleman, V. (2010). From implied to spot volatilities, *Finance and Stochastics*, 14(2), 157–177.

[9] Gatheral, J. (2011). *The Volatility Surface: A Practitioner's Guide*, vol. 357. John Wiley & Sons.

[10] Gatarek, D. and Jabłecki, J. (2019). Towards a general local volatility model for all asset classes, *Journal of Derivatives*, 27(1), 14–30.

[11] Brace, A., Gatarek, D., and Musiela, M. (1997). The market model of interest rate dynamics, *Mathematical Finance*, 7(2), 127–155.

[12] Beveridge, C. and Joshi, M. (2014). The efficient computation of prices and greeks for callable range accruals using the displaced-diffusion lmm, *International Journal of Theoretical and Applied Finance*, 17(1), 1450001.

[13] Chen, A. and Sandmann, K. (2012). In-arrears term structure products: No arbitrage pricing bounds and the convexity adjustments, *International Journal of Theoretical and Applied Finance*, 15(8), 1250054.

[14] Grzelak, L.A. and Oosterlee, C.W. (2012). An equity-interest rate hybrid model with stochastic volatility and the interest rate smile, *The Journal of Computational Finance*, 15(4), 45.

https://doi.org/10.1142/9789811259142_0019

Chapter 19

Thirty Years of Derivatives Market: Originality of the French Experience

N. El Karoui
Emeritus Professor, Sorbonne University
Sorbonne Université/Ecole Polytechnique, Paris
elkaroui@gmail.com

1. Introduction

The French Derivatives market was created much later than the US Market due to political argument. In fact, it was a surprising opportunity, because in addition to using the Anglo-Saxon experience, this allowed the market to take advantage of the computer revolution implied by the Personal Computer. So, the trading activity on the French market places MATIF (1987) and the MONEP (1986) immediately benefited from an innovative technological infrastructure.

The French Derivatives Market, Thirty years already!

A long history peppered with Crises and then Regulation issues

AN EXAMPLE OF ADVANCED FINANCIAL TECHNOLOGY

- Presentation based on many years of consulting activity for derivatives desks in main French Banks.
- Coupled with original training experience in DEA/Master program at Sorbonne-Université/Ecole Polytechnique.
- And with intensive Academic Research in Mathematical-Quantitative finance.

MAIN POINTS

- The French Derivatives Market: the "start up" period (1987–1998).
- The "industrial type" period, and the 2008 crisis (2000–2008).
- The role of the mathematics.
- The Academic formation.
- Personal comments on the role of women in this adventure.

The political context is very important to explain the difference between France and U.S., especially in relation to financial markets. We begin by evoking the crucial event of this period whose impact extended to the whole world, until now.

The Year 1971 in US

The year of deregulation, and the End of Bretton Woods system of fixed exchange rates

HISTORIC DATE

August 15, 1971, Gold Convertibility Ends

- Vietnam War.
- President Nixon's 1971 economic plan, sometimes referred to as "Nixonomics".
- Ended gold convertibility and imposed wage and price controls.

STARTING DATE TO ERA OF THE ECONOMY DRIVEN BY FINANCE

Market Risk

- Great monetary disorder, Deficit spending, Inflation.
- Floating Currencies, Floating Interest rates.
- Speculative estate.
- Savings and Loan Crisis in US.

Market for Future and Options Contracts

FINANCIAL INNOVATION

- Chicago Board of Options Exchange opened in 1973.
- Options contrats and futures become financial instruments with which market risks can be managed.

The Contracts

- *Forward contracts*, transaction shifted at a contractual future date at a fixed price today.
- *Swap contracts* are some extension of forward contract to a series of cash flows in the interest-rates market.
- *Call options* are guarantees again the rise of the underlying.
- Easy instruments for speculation based on anticipation on the future evolution of the underlying.

The political and economic situation in France was radically different. The government had big influence on the economy.

HISTORICAL AND POLITICAL CONTEXT IN FRANCE

Political and Economic context up to 1970s–1980s in France

KEYNESIAN IDEA OF STATE INTERVENTION IN THE POST-WAR PERIOD

- Nationalization of the basic industries.
- As steel and coal producers.
- And three largest deposit banks: BNCI, Crédit Lyonnais et Société générale (SG).
- Pressure of WB and OECD to privatization.

THE 80'S = SOCIALIST PRESIDENT MITTERAND + COHABITATION PERIOD

- Wave of nationalizations in 1982.
- Incompatible with the market liberalization being manifested in the global economy.

- The August 6, 1986, first tentative to a legal regime for privatization of certain public industries.
- First privatization of Banks in 1987 (Société Générale, BNP, Suez).

EVOLUTION OF THE FRENCH CAPITAL MARKET RAFTER THE CRASH OCTOBER

The "ni-ni" Mitterand position

A SLOW EVOLUTION TIRED BY THE EUROPEAN CONSTRUCTION

- "ni-ni" = neither nationalization nor privatization (until 1993).
- but, modernisation of the French Capital Market Clearing Systems.
- End of the monopoly of the exchange agents.
- New regulation for "sociétés de bourse".
- Excellent "financial rating" of the state "France".

Finally, the financial risk markets are created around the years 1986–1987.

The MATIF (February1986)

THE FIRST FRENCH FUTURES MARKET

- Driven by the Debt, with AAA rating of the French State
- Strongly regulated Place

MONEP 1987

- The first French Options Market.
- An event anticipated by the Major French Banks.
- Rapidly, a sophisticated activity very quantitative.

The "Start-Up" period 1988–1998

New Market, New Technology

Computer revolution: IBM Again PC

- In 1988, in big Banks, computer = wholesale IBMs.
- French Banks are betting on technology.
- Engineers and Scientists are request in Derivatives Market.
- Turn delay into technological advantage.

Moore's Law on Power of Computers and Market Volume

- Exponential Growth in Computer Power, and Financial Market.
- Huge impact for the front middle and back office.

Demand in new quantitative tools

- For computer systems to speed up calculations.
- To hedge the market risk, new paradigm.
- For back office, accounting and regulation.

Demand for people

- 1990 = first year of the Master program in "Finance and Application".
- In Probability department at Paris VI University.
- Only for scientific profiles.
- Program: Theoretical Part, Stochastic calculus, PDE, Finance, Stat.
- Applied Part by professionals + 5 months of Training period.

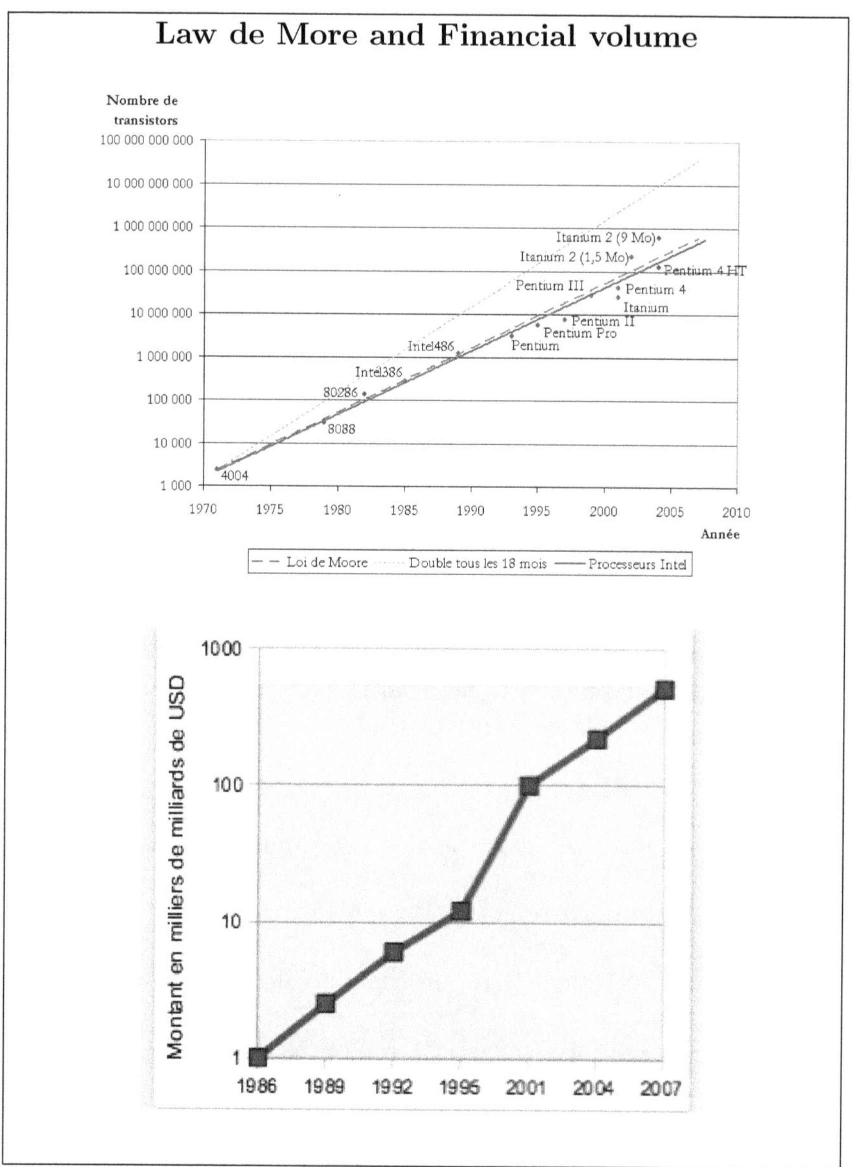

Golden Age of Financial Industry: 1995–2008

Golden age of Financial Innovation

- After 2001, Explosion of the derivatives contracts, with non-tradable underlying: (Volatility, Credit, Subprimes); see Figure 1.
- "Shadow Banking": Hedge-Funds and High-Frequency Trading.
- Banking, investment and finance = a **quantitative and data-driven industry**.

GOLDEN AGE OF QUANTITATIVE FINANCE

- Thousands of scientists, engineers and mathematicians enter the field.
- More that 70 top universities have a degree programs in Financial Mathematics and Engineering.
- Research publications on mathematical problems in investment and finance increase dramatically.

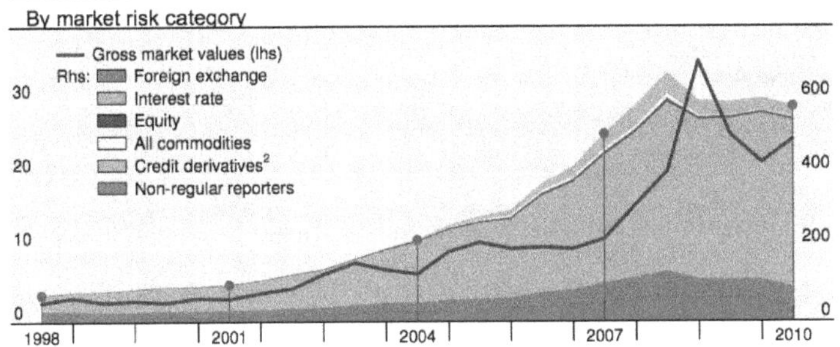

Figure 1: Evolution of notional size of OTC derivatives market.
Source: BIS.

Quantitative Finance: Three Pillars

PRACTICE

- Financial innovation
- Pricing and Hedging portfolio
- Risk management

MATHEMATICS

- Continuous Time Finance
- Stochastic Calculus, and PDEs
- Optimization

NUMERICAL IMPLEMENTATION

- Modeling and Computing (Monte Carlo)
- Calibration
- Risk management in Practice/Regulation/New Challenge

THE BLACK/SCHOLES/MERTON HISTORICAL FORMULA

Pricing and Hedging Methodology

PRICING RULE

- The price of an option contract is the cost of the **hedge**.
- Hedging strategy is based on dynamic *self-financing portfolio* V, written on the tradable asset X.
- With value at T closed to the exposure $V_T \sim h(X_T) = (X_T - K)^+$.

NEW PARADIGM IN RISK MANAGEMENT

- The problem is not to estimate the expected loses.
- Future time is used as tool for risk "diversification".

OPERATIONAL CONSTRAINTS

- The underlying of the contract is tradable in the market.
- Small trade with non-impact on the price of the underlying.
- Liquidity and weak transaction cost.

LIQUIDITY IS THE POSSIBILITY TO TRADE POSITIONS WITHOUT GENERATING MARKET INSTABILITY

It remains for us to briefly introduce the theoretical tools which support this new way of managing risk, without being able to involve a principle of mutualization, and therefore to give priority to statistical distribution of risk.

Examples of financial paths (see Figure 2)

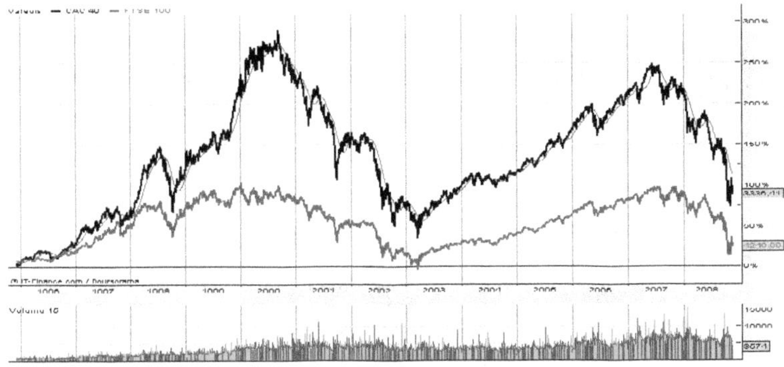

Figure 2: CAC 40 and FTSE between 1996 and 2008.

Brownian motion simulation (see Figure 3)

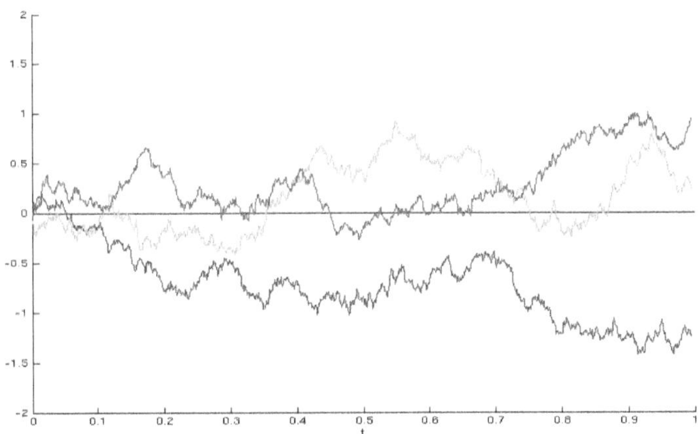

Figure 3: Brownian Path.

Two dimensional Brownian motion, J. F. Colonna (Ecole polytechnique)

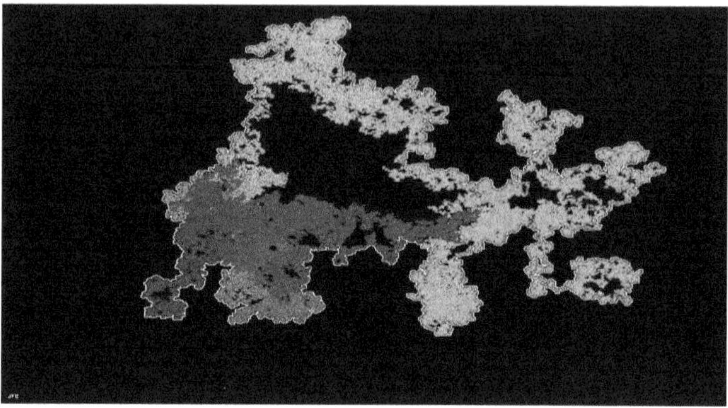

Remember that at this period the computer power was low.

In view of the graph on the variations over time of market prices, the first question was the identification of theoretical models whose behavior over time was also eratic.

The erratic motion of the Brownian process was well known to physicists since Einstein in 1930's. More surprising is that in his thesis, defended at the Sorbonne before H. Poincaré, Louis Bachelier, in 1900 had developed theoretical arguments on the price formula rule which were in favor of such model. We start by paying homage to Pr K. Itô, whose work had an international and multidisciplinary influence since many years.

Stochastic calculus: Itô (1936–1940)

IN HONOR OF PR. K.ITÔ

- Mathematical concepts developed in the 40–50 years with purely maths motivations. There are names
  - stochastic integration w.r t. stochastic process (X_t),
  - stochastic differential calculus,
  - Itô's formula.

- Professor Itô has reintroduced the "paths" in the center of the theory, based on the differential formula $df(X_t)$.
- Less centered around the distribution of the

MATHEMATICAL INTUITION

- The problem is how to negotiate with the functional irregularity of the paths.
- Even it is still possible to give sense to $\sum_{i=0}^{n-1} \delta_{t_i}(X_{t_{i+1}} - X_{t_i}) = V_{t_n}$, it is more subtle to "define" $V_t = \int_0^t \delta_u \, dX_u$.
- The extension of the ordinary differential calculus is a challenge in this context.
- Its works as shown by Itô in a extended sense, with the help of stochastic calculus.

THE MAIN CONCEPT: MARTINGALES M_t

- Concept stable for the stochastic integration.
- The famous Itô formula allows to develop a stochastic differential for $f(V_t)$ using similar stochastic integrals, and other more classical integrals.
- These objects are the *theoretical tools* used by finance theory in 1970's.
- If X_t is the asset price at time t
  - called V_{t_n} is the *gain process* associated with portfolio strategy with δ_{t_i} risky asset at time t_i.
- The integral has the same meaning for continuously traded strategy.

In addition, since Paul Levy in the years 1930's, there is a long French tradition dedicated to the study of stochastic processes in continuous time, with continuous trajectories or with discontinuities, for example the famous Lévy processes, generalizing the Poisson processes.

In the 1970s, in the Laboratoire de Probabilité de Paris VI under the leadership of Prof. Neveu and in Strasbourg of Prof. P. A. Meyer and C. Dellacherie, active and very theoretical research on the application of martingale theory in continuous time to stochastic processes had contributed to consider first the trajectories of the processes in consideration, by playing with them to stop them, reattach them back together, change them over time, and only at the end by "calculating" the probabilities of the events of interest.

Black and Scholes Solution

Self-financing portfolio on tradable underlying X

- The variation of cumulative *gain process* V_t
  - with δ_t shares held at time t.
  - short rate r_t for cash return.
- Has the self-financing dynamics
  - The gain due to the risky investment $\delta_t\, dX_t$,
  - The interest (short rate r_t) due to the residual wealth $V_t - \delta_t X_t$,
  - $dV_t = r_t(V_t - \delta_t X_t)dt + \delta_t dX_t$,
  - $= r_t V_t dt + \delta_t(dX_t - r_t X_t\, dt)$,
  - Terminal constraint $V_T = (X_T - K)^+$.

BS Solution for Geometric BM

- $dX_t = X_t[r\, dt + \sigma(dW_t + \theta dt)], \quad \mu = r + \theta\sigma$
- for Call option$=(X_T - K)^+$
  - No Dependence In The Trend θ.
  - N cumulative distribution for reduite Gaussian variable.
  - $C^{BS}(t, x, r, K, T, \sigma) = x\, N(d_1) - Ke^{-r(T-t)}\, N(d_0)$.
  - Analytic form for d_1 et d_0.

A Stochastic Control Target

- The target $(X_T - K)+$.
- The controlled process is the portfolio V_t^δ.
- The control problem is to find δ such that V_t^δ is self-financing, with terminal condition $V_T^\delta =$ target.

Example of Backward Stochastic Differential Equation (BSDE): A new research domain extended the point of view of "hedging portfolio".

In the graph, the colors have the following meaning:
Blue line = asset path, red line = portfolio value,
greenline = portfolio's risky part

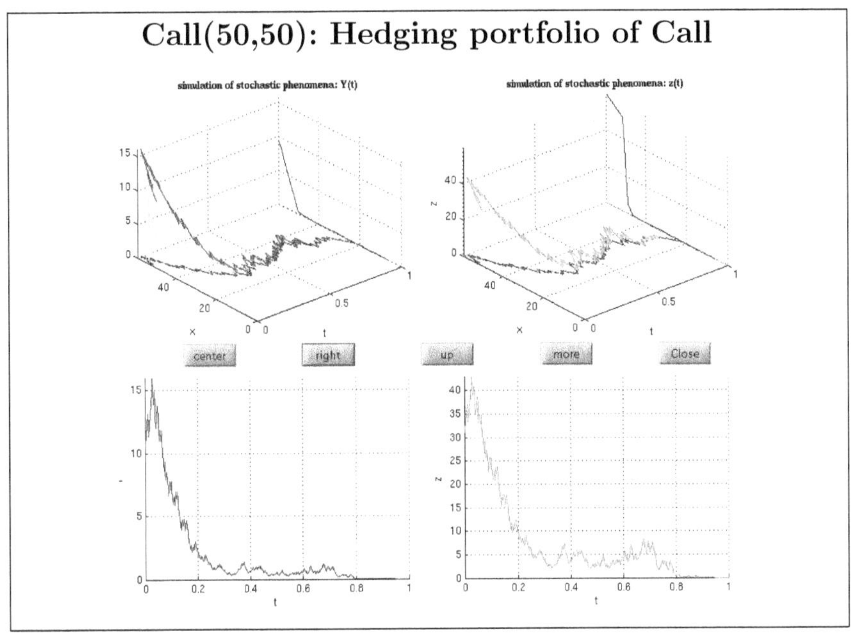

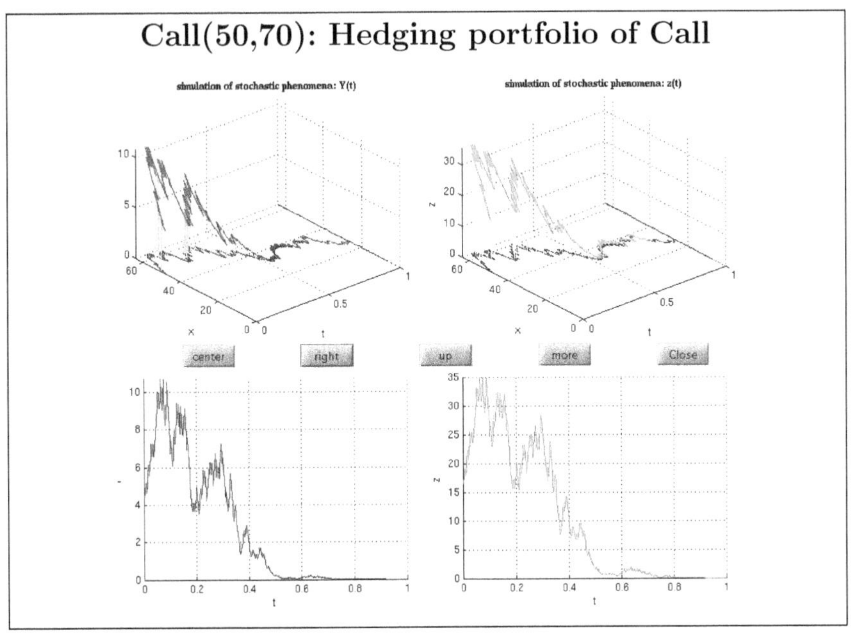

During this period, (years 1970–1980'), I was personally concerned with stochastic control problems, in which an agent act on parameters to modify a trajectory over time in order to optimize a criterion on average. This point of view was very fruitful in approaching the problem of derivatives and their hedging. Following my meeting with the Chinese Pr.S.Peng in 1993 in Paris, we collaborate to unify these different theories with the help of BSDE's.

The problem of calibrating model parameters is fundamental. We have chosen to present it briefly, and to give an example of development associated with the implied volatility. This is very partial given the importance of the problem for professionals and academics.

Calibration Issues: Implied Volatility

FIRST PERIOD: 1973–1987

- Liquid Markets: Exchange Markets, Currencies, etc.
- Quoted option prices are available on the market.
- Hedging rule: One price, one Implied volatility, one hedge.
- Use several times a day at hedging times when market moves.

SECOND PERIOD: 1993–

- More complex derivatives depending on volatility.
- Liquid options contracts are used as hedging instruments.
- **No flat Implied volatility surface.**

QUANTITATIVE FORMULATION

- IMPLIED VOLATILITY $\Sigma^{\text{imp}}_{(t_0,x_0)}(T,K)$
  - from quoted option prices $C^{\text{obs}}_{(t_0,x_0)}(T,K)$
  - by definition, in the BS formula
  - $C^{\text{obs}}_{(t_0,x_0)}(T,K) = C^{BS}(t_0,x_0,T,K,{\Sigma^{\text{imp}}}_{(t_0,x_0)}(T,K))$
- Implied hedging strategy $\delta^{\text{imp}}_{t_0,x_0}(T,K) = \partial_x C^{BS}(t_0,x_0,T,K,{\Sigma^{\text{imp}}}_{(t_0,x_0)}(T,K))$

Implied Volatility and Smile

IMPLIED VOLATILITY SURFACE/SP500

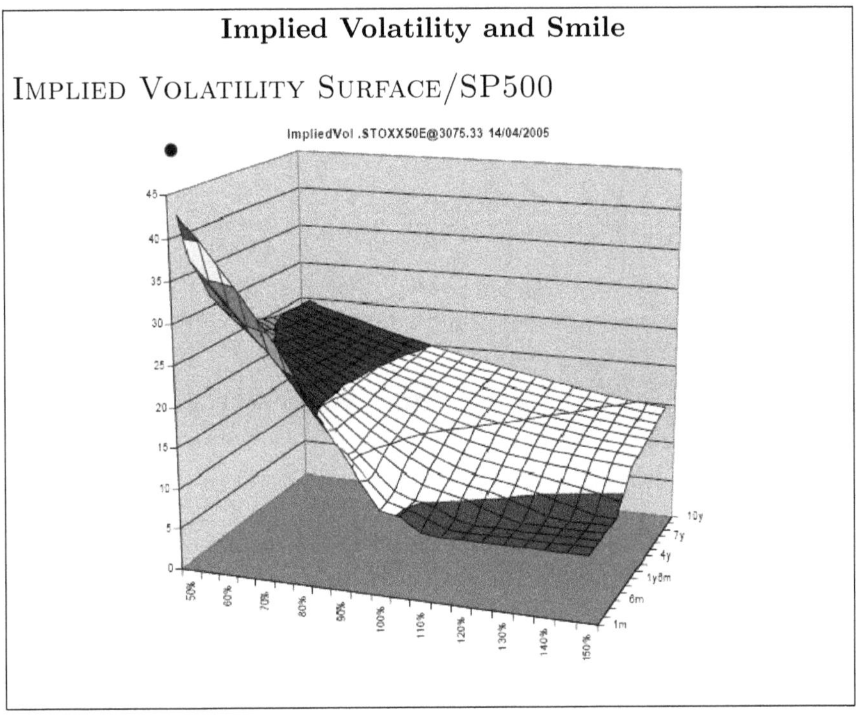

This notion is the starting point for many developments imposed by the existence of a non-flat volatility surface, and the fact that liquid options can be used as hedging instruments. Among the pioneers, we find the "implied diffusion" of Bruno Dupire (1997).

Implied Diffusion

LIQUID MARKETS: The Data set is the family of Call prices for every (T and K)

- First, verify that the coherence of data (convex, $\downarrow K$, and $\uparrow T$ (if $r = 0$)).
- The aim is to price and hedge path dependent options derivatives (barrier options, Asian, Lookback) with these liquid vanilla options, with calibrated Markovian model.

MATHEMATICAL ISSUES (DUPIRE (1996))

- LOCAL VOLATILITY AND DUAL PDE (Dupire (1996)). There exists a function $\sigma^{\mathrm{loc}}_{t_0,x_0}(T,K)$ given by the dual PDE

$$\frac{\partial C}{\partial T} = \frac{1}{2}(\sigma^{\mathrm{loc}}_{t_0,x_0})^2(T,K)K^2\frac{\partial^2 C}{\partial K^2} - rK\frac{\partial C}{\partial K}(T,K).$$

- THE FORWARD START CALL PRICES $C_{t_0,x_0}(t,x,T,K) = v(t,x)$ is solution of the backward PDE, with terminal condition $(x-k)^+$

$$v'_t(t,x) + \frac{1}{2}(\sigma^{loc}_{t_0,x_0})^2(t,x)x^2 v_{xx}(t,x) + rxv_x(t,x) - rv(t,x) = 0.$$

LIMITS OF THE METHOD

- In the market, a finite number of option prices are available, leading to an ill-posed inverse problem. Intensively studied from PDE point of view (penalization, and other methods).
- Do not forget the constraints of the speed of execution (less than 1 mn), and recalibration techniques.
- Often used in currency markets, as convenient to price and hedge barrier options.

SOME LATER MATHEMATIC REFERENCES

- Dupire, B and alii: Formally $(\sigma^{\mathrm{loc}}_{t_0,x_0})^2(T,K) = \mathbb{E}[\tilde{\sigma}^2_t | S_T = K]$
- Brunick, S. (2011). Mimicking an Itô Process by a SDE with same marginals: Multi-dimensional case.
- Guyon, J. and Labordère, P.H. (2011).

This is obviously only a small overview of modeling problems posed by financial markets. Since then, many works, presented in this conference, (M. Rosenbaum for example), have explored new orientations, as Hawkes processes, rough volatility,....

Moreover, we haven't talked about market risk in the interest rates universe. This exciting world cannot be summed up in a few words. In terms of modeling, the key concepts are yield curves, risk-neutral forward universes, and change of "numéraire". Going from one underlying to a underlying curve poses many technical problems.

Apart from the traditional interest rates market, in the years before the crisis, the products on the default of companies or states knew a rapid development, accompanied by a great imagination in financial innovation. The naive application of the tools of traditional derivatives to these new credit derivatives products has largely contributed to the propagation of the crisis.

After the speculative Bubble, the Depression

2007–2008 CREDIT CRUNCH/LEHMAN COLLAPSE

- The *excesses* of the finance industry are dragging down the whole economy.
- *Credit crunch* was based on subprime risks, a lowering of underwriting standards that drew people into mortgages.
- *Diffusion* of the home mortgage crisis in any financial places through securization via MBS.
- *Mortgage-backed securities* (MBS) depend of the performance of hundreds of mortgages.
- *Critical role* of Rating Agency.

THE SPECTRUM OF THE GREAT DEPRESSION (1927)

- Drastic reduction of credit derivatives business.
- Liquidity crisis in the interbank market.
- Multicurves in interest rates modeling, including rating spread.

NEW TRADING RULES, FUNDING WITH COLLATERAL

- Different *bilateral agreement* often as a convex function of the transaction.
- Different *funding* interest rates and *collate* interest rate.

AMONG STRATEGIC RESEARCH PROBLEM POST CRISIS

- Globalisation of financial system: Systemic risk and instability.
- Simulation of counterparty risk.
- Collateralisation, impact and sources of risk.
- Impact of the regulation and transparency.

Over the past 10 years, the world of derivatives has evolved a lot, as described by the other participants.

I would like to end with a question that is particularly close to my heart, the *place of women in this universe*, in particular the French exception, where three Masters of Financial Mathematics (in Sciences), ParisVI, ParisVII, Evry) were created by women.

Program of the Master Degree PVI-Ecole Polytechnique

MASTER DEGREE'S CREATED BY WOMEN, IN 1990. WHY?

- Very negative image of finance in the math community.
- Also the case for stochastic control,....
- Why not for mathematician women ... (as M. Jeanblanc (Evry), L. Elie (PVII), NEK (PVI-X)).
- We realize that it is an exceptional opportunity for students in stochastic process.

PROGRAM OF MASTER FOR "QUANTS"

- Adapted to the demand of the market front office.
- Important evolution of the contents but not the thematic.
- Theoretical part, still with proofs
  - Stochastic process, Numerical methods, Statistics, Algorithmics, Optimization.
  - Introduction to Financial Market, Regulation.
- Practical courses by practitioners, and training period of 5 months in a bank.
- Academic research and links with market professional are the fundamental pillars of the formation.

THE STUDENTS, STILL LARGE DEMAND

- Strong selection based on a good level in mathematics.
- Since the beginning in 1990, about 1,600 graduated students from Paris VI.
- But only 12% of women.
- Famous international reputation of "the french quants".

THE STUDENTS, THIRTY YEARS LATER

- Recently, competition with Master degree's and jobs in Big Data.
- More diversified jobs: in regulation, insurance and accounting firms ... in today's distressed market.
- More concerned by ethical issues (especially for the girls).

Students in Master Degree PVI-X

I SURVIVED ... DEA EL KAROUI, YEAR 2010

As a Conclusion

- Obviously the story did not end with the crisis.
- As developed during these workshop, Financial markets quickly integrated.
- The multiple contributions of new methodologies (Neural networks, AI).
- This beautiful collaborative experience is to be continued.

But the succession is assured!

Thank you to each of you for this exciting adventure

https://doi.org/10.1142/9789811259142_0020

Chapter 20

Option Prices in the Equity, Index and Commodity Markets: The "Message from Markets"

E. I. Ronn
Department of Finance,
McCombs School of Business,
University of Texas at Austin,
Austin, TX, USA
eronn@mail.utexas.edu

Abstract

Hearkening back to the mid part of the previous century, financial economists have focused on financial markets' role in conveying forward-looking information, what may be described as the "Message from Markets".[a]

---

[a]With permission from the respective publishers, this chapter excerpts portions of two of my published papers:

1. "The Valuation and Informational Content of Options on Crude-Oil Futures Contracts" (co-authored with F. Murphy), *Review of Derivatives Research*, 2014.

2. "VIX Implied Volatility as a Time-Invariant, Stationary Assessor of Market Nervousness/Uncertainty", in C. F. Lee, A. Lee and J. Lee (eds.), *Handbook of Investment Analysis, Portfolio Management, and Financial Derivatives*, 2021.

In my December 2018 Conference presentation at the Mount Scopus campus, I included material from a third paper, "Using Equity, Index and Commodity Options to Obtain Forward-Looking Betas and Conditional-CAPM Expected

Capitalizing on the rich content of option markets, this chapter presents and analyzes the informational-content empirical evidence on two financial markets:

1. The informational content of the time-series of VIX, the implied volatility on the S&P 500 Index.
2. Using Merton's [7] Jump-Diffusion Model to Quantify the Jump-Risk in Oil Markets.

Keywords: Informativeness of option markets, Message from markets, Implied vol VIX, Jump-Diffusion model, Crises of 1990/1991 and 2003, Arab spring of 2011.

1. Introduction

In mid-20th century, Nobel Laureate Friedrich A. Hayek [5] wrote:

> Fundamentally, in a system in which the knowledge of the relevant facts is dispersed among many people, ... [w]e must look at the price system as a mechanism for communicating information if we want to understand its real function.

In a similar vein, in their important textbook, Brealey *et al.* [3]

> If [financial markets are] efficient, prices impound all available information. Therefore, if we can only learn to read the entrails,[b] security prices can tell us a lot about the future.

That said, one cannot resist the quip offered by another Nobel laureate, Paul A. Samuelson [11]:

> The stock market has forecast nine of the last five recessions.

It bears repeating that, even those of us who profess efficient financial markets do not pretend these markets are prescient or omniscient.

This chapter is now structured as follows. Section 2 considers a nostalgic look back to the Black–Scholes–Merton 35th Anniversary, held 10 years earlier at Vanderbilt University at the Conference

---

Crude-Oil Spot Prices", *Journal of Energy Markets*, December 2021. The content of that paper is not included in this Conference Proceedings forthcoming.

[b]From Wikipedia: "In the religion of Ancient Rome, the practice of prophecy called for the inspection of the entrails [intestines] of sacrificed animals" to forecast the future.

on Financial Innovation hosted by the Owen Graduate School of Management. Section 3 argues VIX, the implied volatility on the S&P 500 Index, is a time-invariant, stationary assessor of stock market nervousness/uncertainty. In turn, Section 4 uses market prices for crude-oil futures options and the prices of their underlying futures contracts to calibrate the volatility skew using the Merton [7] jump-diffusion option-pricing model, and then proceeds to demonstrate these jump-diffusion parameters bear a close relationship to concurrent economic, financial and geopolitical events. Section 5 concludes.

2. 2008 Black–Scholes–Merton 35th Anniversary, Conference on Financial Innovation, Vanderbilt University

See Figures 1–3.

2.1 *Nobel laureates discuss financial innovation*

Financial market leaders and researchers gathered this past fall for the first-ever Conference on Financial Innovation hosted by the Owen School. The forum focused on such timely topics as volatility, real estate, credit and stock index option markets, as well as real options and share-based compensation contracts. It also assessed the evolution of financial innovation over the past 35 years and explored what might lie ahead.

The conference, which took place October 16–17, commemorated the 35th anniversary of the publication of two landmark financial studies: *The Pricing of Options and Corporate Liabilities* by Fischer Black and Myron Scholes, and *The Theory of Rational Option Pricing* by Robert C. Merton. Originally published in 1973 when options were considered specialized and economically insignificant financial instruments, these two seminal works had an unprecedented influence and came to underlie almost every facet of the theory and practice of modern-day finance. In 1997, Black, Scholes and Merton were awarded the Alfred Nobel Memorial Prize in Economics for their work. Today they are credited with sparking the growth of derivatives markets, whose value now exceeds $600 trillion.

Figure 1: Robert Merton talks about the future of financial innovation during a panel discussion with Myron Scholes and Leo Melamed, far right.

"More than three decades later, we are reminded of the critical relevancy of these pioneering works and how far the ripples of innovation can spread and influence future events", says Robert E. Whaley, Valere Blair Potter Professor of Management and Co-director of the Financial Markets Research Center at the Owen School.

Participating in the conference were finance and economics faculty from more than 40 universities worldwide, including the University of Chicago; the University of California, Los Angeles; New York University; Harvard University; the University of California, Berkeley; Columbia University; and Vanderbilt. Offering the event's keynote address was CME Group Chairman Emeritus Leo Melamed, who is widely recognized as the founder of the financial futures markets. In addition, Scholes, Merton and Melamed participated in a special panel that focused on the direction of financial innovation in the next decade (Figure 1).

"Given the unprecedented financial market volatility and its links to derivative instruments, this new forum and its focus on the derivatives markets couldn't be more timely", Whaley says. "The collective insights of academics and practitioners will prove invaluable as we seek to better understand the past, present and future of financial innovation and its impact on the global financial marketplace".

The 2008 Conference on Financial Innovation was sponsored by the Chicago Board Options Exchange, CME Group, Options Industry Council, Susquehanna International Group LLC, and the Vanderbilt University Law School, which provided facilities for the event. Susquehanna's participation was prompted by Owen alumnus Eric Noll, MBA'90, who serves as the company's Director of Research (Figures 2 and 3).

Despina Leal (http://gamblux.co.cc)
June 2, 2010 (https://wp0.vanderbilt.edu/vanderbiltbusiness/nobel-laureates-discuss-financial-innovation/#comment-50)
nice site bookmark it to come back again

Comments are closed.

Figure 2: One response to "Nobel laureates discuss financial innovation."

RESOURCES

Past editions of *Vanderbilt Business* (https://magazine.owen.vanderbilt.edu/archive/editions/)
Owen Graduate School of Management (http://www.owen.vanderbilt.edu/)
Vanderbilt Alumni Publications (http://www.vuconnect.com/s/1643/start.aspx?sid=1643&gid=2&pgid=61#pubs)

SPRING 2009

More articles from this Issue

CONTRIBUTORS

Nancy Wise (https://wp0.vanderbilt.edu/vanderbiltbusiness/author/nwise/)

Figure 3: Past editions of Vanderbilt Business.

3. VIX: S&P 500 Implied Volatility

One of the most interesting message-from-markets indicator is that of a metric inferred from option prices — the implied volatility that can be extracted from option prices using the famed Black–Scholes [2] option pricing models.

3.1 *Definition of implied volatility*

The key to the seminal contribution of the Black–Scholes–Merton option pricing model is the identification of the parameters which determine option prices. Specifically, for an option on a stock index, the Black–Scholes option pricing model provides the value of an option (c) given the inputs of: The price of the underlying asset (S), strike price (K), riskfree rate (r), time to expiration (T) and prospective volatility (σ) over the remaining time to the option's expiration. It is important to note that of all these parameters, all are observable (the time to expiration and the strike price are *contractual*) save the future volatility σ.

Econometricians have devised numerous ways of estimating prospective volatility using recently-observed returns on the underlying asset (stock or futures). These volatilities are then substituted into the Black–Scholes model to obtain the option's fair market value.

In contrast to using such historically-based volatility estimates, Implied Vol changes the question: Instead of asking,

> What is the value of the option?

the question posed is

> Given the option's observable market price, and assuming the market is using the Black–Scholes model to price options, what volatility number is the 'market' using?

Table 1 provides a useful contrast of implied vol relative to its better-known historical-vol counterpart.

It is useful to note the VIX Index is not actually computed using the Black-Scholes model. The procedure described in https://www.cboe.com/micro/vix/vixwhite.pdf relaxes some of the Black–Scholes assumptions and is more general. But for all intents and purposes

Table 1: Contrasting implied vs historical volatilities.

Descriptor	Historical	Implied
Method of calculation	Standard deviation of rates of return	Inferred from option prices using the Black–Scholes model
Data period for calculation	*Past* History $[-t, 0]$	*Forward*-Looking $[0, T]$, where T is the maturity date of the option
Bias, due to a risk premium, as a measure of volatility	None	Typically perceived as an *upward*-biased measure of future volatility

the Black–Scholes implied volatility for an at-the-money option is sufficient close to what VIX provides.

3.2 *VIX: The implied volatility of the S&P 500 Index*

Our purpose here is to describe VIX, interpret its value and exemplify its application. Consider the following quotes from the CBOE's http://www.cboe.com/micro/vix/faq.aspx#1:

> 1. What exactly is VIX?
>
> In 1993, the Chicago Board Options Exchange® (CBOE®) introduced the CBOE Volatility Index®, VIX®, and it quickly became the benchmark for stock market volatility. It is widely followed and has been cited in hundreds of news articles in the *Wall Street Journal*, Barron's and other leading financial publications. Since volatility often signifies financial turmoil, VIX is often referred to as the 'investor fear gauge'. VIX measures market expectation of near term volatility conveyed by stock index option prices.
>
> 2. Why is VIX called the 'investor fear gauge'?
>
> VIX is based on real-time option prices, which reflect investors' consensus view of future expected stock market volatility. Historically, during periods of financial stress, which are often accompanied by steep market declines, option prices — and VIX — tend to rise. The greater the fear, the higher the VIX level. As investor fear subsides, option prices tend to decline, which in turn causes VIX to decline.

Perhaps VIX's greatest attribute is its time-invariance stationarity,[c] which permits its comparability across different time zones. In contrast, stock prices are not stationary, which makes their levels not comparable across time.

Figure 4 reports a monthly time-series of VIX over the long period January 31, 1990 to January 31, 2007. It is both instructive and interesting to review the different crises through which the world passed over these 17 years, and to see how VIX has quantified each and every one. In turn, Figure 5 updates that time period to a later one, October 1, 2007–July 2, 2018, in essence covering the Great Recession of 2008–2009 and its immediate aftermath. Figure 6 reports the value of VIX's predecessor VXO, the implied volatilty of the S&P 100 Index: The reason for its inclusion here is to demonstrate the

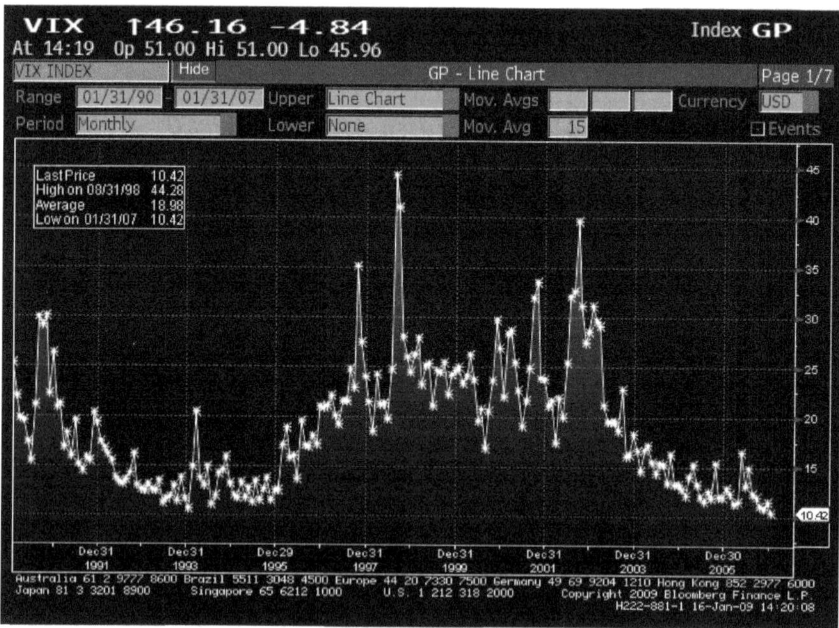

Figure 4: VIX Index from 01/31/1990 to 01/31/2007.

[c]Gagniuc (2017), "In mathematics and statistics, a stationary process is a stochastic process whose unconditional joint probability distribution does not change when shifted in time". Consequently, parameters such as mean and variance also do not change over time.

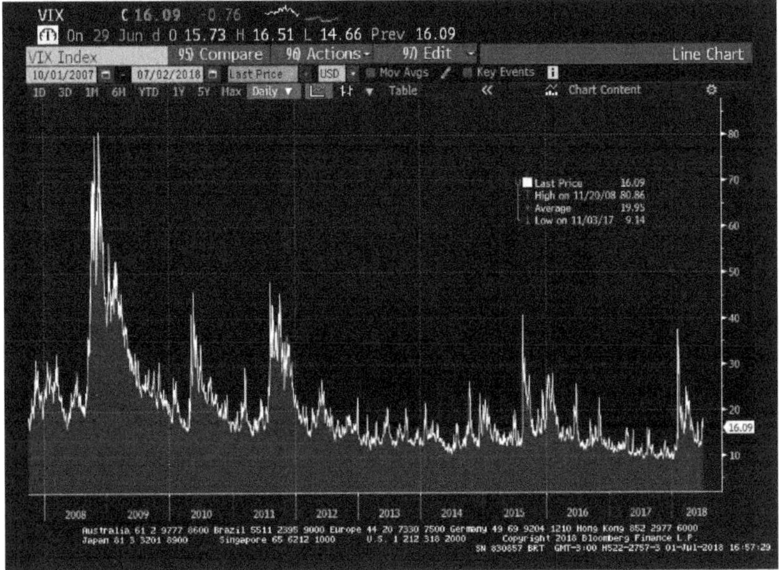

Figure 5: VIX Index from 10/01/2007 to 07/02/2018.

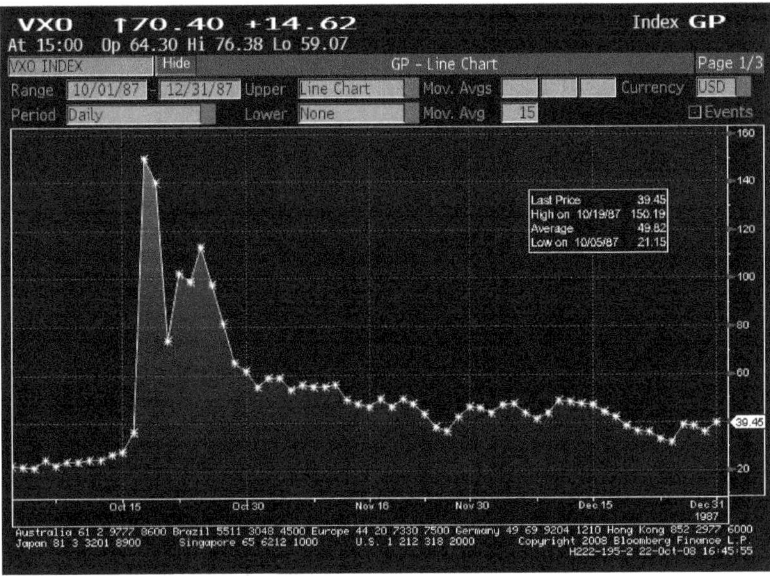

Figure 6: VXO Index from 10/01/1987 to 12/31/1987.

all-time high for implied vol, the October 19, 1987 market crash, at which time VXO exceeded 150%.[d]

We now turn to the heart of our VIX analysis. Whether or not Persian Gulf I and Persian Gulf II were in fact equally "dangerous" to the world is a matter for debate amongst political scientists. Our purpose here is different: We seek to display the peak level of VIX during these two crises. Thus, Figures 7 and 8 graph VIX over the two periods February 28, 1990–February 28, 1991 and November 2, 2002–May 30, 2003, which periods span the two Persian Gulf conflicts.[e] VIX's high-water marks in these two periods are 36.47% on August 23, 1990 and 34.69% on January 27, 2003. Using VIX as the measure of investor uncertainty/nervousness, investors (through VIX) assessed both conflicts as presenting equal risks to the US economy. Although political scientists may take issue with this characterization, I thus infer from VIX a quantitative measure by which to measure any crisis, be it geopolitical, economic or financial.

3.3 *Conclusion: VIX under informationally-efficient financial markets*

In demonstrating the peak value of VIX in two similar crises, we have attempted to address that question by considering the level of VIX implied volatility in the two major Persian Gulf crises of 1990/1991 and 2003.

4. Merton's [7] Jump-Diffusion Model

Perhaps the strongest "evidence" against the standard Black–Scholes–Merton is the empirical evidence of a volatility "skew" — namely, that vol as a function of moneyness (strike price) is not

[d]Although the S&P 100 Index is more volatile than its 500-stock counterpart, VIX did not exist back in 1987.

[e]I submit the term "investor nervousness/uncertainty index" is more appropriate, as "fear" may denote an element of irrationality.

Figure 7: VIX Index from 02/28/1990 to 02/28/1991.

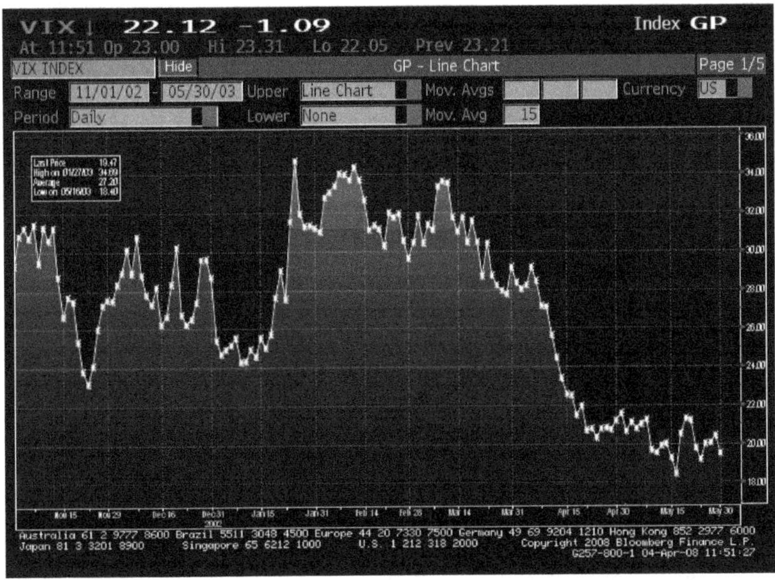

Figure 8: VIX Index from 11/01/2002 to 05/30/2003.

a purely-horizontal line.[f] That vol skew has been with us since October 19, 1987, when the world "discovered" crashes are not a pure manifestation of stock prices in the 1920s and 1930s. Although this skew is manifestly there in terms of both stock prices as well as commodity prices, it is no small tribute to the usefulness of the Black–Scholes–Merton that option prices are still reported in terms of their traditional implied vols, even when a non-flat skew is tantamount to a rejection of one of the model's prescription.

Figure 9 displays the vol skew for options on oil-futures contracts as of June 27, 2018, for maturities of 3, 6, 18 and 24 months. The graph plots implied vol by moneyness, defined as the ratio of the strike price to the prevailing futures for that maturity. The figure clearly displays a non-flat vol skew, with greater concern of a crash

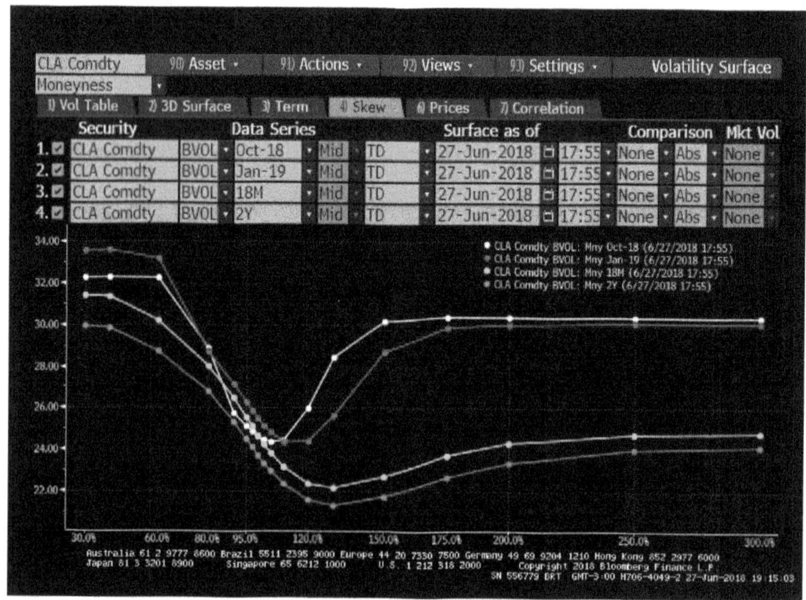

Figure 9: Volatility surface for CLA Commodity (Crude oil) on 06/27/2018.

[f]Although he is not responsible for the model I selected, the inspiration for looking into the issue of precise option valuation is attributable to my luncheon discussion with David Gershon at a Houston conference we both attended over 10 years ago.

(left skewness) than a spike (right skewness): The implied vol for low strike prices is greater than the corresponding vol for high strike prices.

4.1 *The commodity markets version of the Merton (1976) model*

In fitting option on crude-oil futures contracts to the model, we need take cognizance of the fact options on futures contracts require a modification of the original Black–Scholes–Merton model: We need to set the dividend-yield equal to the riskfree rate. This follows from Black's [1] recognition the riskless drift on a costless futures contract is zero.

Ignoring the fact traded options are actually American in style, rather than European, the Merton [7] option pricing model modified to options on futures contracts is given by

$$v_T(K_T) = \sum_{n=0}^{\infty} \frac{e^{-\lambda' T}(\lambda' T)^n}{n!} c_n(F_T, X, T, r_n, q, \sigma_n), \tag{1}$$

where

$v_T(K_T) =$ European call option,
$\lambda' = \lambda(1+\bar{k})$,
$T =$ option expiration,
$c_n\,(F_T, X, T, r_n, q, \sigma_n) =$ Black–Scholes call option value with parameters $\{F_T, X, T, r_n, q, \sigma_n\}$, where q is the *dividend yield*,

$$c_n\,(F_T, X, T, r_n, q, \sigma_n) = F_T\, e^{-qT} N(d) - K e^{-r_n T} N(d - \sigma_n\sqrt{T})$$

$$d \equiv \frac{\ln(F_T/K) + (r_n - q)\,T}{\sigma_n\sqrt{T}} + \tfrac{1}{2}\sigma_n\sqrt{T},$$

$\sigma_n^2 = \sigma^2 + n\delta^2/T$,
$r_n = r - \lambda\bar{k} + n\ln(1+\bar{k})/T$,
$q = r$.

Notes:

1. Although in principle (1) requires a summation over an infinite number of terms, in practice the option value converges after a summation over the first ten terms.

2. The parameters of the jump process are:

$$\begin{aligned}\lambda &= \text{intensity of the jump process,}\\ \bar{k} &= \text{average amplitude of the jump process,}\\ \delta^2 &= \text{variance of the jump process amplitude,}\\ \sigma^2 &= \text{variance of the diffusion process.}\end{aligned}$$

3. $q = r$ in this case, since the F_T's are futures contracts.

The sign of $\bar{k}$ is of critical interest to us: When the market is concerned with crashes, $\bar{k} < 0$ (this is the left skew). Conversely, when the market is concerned with spikes, typically when there are Middle East crises of a political nature, $\bar{k} > 0$ (this is the right skew).

4.2 *Fitting the Merton model to crude-oil futures and option prices*

With observed option prices given by $c_T(K_T)$, and their theoretical (1) counterparts given by $v_T(K_T)$, the objective function is [8]

$$\min_{\{\mathbf{x}\}} \sum_T \sum_K [c_T(K) - v_T(K)]^2, \tag{2}$$

where

$$\mathbf{x} \equiv \{\bar{k}_T, \delta_T, \sigma_T\} \quad \text{for all maturities } T,$$

and using all options with Open Interest > 0 satisfying

$$c_T(K) \geq \max\{0.05, F_T - K + 0.05\}.$$

Our two key assumptions in this estimation procedure were:

1. Given the relevant data's principal-components, set $\lambda = 0.3$ for all T and t;
2. Jump's average amplitude $\bar{k}_T$ and volatility δ_T vary by maturity.

We applied this model to options on crude-oil futures prices for the time period December 17, 2010 to May 3, 2011. We report the empirical results in Table 2.

The empirical sign of $\widehat{\bar{k}}_{T=30\text{ days}}$ during the "Arab Spring of 2011" is telling: Before the onset of the crisis, $\widehat{\bar{k}}_{T=30\text{ days}} < 0$. As the crisis become more acute, and esp. as it progresses from North Africa

Table 2: The sign and magnitude of standardized $\widehat{k}_{T=30\text{ days}}$ during the "Arab Spring of 2011".

Date	Event	Country	Value of $\widehat{k}$ (%)
December 17, 2010	Self-immolation	Tunisia	−23.3
January 18, 2011	President Ben Ali resigns	Tunisia	−22.8
January 25, 2011	Protests in Tahrir Square	Egypt	−32.0
February 11, 2011	President Mubarak resigns	Egypt	−2.76
February 14, 2011	First contagion to Persian Gulf	Bahrain	−0.90
February 22, 2011	Resignation of prime minister	Kuwait	29.7
March 4, 2011			63.0
March 11, 2011	Economic concessions by king	Saudi Arabia	44.3
March 18, 2011	Economic concessions by king	Bahrain	39.2
May 3, 2011			−1.9

Source: Article on the "Arab Spring", http://en.wikipedia.org/wiki/Arab–Spring.

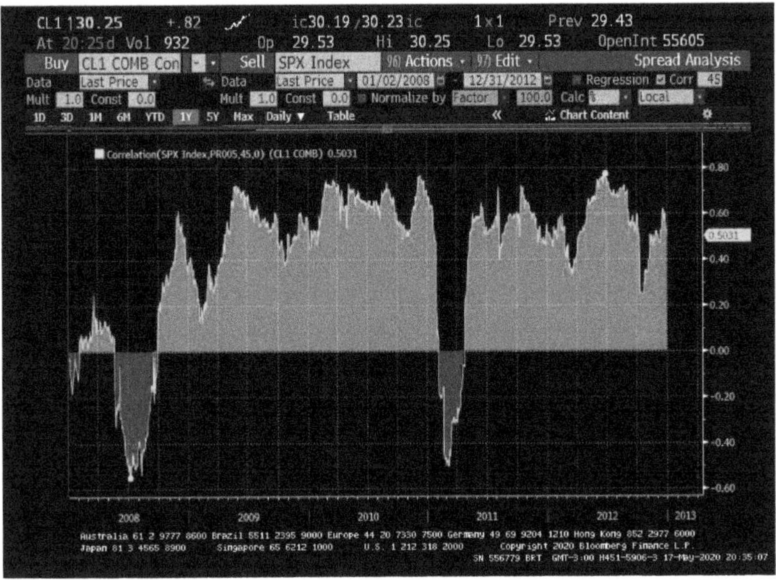

Figure 10: A 45-day moving window for Corr (Oil Prices, S&P 500) from 01/02/2008 to 12/31/2012.

to the more oil price-sensitive Persian Gulf, $\widehat{k}_{T=30\text{ days}}$ becomes increasingly positive. Then, as political actors take remedial actions, the crisis passes. While the political effects of the "Arab Spring" were and are long-lasting, its manifestation in terms of financial markets were short-lived.

We can obtain confirming evidence of this by an empirical examination of a 45-day moving window for Corr (Oil Prices, S&P 500). As can be seen in Figure 10, that Corr was negative for a single quarter in 2011, broadly in agreement with the implications of Table 2.

5. Conclusions

Financial markets in general, and derivative markets in particular, are highly informative. This chapter has focused on the informativeness of option prices in the equity and commodity markets — in an attempt to elicit what may be termed the "Message from Markets".

Applying the Black–Scholes/Merton to options on the S&P 500 Index permitted an invaluable VIX-related quantitative answer to the question, How nervous/uncertain is the financial market? In demonstrating the peak value of VIX in two similar crises, we have attempted to address that question by considering the level of VIX implied volatility in the two major Persian Gulf crises of 1990/1991 and 2003.

In turn, the Merton [7] Jump–Diffusion model demonstrated how crude-oil futures option prices discerned between demand- and supply-side crises. Specifically, upon extracting parameter values from Merton's [7] Jump–Diffusion model, we identified oil markets' spike or crash concerns. We conclude the Merton model conveyed economically important and interesting information regarding the sign and magnitude of a price spike during the spring of 2011.

Acknowledgments

The author acknowledges with thanks the research assistance provided at the University of Texas at Austin, while remaining solely responsible for any errors therein. This chapter was presented at the December 2018 "Options: 45 Years after the Publication of the

Black–Scholes–Merton Model Conference" held at the School of Business Administration, Hebrew University of Jerusalem. I thank the University's Gershon Fintech Center and the organizers, Dan Galai, David Gershon, Alexander Lipton, Mathieu Rosenbaum and Zvi Wiener, for the invitation to address that conference.

References

[1] Black, F. (1976). The pricing of commodity contracts. *Journal of Financial Economics*, 3, 167–179.

[2] Black, F. and Scholes, M. (1973). The pricing of options and corporate Liabilities. *Journal of Political Economy*, 81, 163–175.

[3] Brealey, R.A., Myers, S.C. and Allen, F. (2006). *Principles of Corporate Finance*, McGraw-Hill.

[4] Cboe VIX®. White Paper, Cboe Volatility Index®, https://www.cboe.com/micro/vix/vixwhite.pdf.

[5] Hayek, F.A. (1945). The use of knowledge in society. *American Economic Review*, September.

[6] Gagniuc, P.A. (2017). *Markov Chains: From Theory to Implementation and Experimentation*, John Wiley & Sons, USA, NJ, 1256. ISBN 978-1-119-38755-8.

[7] Merton, R.C. (1976). Option prices when underlying stock returns are discontinuous. *Journal of Financial Economics*, 3, 125–144.

[8] Murphy, F. and Ronn, E.I. (2015). The valuation and informational content of options on crude-oil futures contracts. *Review of Derivatives Research*, 18(2), 95–106.

[9] Ronn, E.I. (2022). VIX implied volatility as a time-invariant, stationary assessor of market nervousness/uncertainty. In C.F. Lee, A. Lee and J. Lee (eds.), *Handbook of Investment Analysis, Portfolio Management, and Financial Derivatives*, World Scientific, Singapore.

[10] Ronn, E.I. (2021). Using equity, index and commodity options to obtain forward-looking betas and conditional-capm expected crude-oil spot prices. *Journal of Energy Markets*, 14(4), 23–56.

[11] Samuelson, P.A. (1966). Science and stocks. *Newsweek Magazine*, September.

https://doi.org/10.1142/9789811259142_0021

Chapter 21

Options Markets in China: The New Frontier

H. Li[*,‡] **and Q. Wang**[†,§]

[*] *Cheung Kong Graduate School of Business, Beijing, China*
[†] *China Financial Futures Exchange, Shanghai, China*
[‡] *htli@ckgsb.edu.cn*
[§] *wangqi21@hotmail.com*

1. Introduction

The publication of the option pricing formula of Black and Scholes [1] and Merton [2] ushered in a great era of developments of the markets of options around the world. Options on stock indices, individual stocks, commodities, interest rates and other financial assets have been widely used by a wide range of market participants around the globe for the purposes of risk management, investment, speculation, and arbitrage.

While options (at least the plain vanilla ones) have become rather standard financial products in developed markets, they have been introduced in China only recently. Stock markets in China were established in the early 1990s: officially, the Shanghai Stock Exchange (SSE) was established on November 26, 1990, and the Shenzhen Stock Exchange (SZSE) on December 1, 1990. Despite the fact that the SSE and SZSE are ranked as the third and the sixth largest stock exchanges in the world with market capitalization of $7.6 trillion and $5.4 trillion, respectively by August 2021, exchanged-traded options were introduced in China only 6 years ago in early 2015.

One of the reasons for the delayed introduction of options is probably due to some widely publicized incidents in early derivatives trading in China in the 1990s. For example, government bond futures were introduced in China in October, 1992 and quickly became a popular vehicle for speculation due to the advantages offered by derivatives trading. In early 1995, speculators bet heavily on government bond futures due to the high inflation that China was experiencing at the time. Some speculators made huge gains based on insider information of government policy on inflation, while others suffered great losses in the order of $1 billion, a huge sum then. The trading havoc resulted in the shutdown of the government bond futures market.

On April 16, 2010, almost 15 years after the government bond futures fiasco, China Financial Futures Exchange (CFFEX) introduced the first equity index futures in China, the CSI 300 index futures. The CSI 300 index is a capitalization-weighted major stock market index of 300 top stocks traded in the SSE and SZSE, with a similar status in the Chinese market as that of the S&P 500 index in the US market. In a market where leverage, short selling, and intraday trading are still heavily restricted (Chines stock trading follows the so-called T + 1 rule, i.e., stocks purchased on one day can only be sold a day later), the CSI 300 index futures quickly became a market favorite by overcoming these obstacles. By the end of 2014, its daily trading volume surpassed one trillion RMB, many times of that of all other commodity futures combined.

After almost 5 years of smooth running of the CSI index futures market without any major hiccups, on February 9, 2015, the SSE introduced the first ever exchanged-traded options in China written on the SSE 50 index ETF. The SSE 50 index is a capitalization-weighted major stock market index of 50 largest and most liquid blue chip stocks traded on the SSE. Representing about a quarter of the total market capitalization of the Chinese equity market, the SSE 50 index has a similar status as the Dow Jones industrial average in the US. The options are written on 10,000 shares of the SSE 50 index ETF managed by the China Asset Management company (China AMC).

Since 2015, more options have been introduced in China, which include options on the CSI 300 index, the CSI 300 index ETFs, and options on about 20 commodity futures. The goal of this chapter is to provide a brief review of exchange-traded options in China. The rest of the chapter is organized as follows. Section 2 provides an overview of exchange-traded options in China. Section 3, discusses several interesting pricing anomalies that reflect the unique institutional structures of the Chinese financial markets, and Section 4 concludes.

2. Exchange-Traded Options

In this section, we provide an overview of exchange-traded options in China. We first discuss financial options, where the underlying assets are either stock market indices or index ETFs, which include the SSE 50 index ETF options, the CSI 300 index ETF options traded on the SSE and the SZSE, as well as the CSI 300 index options traded on the CFFEX. Then we discuss the options on commodity futures traded on the three commodity exchanges in China, i.e., the Dalian Commodity Exchange (DCE), the Zhengzhou Commodity Exchange (ZCE), and the Shanghai Commodity Exchange (SCE). Finally, we will discuss major market participants in Chinese options markets. Most data used in this chapter are from public sources. In particular, The Shanghai Stock [3] provides rich statistics on exchange-traded options.

2.1 *Financial options*

Drawing on the experiences of developed markets, Chinese regulatory authorities can plan the launch of financial options in a more deliberate manner. Table 1 reports the major financial options currently traded in China, with their launch times, underlying assets, and listing exchanges.

Instead of starting with options on individual stocks, exchanges in China started to list options on major market indices. So far two major stock market indices have been considered, the SSE 50 index and the CSI 300 index. As indicated above, the SSE 50 index, which includes 50 blue chip stocks traded on the SSE, is similar to the Dow Jones index, whereas the CSI 300 index, which includes 300 largest stocks traded on the SSE and SZSE, is similar to the S&P 500 index.

Broadly speaking, two types of financial options are available in China now. One is options written on ETFs that track major market indices, which will be referred to as ETF options. Another is options written directly on major market indices, which will be

Table 1: Exchange-traded financial options in China

	ETF Options			Index Options
Products	SSE 50 ETF Option China AMC	CSI 300 ETF Option Huatai-Pinebridge AMC	CSI 300 ETF Option Harvest AMC	CSI 300 Index Option
Launch	2015/2/9	2019/12/23	2019/12/23	2019/12/23
Underlying	SSE 50 ETF China AMC	CSI 300 ETF Huatai-Pinebridge AMC	CSI 300 ETF Harvest AMC	CSI 300 Index
Exchanges	SSE	SSE	SZSE	CFFEX

referred to as index options. While ETF options are listed on stock exchanges (SSE an SZSE), index options are listed on financial futures exchanges (CFFEX). The underlying assets for the ETF options include both the SSE 50 ETF and the CSI 300 ETFs, whereas the only underlying asset for the index options is the CSI 300 index. All options are European with calls and puts listed.

On February 9, 2015, the SSE officially launched the very first financial option in China, the SSE 50 ETF option, where the underlying asset is the SSE 50 ETF managed by the China AMC. However, the launches of other options were significantly delayed by the crash of the Chinese stock market in the summer of 2015 and the circuit breaker disaster in early 2016. Only after the market had been stabilized for a few years, were new financial options started to be introduced. On December 23, 2019, two ETF options and one index option based on the CSI 300 index were introduced. One ETF option is listed on the SSE, whose underlying is the CSI 300 ETF managed by the Huatai-Pinebridge Asset Management Company (Huatai-Pinebridge AMC) and listed on the SSE. The other ETF option is listed on the SZSE, whose underlying is the CSI 300 ETF managed by the Harvest Asset Management Company (Harvest AMC) and listed on the SZSE. The index option is listed on the CFFEX.

The underlying asset of each SSE 50 ETF option is 10,000 shares of the SSE 50 ETF. The SSE 50 ETF options mature on the fourth Wednesday of each of the four maturity months: the current month, the next month, and the following 2 months of the March–June–September–December cycle. Since January, 2018, at the inception of options with each maturity, there are four OTM and ITM options and one ATM option. Before that, there were only two OTM and ITM options and one ATM option.

Figure 1(a) reports daily open interests and trading volume of all the SSE 50 ETF options available on each day from February, 2015 to April, 2021. It is clear that the liquidity of the SSE 50 ETF options market has increased significantly since its launch in early 2015, with daily trading volume reaching a few million contracts per day in recent years. In data not shown here, we see that the ratio between trading volume and open interests since 2017 has been above 50%, suggesting a very active trading market. The price of the SSE 50 ETF ranged between 2 and 4 rmb with an average price of about 3 rmb during this time.

Table 2 reports summary information of open interests and trading volume of the SSE 50 ETF call and put options for the whole year of 2019 and 2020. In 2019 and 2020, the total trading volume of the SSE 50 ETF options is 618 million and 518.5 million contracts, respectively, with an average daily trading volume of 2.53 million and 2.13 million contracts, respectively, and average daily open interests

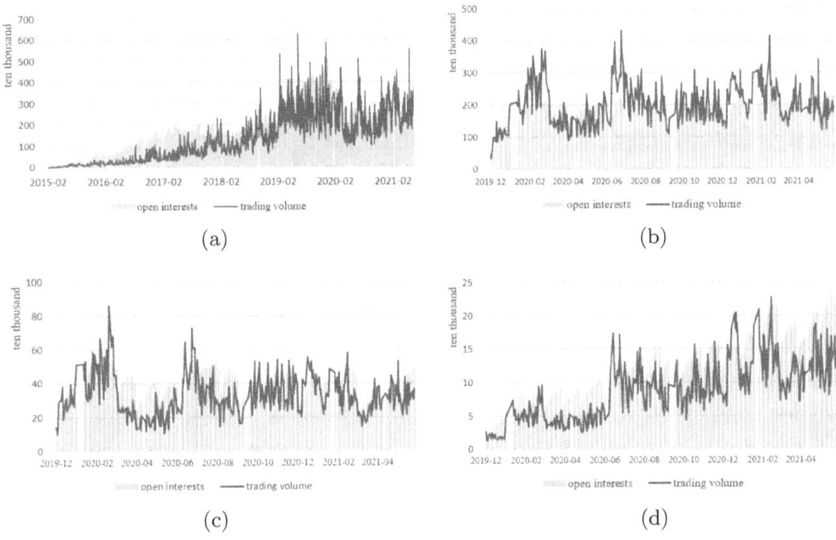

Figure 1: Daily trading volume and open interests of ETF and index options. (a) SSE 50 ETF options; (b) Huatai CSI 300 ETF options; (c) Jiashi CSI 300 ETF options and (d) CSI 300 index options.

of 3.42 million and 2.79 million contracts, respectively. In 2019 and 2020, the total trading volume in terms of notional values is 17.7 trillion rmb and 16.3 trillion rmb, respectively, with an average daily trading volume in terms of notional values of 72.5 billion rmb and 67 billion rmb, respectively, and an average daily trading volume in terms of option premiums of 1.3 billion rmb in both years. In total, there were about 460k contracts exercised in 2019 and 2020, which represent about 85% and 93% of all the ITM options on maturity dates, respectively.

Table 2 clearly shows that the SSE 50 ETF options market has become very liquid, with daily trading volume in terms of notional value (option premium) of about 1 billion US dollars (200 million US dollars), on par with that of some of the most liquid ETF options in the world. Table 2 also shows that call options enjoy higher trading volume and open interests than put options, an interesting phenomenon in China. In general, it is difficult to obtain leverage in Chinese stock market. The built-in leverage of call options, especially deep OTM call options make them very attractive for speculation purpose and consequently increase their usage. Individual investors also like to use calls to "buy the dip" due to the limited downside risk.

Figures 1(b), (c), and (d) present the daily open interests and trading volume of the Huatai-Pinebridge CSI 300 ETF options, the Harvest CSI 300 ETF options, and the CSI 300 index options, respectively. Compared to the SSE 50 index, the CSI 300 index has broader coverage in terms of sectors, industries, and market capitalizations. There are also many more funds that either track or use the CSI 300 index as a benchmark for performance. As a result, the CSI 300 options quickly overtake the SSE 50 options as the most popular index options in China. After their introductions in late 2019, the trading volume and open interests of both CSI 300 ETF options have quickly risen to about 2.5 million contracts per day. While the underlying asset of the CSI 300 ETF options is also 10,000 shares of the CSI 300 ETFs, the price per share ranged between 4 and 6 rmb with an average of about 5 rmb in recent years. Therefore, collectively the trading volume in terms of notional values of the three CSI 300 options is about twice of that of the SSE 50 options. The Huatai-Pinebridge CSI 300 ETF options are more liquid than the Harvest CSI 300 ETF options, mainly because the size of the

Table 2: Open interests and trading volume of the SSE 50 ETF options.

		2020			2019		
		Calls	Puts	Both	Calls	Puts	Both
Trading Volume (10,000 contracts)	Total	28919.19	22930.91	51850.10	33922.89	27880.88	61803.77
	Daily Mean	119.01	94.37	213.37	139.03	114.27	253.29
	Daily Max	—	—	510.12	—	—	626.67
	Daily Min	—	—	96.53	—	—	87.13
Trading Volume (Notional: 100m rmb)	Total	92986.96	69998.52	162985.48	98832.24	78248.33	177080.57
	Daily Mean	382.66	288.06	670.72	405.05	320.69	725.74
	Daily Max	—	—	1656.38	—	—	1810.09
	Daily Min	—	—	266.76	—	—	203.31
Trading Volume (Option Premium: 100m rmb)	Total	1797.10	1390.38	3187.49	1998.46	1360.67	3359.12
	Daily Mean	7.40	5.72	13.12	8.19	5.58	13.77
	Daily Max	—	—	58.01	—	—	38.25
	Daily Min	—	—	4.51	—	—	3.90
Open Interests (10,000 contracts)	Total	129.55	115.87	245.42	199.36	179.78	379.14
	Daily Mean	151.52	127.29	278.81	179.23	162.77	342.00
	Daily Max	—	—	412.46	—	—	515.25
	Daily Min	—	—	179.46	—	—	182.24
Options Exercised	Exercised (10,000 contracts)	25.25	20.75	46.00	27.53	19.29	46.82
	Exercised(%)	92.53%	94.05%	93.21%	80.49%	93.35%	85.34%

underlying Huatai-Pinebridge 300 ETF is much bigger than that of the Harvest 300 ETF. It also helps that the Huatai-Pinebridge 300 ETF is listed on the SSE, a default trading platform for large stocks, whereas the Harvest 300 ETF is listed on the SZSE, a popular choice for trading smaller stocks. The two CSI 300 ETF options are more liquid than the CSI 300 index options, because the notional value of the two ETF options is about one tenth of that of the index options.

2.2 *Commodity options*

As the second largest economy in the world with 1.4 billion people, China has become the largest consumer and importer of raw materials in recent years. Not surprisingly, commodity trading has also become very active in China with three well established commodity futures exchanges: the DCE (established on February 28, 1993), the ZCE (established on October 12, 1990), and the SCE (established on November 26, 1990). According to Statista, in 2019, the trading volume was about 1.3 billion contracts for DCE, 1.1 billion contracts for ZCE, and 1.4 billion contracts for the SCE, whereas the trading volume for the CME group was about 4.8 billion contracts. Collectively with more than 60 listed commodities, the three Chinese commodity exchanges are among the largest commodity markets in the world.

Table 3 reports major commodity options listed on the three commodity exchanges in China with their launching dates.

Table 3: Listed commodity options in China.

Dalian Commodity Exchange (DCE)		Zhengzhou Commodity Exchange (ZCE)		Shanghai Commodity Exchange (SCE)	
Launch	Contract	Launch	Contract	Launch	Contract
2017/3/31	Soybean Meal	2017/4/19	Sugar	2018/9/21	Copper
2019/1/28	Corn	2019/1/28	Cotton	2019/1/28	Rubber
2019/12/9	Iron Ore	2019/12/26	PTA	2019/12/20	Gold
2020/3/30	LPG	2019/12/26	Methanol	2020/8/10	Aluminum
2020/7/6	PP	2020/1/16	Rapeseed Meal	2020/8/10	Zinc
2020/7/6	PVC	2020/6/30	Thermal Coal		
2020/7/6	LLDPE				

While Chinese regulators are very careful in rolling out financial derivatives, they are more willing to introduce commodity derivatives. It is widely perceived that commodity derivatives can help the real economy by providing commodity producers and consumers with important tools for managing risks, whereas financial derivatives are generally perceived as not directly related to the real economy. As a result, within about three and half years after the introduction of the first commodity option in China in March 2017, 17 more commodity options had been listed rather evenly on the three commodity exchanges.

Table 4 reports the daily average of trading volume and open interests of all the commodity options available between 2017 and 2020. Despite the wide varieties, the liquidities of these options are rather poor. For example, the first listed commodity option, the Soybean meal option, is the most liquid among all the options. Yet, its highest average daily trading volume was about 150k contracts and its highest open interest was about 600k contracts, both in 2019. In contrast, the daily average of trading volume and open interests for financial options were in the order of several millions of contracts. Many other contracts are much less liquid, with average daily trading volume and open interests even less than 10k contracts.

2.3 *Market participants*

Chinese regulators impose stringent eligibility requirements that individual investors must satisfy in order to participate in the options market. Table 5 shows that an investor must have 500k rmb cash in his or her account in order to trade index or ETF options and 100k rmb cash to trade commodity options. Investors must have enough experiences of actual or simulated trading in futures or options. They must also demonstrate good command of the knowledge of financial derivatives by passing exams administered by relevant exchanges and show no history of bad credits. As a result, only the most sophisticated individual investors are able to participate in the options market.

Currently the total number of options accounts has surpassed half million. Figure 2(a) shows that 44% of the participants in the SSE 50 ETF options market are individual investors, 35% are market makers, and 21% are institutional investors. Figure 2(b) shows that

Table 4: Daily average of trading volume and open interests of commodity options.

Unit 10,000 Contracts		2017		2018		2019		2020	
		Trading Volume	Open Interests	Trading Volume	Open Interests	Trading Volume	Open Interests	Trading Volume	Open Interests
DCE	Soybean Meal	3.9	23.1	10.3	45.7	14.6	58.1	10.3	49.8
	Corn					6	57.5	4.1	28.7
	Iron Ore					4.3	13.8	4.4	15.1
	LPG							0.6	3.2
	PP							0.9	2.5
	PVC							0.5	1.3
	LLDPE							0.6	1.9
ZCE	Sugar	1.7	11.3	3.8	22.8	5.6	26.3	2.5	14.1
	Cotton					3.1	16.2	1.9	10.1
	PTA					3.2	6	2.6	13.9
	Methanol					2.9	4.7	2.2	10.7
	Rapeseed Meal							1.3	4.3
	Thermal Coal							1.7	4.3
SCE	Copper			3.7	4.4	3.4	6.8	1.8	3.8
	Rubber					0.7	4.1	0.6	3.1
	Gold					1	1.5	0.9	2.9
	Aluminum							0.3	0.8
	Zinc							0.6	0.9

Table 5: Investor eligibility requirements for trading options.

	Cash in Account	Trading Experiences	Professional Tests	Bad Credit
Index options	500,000 rmb	>10 actual trades >20 simulated trades	Pass score: 80	No record
ETF options	500,000 rmb	>6 months active accounts	Pass score depends on the exchange	No record
Commodity options	100,000 rmb	>20 simulated trades	Pass score depends on the exchange	No record

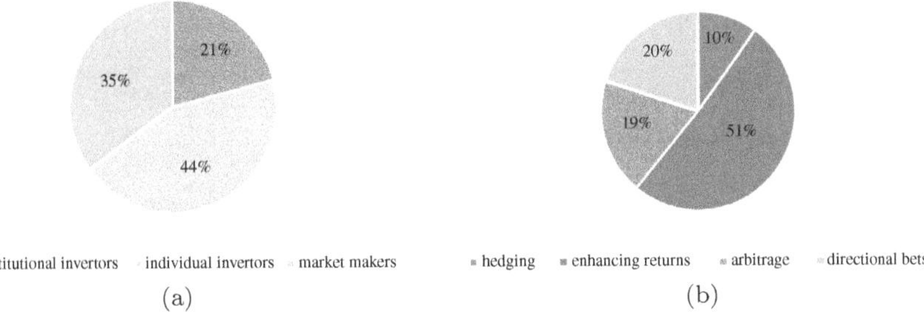

Figure 2: (a) Investors of these SSE 50 ETF options and (b) investment objectives of the SSE 50 ETF options.

51% of the investors in the SSE 50 ETF options have an objective of enhancing returns, 20% directional bets, 19% arbitrage, and 10% hedging. While institutional investors care more about enhancing returns and arbitrage, individual investors are more concerned with enhancing returns and directional bets.

Table 6 reports investor preferences over six different ways of trading options: Open long position, open short position, open covered position, close long position, close short position, and close covered position. It is interesting to see that individual investors are more likely to buy options, whereas institutional investors are likely to short options. About 62% of the opening trades for individual investors are long options, and about 77% of the opening trades for institutional investors are short options. Relatively

Table 6: Trade preferences of individual and institutional investors (2020).

	Individual Investors (%)	Institutional Investors (%)	Both (%)
Open long position	14.22	6.76	20.98
Open short position	8.64	23.86	32.50
Open covered position	0.04	0.02	0.06
Close short position	7.99	20.98	28.97
Close long position	13.26	4.18	17.44
Close covered position	0.03	0.02	0.05
Total	44.18	55.82	100.00

speaking, institutional investors are more likely to trade put options than individual investors.

3. Pricing Anomalies

In this section, we will discuss several interesting pricing anomalies in the Chinese options markets. In particular, we will look into the unique institutional features in China that lead to these anomalies. These results suggest that special attentions must be paid to studying option prices in China.

3.1 *Pricing efficiency*

Figure 3(a)–(c) reports the implied volatilities the SSE 50 ETF options with 30 days to maturity on April 29, 2015 (about 3 months after the first launch) and June 5, 2017. For comparison, it also reports the implied volatilities of the S&P 500 index options on the latter date.

It is interesting to see that the IV curve of the SSE 50 ETF options in early days does not resemble that of matured options markets. Instead, it seems to offer abundant arbitrage opportunities for sophisticated investors. About 2 years later, the IV curve of the SSE 50 ETF options displays the standard smirk as the S&P 500 index options. Since participants in the Chinese options markets

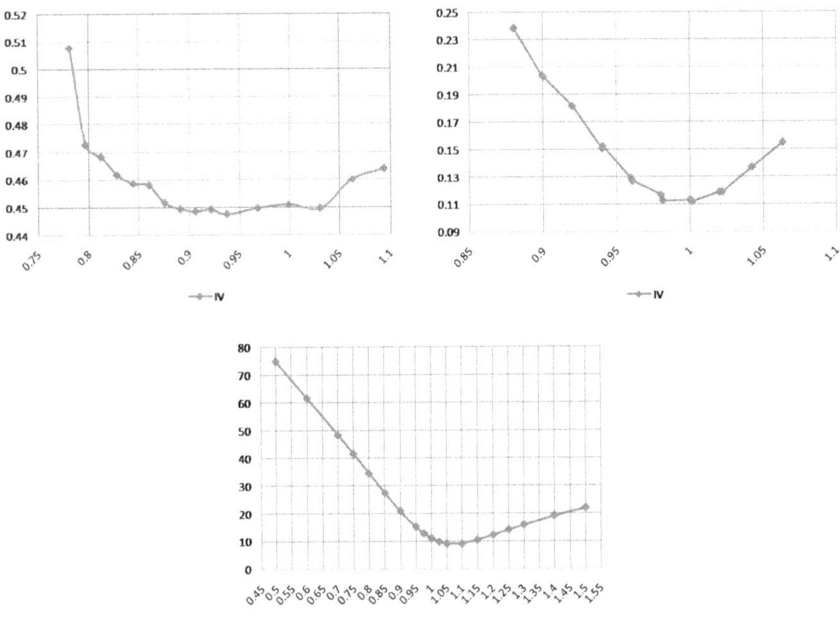

Figure 3: Implied volatilities of 30-day options. (a) IV of 30-day 50 ETF options: 2015/4/29; (b) IV of 30-day 50 ETF options: 2017/6/5 and (c) IV of 30-day S&P 500 options: 2017/6/5.

are either institutional investors or relatively sophisticated individual investors, the market became efficient relatively quickly. In contrast, in the US options market, the smirk emerged only after the 1987 stock market crash.

3.2 *Violation of the put-call parity*

Figure 4 reports the implied volatilities of the SSE 50 ETF calls and puts with 30 days to maturity on June 5, 2017. In a perfect market with no arbitrage, the put-call parity should hold and the implied volatilities of call and put with same maturity and strike should be the same. However, the implied volatilities of the puts are generally higher than that of the corresponding calls. In China, the high borrowing costs for shorting dramatically increase the replication costs of puts, which lead to higher implied volatilities. Since such restrictions

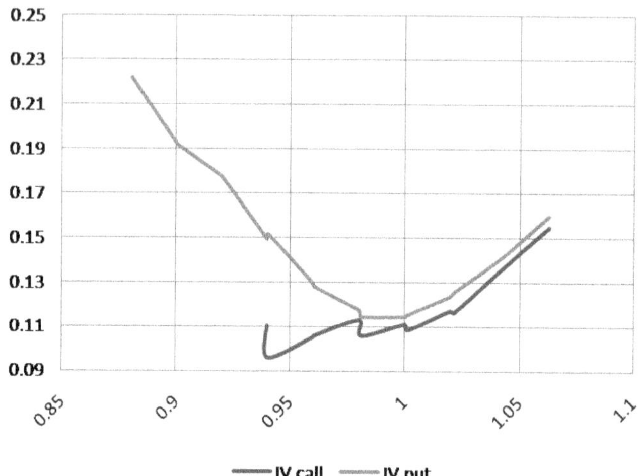

Figure 4: Implied volatilities of 30-day 50 ETF calls and puts: 2017/6/5.

still persist today, one needs to be careful in constructing implied volatilities in China.

3.3 *Negative time value of money*

Table 7 reports the intrinsic values, settlement prices, and close prices of the SSE 50 ETF calls and puts with 6 days to maturity on March 15, 2017. The options include deep ITM and OTM calls and puts. It is interesting to see that for deep ITM calls, their intrinsic values are higher than the corresponding settlement and close prices, implying negative time value of money.

The SSE 50 ETF options mature on the fourth Wednesday of the maturity month, and Wednesday is the last day for exercising the options. However, the owner of the option can only receive the shares on Thursday and has to wait until Friday to sell the shares. Consequently, the owner has to bear the downside risk of the shares for one day, for which effective hedging is not available due to the high cost of shorting. As a result, most owners of deep ITM calls would rather sell the calls before expiration than exercise them, leading to negative time value of money.

Table 7: Time values of money for 6-day 50 ETF options: 2017/3/16.

Intrinsic Value (Call)	Settlement (Call)	Close (Call)	Strike	Close (Put)	Settlement (Put)	Intrinsic Value (Put)
0.315	0.3144	0.3144	2.055	0.0001	0.0002	0
0.266	0.265	0.2649	2.104	0.0001	0.0002	0
0.217	0.2161	0.2161	2.153	0.0001	0.0002	0
0.17	0.1693	0.1693	2.2	0.0002	0.0002	0
0.168	0.1674	0.1674	2.202	0.0001	0.0002	0
0.12	0.1196	0.1196	2.25	0.0004	0.0004	0
0.12	0.1196	0.1196	2.25	0.0002	0.0004	0
0.071	0.0717	0.0717	2.299	0.0006	0.0006	0
0.07	0.07	0.07	2.3	0.0006	0.0006	0
0.022	0.0266	0.0266	2.348	0.0038	0.0036	0
0.02	0.0254	0.0254	2.35	0.0036	0.0036	0
0	0.0043	0.0043	2.397	0.0305	0.0305	0.027
0	0.004	0.004	2.4	0.0321	0.0321	0.03
0	0.0006	0.0006	2.446	0.0769	0.077	0.076
0	0.0006	0.0006	2.45	0.0796	0.081	0.08
0	0.0003	0.0003	2.495	0.1242	0.1263	0.125
0	0.0003	0.0002	2.5	0.1292	0.131	0.13
0	0.0002	0.0002	2.55	0.179	0.181	0.18

3.4 *Correlation between stock price and implied volatility*

Figure 5 plots the daily implied volatility of the SSE 50 ETF options and closing price of the underlying ETF shares, while Table 8 reports the correlation between the two variables in each year since the introduction of the options in early 2015.

We see a significant negative correlation between implied volatility and underlying price in developed markets. However, in China we seem to observe the opposite effects. Out of the 6 years between 2015 and 2021, we observe significant positive correlation in 3 years, and zero correlation in 2 years, and negative correlation in only 2 years.

One of the main reasons for this result is that many individual investors tend to use options, especially calls, for leverage purpose. They rush to buy calls when they think the underlying market is rising, and their interests in options decline in side way markets.

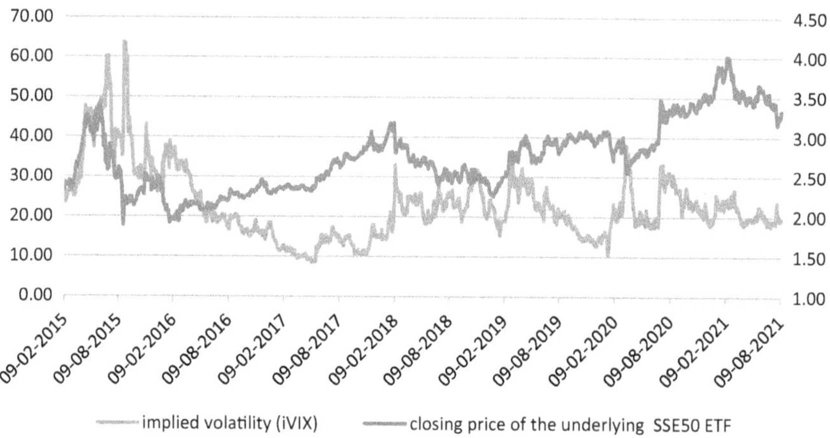

Figure 5: Implied volatility of 50 ETF options and ETF share prices.

Table 8: Correlation between implied volatility of 50 ETF options and ETF share prices.

Year	2015	2016	2017	2018	2019	2020	2021
Correlation	0.38	−0.76	0.69	−0.03	−0.55	0.07	0.62

3.5 *Risk premium of commodity options*

Figure 6 reports the implied volatility and historical volatility of Soybean meal contracts traded on the DCE and the CME between March and August 2017. It is interesting to see at the DCE, there is no significant difference between the implied and historical volatilities, whereas at the CME, the implied volatilities are significantly higher than the historical volatilities. Therefore, while one can earn significant risk premium by selling volatility at the CME, such risk premium does not seem to exist at the DCE.

One main reason for this result is that companies in China with significant hedging demands have not actively participated in the commodities markets for risk management purpose due to various

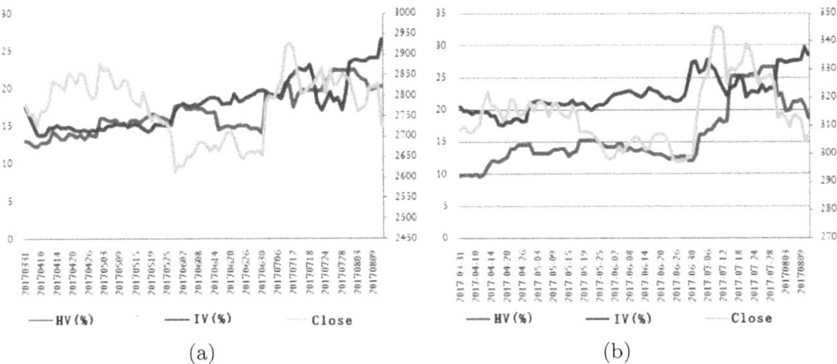

Figure 6: Volatility risk premium of soybean meal options. (a) Main contract (DCE) and (b) Main contract (CME).

concerns. High profile losses due to hedging at several top SOEs make executives reluctant to engage in such programs. Current accounting practices also increase the complexities of hedge programs, especially for publicly traded companies. Without the end buyers of insurance, it is not surprising that insurance premium does not appear in market prices.

4. Conclusion

In this chapter, we have provided a brief overview of the fast growing options markets in China. Compared to other markets, the Chinese options markets are still in their infancy. The most liquid options are a handful of ETF and index options, while options on individual stocks still do not exist. Even though a wide range of commodity options have been introduced, their liquidities are still quite low. However, with continued growth of the Chinese financial markets and the shift of wealth allocation from real estates to financial assets, the potentials for options in China are limitless. The unique institutional features of the Chinese financial markets raise challenges for pricing options in China but also provide excellent opportunities for future research. Therefore, we believe options markets in China provide the most exciting new frontier for both practitioners and academics to explore.

Acknowledgment

We thank the Gershon Fintech Center at the Hebrew University of Jerusalem for the opportunity to present this chapter at the conference, *Options: 45 Years after the Publication of the Black Scholes Merton Model*. We would like to thank the participants of the conference for comments and suggestions. In particular, we would like to thank David Gershon and Alex Lipton for their patience and encouragements.

References

[1] Black, F. and Scholes, M. (1973). The pricing of options and corporate liabilities. *Journal of Political Economy*, 81, 637–654.
[2] Merton, R.C. (1973). Theory of rational of option pricing. *Bell Journal of Economics*, 1, 141–183.
[3] The Shanghai Stock Exchange (2020). *The Shanghai Stock Exchange Annual Report on the Developments of Options Markets (Chinese)*, pp. 1–59.

https://doi.org/10.1142/9789811259142_0022

Chapter 22

Risk Exposure Valuation Using Measure Distortions: An Overview

D. B. Madan

Robert H. Smith School of Business
University of Maryland
College Park, USA

dbm@umd.edu

1. Introduction

Two questions are addressed for which the possibly novel answers provided differ from widely held classical views on these matters. The questions, answers, and applications are the subject matter addressed in much greater detail in Madan and Schoutens [10]. The questions are (1) What is risk? and (2) How to value risk? The classical answer to the first question defines risk as a random variable described by the probabilities for different outcomes. For the second question the value of risk in arbitrage free markets is an expectation conducted under an equivalent change of probability. Numerous papers, books and textbooks make this presentation.

Risk will here not be viewed as an outcome, but an exposure to a potential instantaneous change in value. It is described not by a probability, but by the arrival rate associated to various possible changes. Typically the aggregate arrival rate across all possibilities will be infinite with the very small changes near zero having the possibly infinite measure, thereby encapsulating the idea that it is nothing that happens all the time and interesting things only happen with a finite arrival rate.

For the valuation of risk we take a two price economy perspective as described in Madan and Schoutens [9] and the papers cited therein. Unlike classical valuation that delivers a linear valuation operator on the space of random variables, the two price perspective leads to a nonlinear concave valuation operator on the space of either random variables [9]) or the space of risk exposures Madan and Schoutens [10].

The outline for the rest of this overview is as follows. Section 2 outlines some of the unfortunate consequences of the law of one price. Section 3 introduces the two price economy perspective and its financial relevance. Section 4. introduces distorted expectations as an operational easily implementable conservative vlauation. Section 5 makes the move from random outcomes to risk exposures. Section 6 generalizes distorted expectations to measure distortions to cope with risk exposures. Section 7 presents some illustrative applications. Section 8 concludes.

2. Issues with the Law of One Price

For two random outcomes X, Y in the absence of arbitrage and under the law of one price under which one buy or sell random outcomes at the same price or the value the value of the package $\alpha X + \beta Y$, $V(\alpha X + \beta Y)$ must be

$$V(\alpha X + \beta Y) = \alpha V(X) + \beta V(Y). \tag{1}$$

This required linearity of valuation was noted for example in Ross [12]. Once the linearity is recognized one soon arrives at the classical valuation principle of expectation under a change of probability, that may be termed the pricing probability.

There are some unfortunate consequences of such a valuation principle. For example the value of hedged position is the sum of the value of the target and and the value of the hedge. With a zero cost financed hedge, this value is just the value of the target and there is no value maximizing hedge. Similarly, the value of a portfolio is the sum of the values of the components. For a fixed dollar investment, there is then no value maximizing portfolio.

Hence, some simple and important financial problems have no answers from a value maximizing perspective. In fact, the maximization of market value has long been advocated as an objective for financial decision making with some classic pieces being Milton Freidmans' article in the *New York Times*, September 13, 1970 and Jensen [7]. But there are no solutions interior to a set of possibilities for a linear objective. This has been a classic problem for a theory of the firm [11].

The literature has sought other personalized solutions to the various financial problems, like constructing utility maximizing hedges and portfolios, but such solutions give up on the essential theme of entrusting economic decisions away from persons or committees thereof, towards markets. With a view towards maintaining a market based answer to financial questions we are led to re-evaluate the law of one price itself.

Perhaps the law of one price takes too generous a view of markets. A hint in this direction is offered by the concept of acceptable risks as defined in Artzner *et al.* [1]. Noting that nonnegative random outcomes are acceptable to everyone at zero cost, Artzner *et al.* [1] define acceptable risks more generally as a convex cone of random variables that contains the nonnegative random variables. From this perspective the set of acceptable risks embedded in the law of one price is very large indeed. A purchase/sale at a price below/above the market price is acceptable to all. This makes the set of acceptable risks those with a positive expectation under the pricing probability. Such a convex set is so large that there is no larger convex set and we have what is called a half space. Figure 1 presents a graph illustrating aribtrages, positive values, and more realistic sets of acceptable risks.

Under the law of one price the set of traded claims is closed under negation and this is will not be true for acceptable risks more narrowly defined. If the set of traded claims are modeled by the more narrowly defined acceptable risks then the law of one price fails. If the traded claims form a cone of random outcomes closed under positive scalar multiples then one arrives at a two price economy. If the conic structure is removed then prices will depend on the size of the trade as well. They may be futher made to depend on the time period over which the trade is to be executed, and the credit ratings of the counterparties involved. Given the extensive on the law of one

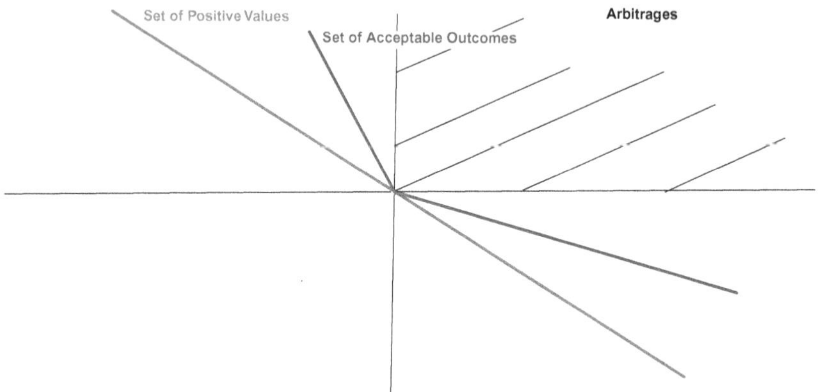

Figure 1: Graph displaying arbitrages, acceptable outcomes, and those with a positive market value.

price we maintain the other assumptions and just entertain a two price framework.

3. The Two Price Framework

It is shown in Artzner *et al.* [1] that all convex cones of acceptable risks are equivalently defined as those having positive expectations under a convex set of test probabilities Q, for all probabilities $Q \in \mathcal{M}$, where $\mathcal{M}$ is the set of all test probabilities. More formally the set of acceptable risks $\mathcal{A}$ is given by

$$\mathcal{A} = \left\{ X | \; E^Q[X] \geq 0, \quad \text{for all } Q \in \mathcal{M} \right\}. \tag{2}$$

Selling X for the price $b(X)$ or buying it for price $a(X)$ requires that the outcomes $X - b(X)$ and $a(X) - X$ be acceptable to the market. It follows that the best of highest price one may sell at, or the best of lowest price one may buy for, are given by

$$b(X) = \inf_{Q \in \mathcal{M}} E^Q[X], \tag{3}$$

$$a(X) = \sup_{Q \in \mathcal{M}} E^Q[X]. \tag{4}$$

The lower or bid price of a two price economy is then a concave function of the random outcomes given the infimum. Similarly, the upper or ask price of a two price economy is a convex function of the outcomes. The former is a candidate for maximizing asset values while the latter is a candidate for minimizing the value of liabilities. Value maximizing hedges and portfolio constructions are then restored.

Furthermore, mathematically the relationship between infima and suprema delivers the equation

$$b(X) = -a(-X). \tag{5}$$

The same may be observed by noting the equivalence between selling X and buying $-X$.

Interestingly, one also obtains an interesting new perspective on efficient frontiers. For an position acquired one may view the reward as the expectation of $E[X]$. The centered variate

$$Z = X - E[X], \tag{6}$$

is then pure risk. To eliminate this risk one has to acquire the negative for its ask price that constitutes a risk charge of

$$\rho(X) = a\left(E[X] - X\right). \tag{7}$$

It follows from equation (5) that the lower value to be maximized is also the reward less the risk charge or

$$b(X) = E[X] - \rho(X). \tag{8}$$

Figure 2 presents a graph of a point on such an efficient frontier that is a value maximizing point.

Additionally, one may define

$$\mathcal{L} = \left\{X \mid E^{Q}[X] = 0, \quad \text{all } Q \in \mathcal{M}\right\}, \tag{9}$$

as the liquid assets for which the law of one price holds and that price is zero. The collection $\mathcal{L}$ is a subspace of the space of all risks and one define two risks to be equivalent if the difference belongs to $\mathcal{L}$. The law of one price then fails for all equivalence classes of risks that may be viewed as the risky outcomes. The class $\mathcal{L}$ is equivalent to zero and thereby not a risk. For all truly risky outcomes the market can only deliver the two prices in any two price economy. There is no longer any sense of a bidirectional price for any risky outcome.

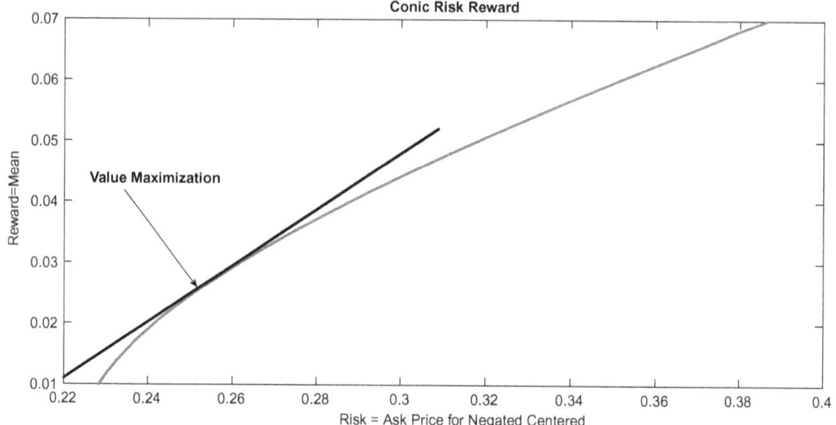

Figure 2: Conic value maximization as a risk reward frontier.

4. Conservative Valuation and Distorted Expectations

Distorted expectations form a particular example of conservative valuations. First one may learn from Kusuoka [5] that if the lower valuation depends solely on the probability law of a risk and furthermore if it is additive for comonotone risks than the lower valuation must be a distorted expectation. The assumption of depending only on the probability law is termed law invariance and the second is termed comonotone additivity. Many classical decision criteria, like expected utility, or mean–variance analysis satisfy law invariance. Comonotone risks are increasing monotonic transformations of each other with little or no possibilities of providing diversification benefits and hence additive of value across such risks is reasonable. Under these two assumptions, the valuation becomes a distorted expectation.

Specifically, there must exist a concave distribution function $\Psi(u)$, defined on the unit interval, $0 \leq u \leq 1$ such that for any random variable or outcome X with distribution function $F_X(x)$ it is the case that

$$b(X) = \int_{-\infty}^{\infty} x \, d\Psi \left(F_X(x) \right). \tag{10}$$

Equivalently one may write

$$b(X) = \int_{-\infty}^{\infty} x\Psi' \left(F_X(x) \right) dF_X(x). \tag{11}$$

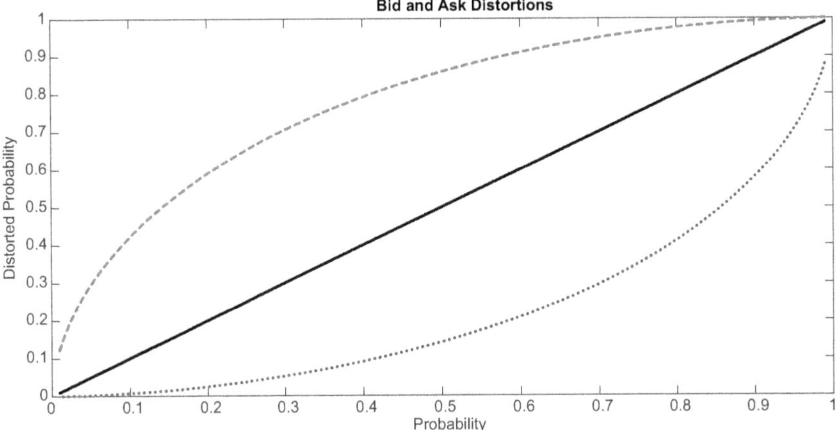

Figure 3: Bid and ask distortions.

One observes from Equation (11) that a distorted expectation is an expectation under the change of probability $\Psi'(F_X(x))$ which lifts the weights on losses when $F_X(x)$ is near zero and reduces the weight on gains when $F_X(x)$ is near unity.

The set of test probabilities $\mathcal{M}$ supporting distorted expectations as a lower valuation of a two price economy is the set of all probability measures Q satisfying

$$Q(A) \leq \Psi(P(A)), \quad \text{for all } A, \text{ with } P(A) > 0. \tag{12}$$

The ask price is also a distorted expectation using the convex, complementary distortion $\widehat{\Psi}(u)$ where

$$\widehat{\Psi}(u) = 1 - \Psi(1-u). \tag{13}$$

Figure 3 presents a graph of a concave distortion and its complementary convex distortion.

5. Risk as Exposure and Its Valuation

Probability is a relativized frequency of events, relativized or normalized by the total probability of all possible events. If we think of the events of interest as the exposure to instantaneous changes in value occurring at different frequencies or arrival rates the total frequency or aggregate arrival rate in models of Lévy processes is infinite. In fact for all limit laws or self decomposible laws as studied by Lévy [6] and Khintchine [3] and explained more recently in Sato [13] it is necessarily infinite. This leads us to consider describing risks more generally by the measure of the unrelativized frequency or arrival rates. We may the describe the exposure by the instantaneous Lévy measure for the arrival rate of moves of different sizes with the aggregate arrival rate being infinity. Of course the infinite measure is concentrated near zero with all finite moves away from zero having a finite arrival rate. The only events happening infinitely often are events near zero, or in other words, we may say that nothing happens all the time.

We therefore replace events as outcomes x described by their probability densities $f(x)$ integrating to unity by exposure to jump sizes $x \neq 0$ described by arrival rates $k(x)$ integrating to infinity. For the parametric bilateral gamma model [4] written as the difference of two independent gamma processes with speed and scale coefficients c_p, b_p and c_n, b_n for the positive and negative moves respectively, the Lévy density is given by

$$k(x) = c_p \frac{e^{-x/b_p}}{x} \mathbf{1}_{x>0} + c_n \frac{e^{-|x|/b_n}}{|x|} \mathbf{1}_{x<0}. \tag{14}$$

The division by x, necessary for limit laws, makes the aggregate arrival rate infinite. We estimate the bilateral gamma model on data for returns on the S&P 500 index for the year 2017 to obtain the parameter values

$$\begin{aligned} b_p &= 0.0030, \\ c_p &= 1.2178, \\ b_n &= 0.0028, \\ c_n &= 0.7130. \end{aligned} \tag{15}$$

If we work with the arrival rate function directly at the instantaneous level one cannot employ probability distortions for conservative valuation as we do not have a probability in place. Madan *et al.* [8] introduced the concept of measure distortions for this purpose. Let G^+, G^- be two increasing functions on the positive half line with G^+

concave and above the identity and G^- convex and below the identity with both zero at zero. The measure distorted lower value of an exposure X on an infinite measure μ is defined as measure distorted variation in Choquet form by

$$b(X) = -\int_0^\infty G^+\left(\mu\left(X < -a\right)\right) da + \int_0^\infty G^-\left(\mu\left(X > a\right)\right) da. \tag{16}$$

The upper value is given by

$$a(X) = -\int_0^\infty G^-\left(\mu\left(X < -a\right)\right) da + \int_0^\infty G^+\left(\mu\left(X > a\right)\right) da. \tag{17}$$

In terms of our Lévy density

$$\mu(A) = \int_A k(x)dx. \tag{18}$$

The measure distorted valuations may be seen as conservative valuations using a set of supporting measures $\mathcal{M}$ by

$$b(X) = \inf_{\widetilde{\nu}\in\mathcal{M}} \int X(\omega)\widetilde{\nu}(d\omega), \tag{19}$$

$$a(X) = \sup_{\widetilde{\nu}\in\mathcal{M}} \int X(\omega)\widetilde{\nu}(d\omega). \tag{20}$$

The set of supporting measures is defined by $\widetilde{\nu} \in \mathcal{M}$ just if

$$G^-\left(\nu(A)\right) \leq \widetilde{\nu}(A) \leq G^+\left(\nu(A)\right), \quad \text{for all } A \text{ with } 0 < \nu(A) < \infty. \tag{21}$$

Figure 4 presents an illustration of a pair of measure distortions.

The parametric measure distortions we employ are

$$G^+(x) = x + a(1 - e^{-cx})^{\frac{1}{1+\gamma}}, \tag{22}$$

$$G^-(x) = x - \frac{b}{c}(1 - e^{-cx}), \tag{23}$$

that were introduced in Eberlein *et al.* [2]. We take as an example $a = b/c$, $b = 1$, $c = 0.5$, and $\gamma = 1$.

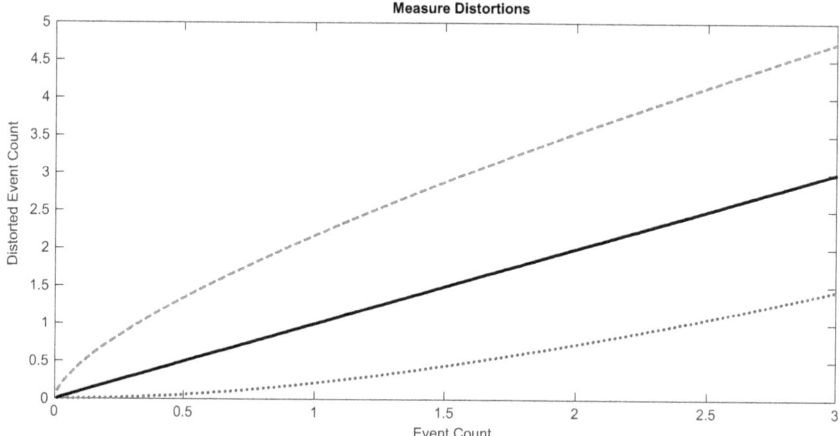

Figure 4: Example of measure distortions.

6. Applications

Two applications are presented in the following subsections. The first deals with hedging an instantaneous exposure. The second optimizes a portfolio exposure.

6.1 *A hedging example*

Consider a negative gamma exposure with liability to a log price relative x of

$$-\frac{1}{2}\left(e^{x}-1\right)^{2}. \tag{24}$$

Consider in addition holding θ units of stock to access the exposure

$$\theta\left(e^{x}-1\right). \tag{25}$$

For the presented bilateral gamma estimated parameters the measure distorted value is maximized at a positive stock position for a zero delta exposure as presented in Figure 5.

6.2 *Portfolio allocation example*

Suppose we have estimated bilateral gamma marginals for a set of n stock returns with marginal parameters $b_{pj}, c_{pj}, b_{nj},$

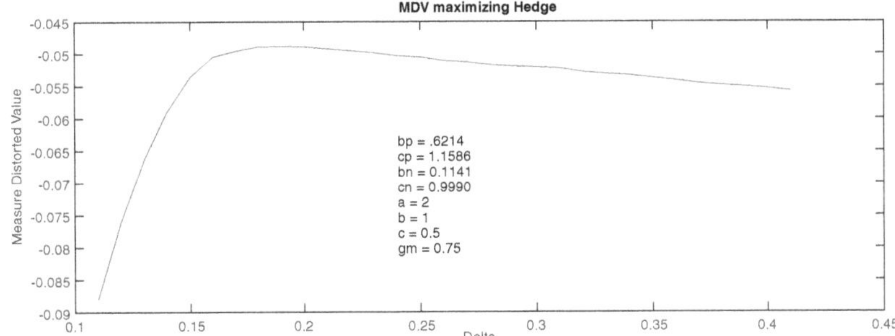

Figure 5: Value maximizing hedge for a unit gamma zero delta exposure in bilateral gamma returns. The bilateral gamma and measure distortion parameters are as reported.

$c_{nj} = b_{jp}, c_{jp}, b_{jn}, c_{jn}$ for $j = 1, \ldots, n$. There exists a multivariate jump arrival rate with full support on $\mathbb{R}^n$ consistent with the marginal jump arrival rates. The resulting model is multivariate VG with independent bilateral gamma shocks added on for each component.

The multivariate VG has the multivariate characteristic function

$$\Phi(u) = \left(\frac{1}{1 - i(\mu' u)\nu + \frac{\nu}{2} u' \Sigma u} \right)^{\frac{1}{\nu}}, \tag{26}$$

that is the characteristic function of multivariate Brownian motion with drift μ and covariance matrix Σ time changed by a gamma process with unit mean rate and variance rate ν. From the prespecified marginal bilateral gamma laws and the selection of ν in excess of the reciprocal of all speed parameters and a correlation matrix C we define the mean and variance rates μ_j,σ_j^2 for the multivariate Brownian motion by

$$\mu_j = \frac{b_{pj} - b_{nj}}{\nu}, \tag{27}$$

$$\sigma_j^2 = \frac{2b_{pj} b_{nj}}{\nu}, \tag{28}$$

and the covariance matrix by

$$\Sigma = \Delta(\sigma) C \Delta(\sigma), \tag{29}$$

where the matrix $\Delta(\sigma)$ is the diagonal matrix with σ_j on the diagonal. The marginal bilateral independent shocks on component j have the same scale parameters as the original prespecified scales and speed reduced by $1/\nu$. The resulting multivariate bilateral gamma characteristic function

$$\phi_{\mathrm{MBG}}(u) = \Phi(u) \times \prod_j \left(\frac{1}{1 - iu_j b_{pj}}\right)^{c_{pj}} \left(\frac{1}{1 + iu_j b_{nj}}\right)^{c_{nj}}.$$

The multivariate Lévy compensator is

$$k(z) = \widetilde{m}(z) + \sum_{j=1}^{n} k_j(z_j) \prod_{i \neq j} \mathbf{1}_{z_i=0},$$

where

$$\begin{aligned}
\widetilde{m}(z) &= \frac{2\exp\left(\mu^T \Sigma^{-1} z\right)}{\nu\,(2\pi)^{n/2-1}\sqrt{|\Sigma|}} \\
&\quad \times \left(\sqrt{\mu^T \Sigma^{-1}\mu + \frac{2}{\nu}}\right)^{\frac{n}{2}} \left(\frac{1}{\sqrt{z'\Sigma^{-1}z}}\right)^{\frac{n}{2}} \\
&\quad \times K_{n/2}\left(\sqrt{\left(\mu^T\Sigma^{-1}\mu + \frac{2}{\nu}\right) z'\Sigma^{-1}z}\right) \cdot k_j(z_j) \\
&= \frac{c_{nj}}{|z_j|}\exp\left(-|z_j|/b_{nj}\right)\mathbf{1}_{z_j<0} + \frac{c_{pj}}{z_j}\exp\left(-|z_j|/b_{pj}\right)\mathbf{1}_{z_j>0},
\end{aligned}$$

and $K_a(x)$ is the modified Bessel function of the second kind.

We form a portfolio of xlf the ETF for the finance sector and the six big banks using a value for ν that is 10% above the lower bound. The maximum short position was set at 20%.We also required the sum of the weights to be unity. The solution for data ending December 21, 2017 was as follows:

XLF	0.2593
JPM	0.1426
WFC	0.0982
BAC	0.0709
C	0.1670
GS	0.1139
MS	0.1470

Instead of maximizing the bid price of the portfolio, a portfolio manager may view the portfolio as a liability promised to shareholders and therefore choose instead to minimize the upper or ask price of the portfolio.The ask price minimizing solution was as follows:

XLF	0.1786
JPM	0.3965
WFC	0.3079
BAC	−0.0097
C	0.0529
GS	0.0505
MS	0.0222

7. Conclusion

Risk may be redefined as exposure described by the arrival rate of instantaneous moves of all sizes with an aggregate arrival rate that is infinite. In valuing and managing risk one has then lost access to probability and one must work with unnormalized measures representing the unrelativized counts of events with no sense to the count of all possible events. Nonlinear conservative valuation from the theory of two price economies modeled by expectations taken under distorted probabilities is then generalized to the use of measure distortions. Financial problems of hedging and portfolio selection are illustrated by either maximizing conservative lower valuations of asset positions or minimizing conservative upper valuations of liability positions. The lower valuations are concave while the upper valuations are convex. The nonlinear conservative valuations deliver market based optimization objectives for financial decision making and bring market value back into decision theory by replacing classical linear valuation operators that are both unsuited to the task and take too generous a view of risk acceptability.

References

[1] Artzner, P., Delbaen, F., Eber, M., and D. Heath (1999). Coherent measures of risk. *Mathematical Finance*, 9, 203–228.

[2] Eberlein, E., Madan, D.B., Pistorius, M., and Yor, M. (2014). Bid and ask prices as non-linear continuous time G-expectations based on distortions. *Mathematics and Financial Economics*, 8, 265–289.

[3] Khintchine, A.Y. (1938). Limit laws of sums of independent random variables. *ONTI*, Moscow (Russian).

[4] Küchler, U. and S. Tappe (2008). Bilateral gamma distributions and processes in financial mathematics. *Stochastic Processes and their Applications*, 118, 261–283.

[5] Kusuoka, S. (2001). On law invariant coherent risk measures. *Advances in Mathematical Economics*, 3, 83–95.

[6] Lévy, P. (1937). *Théorie de l'Addition des Variables Aléatoires*, Gauthier-Villars, Paris.

[7] Jensen, M.C. (2002). Value maximization, stakeholder theory, and the corporate objective function. *Business Ethics Quarterly*, 12, 235–256.

[8] Madan, D.B., Pistorius, M., and Stadje, M. (2017). On dynamic spectral risk measures, a limit theorem and optimal portfolio allocation. *Finance and Stochastics*, 21, 1073–1102.

[9] Madan, D.B. and Schoutens, W. (2016). *Applied Conic Finance*, Cambridge University Press, Cambridge, UK.

[10] Madan, D.B. and Schoutens, W. (2022). *Nonlinear Valuation and Non-Gaussian Risks*, Cambridge University Press, Cambridge, UK.

[11] Milne, F. (1981). The firm's objective function as a collective choice problem. *Public Choice*, 37, 473–486.

[12] Ross, S.A. (1978). A simple approach to the valuation of risky streams. *Journal of Business*, 51, 453–475.

[13] Sato, K. (1999). *Lévy processes and Infinitely Divisible Distributions,* Cambridge University Press, Cambridge UK.

https://doi.org/10.1142/9789811259142_0023

Chapter 23

Insider Trading*

P. Protter

Statistics Department, Columbia University, New York, NY, USA

pep2117@columbia.edu

1. Motivation

Traditionally, one models the evolution of the information of a market via a filtration of σ-algebras. With an asymmetric information model, one has many filtrations: The filtration of the market, the filtration of uninformed traders, the filtration of specialists/analysts, the filtration of people with access to private information. An example of a person with inside access to privileged information and then abusing that knowledge, is that of Collins.

Indeed, Collins, a Republican (former) Representative from New York State, and an early supporter of Donald Trump's bid for the presidency in 2016, provides an example of criminal behavior, related to insider trading. He even made the insider trading calls on the lawn of the White House during a White House picnic! According to the *Washington Post*, "Federal prosecutors charged Rep.

*This little chapter contains the results I presented in my talk at the conference in Jerusalem, in December, 2018, titled "Options: 45 Years after the Publication of the Black Scholes Merton Model", Jerusalem, and organized by Lipton and Rosenbaum. It is based primarily on joint work with Neufcourt. We wish to thank Alex, Mathieu, and Léo.

Collins (R-N.Y.), President Trump's first congressional supporter, with insider trading on Wednesday (August 8, 2018) alleging the New York Republican schemed with his son to avoid significant losses on a biotechnology investment". Collins was a member of the board of the Australian based company **Innate Immunotherapeutics**.

One way to model mathematically the phenomenon of insider trading is via an enlargement of the filtration. This also is appropriate for other applications as we will indicate later. The problem is delicate, but while we would like that semimartingales remain semimartingales in the enlarged filtration, sometimes, more often than not, it is not true.

The issue first arrived in the work of Itô, in 1976 [6]. Itô proposed a type of filtration expansion now known as an **initial expansion**. Itô wanted to be able to treat B_1 as a constant, where B is standard Brownian motion. He wanted to write

$$\int_0^t \mathbf{B_1} H_s dB_s = \mathbf{B_1} \int_0^t H_s dB_s, \tag{1}$$

for a predictable integrand H. Itô created a larger filtration $\mathcal{G}_t = \mathcal{F}_t \vee \sigma(B_1)$ but of course B is no longer a Brownian motion for the filtration $\mathbb{G}$, since it's not a $\mathbb{G}$ martingale. Itô showed, however that B remained a semimartingale in $\mathbb{G}$, and using semimartingale theory he justified the truth of (1).

The "Strasbourg School" of Meyer, Yor, Jeulin, Jacod, and others reformulated Itô's idea in the following way: When can we enlarge a filtration in such a way so that martingales need not stay martingales, but at least remain semimartingales? Put more concisely, we want to expand the filtration in such a way that semimartingales remain semimartingales.

Jacod [7] proved a useful result in this direction which is now known as **Jacod's Criterion:** (See [14] for a pedagogic treatment in English).

Theorem Jacod's Criterion (1987). *Let L be a random variable with values in a standard Borel space $(E, \mathcal{E})$, and let $Q_t(\omega, dx)$ denote the regular conditional distribution of L given $\mathcal{F}_t$, each $t \geq 0$. Suppose that for each t there exists a positive σ-finite measure η_t on $(E, \mathcal{E})$ such that $Q_t(\omega, dx) \ll \eta_t(dx)$ a.s. Then every $\mathbb{F}$ semimartingale X is also an $\mathcal{F} \vee \sigma(L)$ semimartingale.*

A second approach to the expansion of filtrations began with the thesis of Martin Barlow in 1978 [2]. Instead of an initial enlargement à la Itô, he sought a gradual enlargement in order to render a non-negative random variable L a stopping time. The canonical example of a random time of interest that is not a stopping time, is the last exit of a three dimensional Brownian motion from the unit ball. The naive way to accomplish this is to replace the filtration $\mathbb{F}$ by defining $\mathcal{G}_t = \mathcal{F}_t \vee \sigma(L \wedge t)$, and then L is a $\mathbb{G}$ stopping time. The trick, however, is to find conditions on L such that $\mathbb{F}$ semimartingales remain $\mathbb{G}$ semimartingales.

This was the state of the art when Kchia entered the picture. Kchia (in joint work with myself [10]) proposed to expand a filtration $\mathbb{F}$ continuously as time evolves, for example by continuously adding bits of information **arising from another stochastic process**. As always, the trick is to do this in a way that preserves the semimartingale property. The procedure is complicated, and we will give an outline of it. The new contribution presented here, however, is to give a way to describe the new semimartingale decomposition as best as is possible.

In particular, we are interested in the path properties of the new finite variation term under the expanded filtration. First however we will try to explain why these types of results might be interesting or in extreme cases even useful. Indeed, a model of a specialized kind of insider trading is the original motivation for our study. In the US the legality of insider trading is a complicated subject filled with nuance. The US Attorney for the Southern District of New York, formerly Bharara, prosecuted and convicted 85 insider trading cases, before finally losing one.

There are types of trades which are (at least currently) perfectly legal but are most accurately described as insider trading. A dramatic example is provided by the high frequency traders known as co-locators. These companies place their trading machines next to the computers that process the trades of the stock exchange. They rent these co-locations directly from the stock exchanges themselves, and the fiber optics are carefully measured so that no one co-locator has a physical advantage over another (see [11],[13]). Trades take place at intervals of 0.007 seconds.

These co-locators use various specialized orders (such as "immediate or cancel" orders) effectively to "see" the limit order book in the immediate future, and thus determine if a given stock is likely to go up or to go down in the immediate future. With an enlarged filtration we get a new semimartingale decomposition and that affects the collection of risk neutral measures since we need to remove the drift with a Girsanov transformation (if we can), and the point is that the drift has changed. The techniques presented today give a path to the mathematical modeling of such insider trading.

We want to expand the filtration not just initially or with a random time, but dynamically with a stochastic process The results of Kchia *et al.* [9], and El Karoui *et al.* [5], allow us to expand with a not necessarily adapted marked point process. This means to expand with a process X we can approximate it with a sequence of point processes, as time discretizations tend to zero in mesh size. With each point process approximation we expand the filtration, getting a sequence of larger and larger filtrations.

We need the new filtrations to converge (we use the theory of Antonelli and Kohatsu-Higa [1], as well as that of Coquet *et al.*, [4]. We need the semimartingale decompositions to converge, so that we have a semimartingale in the limiting filtration (to do this we use and improve an old result of Barlow and the author [3]). More precisely, we approximate X with a sequence $(X^n)_{n\geq 1}$ of càdlàg processes that are marked point processes with possibly unordered jumps, and then expand with X^n to get a larger filtration $\mathcal{G}_t^n = \mathcal{F}_t \vee \sigma(X_s^n; s \leq t)$ We choose the approximations X^n in such a way that we know that if M is an $\mathbb{F}$ semimartingale, then it is also a $\mathbb{G}^n$ semimartingale, and we can calculate N^n and A^n of its $\mathbb{G}^n$ Doob–Meyer decomposition:

$$M_t = N_t^n + A_t^n. \tag{2}$$

We need some sort of a control on N^n and A^n in (2) as n increases to ∞, to get a convergence of the components of M, which is the original $\mathbb{F}$ semimartingale M, but after the expansion.

We combine the preceding with the (somewhat obscure) theory of the convergence of filtrations.

Lemma 1. *A sequence of σ-fields $\mathcal{A}^n$ converges weakly to a σ-field $\mathcal{A}$ if and only if $E(Z \mid \mathcal{A}^n)$ converges in probability to Z for any integrable and $\mathcal{A}$ measurable random variable Z.*

Lemma 2. *A sequence of filtrations $\mathbb{F}^n$ converges weakly to a filtration $\mathbb{F}$ if and only if $E(Z \mid \mathcal{F}_t^n)_{t\geq 0}$ converges in probability under the*

Skorohod J_1 topology to $E(Z \mid \mathcal{F}_t)_{t\geq 0}$, for any integrable, $\mathcal{F}_T$ measurable random variable Z.

Coquet *et al.*, [4] provide a characterization of weak convergence of filtrations when the limiting filtration is the natural filtration of some càdlàg process X.

Theorem 1. *Let $(\mathbb{F}^m)_{m\geq 1}$ be a sequence of filtrations. Let $\mathbb{F}$ be a filtration such that for all $t \in [0,T]$, $\mathcal{F}_t^m \xrightarrow{w} \mathcal{F}_t$. Define the filtration $\tilde{\mathbb{F}} = (\tilde{\mathcal{F}}_t)_{0\leq t\leq T}$, where $\tilde{\mathcal{F}}_t = \bigvee_m \mathcal{F}_t^m$. Let X be an $\mathbb{F}$ adapted càdlàg process such that X is an $\tilde{\mathbb{F}}$ semimartingale. Then X is an $\mathbb{F}$ semimartingale.*

We next extend an old theorem of Barlow and Protter [3].

Theorem 2. *Let $(\mathbb{G}^n)_{n\geq 1}$ be a sequence of right-continuous filtrations and let $\mathbb{G}$ be a filtration such that $\mathcal{G}_t^n \xrightarrow{w} \mathcal{G}_t$ for all t. Let $(X^n)_{n\geq 1}$ be a sequence of $\mathbb{G}^n$ semimartingales with canonical decomposition $X^n = X_0^n + M^n + A^n$. Assume there exists $K > 0$ such that for all n,*

$$E\left(\int_0^T |dA_s^n|\right) \leq K \quad \text{and} \quad E(\sup_{0\leq s\leq T} |M_s^n|) \leq K$$

Then the following holds.

(i) *Assume there exists a $\mathbb{G}$ adapted process X such that $E(\sup_{0\leq s\leq T} |X_s^n - X_s|) \to 0$. Then X is a $\mathbb{G}$ special semimartingale.*
(ii) *Moreover, assume $\mathbb{G}$ is right-continuous and let $X = M + A$ be the canonical decomposition of X. Then M is a $\mathbb{G}$ martingale and $\int_0^T |dA_s|$ and $\sup_{0\leq s\leq T} |M_s|$ are integrable.*

We say that a semimartingale Y is an $\mathbb{L}$ nicely integrable semimartingale if $Y = N + A$ is its canonical decomposition in $\mathbb{L}$ and there exists a constant K such that

$$E\left(\int_0^T |dA_s|\right) \leq K, \quad \text{and} \quad E\left(\sup_{o\leq s\leq T} |N_s|\right) \leq K. \tag{3}$$

For a given semimartingale X that we are using for our expansion, we approximate X with X^n, where

$$X_t^n = \sum_{i=0}^{n+1} (X_{t_n^i} - X_{t_n^{i-1}}) 1_{\{t \geq t_n^i\}}. \tag{4}$$

Theorem 3 (Generalized Jacod's criterion). *There exists a sequence $(\pi_n)_{n\geq 1} = (\{t_i^n\})_{n\geq 1}$ of subdivisions of $[0,T]$ whose mesh tends to zero and such that for each n, $(X_{t_0^n}, X_{t_1^n} - X_{t_0^n}, \ldots, X_T - X_{t_n^n})$ satisfies Jacod's criterion, i.e., there exists a σ-finite measure η_n on $\mathcal{B}(\mathbb{R}^{n+2})$ such that $P\big((X_{t_0^n}, X_{t_1^n} - X_{t_0^n}, \ldots, X_T - X_{t_n^n}) \in \cdot \mid \mathcal{F}_t\big)(\omega) \ll \eta_n(\cdot)$ a.s*

We let $\mathbb{G}^0$ (resp. $\mathbb{G}$) be the smallest (resp. the smallest right-continuous) filtration containing $\mathbb{F}$ and relative to which X is adapted.

Theorem 4. *Assume X and $\mathbb{F}$ satisfy the Generalized Jacod's Criterion, and that either X is quasi-left continuous, or the sequence of subdivisions $(\pi_n)_{n\geq 1}$ is refining and all fixed times of discontinuity of X belong to $\cup_n \pi_n$.*

Let M be a continuous $\mathbb{F}$ martingale such that $E(\sup_{s\leq T} |M_s|) \leq K$ and $E(\int_0^T |dA_s^{(n)}|) \leq K$ for some K and all n. Then

(i) *M is a $\mathbb{G}^0$ special semimartingale, and*
(ii) *Moreover, if $\mathbb{F}$ is the natural filtration of some càdlàg process Z, then M is a $\mathbb{G}$ special semimartingale with canonical decomposition $M = N + A$ such that N is a $\mathbb{G}$ martingale and $\sup_{0\leq s\leq T} |N_s|$ and $\int_0^T |dA_s|$ are integrable.*

1.1 *New results with Neufcourt*

We want to find the finite variation term A or at least determine its properties. In particular, within the Brownian paradigm, we would like sufficient conditions so that $dA_t \ll dt$ a.s. Such results are necessary conditions for an absence of arbitrage within a Math Finance context. The idea is simple (its analysis is more difficult): Suppose for each decomposition in our sequence we have $X_t^n = M_t^n + \int_0^t \alpha_s^n \, ds$ for a filtration $\mathbb{G}^n$ We call the integrand processes $(\alpha_s^n)_{s\geq 0}$ the **information drifts**.

We look for conditions such that $\int_0^t \alpha_s^n ds$ converge to a process of the form $\int_0^t \alpha_s ds$ An old example due to Jeulin [8] shows that this need not be the case; that is, the limiting process A_t can have paths that are a.s. singular with respect to Lebesgue measure, similar to the paths of a local time

We say that a sequence of σ algebras $(\mathcal{H}^n)_{n\geq 1}$ **converges to a σ algebra $\mathcal{H}$ in L^p if**

For any $Z \in L^p(\mathcal{H}, P)$ we have $E(Z|\mathcal{H}^n) \to Z$ in L^p as $n \to \infty$.

We have an analogous notion for the convergence of filtrations in L^p.

Let Z be a Bessel 3 process, $\mathbb{F}$ its natural filtration, $X_t = \inf_{s>t} Z_s$ and $\mathbb{G}$ the progressive expansion of $\mathbb{F}$ with X. This example has been studied in detail by both Jeulin [8] and Pitman [12] using different techniques. Let $B_t = Z_t - \int_0^t \frac{ds}{Z_s}$. It is a classical result that B is an $\mathbb{F}$ Brownian motion. Using Williams' path decomposition for Brownian motion, Pitman [12] proved in 1975 that $B_t - (2X_t - \int_0^t \frac{ds}{Z_s})$ is a $\mathbb{G}$ Brownian motion. Using filtration expansion results, Jeulin [8] showed in 1980 the $\mathbb{G}$ semimartingale property of B, and he provided its decomposition simultaneously. However, these two techniques do not generalize.

In the technique of Kchia and Protter [10] all of the intermediary processes $(A_s^n)_{s\geq 0}$ a.s. have paths that are absolutely continuous with respect to ds, yet as we see in the limit, thanks to the results of Jeulin and Pitman, that the $\mathbb{G}$ decomposition B is given by

$$B_t = \left(B_t - \left(2X_t - \int_0^t \frac{ds}{Z_s}\right)\right) + \left(2X_t - \int_0^t \frac{ds}{Z_s}\right), \tag{5}$$

where Z is a Bessel (3) process The finite variation term of (5) is $2X_t - \int_0^t \frac{ds}{Z_s}$. We note that the process X is non-decreasing but dX_s has support on a random set which has Lebesgue measure 0 a.s. Due to the presence of a singular term in the decomposition (5) we cannot find an equivalent probability measure that turns B into a $\mathbb{G}$ (local) martingale.

So we are in the situation where each approximating term is well behaved, but in the limit the process we are after cannot be transformed into a local martingale and this example shows that we cannot have NFLVR, implying the absence of arbitrage opportunities.

Intuitively, this filtration expansion introduces arbitrage opportunities into the market where an insider discovers the extra information X_t progressively and obtains an arbitrage opportunity that is hidden from the rest of the market.

Caveat: Brownian motion is not a good model of a stock price (for example it does not remain positive) but an extension of the above could also be treated.

1.2 *Convergence of the information drifts*

Theorem 5. *Let $(\mathbb{G}^n)_{n\geq 1}$ be a non-decreasing sequence of filtrations and suppose that M is a $\mathbb{G}^n$ semimartingale with decomposition $M = M^n + \int_0^t \alpha_s^n d[M,M]_s$ for every $n \geq 1$ for some $\mathbb{G}^n$ adapted process α^n. If $\mathbb{G}^n \to \mathbb{G}$ in L^2 and if*

$$\sup_{n\geq 1} \int_0^T (\alpha_s^n)^2 d[M,M]_s < \infty, \tag{6}$$

then M is also a $\mathbb{G}$ semimartingale with decomposition

$$M = \tilde{M} + \int \alpha_s d[M,M]_s, \tag{7}$$

for a $\mathbb{G}$ adapted process α.

Theorem 6. *Suppose a process X is continuous. Suppose for a sequence of finite partitions π^n with final element $\ell(n)+1$ we have that*

$$(X_{t_0^n}, X_{t_1^n} - X_{t_0^n}, \ldots, X_{t_{\ell(n)+1}^n} - X_{t_{\ell(n)}^n})$$

satisfies the generalized Jacod's condition, and let α^n be the information drift of the nth decomposition.

(a) *If $\sup_{n\geq 1} E \int_0^T |\alpha_s^n| d[M,M]_s < \infty$ then M is a continuous $\mathbb{G}$ semimartingale;*

(b) *If $\sup_n E \int_0^T (\alpha_s^n)^2 d[M,M]_s < \infty$, then M is a continuous $\mathbb{G}$ semimartingale decomposition.*

$$M = \tilde{M} + \int \alpha_s d[M,M]_s,$$

and $E \int_0^T (\alpha_s^n - \alpha_s)^2 d[M,M]_s \to 0$ as $n \to \infty$.

The example of the Bessel (3) process of Pitman and Jeulin applies to case (a) of the previous theorem. In case (b) we can show explicitly that the information drifts α^n have the property that

$$E\int_0^T (\alpha_s^n)^2 d[M,M]_s = \int_0^t E\left(1_{\{\varepsilon_n \le Z_s\}}\frac{1}{Z_s^2}\right) ds \to \infty.$$

Remark. The previous theorem has a version with X càdlàg and quasi-left continuous, such as occurs for example with a Hunt process. As examples we can take a class of Hunt processes of a special form: Let Z be a Lévy process and let X be the solution of an SDE of the form

$$X_t = X_0 + \int_0^t \sigma(X_{s-})dZ_s + \int_0^t b(X_s)ds, \tag{8}$$

where σ and b are (for example) Lipschitz continuous. Then X is a Hunt process.

For examples using this technique we first point out there are several interesting examples worked out by hand by Jeulin [8] and Yor, long ago, and more recently Corcuera, Imkeller, Kohatsu and Higa, and Jacod-Protter among others. We can reprove and sometimes improve them using these techniques. We also have some improvements of the old examples and a new example.

1.3 *A new example*

In order to find expansions with a continuous anticipation satisfying the information drift property we must consider the right speed of anticipation. Let ϕ be a continuous time change, i.e., a non-decreasing stochastic process with continuous paths, independent from W, and let $X_t := W_{t\wedge\phi_t}$. The natural expansion of $\mathcal{F}$ with the process X is the filtration $\check{\mathcal{G}}$ given by $\check{\mathcal{G}}_t := \mathcal{F}_t \vee \sigma(X_s, s \le t)$. It is equivalent and useful for applications to consider the right-continuous filtration $\mathcal{G}_t := \bigcap_{u>t}(\mathcal{F}_u \vee \sigma(X_s, s \le u)), t \in I$.

Theorem 7. *For every $s \ge t$ define the random time $\tau(s,t) := \inf\{0 \le u \le s : u \vee \phi_u = t\}$ and suppose that it admits a $\mathcal{G}_s$-conditional density $u \mapsto f(u;s,t)$, with respect to Lebesgue measure, which is* *continuously differentiable in* (st). *Then the* $\mathcal{G}$*-information drift* α *of the Brownian motion* W *is given by*

$$\alpha_s = \int_0^s W_{\phi_u} \partial_t f(u; s, t)\Big|_{t=s} du.$$

Acknowledgment

Supported in part by NSF Grant DMS-2106433.

References

[1] Antonelli, F. and Kohatsu-Higa, A. (2000). Filtration stability of backward SDE's. *Stochastic Analysis and Applications*, 18(1), 11–37.

[2] Barlow, M. (1978). Study of a filtration expanded to include an honest time, *Z. Wahrtscheinlichkeitstheorie Verw. Gebeite*, 44, 307–323.

[3] Barlow, M. and Protter, P. (1990). *On Convergence of Semimartingales*, Séminaire de Probabilités XXIV, Springer Lecture Notes in Mathematics, Vol. 1426; pp. 188–193.

[4] Coquet, F., Mémin, J., and Słominski, L. (2001). On weak convergence of filtrations. *Séminaire de Probabilités*, 35, 306–328.

[5] El Karoui, N., Jeanblanc, M., and Jiao, Y. (2015). Density approach in modeling successive defaults. *SIAM Journal on Financial Mathematics*, 6, 1–21.

[6] Itô, K. (1978). Extension of stochastic integrals. In: *Proceedings of International Symposium on Stochastic Differential Equations*, New York, Wiley, pp. 95–109.

[7] Jacod, J. (1985). Grossissement initial, hypothèse (H'), et théorèm de Girsanov, in *Grossissements de Filtrations, Exemples et Applications*, Vol. 1118 of *Lecture Notes in Mathematics*, Springer, Berlin.

[8] Jeulin, Th. (1980). Comportement des semi-martingales dans un grossissement de filtration, *Probability Theory and Related Fields*, 52(2), 149–182.

[9] Kchia, Y., Larsson, M., and Protter, P. (2013). Linking progressive and initial filtration expansions. *Malliavin Calculus and Stochastic Analysis*, Vol. 34, Springer Proceedings in Mathematics & Statistics, pp. 469–487.

[10] Kchia, Y. and Protter, P. (2015). On progressive filtration expansions with a process; Applications to insider trading. *International Journal of Theoretical and Applied Finance*, 18(04), 1–48.

[11] Lewis, M. (2015). *Flash Boys*, W.W. Norton & Company.
[12] Pitman, J. (1975). One-dimensional Brownian motion and the three-dimensional Bessel process, *Advances in Applied Probability*, 7, 511–526.
[13] Protter, P. (2015). Flash boys: Cracking the money code. *Quantitative Finance*, 15(2). DOI: 10.1080/14697688.2015.1007472.
[14] Protter, P. (2005). *Stochastic Integration and Differential Equations*, 2nd Edition, *Version 2.1*, Springer-Verlag, Heidelberg.

https://doi.org/10.1142/9789811259142_0024

Chapter 24

Contingent Claims Analysis in Corporate Finance

M. Crouhy,[*,‡] **D. Galai**[†,§]**, and Z. Wiener**[†,‖]

[*]*Natixis, France*

[†]*Jerusalem School of Business, The Hebrew University, Israel*

[‡]*Michel.Crouhy@gmail.com*

[§]*Dan.Galai@huji.ac.il*

[‖]*Zvi.Wiener@huji.ac.il*

Abstract

The Contingent Claims Analysis (CCA) is a general approach to analyze the stakeholders of a corporation who have contingent claims on the future, uncertain cash-flows generated by the operations of the firms. The CCA allows valuing each stakeholder's claim and also to assess the risk incurred by the stakeholders. The CCA highlights the potential conflicts of interest among the various claimholders. In this paper, we review applications of CCA including valuation of various forms of debt, rating, credit spread, probability of default and corporate events like dividends, employee stock options and M&A. The CCA framework is shown to be useful to address all these financial questions. In this approach the starting point is that the value and the risk of the firm's assets are given. The future distribution of the assets' rates of return is also known and given. The focus is on the liability side of the balance sheet, i.e., the funding sources of the activity of the firm, and more generally on the financial claims of the various claimholders of the firm.

Keywords: Contingent claims, Merton model, dividends, debt, credit spread, corporate finance, bankruptcy, equity valuation, covenants, convertible securities, volatility, sovereign debt.

1. Introduction

The contingent claims analysis (CCA) is a general approach to analyze the stakeholders of a corporation who have contingent claims on the future, uncertain cash-flows generated by the operations of the firms. The CCA allows valuing each stakeholder's claim and also to assess the risk incurred by the stakeholders. The CCA can also help to better understand the potential conflicts of interest among the various claimholders, and hence to better address corporate governance issues.

In this approach the starting point is that the value and the risk of the firm's assets are given. The future distribution of the assets rates of return is also known and given. Usually, for computational convenience, it is assumed that the value of the firm's assets is lognormally distributed, and, therefore, the assets rates of return are normally distributed, in continuous time. The fundamental assumption is that the assets can be analyzed using the CAPM model of Sharpe [1] and Lintner [2,3], as it is well documented in Fama and Miller [4] book. This framework can be extended with the APT and the multi-index analysis. The focus is on the liability side of the balance sheet, i.e., the funding sources of the activity of the firm, and more generally on the financial claims of the various claimholders of the firm.

The starting point is to recognize that a firm, like a coin, has two sides, i.e., the asset side and the liability side. They are identical in overall value and risk. The balance sheet of the firm is well balanced in economic terms, i.e., at each instant the value of the assets is equal to the value of equity and the liabilities. There cannot be any gap between the two sides of the balance sheet. Hence, the value of the firm and its risk, are fully divided among the claimholders. The driving force of corporate events is usually on the assets' side while the liability side reflects the changes and adjusts itself. Both changes in the value or in the riskiness of the assets have an impact on the liabilities. The CCA provides a theoretical framework that dynamically connects the two sides of the balance sheet. Many questions, like analysis of various forms of debt, dividends, effect of corporate tax codes, or M&A as well as many other corporate events can be analyzed in the framework of CCA.

The firm is like a pizza with each claimholder having a claim on the pizza that is fully consumed by all the stakeholders. The conflicts of interest are on who gets its slice first, and how big is the size of the slice. The stakeholders favor a larger size of the pizza, i.e., the size of the firm, as long as it increases their share. Many corporate decisions have an impact on the distribution of the value among stakeholders and not only on the size of the whole firm.

When we analyze the value of the stakeholders' specific claims, we take as given all the factors that drive the value of the firm. This is in the spirit of Modigliani and Miller (M&M) [5] analysis of the firm, in an economy with no corporate taxes. They show that under assumptions of perfect capital markets (PCM) the value of the firm is not a function of its capital structure. Actually, the CCA premise is that the value of the assets of the firm is fully distributed among all the claimholders. Merton [6] proves that the M&M propositions also hold for the case of bond default.

In this approach, if we add corporate taxes, the government, as a tax collector, is also a stakeholder and the tax claim should be endogenized; it implies that the assets of the firm should be considered on a before tax basis. Not only is the CCA consistent with M&M as it asserts that the pizza is fully eaten, and equity holders are entitled to get the residual value as long as it is non-negative. Again, the firm is like a coin that has two identical sides in terms of overall value and risk. Hence, there is no need to prove the M&M theorems.

Another important distinction between the two sides of the balance sheet (defined in economic rather than accounting terms) is that while we commonly assume that the value of the assets follows a stationary lognormal process, the value of the claims of the stakeholders doesn't necessarily follow a stationary distribution. Therefore, asset pricing models like the CAPM cannot be used to price the non-stationary claims of the stakeholders as shown by Galai and Masulis [7]. In the simple case of a firm, financed with equity and a pure discount bond, as analyzed by Merton [8], the option pricing model (OPM) can be used to price simultaneously equity and debt.

In the literature on valuation of liabilities many assumptions are made, either explicit or implicit. The first set of assumptions is related to the asset side, e.g., the nature of assets' value uncertain behavior, and, the use of proceeds if money is currently raised.

The second set of assumptions relates to the equity and liability side of the balance sheet, e.g., the current capital structure and whether it is going to change. Authors, dealing with warrants valuation, for example, used different set of assumptions: some analyzed companies with equity and warrants only, and for such companies, whether dividends are expected to be paid out or not. And even then, we can ask whether dividends are fully expected or not, remembering that dividends, *per se*, reduce the asset size of the firm. Also, how the proceeds from the potential exercise of the warrants can affect the valuation models whether the proceeds are used for a scale expansion of the firm, to retire debt, or to pay dividends (or, any combination of the above).

One very important assumption concerns corporate taxes. Many papers (e.g., [5,7,8] paper and assume the corporate tax rate is zero. However, other authors (e.g., [9,10]) assume the existence of corporate taxation. And even in the tax case some assume it is a full offset tax while others assume only partial offsetting or, no offsetting. Also, some assume the coupon payment is fully deducted as an expense as compared to the effective yield, taking the discount or premium on the debt value into account.

2. CCA has Revolutionized the Field of Corporate Finance

- The CCA is the application of OPM to analyzing the stakeholders of a corporation who have contingent claims on the future, uncertain cash-flows generated by the operations of the firm.
- CCA has been useful to address financial issues: Valuation of equity, various forms of debt, ratings, credit spreads, probability of default, corporate events (dividends, stock options, M&A), conflicts of interest among stakeholders, corporate governance issues s.a. dividend policy, compensation, sharing of voting rights.
- To celebrate this great achievement over the last 46 years following the publication of Black–Scholes–Merton (BSM) OPM model, we produced a four volume anthology of the major contributions in the applications of CCA to corporate finance; see Figure 1.

Figure 1: World Scientific Reference on Contingent Claims Analysis in Corporate Finance.
Source: https://www.worldscientific.com/worldscibooks/10.1142/9857.

3. Corporate Finance

- Corporate finance deals with the two sides of the balance sheet: (1) selecting and evaluating assets, and (2) analyzing the capital structure and the costs of the sources of financing the firm.
- The CCA deals with the latter: how to price equity, debt and other stakeholders' claims, deriving their cost, and highlighting the potential conflicts of interest.
- While the CAPM and its extensions can be useful for investment decisions, the CCA is the only approach to deal with the financing aspects of the corporation; see Figure 2.

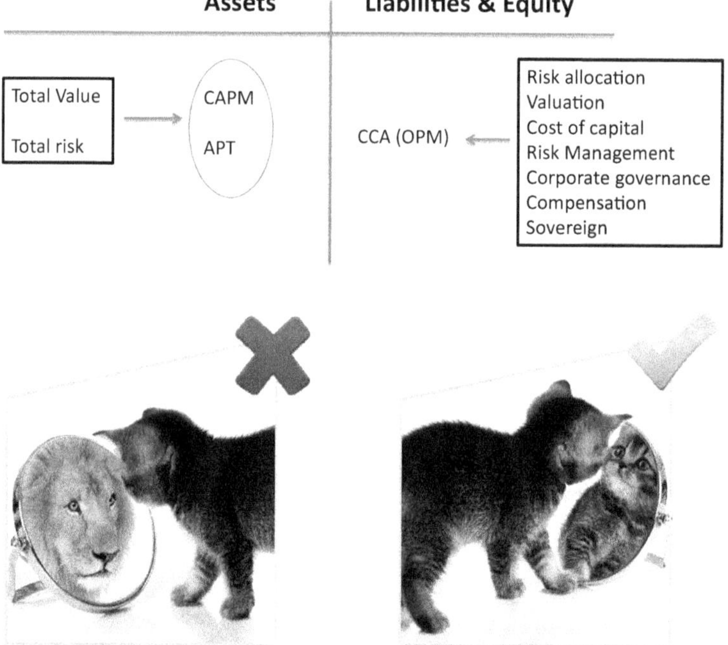

Figure 2: CCA is the only approach to deal with the financing aspects of the corporation.

4. Agenda

- Foundations.
- Pricing of debt and equity.
- Pricing of warrants, convertible securities, preferred stocks.
- CCA and various corporate issues: dividends, employee stock options (ESO).
- CCA for banks and sovereign debt.

4.1 *Foundations*

- BSM is mostly associated with the pricing of traded options, trading strategies replicating payoffs, and market risk mitigation.
- In this presentation, we focus on BSM contributions to the field of Corporate Finance:
  - We believe that teaching of corporate finance should be reconsidered to reflect the insights of CCA.

- CCA has also significant implications for corporate governance (e.g., dividend policy, compensation, alternative ways to share voting rights in a corporation).

- Black and Scholes [11] and Merton [8,12] — hereafter referred to as BSM, introduced the CCA to the pricing of stock options with the insight that corporate liabilities are analogous to options and can be valued in a similar manner.
- BSM introduced the *structural approach* to credit risk analysis, where default is endogenously generated within the model.
- The alternative approaches are:
  - Credit rating systems of S&P, Moody's, Fitch and others.
  - The "reduced-form approach" of Jarrow-Turnbull/Duffie-Singleton is used, for example, to price CDS and other credit derivatives.
  - The Credit Migration Approach of CreditMetrics based on migration of ratings on an annual basis.
- BSM provide the fundamental version of the structural model, where default is assumed to occur when the firm's net assets falls below the market value of its liabilities — *the firm is insolvent*; see Figure 3.
- In a regime of limited liability, the firm's shareholders have the option to default on the firm's debt; see Figures 4 and 5.
  - Equity can then be viewed as a European call option on the assets of the firm with a strike price equal to the face value of the firm's debt.
  - Debt holders, on the other hand, are short a put option on the assets of the firm with a strike equal to the face value of debt. The credit spread is simply the value of this put option.

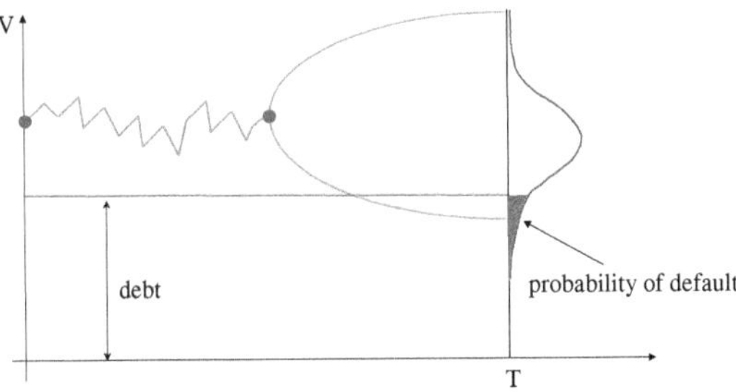

Figure 3: Merton's structural default model.

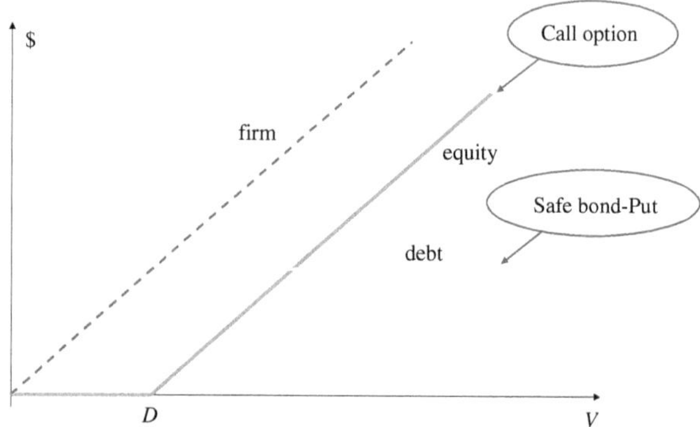

Figure 4: Merton's model of equity and debt represented as financial options on the value of the assets.

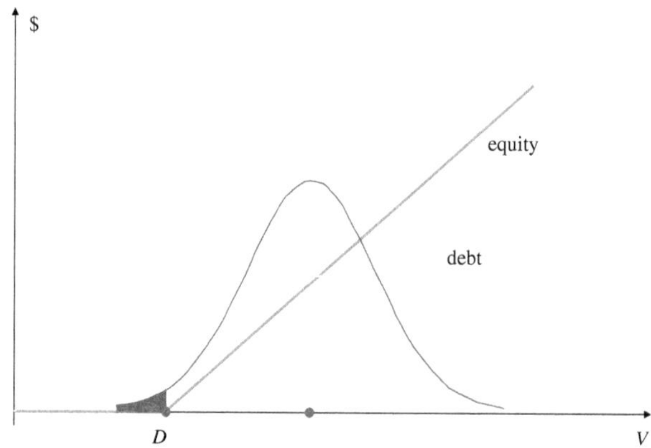

Figure 5: Probability distribution of the final value of the assets and the default area marked below the debt (D).

- Ultimately, CCA can be used to value all the components of the firm's liabilities: equity, debt, convertible bonds, warrants, CoCos, etc. The value of each component of the liability mix will depend upon:
  - the stochastic process followed by the assets of the firm, interest rate dynamics,
  - the payout policy (dividends, coupons, etc.) to the various stakeholders,
  - the level of subordination of the various debt components,
  - the default trigger, and
  - the reorganization process in case of default.

- CCA is a powerful framework to analyse the linkage between the firm's capital structure, the valuation of corporate liabilities and credit spreads.
- The key idea is that the value of the assets defines the sum of all the claims of the stakeholders:
  - shareholders, various debt holders with specific terms, etc.
- The basic insight is that the total *value* and total *risk* of the assets are shared and transferred between the various stakeholders in the firm, which is consistent with M&M.
- In four volumes, our anthology contains 70 key articles that expand, the BSM framework to many applications such as:
  - the pricing of equity, warrants and convertible bonds,
  - the impact of taxation, stochastic interest rates, dividend policy and the reorganization or liquidation process in case of default.
- CCA can also address issues related to:
  - banking regulation, such as deposit insurance and contingent capital (CoCos), as well as,
  - macroeconomic and international finance issues, including the pricing of sovereign debt.
- The CCA was also subject to empirical studies, especially related to bonds and their spreads over the risk-free bonds.

4.2 *The pricing of debt and equity*

- Within BSM framework we can derive:
  - the credit spread: $\pi_T = -1/Tln[N(d_2) + V/Fe^{-rT}N(-d_1)]$,
  - the risk-neutral probability of default: $N(-d_2)$, and
  - the expected discounted recovery rate: V, $V \leq F$.
- All these values are endogenously determined and depend on both the firm's capital structure and the dynamics of its asset value.
- **The credit risk of the corporate bond is fully incorporated in the put option on the value of the firm with the strike price equal to the face value of the debt: Crouhy *et al.* [13]** show that the value of the put option can be decomposed into the expected shortfall, conditional on the firm being bankrupt at maturity, and the expected probability of such an event.

- **Crouhy and Galai [14]** examine the relation between the risk-neutral and physical probabilities of default, noting that the two can differ substantially.
- The first major extension of Merton's model is by:
  - **Black and Cox [15]** who let default occur prior to the bond's maturity by introducing a "safety covenant" that allows debt holders to trigger default, any time, when the asset value falls below a predetermined threshold known as a "default boundary"; see Figure 6.

    Equity is no longer a European call on the firm's assets, but rather a "down-and-out" call option on them. The probability of default is higher. There is a transfer of value from shareholders to the debt holders which translate into a lower credit spread.

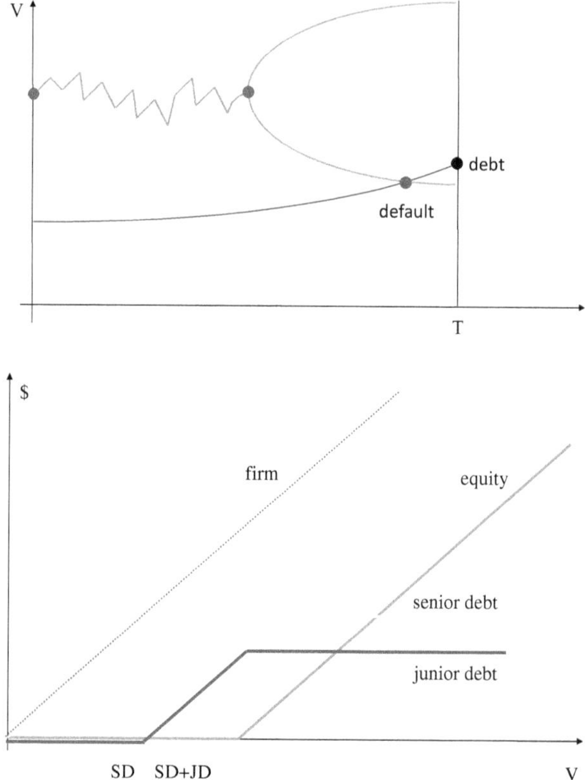

Figure 6: (a) Path dependent covenants; (b) Senior and junior debts and (c) Valuation of corporate debt.

- More extensions of Merton's model.
  - **Geske [16]** derives the value of the bond for risky coupon–paying debt, using the compound option model. The firm can default at any coupon paying date if the firm's assets fall below the coupon at that date.
  - **Leland [10]** extends Merton's model to account for taxes, bankruptcy costs, continuous coupon payments and bond covenants. This model allows to determine the optimal capital structure, the debt capacity, and credit spreads. Leland derives the optimal default boundary and the value maximizing optimal capital structure. Leland's endogenous default boundary is a generalization of Black–Cox [15].
- More extensions of Merton's model:
  - **Leland and Toft [17]** expand Leland model by seeking an endogenous solution for the capital structure and debt maturity. Optimal debt maturity is determined by striking a balance between the tax advantage of long-term debt and the disadvantages engendered by bankruptcy and agency costs.
  - **Mella-Barral and Perraudin [18]** investigate strategic debt service, whereby equity holders under distressed conditions renegotiate the terms of the debt.

Valuation of Corporate Debt Liquidation triggers

The value of equity and debt is analyzed under alternative assumptions about the default process.

- **Moraux [19]** extends the Leland and Toft [17] model to allow for a delay between the default trigger and the liquidation of the firm's assets. Liquidation occurs when the total time that the firm's assets spends under the distress threshold exceeds some pre-determined grace period. He then looks at the ex-ante pricing of corporate liabilities.
- **Francois and Morellec [20]** complement Moraux [19] and examine whether the so-called exclusivity period defined by Chapter 11 of the U.S. bankruptcy code impacts asset prices, the choice of the capital structure and the decision to default.
- **Galai *et al.* [21]** extend both previous models by taking into account the effect of the severity of the distress event on the decision to liquidate the firm's assets. The intensity of the distress

event affects the valuation of the debt, though, there is no closed form solution.

Pricing of Debt and Equity Systematic Risk

- While **Merton** [8] focus on the valuation of corporate debt and its credit spread, **Galai and Masulis** [7] combine the CAPM and OPM to value equity and the systematic risk of both equity and debt.
  - Systematic risk is non-stationary and non-stationarity increases with leverage.
  - They also analyse the effects of mergers, spin-offs and increase volatility on the values and risks of the stakeholders' claims.

Valuation of Corporate Debt Modigliani-Miller and CCA

- **Merton** [6] proves that the M&M propositions also hold for the case of bond default.
  - The importance of M&M to CCA is the idea that the value of the enterprise is determined by the assets of the firm and not from the liabilities. The value of the enterprise is shared by all stakeholders, and if one class of stakeholders is increasing its value, it must be at the expense of other liabilities.
- **Galai** [22] introduces corporate taxes and the government as a stakeholders on the firm's assets. Then, the M&M propositions can be re-derived in this extended framework. The firm should be analysed on before-tax basis.

Taxation and Accounting

- **Brennan and Schwartz** [9], in the CCA framework, relate the value of a levered firm to the value of an unlevered firm, the amount of debt, and the time to maturity of the debt. They address conflicting effects of an increase in the leverage of the firm that increases the tax savings as long as the firm is alive, but also increases the probability of default. Then, an optimal capital structure can be derived.

- **Galai** [23] allows for the adjustment of interest rates to account for the risk of default and show that in that case there is no optimal capital structure.
- **Barth *et al.*** [24] adopt the CCA approach to assess the fair value of corporate bonds taking into account conversion, call, put and sinking fund features as required by the FASB accounting standards.

Stochastic Interest Rates

- **Shimko *et al.*** [25] extend Merton [8] model to value risky debt for the case of stochastic interest rates. In their model interest rates follow a mean-reverting process with constant volatility known as the Vasicek Model.
- **Longstaff and Schwartz** [25] extend the Black–Cox [15] model by introducing stochastic interest rates following the Vasicek process, and deviation from the strict absolute priority rule with default occurring when the value of assets falls below a constant threshold.
- **Briys and de Varenne** [27] extend the previous model to allow for variable default barrier that is the discounted value of a fixed quantity. When this barrier is crossed the bondholders receive an exogenous specified fraction of the remaining assets.
- **Duffie and Lando** [28] extend the previous literature to the case of incomplete secondary-market information about the credit quality of the firm's debt. They solve for the optimal capital structure and default policy, and derive the conditional distribution of the firm's assets, given incomplete accounting information, along with the associated probability of default, the default arrival intensity and the credit spreads.

Moody's KMV Model

- The initials KMV stand for the first letter of the last names of Stephen Kealhofer, John McQuown and Oldrich Vasicek who founded KMV Corporation in 1989. S. Kealhofer and O. Vasicek are two former academics from U.C. Berkeley. In 2002, Moody's Corporation acquired KMV and it is now referred to as Moody's KMV.

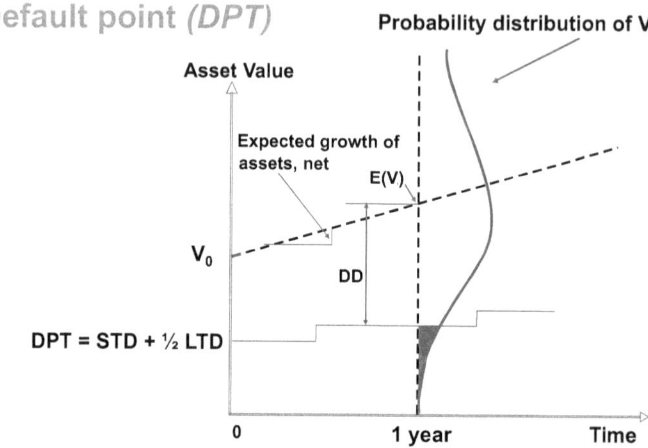

Figure 7: KMV: EDFs Expected Default Frequencies.

- KMV produces EDF, or Expected Default Frequency, of traded companies, which are proxies for default probabilities (DPs). While Merton [8], offers an analytical model, KMV proposes a model which is more heuristic and empirically based; see Figure 7.
- **Vasicek [29]**, **Sundaram [30], Kealhofer [31]** and **Bohn and Crosbie [32]** discuss several issues related to the practical implementation of Merton's model, as reflected in the KMV approach.

Derivation of the probabilities of default from the distance to default.

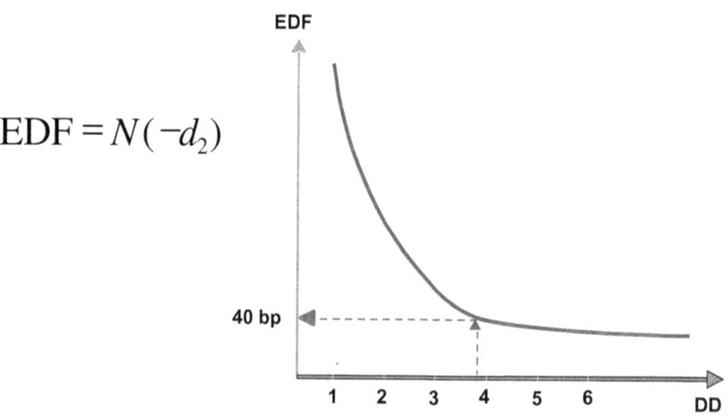

Figure 8: EDF vs. the distance to default.

KMV also uses historical data to compute EDFs; see Figure 8.

4.3 *The pricing of warrants, convertible securities, preferred stocks*

4.3.1 *Pricing of warrants*

- Warrants are similar to call options except that they are issued by the firm. The introduction of warrants as a source of financing complicates the valuation of equity since now we must take into account the cash injection into the firm when warrants are exercised, leading to potential dilution of current shareholders.
- Warrants are similar to issuing equity and supplying loans to the warrant holders: it creates negative leverage.
- **Galai and Schneller [33]** proposes the first pricing model for warrants for an all equity firm which takes potential dilution from warrant exercise explicitly into account in a firm's valuation.
- Extensions of this model are:

  - The optimal exercise strategy for American warrants [34].
  - Sequential exercise strategies by warrant holders [35,36].
  - Pricing of warrants in a firm financed by both equity and debt, and assume that the proceeds from warrrant exercise are reinvested in the firm [37].
  - **Simonato [38]** generalizes Crouhy–Galai by assuming that the maturity of the warrants differs from debt maturity. He assumes pricing errors in the equity model. He derives simultaneously the non-observable asset value of the firm together with the asset return volatility.

4.3.2 *Pricing of convertible securities*

- **Ingersoll [39,40]** is one of the pioneering works on the valuation of hybrid securities. Ingersoll develops a method for determining optimal call and conversion strategies and affirms the validity of the Black–Scholes model for pricing both callable and non-callable convertible bonds, as well as preferred stock; see Figure 9.
- **Brennan and Schwartz [41]** offer a more general algorithm for determining the value of callable convertible bonds.

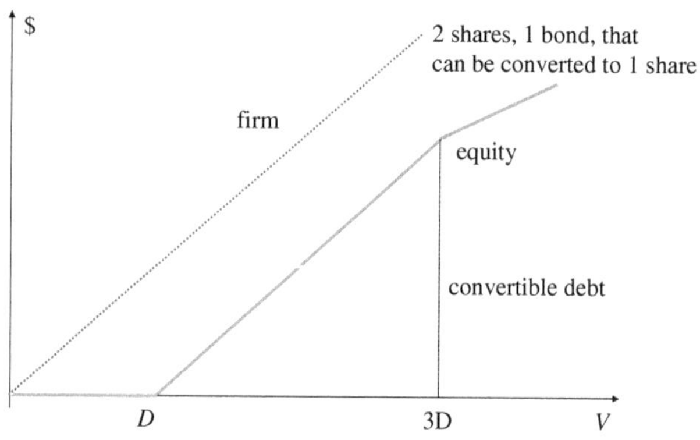

Figure 9: Convertible bond.

- **Dorion *et al.* [42]** focus on the agency conflict between shareholders and bondholders. They show that properly designed convertible bonds can reduce this agency conflict, since conversion forces existing shareholders to share the firm's upside potential with bondholders.

4.4 *CCA and various corporate issues*

In this section, CCA is used to analyze various securities or contracts issued by corporations to achieve specific goals:

- Corporations issue special employee stock options (ESO) to executives and key personnel, and the employees become equity stakeholders in the corporation.
- Firms acquire know how and other intellectual property for which they pay royalties, which may take various forms.
- CCA can also apply to corporate governance, concerning dividend policy, compensation, and alternative ways to share voting power in major corporate decision-making.

This section highlights several cases in which the use of CCA goes beyond the assessment of credit spreads and the valuation of equity and debt.

- **Cooper and Mello [43]** show that in perfect markets, risky swaps transfer wealth from shareholders to debtholders. They obtain a closed-form solution, under simplifying assumptions, for the value of default risk in swaps.

- **Galai and Ilan** [44] apply the CCA to the economic evaluation of remuneration from patents and licensing activity. They derive a fair transaction price for the technology transfer between licensors and the licensees based on Merton's [6] approach to the valuation of deposit insurance. The elasticity of demand for the licensed product plays a major role in determining the royalty scheme.
- **Cvitanic *et al.*** [45], propose an analytical pricing formula which incorporates special features of ESO, like vesting, forfeitures and voluntary exercise. This analytic formula became particularly important after accounting standards adopted fair value reporting of stock-based compensation.
- **Galai and Wiener** [46] propose a new approach to dynamic representation of various groups of stakeholders on corporate boards and general meetings. This approach is based on Merton's model, dividing voting rights proportionally to the marginal value of the corresponding contingent claim, i.e., the "delta" ratio of each stakeholder.
- **Goshen and Wiener** [47] develop an option-like valuation of contractual freeze-out clauses — an important legal right given to majority shareholders to compel minority shareholders to liquidate their shares under certain circumstances. Minority shareholders have an offsetting right to demand for an entire fairness test. The model shows how to incorporate these features into equity pricing.

4.4.1 *Dividends as contingent claims*

This section deals with how dividends can be treated as contingent claims on the corporation. Dividends are a component in equity valuation, and as such, constitute a claim on a firm's future cashflow.

- **Garbade** [48] articulates the valuation of debt and equity for a firm that pays periodic coupons to debt holders as well as cash dividends to shareholders; see Figure 10.
- **Galai and Wiener** [49] highlight potential conflicts of interest between equity holders and debt holders surrounding dividend payments. If dividends are withheld, even when the company has the

resources, the value of debt may increase, shifting value from equity to debt. If too much is paid in dividends, there may be a shift of value from debt to equity. These arguments are presented in a simple binomial, two-period framework.

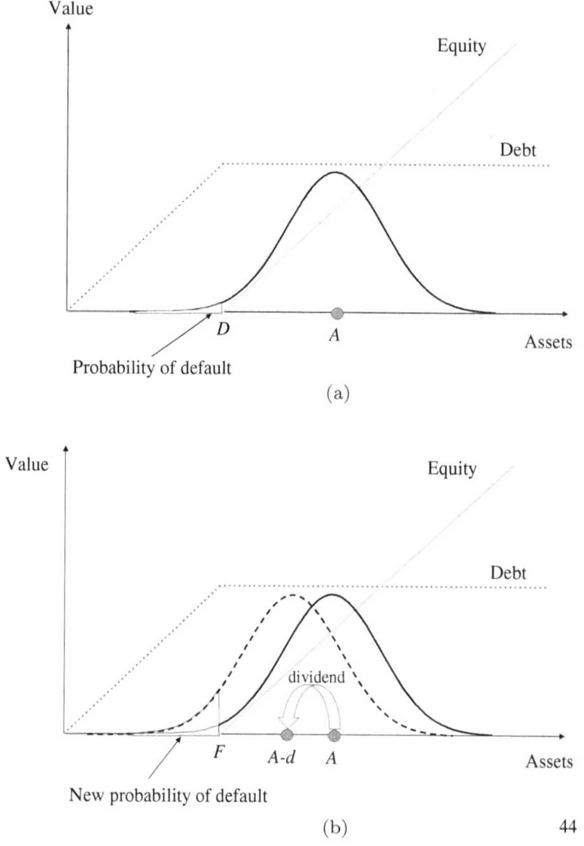

Figure 10: Dividends and PD. Probability of default before and after a cash dividend payment.

4.5 *CCA for banks and sovereign debt*

4.5.1 *CCA for banks*

Banking Models

CCA is also useful to address banking issues related to regulation such as deposit insurance, contingent bank capital (CoCos) as well as international finance issues such as the pricing of sovereign debt.

- **Merton [6]** looks at guarantees, such as deposit insurance and loan guarantees, as liabilities or costs to the guarantor. Merton prices the economic value of the guarantee using CCA. More precisely, he establishes the correspondence between deposit insurance and loan guarantees, and a put option on the assets of the bank.
- **Ronn and Verma [50]** adapt Merton's model to account for the fact that the FDIC forces bank closure only when the value of the assets of the bank falls below a fraction of total debt, after having tried to rescue the troubled bank by the infusion of funds.
- **Crouhy and Galai [51]** use the CCA for bank stakeholders exposed to three types of risks: interest rate risk, financial risk due to the leveraged position of the bank, and default risk. They derive the equilibrium price of equity, the fair interest rate that depositors should require to be fully compensated for the financial and default risks they face. They also derive the equilibrium deposit insurance premium as a function of the capital ratio. They also investigate the interactions among regulatory measures such as capital adequacy requirement and interest rate ceiling, and show that when both are imposed one of them is ineffective.
- **Dermine and Lajeri [52]** extend Merton [6] model of deposit insurance by explicitly linking the corporate loans on the balance sheet of the bank to the balance sheet of the borrowing firms. The credit risk exposure of the bank then depends specifically on the default risk of the borrowing firms. The valuation of the deposit insurance is similar to the put option discussed in the literature, except that the underlying asset is the one of the borrower, not the one of the bank.

Contingent Convertibles (CoCos)

After the GFC, new capital instruments called, contingent capital or contingent convertibles (CoCos) have been proposed with the goal of reducing the likelihood that banks experience financial distress and also to avoid future government bailouts. These instruments are debt that converts to common shareholders equity if a bank's original equity or capital is depleted. It is a mechanism for automatic capital restructuring that extinguishes debt and replaces it with new common equity.

- **Pennacchi [53]** adopts the CCA to determine the yields that contingent capital investors should require to be fairly compensated for the risk they face for different contractual terms. Pennacchi extends the convertible model of Leland [10] by assuming that the market value of the bank's assets follows a jump-diffusion process, interest rates are stochastic, deposits are an overnight source of funding and can be adjusted daily to meet a target asset-to-deposit ratio. In his set-up the bank is closed when the value of the assets falls below the promised value of deposits. Various conversion triggers are analyzed, the most common one being the bank's capital falling below a threshold.

- **Glasserman and Nouri** [54] analyze the problem of existence and uniqueness of equilibrium values for a firm's liabilities when the bank issues CoCos, or in other words that there exists values for the banks's liabilities consistent with a market-price trigger for CoCos. They show that such equilibrium exists and is unique for triggers high enough so that existing shareholders are diluted.
- **De Spiegeleer and Schoutens** [55] consider the CoCos as a derivative security with a trigger expressed as a barrier on the equity price. They, show that the CoCos are equivalent to long position in a corporate bond, plus a knock-in forward option together with a short position in a binary-down- and- in option. Then, using the BSM framework they are able to derive closed form solutions for the price of CoCos with different characteristics.
- **Sundaresan and Wang** [56] also consider CoCos with a market trigger for mandatory conversion. They show that when CoCos with a market trigger is used it may introduce the potential for price uncertainty, market manipulation and inefficient capital allocation. To obtain a unique equilibrium the conversion rule must ensure that, at the trigger price, conversion does not change the value of the security (equity) on which the trigger is placed. Sundaresan and Wang propose modifying the terms of the contingent capital contract to eliminate the possibility of a value transfer and thus to ensure a unique equilibrium.

4.5.2 *CCA for sovereign debt*

International and Sovereign Debt

- **Gapen *et al.*** [57] apply CCA to the balance sheet of the combined government and monetary authorities to analyze sovereign risk. They extend the Merton/KMV framework to the analysis of sovereign debt. This paper develops a set of key credit risk indicators to measure sovereign balance sheet risk. These include the distance to distress, probability of default, credit spreads, and the market value of risky foreign currency-denominated debt.

- **Gray *et al.* [58]** extend the Gapen *et al.* model to explore actual and potential applications of the CCA framework for investment management: (i) valuing, investing, and trading sovereign securities including Sovereign Capital Structure Arbitrage trading strategies; (ii) design and management of sovereign wealth funds; and, (iii) design and valuation of new sovereign risk transfer instruments and contracts.
- **Gray *et al.* [59]** build on the previous framework based on CCA to develop early warning indicators of financial crisis and apply them to the subprime mortgage crisis of 2007–2008. They show how the CCA framework can trace the amplification of risk from household mortgages via structured products to off-balance-sheet entities, to banks by using a system of interlinked risk-adjusted balance sheets. They show how the CCA framework can measure and analyze contingent liabilities of the government and central bank. They propose new metrics for financial vulnerability to help analyze systemic risk and how these risk indicators can be incorporated in monetary policy models to better evaluate the relationships between financial stability, monetary policy, and economic growth.
- **Gray *et al.* [60]**, as in their previous model, view the sectors of the economy as interconnected portfolios of assets, liabilities, and guarantees. By linking the balance sheets of the different sectors of the economy they can analyze different types of risk transmission channels. The CCA framework provides a forward-looking market-based set of indicators to measure the vulnerability of various sectors of the economy and to quantify the effects of asset-liability mismatches within and across institutions.
- **Galai and Wiener [61]** use the CCA framework to show that in a multicurrency environment, a firm wishing to minimize the probability of insolvency (and thus the costs of financing) may select to finance activities with a currency that is highly correlated with the rate of return on the firm's assets. Their model applies

directly to a bank that lends in local currency but obtains financing in foreign currency either from abroad or from local depositors.

- **Belev and diBartolomeo [62]** develop a structural model of a sovereign country in order to analyze sovereign credit risk. They apply their analysis to European countries, the U.S. and Japan and find consistency with observed variables and real world events.

Acknowledgment

We thank Zvi Bodie for his insights, suggestions and fruitful discussions, as well as the participants of the IRMC 2019 conference in Milan, the "Options — 45 Years Since the Publication of the Black Scholes Merton Model" conference in Jerusalem, the *17th Finance, Risk and Accounting Perspectives* conference in Helsinki, the *Analytics for Management and Economics Conference* in St. Petersburg and the *Multinational Financial Society (MFS)* conference 2019. We acknowledge financial support from the Zagagi Center and the Krueger Center at the Jerusalem School of Business at The Hebrew University as well as the Sanger Family Chair in Banking and Risk Management (Wiener).

References

[1] Sharpe, W.F. (1964). Capital asset prices: A theory of market equilibrium. *Journal of Finance*, 19(3), 425–442.
[2] Lintner, J. (1965a). Security prices, risk and maximal gains from diversification. *Journal of Finance*, 20(4), 587–615.
[3] Lintner, J. (1965b). The valuation of risk assets and the selection of risky investments in stock portfolios and capital budgets. *Review of Economics and Statistics*, 47(1), 13–37.
[4] Fama, E. and Miller, M. (1972). *The Theory of Finance*, Dryden Press.
[5] Modigliani, F. and Miller, M.H. (1958). The cost of capital, corporation finance and the theory of investment. *American Economic Review*, 48, 261–297.
[6] Merton, R.C. (1977). On the pricing of contingent claims and the Modigliani-Miller Theorem. *Journal of Financial Economics*, 5(2), 241–249. A later version of this paper appeared as Chapter 12 in the book, R.C. Merton, *Continuous Time Finance*, Wiley Blackwell, 1992.

[7] Galai, D. and Masulis, R.W. (1976). The option pricing model and the risk factor of stock. *Journal of Financial Economics*, 3, 53–81.
[8] Merton, R.C. (1974). On the pricing of corporate debt: The risk structure of interest rates. *Journal of Finance*, 29(2), 449–470.
[9] Brennan, M.J. and Schwartz, E.S. (1978). Corporate income taxes, valuation, and the problem of optimal capital structure. *The Journal of Business*, 50(1), 103–114.
[10] Leland, H.E. (1994). Corporate debt value, bond covenants, and optimal capital structure. *Journal of Finance*, 49(4), 1213–1252.
[11] Black, F. and Scholes M. (1973). The pricing of options and corporate liabilities. *Journal of Political Economy*, 81(3), 637–654.
[12] Merton, R.C. (1973). Theory of rational option pricing. *The Bell Journal of Economics and Management Science*, 4(1), 141–183.
[13] Crouhy, M., Galai, D., and Mark, R. (1998). Credit risk revisited. *Risk magazine, Credit Risk Supplement*, pp. 40–44.
[14] Crouhy, M. and Galai, D. (2018). The relationship between the risk-neutral and physical probabilities of default. In: M. Crouhy, D. Galai and Z. Wiener (Eds.), *Contingent Claims Analysis in Corporate Finance*, Vol. 1, World Scientific, pp. 183–186.
[15] Black, F. and Cox, J.C. (1976). Valuing corporate securities: Some effects of bond indenture provisions. *Journal of Finance*, 31(2), 351–367.
[16] Geske, R. (1977). The valuation of corporate liabilities as compound options. *The Journal of Financial and Quantitative Analysis*, 12(4), 541–552.
[17] Leland, H.E. and Toft, K.B. (1996). Optimal capital structure, endogenous bankruptcy, and the term structure of credit spreads. *Journal of Finance*, 51(3), 987–1019.
[18] Mella-Barral, P. and Perraudin, W. (1997). Strategic debt service. *Journal of Finance*, 52(2), 531–556.
[19] Moraux, F. (2002). Valuing Corporate Liabilities When the Default Threshold is not an Absorbing Barrier, Working Paper, Universite de Rennes 1, France.
[20] Francois, P. and Morellec, E. (2004). Capital structure and asset prices: Some effects of bankruptcy procedures. *The Journal of Business*, 77(2), 387–411.
[21] Galai, D., Raviv, A., and Wiener, Z. (2007). Liquidation triggers and the valuation of equity and debt. *Journal of Banking & Finance*, 31(12), 3604–3620.
[22] Galai, D. (1998). Taxes, M-M propositions and government's implicit cost of capital in investment projects in the private sector. *European Financial Management*, 4(2), 143–157.

[23] Galai, D. (1988). Corporate income taxes and the valuation of the claims on the corporation. *Research in Finance*, 7, 75–90.

[24] Barth, M.E., Landsman, W.R., and Rendleman, R.J. Jr. (1998). Option pricing-based bond value estimates and a fundamental components approach to account for corporate debt. *The Accounting Review*, 73(1), 73–102.

[25] Shimko, D.C., Tejima, N., and van Deventer, D.R. (1993). The pricing of risky debt when interest rates are stochastic. *The Journal of Fixed Income*, 3(2), 58–65.

[26] Longstaff, F.A. and Schwartz, E.S. (1995). A simple approach to valuing risky fixed and floating rate debt. *Journal of Finance*, 50(3), 789–819.

[27] Briys, E. and de Varenne, F. (1997). Valuing risky fixed rate debt: An extension. *The Journal of Financial and Quantitative Analysis*, 32(2), 239–248.

[28] Duffie, D. and Lando, D. (2003). Term structures of credit spreads with incomplete accounting information. *Econometrica*, 69(3), 633–664.

[29] Vasicek O.A. (1984). Credit Valuation, White Paper, *Diversified Corporate Finance.*

[30] Sundaram, R.K. (2001). The Merton/KMV Approach to Pricing Credit Risk. This article originally appeared in *Extra Credit*, a former publication of Merrill Lynch.

[31] Kealhofer, S. (2003). Quantifying credit risk I: Default prediction. *Financial Analysts Journal*, 59(1), 30–44.

[32] Crosbie, P. and Bohn, J. (2003). *Modeling Default Risk, Moody's KMV "White Paper"* series.

[33] Galai, D. and Schneller, M.I. (1978). Pricing of warrants and the value of the firm. *Journal of Finance*, 33(5), 1333–1342.

[34] Emanuel, D.C. (1983). Warrant valuation and exercise strategy. *Journal of Financial Economics*, 12(2), 211–235.

[35] Constantinides, G.M. (1984). Warrant exercise and bond conversion in competitive markets. *Journal of Financial Economics*, 13(3), 371–397.

[36] Spatt, C.S. and Sterbenz, F.P. (1988). Warrant exercise, dividends, and reinvestment policy. *Journal of Finance*, 43(2), 493–506.

[37] Crouhy, M. and Galai, D. (1994). The interaction between the financial and investment decisions of the firm: The case of issuing warrants in a levered firm. *Journal of Banking & Finance*, 18(5), 861–880.

[38] Simonato, J.G. (2015). New warrant issues valuation with leverage and equity model errors. *Journal of Financial Services Research*, 47(2), 247–272.

[39] Ingersoll, J.E. Jr. (1977a). A Contingent-claims valuation of convertible securities. *Journal of Financial Economics*, 4(3), 289–321.

[40] Ingersoll, J.E. Jr. (1977b). An examination of corporate call policies on convertible securities. *Journal of Finance*, 32(2), 463–478.
[41] Brennan, M.J. and Schwartz, E.S. (1977a). Convertible bonds: Valuation and optimal strategies for call and conversion. *Journal of Finance*, 32(5), 1699–1715.
[42] Dorion, C., P. Francois, P., Grass, G., and Jeanneret, A. (2014). Convertible debt and shareholder incentives. *Journal of Corporate Finance*, 24, 38–56.
[43] Cooper, I.A. and Mello, A.S. (1991). The default risk of swaps. *Journal of Finance*, 46(2), 597–620.
[44] Galai, D. and Ilan, Y. (1995). Economic evaluation of remuneration from patents and technology transfers. *International Review of Financial Analysis*, 4(2/3), 107–121.
[45] Cvitanic, J., Wiener, Z., and Zapatero, F. (2008). Analytic pricing of employee stock options. *The Review of Financial Studies*, 21(2), 683–724.
[46] Galai, D. and Wiener, Z. (2008). Stakeholders and the composition of the voting rights of the board of directors. *Journal of Corporate Finance*, 14, 107–117.
[47] Goshen, Z. and Wiener, Z. (2004). The Value of the Freezeout Option, paper originally published in the Columbia Law and Economics Working Paper Series (No. 260).
[48] Garbade, K.D. (2001). Dividend-Paying Stock, originally published as Chapter 14 in the book. In: K. Garbade (Ed.), *Pricing Corporate Securities as Contingent Claims*, MIT Press, pp. 273–282.
[49] Galai, D. and Wiener, Z. (2018). Dividend policy relevance in a levered firm — The binomial case. *Economic Letters*, 172, 78–80.
[50] Ronn, E.I. and Verma, A.K. (1986). Pricing risk-adjusted deposit insurance: An option-based model. *Journal of Finance*, 41(4), 871–895.
[51] Crouhy, M. and Galai, D. (1991). A contingent claim analysis of a regulated depository institution. *Journal of Banking and Finance*, 15, 73–90.
[52] Dermine, J. and Lajeri, F. (2001). Credit risk and the depository insurance premium: A note. *Journal of Economics and Business*, 53(5), 497–508.
[53] Pennacchi, G. (2010). A Structural Model of Contingent Bank Capital, Federal Reserve Board of Cleveland Working Paper No. 10-04.
[54] Glasserman, P. and Nouri, B. (2012). Contingent capital with a capital-ratio trigger. *Management Science*, 58(10), 1816–1833.
[55] De Spiegeleer, J. and Schoutens, W. (2012). Pricing contingent convertibles: A derivatives approach. *The Journal of Derivatives*, 20(2), 27–36.

[56] Sundaresan, S. and Wang, Z. (2015). On the design of contingent capital with a market trigger. *Journal of Finance*, 70(2), 881–920.

[57] Gapen, M.T., Gray, D.F., Lim, C.H., and Xiao, Y. (2008). Measuring and analyzing sovereign risk with contingent claims. *IMF Staff Papers*, 55(1), 109–148.

[58] Gray, D.F., Merton, R.C., and Bodie, Z. (2007). Contingent claims approach to measuring and managing sovereign credit risk. *Journal of Investment Management*, 5(4), 5–28.

[59] Gray, D.F., Merton, R.C., and Bodie, Z. (2008). A Contingent Claims Analysis of the Subprime Credit Crisis of 2007–2008, *CREDIT 2008 Conference on Liquidity and Credit Risk*.

[60] Gray, D.F., Merton, R.C., and Bodie, Z. (2011). Measuring and managing macrofinancial risk and financial stability: A new framework. *Financial Stability Monetary Policy and Central Banking*, Central Bank of Chile.

[61] Galai, D. and Wiener, Z. (2012). Credit risk spreads in local and foreign currencies. *Journal of Money, Credit and Banking*, 44(5), 883–901.

[62] Belev, E. and di Bartolomeo, D. (2015). Finance meets macroeconomics: A structural model of sovereign credit risk, society of actuaries enterprise risk management symposium: A Structural Model of Sovereign Credit and Bank Risk.

[63] Crouhy, M., Galai, D., and Wiener, Z. (Eds.) (2019). *Contingent Claims Analysis in Corporate Finance*, 4 volumes. Volume 1: *Foundations of CCA and Equity Valuation*; Volume 2: *Corporate Debt Valuation with CCA*; Volume 3: *Empirical Testing and Applications of CCA*; Volume 4: *Contingent Claims Approach for Banks and Sovereign Debt*, World Scientific.

https://doi.org/10.1142/9789811259142_bmatter

Index

T

U

V

W

Y

Z